W9-CPF-161

Catalyst 2.0

Use this registration card to access *Catalyst 2.0: the premier online resource for writing, research, and editing.* Available free with every student and instructor copy of *The New McGraw-Hill Handbook*, online access includes:

- A complete interactive ebook of the text
- The *Factiva* online database with thousands of full text articles and images from periodicals and journals
- Interactive tutorials on document design and visual rhetoric
- Guides for avoiding plagiarism and evaluating sources
- Electronic writing tutors for composing informative, interpretive, and argumentative papers
- *Bibliomaker* software for the MLA, APA, Chicago, and CSE styles of documentation
- More than 4,500 exercises with feedback in grammar, usage, and punctuation

In addition, *Catalyst 2.0* offers writing instructors a new, state-of-the-art course management and peer review system that allows users to do the following:

- Embed comments and links contextually alongside reviewed papers
- Create and select from lists of 'favorite' comments
- Drag and drop editing abbreviations and symbols into papers that link to *Catalyst* grammar coverage online
- Create and comment on multiple drafts among groups of student reviewers
- Use instructor-created review questions to respond to drafts

The New
McGraw-Hill
Handbook

The New McGraw-Hill Handbook

Elaine P. Maimon
University of Alaska Anchorage

Janice H. Peritz
Queens College,
City University of New York

Kathleen Blake Yancey
Florida State University

With notes for multilingual students
and *Guide for Multilingual Writers* by
Maria Zlateva, *Boston University*

Boston Burr Ridge, IL Dubuque, IA Madison, WI New York
San Francisco St. Louis Bangkok Bogotá Caracas Kuala Lumpur
Lisbon London Madrid Mexico City Milan Montreal New Delhi
Santiago Seoul Singapore Sydney Taipei Toronto

The McGraw·Hill Companies

Higher Education

Published by McGraw-Hill, an imprint of The McGraw-Hill Companies, Inc., 1221 Avenue of the Americas, New York, NY 10020. Copyright © 2007. All rights reserved. No part of this publication may be reproduced or distributed in any form or by any means, or stored in a database or retrieval system, without the prior written consent of The McGraw-Hill Companies, Inc., including, but not limited to, in any network or other electronic storage or transmission, or broadcast for distance learning.

1 2 3 4 5 6 7 8 9 0 DOC DOC 0 9 8 7 6 5

Hardcover:
ISBN-13:   978-0-07-298050-9
ISBN-10:   0-07-298050-8

Softcover:
ISBN-13:   978-0-07-321687-4
ISBN-10:   0-07-321687-9

Editor-in-chief: *Emily Barrosse*
Publisher: *Lisa Moore*
Sponsoring editor: *Christopher Bennem*
Director of development: *Carla Kay Samodulski*
Development editor: *David Chodoff*
Marketing manager: *Lori DeShazo*
Media producer: *Alex Rohrs*
Managing editor: *David M. Staloch*
Art director: *Jeanne M. Schreiber*

Senior designer: *Cassandra Chu*
Interior and cover designer: *Maureen McCutcheon*
Art manager: *Robin Mouat*
Lead production supervisor: *Randy Hurst*
Photo research coordinator: *Alexandra Ambrose*
Photo researcher: *Christine Pullo*
Composition: *Thompson Type*
Printing: *R.R. Donnelley & Sons*

Cover images: (from left to right) © *Philadelphia Museum of Art/CORBIS;* © *NASA/Roger Ressmeyer/CORBIS; Nevros/Folio, Inc.;* © *Jon Hicks/CORBIS*

Credits: *The credits section for this book begins on page C-1 and is considered an extension of the copyright page.*

Library of Congress Cataloging-in-Publication Data
Maimon, Elaine P.
  The new McGraw-Hill handbook / Elaine P. Maimon, Janice H. Peritz, Kathleen Blake Yancey.
    p. cm.
    Includes index.
    ISBN-13: 978-0-07-298050-9; ISBN-10: 0-07-298050-8
  English language—Rhetoric—Handbooks, manual, etc. 2. Academic writing—Handbooks, manuals, etc. 3. Report writing—handbooks, manual, etc.
  I. Peritz, Janice. II. Yancey, Kathleen Blake, III. Title

PE1408.M3364 2005
808'.042—dc22   2005054416

The Internet addresses listed in the text were accurate at the time of publication. The inclusion of a Web site does not indicate an endorsement by the authors or McGraw-Hill, and McGraw-Hill does not guarantee the accuracy of the information presented at these sites.

www.mhhe.com

Contents

Part 1 ▪ Writing and Designing Papers

v

Part 2 ▪ Common Assignments across the Curriculum

Part 3 ▪ Researching

Part 4 ■ Documenting across the Curriculum

Part 5 ■ Writing beyond College

Part 6 ▪ Grammar Basics

Part 7 ▪ Editing for Grammar Conventions

36 Problems with Pronouns 638

Part 8 ▪ Editing for Clarity

Part 9 ■ Editing for Word Choice

Part 10 ■ Sentence Punctuation

Part 11 ▪ Mechanics and Spelling

Part 12 ▪ Guide for Multilingual Writers

Part 13 ▪ Further Resources for Learning

Preface

Writing and research have changed dramatically since the first hardcover English handbooks appeared, and so have students. Today's students don't just write papers; they create multimedia presentations. They don't just do research; they sift through a mountain of online information. They don't just read print texts; they analyze visual information of all kinds. They don't just come to class; they participate in an extended online learning community. Their perspectives on college life are different from those of previous generations, as are their expectations.

These changes were uppermost in our minds when we started work on *The New McGraw-Hill Handbook.* They have put new demands on composition courses, demands that we designed the book to meet.

Features of *The New McGraw-Hill Handbook*

Comprehensive but accessible, *The New McGraw-Hill Handbook* provides students with tools for learning, writing, researching, and editing that reflect the challenges and opportunities they face today, in the classroom and beyond. The book also provides students and teachers with online access to several powerful technological resources.

Learning

The New McGraw-Hill Handbook is unique in the amount of support it provides students to help them meet the challenges of learning in college.

- **An introduction to learning in college**

  Chapter 1: Learning across the Curriculum provides an introduction to learning in college that emphasizes the importance of writing as a learning tool and the rewards and challenges of learning in a multimedia world.

- **Further resources for learning**

  The innovative final section of the book (Part 13: Further Resources for Learning) provides students with a variety of resources—a glossary of terms from across the curriculum, a timeline of world history, a world map, a Quick Reference for ESL Writers, and a Guide to Weights and Measures—that will help them with learning throughout their college years and beyond.

- **Abundant resources for multilingual writers**

  The last section of Chapter 1 is devoted to the particular challenges to learning in college faced by multilingual students. Numerous *For Multilingual Students* boxes throughout the book (prepared by Maria Zlateva, Director of ESL at Boston University) provide targeted advice on every stage of the writing process. A three-chapter "Guide for Multilingual Writers" (Part 12), also prepared by Maria Zlateva, addresses common problems multilingual students encounter as they master English grammar and usage. A separate index for multilingual writers follows the main index. The handy grammar tips in the pull-out section in Part 13: Further Resources for Learning, provide a quick reference that is easy for students to carry as they attend classes or work in the library.

- **Boxes that offer support for today's diverse student population**

  The boxes in *The New McGraw-Hill Handbook* supplement the text discussion with important information and helpful advice.

  Learning in College: Featured throughout the text, these boxed tips offer students information and strategies that will help them become better learners and writers.

  Charting the Territory: These boxes present relevant information on such topics as interpretive assignments in different disciplines and the function of the passive voice in scientific writing, giving students a sense of how requirements and conventions vary across the curriculum.

  TextConnex: Offering advice on using electronic resources and composing on a computer, as well as lists of useful Web sites, the TextConnex boxes help today's hyper-connected students take full advantage of the technology available to them.

  Writing beyond College: These boxes alert students to connections between topics covered in the chapters and a variety of related writing situations beyond college.

Boxes for Multilingual Students: These boxes offer advice on learning in college, writing, research, and selected points of grammar.

Writing

The New McGraw-Hill Handbook recognizes the importance of critical thinking and academic writing in first-year composition.

- **A focus on critical thinking and effective writing across the curriculum**

   Although instructors in various disciplines may approach subject matter differently, thinking critically and writing logically are underlying expectations across the curriculum. For this reason, *The New McGraw-Hill Handbook* follows its thorough coverage of the writing process (in Part 1: Writing and Designing Papers) with a chapter on critical reading, thinking, and writing at the beginning of Part 2: Common Assignments across the Curriculum. Reading and thinking critically lead to writing critically and presenting persuasive arguments. Subsequent chapters in Part 2 give students advice on writing the three most commonly assigned types of papers—informative reports, interpretive analyses (including literary analyses), and arguments—as well as guidance on such other common assignments as personal essays, in-class essay exams, and oral presentations.

- **A chapter on multimedia assignments**

   Many students will be asked, or have already been asked, to move beyond traditional college assignments and to write in media other than the printed page. Part 2: Common Assignments concludes with a chapter (14: Multimedia Writing) with information on a variety of multimedia assignments, including instruction on creating photo and hypertext essays with a word processing program, using presentation software to create multimedia presentations, and designing effective Web sites and blogs.

- **Strong, integrated coverage of visual rhetoric**

   The New McGraw-Hill Handbook integrates its extensive coverage of visual rhetoric into its coverage of the writing process and academic writing in Parts 1 and 2. This integration encourages students to think about design issues and the use of visuals as a natural part of the writing process. All the chapters on the writing process (2–5) provide advice on the selection and appropriate use of photos, charts, and graphs in papers. Chapter 7, on critical reading, thinking, and writing, integrates a discussion of the critical analysis of images with its discussion of the critical analysis of written texts. A separate chapter (Chapter 6: Designing Academic Papers) provides guidelines for using design to enhance written communication.

- **More sample papers and samples of writing than any other handbook**

  Because students learn best from practical models that relate to their actual experience, *The New McGraw-Hill Handbook* provides plentiful samples of student and professional writing for a variety of purposes—to inform, interpret, and argue—from a wide range of disciplines. To show the realities of the processes of drafting, revising, and research, the writing process chapters follow the development of a student essay from conception to final draft, the common assignments chapters include eight student papers, and the MLA and APA documentation chapters each feature a complete student research report.

- **Plenty of advice on using technology**

  Today's student has more opportunities to write than ever before. E-mail, Web sites, chat rooms, and blogs all supplement the traditional occasions for writing offered by college coursework. Because we recognize that writing in college and in the world of work has become less and less a matter of the writer alone at a desk and more and more a matter of using technology effectively, we attend to technology throughout the text, with advice on using online tools for learning in Chapter 1; specific, practical suggestions for using online resources to collaborate with peer reviewers and revise papers in Chapter 5; advice on designing academic papers and preparing print and online portfolios in Chapter 6; advice for writing scannable résumés in Chapter 29; and TextConnex boxes with advice on technology and useful links to online resources.

- **Preparation for writing at work and in the community**

  Part 6: Writing beyond College demonstrates how writing in college prepares students for success in the professional world. Special topics include applying for internships, producing résumés in scannable and traditional formats, service learning, and creating brochures and posters. In addition, *Writing beyond College* boxes throughout the book illustrate the variety of writing situations students are likely to encounter outside of college.

Researching

The New McGraw-Hill Handbook helps students navigate the complexities of research in a wired world.

- **Support for conducting research and managing information**

  The library's shelves are only the beginning of research for students today. The process continues on the Internet and in the field, the archive, and the lab. To assist students in these varied venues, Part 3 of *The New McGraw-Hill Handbook* (Researching) provides abundant guidance on posing research questions, understanding the role of ethics in research, conducting keyword searches in the library and on the Web, and thinking critically about sources. We also offer a detailed directory of sources from different disciplines in Chapter 23.

- **Exceptional coverage on note taking and avoiding plagiarism**

  Because students are confronted with more sources than ever before, they need more help with note taking strategies and clear, straightforward advice on how to join the academic conversation without plagiarizing sources. *The New McGraw-Hill Handbook* devotes two full chapters to this critical concern. Chapter 20: Plagiarism, Copyright, and Intellectual Property, which is unique to this book, provides an overview of the issues of copyright, plagiarism, and fair use. Chapter 21: Working with Sources and Avoiding Plagiarism gives students practical instruction on taking notes that summarize, paraphrase, and quote sources as well as on how to integrate those sources into a paper without plagiarizing.

- **A unique chapter on finding and creating effective visuals**

  Chapter 17: Finding and Creating Effective Visuals helps students make critical choices about the kinds of visual sources to include in their papers and the forms those sources can take. The chapter includes discussions of why and when students should—or shouldn't—use images to reinforce a point and gives them practical advice on displaying information visually.

- **Documentation flowcharts**

  As they conduct research, students today are confronted with more types of sources than ever before. The chapters on MLA and APA documentation (24 and 25) feature decision-tree-like diagrams that help students identify the kind of source they are dealing with and where to find the proper format for documenting it.

- **Visual guides for documenting sources**

  To show busy students where to find the information they need to cite their sources properly, Chapters 24 and 25 also feature facsimile pages from books, periodicals, and Web sites that illustrate where students can find the author's name, the date of publication, and so on.

Editing

The New McGraw-Hill Handbook helps today's students see how grammar fits into the writing process, so they can learn to become effective editors of their own work.

- **Grammar in the context of editing.**

  Most of the chapters in Parts 7–9, which cover the conventions of English grammar, usage, punctuation, and mechanics, are structured first to teach students to identify a particular problem and then to edit to eliminate the problem in a way that strengthens their writing.

- **Boxes that help students recognize and correct errors**

  The "Identify and Edit" boxes, which appear in key grammar, style, and punctuation chapters in Parts 7, 8, and 10, give students—especially visual learners—strategies for identifying and correcting their most serious sentence problems and are especially useful for quick reference.

- **Boxes that help students use grammar and style checkers**

  Boxes appearing near the beginning of each chapter in Parts 7, 8, 10, and 11 warn students of the pitfalls of relying too much on computer grammar and style checkers when editing their work, empowering students to become their own "grammar checkers."

- **"Test Yourself" quizzes**

  Appearing at the beginning of Parts 6–8 and 10–11, these diagnostic tests help students pinpoint aspects of grammar, style, punctuation, and mechanics that give them trouble. Scratch off answer keys at the end of the book reveal solutions and direct students to additional help in the handbook. Additional diagnostic tests are available on *Catalyst.*

- **Practice exercises**

  Practice exercises appear throughout the book, with content drawn from subjects across the curriculum that students are likely to encounter in their first-year courses. For students who need even more practice, *Catalyst* offers more than 4,500 additional exercises with immediate explanatory feedback in response to incorrect answers.

Technology

The New McGraw-Hill Handbook provides online access to valuable technological resources.

- *Catalyst 2.0: The premier online tool for writing and research*

  Catalyst 2.0 provides online support for today's tech-savvy students, or for those students who need to become savvy about technology, with a variety of study tools, including an interactive tutorial on visual rhetoric and document design; more than 4,500 exercises on grammar and usage at several levels of difficulty, with instant feedback; ten interactive writing guides; a tutorial on avoiding plagiarism, and *Bibliomaker* documentation software.

- **Online peer review and course management utilities**

  Available for instructors who wish to use them, class tools for electronic peer review and course management, provided by *Catalyst 2.0,* may be activated for free online. Students can gain access to the course with the *Catalyst* registration code that comes free with every text. Instructors can have their students share and comment on drafts of one another's papers, view their grades online, and link to all the resources in *Catalyst* without ever having to worry about ordering special packages.

- **Integrated e-book and Interactive Annotated Instructor's Edition**

  For ease of use at a home computer or in a lab, a complete e-book is available for students on the text's Web site, with hyperlinks to *Catalyst 2.0* throughout. In addition, the Web site features the first-ever Interactive Annotated Instructor's Edition, with hundreds of pop-up assignment suggestions and "Teacher to Teacher" advice as well as hyperlinks to online sources, links and suggestions for using the resources within *Catalyst 2.0,* and hyperlinks to our Partners in Teaching online resource for Teaching Composition.

Supplements for *The New McGraw-Hill Handbook*

Catalyst 2.0: A Tool for Writing and Research (www.mhhe.com/nmhh)

Throughout *The New McGraw-Hill Handbook,* Web references in the margin let students know where they can find additional resources on the text's comprehensive Web site. Access to the site—which is powered by *Catalyst 2.0,* the premier online resource for writing, research, and editing—is free with every student and instructor copy of *The New McGraw-Hill Handbook.* The site includes the following resources for students:

- A complete interactive e-book of the text
- Factiva online database with thousands of full text articles and images from periodicals and journals
- Interactive tutorials on document design and visual rhetoric
- Guides for avoiding plagiarism and evaluating sources
- Electronic writing tutors for composing informative, interpretive, and argumentative papers
- *Bibliomaker* software for the MLA, APA, Chicago, and CSE styles of documentation
- More than 4,500 grammar exercises

In addition, *Catalyst 2.0* offers writing instructors a new, state-of-the-art course management and peer review system that allows users to do the following:

- Embed comments and links contextually alongside reviewed papers
- Create and select from lists of favorite comments
- Drag and drop editing abbreviations and symbols that link to *Catalyst* grammar coverage into papers
- Create and comment on multiple drafts among groups of student reviewers
- Use instructor-created review questions to respond to drafts

Interactive Annotated Instructor's Edition
**Deborah Coxwell Teague, Florida State University and
Dan Melzer, California State University, Sacramento**
Accessible through *Catalyst,* this online interactive instructor resource will include a complete e-book of the text with the following features:

- Icons in the margins that link to pop-up suggestions for using the text in class
- Links to *Catalyst* and suggestions for using online assets in class
- Links to online resources for writing and research
- Links to the *McGraw-Hill Partners in Teaching* Web site, featuring discussion modules by dozens of the best academics on topics ranging from plagiarism to writing across the curriculum and more
- A printable version of the Instructor's Manual

The Partners in Teaching/Teaching Composition Website and Listserv
Moderated by Chris Anson, North Carolina State University
Offered by McGraw-Hill as a service to the composition community, this listserv brings together senior members of the college composition community with newer members—junior faculty, adjuncts, and teaching assistants—through an online newsletter and accompanying discussion group to address issues of pedagogy, both in theory and in practice.

The McGraw-Hill Exercise Book (ISBN 0-07-232890-8)
Santi Buscemi, Middlesex College and Susan Popham, University of Memphis
Featuring numerous sentence-level and paragraph-level editing exercises, as well as exercises in research, documentation, and the writing process, this workbook can be used for any composition course.

The McGraw-Hill Exercise Book for Multilingual Writers (ISBN 0-07-326030-4)
Maggie Sokolik, University of California, Berkeley
This workbook features numerous sentence-level and paragraph-level editing exercises tailored specifically for multilingual students.

The McGraw-Hill Writer's Journal (ISBN 0-07-326031-2)
Lynée Gaillet, Georgia State University
This elegant, spiral-bound journal for students includes quotations on writing from famous authors, as well as advice on the writing process.

The McGraw-Hill Student Planner (ISBN 0-07-322205-4)
This practical, spiral-bound date book and planner for students is organized around the academic year, offering them a handy tool to structure and plan their work. It includes a brief almanac at the back with important facts from a variety of disciplines.

Dictionary and Vocabulary Resources

Random House Webster's College Dictionary (ISBN 0-07-240011-0)
This dictionary includes over 160,000 entries and 175,000 definitions.

The Merriam-Webster Dictionary (ISBN 0-07-310057-9)
Based on the best-selling Merriam-Webster's Collegiate Dictionary, the paperback dictionary contains over 70,000 definitions.

The Merriam-Webster Thesaurus (ISBN 0-07-310067-6)
This handy paperback thesaurus contains over 157,000 synonyms, antonyms, related and contrasted words, and idioms.

Merriam-Webster's Vocabulary Builder (ISBN 0-07-310069-2)
This handy paperback introduces 3,000 words, and includes quizzes to test progress.

Merriam-Webster's Notebook Dictionary (ISBN 0-07-299091-0)
An extremely concise reference to the words that form the core of English vocabulary, this popular dictionary, conveniently designed for 3-ring binders, provides words and information at students' fingertips.

Merriam-Webster's Notebook Thesaurus (ISBN 0-07-310068-4)
Conveniently designed for 3-ring binders, this thesaurus helps the student search for words they might need today. It provides concise, clear guidance for over 157,000 word choices.

Merriam-Webster's Collegiate Dictionary and Thesaurus, Electronic Edition (ISBN 0-07-310070-6)
Available on CD-ROM, this online dictionary contains thousands of new words and meanings from all areas of human endeavor, including electronic technology, the sciences, and popular culture.

Acknowledgements

When we wrote *The New McGraw-Hill Handbook,* we started with the premise that it takes a campus to teach a writer. It is also the case that it takes a community to write a handbook. This text has been a major collaborative effort for all three of us. Over the years, that ever-widening circle of collaboration has included reviewers, editors, librarians, faculty colleagues, and family members.

Let us start close to home. Mort Maimon brought to this project his years of insight and experience as a writer and as a secondary and post-secondary English teacher. Gillian Maimon, a teacher, a Ph.D. candidate, and a writing workshop leader, and Alan Maimon, a journalist who is expert in using every resource available to writers, inspired and encouraged their mother in this project. Alan also presented a new inspiration to the second edition—first granddaughter Annabelle Elaine Maimon, who already shows promise of becoming a writer. Rudy Peritz and Lynne Haney reviewed drafts of a number of chapters, bringing to our cross-curricular mix the pedagogical and writerly perspectives of, respectively, a law professor and a sociologist. Jess Peritz, a current college student, was consulted on numerous occasions for her expert advice on making examples both up-to-date and understandable.

At Arizona State University West, Beverly Buddee, executive assistant to the provost, worried with us over this project for six years.

Our deepest gratitude goes to Lisa Kammerlocher and Dennis Isbell for the guidelines on critically evaluating Web resources in Chapter 18, as well as to Sharon Wilson. Thanks, too, go to C. J. Jeney and Cheryl Warren for providing assistance. ASU West professors Thomas McGovern and Martin Meznar shared assignments and student papers with us. In the Chancellor's office at the University of Alaska Anchorage, Denise Burger, Rosanne Kruckenburg, and Christine Tullius showed admirable support and patience.

Several colleagues at Queens College and elsewhere not only shared their insights on teaching and writing, but also gave us valuable classroom materials to use as we saw fit. Our thanks go to Fred Buell, Stuart Cochran, Nancy Comley, Ann Davison, Joan Dupre, Hugh English, Sue Goldhaber, Marci Goodman, Steve Kruger, Eric Lehman, Norman Lewis, Charles Molesworth, Beth Stickney, Amy Tucker, and Stan Walker. We are also grateful to the following faculty from other institutions who contributed valuable materials and advice: Jane Collins, Jane Hathaway, Jan Tecklin, Christine Timm, Scott, Zaluda, Diane Zannoni, and Richard Zeikowitz. The Queens College librarians gave us various kinds of help with the researching and documentation chapters, and we thank them, especially Sharon Bonk, Alexandra DeLuise, Izabella Taler, and Manny Sanudo.

We want to give special thanks to the students whose papers we include in full: Rajeev Bector, Nicholas Buglione, Diane Chen, Sam Chodoff, McKenna Doherty, Audrey Galeano, Josephine Hearn, Esther Hoffman, Carlos Jasperson, Ignacio Sanderson, and Joseph Smulowitz. We also want to acknowledge the following students who allowed us to use substantial excerpts from their work: Ilona Bouzoukashvili, Lara Deforest Baz Dreisinger, Sheila Foster, Jacob Grossman, Jennifer Koehler, Holly Musetti, and Umawattie Roopnarian.

Our thanks also go to Judy Williamson and Trent Batson for contributing their expertise on writing and computers as well as for sharing what they learned from the Epiphany Project. We also thank Rich Rice of Texas Tech for reviewing the technology coverage and for suggesting the image interpretation assignment in Chapter 14, as well as Dene Grigar of Texas Woman's University, Donna Reiss of Tidewater Community College, Cheryl Ball of Utah State University, and Elizabeth Nist of Anoka-Ramsey Community College for their advice on technology and for the chapter on multimedia assignments. We are grateful to Harvey Wiener and the late Richard Marius for their permission to draw on their explanations of grammatical points in the *McGraw-Hill Handbook*. We also appreciate the work of Andras Tapolcai, who collected many of the examples used in the documentation chapters, and the contributions of Maria Zlateva, Boston University, for her work on Part 12, A Guide for Multilingual Writers and on the For Multilingual Students boxes that appear throughout the text. Thanks to Charlotte

Smith of Adirondack Community College for her help on several sections of the book. Thanks also go to librarians Debora Person, University of Wyoming, and Ronelle K. H. Thompson, Augustana College, who provided us with helpful comments on Part 3: Researching. Our colleague Don McQuade has inspired us, advised us, and encouraged us throughout the years of this project.

Within the McGraw-Hill organization, many wonderful people have been our true teammates. Tim Julet believed in this project initially and signed us on to what has become a major life commitment. From 1999, Lisa Moore, first as executive editor for the composition list, then as publisher for English, has creatively, expertly, and tirelessly led the group of development editors and in-house experts who have helped us find the appropriate form to bring our insights as composition teachers to the widest possible group of students. We have learned a great deal from Lisa. Thanks too to Christopher Bennem, who had the challenging job of filling Lisa's shoes as sponsoring editor. This book has benefited enormously from two extraordinary development editors: Carla Samodulski, director of development for English, and David Chodoff. Both were true collaborators; as the chapters on editing show, the book has benefited enormously from their care and intelligence. Other editorial kudos go out to Cynthia Ward, whose influence can be felt throughout the book, Betty Chen for her tireless work on this project over the last two years, and to Margaret Manos, Laura Olson, James Marquand, and Meg Botteon. Thanks to Paul Banks, Todd Vaccaro, Alex Rohrs, and Manoj Mehta, without whom there would be no *Catalyst 2.0*. David Staloch, managing editor, monitored every detail of production; Cassandra Chu, senior designer, supervised every aspect of the striking text design and cover; Randy Hurst coordinated manufacturing of all components. Lori DeShazo marketing manager, and Ray Kelley, Paula Radosevich, Byron Hopkins, Lisa Berry, Audra Buchanan, and Brian Gore, field publishers, have worked tirelessly and enthusiastically to market *The New McGraw-Hill Handbook*. We also appreciate the hands-on attention of McGraw-Hill senior executives Emily Barrosse, editor-in-chief; and Steve Debow, president of the Humanities, Social Science, and Languages group.

Finally, many, many thanks go to the reviewers who read various versions of this text, generously shared their perceptions, and had confidence in us as we shaped this book to address the needs of their students.

Kirk Adams, Tarrant County College Southeast

Paul Andrews, St. John's River Community College

Sonya Bagby, State University of West Georgia

Mark Balhorn, University of Wisconsin, Stevens Point

Joseph Bizup, Columbia University

J. Blackwell, Thomas Nelson Community College

Monica Bosson, City College of San Francisco

Suzanne Britt, Meredith College

Harryette Brown, Eastfield College

Alexander Bruce, Florida Southern College

Albino Carrillo, University of Dayton

Susanna Childress, Florida State University

Margaret Clark , Florida Community College at Jacksonville

Brian Cliff, Georgia Tech

Adrian Cloete, DeVry University

Robin Colby, Meredith College

Penny Colgazier, Tulsa Community College

Genevieve Coogan, Houston Community College

Howard Cox, Angelina College

Deborah Coxwell-Teague, Florida State University

James Crawford, Walters State Community College

Carole Creekmore, Georgia Perimeter College

Gita DasBender, Seton Hall University

Rose Day, Albuquerque TVI Community College

Michel de Benedictis, Miami Dade College Kendall

William Epperson, Oral Roberts University

Caroline Fitzpatrick, Alvernia College

Lynée Lewis Gaillet, Georgia State University

Joanna Gibson, Texas A&M University

Travis Gordon, Midlands Tech College

Dene Grigar, Texas Woman's University

M. Katherine Grimes, Ferrum College

Michael Haddock, Florida Community College at Jacksonville

Joe Hardin, Western Kentucky University

Melody Hargraves, St. John's River Community College

Lory Hawkes, DeVry University

Georgina Hill, Western Michigan University

Amanda Himes, John Brown University

Jonathan Himes, John Brown University

Thomas Holmes, East Tennessee State University
Laura Jeffries, Florida Community College at Jacksonville
Carol Johnson, Tulsa Community College
Larry Juchartz, Mott Community College
Salwa Khoddam, Oklahoma City University
Peggy Kilgore, Tennessee Tech University
Craig Kleinman, City College of San Francisco
Melissa Knous, Angelina College
Mary Sue Koeppel, Florida Community College at Jacksonville
Cynthia Kuhn, Metropolitan State College of Denver
Rachel Langille, Mott Community College
Paul Matsuda, University of New Hampshire
William Matta, McLennan College
Michael Matto, Adelphi University
Shirley McBride, Collin Count, Community College
Elise McClain, St. John's River Community College
Melissa McCool, Mississippi State University
Laura McCullough, Vance Granville Community College
Patrick McMahon, Tallahassee Community College
Jeannine Morgan, St. John's River Community College
Susan Nash, Florida Community College at Jacksonville
Donna Nelson-Beene, Bowling Green State University
Elizabeth Nist, Anoka-Ramsey Community College
Sandra Offiah-Hawkins, Daytona Beach Community College
Amy Pardo, Mississippi University for Women
Matthew Parfitt, Boston University
Francisco Perez, Tarrant County College Northeast
Terry Phelps, Oklahoma City University
Susan Popham, University of Memphis
Delma Porter, McNeese State University
Brian Reeves, Tomball College
Melissa Richardson, Central Texas College
James Richey, Tyler Junior College
Peggy Ruff, DeVry University
Arvis Scott, McLennan College

Phillip Sipiora, University of South Florida
Susan Slavicz, Florida Community College at Jacksonville
Bonnie Kathryn Smith, Belmont University
Allison Smith, Middle Tennessee State University
Maggie Sokolik, University of California Berkeley
Jacqueline Thomas, University of Texas at Austin
Carla Todaro, Walters State Community College
Tammy Townsend, Jones County Junior College
Janet Turk, Lamar University
Keri Turner, Nicholls State University
Christopher Twiggs, Florida Community College at Jacksonville
William Vaughn, Central Missouri State University
Thomas Veale, United States Military Academy at West Point
Ann Westrick, Bowling Green State University
Lana A. Whited, Ferrum College
Nancy Wilson, Texas State University
Sallie Wolf, Arapahoe Community College
Margaret Wye, Rockhurst College
Maria Zlateva, Boston University

Elaine P. Maimon
Janice H. Peritz
Kathleen Blake Yancey

About the Authors

Elaine P. Maimon is Chancellor of the University of Alaska Anchorage, where she is also Professor of English. Previously she was Provost (Chief Campus Officer) at Arizona State University West and Vice President of Arizona State University as a whole. In the 1970s, she initiated and then directed the Beaver College writing-across-the-curriculum program, one of the first WAC programs in the nation. A founding Executive Board member of the National Council of Writing Program Administrators (WPA), she has directed national institutes to improve the teaching of writing and to disseminate the principles of writing across the curriculum. With a PhD in English from the University of Pennsylvania, where she later helped to create the Writing Across the University (WATU) program, she has also taught and served as an academic administrator at Haverford College, Brown University, and Queens College.

Janice Haney Peritz is an Associate Professor of English who has taught college writing for more than thirty years, first at Stanford University, where she received her PhD in 1978, and then at the University of Texas at Austin; Beaver College; and Queens College, City University of New York. From 1989 to 2002, she directed the Composition Program at Queens College where in 1996 she also initiated the College's writing-across-the-curriculum program and the English Department's involvement with the Epiphany Project and cyber-composition. She also worked with a group of CUNY colleagues to develop The Write Site, an online learning center, and more recently directed the CUNY Honors College at Queens College for three years. Currently, she is back in the English Department doing what she loves most: full-time classroom teaching of writing, literature, and culture.

Kathleen Blake Yancey is the Kellogg W. Hunt Professor of English at Florida State University. She has taught at Virginia Tech, Purdue University, the University of North Carolina at Charlotte, and Clemson University, where she held the Pearce Professorship and directed the Pearce Center for Professional Communication. In 2004 she served as Chair for the Conference on College Composition and Communication (CCCC) and has also served as President of the Council of Writing Program Administrators and as Chair of the NCTE College Forum. She is currently the Vice-President Elect of the NCTE. A co-founder and co-leader of the National Coalition on Research into Electronic Portfolios, she consults on curriculum, assessment, and portfolio efforts internationally.

The way the butterfly in this image emerges on a computer screen, as if from a cocoon of written text, suggests the way writers transform words and visuals into finished works through careful planning, drafting, revision, and design.

I like to do first drafts at night, when I'm tired, and then do the surgical work in the morning when I'm sharp.
—ALEX HALEY

Writing and Designing Papers

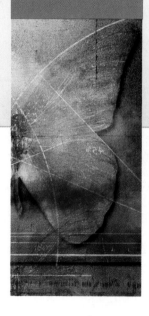

1 Learning across the Curriculum

1a Use writing to learn as you learn to write.

College is a place for exploration. During your studies, you will travel through many courses, participating in numerous conversations—oral and written—about nature, society, and culture. As you navigate your college experience, use this book as your map and guide.

- As a map, this text will help you understand the different approaches to knowledge you may encounter as you move from course to course and see how your studies relate to the larger world of learning.

- As a guide, this text will help you write everything from notes to exams to research papers—the record of your participation in the culture of your campus.

www.mhhe.com/
nmhh

For discipline-related resources, go to

Learning > Links across the Curriculum

1. Studying the world through a range of academic disciplines

Each department in your college represents a specialized territory of academic study, or area of inquiry, called a **discipline.** A discipline has its own history, terminology, and characteristic concerns. The discipline of sociology, for example, is concerned with the conditions, patterns, and problems of people in groups and societies. Sociologists collect, analyze, and interpret data about groups and societies; they also debate the data's reliability and the credibility of various interpretations. These debates occur in journals, books, conferences, and classrooms—sites where knowledge is produced and communicated.

Each discipline is composed of diverse communities or social groups. All economists do not see and say things in the same way. Although they belong to the same discipline—the discipline of economics—economists identify with various groups within their discipline based on their approaches to economic theory.

Your college curriculum is likely to include distribution requirements that will expose you to a range of disciplines. You may be asked to take one or two courses in the humanities (the disciplines of literature, music, and philosophy, for example), the social sciences (sociology, economics, and psychology, for example), and the natural sciences (physics, biology, and chemistry, for example). When you write in each disci-

CHARTING the TERRITORY

Getting the Most from a Course

When you take a course, your purpose is not just to amass information about this or that topic. Your purpose is also to understand the kinds of questions people who work in the discipline ask.

- In an art history class, for example, you might ask how a work relates to an artist's life and times.
- In a math class, you might ask what the practical applications of a particular concept are.
- In a sociology class, you might ask how race or gender relates to income.

pline—taking notes, writing papers, answering essay-exam questions—you will join the academic conversation and deepen your understanding of how knowledge is constructed. In doing so, you will be learning to see and think about the world from different vantage points.

2. Using writing as a tool for learning

One important goal of this handbook is to help you research and write your papers well. As you go from course to course, however, remember that writing itself is a great aid to learning. Travelers often keep journals and write letters to record what they have seen, heard, and done; to react to their experiences; and to reflect on the meaning of it all. Think of the way a simple shopping list aids your memory once you get to the store, or recall the last time you were asked to keep the minutes of a meeting. Because of your heightened attention, you undoubtedly knew more about what happened at that meeting than did anyone else who attended it. Writing helps you remember, understand, and create.

www.mhhe.com/
nmhh
For more on learning
in college, go to
Learning

www.mhhe.com/
nmhh
For activities to help
strengthen your use of
writing as a tool for
learning, go to
Learning > Writing
to Learn Exercises

- **Writing aids memory.** From taking class notes (*see Figure 1.1*) to jotting down ideas for later development, writing ensures that you will be able to retrieve important information. Many students find it useful to use an informal outline for lecture notes (*see the illustration on p. 4*) and then go back and fill in details after class. Write down ideas inspired by your course work—in any form or order—so that you will not forget them. These ideas can be the seeds for a research project or other critical inquiry.

- **Writing sharpens observations.** When you record what you see, hear, taste, smell, and feel, you increase the powers of

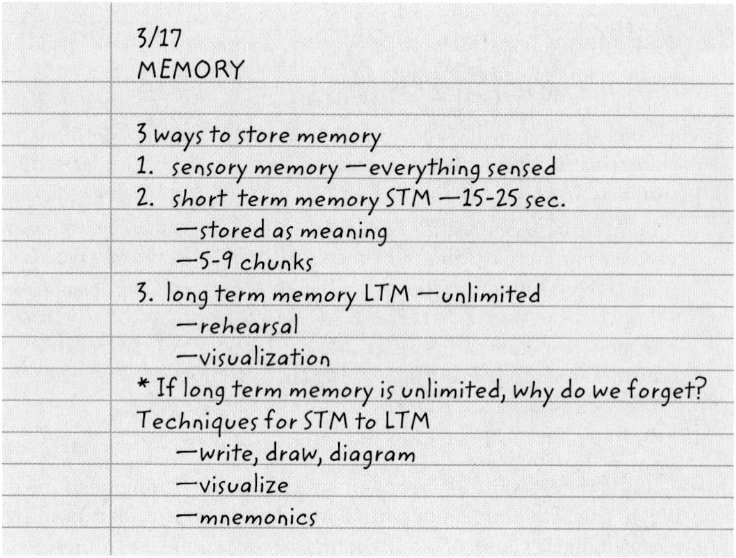

```
3/17
MEMORY

3 ways to store memory
1. sensory memory —everything sensed
2. short term memory STM —15-25 sec.
     —stored as meaning
     —5-9 chunks
3. long term memory LTM —unlimited
     —rehearsal
     —visualization
* If long term memory is unlimited, why do we forget?
Techniques for STM to LTM
     —write, draw, diagram
     —visualize
     —mnemonics
```

FIGURE 1.1 **Lecture notes.** Jotting down the main ideas of a lecture and the questions they raise helps you become a more active listener.

your senses. Write down each place where a flute is heard in a piece of music, and you will hear the instrument more clearly. Note the smells during a chemistry experiment, and you will more readily detect changes caused by reactions.

■ **Writing clarifies thought.** "How do I know what I think until I see what I say?" E. M. Forster's oft-quoted question reminds us that we frequently write our way into a topic. Writing and then carefully reading your own early drafts help you pinpoint what you really want to say. The last paragraph of a first draft often becomes the first paragraph of the next draft.

■ **Writing uncovers connections.** Maybe a character in a short story reminds you of your neighbor, or an image in a poem makes you feel sad. What is it about your neighbor that is similar to the fictional character? What is it about the poetic image that evokes memories of loss? Writing down answers to questions like these can help you learn more about the short story, and possibly more about yourself.

- **Writing improves reading.** When you read, taking notes on the main ideas and drafting a brief summary of the writer's points sharpen your reading skills and helps you retain what you have read. Writing a personal reaction to the reading enhances your understanding. (*For a detailed discussion of critical reading and writing, see Chapter 7.*)
- **Writing strengthens argument.** In the academic disciplines, an argument is not a fiery disagreement but rather a path of reasoning to a position. When you write an argument, you work out the connections between your ideas—sometimes uncovering flaws that force you to rethink your position and at other times finding new connections that make your position stronger. Writing also requires you to consider your audience and the objections they might raise. In all these cases, the process of writing challenges you to think more deeply about your positions. (*For a detailed discussion of argument, see Chapter 10.*)

3. Taking responsibility for reading, writing, and research

www.mhhe.com/nmhh
For more on study skills, go to
Learning > Study Skills Tutor

The academic community of college assumes that you are an independent learner, capable of managing your workload without supervision. For most courses, the course syllabus will be the primary guide to what is expected of you, serving as a contract between you and your instructor. It will tell you what reading you need to do in advance of each class, when tests are scheduled, and when papers or stages of papers (for example, topic and research plan, draft, and final paper) are due. Use the syllabus to map out your weekly schedule for reading, research, and writing. (*For tips on how to schedule a research paper, see Chapter 15.*)

If you are collaborating with a group on a project, it is essential to schedule a series of meetings well in advance to avoid schedule conflicts. It is just as important, however, to schedule time for your solo projects, time away from the distractions of phones, e-mail, and visitors. You will be much more efficient if you work in shorter blocks of concentrated time than if you let your reading and writing drag on for hours filled with interruptions.

4. Recognizing that writing improves with practice

Composition courses are extremely valuable in helping you learn to write at the college level, but your development as a writer does not end there. Writing in all your courses, throughout your academic career, will enable you to mature as a writer while preparing you for more writing after college.

LEARNING in COLLEGE

Dealing with Stress

Whether academic pursuits are a struggle or come easily to you, whether you are fresh out of high school or graduated years ago, college is a challenge. It helps to develop responses to the stress that often results.

- **Make flexible schedules.** Schedules help you control your time and avoid procrastination by breaking big projects into manageable bits. Be sure to leave room for the unexpected so that the schedule itself does not become a source of stress.
- **Take care of yourself.** Eating healthy food, exercising regularly, and getting plenty of sleep are well-known stress relievers. Some people find meditation to be very effective.
- **Reach out for support.** If you find it difficult to cope with stress, seek professional help. Colleges have trained counselors on staff as well as twenty-four-hour crisis lines.

Exercise 1.1 Examining a syllabus

Refer to the sample syllabus on page 7 (*Figure 1.2*) to answer the true-false questions below.

1. You can make up a missed exam for any reason. _____
2. The short papers are worth 30 percent of your final grade. _____
3. The papers can be on any topic you choose. _____
4. Late papers get partial credit. _____

1b Explore ways of learning in a multimedia world.

You are likely to register for courses through your college's Web site, conduct research on the Web, and perhaps even attend lectures in "smart classrooms" equipped to display images from the instructor's computer and DVD/VCR. In this multimedia environment, you will be dealing with images as well as spoken and written texts to a greater degree than any previous generation. Composing, too, will involve images as well as words.

1. Becoming aware of the persuasive power of images

As a student, you will be analyzing images as well as creating them. We live in a world in which images—in advertising, in politics, in books

History 1000
Survey of World History to 1500
Fall 2006

Instructor: Professor Chodoff
Office: MHB 304
Office Hours: Tuesday and Thursday, 11:00–12:00 or by
   appointment

Required Texts:
Bentley and Ziegler, *Traditions and Encounters*, Volume I, second
   edition, McGraw-Hill, 2003
Scudder, *World Civilization Reader,* Volume I, McGraw-Hill, 2003

Description: This course traces the history and interaction of the
world's civilizations from the beginning of agriculture and the
appearance of the first cities to the eve of Europe's global
expansion in the fifteenth century.

Grading and Due Dates:

	Percent of final grade	Date
Class participation	15%	
Short paper 1	15%	September 29
Midterm exam	20%	October 13
Short paper 2	15%	December 1
Final exam	35%	December 15

Short Papers: You are required to write two short (750- to 1250-
word) papers relating a primary source document from the
Scudder reader to its historical context. Late papers will not be
accepted.

Make-up Exams: Make-up exams will be scheduled only for
students who miss the scheduled exam for a documented family
or medical emergency.

FIGURE 1.2 **A sample syllabus.**

and classrooms—join with words as tools of persuasion as well as instruction. Images, like words, require careful, critical analysis. A misleading graph (*see Figure 1.3, p. 9*) or an altered photograph can easily distort your perception of a subject. The ability not only to understand visual information but also to evaluate its credibility is an essential tool for learning and writing. (*For details on evaluating visuals, see Chapter 7: Reading, Thinking, Writing, pp. 142–60.*)

Exercise 1.2   Recognizing misleading images

Conduct a Web search using the keywords "misleading images" and "misleading charts," and collect examples of three different types of misleading visuals. Be prepared to share your examples with the class.

---

2. Making effective use of multimedia elements

Technology is making it possible for you to include images and other nonverbal elements in your writing. Not too long ago, most students wrote their papers on a typewriter. If they needed to include any special notation—an equation, say, in a paper for a math or science class or a musical example in a paper for a music class—they would probably have written it out by hand on a separate sheet of paper. Including a photograph was out of the question, except perhaps as a fuzzy black-and-white photocopy on a separate page.

Computers now let you create these elements yourself or import them from other sources and place them where you want them in your writing. This passage from Beethoven's Fifth Symphony is one example:

A photo or diagram or chart can contain information that adds details, makes relationships clearer, and provides an extra dimension to the otherwise flat, printed page. In a paper for a geography course, for example, "before" and "after" photographs, like the ones on page 10 (*Figure 1.4*), can illustrate at a glance the effects of a hurricane on a coastline.

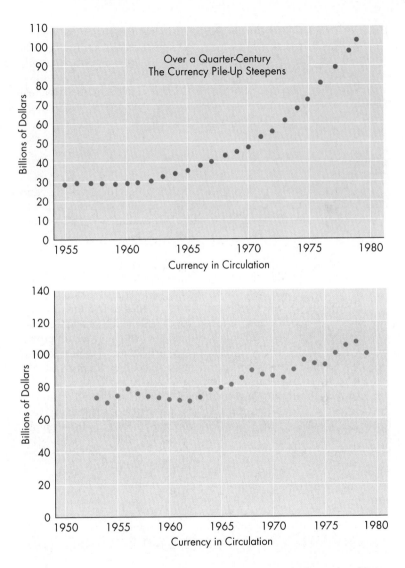

FIGURE 1.3 **A misleading graph.** The graph on top, which appeared in a 1979 article in the *Wall Street Journal,* shows a dramatic and accelerating increase in currency in circulation in the United States between 1953 and 1979. As a measure of the purchasing power of the individual Americans who held the currency, however, the graph is misleading because it fails to take inflation into account. The second graph, corrected for inflation (based on the dollar's purchasing power in 1979), reveals a generally steady but far less dramatic rate of increase.

Before Hurricane Bertha

After Hurricane Bertha

FIGURE 1.4 **The effects of a hurricane.**

A graph (*see Figure 1.5*) can effectively illustrate important trends for a history paper. A timeline, like the one in the Further Resources for Learning section at the end of this book, can help your readers grasp the relationships among important events.

If you can post your paper online or deliver it as an electronic file to be read on the computer, you can include an even greater variety

Total U.S. Resident Population 1800–1900, by decade (in thousands)

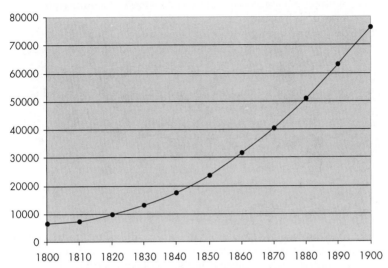

FIGURE 1.5 A line graph showing trends over time. To learn how to create a graph like this one, see Figure 17.2.

of media. You could supplement a musical passage, for example, with a link to an audio file of the passage. You could supplement a paper about political speeches for an American Government course with a link to a video clip of a politician giving a speech.

(For details on creating effective visuals, see Chapter 3: Planning and Shaping the Whole Essay, Chapter 4: Drafting Paragraphs and Visuals, and Chapter 5: Revising and Editing. For information on creating multimedia presentations, see Chapter 14: Multimedia Writing. For help with finding appropriate visuals, see Chapter 17: Finding and Designing Effective Visuals.)

www.mhhe.com/
nmhh
For an interactive tutorial on using visuals, go to

Writing > Visual Rhetoric Tutorial > Visualizing Data

Exercise 1.3 Deciding when to use visuals

1. Decide whether each of the following would be best presented as a visual, as written text, or both. For those that call for a visual, which type of visual would you use?
   a. Instructions for constructing a birdhouse
   b. An inventory of the different species of birds that appear in your yard during a one-month period

    c. A description of a songbird's call

    d. A discussion of how a bird's wings enable it to fly

    e. A proposal on ways to protect endangered songbirds from predation by cats

2. Go to the Further Resources for Learning section at the end of this book, read the entry for the term *Aristotelian* in the glossary of Selected Terms from across the Curriculum (*p. FR-18*), and note the entry for Aristotle on the Timeline of World History (*p. FR-3*). How does the timeline help you place the term in historical context? What can you learn from the timeline about significant developments in geometry, theater, physics, and religion that occurred within a few hundred years of Aristotle's lifetime?

www.mhhe.com/
nmhh
For more about
online learning
resources, go to

Additional Links
on Learning

3. Taking advantage of online and other electronic tools for learning

Technology now makes it possible to transcend the constraints of the clock, the calendar, and the car and to engage in educational activities 24/7, or twenty-four hours a day, seven days a week.

■ **E-mail.** E-mail, the medium for sending messages and document attachments over the Internet, is the common currency of the electronic frontier and the most frequently used form of written communication in the world today. In some classes, you can use e-mail to communicate with your professor, other students, or a consultant in your school's writing center. Remember, however, that although e-mail is (almost) always available, people are not. Just as your professor may schedule office hours in a campus building, she or he may tell you that you can send e-mail anytime but that you should expect an answer only during certain periods.

■ **Instant messaging.** Instant messaging (IM) allows you to engage in real-time conversations with individuals who are connected to the Internet at the same time as you. It can be used to further your learning in much the same way as e-mail, although you cannot attach papers to an IM. Instant messaging should be used sparingly in an academic setting, however. It can distract you from work you need to concentrate on and is rarely appropriate for addressing instructors.

■ **Course Web sites.** Your instructor may have a Web site for your course (*see Figure 1.6*). If so, check it for late-breaking announcements, the course syllabus, assignments (and their due dates), and course-related links as well as other Web resources.

TextConnex

Netiquette

The term *netiquette* combines the words *Internet* and *etiquette* to form a new word that stands for good manners in cyberspace. Here are some netiquette guidelines:

- **Remember that you are interacting with real humans,** not machines, and practice kindness, patience, and good humor.
- **Use accurate subject headers to indicate your topic.**
- **Limit each e-mail to a single topic,** particularly if you are sending e-mail to lists, news groups, or conferences.
- **Use words economically, and edit carefully.** Readers' eyes tire and patience evaporates when they encounter all lowercase letters or text that lacks appropriate punctuation.
- **Bear in mind that without cues such as facial expressions, body language, and vocal intonation, your message can easily be misunderstood in a virtual setting.** Be extra careful about humor that could be misread as sarcasm. Misunderstandings can escalate quickly into *flaming,* the sending of angry, inflammatory posts that use heated language.
- **Avoid ALL CAPS.** Typing in all caps is considered shouting.
- **Remember that your e-mail message can be reproduced.** Avoid saying anything you would not want attributed to you or forwarded to others.
- **Include a sufficient portion of the previous text** when responding to an e-mail, or use a dash to keep the conversation flowing and to provide context.
- **Always seek permission to use other people's ideas.** Electronic text makes sharing ideas easy. If you use another person's online thoughts or words, seek permission first, and always acknowledge the other person properly. Never forward another person's words without consent.
- **Never copy other people's words and present them as your own.** This practice, known as *plagiarism,* is always wrong. (*See Part 4: Documenting across the Curriculum, for help with citing Internet sources.*)
- **Include your name and contact information at the end of every e-mail you send.**

- **Networked classrooms and virtual classrooms.** Some colleges and instructors are experimenting with **networked classrooms**—classrooms in which each student works at one of a network of linked computers. Instructors, for example, can

13

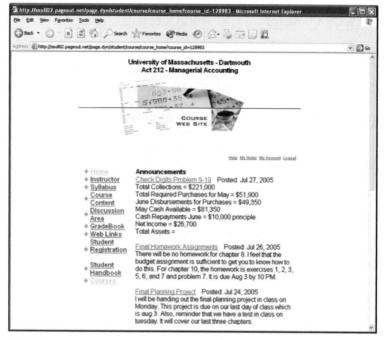

FIGURE 1.6 The home page for a course in accounting at the University of Massachusetts, Dartmouth.

post daily assignments and discussion topics, and students might be assigned to work collaboratively on a writing project. Because you are interacting in writing rather than in spoken discussion, you can more easily save ideas and comments and use them in the first draft of a paper. Online interactive class sessions also help you become more aware of audience and purpose in your writing because the audience is writing back to you and can ask you for clarifications (*see Chapter 2: Understanding Writing Assignments*). Computers and the Internet also make it possible for students to engage in distance learning—from almost anywhere in the world—in classes conducted entirely online in **virtual classrooms.**

■ **Blogs.** Weblogs (or blogs) provide another forum for online discussion and interaction. A **blog** is a personal online journal. Blog authors might post dated entries with personal commentary on a variety of topics, include links to Web sites the authors find interesting, and (sometimes) provide a way for readers to add comments of their own. Software and online services now exist that make it possible for almost anyone to create a blog.

4. Using peer review software such as *Catalyst*

E-mail, IM, networked classrooms, blogs, and many other electronic resources (such as bulletin boards and discussion groups) provide a variety of forums for you and your peers to discuss assignments and other topics that come up in your classes. These discussions can help you test ideas and clarify your thoughts as you respond to assignments and work through writing projects.

Peer review is a structured process that goes a step beyond these informal discussions. Often encouraged or required by instructors, peer review gives students the opportunity to respond to one another's work at various designated stages in the writing process, to identify and iron out problems, and to hone arguments.

Peer review is, of course, possible without computers and the Internet. Specialized software like the writing environment in the *Catalyst* Web site that accompanies this book, however, makes peer review an efficient and accessible learning tool. The *Catalyst* software permits you and the other members of your assigned peer group to make comments about one another's writing and to view and respond to those comments (*see Figure 1.7*). You can write directly into the program's own word processor, or copy and paste work from another word-processing program.

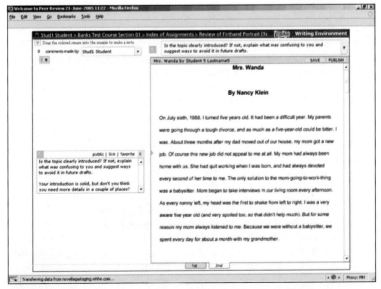

FIGURE 1.7 **A paper undergoing peer review in *Catalyst*.**

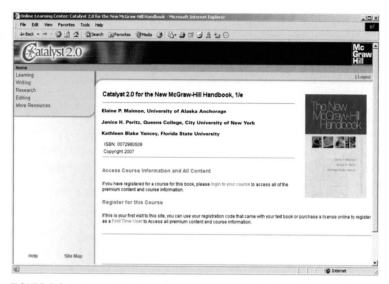

FIGURE 1.8 **The *Catalyst* student home page for *The New McGraw-Hill Handbook*.**

www.mhhe.com/
nmhh

To explore
Catalyst, go to

Home

Exercise 1.4   Using *Catalyst*

Go to *Catalyst,* the Web site that supports this text (*see Figure 1.8*). Your registration code is included with this book. Click on First Time User(s) and follow the on-screen instructions to set up your *Catalyst* account. Once you have entered the student home page (it should look like the preceding illustration), explore the site's five resource areas: Learning, Writing, Research, Editing, and More Resources. If you have a personal digital assistant (PDA), you can download a reference version of the grammar and documentation portions of this handbook from the site. Indicate where you would look for help with the following:

1. Choosing a topic to research
2. Deciding if a sentence you have written has a comma splice
3. Evaluating the source of some demographic data about your town
4. Searching for online sources for a psychology paper
5. Writing an interpretive paper about a short story
6. Developing a thesis for a paper
7. Avoiding plagiarism when you make use of sources in a research paper

1c Use strategies for learning when English is your second language.

To some extent, college presents everyone with an unfamiliar culture and its languages. The language of anthropology, for example, probably sounds strange and new to most students, including those who have been speaking English all their lives. If English is your second language (ESL) or if you are multilingual, you already have experience trying to feel at home in a new culture and working to acquire a new language.

Asking questions of your professors and others, as well as consulting guidebooks like your course textbooks, can help you orient yourself. So too can recognizing specialized vocabulary, including common English words that have a special meaning when they are used within a discipline. Like all students, you will have to engage in writing to learn and in critical reading and thinking to succeed in college.

1. Becoming aware of cultural differences in communication

If you are familiar with at least two languages and cultures, you already know that there is more than one way to interact politely and effectively with other people. In fact, you may wonder about the way people communicate in U.S. college classrooms. Your classmates may pride themselves on being direct, but you may think that they sound almost impolite in their enthusiasm to make a point. They may consider themselves to be explicit and precise; you may wonder why they are explaining things that attentive people should be able to figure out for themselves.

Colleges in the United States emphasize openly exchanging views, clearly stating opinions, and explicitly supporting judgments with examples, observations, and reasons. You may be reluctant to participate because you are worried about an "accent" or about the fine points of grammar or pronunciation. Don't worry. Communication is your first priority, so gather up your confidence and join the conversation. As a student, you are expected to do the following:

- Participate actively in small-group discussions.
- Ask and answer questions during class discussions.
- Approach instructors and fellow students outside of class when you need additional help.

2. Using writing to learn more about English

To develop your fluency in English, get into the habit of writing every day.

17

- **Write a personal journal.** Using English to explore your thoughts, feelings, and questions about your studies and your life in college will help make you feel more at home in the language.

- **Keep a writer's notebook.** Every day, write down a quotation from something you have read, and then either comment on it or put the idea into your own words. Write down bits of dialogue you overhear. Make lists of words and phrases that are new to you; many of these will turn out to be English **idioms,** words and phrases with special meanings not necessarily included in a simple dictionary definition. Go over these lists with your writing group, a friend, or a tutor in the writing center.

- **Write letters in English.** Letters are a good way to practice the informal style used in conversation. Write to out-of-town acquaintances who do not speak your first language. Write a letter to the college newspaper about some change you think needs to be made at the college or about what someone else has suggested in a letter to the editor. You can also write brief notes either on paper or through e-mail to instructors, tutors, librarians, secretaries, and other native speakers of English. Write notes to your roommates, dorm manager, repair person, and others whom you encounter on campus and off. Written communication will sometimes help you achieve your purpose more efficiently than leaving telephone messages.

www.mhhe.com/
nmhh
For access to online
dictionaries and
thesauri, go to

Dictionaries
and Thesauri

3. Using learning tools that are available for multilingual students

The style of written communication favored in U.S. colleges is often re-ferred to simply as "good writing." This handbook explains this aca-demic style and its variations. This style—which is sometimes described as analytical and argumentative—reflects the Western cultural tradi-tion, one of many traditions in the world.

The following reference books can also help you as you write pa-pers for your college courses. You can purchase them in your college's bookstore or find copies in the reference room of your college's library.

ESL dictionary   A good dictionary designed especially for second-language students can be a useful source of information about word meanings. Ordinary dictionaries frequently define difficult words with other difficult words. In the *American Heritage Dictionary,* for example, the word *haze* is defined as "atmospheric moisture, dust, smoke, and vapor suspended to form a partially opaque condition." An ESL dictionary defines it more simply as "a light mist or smoke."

Do not confuse ESL dictionaries with bilingual or "translation" dictionaries. Translation dictionaries frequently oversimplify word meanings. So too do abridged dictionaries that do not indicate shades of meaning.

Like all standard English dictionaries, an ESL dictionary includes instructions for its use. These instructions explain the abbreviations used in the entries. They also list the special notations used for words classified as slang, vulgar, informal, nonstandard, or other categories worthy of special attention. In the ESL/Learner's Edition of the Random House Webster's Dictionary of American English (1997), you will find "pig out" as the sixth entry under the word pig:

> **Pig out** (no obj) Slang. to eat too much food: *We pigged out on pizza last night.*

The entry tells you that "pig out" does not take a direct object ("no obj") and that its use is very informal ("Slang"), appropriate in talking with classmates but not in writing formal papers. You will hear a great deal of slang on your college campus, on the radio, and on TV. Make a list of slang phrases, and look them up later. If you don't find them listed in your standard or ESL dictionary, check for them in a dictionary of American slang.

The dictionary will help you with spelling, syllabication, pronunciation, definitions, word origins, and usage. The several meanings of a word are arranged first according to part of speech and then from most common to least common meaning. Examine the entry for the word academic in the ESL/Learner's Edition:

> **ac.a.dem.ic** / ˌækəˈdɛmɪk/ *adj.* **1.** (before a noun) of or relating to a school, esp. one for higher education: *an academic institution.* **2.** Of or relating to school subjects that teach general intellectual skills rather than specific job skills: *academic subjects like English and mathematics.* **3.** Not practical or directly useful: *Whether she wanted to come or not is an academic question because she's here now.*—*n.* (count) **4.** A student or teacher at a college or university —**ac'a.dem'i.cal.ly,** *adv.*

Note that nouns are identified as count or noncount, indicating whether you can place a number in front of the noun and indicate a plural. You can say "Four academics joined the group," so when *academic* is used as a noun, it is a count noun. *Honesty* is a noncount noun.

When you look up words or phrases in the dictionary, add them to your personal list. Talk the list over with classmates. They will be happy to explain particular, up-to-date uses of the words and phrases you are learning. To expand your vocabulary, consult a thesaurus for synonyms and use the most precise term.

Dictionary of American idioms As we explained earlier, an idiom is an expression that is peculiar to a particular language and cannot be understood by looking at the individual words. "To catch a bus" is an idiom.

Desk encyclopedias You will find one-volume encyclopedias on every subject from U.S. history to classical or biblical allusions in the reference room of your college's library. You may find it useful to look up people, places, and events that are new to you, especially if the person, place, or event is referred to often in U.S. culture.

Exercise 1.5 Using learning tools

Choose one of the following statements and use one of the learning tools discussed in this section to determine what any unfamiliar terms or concepts in the statement mean.

1. "Like those typical New Deal liberals, Smith wants to remake the way we do things in this hospital!"
2. "I need to get the straight dope on that situation before I can proceed."
3. "I plan to sign up for another tour of duty in the Navy."
4. "Let's not pour any more money down that rat hole."
5. "We need to protect our rights under the Fourteenth Amendment."

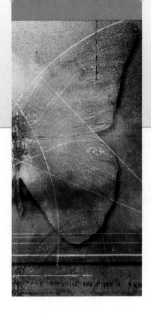

2 Understanding Writing Assignments

No matter what your course of study, writing will be an important part of your college experience. Most college courses require at least some writing. Writing assignments are designed to help you learn about a topic in a field of study and to demonstrate what you have learned. Understanding what is being asked of you as a writer is a critical ingredient in your success.

2a Recognize that writing is a process.

www.mhhe.com/
nmhh
For help with the
writing process, go to
Writing > Writing
Tutors

There may be students who dive into a new writing project with glee. For many of us, however, any excitement we may feel is tempered by anxiety. Words do not flow effortlessly from the pens—or keyboards—of even the most experienced writers. As you begin working on a paper, you will find it helpful to remember that writing is a process, a series of manageable activities that result in a finished product. Although **writing processes** vary in scope and sequence from writer to writer and assignment to assignment, the following activities should be part of every lengthy writing project:

- **Understand the assignment** (Chapter 2). Begin by analyzing the assignment so that you are clear about your **writing situation:** your topic and purpose as well as the audience you will address, the tone you will take, and the genre—or type of writing—you will produce. Examine the assignment for other important details about deadline, length, and format.

- **Generate ideas and plan your approach** (Chapter 3). Give yourself time to explore your topic, using a variety of brainstorming techniques suitable for academic papers. Decide on a working thesis that will help you focus your first draft, and sketch an informal or a formal plan for the sequence of ideas in your paper.

- **Draft paragraphs and visuals** (Chapter 4). Think about paragraph development as a way of moving your writing forward. Use various strategies such as description and comparison to develop and shape your ideas. Consider when visuals

21

Writing Skills in College and beyond

The writing that you do in college is excellent preparation for your professional life, even if you do not choose a career in academia. Business leaders say that strong writing skills are an essential component of job performance, and the amount of writing increases with job advancement. The skills you develop by responding to college writing assignments—analyzing the writing situation, gathering information, generating ideas, drafting unified and coherent paragraphs, and revising and editing with your audience in mind—will serve you well after graduation.

such as tables and graphs will be an efficient way to present data and support your ideas. After the body of your paper is drafted, take time to develop an effective introduction and conclusion.

■ **Revise, edit, and proofread** (Chapter 5). Once you have a first draft, you can develop and tailor it for your readers in one or more subsequent drafts. Analyze the overall development of your paper as it moves from paragraph to paragraph, then look at individual paragraphs, sentences, and words. Revising and editing checklists will assist you in this process.

■ **Design your document** (Chapter 6). A clear, uncluttered format will make your paper more appealing to readers. Lists and headings may help them see the structure of longer papers.

Exercise 2.1   Exploring your writing process

We can learn about ourselves as writers, about what holds us back and what motivates us, by telling the story of our writing experiences. Write a brief narrative about your own experiences as a writer. The following questions will help you get started.

1. How were you taught to write in school? Were you encouraged to explore ideas and use your imagination, or was the focus primarily on writing correct sentences? Did you struggle with writing assignments, or did they come easily to you? Have you ever written for pleasure, not just in response to a school assignment?

2. Describe the writing process you use for academic papers. Does your writing process vary according to the assignment? If so,

how? Do you engage in all the activities described in the earlier bulleted list? If not, which ones do you skip? Which activities are the most difficult for you? Why? Which are the easiest? Why?

 LEARNING in COLLEGE

Scanning Assignments

When you receive a writing assignment, scan it to make sure that you can answer the following questions:

- **How long is the paper supposed to be, and when is it due?** The length of the paper and the amount of time you are given to complete it are good indications of the importance of the assignment. For some complex or important assignments, your instructor may include due dates for progress reports or first drafts. So that you can complete your paper on time and within the specified number of pages, you may need to narrow your topic further.
- **What format is required for the assignment?** For some assignments, like a laboratory report, you must follow a conventional format. If your paper requires the use of sources, instructors generally prefer a particular style of documentation. If you are not sure which style to use, check with your instructor. (*See Part 4 on documentation styles.*)

2b Find an appropriate topic.

Many college writing assignments allow students to find a topic of interest to them within the framework of the course. The following assignment lets students choose which photographer and photographs they will write about:

ASSIGNMENT   Visit a local photography exhibit or check out the photography archives in the library. Choose one or more photographs to analyze, and discuss the role of the photographer. Consider the formal elements of the photograph(s) as well as the social context.

FIGURE 2.1 **The Web site for a photography exhibit.** Diane Chen found this Web site about Sebastião Salgado's exhibit *Migrations: Humanity in Transition.*

After locating some photography exhibits in her area, reading a few reviews of them, and exploring information about them on the Web, Diane Chen selected an exhibit called *Migrations: Humanity in Transition (Figure 2.1)* because of its relevance to her family's immigrant history. (We will follow Diane Chen's work on this paper from start to finish in the following chapters.) A topic does not need to have personal relevance to be intellectually interesting, of course. A student with an interest in science who is assigned to write about one factor in the decline of the Roman Empire might focus on the epidemics that ravaged the Roman population. Someone interested in military history might focus instead on the instability caused by a succession of military emperors who seized power by force.

1. Finding a manageable topic

To generate ideas on a subject, it helps to write about a question. To develop questions, play the "I wonder/They say/I think" game:

- **I wonder:** Taking the subject matter of the course or the assignment as your point of departure, list concepts and issues that you wonder about.

- **They say:** Reviewing your class notes, course reading, online postings to discussion groups, and scholarly bibliographies, check to see what topics and issues others in the field say are important. Jot down relevant information, ideas, and issues.

- **I think:** Choosing an item or two that you have listed, figure out what you think about it, giving your curiosity free rein. Connect your interests to what you are learning in the course.

2. Narrowing your topic

When choosing a topic to write about, you will need to consider whether it is narrow enough to fit the length of your assignment. A topic such as Thomas Jefferson's presidency would be appropriate for a book-length treatment but could not be covered in adequate detail in an essay. Narrowing the topic allows you to make the assignment your own as you tailor it to your intellectual interests. Consider the following examples:

BROAD TOPICS	NARROW TOPICS
Sports injuries	The most common types of field injuries in soccer and how to administer emergency care
Reading problems	Approaches to treating dyslexia in middle-school students
"A Modest Proposal" by Jonathan Swift	Satire of English attitudes toward the Irish in Jonathan Swift's "A Modest Proposal"

The following strategy can help you narrow your subject area:

1. Think of a specific question, browsing through course texts and your class notes to get ideas. To make a question more specific, use the "five *w*'s and an *h*" strategy by asking about the *who, what, why, when, where,* and *how* of a topic (*see Chapter 3, p. 39*).

2. Make sure that you are posing a challenging question that will interest your readers. If a question can be answered with a simple yes or no, a dictionary-like definition, or the kind of

25

presentation you would find in a textbook, you should rework it or choose another question.

3. Speculate about the answer to your question, which will give you a hypothesis to work with during the research process. A **hypothesis** is a speculation, or guess, that must be tested and revised as you explore your topic.

Exercise 2.2 Narrowing a topic

Narrow the topics below so that they would be appropriate for a paper of approximately ten double-spaced pages.

1. For a course in criminal justice: crime-prevention programs
2. For a psychology course: studies on memory
3. For a nutrition course: obesity in the United States
4. For a film course: filmmaking in the 1990s
5. For a history course: Civil War battles

2c Be clear about the purpose of your assignment.

If your instructor has provided a written description of the assignment, look for key terms that might give you a clue about its **purpose.** Are you expected to inform, interpret, or argue? Each of these purposes is linked to a common writing assignment found in many different disciplines.

- In an **informative report,** the writer's purpose is to pass on what he or she has learned about a topic or issue. The following terms are often associated with the task of informing:

  Classify
  Illustrate
  Report
  Survey

  EXAMPLE   A psychology student might *survey* recent research on the topic of the effects on adolescents of violence in computer games.

  EXAMPLE   A business major might *illustrate* the theory of supply-side economics with an example from recent history.

CHARTING the TERRITORY

Posing Discipline-Specific Questions

The particular course you are taking defines a range of questions that are appropriate within a given discipline. Here are examples of the way your course would help define the questions you might ask if, for example, you were writing about Thomas Jefferson:

U.S. history: How did Jefferson's ownership of slaves affect his public stance on slavery?

Political science: To what extent did Jefferson's conflict with the courts redefine the balance of power among the three branches of government?

Art history: What architectural influences do you see at work in Jefferson's design for his home at Monticello?

- **Interpretive analyses** explore the meaning of written documents, cultural artifacts, social situations, and natural events. The following terms are likely to appear when the purpose is interpreting:

Analyze
Compare
Explain
Reflect

EXAMPLE A philosophy student might *explain* the allegory of the cave in Plato's *Republic*.

EXAMPLE A science student might *analyze* satellite images in order to make weather predictions.

- **Arguments** are valued in all fields of study. An argument proves a point or supports an opinion through logic and concrete evidence. The following terms usually indicate that the purpose of a paper is to argue a position:

Agree
Assess
Defend
Refute

EXAMPLE A political science student might *defend* the electoral college system.

EXAMPLE A nutrition student might *refute* the claims of low-carb weight-loss diets.

27

CHARTING the TERRITORY

Writing to Express: Personal Essays

Another purpose for writing is to express thoughts on and feelings about personal experiences. Your first writing assignment for college—the essay required by the Admissions Department as part of your college application form—probably had this purpose. The personal essay is one of the most literary kinds of writing. Not surprisingly, therefore, personal essays are most frequently assigned in English composition courses. (*For more on personal essays and writing with an expressive purpose, see Chapter 11, pp. 237–41.*)

Exercise 2.3 Identifying the purpose

For each of the following assignments, state whether the primary task is to inform, interpret, or argue a position.

1. Defend or refute the claim that the colonies would inevitably have declared independence no matter how Britain had responded to their demands.
2. Explain the Declaration of Independence as a product of the European Enlightenment.
3. Survey and classify the variety of ways in which Americans responded to the Declaration of Independence and the outbreak of the Revolutionary War.

2d Use the appropriate genre.

Genre simply means kind of writing. Poems, stories, and plays are genres of literature, and audiences have different expectations for each. Most of the writing you will be asked to produce in college will be nonfiction, that is, writing about real events, people, and things for the purpose of argument, information, or interpretation. Within nonfiction, however, there are many additional genres of writing. You encounter some genres, such as letters, brochures, and Web sites, in your everyday life. Others, such as case studies, lab reports, or literary analyses, you will typically encounter for the first time in college. Different genres of writing predominate in different disciplines. Some types of writing, like the case study, are common in a particular field such as sociology, but not in all disciplines across the curriculum. Understanding the genre that an assignment calls for is an important step in successfully fulfilling it. If you are supposed to be writing a description of a snake for a field guide, you will not be successful if you write a poem—even a very good poem—about a snake.

Some Common Genres of Writing

Letters	Profiles	Brochures
Memoirs	Proposals	Oral presentations
Essays	Instructions	Web sites
Reviews	Reports	

Sometimes an assignment will specify the genre you are expected to produce. For example, you may be asked to write a report (an informative genre), a comparative analysis (an interpretive genre), or a critique (an argumentative genre). In other instances you might be asked to select the genre yourself. If so, give careful consideration to the advantages and disadvantages that each genre offers. Make sure the one you choose—whether it be a Web site, a multimedia presentation, or a researched essay—is appropriate to the purpose of your writing assignment.

Frequently, you will find that a particular genre has very specific conventions for formatting and design. If you are writing a typical academic research paper, for instance, you will have to follow the formatting requirements of the documentation style you use for that project. Whether you need to follow the style recommended by the Modern Language Assocation (MLA), the American Psychological Association (APA), the editors of *The Chicago Manual of Style,* the Council of Science Editors (CSE), or some other authority will depend largely on the discipline you are writing for. Your instructor will typically let you know which style you should use. You can find coverage of the MLA, APA, Chicago, and CSE styles in Part 4: Documenting across the Curriculum. *(For more on when to use a specific documentation style for a discipline, see Chapter 22: Writing the Paper, pp. 368–72.)*

If you are unfamiliar with the conventions of a particular genre, seek out examples from your instructor or college writing center. Many genres of academic writing are covered in Part 2: Common Assignments across the Curriculum; additional genres are covered in Part 5: Writing beyond College.

2e Ask questions about your audience.

Whether we realize it or not, most of us are experts at adjusting what we say to suit the audience we are addressing. In everyday conversation, for example, your description of a car accident would be different if you were talking to a young child instead of an adult. When you

Purposes and Genres

The common purposes of academic writing are also the common purposes for most genres of communication that you will encounter outside of college. (*See Part 5: Writing beyond College.*)

- A blog presents an individual's interpretation of world events.
- A brochure can inform its reader about a particular subject.
- A grant proposal argues for an allocation of funds or other resources.

write informally to friends and family, you add and subtract details, adjust your word choice, and make decisions about content appropriateness based on your understanding of your audience. For most college assignments, however, the situation is more complex. Your instructor is your primary audience, but he or she also represents a larger group of readers who have an interest or stake in your topic. Here are two questions to ask about your audience:

1. **Are your readers specialists, or are they a general audience?** How much prior knowledge and specialized vocabulary can you assume your audience has? An education professor, for example, might ask you to write for a general audience of your students' parents or your community board. You can assume that they have a general knowledge of your subject, such as might be gained by watching TV news reports or reading the local newspaper, but that you will need to explain concepts such as "authentic assessment" or "content standards." If you were writing a paper to present to a specialist audience of school principals or educational psychology researchers, you would not need to define these common terms from within the discipline.

   Consider, for example, how audience accounts for the differences in these two passages about snakes:

   > Many people become discouraged by the challenge of caring for a snake which just grows and grows and grows. Giant pythons can get bigger than their owners, eat bunnies, and need large cages, plus it's hard to find pet sitters for them when you go out of town.

   > —DANA PAYNE, Woodland Park Zoo Web Site

The skull of *Python m. bivittatus* is very highly ossified, with dense bone and complex sutures. Like other snakes, it has lost the upper temporal bar, jugal, squamosal, and epipterygoid. A bony interorbital septum is present.

—SUSAN EVAN, NSF Digital Library at UT Austin

The first passage, written for a general audience, gives practical advice in simple, nontechnical language and with a humorous tone. The second passage focuses on physical details of primary interest to other scientists who study snakes and uses technical language and a serious tone.

2. **Are the demographics** (age, gender, sexual orientation, race, ethnicity, cultural background, religion, group membership) **of your audience relevant to your presentation?** What experiences, assumptions, interests, opinions, and attitudes might your audience members have in common? Will any of your ideas be controversial with them? Especially when you are writing an argument, this kind of background information may be helpful so that you can build rapport with your audience and anticipate any objections they may have. In some high-stakes situations, writers may interview representatives of their potential audience or gather information about them using questionnaires. More typically, writers use peer review to gauge audience reactions and make adjustments (*see Learning in College: An Audience of Your Peers on p. 32*).

2f Determine the appropriate tone.

When you speak, you use your voice to register tone. The sentence "I am surprised at you" could express anger, excitement, or disappointment depending on your tone of voice. In writing, content, style, and word choice communicate **tone.**

Consider the differences in tone in the following passages on the subject of a cafeteria makeover:

SARCASTIC "I am special," the poster headline under the smirking face announces. Well, good for you. And I'm specially glad that cafeteria prices are up because so much money was spent on motivational signs and new paint colors that could make you lose your lunch.

SERIOUS Although the new colors in the cafeteria are electric and clashing, color in general

Tips

LEARNING in COLLEGE

An Audience of Your Peers

In some courses, you may have the opportunity to get feedback on your drafts from a peer audience—other classmates with similar levels of expertise in the course content. Getting responses to a paper from classmates gives you the chance to test your writing with a real audience before you finalize it. Comments from readers can help you see where passages are unclear, paragraphs need more detail, and sentences delight or offend. You will find that audiences are not monolithic: opinions vary; individuals react to and notice different things. Although you may not be able to respond to each classmate's critique, you should look for recurring comments and common themes among the responses. You may want to address those issues before submitting your paper to its final audience.

does brighten the space and distinguish it from the classrooms. The motivational posters didn't inspire students; instead, many students mocked them, so the manager took them down.

The tone in the first passage is sarcastic. It is obviously intended for other students. An audience of, say, school administrators probably would not appreciate the slang or the humor. The second passage is more serious and respectful in tone while still offering a critique.

For most college writing, your tone should reflect seriousness about the subject matter and purpose, as well as respect for your readers. You can indicate your seriousness by stating information accurately, presenting reasonable arguments and interpretations, dealing fairly with opposing views, and citing sources for your ideas. Unless you are writing a personal essay, the topic, not yourself or your feelings, should be the center of attention.

Writing with seriousness and authority does not mean being condescending or pompous to readers, as in the following examples:

CONDESCENDING   Along with many opportunities, obstacles exist that have restricted the amount of foreign direct investment, as I already explained to you.

POMPOUS   It behooves investors to cogitate over the momentousness of their determinations.

These sentences use a more appropriate tone for college writing:

APPROPRIATE   Along with many opportunities, obstacles exist that have restricted the amount of foreign direct investment, as noted earlier.

APPROPRIATE   Investors should consider the consequences of their decisions.

(For more on appropriate language, see Chapter 48.)

Exercise 2.4 Analyzing audience and tone

Find an article from one of the following sources, and rewrite a paragraph in the article for the specified audience.

1. An article on a diet or exercise that appears in a magazine for teenagers (30- to 40-year-old adults)
2. An article on a celebrity's court trial that appears in a supermarket tabloid (the audience of a highly respected newspaper such as the *New York Times* or the *Wall Street Journal*)
3. A discussion of clinical depression from a psychology journal (your classmates)

2g Meet early to discuss coauthored projects.

A project is coauthored when more than one person is responsible for producing it. In many fields, such **collaborative writing** is essential. Here are some suggestions to help you make the most of this challenge:

- Working with your partners, decide on some ground rules, including meeting times, deadlines, and ways of reconciling differences. Will the majority rule, or will you make decisions in some other way? Is there an interested and respected third party who can be consulted if the group's dynamics break down?

- Divide the work fairly so that everyone has a part to contribute to the project. Keep in mind that each group member should do some researching, drafting, revising, and editing.

- In your personal journal, record, analyze, and evaluate the intellectual and interpersonal workings of the group as you see and experience them. If the group's dynamics begin to break down, seek the assistance of a third party.

LEARNING in COLLEGE

For Coauthoring Online

Computer networks make it easier for two or more writers to co-author texts. With e-mail, you can preserve your individual contributions to the final paper and, if need be, share them with your instructor. You will also have a record of how the piece developed and how well you and your coauthor(s) worked as a team.

2h Gather the tools you need to get started.

Along with access to a good library and a quiet place to think, you should have the following resources when you get started on a paper.

1. For researching and composing, you will need **access to a computer with a word-processing program** that includes spelling and grammar checkers. Note, however, that spelling and grammar checkers are useful for flagging words or passages that might be incorrect, but they are no substitute for careful proofreading. See the Grammar Checker boxes in the editing chapters (*Parts 6 through 11*) for details on the limitations of these programs. For many assignments, you will also need **access to the Internet,** as well as the **ability to handle graphics.**

2. **A college desk dictionary and a thesaurus** will help you find, pronounce, and spell the words you will need to make your writing more precise, compelling, and evocative. Chapter 47: Dictionaries and Vocabulary explores these essential tools in greater depth.

3. Keep **this handbook** nearby to help with researching, generating ideas, drafting, designing, and revising. Use the index to look up answers to questions about grammar, usage, style, punctuation, and mechanics that may come up as you are editing.

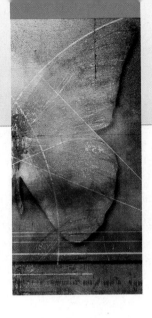

3 Planning and Shaping the Whole Essay

Writing helps you discover new ideas and connect them to other ideas and to what you already know. This chapter will help you get started on writing the first draft of your essay. It offers strategies for exploring your topic, developing a thesis, and planning a preliminary structure for your paper. These strategies are useful at the beginning of the writing process, but you may also need to return to them at a later stage of your project, especially if you find yourself staring at a blank screen. Writing is a messy business, and planning, drafting, revising, and designing rarely proceed in a straight line; writers often need to circle back to an earlier stage.

3a Explore your ideas.

www.mhhe.com/nmhh
For help generating ideas, go to
Writing >
Paragraph/Essay
Development >
Prewriting

The following strategies, sometimes called **invention techniques** or **prewriting activities,** are designed to get you thinking and writing about your topic. Remember that what you write at this stage is for your eyes only—no one will be judging your work. You can do much of your exploratory writing in a **journal,** which is simply a place to record your thoughts on a routine basis. (*For more on journals see p. 41.*) Your class notes constitute a type of academic journal, as do the notes you take on your reading and research.

As you explore, turn off your internal critic and generate as much material as possible. Later you can select the best ideas from what you produce.

1. Reviewing your notes and annotations

If your assignment involves reading one or more texts or researching multiple sources, review your notes and annotations. (*For details on annotating, see Chapter 7. For details on researching and keeping a research journal, see Chapter 21.*) If you are writing about something you have observed, review any notes or sketches you have made (*see Figure 3.1*). These immediate comments and reactions are one of your best sources for ideas. Look for patterns.

CHECKLIST

Activities for Exploring Your Ideas

☐ 1. Review your notes and annotations.

☐ 2. Freewrite.

☐ 3. List.

☐ 4. Cluster.

☐ 5. Question.

☐ 6. Keep a journal.

☐ 7. Browse in the library.

☐ 8. Search the Internet.

☐ 9. Exchange ideas.

FIGURE 3.1 Sketching to record observations. Diane Chen sketched this drawing of the photograph she planned to write about. The sketch helped her see elements of the photograph more clearly.

CHARTING the TERRITORY

Varieties of Notes

The writing that you do as you gather information about your topic will help you develop your observational skills within the context of different disciplines. Here are some examples of the different kinds of notes you might take for courses in three different disciplines:

- **For a paper on conflict resolution** among four-year-olds for a course in human development, you observe and record the play activities of one child during several play periods in a preschool class. Your careful written observations will help you understand principles in the course text and may later contribute to a case study (*see Chapter 11*).

- **For an article on journalistic styles** for a news reporting class, you read an account of the same event in the *New York Times,* the *Arizona Republic,* and *Time* magazine, annotating each with notes on its style and point of view. Analyzing the treatment of the same story in different publications will help you identify stylistic differences.

- **For a review of a play** for a theater course, you take notes on the set, lighting, costumes, makeup, and acting as well as on the characters, dialogue, and action of the play. You use these notes to think about the choices made by the play's director and company.

2. Freewriting

To figure out what you are thinking, try **freewriting.** Just write whatever occurs to you about a topic. If nothing comes to mind, then write "nothing comes to mind" until something else occurs to you. The trick is to keep pushing forward without stopping. It is especially important not to worry about spelling, punctuation, or grammar rules as you freewrite. Your objective is to explore ideas freely and to "loosen up" in the same way that a jogger might perform stretches before a long run. Usually, you will discover some implicit point in your seemingly random writing.

Once you have some ideas down on paper, you might try doing some **focused freewriting.** When you do focused freewriting, you begin with a point or a specific question. You might explore more deeply one of the ideas or questions that you discovered while freewriting. The following is a portion of Diane Chen's freewriting about her photography paper:

> I want to talk about what it's like to look at all these pictures of people suffering, but to also admire how beautifully the photographs have been composed. Those two things feel like they shouldn't go together. But it's also what makes the photographs so great—because you're feeling two different emotions at the same time. It makes it harder to stop looking at what it is he's trying to show us.

Looking at Diane Chen's focused freewriting, you can see ideas beginning to take shape that she might be able to use in her paper. She needed several sessions of general freewriting, however, before she was able to reach this point.

3. Listing

Another strategy is to **brainstorm** by starting with a topic and listing the words, phrases, images, and ideas that come to mind. Later, you can review this list and highlight the items you would like to explore. When you brainstorm in this way, try to be as exhaustive as you can. Don't worry about whether the individual thoughts or ideas are "right." Just get them down on paper or into an electronic file.

Once you have composed a fairly lengthy list, go through it looking for patterns and connections. If you have written your list on paper, highlight or connect related ideas. If you have typed them into a document, group related material together. Move apparently extraneous material or ideas to the end of the list or to a separate page.

After you have sorted through the items in your list, zero in on the areas of most interest, and add any new ideas that occur to you. Arrange the items into main points and subpoints if necessary. Later, this material may form the basis of an outline for your paper.

Here is part of a list that Diane Chen produced for her paper about a photography exhibit:

Migrations—still photographs, dynamic subject
why migrate/emigrate?

my family—hope of a better life
fear & doubt in new places; uprooting
beautiful photos but horrible reality
Salgado as photojournalist
black & white pictures
strong vertical & horizontal lines
lighting choices are meaningful

4. Clustering

Having something down in writing enables you to look for categories and connections. **Clustering,** sometimes called **mapping,** is a brainstorming technique that generates categories and connections from the beginning. To make an idea cluster, do the following:

- Write your topic in the center of a piece of paper, and draw a circle around it.
- Surround the topic with subtopics that interest you. Circle each, and draw a line from it to the center circle.
- Brainstorm more ideas. As you do so, connect each one to a subtopic already on the sheet, or make it a new subtopic of its own.

As she explored her ideas about the Salgado exhibit, Diane Chen prepared the cluster that appears in Figure 3.2 on the next page.

5. Questioning

Asking questions is a good way to explore a topic further. The journalist's five *w*'s and an *h* (*who? what? where? when? why?* and *how?*) can help you find specific ideas and details. For example, here are some questions that would apply to the photography exhibit:

- Who is the photographer, who are his subjects, and who is his audience?
- What is the photographer's attitude toward his subjects?
- Where were these pictures shot and first published?
- When did these events take place?
- Why are the people in these pictures migrating?
- How did I react to these images?

Other questioning techniques include the following:

- Looking at a topic dramatically, as an action (*what*) with actors (*who*), a scene (*where*), means (*how*), and purpose (*why*)

39

FIGURE 3.2 Diane Chen's cluster about the Salgado exhibit.

- Looking at a topic as a static thing—a particle—that has its own distinguishing features and parts, as a wave that changes over time, and as a field that operates as a system

STATIC THING   What facial expressions do the people in the photographs have? Are they standing alone or in groups? What are they carrying or holding?

WAVE   What changes take place in refugees and immigrants over time? Do refugees lose their sense of belonging even after they are allowed to return home? What are the differences between first-generation immigrants and the children that are born and raised in the adopted country?

FIELD   How do refugees and immigrants affect the country they migrate to? How are they treated by members of the new society? How should they be treated?

For other questioning ideas, take note of the problems or questions your professor poses to get class discussion going. If you are using a textbook in your course, check out the study questions.

CHARTING the TERRITORY

Different Questions Lead to Different Answers

Always consider what questions make the most sense in the context of the course you are taking. Scholars in different disciplines pose questions related to their fields.

- **Sociology:** A sociologist might ask questions about the ways recent immigrants interact with more established immigrants from the same country.
- **History:** A historian might ask how and why immigration to the United States has changed over the past century.
- **Economics:** An economist might wonder what effect refugees have on the economy of their host country.

TEXTCONNEX

Electronic Journals

A journal need not be a fancy leatherbound book; in fact, it need not be a book at all. You can use the notes section of a personal digital assistant (PDA) to jot down your thoughts, and a word-processing file works well for longer journal entries. Be sure to label your files so that you can retrieve and review your entries quickly. For a PDA such as a Palm, consider creating a new category called Academic Journal in the Note Pad.

6. Keeping a journal

As noted, you can record your notes and ideas in a journal (*see Figure 3.3*). However, you may find it helpful to go beyond note taking and start recording ideas and questions inspired by your classes or your exploratory writing. For example, you might write about connections between what has happened in your personal life and your academic subjects, connections among your subjects, or ideas touched on in class that you would like to know more about. Jotting down one or two thoughts at the end of class and taking a few minutes later in the day to explore those ideas at greater length will help you build a store of essay ideas.

> Prof. says some Civil War photographers posed the corpses on the battleground. Does that change the meaning or value of their work? Did their audiences know they did this, and if so, what did they think of the practice?

41

FIGURE 3.3 Leonardo's notebook. The Renaissance artist, scientist, and inventor Leonardo da Vinci filled more than a thousand pages with observations and illustrations. Scholars believe that his original intention was to gather material for a paper on mechanics.

For MULTILINGUAL STUDENTS

Private Writing in English

Multilingual students can also use a journal to develop fluency in thinking and writing in English. Keep in mind that no one will be correcting your work, so you can focus on writing as much as possible. You can also use your journal to collect and comment on idioms and to express your thoughts on your experience as a multilingual student.

Exercise 3.1   Keeping an academic journal

Start a print or electronic journal and write in it daily for at least two weeks. Using your course work as a springboard, record anything that comes to mind, including personal reactions and memories. At the end of the two weeks, reread your journal and write about the journal-keeping experience. Does your journal contain any ideas or information that might be useful for the papers you are writing? Has the journal helped you gain any insight into your courses or your life as a student?

7. Browsing in the library

Your college library is filled with ideas—and it can provide inspiration when you need to come up with your own. Sometimes it helps to take a break: leave your study carrel, stretch your legs, and browse the bookshelves.

8. Searching the Internet

Exploring a subject on the World Wide Web is the electronic equivalent of browsing in the library. Type keywords related to your topic into a search engine such as *Google,* and visit several sites on the list that results. (*See Chapter 16: Finding and Managing Print and Online Sources, pp. 295–312.*) When Diane Chen searched *Google* using the keywords "Salgado" and "migrations," for example, she got the results in Figure 3.4.

FIGURE 3.4 Initial results of an Internet search. This screen shows the first six results of Diane Chen's search on *Google.*

9. Exchanging ideas in person or online

If you read the acknowledgments in the books on your shelves, you will see that writing is a social activity. Most authors thank family members, editors, librarians, and colleagues for help on work in progress. Likewise, you should welcome opportunities to talk about your writing with your classmates, friends, and family.

- Brainstorm within your peer response group, if your instructor has set up such groups. Come prepared with ideas and information on your topic to get the discussion started.

- Seek out students who have taken the course in previous semesters and discuss with them their approaches to writing assignments.

- Find out if your college has a writing center that welcomes students for discussions of work in progress.

The online tools that are available to writers offer another way for you to collaborate with others on your papers. Discuss your assignments by exchanging e-mail. Especially if your course has a class Web site, you might exchange ideas in chat rooms. Other options for exploring your topic and gathering ideas include instant messaging (IM) and virtual environments.

Writing e-mail　When you work on papers with classmates, you can use e-mail in the following ways:

- To check out your understanding of the assignment
- To try out various topics
- To ask each other useful questions about ideas
- To share your freewriting, listing, and other exploratory writing
- To respond to each other's ideas, including requests for clarification and additional information

Chatting with each other about ideas　You can also use online chats as well as other virtual spaces to share ideas. Your instructor may include **chat room** activities, where you go into virtual rooms to work on assignments in small groups or visit and interact with other classes at other colleges. Some people find that chatting in such virtual rooms, or synchronous spaces, prompts them to become more creative. In the exchange in Figure 3.5, for example, two students share ideas about work.

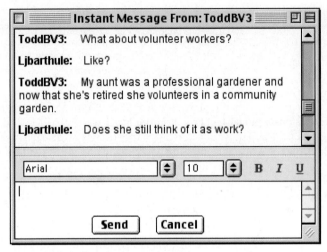

FIGURE 3.5 Exchanging ideas in an online chat.

Exercise 3.2   Generating ideas

Most people do not use all of the invention techniques described in the preceding section when they begin a paper. However, you can take this opportunity to experiment with these techniques to see which of them work best for you. For a paper that you are currently writing or a topic you are interested in, apply the following techniques to brainstorm about your topic: listing, clustering, freewriting, questioning, and searching the Internet or browsing in the library. Be sure to put your responses in writing, even if your instructor will not be reading your work. If possible, exchange ideas with classmates, either in person or online.

3b   Decide on a thesis.

The **thesis** is the central idea of your paper. It needs to communicate a specific point about your topic and suit the purpose of the assignment. As you explore your topic, ideas for your thesis will begin to emerge. You can focus these ideas by drafting a preliminary, or working, **thesis statement,** which can be one or more sentences long. A preliminary thesis is just that: preliminary. As you draft and revise your paper, you may revise or even change your thesis several times. Nonetheless, having a strong thesis statement will help you get started on your first draft.

www.mhhe.com/
nmhh
For help with developing a thesis, go to
Writing >
Paragraph/Essay Development >
Thesis/Central Idea

45

CHECKLIST

A Strong Thesis

A strong thesis does the following:

- [ ] 1. It fits the purpose of the assignment.

- [ ] 2. It makes a specific point about the topic and gives readers a sense of the direction of your paper.

- [ ] 3. It asserts something that could make a difference in what readers know, understand, or believe.

1. Making sure your thesis fits the purpose of the assignment

All theses are argumentative in the sense that they make an assertion. A thesis for an argument takes a clear position on an issue or recommends an action. A thesis for an informative or interpretive paper often previews the paper's content or expresses the writer's insight into the topic. If your purpose is to analyze a short story, for example, a one-sentence summary of the plot or the author's biography will not work as a thesis. If you are asked to write an informative paper detailing the factors behind large-scale population migrations in the 1990s, your thesis should not state your position on immigration reform. (*For information on assignment purposes, see 2c, p. 26.*)

THESIS TO INFORM	The exhibit *Migrations* offers images of the world's poor people.
THESIS TO INTERPRET	Sebastião Salgado's photographs ask us to understand the pain and suffering that refugees experience.
THESIS TO ARGUE	Military intervention by the United States and other nations can prevent further increases in the number of refugees.

2. Making sure that your thesis is specific

Vague theses usually lead to weak, unfocused papers. Watch out in particular for thesis statements that simply announce your topic, state an obvious fact about it, or offer a general observation:

ANNOUNCEMENT	I will discuss the photography exhibit *Migrations* by Sebastião Salgado. [*What is the writer's point about the photography exhibit?*]
STATEMENT OF FACT	The exhibit of photographs by Sebastião Salgado is about people in migration. [*This thesis gives us information about the exhibit, but it does not make a specific point about it.*]
GENERAL OBSERVATION	Sebastião Salgado's photographs of people in migration are beautiful and informative. [*Although this thesis makes a point about the photographs, the point could apply to many photographs. What makes these photographs special?*]

By contrast, a specific thesis signals a focused, well-developed paper.

SPECIFIC	Like a photojournalist, Salgado brings us images of newsworthy events, but he goes beyond objective reporting, imparting his compassion for refugees and migrants to the viewer.

In this example, the thesis expresses the writer's particular point—Salgado's intention to move the viewer.

Note: A thesis statement can be longer than one sentence (if necessary) to provide a framework for your main idea. All of the sentences taken together, though, should build to one specific, significant point that fits the purpose of your assignment. (Some instructors may prefer that you limit your thesis statements to one sentence.)

---

3. Making sure your thesis is significant

A significant thesis makes an assertion that could potentially change what readers know, understand, or believe. Chances are that what makes a difference to you will also make a difference to your readers. When you are looking for possible theses, be sure to challenge yourself to develop one that you care about.

Exercise 3.2 Evaluating thesis statements

Evaluate the thesis statements that accompany each of the following assignments. If the thesis statement is inappropriate or weak, explain why and suggest how it could be stronger.

1. *Assignment:* For a social ethics course, find an essay by a philosopher on a contemporary social issue, and argue either for or against the writer's position.
   Thesis: In "Active and Passive Euthanasia," James Rachels argues against the standard view that voluntary euthanasia is always wrong.
2. *Assignment:* For an economics course, find an essay on the gap between rich and poor in the United States, and argue either for or against the writer's position.
   Thesis: George Will's argument that economic inequality is healthy for the United States depends on two false analogies.
3. *Assignment:* For a nutrition course, report on recent research on an herbal supplement.
   Thesis: Although several researchers believe that echinacea supplements may help reduce the duration of a cold, all agree that the quality and the content of these supplements vary widely.
4. *Assignment:* For a literature course, analyze the significance of setting in a short story.
   Thesis: William Faulkner's "A Rose for Emily" is set in the fictional town of Jefferson, Mississippi, a once-elegant town that is in decline.
5. *Assignment:* For a history course, describe the factors that led to the fall of the Acheamenid Empire.
   Thesis: Goverments that attempt to build far-flung empires will suffer the same fate as the Achaemenids.

Exercise 3.3 Thinking about your own thesis statements

Identify the thesis statements in two of your recent papers, and evaluate how well they meet the criteria for thesis statements given in the checklist on page 46. Freewrite about the process of arriving at a thesis in those papers: Did you start drafting your paper with a preliminary thesis? If not, do you think that having a working thesis would have made it easier or harder to produce a first draft? At what point did you arrive at the final thesis? Did your thesis change over the course of several drafts?

LEARNING in COLLEGE

Finding a Thesis through Questioning

It may help to think of the thesis as an answer to a question. In each of the following three examples, the topic of the thesis is in italics and the assertion about that topic is underlined.

QUESTION	What makes a photograph significant?
THESIS	*The significance of a photograph* <u>depends on both its formal and its documentary features.</u>
QUESTION	What did Alfred Stieglitz contribute to the art of photography?
THESIS	*Alfred Stieglitz's struggle to promote photography as an art* <u>involved starting a journal, opening a gallery, and making common cause with avant-garde modernist artists.</u>
QUESTION	Is Susan Sontag right that photography obstructs critical thinking?
THESIS	*Susan Sontag's critique of photography* <u>is unconvincing, partly because it assumes that most people are visually unsophisticated and thoughtlessly voyeuristic.</u>

3c Plan a structure that suits your assignment.

Many writers feel that they are more efficient when they know in advance how to develop their thesis and where to fit the information they have gathered. For some, that means organizing their notes into a sequence that makes sense. Others prefer to sketch out a list of ideas in a rough outline; still others prefer to prepare a formal outline. Whether the plan is loose or exact, it helps to have some kind of guide as you work your way through the first draft of your paper.

Every paper needs the following components:

- A beginning, or **introduction,** that hooks the reader and usually states the thesis
- A middle, or **body,** that develops the main idea of the paper in a series of paragraphs—each making a point that is supported by specific details
- An ending, or **conclusion,** that gives the reader a sense of completion, often by offering a final comment on the thesis

1. Deciding on an organizational scheme

Give some thought to how you will lay out the body of the paper, using one or a combination of the following organizational schemes:

- **Chronological organization:** Common in history writing, a chronological organization takes the reader through a series of events while explaining their significance to the thesis. A variation on this scheme is used in science writing, where the steps of an experiment are detailed and the results over time are described. A paper that walks the reader scene by scene through a movie or play employs a chronological scheme, as does a biography or a case study. A survey of the literature for an informative report might also proceed chronologically, from the earliest to the most recent articles on a topic.

- **Problem-solution organization:** In proposals, a type of argument common in business writing as well as in public administration, the problem-solution scheme is an efficient way to present a rationale for change. For example, an argument paper for a U.S. government course could explain the problems with electronic voting devices and then describe solutions for overcoming each of them.

- **Thematic organization:** In a sense, all papers have a thematic organization in that they elaborate on a subject or theme. However, in contrast to a chronological or problem-solution organization, a thematic structure takes the reader through a series of examples that build from simple to complex, from general to specific, or from specific to general. For example, in her paper about the *Migrations* exhibit, Diane Chen begins with a general discussion of Salgado's work and then focuses on one specific photograph.

2. Deciding on a type of outline

www.mhhe.com/
nmhh
For more on outlines,
go to

Writing >
Paragraph/Essay
Development >
Outlines

It is not essential to have an outline before you start drafting; indeed, some writers prefer to discover how to connect and develop their ideas as they compose. However, even if you prefer to work out your ideas through drafting, outlining still has a place in the writing process. An outline of your first draft will help you spot organizational problems or places where the support for your thesis is weak.

A **scratch outline** is a simple list of points, without the levels of subordination that are found in more complex outlines. Scratch outlines are useful for briefer papers. Here is a scratch outline for Diane Chen's paper on the *Migrations* exhibit:

1. Photojournalism should be factual and informative, but it can be beautiful and artful too, as Salgado's *Migrations* exhibit illustrates.

2. The exhibit overall—powerful pictures of people uprooted, taken in 39 countries over 7 years. Salgado documents a global crisis: over 100 million displaced due to war, resource depletion, overpopulation, natural disasters, extreme poverty.
3. Specific picture—"Orphanage"—describe subjects, framing, lighting, emotions it evokes.
4. Salgado on the purpose of his photographs. Quote.

A **do/say plan** is a more detailed type of informal outline. To come up with such a plan, review your notes and other relevant material. Then write down your working thesis, and list what you will say for each of the following "do" categories: introduce, support and develop, conclude. Here is an example:

Thesis: George Will is wrong about economic inequality being good for the United States.

1. **Introduce** the issue and my focus.
   - Use two examples to contrast rich and poor: "approximately 17,000 Americans declared more than $1 million of annual income on their 1985 tax returns" (Mantsios 196). Between 1979 and 1992, there was a 15% decrease in the manufacturing workforce, and in 1993, Sears eliminated 50,000 merchandising jobs (Rifkin 2).
   - Say that the issue is how to evaluate increasing economic inequality, and introduce George Will's article "Healthy Inequality." Summarize Will's argument.
   - Give Will some credit for raising issue, but then state my thesis: he's wrong about more inequality being good for the United States.

2. **Support and develop** my thesis that Will's argument is wrong.
   - Point out that Will relies on the economic interpretations of Greenwood and Yorukoglu. They see decline ("modest") in labor productivity beginning in 1974. But Rifkin says "manufacturing productivity is soaring"—up 35%.
   - Point out one thing Will and Rifkin agree on: computer revolution is affecting economy/jobs. But Will thinks the effects are like "economic turbulence" caused in 1770 by steam engine and in 1840 by electricity.
   - Show that these analogies aren't convincing. Too many differences. Use Aronowitz on "jobless future" and Rifkin for support.
   - Say that Will makes fun of those who "decr[y] . . . injustice," people like Rifkin and Aronowitz. Will thinks inequality motivates people to learn new skills so that they can compete. A skilled workforce makes our society better/healthy.
   - Will's idea of the healthy society is narrow. It is an economic idea only. And he thinks that an unemployed worker can just get more

51

skilled—can learn the new technology. But who will pay for the training?

3. **Conclude** that Will doesn't ask or answer such key questions because he denies that there is any problem. Earlier he says "suffering is good." Where would he draw the line? Maybe quote from Max Weber?

In outlining his plan, this student has already begun drafting because as he works on the outline, he gets a clearer sense of what he thinks is wrong with Will's argument. He starts writing sentences that he is likely to include in the first complete draft.

A **formal outline** classifies and divides the information you have gathered, showing main points, supporting ideas, and specific details by organizing them into levels of subordination. You may be required to include a formal outline for some assignments.

Formal outlines come in two types. A formal **topic outline** uses single words or phrases; a formal **sentence outline** states every idea in a sentence. Because the process of division always results in at least two parts, in a formal outline every I must have a II; every A, a B; and so on. Also, items placed at the same level must be of the same kind; for example, if I is London, then II can be New York City but not the Bronx or Wall Street. Items at the same level should also be grammatically parallel; for example, if A is "Choosing Screen Icons," then B can be "Creating Away Messages" but not "Away Messages" (unless the writer changes A to "Screen Icons").

Here are two outlines for Diane Chen's paper on the *Migrations* exhibit, a formal topic outline first, followed by a formal sentence outline:

www.mhhe.com/
nmhh
For help with outlining,
go to

Writing >
Outlining Tutor

FORMAL TOPIC OUTLINE

Thesis: Like a photojournalist, Salgado brings us images of newsworthy events, but he goes beyond objective reporting, imparting his compassion for refugees and migrants to the viewer.

 I. Sophistication of Salgado's photographs
 II. Power of "Orphanage attached to the hospital" photo
   A. Three infant victims of Rwanda War
     1. Label: abstract statistics
     2. Photo: making abstractions real
   B. Documentary vividness and dramatic contrasts of black and white
     1. Black-and-white stripes of blankets
     2. White eyes and dark blankets
     3. Faces
       a. Heart-wrenching look of baby on left

      b. Startled look of baby in center

      c. Glazed and sickly look of baby on right

   C. Intimate vantage point

     1. A parent's perspective

     2. Stress on innocence and vulnerability

III. Salgado's ability to illustrate big issues with intimate images

FORMAL SENTENCE OUTLINE

Thesis: Like a photojournalist, Salgado brings us images of newsworthy events, but he goes beyond objective reporting, imparting his compassion for refugees and migrants to the viewer.

I. The images in *Migrations,* an exhibit of his work, suggest that Salgado does more than simply point and shoot.

II. Salgado's photograph "Orphanage attached to the hospital at Kibumba, Number One Camp, Goma, Zaire" illustrates the power of his work.

   A. The photograph depicts three infants who are victims of the war in Rwanda.

     1. The label indicates that there are 4,000 orphans in the camp and 100,000 orphans overall.

     2. The numbers are abstractions that the photo makes real.

   B. Salgado's use of black and white gives the photo a documentary feel, but he also uses contrasts of light and dark to create a dramatic image of the babies.

     1. The vertical black-and-white stripes of the blanket direct viewers' eyes to the infants' faces and hands.

     2. The whites of the infants' eyes stand out against the darkness of the blankets.

     3. The camera's lens focuses sharply on the babies' faces, highlighting their expressions.

       a. The baby on the left has a heart-wrenching look.

       b. The baby in the center has a startled look.

       c. The baby on the right has a glazed and sunken look and appears to be near death.

   C. The vantage point of this photograph is one of a parent standing directly over his or her child.

     1. The infants seem to belong to the viewer.

     2. The photo is framed so that the babies take up the entire space, consuming the viewer with their innocence and vulnerability.

III. Salgado uses his artistic skill to get viewers to look closely at painful subjects, illustrating a big, complex topic with a collection of intimate, intensely moving images.

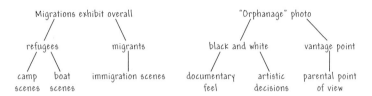

FIGURE 3.6 A tree diagram of Diane Chen's topic ideas.

A **tree diagram** is a nonlinear method of planning your paper's organization. In a tree diagram (*see Figures 3.6 and 3.7*), you can see the relationship between topics and subtopics, but the sequence of topics is not specified. Tree diagrams are useful when you want to group your ideas but prefer to make decisions about their sequence as you draft.

LEARNING in COLLEGE

Formatting Rules for Formal Outlines

- Place the thesis statement at the beginning of the outline. It should not be numbered.
- Start the outline with the first body paragraph. Do not include the introduction or conclusion.
- For a topic outline, capitalize the first word of each new point and all proper nouns. Do not use periods to end each point.
- For a sentence outline, capitalize and punctuate each item as you would any sentence.
- Different styles of numbers and letters indicate levels of generality and importance, as in the example on pages 52–53. Use capital Roman numerals (I, II, III) for each main point, capital letters (A, B, C) for each supporting idea, arabic numbers (1, 2, 3) for each specific detail, and lowercase letters (a, b, c) for parts of details. Place a period and a space after each number or letter.
- Indent consistently. Roman numerals should line up under the first letter in the thesis statement. Capital letters should line up under the first letter of the first word of the main point, and so on. See the example on page 53 for a model of outline format.

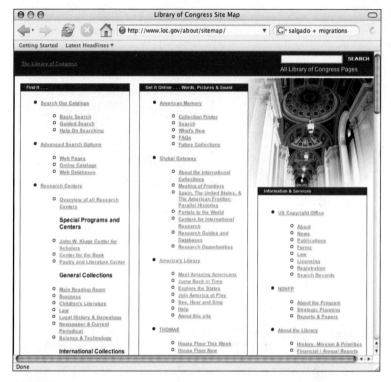

FIGURE 3.7 A site map. Site maps such as this one for the Library of Congress Web site are a kind of tree diagram.

TEXTCONNEX

Formatting an Outline

Most word-processing software has a feature that will indent and number your outline automatically. Spend a little time investigating this feature before you attempt to set up a numbered outline so that the program can help rather than hinder your efforts.

WRITING CONNECTIONS

Storyboards

In preparation for filming, some directors make storyboards—comic strip-like sketches that outline major changes of action in a scene sequence.

Developers who work in other visual media have begun to adapt storyboards to their own ends. Web designers, for example, may use storyboards to plan Web sites, and CD-ROM developers may create a storyboard for each screen.

Exercise 3.4   Shaping notes into an outline

Arrange the following items into a properly formatted formal topic outline, with several levels of subordination.

> thesis: used with supervision, instant messaging can offer many advantages to adolescents
>
> build social ties
>
> strengthen existing friendships
>
> maintain long-distance relationships
>
> chat with several friends simultaneously
>
> extend social network
>
> meet friends' friends
>
> talk to new classmates
>
> explore identity
>
> create an online persona

pick screen icon
create screen name
experiment with multiple personas
public screen name
private or secret screen name

Exercise 3.5 Reflecting on your own work: Outlining

Generate an outline for one of your current assignments—before or after you write your first draft—and freewrite about your experiences. Were you able to generate an outline before you started drafting paragraphs? If so, did you stick with your outline, or did you deviate from it? What kind of outline, are you most comfortable with? If you were not able to create an outline before you started drafting, why not?

3d Consider using visuals.

As you plan your paper, you should consider whether one or more visuals would help support your thesis. Used judiciously, visuals such as tables, charts, and graphs provide clarity. Effective visuals are used for a specific purpose, not for decoration, and each type of visual illustrates some kinds of material better than others. For example, compare the table on page 58 and the line graph on page 60. Both present similar types of data, but do both have the same effect on you? Does one strike you as clearer or more powerful than the other?

Effective visuals are simple and clear. If a chart is overloaded with information, separate it into several charts instead.

> *Caution:* Because the inclusion of visual elements in papers is more accepted in some fields than in others, you may want to ask your instructor for advice before planning to include visuals in your paper.

1. Tables

Tables are used to display information so that the reader can scan it easily. Tables are made up of rows and columns of cells; each cell presents an element of textual, numeric, or graphic information. Tables organize data for readers. Consider the example in Figure 3.8 taken from the Web site of the U.S. Environmental Protection Agency. It

U.S. Emissions of Criteria Pollutants, 1989–1996
(million metric tons of gas)

SOURCE	1989	1990	1991	1992	1993	1994	1995	1996
Carbon monoxide	93.5	91.3	88.3	85.3	85.4	89.6	83.5	NA
Nitrogen oxides	21.1	20.9	20.6	20.7	21.1	21.5	19.7	NA
Nonmethane VOCs	21.7	21.4	20.8	20.3	20.5	21.1	20.7	NA

NA = not available.

Note: Data in this table are revised from the data contained in the previous EIA report *Emissions of Greenhouse Gases in the United States 1995,* DOE/EIA-0573(95) (Washington, DC, October 1996).

SOURCE: U.S. Environmental Protection Agency, Office of Air Quality Planning and Standards, National Air Pollutant Emission Trends, 1900–1995, EPA-454/R-96-007 (Research Triangle Park, NC, October 1996), pp. A-5, A-9, and A-16.

FIGURE 3.8 A table.

would be more difficult to compare the numbers for different years if these data were presented in paragraph form, and because the measurements include decimals, it would also be difficult to place them precisely on a graph. A table is ideal for displaying this type of exacting data.

TEXTCONNEX

Preparing Tables

You can usually create and edit tables in your word-processing program. If you use Microsoft Word, for example, the program allows you to size columns proportionally to avoid distorting their contents and to make them fit your text. Under the Table pulldown menu, select Insert, then click on Table. You will see a dialogue box. Choose Autofit to Content instead of Fixed Column Width. As you create the table, the borders will automatically increase. You can also create tables using database, spreadsheet, presentation, and Web-site-construction software.

2. Bar graphs

Bar graphs show relationships and highlight comparisons between two or more variables, such as the cost of tuition and fees at eight different public universities (*Figure 3.9*). Tables can accomplish the same goal, but bar graphs allow the reader to see relative sizes quickly.

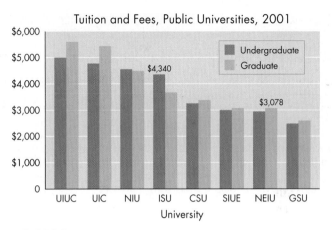

FIGURE 3.9 **A bar graph.**

3. Pie charts

Pie charts are circles divided into segments. They are useful for showing differences between parts in relation to a whole, as long as the differences are significant and there aren't too many parts. Pie charts can show only static data, not changes in data over time. The segments of a pie chart should add up to 100 percent of something, such as the sources of water contamination (*Figure 3.10*).

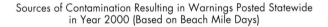

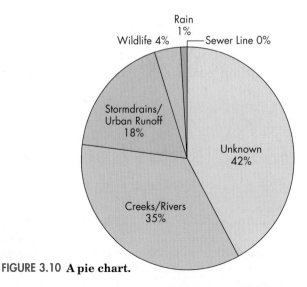

FIGURE 3.10 **A pie chart.**

TextConnex

Preparing Pie Charts

Several types of computer programs allow you to create pie charts. To create a pie chart in PowerPoint, for example, just open a "blank presentation." A group of different slide layouts will appear. Click on the pie chart layout, and you will see a premade slide with numbers already in the segments of the circle. Replace those numbers with your own by deleting the text in the little spreadsheet that is displayed along with the pie chart and typing in your own numbers. Relabel the categories and insert them in the slide. You can then copy and paste the pie chart into your text.

4. Line graphs

Line graphs or charts are used to show changes over time or to show the relationship between two or more variables over time, such as three sources of nitrous oxide emissions over a sixteen-year period (*Figure 3.11*).

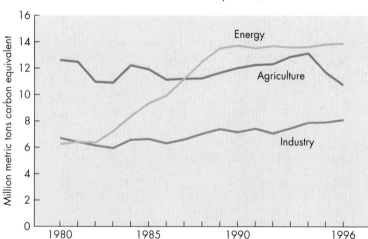

FIGURE 3.11 **A line graph.**

5. Diagrams

Used to show processes or structures visually, diagrams include such visuals as timelines, organization charts, and decision trees. The diagram in Figure 3.12 shows the factors involved in the decision to commit a burglary.

6. Photographs and illustrations

Photographs and illustrations can reinforce a point you are making in your text in ways that words cannot, showing readers what your subject actually looks like or how it has been affected or changed. For example, the illustration reproduced in Diane Chen's paper on the *Migrations* photography exhibit is central to her discussion (*see Chapter 5: Revising and Editing, p. 123*). The picture in Esther Hoffman's paper on Louis Armstrong and his manager (*see Chapter 24: MLA Documentation Style, p. 423*) provides further evidence of the relationship Hoffman is describing.

You should be aware that different photographs on the same subject can serve different purposes. For example, compare the image on page 62 (*Figure 3.13*) with those on page 10 in Chapter 1. As illustrations of the impact of hurricanes, all three are effective, but they communicate different information. Whereas the satellite photo vividly

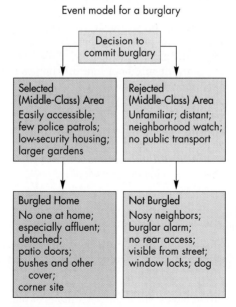

Event model for a burglary

FIGURE 3.12 A diagram.

FIGURE 3.13 Hurricane Frances on September 5, 2004.

illustrates the size of Hurricane Frances and the region it affected
when it struck the United States, the before-and-after photos of the
coastal area ravaged by Hurricane Bertha convey the destructive
power of the storm and the physical effects of its landing. One image
might work well in an informative paper; the other might provide
vivid support for an argument about building homes in coastal areas
that regularly experience hurricanes.

When you use photographs or illustrations, always credit your
source, and be aware that most photographs and illustrations are
protected by copyright. If you plan to use a photograph as part of a Web
page, for example, you will usually need to obtain permission from the
copyright holder. (*The credit information for most illustrations in this
book appears in the Credits list at the back of the book.*)

www.mhhe.com/
nmhh
For an interactive
tutorial on using
visuals, go to:

Writing > Visual
Rhetoric Tutorial >
Visualizing Data

Exercise 3.6   Using visuals

For each of the following kinds of information, decide which type of
visual would be most effective. (You do not need to prepare the visual
itself.)

1. For an education paper, show the percentage of teaching
   time per week devoted to math, language arts, science, social

studies, world languages, art, music, and physical education using a _____.

2. For a business paper, show the gross domestic product (GDP) for ten leading industrial countries over a five-year period using a _____.

3. For a criminal justice paper, compare the incidence of three different types of crime in one precinct during a three-month period using a _____.

4. For a health paper, chart the number of new cases of AIDS in North America and Africa over a ten-year period in order to show which continent has had the greater increase using a _____.

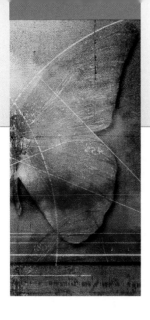

4 Drafting Paragraphs and Visuals

Unless you are writing for an in-class exam, you will usually be able to refine your essay by working through several drafts. (*See Chapter 5: Revising and Editing for an example of a paper in successive drafts.*) Think of your first draft as an attempt to discover a beginning, a middle, and an end for what you have to say, but remember that it is preliminary. Avoid putting pressure on yourself to make it perfect the first time through.

This chapter offers strategies for developing paragraphs, the building blocks of an essay. It will also help you decide when to use visuals to present information and what kinds of visuals suit different purposes. In Chapter 5, we will look at strategies for revising your work. Keep in mind, though, that all writing activities are interconnected—and that you may move back and forth between drafting and revising.

www.mhhe.com/ nmhh
For more on drafting and revising, go to

Writing >
Paragraph/Essay
Development >
Drafting and
Revising

4a Use electronic tools for drafting.

If you did not set up a folder for your paper as you were researching and generating ideas, be sure to do so before you start drafting. The following tips will make this process go smoothly:

1. **Save your work.** Always protect your creativity and hard-won drafts from power surges and other acts of technological treachery. Save often, and make backups.

2. **Label revised drafts with different file names.** Use a different file name for each successive version of your paper. For example, Diane Chen could have saved drafts of her paper as Migrations1, Migrations2, Migrations3, and so on.

3. **Print hard copies early and often.** If you save and print the original, you can feel free to experiment.

When you are collaborating with other students on a paper, you can use the Versions feature in the File menu of Microsoft Word to save various drafts of text. Too many versions can get confusing, though, so you should create versions only when your project requires it.

www.mhhe.com/
nmhh
For more on
paragraph unity,
go to

Writing >
Paragraph/Essay
Development >
Unity

Tips LEARNING in COLLEGE

Avoiding Writer's Block

Although it is important to allot time for generating and organizing your ideas, do not put off writing the first draft. If you find it difficult to get started, consider the tips below.

1. **Resist the temptation to be a perfectionist.** The poet William Stafford said, "There's no such thing as writer's block for writers whose standards are low enough." Reserve your high standards for the revising and editing stages of your paper. For your first draft, do not worry about getting the right word, the stylish phrase, or even the correct spelling.

2. **Take it "bird by bird."** Writer Anne Lamott counsels students to break down writing assignments into manageable units and then make a commitment to finishing each unit in one session. She passes along her father's advice to her brother, who had procrastinated on a report about birds and was frozen by the enormity of the project: "Bird by bird, buddy. Just take it bird by bird."

3. **Start anywhere.** If you are stuck on the beginning, pick a section where you have a clearer sense of what you want to say. You can go back later and work out the transitions.

4. **Generate more ideas.** If you hit a section where you are drawing a blank, it may be that you need to do more reading, research, or brainstorming. Be careful, though, not to use reading and research as a stalling tactic.

4b Write focused paragraphs.

A **paragraph** is a set of sentences that develop an idea or example in support of the thesis. Paragraphs break the text into blocks for your readers, allowing them to see how your essay builds step by step. A paragraph indent of one-half inch is typically used in academic writing. In business writing and publishing, a line space above the paragraph may be used instead of an indent.

1. Focusing on one main point or example

In a strong paragraph, the sentences form a unit that explores one main point or elaborates on one main example. When you are drafting, start a new paragraph when you introduce a new reason that supports your thesis, a new step in a process, or a new element in an analysis. The paragraphs in your first draft may not all be perfectly unified, and you will likely need to revise for paragraph unity later on (*see Chapter 5: Revising and Editing*). However, if you bear in mind as you draft that a paragraph develops a main point or example, then ideas will flow and revising will be easier.

The paragraph in the following example focuses on a theory that the writer will refer to later in his essay. The main idea is highlighted:

The main idea is introduced in the high- lighted sen- tences.

Details of attachment theory are developed in the rest of the paragraph.

> Current thinking on the topic of loss and mourning rests on foundations constructed by the British psychiatrist John Bowlby. Using examples from animal and human behavior, Bowlby (1977) posited "attachment theory" as a means of understanding the powerful bonds between humans and the disruption that comes when the bonds are jeopardized or destroyed. The bonds are formed because of a need for security and safety, are developed early in life, are long enduring, and are directed toward a few special individuals. In normal maturation, the child becomes ever more independent, moving away from the figure of attach- ment, and returning periodically for safety and security. If the bonds are threatened, the individual will try to restore them through crying, clinging, or other types of coercion; if they are destroyed, withdrawal, apathy, and despair will follow.
>
> —JONATHAN FAST, "After Columbine:
> How People Mourn
> Sudden Death"

2. Signaling the main idea of your paragraph with a topic sentence

A **topic sentence** is not always essential, but it can be a helpful start- ing point as you draft a paragraph. In the paragraph below, the topic sentence (highlighted) provides the writer with a launching point for a series of details:

The topic sentence announces that the para- graph will focus on a certain kind of evidence.

> The excavation also revealed dramatic evidence for the com- memorative rituals that took place after the burial. Four cattle had been decapitated and their skulls symbolically placed in a ditch enclosing the burial pit. In the soil above the skulls ar- chaeologists found the butchered bones of at least 250 slaugh- tered cattle, evidence for a huge ceremonial feast. Clearly this was an expensive way to commemorate a leader. Indeed, the huge quantity of meat suggests that the entire tribe may have

gathered at the grave to take part in a ritual feast. Perhaps this was one way the bonds between scattered communities were strengthened.

—DAMIAN ROBINSON, "Riding into the Afterlife"

Sometimes the sentences in a paragraph will lead to a unifying conclusion, a form of topic sentence, as in this example:

Table 1 presents the 15 mechanisms for gaining prestige that were reported for girls and for boys. There were few differences in the avenues to prestige between those in public and private high schools, particularly for girls. Avenues to prestige for girls that focus on their physical attributes, such as attractiveness, popularity with boys, clothes, sexual activity, and participation in sports, were more prominent in public schools than in private schools. In private schools the avenues more indicative of personality attributes, such as general sociability, having a good reputation/virginity, and participating in school clubs/government and cheerleading, were more prominent. Contrary to what parents may expect, avenues considered to be more negative, such as partying and being class clown, appeared more prevalent in private schools than in public schools. However, only clothes remained a significantly more important route to prestige for girls in public schools compared to girls in private schools once controls were introduced for region, size of community, year of graduation, and gender of respondent. Thus, taken together, type of high school had little effect on the ways in which girls accrued prestige in high school.

—J. JILL SUITOR, REBECCA POWERS, AND RACHEL BROWN, "Avenues to Prestige among Adolescents"

If a topic sentence would simply state the obvious, it can be omitted. In the following example, it is not necessary to state that the paragraph is about Igor Stravinsky's early life:

Stravinsky was born in Russia, near St. Petersburg, grew up in a musical atmosphere, and studied with Nikolai Rimsky-Korsakov. He had his first important opportunity in 1909, when the great impresario Sergei Diaghilev heard his music.

—ROGER KAMIEN, *Music: An Appreciation*

Exercise 4.1   Paragraph unity

Underline the topic sentences in the following paragraphs. If there is no topic sentence, state the main idea.

1.   Based on the results of this study, it appears that a substantial amount of bullying by both students and teachers may be occurring in college. Over 60% of the students reported having observed a student being bullied by another student, and over 44% had seen a teacher bully a student. More than 6% of the students reported having been bullied by another student occasionally or very frequently, and almost 5% reported being bullied by a teacher occasionally or very frequently, while over 5% of the students stated that they bullied students occasionally or very frequently.

—MARK CHAPELL ET AL., "Bullying in College by Students and Teachers"

2.   ARS [the Agricultural Research Service] launched the first areawide IPM [Integrated Pest Management] attacks against the codling moth, a pest in apple and pear orchards, on 7,700 acres in the Pacific Northwest. Other programs include a major assault against the corn rootworm on over 40,000 acres in the Corn Belt, fruit flies in the Hawaiian Islands, and leafy spurge in the Northern Plains area. In 2001, an areawide IPM project began for fire ants in Florida, Mississippi, Oklahoma, South Carolina, and Texas on pastures using natural enemies, microbial pesticides, and attracticides.

—ROBERT FAUST, "Integrated Pest Management Programs Strive to Solve Agricultural Problems"

3.   As far as the starting point of investigating the Dao of the universe is concerned, Feng and Kant have something in common. Contrary to advocates of positivism, Feng, like Kant, does not reject the discussion of ontological problems. However, he has not endeavored to construct an ontological system outside the human knowing process. As mentioned earlier, his theory of wisdom can be characterized as a theory about the nature of human beings and the Dao of the universe. However, the main content of the theory is how to know the world and know oneself. It is by no means accidental that the first volume of his Trilogy on Wisdom, which set the guidelines for the whole work, is titled Knowing the World and Knowing

the Self. Therefore, in Feng's eyes, the theory of the Dao
of the universe, although an ontological problem, is essentially a question of knowing the world.

—YANG GUORONG, "Transforming
Knowledge into Wisdom"

4c Write paragraphs that have a clear organization.

The sentences in your final draft need to be clearly related to one another. As you are drafting, make connections among your ideas and information as a way of moving your writing forward. One way to make
your ideas work together is to organize them using one of the common
organizational schemes for paragraphs. (*For advice on using repetition, pronouns, and transitions to relate sentences to one another, see
Chapter 5.*)

1. Developing a chronological or spatial organization

The sentences in a paragraph with a **chronological organization** describe a series of events, steps, or observations as they occur in time: this
happened, then that, and so on. The sentences in a paragraph with a
spatial organization present details as they appear to a viewer: from
top to bottom, outside to inside, east to west, and so on. In the following
example, the authors use a chronological organization to describe how
they found research subjects for their study:

> Recruitment of students with ADHD and their teachers oc-
> curred through two mechanisms. The first mechanism involved
> making initial contact with school systems and/or principals to   *First step.*
> determine potential interest for participation. Contacts were
> made with administrators (principals, special education direc-
> tors, or superintendents) from school systems in the Boston sub-
> urban area. Approximately half of the contacted school systems
> expressed initial interest in participating. The principal investi-   *Result of first step.*
> gator described the study at faculty meetings at the schools
> within each system to solicit the participation of teachers. To
> protect against potential confounds (i.e., differences between   *Second step.*
> teachers who agreed and did not agree to participate), all teach-
> ers in each school had to agree to participate for the school to be
> included in the study. Approximately 85% of schools agreed to   *Result of second step.*
> participate after hearing the project described.

—ROSS GREENE ET AL., "Are Students with ADHD
More Stressful to Teach?"

You can see an example of spatial organization in paragraphs 4–6 of Diane Chen's student paper about Sebastião Salgado, on pages 123–24.

2. Developing a general-to-specific organization

As we have seen, paragraphs often start with a general topic sentence that states the main idea and then proceed with specifics that elaborate on that idea. The general topic sentence can include a question that the paragraph then answers or a problem that the paragraph goes on to solve. A variation of the general-to-specific organization includes a **limiting sentence** that seems to oppose the main idea. This structure allows you to bring in a different perspective on the main idea but then go on to defend it with specific examples, as in this paragraph:

General topic sentence.
Limiting sentence.
Specifics.

> Parents do not have the moral right to make decisions for their children simply because of their status as parents. This idea may seem to go against our basic understanding of how families should operate. However, there are a number of actual cases that illustrate the weaknesses in the argument for absolute parental rights. [*The following paragraphs present a series of examples.*]
>
> —SHEILA FOSTER, "Limiting Parental Rights," student paper

3. Developing a specific-to-general organization

We have also seen that the general topic sentence can come at the end of the paragraph, preceded by the specific details leading up to that general conclusion (*see the paragraph from "Avenues to Prestige among Adolescents," p. 67*). This organizational scheme is especially effective when you are preparing your reader for a revelation. The following example is a variation on this organization; the paragraph begins and ends with general statements that offer an interpretive framework:

Introductory general statement.

Specific details.

> Even the subtlest details of Goya's portrait convey tension between revealing and concealing, between public and private personae. Dona Josefa's right eye avoids our gaze while her left eye engages it. Half of her ear is revealed while half is obscured by her hair. Above the sitter's arms, her torso faces us directly; her legs, however, turn away from us toward the left. The closed fan that Dona Josefa holds atop her stomach, pointed toward her enclosed womb, seems a mere trapping of formality in an otherwise informal setting. The fan reminds viewers that though we intrude on a private domain, Dona Josefa remains aware that

she is indeed receiving company. Thus while our glimpse of her is, in many ways, an intimate one, Goya never allows us to forget that through the act of portraiture, this private self is being brought into the social sphere—and that our voyeurism has not gone unnoticed.

Concluding
general
statement.

—BAZ DREISINGER, "The Private Made Public:
Goya's *Josefa Castilla Portugal de
Garcini y Wanasbrok*," student paper

Exercise 4.2   Paragraph organization

Go back to the paragraphs in Exercise 4.1 (*pp. 68–69*) and identify the organizational strategy used in each one.

4d   Develop ideas and use visuals strategically.

www.mhhe.com/
nmhh
For more information
on developing
paragraphs, go to
Writing >
Paragraph
Patterns

When you develop ideas, you give your writing texture and depth. The following strategies can help you develop the ideas that support your thesis into a complete draft. Depending on the purpose of your paper, you may use a few of these strategies throughout or a mix of all of them.

Photographs and other kinds of visuals can also support your ideas. As with paragraphs, you can use a mix of visuals in a paper. Keep in mind, though, that any visuals you use should always serve the overall purpose of your work. (*See 3d, pp. 57–63, for more on types of visuals and their purposes.*)

1. Narration

When you narrate, you tell a story. (*See Figure 4.1 for an example of a narrative visual.*) The following paragraph comes from a personal essay on the goods that result from "a lifetime of production":

My dad changed too. He had come to that job feeling—as I do now—that everything was still possible. He'd served his time in the air force during the Korean War. Then, while my mother worked as a secretary to support them, he earned a college degree courtesy of the GI Bill. After graduation, my father painted houses for a season until he was offered a position scheduling the production of corrugated board. He took it, though he has told me that he never planned to stay. It was not something he envisioned as his life's work. I try to imagine what it is like

FIGURE 4.1 Visuals that narrate. Using images that narrate can be a powerful way to reinforce a message or portray events you discuss in your paper. Images like this one help tell one of many stories about the conflict in Iraq.

suddenly to look up from a stack of orders and discover that the job you started one December day has watched you age.

—MICHELLE M. DUCHARME, "A Lifetime of Production"

www.mhhe.com/
nmhh
For help with use of narration, go to

Writing > Writing
Tutors > Narration

Notice that Ducharme begins with two sentences that state the topic and point of her narration. Then using the past tense, she recounts in chronological sequence some key events that led to her father's taking a job in the box manufacturing business.

2. Description

To make an object, a person, or an activity vivid for your readers, describe it in concrete, specific words that appeal to the senses of sight,

FIGURE 4.2 Visuals that describe. Although it may seem obvious that images can serve a descriptive purpose, you should pay careful attention to the effect your selection will have on your paper. This photograph of Kurt Cobain, for example, could add dimension to a portrayal of the musician as a talented but conflicted artist.

sound, taste, smell, and touch. (*See Figure 4.2 for an example of a descriptive visual.*) In the following example, Diane Chen describes her impression of a photograph:

> The vertical black-and-white stripes of the blanket direct our eyes to the infants' faces and hands, which are framed by a horizontal white stripe. The whites of their eyes in particular stand

www.mhhe.com/
nmhh
For help with the use
of description, go to

Writing > Writing
Tutors >
Description

73

out against the darkness created by the shell of the blankets. The camera's lens also seems to be in sharper focus on the faces than on the blankets, again drawing our attention to the babies' expressions.

—DIANE CHEN, "The Caring Eye of Sebastião Salgado," student paper

www.mhhe.com/
nmhh
For help with the
use of classification,
go to

Writing >
Writing Tutors >
Classification

3. Classification

Classification is a useful way of grouping individual entities into identifiable categories (*see Figure 4.3*). Classifying occurs in all academic disciplines and often appears with its complement—**division,** which breaks a whole entity into its parts.

[M]ost of America's traditional, routinized manufacturing jobs will disappear. So will routinized service jobs that can be done from remote locations, like keypunching of data transmitted by satellite. Instead, you will be engaged in one of two broad categories of work: either complex services, some of which will be sold to the rest of the world to pay for whatever Americans want to buy from the rest of the world, or person-to-person services, which foreigners can't provide for us because (apart from new immigrants and illegal aliens) they aren't here to provide them.

Complex services involve the manipulation of data and abstract symbols. Included in this category are insurance, engineering, law, finance, computer programming, and advertising. Such activities now account for almost 25 percent of our GNP, up from 13 percent in 1950. They have already surpassed manufacturing (down to about 20 percent of GNP). Even *within* the manufacturing sector, executive, managerial, and engineering positions are increasing at a rate almost three times that of total manufacturing employment. Most of these jobs, too, involve manipulating symbols.

—ROBERT REICH, "The Future of Work"

To make his ideas clear, Reich first classifies future work into two broad categories: complex services and person-to-person services. Then in the next paragraph, he develops the idea of complex services in more detail, in part by dividing that category into more specific—and familiar—categories like engineering and advertising.

4. Definition

You should define any concepts that the reader must understand to follow your ideas. (*See Figure 4.4 for an example of the use of a visual to define.*) Interpretations and arguments often depend on one or two key

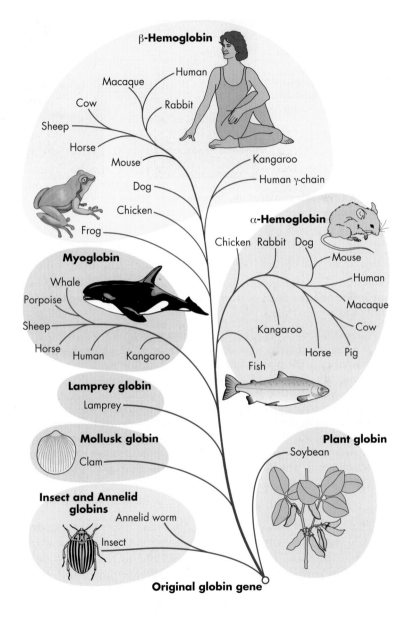

FIGURE 4.3 Visuals that classify or divide. An image can help you make the categories in or parts of complex systems or organizations easier for your reader to understand. The image shown here, for example, helps readers comprehend the evolution of a common gene.

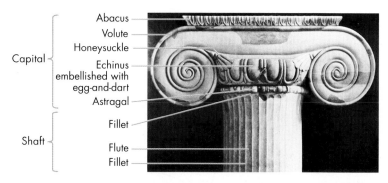

FIGURE 4.4 Visuals that define. Visuals can be extremely effective when used to support a written definition or to identify parts of a whole. This image uses labels and leader lines to identify the characteristics of an Ionic column, an example of one of the five orders of classical architecture.

www.mhhe.com/
nmhh
For help with the
use of definition,
go to

Writing >
Writing Tutors >
Definition

ideas that cannot be quickly and easily defined. In the following example, John Berger defines "image," a key idea in his televised lectures on the way we see things:

> An image is a sight which has been recreated or reproduced. It is an appearance, or a set of appearances, which has been detached from the place and time in which it first made its appearance and preserved—for a few moments or centuries. Every image embodies a way of seeing. Even a photograph. For photographs are not, as is often assumed, a mechanical record. Every time we look at a photograph, we are aware, however slightly, of the photographer selecting that sight from an infinity of other possible sights. This is true even in the most casual family snapshot. The photographer's way of seeing is reflected in his choice of subject.
>
> —JOHN BERGER, *Ways of Seeing*

5. Illustration

No matter what your purpose and point may be, to appeal to readers you have to show as well as tell. Detailed examples (and well-chosen visuals—see Figure 4.5) can make abstractions more concrete and generalizations more specific, as the following paragraph shows:

> As Rubin explains, "for much of the Accord era, the ideal-typical family . . . was composed of a 'stay-at-home-mom,' a working father, and dependent children. He earned wages; she cooked, cleaned, cared for the home, managed the family's social

Neutral nations	
Axis nations	
Axis-occupied areas	
Allied areas	
Allied with Germany	

FIGURE 4.5 Visuals that illustrate. This map illustrates the territorial contours of Allied and Axis powers in Europe at the height of World War II.

life, and nurtured the family members" (97). Just such an arrangement characterized my grandmother's married life. My grandmother, who had four children, stayed at home with them, while her husband went off to work as a safety engineer. Sadly, when he died, she was left with nothing. She needed to support herself, yet had no work experience, no credit, and little education. But even though society frowned on her for seeking employment, my grandmother eventually found a clerical position—a low-level job with few perks.

—JENNIFER KOEHLER, "Response to Exercise 6," student paper

www.mhhe.com/ nmhh
For help with the use of illustration, go to

Writing >
Writing Tutors >
Exemplification

Caution: To some extent, the primary function of any image you choose to include in your paper will be illustrative. Images should not function merely as decoration, however. For each image you are considering, ask yourself if it truly adds information to your paper. If the answer is no, then its purpose is probably more decorative than illustrative, and you should reconsider including it.

www.mhhe.com/
nmhh

For help with the use of comparison and contrast, go to

Writing >
Writing Tutors >
Comparison/
Contrast

6. Comparison and contrast

When you *compare,* you explore the similarities and differences among various items. When the term *compare* is used along with the term *contrast,* however, then *compare* has a narrower meaning: "to spell out key similarities." *Contrast* always means "to itemize important differences." (*See Figure 4.6.*)

In the following example, the student writer uses a **subject-by-subject** pattern to contrast the ideas of two social commentators, Jeremy Rifkin and George Will:

> Rifkin and Will have different opinions about unemployment due to downsizing and the widening income gap between rich and poor. Rifkin sees both the decrease in employment and the increase in income disparity as evils that must be immediately dealt with lest society fall apart: "If no measures are taken to provide financial opportunities for millions of Americans in an era of diminishing jobs, then . . . violent crime is going to increase" (3). Will, on the other hand, seems to believe that both unemployment and income differences are necessary to the health of American society. Will writes, "A society that chafes against stratification derived from disparities of talents will be a society that discourages individual talents" (92). Apparently, the society that Rifkin wants is just the kind of society that Will rejects.

> —JACOB GROSSMAN, "Dark Comes before Dawn,"
> student paper

Notice that Grossman comments on Rifkin first and then turns to his second subject, George Will. To ensure paragraph unity, he begins with a topic sentence that mentions both subjects.

In the following paragraph, the student writer organizes her comparison of two photographs **point by point** rather than subject by subject. Instead of saying everything about Smith's picture before commenting on the Associated Press (AP) photo, the writer moves back and forth between the two images as she makes and supports two points: first, that the images differ in figure and scene and second, that they are similar in theme.

Divided by an ocean, two photographers took pictures that at first glance seem absolutely different. W. Eugene Smith's well-known *Tomoko in the Bath* and the less well-known AP photo *A Paratrooper Works to Save the Life of a Buddy* portray distinctively different settings and people. Smith brings us into a darkened room where a Japanese woman is lovingly bathing her malformed child, while the AP staff photographer captures two soldiers on the battlefield, one intently performing CPR on his wounded friend. But even though the two images seem as different as women and men, peace and war, or life and death, both pictures show something similar: a time of suffering. It is the early 1970s—a time when the hopes and dreams that modernity promoted are being exposed as deadly to human beings. Perhaps that is why the bodies in both pictures seem humbled. Grief pulls you down onto your knees. Terror impels you to crawl along the ground.

—ILONA BOUZOUKASHVILI, "On Reading Photographs," student paper

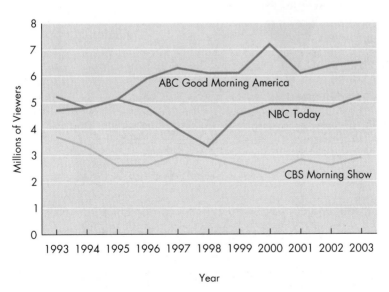

FIGURE 4.6 Visuals that compare and contrast. Graphs and charts are effective ways of comparing parallel sets of data. This line graph tracks the population of viewers for the three most popular morning shows over ten years.

79

7. Analogy

An analogy compares topics that at first glance seem quite different (*see Figure 4.7*). A well-chosen analogy can make unfamiliar or technical information seem more commonplace and understandable.

The human eye provides a good starting point for learning how a camera works. The lens of the eye is like the *lens* of the

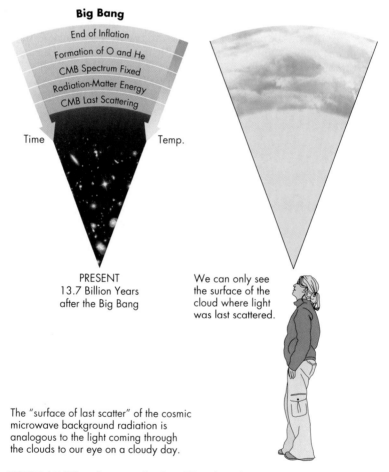

Big Bang

End of Inflation

Formation of O and He

CMB Spectrum Fixed

Radiation-Matter Energy

CMB Last Scattering

Time   Temp.

PRESENT
13.7 Billion Years
after the Big Bang

We can only see
the surface of the
cloud where light
was last scattered.

The "surface of last scatter" of the cosmic
microwave background radiation is
analogous to the light coming through
the clouds to our eye on a cloudy day.

FIGURE 4.7 Visuals as analogies. Visual analogies operate in the same way as written analogies. This graphic uses an analogy to explain the concept of "surface of last scatter," which physicists use in describing the Big Bang.

camera. In both instruments the lens focuses an image of the surroundings on a *light-sensitive surface*—the *retina* of the eye and the *film* in the camera. In both, the light-sensitive material is protected within a light-tight container—the *eyeball* of the eye and the *body* of the camera. Both eye and camera have a mechanism for shutting off light passing through the lens to the interior of the container—the *lid* of the eye and the *shutter* of the camera. In both, the size of the lens opening, or *aperture,* is regulated by an *iris diaphragm.*

—MARVIN ROSEN, *Introduction to Photography*

8. Process

To explain how to do something or show readers how something is done, you use process analysis (*see Figure 4.8*), explaining each step of the process in chronological order, as in the following example:

> To end our Hawan ritual of thanks, *aarti* is performed. First, my mother lights a piece of camphor in a metal plate called a *taree.* Holding the taree with her right hand, she moves the fire in a circular, clockwise movement in front of the altar. Next, she stands in front of my father and again moves the fiery *taree* in a circular, clockwise direction. After touching his feet and receiving his blessing, she attends to each of us children in turn, moving the fire in a clockwise direction before kissing us, one by one. When she is done, my father performs his *aarti* in a similar way, and then my sister and I do ours. When everyone is done, we say some prayers and sit down.

—U. ROOPNARIAN, "Family Rituals," student paper

www.mhhe.com/
nmhh
For help with
describing a process,
go to

Writing > Writing
Tutors > Process
Analysis

9. Cause and effect

Use a cause-and-effect strategy when you need to trace the causes of some event or situation, to describe its effects, or both (*see Figure 4.9*). In the following example, Rajeev Bector explains the reasons for a character's feelings and actions in a short story:

> Given the differences between Mrs. Chestny's and her son's values, as well as the oppressiveness of Mrs. Chestny's racist views, we can understand why Julian struggles to "teach" his mother "a lesson" (185) throughout the entire bus ride. Goffman would point out that "each individual is engaged in providing

www.mhhe.com/
nmhh
For help analyzing
cause and effect,
go to

Writing > Writing
Tutors > Causal
Analysis

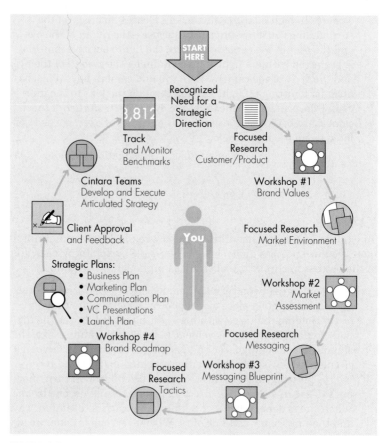

FIGURE 4.8 Visuals that show a process. Flow charts and diagrams such as this one, developed by Cintara Corporation, are especially useful when illustrating a process. © Cintara Company. Reprinted with permission.

evidence to establish a definition of himself at the expense of what can remain for the other" (29). But in the end, neither character wins the contest. Julian's mother loses her sense of self when she is pushed down to the ground by a "colored woman" wearing a hat identical to hers (187). Faced with his mother's breakdown, Julian feels his own identity being overwhelmed by "the world of guilt and sorrow."

—RAJEEV BECTOR, "The Character Contest in Flannery O'Connor's 'Everything That Rises Must Converge,'" student paper

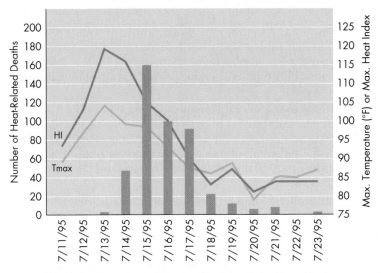

Heat-Related Deaths – Chicago, July 1995
Maximum Temperature and Heat Index

This graph tracks maximum temperature (Tmax), heat index (HI), and heat-related deaths in Chicago each day from July 11 to 23, 1995. The orange line shows maximum daily temperature, the green line shows the heat index, and the bars indicate number of deaths for the day.

www.mhhe.com/
nmhh
For more information
on how to work with
visuals, go to

Writing > Visual
Rhetoric Tutorial >
Understanding
Images

FIGURE 4.9 Visuals that show cause and effect. Visuals can provide powerful evidence when you are writing about causes and effects. However, although graphs like this one may seem self-explanatory, you still need to analyze and interpret them for your readers.

Caution: When you use graphs or other visuals to summarize numeric data or show possible causal relationships, you need to discuss the visuals in the body of your text. Sometimes explaining the data may be your primary objective. In other situations, the data may serve as only one piece of evidence in support of your thesis.

Exercise 4.3   Developing ideas

Experiment with the development strategies just discussed—narration, description, classification, definition, illustration, comparison and contrast, analogy, process, and cause and effect—in a paper you are currently drafting. Are some strategies inappropriate to your assignment? Have you combined any of the strategies in a single paragraph?

www.mhhe.com/
nmhh
For an interactive
tutorial on using
visuals, go to

Writing > Visual
Rhetoric Tutorial >
Document Design

4e Integrate visuals effectively.

If you decide to use a table, chart, diagram, or photograph in your paper, keep this general advice in mind:

1. **Number tables and other figures** consecutively throughout your paper, and label them appropriately: Table 1, Table 2, and so on. Do not abbreviate *Table*. *Figure* may be abbreviated as *Fig.*

2. **Refer to the visual element in your text** before it appears, placing the visual as close as possible to the text in which you state why you are including it. If your project contains many visuals or complex tables, you may want to group them in an appendix. Always refer to a visual by its label: for example, "See Fig. 1."

3. **Give each visual a title or caption** that clearly explains what the visual shows. A visual with its caption should be clear without the discussion in the text, and the discussion of the visual in the text should be clear without the visual itself.

4. **Include explanatory notes below the visuals.** If you want to explain a specific element within the visual, use a super-script *letter* (not a number) both after the specific element and before the note. This is essentially a footnote, but the explanation should appear directly beneath the graphic, not at the foot of the page or at the end of your paper. Do not use your word processor's Insert/Footnote commands to create the footnote because the program will put the note in one of those two places.

5. **Credit sources for visuals.** If you use a visual element from a source, you need to credit the source. Unless you have specific guidelines to follow, you can use the word *Source,* followed by a colon and complete documentation of the source, including the author, title, publication information, and page number if applicable. Note that book publishers typically provide source information for visuals near the beginning or end of the book.

Note: The Modern Language Association (MLA) and the American Psychological Association (APA) provide guidelines for figure captions and crediting sources of visuals that differ from the previous guidelines (*see Chapter 24: MLA Documentation Style, p. 415, and Chapter 25: APA Documentation Style, pp. 453–54*).

4f   Craft an introduction that establishes your purpose.

www.mhhe.com/
nmhh
For more information
on crafting
introductions, go to
Writing >
Paragraph/Essay
Development >
Introductions

As you begin your first draft, you may want to skip over the introduction and start by writing the body of your paper. After your paper has taken shape, you can then go back and sketch out the main ideas for your introduction.

For most types of papers, your opening paragraph or paragraphs will include your thesis statement, either stated at the beginning or held until the end of the introduction. An introduction that begins with broad assertions and then narrows the focus to conclude with the thesis is called a **funnel opener.** In addition to the placement of your thesis, you will need to consider if or how your thesis has changed in the course of writing your first draft and adjust it if necessary.

Some papers, however, will not include a thesis statement in the introduction. If your purpose is analytic, you may prefer to build up to your thesis, placing it near the end of the paper. Some types of writing, such as narratives, may not require an explicitly stated thesis if the main idea is obvious without it.

Once you are clear on the main ideas you want to include in your introduction, focus on presenting them in a way that will hook readers. Because the introduction establishes your credibility, avoid either understating or overstating your authority ("I'm not completely sure about this, but . . ."; "As an expert on the topic, I think . . ."). Instead, encourage readers to share your view of the topic's importance, rather than simply telling them what you think. An introduction that begins by referring to the paper title or that baldly states "The purpose of my essay is . . ." could benefit from a creative approach. Here are some opening strategies:

- Tell a brief story related to the question your thesis answers.

- Begin with a relevant and attention-getting quotation.

- Begin with a paraphrase of a commonly held view that you immediately question.

- State a working hypothesis.

- Define a key term, but avoid the tired opener that begins "According to the dictionary. . . ."

- Pose an important question.

Each of the opening paragraphs that follow combines several of these strategies.

These paragraphs from an informative essay begin with an attention-getting fact, followed by a definition of key terms, a key question, and a working hypothesis:

> Every year huge rotating storms packing winds greater than 74 miles per hour sweep across tropical seas and onto shore-lines—often devastating large swaths of territory. When these roiling tempests—called hurricanes in the Atlantic and the eastern Pacific oceans, typhoons in the western Pacific and cyclones in the Indian Ocean—strike heavily populated areas, they can kill thousands and cause billions of dollars of property damage. And nothing, absolutely nothing, stands in their way.
>
> But must these fearful forces of nature be forever beyond our control? My research colleagues and I think not. Our team is investigating how we might learn to nudge hurricanes onto more benign paths or otherwise defuse them. Although this bold goal probably lies decades in the future, we think our results show that it is not too early to study the possibilities.
>
> —Ross N. Hoffman, "Controlling Hurricanes"

These paragraphs from an analytical essay begin with a vivid quotation that illustrates a commonly held view. The writer then calls that view into question:

> "Loathsome hordes, dark swarms of worms that emerge from the narrow crevices of their holes when the sun is high, preferring to cover their villainous faces with hair rather than their private parts and surrounding areas with clothes." So wrote the sixth-century British churchman Gildas, lamenting the depredations of Pictish and other Scotland-based barbarian "butchers" a century earlier following Rome's abandonment of its British provinces in A.D. 410. This characterization of the Picts as illiterate, uncivilized, scantily clothed, and promiscuous heathens has clung to them to the present day. Although over the past half century scholars have regarded the cleric Gildas as a somewhat biased commentator, most haven't tended to see the Picts as outstandingly civilized either.
>
> Now, however, one of the most detailed surveys of their art has revealed that these archetypal barbarians actually developed a deep knowledge of the Bible and of some aspects of Roman classical literature. . . .
>
> —David Keys, "Rethinking the Picts"

TEXTCONNEX

Beginnings, Middles, and Ends

If you are creating a Web site, remember that readers may enter it in the "middle" and never find the "end." Web sites simply do not have the kind of linear structure that papers do, and readers tend to want information in short chunks rather than in lengthy paragraphs. However, readers visiting a Web site still expect to be able to go to an introductory page, or *home page,* that makes the overall purpose and contents of the site clear. Make sure that your home page loads quickly—in ten seconds or less with a 56K modem. Provide clear navigational links on every page of the site, and always include one link that returns the user to the home page.

4g Conclude by answering "So what?"

www.mhhe.com/
nmhh
For more information
on conclusions, go to
Writing >
Paragraph/Essay
Development >
Conclusions

Just as a paper's opening makes a first impression and motivates the reader to continue reading, its closing makes a final impression and motivates the reader to think further. The purpose of the conclusion is to bring your paper to an interesting end. You should not merely repeat the main idea that you introduced at the beginning of the paper, and you should also avoid introducing a completely new topic. Your conclusion should remind readers of the paper's significance and satisfy those who might be asking, "So what?" Here are some common strategies for concluding a paper effectively:

- Refer to the story or quotation you used in your introduction.
- Answer the question you posed in your introduction.
- Summarize your main point.
- Call for some action on your reader's part.
- Present a powerful image or forceful example.
- Suggest some implications for the future.

The following conclusion refers to a quotation used in the introduction (*see p. 86*) as it summarizes the main point:

> Burghead, the current excavations at Tarbat, and new art-history research demonstrate the extraordinary diversity and sophistication of Dark Age Pictish culture. Even if the Picts had once been scantily clothed "butchers," as Gildas and others no doubt perceived them, they evolved into something quite different.
>
> —DAVID KEYS, "Rethinking the Picts"

This research report concludes with recommendations for action:

> The results of this study support the conclusions of Rome et al. (2003) that early detection and treatment helps decrease eating disorder morbidity in the adolescent population. School systems, administrators, athletic directors, coaches, and teachers must make every effort to ensure that their policies, programs, and personnel support a healthy environment for their students. Through primary prevention dialogue with parents, students, health professionals and community members, the prevention and early detection of eating disorders could be better realized. Within the limits of what is possible, every effort must be made to create an environment that counteracts a toxic culture.
>
> —SUSAN WOODS, "Untreated Recovery from Eating Disorders"

If your paper is brief—five hundred words or fewer—a few concluding sentences may be enough to satisfy the reader. You might also end a brief paper with a powerful supporting point and vivid image. A short essay presenting two sides of the argument over whether cell phones make us more secure concludes with a quotation supporting the pro–cell phone side:

> "If you are left to your own, what would you think about?" said Kenneth J. Gergen, a professor of psychology at Swarthmore College, and author of *The Saturated Self.* "You have to have other voices, reports and news. The best decisions are made in a whole set of dialogues."
>
> —KEN BELSON, "Saved, and Enslaved, by the Cell"

For MULTILINGUAL STUDENTS

Special Features of Introductions and Conclusions

English readers have specific expectations about the role of the different paragraphs in a piece of writing. They expect introductory paragraphs to tackle the topic directly. Therefore, you should avoid offering long background explanations or making broad generalizations, which may be typical of opening paragraphs in your culture. Readers expect the concluding paragraph to revisit the thesis and, for complex papers, to summarize the main points. Summarizing may seem repetitive to you, but it is seen as yet another chance for the reader to grasp the gist of your message.

Exercise 4.4	Analyzing introductions and conclusions

Find an essay that has an introduction or a conclusion that engaged you and one with an introduction or conclusion that failed to draw you in. What strategies did the successful essay employ? What strategies could the writer of the unsuccessful essay have used? Next look at the introduction and conclusion of an essay you are currently writing. Do these paragraphs use any of the strategies discussed in this section? If not, try one of the strategies when you revise.

5 Revising and Editing

Once you have a draft of your paper, you can approach it with a critical eye. In the **revising** stage of the writing process, you review the whole paper and its parts, adding, deleting, and moving text as necessary. After you are satisfied with the substance of your paper, **editing** begins. When you edit, you polish sentences so that you say what you want to say as effectively as possible.

This chapter focuses on revising and includes a complete student essay in several drafts. It also introduces the concepts and principles of editing, which are covered in much greater detail in Parts 6 through 12.

5a Get comments from readers.

Asking actual readers to comment on your draft is the best way to get fresh perspectives on your writing. (Be sure that your professor allows this kind of collaboration.) Because you can send drafts to readers by e-mail or post them on a class Web site, computers can make it easier to get comments and use them to revise your work.

1. Trying peer review

Whether it is required or optional, **peer review** is a form of **collaborative learning** that involves reading and critiquing your classmates' work while they review yours. When you have a fairly solid draft to share, you can send it to your peer reviewers by e-mail (also print out a hard copy for yourself), or you can meet in person to exchange and read drafts. Consider including printouts of some of your peers' responses with your final draft so that your teacher knows you have taken the initiative to work with other writers. If you meet in person, you can ask your peer reviewers to write out their responses and then include these written responses with your final draft.

Most readers genuinely want to be helpful. When sharing your drafts with your peers, help them give you the assistance you need by asking them specific questions. The best compliment they can pay you is to take your work seriously enough to make constructive suggestions. When you share a draft with readers, give them the answers to the following questions:

LEARNING in COLLEGE

Re-Visioning Your Paper

Revising is a process of "re-visioning"—of looking at your work through the eyes of your audience. Here are some tips for getting a fresh perspective on your paper:

1. **Get feedback from other readers.** Candid, respectful feedback can help you discover the strong and weak areas of your paper. See section 5j (*pp. 115–18*) for advice on making use of readers' reactions to your drafts.

2. **Let your draft cool.** Whenever possible, try to schedule a break between drafting and revising. A good night's sleep, a movie break, or some physical exercise will help you view your paper more objectively.

3. **Read your paper aloud.** Some people find that reading aloud helps them hear their paper the way their audience will.

4. **Use revising and editing checklists.** The checklists on pages 95, 110, and 116 will assist you in evaluating your paper systematically.

- **What is your assignment?** Readers need to understand the context for your paper—especially your intended purpose and audience.

- **How close is the project to being finished?** Your answer to this question helps readers understand where you are in the writing process and how best to assist you in taking the next step.

- **What steps do you plan to take to complete the project?** If readers know your plans, they can either question the direction you are taking or give you more specific advice, such as the titles of additional books or articles that you might consult.

- **What kind of feedback do you need?** Let your readers know what you are looking for. Do you want readers to summarize your main points so you can determine if you have communicated with them clearly? Do you want to know what readers were thinking and feeling as they read or heard your draft? Do you want a response to the logic of your argument or the development of your thesis?

Reading other writers' drafts will help you view your own work more objectively, and comments from readers will help you see your own

GIVING and RECEIVING FEEDBACK

Guidelines for Giving Feedback

1. **Focus on strengths as well as weaknesses.** Writers need to know what parts of their paper are strongest so that they can retain those sections when they revise and use those sections as models as they work to improve weaker sections. At the same time, do not withhold constructive criticism, or you will deprive the writer of an opportunity to improve the paper.

2. **Be specific.** Give examples to back up your general reactions.

3. **Be constructive.** Phrase negative reactions in a way that will help the writer see a solution. For example, instead of saying that an example is a bad choice, explain that you did not understand how the example was connected to the main point and suggest a way the writer could make the connection clearer.

4. **Ask questions.** Jot down any questions that occur to you as you read. Ask for clarification, or note an objection that readers of the final version might make.

Guidelines for Receiving Feedback

1. **Resist being defensive.** Keep in mind that readers are discussing your paper, not you, and their feedback offers a way for you to see your paper differently. Be respectful of their time and efforts.

2. **Ask for more feedback if you need it.** Some students may be hesitant to share all of their reactions, and you may need to do some coaxing.

3. **Try not to be frustrated by conflicting comments.** When you have two or more readers, you will receive differing—and sometimes contradictory—points of view on your work. Instead of looking to peer reviewers for "the truth" about your paper, examine points of conflict and rethink the parts of your paper that have caused them. You, not your reviewers, are in charge of decisions about your paper.

writing as others see it. As you gain more objectivity, you will become more adept at revising your work. In addition, the approaches that you see your classmates taking to the assignment will broaden your perspective and give you ideas for new directions in your own writing.

Peer review is possible without computers and the Internet, of course, but specialized software, like the writing environment in the *Catalyst* Web site that accompanies this book, can make it easier for

For MULTILINGUAL STUDENTS

Peer Review

Peer editing is a part of many American writing classes and is frequently used to teach editing skills and to cultivate collaboration in a student writing community. As a multilingual writer, you will find peer editing helpful in many ways. It will show you that many errors you make are quite common. It will help you improve your ability to detect mistakes and to decide which mistakes to address first. It will also challenge you to look at your writing with a critical eye and to present your ideas to a diverse audience. Don't be surprised to find that you know as much as, if not more than, your fellow students about a variety of topics, including English grammar.

you to obtain and review comments from your readers. (*For more on this feature of* Catalyst, *see Chapter 1, p. 15.*)

2. Responding to readers

Consider and evaluate your readers' suggestions, but remember that you are under no obligation to do what they say. Sometimes you will receive contradictory advice. One reader may like a particular sentence; a second reader may suggest that you eliminate the very same sentence. Is there common ground? Yes. Both readers stopped at that sentence. Ask yourself why—and if you want readers to pause there. Remember that you are the one who is ultimately responsible for your paper, so you need to make decisions that you are comfortable with.

5b   Use online tools for revising.

www.mhhe.com/
nmhh
For help with revising, go to

Writing >
Paragraph/Essay
Development >
Drafting and
Revising

Word-processing programs can make your text look beautiful, with a pleasing format and an easy-to-read typeface. Even though a first draft may look finished, however, it is still a first draft. Be sure to check below the surface for problems in content, structure, and style. Move paragraphs around, add details, and delete irrelevant sentences. The computer makes these changes almost effortless. However, it is always a good idea to print out a copy of your draft because hard copy, unlike the computer screen, allows you to see the big picture—your paper as a whole.

So that you can work efficiently, you should become familiar with the revising and editing tools in your word-processing program.

93

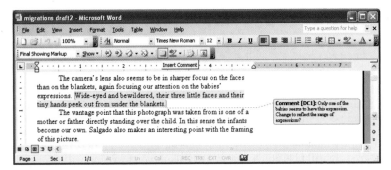

FIGURE 5.1 **Using Microsoft Word's Comments feature.**

- **Comments:** Many word-processing programs have a Comments feature (*see Figure 5.1*) that allows you to add notes that pop up when readers run the cursor over highlighted text. This feature is very useful for giving feedback on someone else's draft. Some writers also like to use it to make notes to themselves.

- **Track Changes:** The Track Changes feature (*see Figure 5.2*) allows you to edit a piece of writing—either yours or another writer's—while maintaining the original text. Usually, strikethrough marks show what you have deleted or replaced. Because you can still see the original text, you can judge whether a change has improved the paper and whether any vital information was lost when the change was made. If you change your mind, you can restore the deleted text. When collaborating with another writer, you should keep the original text intact while suggesting changes. To do this, track changes onscreen only.

5c Focus on the purpose of your writing.

As you reread your paper and decide how to revise it, base your decisions on the purpose of your paper. Is your primary purpose to inform, to interpret, or to argue? (*For more on assignment purposes, see Chapter 2, pp. 26–28.*)

Clarity about your purpose is especially important when an assignment calls for interpretation. A description is not the same as an interpretation. With this principle in mind, Diane Chen read over the first draft of her paper on the *Migrations* photography exhibit. Here is part of her description of the photograph she chose to discuss in detail:

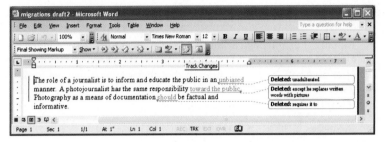

FIGURE 5.2 **Showing revisions with Track Changes.**

CHECKLIST

Revising Your Draft for Content and Organization

☐ 1. **Purpose:** Is my purpose for writing clear? If not, how can I revise to make my purpose apparent?

☐ 2. **Thesis:** Is my thesis clear and specific, and do I introduce it early in my draft? If not, do I have a good reason for withholding it or not stating it at all?

☐ 3. **Order:** Are my key points arranged effectively? Would another order support my thesis better?

☐ 4. **Paragraphs:** Is each paragraph well developed, unified, and coherent?

☐ 5. **Visuals:** If I am using visuals, do they communicate what I intend them to without unnecessary clutter?

FIRST DRAFT

The photograph is black and white, as are the others in the show. The faces of the babies are in sharp focus while the blanket is a bit defocused. Light, which is essential to photography, is disseminated from a single source coming from the upper left-hand corner of the picture. The light source is not too bright as to bathe the babies in light, but just bright enough to illuminate their faces, which have expressions of interest and puzzlement. Perhaps they are wondering who Salgado is or what is that strange contraption he is holding.

Keeping her purpose in mind, Chen realized that she needed to discuss the significance of her observations—to interpret the details and offer an analysis. She wanted to show her readers how the formal elements of the photograph functioned. Her revision makes this interpretation clearer.

REVISION

The orphanage photograph is shot in black and white, as are the other images in the show, giving it a documentary feel that emphasizes the truth of the situation. But Salgado's choice of black-and-white photography is also an artistic decision. He uses the contrasts of light and dark to create a dramatic image of the three babies.

The vertical black-and-white stripes of the blanket direct our eyes to the infants' faces and hands, which are framed by a horizontal white stripe . . .

www.mhhe.com/
nmhh
For help developing
a strong thesis,
go to

Writing >
Paragraph/Essay
Development >
Thesis/Central
Idea

5d Make sure you have a strong thesis.

Remember that a thesis makes an assertion about a topic. It links the *what* and the *why.* Is your thesis evident on the first page of your draft? Before readers get very far along, they expect an answer to the question, "What is the point of all this?" If you do not find the point on the first page, its absence is a signal to revise, unless you are deliberately waiting until the end to reveal your thesis. (*For more on strong theses, see Chapter 3, pp. 45–48.*)

When Diane Chen looked over the first draft of her paper, she decided that she needed to strengthen her thesis statement. She had included two sentences that could serve as a thesis, and it wasn't clear which one was to be the central idea of her paper:

POSSIBLE THESIS

[A] photograph taken with an aesthetic awareness does not debase the severity of war and worldwide suffering.

POSSIBLE THESIS

Whether capturing the millions of refugee tents in Africa that seem to stretch on for miles or the disheartened faces of small immigrant children, Salgado brings an artistic element to his pictures that suggests he does so much more with his camera than just point and shoot.

LEARNING in COLLEGE

Selecting a Title

Your essay title should engage your readers' interest and prepare them for the thesis of your paper. The title should not simply state a broad topic ("Lake Superior Zooplankton") but rather should indicate your angle on that topic ("Changes in the Lake Superior Crustacean Zooplankton Community"). Here are some suggestions for strengthening your title:

1. Include a phrase that communicates the purpose of your paper.
   - Alcohol Myopia Theory: A Review of the Literature
   - From Palm to Blackberry: A Brief History of PDAs
   - Punishment to Fit the Crime: An Argument for the Death Penalty
2. Use a question to indicate that your paper weighs different sides of an argument.
   - Does the Patriot Act Strengthen America?
   - Performance-Based Funding for the Arts: Wise Fiscal Policy or Unwise Gamble?
3. Use a quotation and/or a play on words or a vivid image.
   - Much Ado about "Noting": Perception in Shakespeare's Comedy
   - Many Happy Returns: An Inventory Management Success Story
   - A Fly Trapped in Amber: On Investigating Soft-Bodied Fossils

Chen decided to change her introduction to sharpen the focus on one main idea:

FINAL THESIS   Like a photojournalist, Salgado brings us images of newsworthy events, but he goes beyond objective reporting, imparting his compassion for refugees and migrants to the viewer.

(*To compare Diane's first and second drafts, see pp. 118 and 120.*)

Many writers start with a working thesis, which evolves into a more specific, complex assertion as they develop their ideas. Sometimes writers find that their ideas change altogether, and the working thesis needs to be completely revised.

Your thesis should be developed throughout the paper. Readers need to see a statement of the main idea on the first page, but they also expect the writer to return to the thesis near the end. Here is Diane Chen's restatement of her thesis from the end of her revised draft:

> Salgado uses his skills as an artist to get us not only to look at these difficult subjects, but also to feel compassion for them. He is able to bring a story as big and complex as the epic displacement of the world's people to us through a collection of intimate and intensely moving images. As he says in his introduction to the exhibit catalog, "We hold the key to humanity's future, but for that we must understand the present. We cannot afford to look away" (15).

Exercise 5.1   Revising thesis statements

Examine some of your recent papers to see if the thesis is clearly stated. Is the thesis significant? Can you follow the development of this idea throughout the paper? Does the version of your thesis in the conclusion answer the "so what?" question?

5e   Review the structure of your paper as a whole.

In a first draft, you are wise to think broadly about the different parts of your paper and how you should order them. Does the paper have a beginning, a middle, and an end, with bridges between those parts? When you revise, however, you can refine and even change this structure so that it supports what you want to say more effectively.

One way to review the structure is by outlining your first draft. (*For help with outlining, see Chapter 3, pp. 50–54.*) An outline makes clear the overall pattern of your thinking. Try listing the key points of your draft in sentence form; whenever possible, use sentences that actually appear in the draft. This kind of point-by-point outlining will allow you to see the logic (or lack of it) in your draft. Ask yourself if the key points are arranged effectively or if another arrangement would work better. The following structures are typical ways of organizing papers:

- An *informative structure* sets out the key parts of a topic.

- An *exploratory structure* begins with a question or problem and works step by step to discover or explain an answer or a solution.

- An *argumentative structure* presents a set of linked reasons plus supporting evidence.

5f Revise your essay for paragraph development, paragraph unity, and coherence.

The structure you choose for your paper should be appropriate to the assignment, your purpose, and your thesis, and the paper's parts should develop your ideas in an orderly way. As you revise, examine each paragraph, asking yourself what role it plays—or should play—in the paper as a whole. Keeping this role in mind, check the paragraph for development and unity. You should also check each paragraph for coherence—and consider whether all of the paragraphs taken together contribute to the paper as a whole.

1. Paragraph development

As you revise your paper, ask yourself: Does each paragraph provide enough detail? Paragraphs in academic papers are usually about a hundred words long. Although sometimes you will deliberately use a one- or two-sentence paragraph for stylistic emphasis, when paragraphs are short for no apparent stylistic reason, they may need to be developed more fully. Would more information make the point clearer? Perhaps a term should be defined. Do generalizations need to be supported with examples?

Note how this writer developed one of her draft paragraphs, adding details and examples to make her argument more clearly and effectively:

FIRST DRAFT

A 1913 advertisement for Shredded Wheat illustrates Kellner's claim that advertisements sell self-images. The ad suggests that serving Shredded Wheat will give women the same sense of accomplishment as gaining the right to vote.

REVISION

According to Kellner, "advertising is as concerned with selling lifestyles and socially desirable identities . . . as with selling the products themselves" (193). A 1913 ad for Shredded Wheat shows how the selling of self-images works. At first glance, this ad seems to be promoting the women's suffrage movement. In big, bold letters, "Votes for Women" is emblazoned across the top of the ad. But a closer look reveals that the ad is for Shredded Wheat cereal. Holding a piece of the cereal in her hand, a woman stands behind a large bowlful of Shredded Wheat biscuits that is made to look like a voting box. The text claims that "every biscuit is a vote for health, happiness and domestic freedom." Like the rest of the advertisement, this claim suggests that serving Shredded Wheat will give women the same sense of accomplishment as gaining the right to vote.

—HOLLY MUSETTI, student paper

www.mhhe.com/
nmhh
For help developing
paragraph unity,
go to

Writing >
Paragraph/Essay
Development >
Unity

2. Paragraph unity

A unified paragraph has a single, clear focus. To check for **unity,** identify the paragraph's topic sentence (*see p. 66*). Everything in the paragraph should be clearly and closely connected to the topic sentence.

Compare the first draft of the following paragraph with its revision, and note how the addition of a topic sentence (in bold in the revision) makes the paragraph more clearly focused and therefore easier for the writer to revise further. Note also that the writer deleted ideas that did not directly relate to the paragraph's main point (underlined in the first draft):

FIRST DRAFT

Germany is ranked first on worldwide production levels. Automobiles, aircraft, and electronic equipment are among Germany's most important products for export. As the standard of living of the citizens of what was formerly East Germany increases due to reunification, their purchasing power and productivity will increase. A major problem is that east Germany is not as productive or efficient as west Germany, and so it would be better if less money were invested in the east. Germany is involved in most global treaties that protect business interests, and intellectual property is well protected. A plus for potential ventures and production plans is its highly skilled workforce. Another factor that indicates that Germany will remain strong in the arena of productivity and trade is its physical location in the world. "Its terrain and geographical position have combined to make Germany an important crossroads for traffic between the North Sea, the Baltic, and the Mediterranean. International transportation routes pass through all of Germany," thus utilizing a comprehensive and efficient network of transportation, both on land and over water ("Germany," 1995, p. 185). Businesses can operate plants in Germany and have no difficulties transporting goods and services to other parts of the country. Generally, private enterprise, government, banks, and unions cooperate, making the country more amenable to negotiations for business entry or joint ventures.

REVISION

For many reasons, Germany is attractive both as a market for other nations and as a location for production.

As the standard of living of the citizens of what was formerly East Germany increases due to reunification, their purchasing power and productivity increase. Intellectual property is well protected, and Germany is involved in most global treaties that protect business interests. Germany's highly skilled workforce is another plus for potential ventures and production plans. Generally, private enterprise, government, banks, and unions cooperate, making the country amenable to negotiations for business entry or joint ventures. Germany also has an excellent physical location that makes it an "important crossroads for traffic between the North Sea, the Baltic, and the Mediterranean" ("Germany," 1995, p. 185). Equally important, a comprehensive and efficient transportation system allows businesses to operate plants in Germany and easily transport their goods and services to other parts of the country and the world.

> —JENNIFER KOEHLER, "Germany's Path to Continuing Prosperity"

3. Coherence

The sentences in a paragraph should "cohere," or stick together as a unit. Likewise, each paragraph should be clearly related to the rest of the essay. A coherent paragraph flows smoothly, with an organization that is easy to follow and with each sentence clearly related to the next. (*See Chapter 4, pp. 69–83, for tips on how to develop well-organized paragraphs.*) You can improve the **coherence** both within and among the paragraphs in your draft by using repetition, pronouns, parallel structure, and transitions.

www.mhhe.com/
nmhh
For help writing
coherent paragraphs,
go to
Writing >
Paragraph/Essay
Development >
Coherence

Use repetition to emphasize the main idea   Repeating key words helps your readers stay focused on the topic of your paper and can serve to reinforce your thesis. In the example that follows, Rajeev Bector opens his paper with a paragraph that uses repetition (highlighted) to define a key term that is central to his essay:

> Sociologist Erving Goffman believes that every social interaction establishes our identity and preserves our image, honor, and credibility in the hearts and minds of others. Social interactions, he says, are in essence "character contests" that occur not only in games and sports but also in our everyday dealings with strangers, peers, friends and even family members. Goffman defines character contests as "disputes [that] are sought out and indulged in (often with glee) as a means of establishing where ones boundaries are" (29). Just such a contest

occurs in Flannery O'Connor's short story "Everything That
Rises Must Converge."

—RAJEEV BECTOR, "The Character Contest in Flannery
O'Connor's 'Everything That Rises Must Converge,' "
student paper

*(To see Bector's complete essay, turn to p. 195 in Chapter 9: Interpretive
Analyses.)*

Use pronouns to avoid unnecessary repetition When used se-
lectively, repetition can be an effective tool for building coherent paragraphs. Be careful not to overdo it, however. Too much repetition can
make your sentences sound clumsy and your paragraphs seem monotonous. Use pronouns to stand in for nouns where needed, and to
form connections between sentences.

In the paragraph below, Diane Chen uses pronouns (highlighted)
to create smooth-sounding sentences that hold the paragraph together:

> Salgado uses his skills as an artist to get us not only to look at these
> difficult subjects, but also to feel compassion for them. He is able to
> bring a story as big and complex as the epic displacement of the world's
> people to us through a collection of intimate and intensely moving
> images. As he says in his introduction to the exhibit catalog, "We hold
> the key to humanity's future, but for that we must understand the
> present. We cannot afford to look away."

Use parallel structure to emphasize connections When you repeat sentence structures instead of key words, the parallel structure
you create helps to form connections within and between the sentences
of your paragraph. In the following sentence, for example, the three
clauses are grammatically parallel, each consisting of a pronoun (P)
and a past-tense verb (V):

<pre>
      P - V   P - V   P - V
</pre>
➤ **We came, we saw, and we conquered.**

Within paragraphs, two or more sentences can have parallel
structures, as in the following example:

➤ **Because the former West Germany lived through a generation of prosperity, its people developed high expectations of material comfort. Because the former East
Germany lived through a generation of deprivation, its
people developed a disdain for material values.**

Too much parallelism can seem repetitive, though, so save this device
for ideas that can be meaningfully paired. (*For more information on*

TRANSITIONAL EXPRESSIONS

Transitional Expressions

- **To show relationships in space:** above, adjacent to, against, alongside, around, at a distance from, at the . . . , below, beside, beyond, encircling, far off, forward, from the . . . , in front of, in the rear, inside, near the back, near the end, nearby, next to, on, over, surrounding, there, through the . . . , to the left, to the right, up front
- **To show relationships in time:** afterward, at last, before, earlier, first, former, formerly, immediately, in the first place, in the interval, in the meantime, in the next place, in the last place, later on, latter, meanwhile, next, now, often, once, previously, second, simultaneously, sometime later, subsequently, suddenly, then, therefore, third, today, tomorrow, until now, when, years ago, yesterday
- **To show something added to what has come before:** again, also, and, and then, besides, further, furthermore, in addition, last, likewise, moreover, next, too
- **To give examples that intensify points:** after all, as an example, certainly, clearly, for example, for instance, indeed, in fact, in truth, it is true that, of course, specifically, that is
- **To show similarities:** alike, in the same way, like, likewise, resembling, similarly
- **To show contrasts:** after all, although, but, conversely, differ(s) from, difference, different, dissimilar, even though, granted, however, in contrast, in spite of, nevertheless, notwithstanding, on the contrary, on the other hand, otherwise, still, though, unlike, while this may be true, yet
- **To indicate cause and effect:** accordingly, as a result, because, consequently, hence, since, then, therefore, thus
- **To conclude or summarize:** finally, in brief, in conclusion, in other words, in short, in summary, that is, to summarize

editing for parallelism in your writing, turn to Chapter 42: Faulty Parallelism.)

Use transitional words and phrases   One-word **transitions** and **transitional expressions** link one idea to another, helping readers understand your logic. (*See the box above for a list of common transitional expressions.*) Compare the following two paragraphs, the first version without transitions and the second, revised version with transitions (in bold type) that connect one thought to another:

103

FIRST DRAFT

Glaser was in a position to powerfully affect Armstrong's career and his life. Armstrong acknowledged Glaser's importance, referring to him at one point as "the man who has guided me all through my career" (qtd. in Jones and Chilton 202). There is little evidence that the musician submitted to whatever his business manager wanted or demanded. Armstrong seemed to recognize that he gave Glaser whatever power the manager enjoyed over him. Armstrong could and did resist Glaser's control when he wanted to. That may be one reason why he liked and trusted Glaser as much as he did.

REVISION

Clearly, Glaser was in a position to affect Armstrong's career and his life powerfully. Armstrong acknowledged Glaser's importance, at one point referring to him as "the man who has guided me all through my career" (qtd. in Jones and Chilton 202). **However,** there is little evidence that the musician submitted to whatever his business manager wanted or demanded. **In fact,** Armstrong seemed to recognize that he gave Glaser whatever power the manager enjoyed over him. When he wanted to, Armstrong could and did resist Glaser's control, and that may be one reason why he liked and trusted Glaser as much as he did.

—ESTER HOFFMAN, "Louis Armstrong and Joe Glaser"

(To see Hoffman's complete essay, turn to pp. 416–26 in Chapter 24: MLA Documentation Style.)

Use coherence strategies to show how paragraphs are related
You can also use repetition, pronouns, parallelism, and transitions to show how paragraphs in an essay are related to one another. In addition, you can use **transitional sentences** both to refer to the previous paragraph and at the same time to move your essay on to the next point. Notice how the first sentence at the beginning of the second paragraph below, from Diane Chen's essay about Sebastião Salgado, both refers to the babies described in the previous paragraph and serves as a topic sentence for the second paragraph.

The vertical black-and-white stripes of the blanket direct our eyes to the infants' faces and hands, which are framed by a horizontal white stripe. The whites of their eyes in particular stand out against the darkness created by the shell of the blankets. The camera's lens also seems to be in sharper focus on the faces than on the blankets, again focusing our attention on the babies' expressions.

Each baby has a different response to the camera. The baby on the left returns our gaze with a heart-wrenching look. The baby in the center, whose eyes are open extra-wide, appears startled and in need of comforting. But the baby on the right, whose eyes are glazed and sunken, doesn't even notice the camera. We glimpse death in that child's face.

Exercise 5.2 Revising paragraphs

Revise the paragraphs below to improve their unity, development, and coherence.

1. Vivaldi was famous and influential as a virtuoso violinist and composer. Vivaldi died in poverty, having lost popularity in the last years before his death. He had been acclaimed during his lifetime and forgotten for two hundred years after his death. Many composers suffer that fate. The baroque revival of the 1950s brought his music back to the public's attention.

2. People who want to adopt an exotic pet need to be aware of the consequences. Baby snakes and reptiles can seem fairly easy to manage. Lion and tiger cubs are playful and friendly. They can seem as harmless as kittens. Domestic cats can revert to a wild state quite easily. Adult snakes and reptiles can grow large. Many species of reptiles and snakes require carefully controlled environments. Big cats can escape. An escaped lion or tiger is a danger to itself and to others. Most exotic animals need professional care. This kind of care is available in zoos and wild-animal parks. The best environment for an exotic animal is the wild.

Exercise 5.3 Writing well-developed, coherent paragraphs

Using the strategies for paragraph development and coherence discussed in section 5f, write a paragraph for one of the following topic sentences. Working with two or more classmates, decide where your paragraph needs more details or improved coherence.

1. Awards shows on television often fail to recognize creativity and innovation.

2. Most people learn only those aspects of a computer program that they need to use every day.

3. First-year students who also work can have an easier time adjusting to the demands of college life than nonworking students.

4. E-mail messages that circulate widely can be broken down into several categories.

**www.mhhe.com/
nmhh**
For more on using
visuals, go to
Writing > Visual
Rhetoric Tutorial >
Visualizing Data

5g Revise visuals.

If you have used visuals in your paper to present information, you should return to them during the revision stage to eliminate what scholar Edward Tufte calls **chartjunk,** or distracting visual elements. The following are Tufte's suggestions for editing visuals so that your readers will focus on your data rather than your "data containers."

- **Eliminate grid lines or, if the lines are needed for clarity, lighten them.** Tables should not look like nets, with every number enclosed. Vertical rules are needed only when space is extremely tight between columns.

DRAFT

Average and Beginning Teacher Salaries in New England, 1999–2000

STATE	AVERAGE SALARY	BEGINNING SALARY
Connecticut	$52,410	$30,466
Rhode Island	48,138	27,286
Massachusetts	46,955	30,330
New Hampshire	37,734	24,650
Vermont	36,402	25,791
Maine	35,561	22,942

REVISION

Average and Beginning Teacher Salaries in New England, 1999–2000

STATE	AVERAGE SALARY	BEGINNING SALARY
Connecticut	$52,410	$30,466
Rhode Island	48,138	27,286
Massachusetts	46,955	30,330
New Hampshire	37,734	24,650
Vermont	36,402	25,791
Maine	35,561	22,942

- **Eliminate unnecessary three-dimensional renderings.**
  Cubes and shadows can distort the information in a visual.
  For most charts, including pie charts, a flat image makes it
  easier for readers to compare parts. (*See Figure 5.3.*)

DRAFT

Annual Expenses for Everson Chemical, 2004

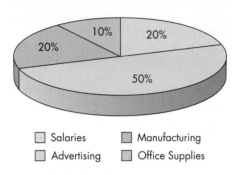

REVISION

Annual Expenses for Everson Chemical, 2004

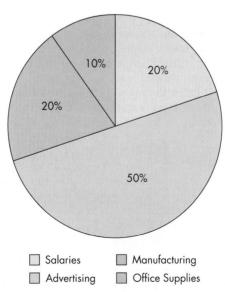

FIGURE 5.3 **Revising a pie chart to increase clarity.**

- **Label data clearly,** avoiding abbreviations and legends, if possible. Make sure that your visual has an informative title.

- **Use bright colors sparingly,** to focus attention on the key data. If you are including a map, use muted colors over large areas, and save strong colors for emphasis.

- **Avoid decorating your visual with distracting pictures.** Clip art and other decorative elements seldom make data more interesting, nor do they make it appear more substantial.

- **Look out for and correct distortions of the data.** In the draft version of the graph in Figure 5.4 (*on the facing page*), eight months of the year are plotted separately, with the months of January, February, March, and April grouped together. This creates a misleading impression of hurricane activity by month. The revision corrects this distortion.

www.mhhe.com/
nmhh
For additional help
with editing, go to
Editing

5h Edit sentences.

When you are satisfied with the overall placement and development of your ideas, then you can turn your attention to individual sentences and words. Parts 7, 8, and 9 of this handbook address the many specific questions that writers have when they are editing for grammar conventions, clarity, and word choice. The section that follows gives you an overview of editing concerns and techniques.

1. Editing for grammar conventions

Many of us use the rules of English grammar unconsciously to generate sentences that other English speakers can easily understand. Sometimes, however, we will construct a sentence or choose a word form that does not follow the rules of standard written English. In academic writing, these kinds of errors are distracting to readers and can obscure your meaning.

DRAFT

Photographs of illegal immigrants being captured by the United States border patrol, of emotional immigrants on the plane to their new country, and of villagers fleeing rebel gangs. [*This is a sentence fragment because it lacks a verb. It also omits the writer's point about these images.*]

EDITED SENTENCE

Photographs of illegal immigrants being captured by the United States border patrol, of emotional immigrants on the plane to their new country, and of villagers fleeing rebel gangs exemplify the range of migration stories.

DRAFT

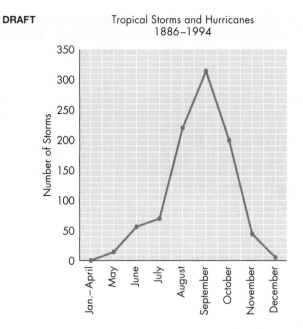

REVISION

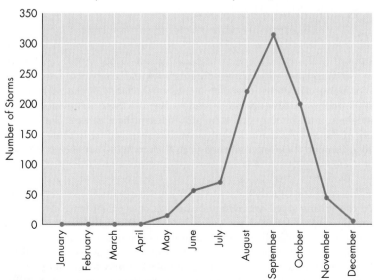

FIGURE 5.4 Eliminating distortion in a line graph.

CHECKLIST

Editing Your Sentences and Words

Most writers are prone to problems with some aspects of the conventions of written English. The diagnostic "Test Yourself" quizzes that begin Parts 7 and 8 of this handbook, the exercises in the chapters in Parts 7 through 9, and the editing checklists that close each part can help you determine which conventions give you trouble. To create a personalized editing checklist, fill in the boxes next to your trouble spots in the list that follows.

1. **Editing for grammar conventions** (*Part 7*): Does my paper contain any of the common errors that may confuse or distract readers?

   ☐ Sentence fragments
   ☐ Comma splices
   ☐ Run-on sentences
   ☐ Subject-verb agreement problems
   ☐ Incorrect verb forms
   ☐ Inconsistent verb tenses
   ☐ Pronoun-antecedent agreement problems
   ☐ Incorrect pronoun forms
   ☐ Misused adjectives or adverbs
   ☐ Other: _____

Professional editors use abbreviations and symbols to note errors in a manuscript; a list of common ones can be found at the back of this book. Your instructor and other readers may use these abbreviations and symbols, and you may find it helpful to learn them as well. Some writers prefer simply to mark sentences that seem wrong to them as they read through their text and then to go back to figure out each error.

2. Editing for clarity

At the editing stage, you will also want to focus on sentence style, aiming for clearly focused yet varied writing. Some of your sentences, though grammatically correct, can probably be improved at this stage. A volley of short, choppy sentences, for example, distracts readers from what you have to say, whereas an unbroken stream of long, complicated sentences is likely to dull their senses. In the example that follows,

2. **Editing for clarity** (*Part 8*): Is every sentence clear and direct? Does my paper contain any of the following common causes of unclear sentences?

   ☐ Wordiness
   ☐ Missing words
   ☐ Mixed constructions
   ☐ Confusing shifts
   ☐ Faulty parallelism
   ☐ Misplaced or dangling modifiers
   ☐ Problem with coordination and subordination
   ☐ Other: _____

3. **Editing for word choice** (*Part 9*):

   ☐ Have I avoided slang, biased language, clichés, and other inappropriate usages?
   ☐ Is my choice of words as precise as it could be?
   ☐ Have I misused any commonly confused words (for example, *advice* vs. *advise*) or used any nonstandard expressions (for example, *could of*)?

If you are in the process of developing fluency in English, consult Part 12: Guide for Multilingual Writers for additional editing advice specific to multilingual writers.

notice how the revised version connects ideas for readers and, consequently, is easier to read.

DRAFT   My father was a zealous fisherman. He took his fishing rod on every family outing. Often he spent the whole outing staring at the water, waiting for a nibble. He went to the kitchen as soon as he got home. He usually cleaned and cooked the fish the same day he caught them.

REVISED   A zealous fisherman, my father took his fishing rod on every family outing. He would often spend the whole afternoon by the shore, waiting for a nibble, and then hurry straight to the kitchen to clean and cook his catch.

TEXTCONNEX

The Pros and Cons of Grammar Checkers and Spell Checkers

Grammar checkers and spell checkers can help you spot some errors, but they miss many others and may even flag correct sentences. Consider the following example:

➤ **Thee neighbors puts there cats' outsider.**

A spelling and grammar checker did not catch the five real errors in the sentence. (Correct version: *The neighbors put their cats outside.*) The software also flagged the following grammatically correct and eloquent sentence by Alice Walker and suggested the nonsense substitution below.

WALKER'S SENTENCE

➤ **Consider, if you can bear to imagine it, what might have been the result if singing, too, had been forbidden by law.**

GRAMMAR CHECKER'S SUGGESTION

➤ **Consider, if you can bear to imagine it, law if singing, too, had forbid what might have been the result.**

If you are aware of your program's deficiencies and its obvious inability to think like an English speaker, then you can make some use of it as you edit your manuscript. Be sure, however, to review the manuscript carefully yourself. Throughout the grammar chapters of this book, Grammar Checker boxes warn you of potential pitfalls in using these tools.

Grammatically correct sentences can also be weak if they are wordy and lack a clear subject and a vivid verb. The editing stage is the best time to condense and focus these kinds of sentences:

DRAFT   Although both vertebral and wrist fractures cause deformity and impair movement, hip fractures, which are one of the most devastating consequences of osteoporosis, significantly increase the risk of death, since 12%–30% of patients with a hip fracture die within one year after the fracture, while the mortality rate climbs to 40% for the first two years post fracture.

REVISED   Hip fractures are one of the most devastating consequences of osteoporosis. Although vertebral and wrist fractures cause deformity and impair movement, hip fractures significantly increase the risk of death. Within one year after a hip fracture, 12%–20% of the injured die. The mortality rate climbs to 40% after two years.

DRAFT   *There are stereotypes* from the days of a divided Germany that must be dealt with.

REVISED   *Stereotypes* formed in the days of a divided Germany *persist* and must be dealt with.

3. Editing for word choice

Finding precisely the right word and putting that word in the best place is an important part of revision. In a sense, different disciplines and occupations have their own dialects that members of the community are expected to know and use. The word *significant,* for example, has a mathematical meaning for the statistician that it does not have for the literary critic. When taking courses in a discipline, you should use its terminology or dialect, not to impress the instructor but to be understood accurately. Whenever you are unsure of a word's denotation (its exact meaning), be sure to consult a dictionary.

As you review your draft, look for general terms that might need to be made more specific:

DRAFT   Foreign direct investment (FDI) in Germany will probably remain low because of several *factors.* [Factors *is a general word that should signal you to get specific by answering the question, "What factors?"*]

REVISED   Foreign direct investment (FDI) in Germany will probably remain low because of *high labor costs, high taxation, and government regulation.*

Your search for more specific words can lead you to a dictionary and a thesaurus, two essential tools for choosing precise words. A dictionary gives the exact definition of a word, its history (etymology), and the parts of speech it belongs to. A thesaurus provides its synonyms, words with the same or nearly the same meaning. (*For more on using a dictionary and a thesaurus, see Chapter 47.*)

One student used both a thesaurus and a dictionary as aids in revising the following sentence:

DRAFT   Malcolm X had a special kind of power.

Dissatisfied with the precision of the word *power,* this writer checked a thesaurus and found the word *influence* listed as a synonym for *power* and the word *charisma* given as a special kind of influence. Going back to the dictionary, she found that *charisma* means a "divinely conferred" power and has an etymological connection with *charismatic,* a term used to describe ecstatic Christian experiences like speaking in tongues. *Charisma* was exactly the word she needed to convey both the spiritual and the popular sides of Malcolm X:

REVISED   Malcolm X had a special kind of charisma.

As you edit for word choice, you will also want to make sure that your tone is appropriate for academic writing (*see Chapter 2, p. 31*) and that you have avoided biased language, such as the use of *his* to refer to women as well as men:

BIASED

Every student who wrote *his* name on the class list had to pay a copying fee in advance and pledge to attend every session.

REVISED AS PLURAL

Students who wrote *their* names on the class list had to pay a copying fee in advance and pledge to attend every session.

REVISED TO AVOID PRONOUNS

Every student who signed up for the class had to pay a copying fee in advance and pledge to attend every session.

REVISED WITH *HIS OR HER*

Every student who wrote *his or her* name on the class list had to pay a copying fee in advance and pledge to attend every session.

(*See Chapter 48: Appropriate Language for advice on editing to eliminate biased language.*)

Exercise 5.4   Editing sentences

Type the following sentences into your word processor and activate the grammar and spell-checker feature. Copy the sentence suggested by the software, and then write your own edited version of the sentence.

1. Lighting affects are sense of the shape and texture of the objects depict.
2. A novelist's tells the truth even though he invent stories and characters.
3. There are the question of why bad things happen to good people, which story of Job illustrate.
4. A expensive marketing campaign is of little value if the product stinks.
5. Digestive enzymes melt down the nutrients in food so that the body is able to put in effect a utilization of those nutrients when the body needs energy to do things.

5i Proofread carefully before you turn in your paper.

Once you have revised your paper at the whole essay, paragraph, and sentence levels, it is time to give your work one last check to make sure that it is free of typos and other mechanical errors.

Many writers prefer to **proofread** their paper when it is in its final format. If you are required to submit your writing assignment on paper, then you should proofread a printout. Even if you are submitting an electronic version of your paper, it is still a good idea to proofread a printed version. Placing a ruler under each line as you proofread can make it easier to focus. Another proofreading technique that helps you slow down and focus is to start at the end of the paper and proofread your way backwards to the beginning, sentence by sentence.

5j Use resources available on your campus, on the Internet, and in your community.

www.mhhe.com/ nmhh
For links to online resources on writing, go to
Writing > Writing Web Links

As you revise and edit your paper, you can call on a number of different resources outside of the writing classroom for help.

1. Using the campus writing center
Many campuses maintain writing centers, staffed by tutors, that offer help at every stage of the writing process. Tutors in the writing center can read and comment on drafts of your work. They can also help you find and correct problems with grammar, punctuation, and mechanics.

2. Using online writing labs, or OWLs
Most OWLs present information about writing that you can access anytime, including lists of useful online resources. Some OWLs are

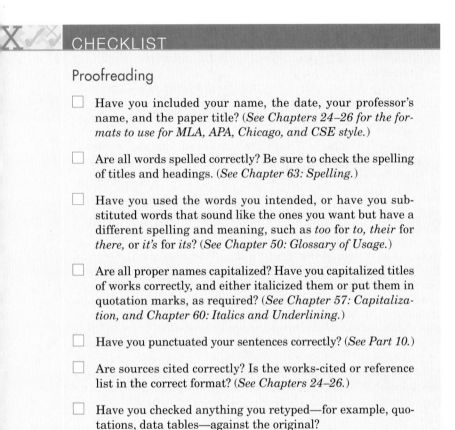

CHECKLIST

Proofreading

☐ Have you included your name, the date, your professor's name, and the paper title? (*See Chapters 24–26 for the formats to use for MLA, APA, Chicago, and CSE style.*)

☐ Are all words spelled correctly? Be sure to check the spelling of titles and headings. (*See Chapter 63: Spelling.*)

☐ Have you used the words you intended, or have you substituted words that sound like the ones you want but have a different spelling and meaning, such as *too* for *to, their* for *there,* or *it's* for *its*? (*See Chapter 50: Glossary of Usage.*)

☐ Are all proper names capitalized? Have you capitalized titles of works correctly, and either italicized them or put them in quotation marks, as required? (*See Chapter 57: Capitalization, and Chapter 60: Italics and Underlining.*)

☐ Have you punctuated your sentences correctly? (*See Part 10.*)

☐ Are sources cited correctly? Is the works-cited or reference list in the correct format? (*See Chapters 24–26.*)

☐ Have you checked anything you retyped—for example, quotations, data tables—against the original?

staffed by tutors who support students working on specific writing assignments. OWLs with tutors can be useful in the following ways:

▪ You can submit a draft by e-mail for feedback. OWL tutors will return your work, often within forty-eight hours.

▪ OWLs may post your paper in a public access space where you will receive feedback from more than just one or two readers.

▪ You can read papers online and learn how others are handling writing issues.

You can learn more about what OWLs have to offer by checking out the following Web sites:

- *Purdue University's Online Writing Lab (Figure 5.5)* <http://owl.english.purdue.edu>
- *Writing Labs and Writing Centers on the Web* (visit almost 50 OWLs) <http://owl.english.purdue.edu/internet/owls/writing-labs.html>
- *Washington State University's Online Writing Lab* <http://owl.wsu.edu>

3. Working with experts and instructors

In addition to sharing your work with peers in class, through e-mail, or in online environments, you can use e-mail to consult experts. Suppose, for example, that a friend at another college is an expert on the topic of your paper. You can use e-mail to interview that friend, and then include parts of the interview in your paper. As always, you must properly credit your source. (*See Part 4 on documentation styles.*)

You can also consult your instructor or other experts. Many students don't think to ask their instructor questions by e-mail. If your instructor is willing, you can quote from his or her response in your paper, giving it a proper citation, of course.

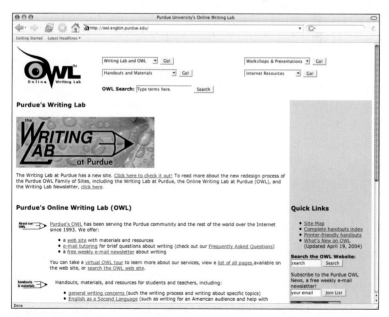

FIGURE 5.5 **The Purdue Online Writing Lab.**

Your instructor's comments on an early draft are especially valuable. He or she will raise questions and make suggestions, but remember, it is not your instructor's job to "solve" the paper for you and to tell you everything you need to do to get an A in the course. It is your responsibility to address the issues your instructor raises and to revise your work.

5k Learn from one student's revisions.

In this section we will look at several drafts of Diane Chen's paper on the *Migrations* photography exhibit. The photograph that she is discussing can be seen in the final version of her paper, on page 123.

1. First draft, with revision comments
In Chapter 2, we saw Diane Chen choose the exhibit of photographs by Sebastião Salgado as the topic for a paper she needed to write in response to a writing assignment (*see 2b, p. 23*). In Chapter 3, we saw her explore this topic (*see 3a, pp. 35–44*), develop a working thesis (*see 3b, pp. 45–47*), and plan her organization (*see 3c, pp. 50–54*). Here is Diane Chen's first draft, along with notes about general and paragraph-level concerns that she received at her school's writing center.

Consider using a title that is related to your thesis.

Sebastião Salgado

Migrations: Humanity in Transition

The role of a photojournalist is to inform and educate the public in an unbiased manner. Photography as a means of documentation requires it to be factual and informative. However, a photograph taken with an aesthetic awareness does not debase the severity of war and worldwide suffering.

Can you connect this idea to the exhibit sooner for a clearer focus?

In a recent exhibition of Sebastiao Salgado's work entitled, "Migrations: Humanity in Transition," the noted photographer displayed his documentation of the plight of migrants and refugees through beautiful and artful photographs. Whether capturing the

OK?

Why is this artistic element significant?

millions of refugee tents in Africa that seem to stretch on for miles or the disheartened faces of small immigrant children, Salgado brings an artistic element to his pictures that suggests he does so much more with his camera than just point and shoot.

So many photographs in Salgado's show are certain to impress and touch the viewers with their subject matter and sheer beauty. However, "Orphanage attached to the hospital at Kibumba, Number One Camp, Goma, Zaire," was my favorite photograph. It depicts three apparently newborn or several month old babies, who are victims of the genocidal war in Rwanda, arranged neatly in a row, wrapped in a mass of stripe-patterned clothes or blankets. Wide-eyed and bewildered, their three little faces and their tiny hands peek out from under the blankets. The whites of their eyes stand out against the darkness created by the shell of the blankets.

> *This phrase doesn't seem quite appropriate to the subject.*

> *Does this apply to all three faces?*

The photograph is black and white, as are the others in the show. The faces of the babies are in sharp focus while the blanket is a bit defocused. Light, which is essential to photography, is disseminated from a single source coming from the upper left-hand corner of the picture. The light source is not too bright as to bathe the babies in light, but just bright enough to illuminate their faces, which have expressions of interest and puzzlement. Perhaps they are wondering who Salgado is or what is that strange contraption he is holding. The lighting also creates contrasts of light and dark in the peaks and valleys created by the folds in the blanket.

> *Nice observation, but how is it connected to the rest of the paragraph?*

> *Excellent descriptions but tie them to analyses.*

What I find most impress*ive* in this picture is Salgado's ability to find the beauty of human life amidst the ugliness of warfare. The vantage point that this photograph was taken from is one of a mother or father directly standing over the child. In this sense the infants become our own. Salgado also makes an interesting point with the framing of this picture. The babies and the blanket occupy the entire photo. The beauty of the infants consumes the viewer. It is unclear if any part of this composition was posed. Logically, a true photojournalist would not manipulate his subject but photograph it as is.

> *Do the details that follow support this particular idea?*

> *Point is not related to rest of paragraph.*

Perhaps such aesthetic consciousness is necessary in order for the audience to even be able to look at the photographs. Hardly anyone enjoys looking at gruesome or explicit pictures, an issue newspaper editors have to grapple with in every copy. As art, Salgado's

119

meaning?

photographs transport us in grand and abstract way. As a photojournalist, Salgado needs to tell it like it is. Finding the right balance between the two means atracting the eye of the viewer while

What is it?

conveying a strong message. Salgado never lets us forget that it is after all, refugee camps and remnants of bloody tribal gang warfare that we are looking at. Beauty needs to accompany truth for it to be bearable.

Diane,
Your paper is full of great observations about the Salgado picture, but I wasn't sure of your thesis. There seemed to be one at the end of the first paragraph and another at the end of the second. A clear thesis would give you a focus for discussing the significance of your observations. I look forward to reading the next draft.
Seth

2. Second draft, with edits

For her second draft, Chen revised her introduction and sharpened her thesis statement. She changed the focus of her essay somewhat, from the beauty of the picture to the way that the picture forces the viewer to look closely into the babies' faces and feel compassion for them. She also tightened the focus of her descriptive paragraphs so that the details in each one served her analytic purpose. After revising her paper overall, she edited her second draft. (*A key to the editing symbols used here can be found at the back of this book.*)

The Caring Eye of Sebastião Salgado

Photographer Sebastião Salgado spent seven years ~~of his life~~ *along migration routes and* traveling to city slums, refugee camps~~, and migration routes~~ in order to document the lives of people uprooted from their homes. *land* A selection of his photographs can be seen in the exhibit, "Migrations: Humanity in Transition." Like a photojournalist, Salgado brings us images of newsworthy events, but he goes beyond objective reporting, imparting his compassion for refugees and migrants to the viewer.

M of the So many photographs in Salgado's show are certain to ~~impress~~ *viewers.* ~~and touch the viewers with their subject matter and sheer beauty.~~ *thousands* Whether capturing the ~~millions~~ of refugee tents in Africa that seem to stretch on for miles or the disheartened faces of ~~small~~ immigrant children, *the images in Migrations* ~~Salgado brings an artistic element to his pictures that~~ suggests *that Salgado* he does so much more with his camera than ~~just~~ point and shoot.

Salgado's photograph of the most vulnerable of these refugees illustrates the power of his work. "Orphanage attached to the hospital at Kibumba, Number One Camp, Goma Zaire," depicts three _(Fig. 1)_ _infants_ ~~apparently newborn or several month old babies,~~ who are victims of the genocidal war in neighboring Rwanda. The label for the photograph _reveals_ ~~tells us~~ that there were 4,000 orphans at this camp and an estimated 100,000 Rwandan orphans overall. Those numbers are mind-numbing, _abstractions_ but this picture is not.

The orphanage photograph is shot in black and white, as are the others in the show, ~~and provides the audience with~~ _giving it_ a ~~very~~ documentary, ~~newspaper type of~~ feel that emphasizes that this is a real~~, newsworthy~~ situation ~~that we need to be aware of~~. _deserving our attention_ But Salgado's choice of black-and-white photography is also an artistic decision. He uses the contrasts of light and dark to create a dramatic image of the three babies.

The vertical black-and-white stripes of the blanket direct our eyes to the infants' faces and hands, which are framed by a horizontal white stripe. The whites of their eyes in particular stand out against the darkness created by the shell of the blankets. The camera's lens also seems to be in sharper focus on the faces than on the blankets, again focusing our attention on the babies' expressions. ¶Each baby has a different response to the camera. The center baby, with his or her extra-wide eyes, appears startled and in need of comforting. The baby to the right is oblivious to the camera and in fact seems to be starving or ill. The healthy baby on the left returns our gaze.

_of_ The vantage point ~~that~~ this photograph ~~was taken from is~~ _is_ one of a _parent_ _his or her_ ~~mother or father~~ directly standing over the child. In this sense the _frames_ infants become our own. Salgado also ~~makes an interesting point with~~ _strategically_ ~~the framing of~~ this picture. The babies in their blanket consume the entire space, so that their innocence and vulnerability consumes the viewer.

Salgado uses his skills as an artist to get us ~~not only~~ to look at these difficult subjects, ~~but also to feel compassion for them.~~ He is able

Reorganize —move from left to right across the picture for a more dramatic conclusion.

to bring a story as big and complex as the epic displacement of the world's people to us through a collection of intimate and intensely moving images. As he says in his introduction to the exhibit catalog, "We hold the key to humanity's future, but for that we must understand the present. We cannot afford to look away."

Add citation and work cited.

3. Final draft

After editing her paper, Chen printed it out, proofread it, corrected some minor errors, and then printed the final version, which is reprinted below. (Chen formatted her paper using the MLA style. The version here, however, does not reflect all the MLA conventions for page breaks, margins, and line spacing. For details on the proper formatting of a paper in MLA style, see Chapter 26 and the sample that begins on p. 416.)

Diane Chen
Professor Bennet
Art 258: History of Photography
5 December 2004

The Caring Eye of Sebastião Salgado

Photographer Sebastião Salgado spent seven years traveling along migration routes to city slums and refugee camps in order to document the lives of people uprooted from their homelands. A selection of his photographs can be seen in the exhibit Migrations: Humanity in Transition. Like a photojournalist, Salgado brings us images of newsworthy events, but he goes beyond objective reporting, imparting his compassion for refugees and migrants to the viewer.

Chen identifies the topic of her essay and then states her thesis.

Many of the photographs in Salgado's show are certain to touch viewers. Whether capturing the thousands of refugee tents in Africa that seem to stretch on for miles or the disheartened faces of immigrant children, the images in Migrations suggest that Salgado does so much more than point and shoot.

Chen provides background information about the exhibit.

Salgado's photograph of the most vulnerable among these refugees illustrates the power of his work. "Orphanage attached to the hospital at Kibumba, Number One Camp, Goma, Zaire" (Fig. 1) depicts three infants who are victims of the genocidal war in neighboring

The text of the paper includes a reference to the photograph that Chen discusses.

122

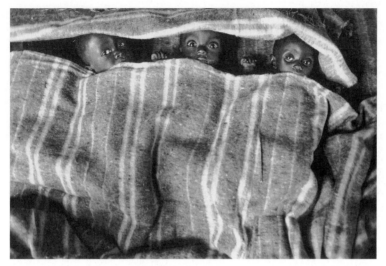

Fig. 1. Sebastião Salgado, Migrations, "Orphanage attached to the hospital at Kibumba, Number One Camp, Goma, Zaire."

Rwanda. The label for the photograph reveals that there were 4,000 orphans at this camp and an estimated 100,000 Rwandan orphans overall. Those numbers are mind-numbing abstractions, but this picture is not.

The orphanage photograph is shot in black and white, as are the others in the show, giving it a documentary feel that emphasizes that this is a real situation deserving our attention. But Salgado's choice of black-and-white photography is also an artistic decision. He uses the contrasts of light and dark to create a dramatic image of the three babies.

The fourth paragraph focuses on the image that Chen uses to illustrate her main point.

The vertical black-and-white stripes of the blanket direct our eyes to the infants' faces and hands, which are framed by a horizontal white stripe. The whites of their eyes in particular stand out against the darkness created by the shell of the blankets. The camera's lens also seems to be in sharper focus on the faces than on the blankets, again focusing our attention on the babies' expressions.

Chen describes the photograph in the next three paragraphs, using a spatial organization for her details.

123

Each baby has a different response to the camera. The baby on the left returns our gaze with a heart-wrenching look. The baby in the center, whose eyes are open extra-wide, appears startled and in need of comforting. But the baby on the right, whose eyes are glazed and sunken, doesn't even notice the camera. We glimpse death in that child's face.

The vantage point of this photograph is one of a parent standing directly over his or her child. In this sense the infants become our own. Salgado also frames this picture strategically. The babies in their blanket consume the entire space, so that their innocence and vulnerability consume the viewer.

The concluding paragraph restates the thesis.

Salgado uses his skills as an artist to get us to look closely at these difficult subjects. He is able to bring a story as big and complex as the epic displacement of the world's people to us through a collection of intimate and intensely moving images. As he says in his introduction to the exhibit catalog, "We hold the key to humanity's future, but for that we must understand the present. We cannot afford to look away" (15).

Paper ends with a compelling quotation.

————————————[new page]————————————

The work-cited entry appears on a new page.

Work Cited

Salgado, Sebastião. Migrations. New York: Aperture, 2000.

Chen lists the source of the quotation that she uses to end her essay.

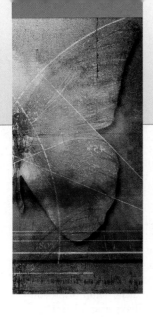

6 Designing Academic Papers and Preparing Portfolios

As noted in Chapter 5, one of your final writing tasks is to proofread your paper to make sure it is free of distracting errors. Another is to format your text so that readers can "see" your ideas clearly. In this chapter, the main focus is on designing academic papers. (*Advice on designing multimedia presentations and Web sites is in Chapter 14: Multimedia Writing, and advice on designing brochures, newsletters, résumés, and other documents is in Part 5: Writing beyond College.*)

In your writing courses, as well as in other courses and in your professional life, you may be called on to compile a **portfolio,** a collection of your writing and related work. This chapter offers guidelines for designing print and electronic portfolios that showcase your work effectively.

6a Consider audience and purpose when making design decisions.

www.mhhe.com/ nmhh
For links to information on document and Web design, go to

Writing > Writing Web Links > Annotated Links on Design

Like writing decisions, effective design decisions take into account your purpose for writing. As you plan your document, consider your purpose as well as the needs of your audience. If you are writing an informative paper for a psychology class, your instructor—your primary audience—will probably prefer that you follow the guidelines provided by the American Psychological Association (APA). If you are writing a lab report for a biology or chemistry course, you will very likely need to follow a well-established format and use the documentation style recommended by the Council of Science Editors (CSE) to cite any sources you use. A history paper might call for use of the Chicago style. If you are responding to an assignment in a creative nonfiction course, you might have more freedom in making design decisions, though if you cite sources you will need to use the style recommended by the Modern Language Association (MLA). In any paper, however, your goal is to enhance the content of your text, not decorate it. (*For help with these documentation styles, see Chapter 24: MLA Documentation Style, Chapter 25: APA Documentation Style, and Chapter 26: Chicago and CSE Documentation Styles.*)

6b   Use the toolbars available in your word-processing program.

Your word-processing program's toolbars give you a range of options for editing, sharing, and designing documents. A variety of toolbars are available in most widely used word-processing programs. Figure 6.1, for example, shows Microsoft Word with three toolbars open: standard, drawing, and reviewing. The standard toolbar allows you to choose different typefaces; bold, italic, or underlined type; numbered or bulleted lists; and so on. The drawing toolbar allows you to insert boxes, drawings, and clip art into your text; and the reviewing toolbar enables you to mark changes, add comments, and even send your document to a reader.

If you are using a word-processing program other than Microsoft Word, take some time to learn the different toolbars and formatting options that are available to you.

6c   Think intentionally about design.

For any document that you create, whatever its purpose or audience, you need to apply the same basic design principles:

- Organize information for readers.
- Choose typefaces and use lists and other graphic options to make your text readable and to emphasize key elements.
- Format related design elements consistently.
- Use headings to organize long papers.
- Use restraint.

www.mhhe.com/
nmhh
For more on designing your paper, go to

Writing > Visual Rhetoric Tutorial > Document Design

A sample page from a student's report on a local food bank, which includes information that she gathered while serving as a volunteer, illustrates these principles. The content in Figure 6.2 on page 128 is at

FIGURE 6.1 **Three word-processing toolbars.**

a disadvantage because the author has not adhered to these principles. By contrast, the same content in Figure 6.3 on page 129 is clearer and easier for readers to understand because of its design.

1. Organizing information for readers

You can organize information visually and topically by grouping related items using boxes, indents, headings, spacing, and lists. For example, in this book headings help to group information for readers, and bulleted and numbered lists such as the bulleted list on the preceding page present related points. These variations in text appearance help readers scan, locate information, and dive in when they need to know more about a topic. If a color printer is available to you and your instructor allows you to use color in your paper, then it can serve this purpose as well.

You can also use **white space,** areas of a document that do not contain type or graphics, to help organize information for your readers. Allowing generous margins and plenty of white space above headings and around other elements makes text easier to read.

You should also introduce any visuals within your text and position them so that they appear near—but never before—this text reference. Strive for a pleasing balance between visuals and other text elements; for example, don't try to cram too many visuals onto one page.

2. Using type style and lists to make your text readable and to emphasize key elements

Typefaces are designs that have been established by printers for the letters in the alphabet, numbers, punctuation marks, and special characters. **Fonts** are all of the variations available in a certain typeface and size (for example, 12-point Times New Roman is available in **bold** and *italics*). Serif typefaces have tiny lines at the ends of letters such as n and y; sans serif typefaces do not have these lines. Standard serif typefaces such as the following are widely used for basic text because they are easy to read:

Times New Roman   Courier
Bookman Old Style   Palatino

For most academic papers, you should choose a standard, easy-to-read typeface and use a 10- or 12-point size. Sans serif typefaces such as the following are sometimes used for headings because they offer a pleasing contrast:

Arial
Verdana

(*Text continues on page 130.*)

127

Emphasis wrong: Title of report is not as prominent as the heading within the report.

The Caring Express Food Bank

The Caring Express Food Bank serves a varied population of clients, including chronically homeless people, temporarily homeless people, recent immigrants, elderly people on fixed incomes, and people in need of temporary services.

Margins are not wide enough, making the page look crowded.

Bar chart is not introduced in the text and does not have a caption.

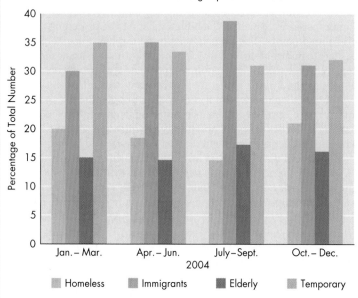

Clients of the Caring Express Food Bank

While the number of homeless, both temporary and permanent, that Caring Express assisted in 2004 decreased during the summer months, the number of immigrant workers increased. The percentage of elderly people and people in need of temporary services remained fairly stable throughout the year.

Description of procedure is dense, not easy to follow.

How Caring Express Helps Clients

When new clients come to Caring Express, a volunteer fills out a **form** with their **address** (if they have one), their **phone number,** their **income,** their **employment situation,** and the help they are receiving, if any, from the local department of human services. Clients who do not live in Maple Valley are referred to a food bank or outreach program in their area. Clients who qualify check off the food they need from a list, and then that food is packed and distributed to them.

Use of bold type and different typeface for no reason.

FIGURE 6.2 **Example of a poorly designed report.**

The Caring Express Food Bank

The Caring Express Food Bank serves a varied population of clients, including chronically homeless people, temporarily homeless people, recent immigrants, elderly people on fixed incomes, and people in need of temporary services. As Figure 1 shows, while the number of homeless, both temporary and permanent, that Caring Express assisted in 2004 decreased during the summer months, the number of immigrant workers increased. The percentage of elderly people and people in need of temporary services remained fairly stable throughout the year.

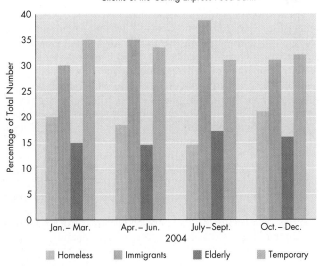

Figure 1. Percentage of clients in each group during 2004

How Caring Express Helps Clients

When new clients come to Caring Express, the volunteers follow this procedure:

1. The volunteer fills out a form with the client's address (if he or she has one), phone number, income, and employment situation.
2. Clients who do not live in Maple Valley are referred to a food bank or outreach program in their area.
3. Clients who qualify check off the food they need from a list.
4. The food is packed and distributed to them.

Title is centered and in larger type than text and heading.

Bar chart is introduced and explained.

White space above and below figure sets it off.

Caption explains figure.

Heading is subordinate to title.

Procedure is explained in a numbered list. Writer uses parallel structure for list entries.

FIGURE 6.3 Example of a well-designed report. **129**

Tips

LEARNING in COLLEGE

The Basics: Margins, Spacing, Type, Page Numbers, and Printing

Here are a few basic guidelines for formatting academic papers.

- **First page:** In a paper that is no longer than five pages, you can usually place a header with your name, your professor's name, your course and section number, and the date on the first page, preceding the text. (*For an example, see the final draft of Diane Chen's paper on p. 122.*) If your paper exceeds five pages, page one is usually a title page. (*For an example of a title page for a paper written in APA style, see the first page of Audrey Galeano's paper on p. 455.*)

- **Type:** Select a common typeface, or font, such as Courier, Times New Roman, or Bookman, and choose a 10- or 12-point size.

- **Margins:** Use one-inch margins on all four sides of your text. Adequate margins make your paper easier to read and give your instructor room to write comments and suggestions.

- **Margin justification:** Line up, or justify, the lines of your document along the left margin but not along the right margin. Leaving a "ragged-right"—or uneven—right margin enables you to avoid odd spacing between words.

- **Spacing:** Always double-space your paper unless you are instructed to do otherwise, and indent each paragraph five spaces. Use the ruler at the top of your screen to set this indent automatically. (Many business documents are single spaced, with an extra line space between paragraphs.) Allow one space after periods, question marks, exclamation points, commas, semicolons, and colons. Add a space before and after an ellipsis mark. Do not allow extra space before or after dashes, hyphens, apostrophes, quotation marks, parentheses or brackets, or a mark that is immediately followed by another mark, such as a comma followed by a quotation mark. (*For more on these punctuation marks, see Part 10.*)

- **Page numbers:** Page numbers typically appear in the upper right-hand corner of the page. Some documentation styles require a header next to the page number—see Chapters 24–26 for the requirements of the style you are following.

- **Printing:** Print final drafts of your academic papers on a laser or an ink-jet printer.

You should make sure, however, that your instructor approves of their use before including them in an academic paper.

Many typefaces available on your computer are known as *display fonts,* for example:

Curlz

Lucinda Sans

Old English

Monotype Corsiva

These should be used rarely, if ever, in academic papers, on the screen, or in presentations. They can be used effectively in other kinds of documents, however, such as brochures, fliers, and posters.

You can emphasize a word or phrase in your text by selecting it and making it **bold,** *italicized,* or underlined. Numbered or bulleted lists help you cluster larger amounts of information and make the material easier for readers to understand. Because they stand out from your text visually, lists help readers see that ideas are related. You can use a numbered list to display steps in a sequence, present checklists, or suggest recommendations for action.

Format text as a numbered or bulleted list by choosing the option you want from your word-processing program's formatting commands. Use parallel structure in your list, introduce it with a complete sentence followed by a colon, and put a period at the end of each entry if the entries are complete sentences. If they are not complete sentences, no punctuation is necessary.

Putting information in a box emphasizes it and also makes it easier for readers to find if they need to refer to it again. Most word-processing programs offer several ways to enclose text within a border or box.

3. Formatting related design elements consistently

In design, simplicity, contrast, and consistency matter. If you emphasize an item by putting it in italic or bold type or in color, or if you use a graphic element such as a box to set it off, consider repeating this effect for similar items to give your document a unified look. Even a simple horizontal line can be a purposeful element in a long document when used consistently to help organize information.

4. Using headings to organize long papers

In short papers, headings can disrupt the text and are usually not necessary. In longer papers, though, they can help you organize complex information.

Effective headings are brief and descriptive. The headings in academic papers are usually in the form of phrases, although they might be in the form of questions or even imperative sentences. Make sure that your headings are consistent in grammatical structure as well as formatting:

Phrases beginning with –*ing* words
Fielding Inquiries
Handling Complaints

Nouns and noun phrases
Customer Inquiries
Complaints

Questions
How Do I Field Inquiries?
How Do I Handle Complaints?

Imperative sentences
Field Inquiries Efficiently
Handle Complaints Calmly and Politely

Headings at different levels can be in different forms. For example, in this text, the first-level headings are imperative sentences; the second-level headings usually begin with –*ing* words.

Place and highlight headings consistently throughout your paper. If you have not already done so, preparing a formal topic outline will help you decide what your main points and second-level points are and where headings should go. (*For help with topic outlines, see Chapter 3, pp. 50–55.*) You might center all first-level headings—which correspond to the main points in your outline—and put them in bold type. If you have second-level headings—your supporting points—you might align them at the left margin and underline them. Third-level headings, if you have them, could be aligned at the left margin and in plain type.

Tips

LEARNING in COLLEGE

Standard Headings and Templates

Some types of papers, such as lab reports and case studies, have standard headings, such as Introduction, Abstract, and Methods and Materials for a lab report (*see Chapter 8, pp. 171–79*). These headings give you a head start in organizing your writing.

For some types of documents, *templates,* or preformatted styles, establish the structure and settings for the document and apply them automatically. If you know you will need to produce on a regular basis a certain kind of paper that requires a specific kind of formatting—such as a lab report—you might consider creating a template for it.

First-Level Heading
Second-Level Heading
Third-Level Heading

A heading should never appear at the very bottom of a page. If a heading falls in that position, move it to the top of the next page.

5. Using restraint

If you include too many graphics, headings, bullets, boxes, or other elements in a document, you risk making it as "noisy" as a loud radio. Certain typefaces and fonts have become standard because they are easy on the eye. Variations from these standard fonts jar the eye. Bold or italic type, underlining, or any other graphic effect should not continue for more than one or two sentences at a time.

Refrain from relying too much on bold and italics to emphasize ideas in your sentences. Instead, use structure and word choice to let your readers know what is important.

6d Compile a print or an electronic portfolio that presents your work to your advantage.

When presenting their written work for final submission, students are often asked to collect it in a portfolio. Likewise, when applying for a position that calls for a great deal of writing, job candidates are usually asked to provide a portfolio of their writing. Although most portfolios consist of a collection of papers in print form, portfolios can be created in different media. Many students create writing portfolios that are available electronically.

Portfolios, regardless of medium, share at least three common features:

- They are a *collection* of work.
- They offer a *selection*—or subset—of a larger body of work.
- Once assembled, they are introduced, narrated, or commented on by a document that offers the writer's *reflection* on his or her work.

As with any type of writing, both print and electronic portfolios serve a purpose and address an audience. For example, you may be asked to prepare a "showcase" or "best-work" portfolio, intended to exhibit your best writing. You would present such a portfolio in a situation where you need to demonstrate writing proficiency, such as in a job interview. You might be asked to create a portfolio that documents how your writing has improved during a course or a term; sometimes such a portfolio counts toward a course grade. At other times, you might use a portfolio for planning purposes, to give yourself an opportunity to look back over your written work to identify successes and set new writing goals.

1. Assembling a print portfolio

Course requirements vary, so if you are assembling a writing portfolio for a course, you should always follow the guidelines your instructor provides. Nevertheless, when creating a print writing portfolio, you will usually need to complete the following five activities:

Assembling a Print Portfolio

1. Gather all your written work.
2. Make appropriate selections.
3. Arrange the selections.
4. Include a reflective essay or letter.
5. Polish your portfolio.

Gathering your writing   To organize your portfolio, it is often useful to create a list, or inventory, of the writing that you are including. You can use this list to make sure that you have included every piece of writing that you want or need to provide. If you are preparing a portfolio for a writing course, you may need to provide your exploratory writing, notes, and comments from peer reviewers as well as all your drafts for one or more of the papers you include. Make sure all of your materials have your name on them and that the copy of your final draft does not include any errors.

Reviewing your written work and making the appropriate selections   As you review your work, keep the purpose of the portfolio in mind as well as the criteria that will be used to evaluate it. If you are assembling a "showcase" portfolio, then you want to select your very best work. If you are demonstrating your improvement as a writer, you want to select papers that show your development and creativity. You might provide all the exploratory writing, peer comments, and drafts for a particular paper to show how your writing process developed and how it contributed to the success of the final version.

   If no criteria have been provided, consider the audience for the portfolio when deciding which selections will be most appropriate.

If you include multiple drafts in your portfolio, you might use one or more of the following strategies to demonstrate improvement from one draft to the next:

- Use a highlighter to note changes you made from one draft to the next.
- Annotate changes to explain why you made them—because you wanted to provide additional evidence, for instance, or to clarify a complex point.
- Choose two texts, completed at different times, to demonstrate how your writing has improved over the course of a term or year.

Who will read the portfolio? What qualities will they be looking for as they read your work?

Arranging the selections deliberately   In some situations, you will have specific guidelines for how to arrange your portfolio. For instance, sometimes the reader or readers will ask you to arrange your work in the order in which you wrote it, that is, in chronological order. If you have not been told how to organize your portfolio, however, you can think of it as if it were a single text and decide on an arrangement that will serve your purpose. Does it make sense to organize your work from weakest to strongest? Alternatively, given your purpose and audience, does it make sense to move from a less important paper to a more important paper? How will you determine importance?

Whatever arrangement you choose, you will need to explain your rationale for it to your reader. You can include this information in a letter to the reader, in a brief introduction, or in your table of contents listing the papers in your portfolio. For each paper, you can provide an *annotation,* a brief explanation, that indicates why it has been included.

Writing a reflective essay or letter   The reflective statement is one of the most important pieces of writing in a portfolio. It may take the form of either an essay or a letter, depending on your purpose or the requirements you have been given. Sometimes, the reflective essay will be the last one in a portfolio so that the reader can review all of the work first and then read the writer's interpretation at the end. At other times, you will provide your reflections on your work in a letter that opens the portfolio. Regardless of its genre or placement, however, the reflective text gives you an opportunity to explain something about your writing or about yourself as a writer. Common topics in the reflective text include the following:

- How you developed various papers
- Which papers you believe are particularly strong and why
- What you learned as you worked on these assignments
- Who you are now as a writer

As for all of your writing, you should follow the stages of the writing process in preparing your reflective essay or letter. Once you have completed it, you can assemble all of the components of your portfolio in a folder.

Polishing your portfolio   Although the steps in preparing a portfolio are listed in a sequence, many students find that, as they work through them, they need to backtrack to an earlier step. In the process of writing the reflective letter or essay, for example, you might discover a better way to arrange your work, or as you arrange your portfolio, you might find that you would like to review all your work again. Do not be surprised if you find yourself repeating some of these tasks.

If you want a portfolio that presents you and your work in the best light, it is also wise to share it with classmates or colleagues before submitting it for a class grade, a writing requirement, or a job interview. As with any writing, a portfolio will improve if it is revised based on peer review.

The good news is that most students learn about themselves and their writing as they compile their portfolios and write reflections on their work. The process not only makes them better writers, it helps them learn how to demonstrate their strengths as well.

2. Preparing an electronic portfolio

For some courses or professional purposes, you will need to present your work in an electronic format. For example, an education student might be required to provide an electronic portfolio of lesson plans, class handouts, and other instructional materials that he or she has developed. Electronic portfolios can be saved on a CD-ROM, or they can be published on a Web site.

Writers creating electronic portfolios need to collect, select, and reflect on their work, just as writers creating print portfolios do. Because digital portfolios allow you to include different kinds of texts, such as audio files and video clips; because they can be connected to other texts using hyperlinks; and because their success depends on the use of visual elements, you will need to follow this five-step process in preparing an electronic portfolio:

Creating an Electronic Portfolio

1. Gather all your written work and audio, video, and visual texts.
2. Decide on an arrangement and presentation for your selections.
3. Add links.
4. Include a reflective essay or letter.
5. Test your portfolio for usability.

Gathering your written work as well as your audio, video, and visual texts   Depending on your purpose, you may need to collect exploratory writing, peer comments, and all drafts, just as you would for a print portfolio. Because you are collecting different kinds of texts, you will need to make up to four inventories:

- A verbal inventory, consisting of your written work (be sure to scan in any handwritten work that you will not be providing as a digital text)
- An audio inventory (examples: speeches, music)
- A video inventory (examples: movie clips, videos you have created)
- A visual inventory (examples: photographs, drawings)

The most important—and typical—components of an electronic writing portfolio tend to be the verbal and visual texts. Even if you don't have many visuals, you should collect some as you begin to work on your portfolio because they can help you think about the images you will want to use to describe your work visually. One writer, for instance, might use a photograph of a flower to express the idea of development over time; another writer might use images of everyday life in two countries to show that she has included texts in two languages in her portfolio.

Selecting appropriate texts and deciding how to arrange and present them   As in a print portfolio, your work can be arranged in a variety of ways: in chronological order, in order of importance, or in another way that suits your purpose. Once you have decided on a basic arrangement, you will need to decide how to help your reader navigate it. Because you are working in a digital environment, you can use links to help your reader move within your digital portfolio (*see Figure 6.4 on p. 138*).

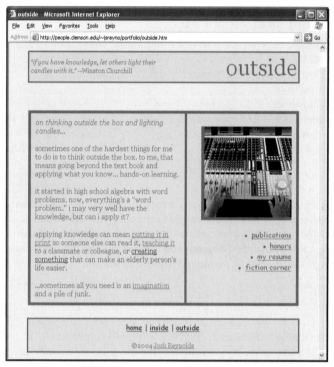

FIGURE 6.4 A screen from a student's electronic portfolio.
Note the many links for easy navigation.

One very simple, intuitive method for helping readers navigate the portfolio is to provide a table of contents with links to the text for each item. You might then provide links from each final draft to exploratory writing, drafts in progress, and comments from peer reviewers. Alternatively, you might decide to make the table of contents part of an introductory page that also gives information about you and explains the course. As with a print portfolio, you might decide to open with a reflective letter embedded with links that take readers to your written work and other texts.

Regardless of the navigational method you choose, you should think about the opening screen: what it will look like, how it will establish your purpose and appeal to your audience, and what kind of guidance you will provide for the reader. You will want to choose colors, images for the front page and successive pages, and typefaces that visually suggest who you are as a writer. As you plan this opening screen, you might create a flowchart that shows each item in your portfolio and how it is linked to others. Once you have a complete visual plan, you can begin to think about adding links to your selections.

Adding links to your selections and backup materials After you have selected the written works and other texts you want to present as part of your portfolio and planned its structure, you need to decide what kind of hyperlinks you will add. Many word-processing programs have a Hyperlink function that allows you to add links to your text. Choose links that will help the portfolio reader better understand you and your writing.

Two kinds of links are common in electronic portfolios: internal and external. Internal links are used to connect one piece of writing to another. For instance, a writer might link an earlier draft to a later one or link a PowerPoint presentation to a paper on the same topic, to show the connections between them. External links connect the reader to related files that are external to the work in the portfolio but relevant to it. For instance, if you collaborated with another colleague on a project, you might link to that person's electronic portfolio. If you used resources from a particular library, you might link to that institution or to the resource itself. (*For more on the use of links in multimedia writing, see Chapter 14: Multimedia Writing, p. 259.*)

Writing a reflective text As in a print portfolio, the reflective text explains to the reader what the writer wants him or her to know about the selections. A digital environment, however, offers you more possibilities for presenting this reflection. You can make it highly visual; for example, you might have it cascade across a series of screens. Another option would be to link to an audio or video file in which you talk directly to the reader.

Testing your electronic portfolio before sharing it with the intended audience Make sure your portfolio works—both conceptually and structurally—before releasing it. You should navigate all the way though your portfolio yourself before asking your reader to do so. Sometimes links fail to work, or files don't open, so this step is very important. In addition, going through the portfolio yourself is the only way you can make sure it will be easy for your reader to navigate and to understand.

Auguste Rodin's sculpture The Thinker *evokes the psychological complexity of human thought and suggests the spirit of critical inquiry common to all disciplines across the curriculum.*

PART 2

> Anybody who is involved in working across the disciplines is much more likely to have a lively mind and a lively life.
>
> —MARY FIELD BELENKY

Common Assignments across the Curriculum

7 Reading, Thinking, Writing: The Critical Connection

Most of the common assignments you will tackle in college—informative reports, interpretive analyses, and arguments—begin with reading. Indeed, the exchange of ideas in every discipline happens as scholars read and respond to one another's work. This chapter introduces you to the process of critical reading as a way of getting intellectually involved with your studies. In this context, the word *critical* means thoughtful. When you read critically, you recognize the literal meaning of the text, make inferences about implicit or unstated meanings, and then make your own judgments in response.

When they talk about reading texts, most people are thinking of words on a printed page. However, in this chapter we have a broader meaning in mind. Advances in technology have made it easier than ever to receive information in a variety of ways, so it is essential now to be able to "read" critically, not just written texts, but visuals, sounds, and spoken texts as well. We use the word *text,* then, to refer to works that readers, viewers, or listeners invest with meaning and that can be critically analyzed.

7a Recognize that critical reading is a process.

Critical reading is a process just as writing is a process. As with writing, you will find yourself moving back and forth among the steps in this process.

Critical readers don't just read; they reread. The writer Ray Bradbury claims that he read Herman Melville's *Moby Dick* eighty to ninety times before he understood it well enough to write the screenplay for John Huston's movie adaptation. Bradbury is certainly an extreme example of devotion to critical reading, but you will find that going back over a text more than once deepens your understanding. Your goals for your reading (from simply checking a fact to undertaking a full-scale evaluation of a text) will determine how much time you need to spend.

Writing at every stage of the critical reading process also helps to deepen your involvement with the text. If you are reading a book that you own, write in it as you read, highlighting key ideas and terms and

LEARNING in COLLEGE

Reading Critically

- **Preview** the piece before you read it.
- **Read** the selection for its topic and point.
- **Analyze** the who, what, and why of the piece by **annotating** it as you reread it and **summarizing** what you have read.
- **Synthesize** through making connections.
- **Evaluate** what you've read.

noting your questions or objections. If you are reading a library book, a Web page, or a nonprint text, keep notes in a journal—paper or electronic—to help you remember what you have read and reflect on its significance. (*See the TextConnex box on p. 152 for other tips on annotating electronic texts.*)

7b Preview the text or visual.

Critical reading begins with **previewing:** looking over the text's author and publication information and quickly scanning its contents to gain a context for understanding and evaluating it.

If the text is a possible source for a paper, you will also need to determine whether it is a **primary source** or a **secondary source**—that is, whether it is a firsthand (primary) account of an event or research or someone else's (secondary) interpretation of that firsthand account. Research reports in the sciences are primary sources; textbooks and encyclopedia articles are secondary sources. Original works of art, literature, theater, film, and music are also primary sources; critical analyses and reviews are secondary sources.

1. Asking questions as you preview a text

As you preview a text, ask questions to gather information about it that will alert you to any biases and help you judge the credibility of the evidence and arguments the piece presents. Preview questions will also help you get a sense of the whole text so that you have a framework for your reading.

www.mhhe.com/
nmhh
For more on
evaluating sources,
go to

Research > CARS
Source Evaluation
Tutor

Author

- Who wrote this piece?
- What are the author's credentials?
- Who is the author's employer?
- What is the author's occupation?
- What do you know about the author's interests and values?

Purpose

- What do the title and first and last paragraphs tell you about the purpose of this piece?
- Do the headings provide clues to the purpose of the piece?
- What do the visuals suggest about the purpose of this piece?
- What might have motivated the author to write the piece?
- Do you think the main purpose will be to inform, to interpret, to argue, or something else (to entertain or to reflect, for instance)?

Audience

- Whom do you suspect the author is trying to inform or persuade?
- If the piece includes boldfaced terms or a glossary, do the terms give you a sense of what kind of knowledge the author expects his or her audience to have?
- Is the author addressing you and others like you?

Content

- What does the title tell you the piece is about?
- Does the first paragraph include the main point?
- Do the headings give you the gist of the piece?
- Does the conclusion tell you what the author is trying to inform you about, interpret for you, or argue?

Context

- When was the piece published? Is it current? Does the date matter?
- What kind of publication is it? Is it a book, an article in a periodical or library database, a Web page?
- Where and by whom was the piece published? If it was published electronically, was it posted by the author or by an organization with a special interest?

LEARNING in COLLEGE

Evaluating Context in Different Kinds of Publications

- **For a book:** Are you looking at the original publication, or is this material reprinted from another source? What is the publisher's reputation? University presses, for example, are very selective about the books they publish, usually concentrating on scholarly works. Vanity presses—which require authors to pay to publish their work—are not selective at all.
- **For an article in a periodical:** Look at the list of editors and their affiliations. What do you know about the journal, magazine, or newspaper in which this writing appears? Are the articles that appear in it reviewed by experts in a particular field before they are published?
- **For a Web page:** Who created the page? A Web page named for a political candidate, for example, may actually have been put on the Web by his or her opponents. (*See the TextConnex box, Using the CARS Checklist to Evaluate Web Sites, in Chapter 18: Evaluating Sources, p. 328.*)

2. Asking questions as you preview a visual

You can use most of the previewing questions for texts to preview visuals. Here are some additional questions you should ask:

www.mhhe.com/
nmhh
For an interactive
tutorial on analyzing
visuals, go to
Writing > Visual
Rhetoric Tutorial >
Understanding
Images

- In what context does the visual appear? Was it intended to be viewed on its own (as an artistic photograph or painting) or as part of a larger work (an image in a magazine ad, a graph in a research report, an illustration in a book)? Is there an even broader context for the image (is it part of a television commercial, for example)?
- Does the visual consist of a single image, or is it part of a series of images (for example, a graphic novel, a music video, a film)?
- Does the visual represent a real event, person, or thing (a news photo, a portrait), or is it fictional (an illustration in a story)?
- What does the visual depict? Is its literal meaning immediately clear, or do you need to spend time looking at it to figure it out?
- Is the visual accompanied by audio or printed text?

FIGURE 7.1 Previewing a visual. The text superimposed on this photograph reads: "I AM NOT AN AMERICAN WHO BELIEVES WE SHOULD ALL HAVE THE SAME OPINIONS. I AM AN AMERICAN who believes that our right to have lively discussion and thorough investigation are the things that make our country great. I AM AN ACLU MEMBER because free speech is the foundation of freedom. Keep America SAFE & FREE. SIGN ON AT: WWW.ACLU.ORG."

A preview of Figure 7.1 (above) might produce these answers:

- **In what context does the visual appear?** This advertisement appeared in the *New York Times Magazine,* among other publications. The ad doesn't have an "author," but it is clearly the product of the American Civil Liberties Union (ACLU), as the bright box in the lower right-hand corner indicates. The box also indicates the purpose of the ad: to persuade viewers to join the organization.

- **Does the visual consist of a single image, or is it part of a series of images?** There is one image: a black-and-white photograph that shows the actor Kristin Davis, best known for playing Charlotte on the television series *Sex and the City.*

- **Does the visual represent a real event, person, or thing, or is it fictional?** The image appears to be nonfiction (even though Davis almost certainly has been posed by the photographer). Davis appears as herself, not "Charlotte."

- **What does the visual depict?** Davis is standing in what appears to be a gritty urban location.

- **Is the visual accompanied by audio or printed text?** Printed text appears over Davis's image, suggesting that the words are hers. Some of those words are emphasized with capital letters.

The meaning of this image is not immediately clear from a preview. We will need to read it more closely to grasp its message fully.

7c   Read and record your initial impressions.

A first reading is similar to a first draft—your primary purpose is to get a sense of the whole. Read the selection for its literal meaning. Identify what the text is about and the main point the writer makes about the topic. Try to read the work in one sitting, if possible. Note unclear or difficult passages to come back to later, as well as ideas that grab your attention. Record your initial impressions:

- If the text or image is an argument, what opinion is being expressed? Were you persuaded by the argument?
- Did you have an emotional response to the text or image? Were you surprised, amused, or angered by anything in it?
- What was your initial sense of the writer or speaker?
- What key ideas did you take away from the work?

Exercise 7.1   Preview and first reading of an essay

On the following pages is an essay that appeared in the *Village Voice,* a weekly journal of opinion and commentary published in New York City.

1. Preview the essay, using the questions in 7b.
2. Read through the essay in one sitting, then record your initial impressions, using the questions in 7c.

Misguided Multiculturalism

NAT HENTOFF

An American-history requirement hallows ethnocentrism just as everyone else is embracing internationalism and preparing students to become citizens of the world.

> —Joanne Reitano, history professor and chair of the
> Community College Caucus, *New York Post,* May 28 [2000]

Both my parents were immigrants from Russia. In my neighborhood, Yiddish was a first and second language. I grew up in the depths of the **147**

Great Depression. There were weeks when my father came home with $5 or less. My mother walked blocks to save a few cents on food.

I went to public school. Some of my friends were sent to the yeshiva—an Orthodox Jewish religious school—but my parents, having experienced the vicious, pervasive anti-Semitism in the Old Country, wanted me to learn what America was all about.

At Boston Latin School and Northeastern University—a working-class college—I took classes that taught a great deal about the fundamental rights and liberties that had to be fought for during this still "unfinished American revolution," as Thurgood Marshall called it. These were required courses, and inspired my lifelong involvement in civil rights and civil liberties.

This is a personal prelude to an intense controversy over a proposed four-year master plan for the City University of New York by CUNY's Board of Trustees, which will be voted on by the New York State Board of Regents in September. The leading, and impassioned, advocate of the part of the plan that I'm focusing on here is Herman Badillo, chairman of CUNY's Board of Trustees.

5   A key element in the plan is its call for a core curriculum, including a required course in American history—which is already in place in the state university system. A number—not all—of the faculty members on the various campuses vigorously object. Some say trustees have no business meddling in what should be the prerogative of the faculty. Others call the very idea of a required course in American history absurd. "The assumption," says professor Joanne Reitano, "is that our immigrant students need to be taught what it means to be an American."

Over the years, I have given classes in this city's public schools, from elementary grades through high school. And as a reporter, I have spent considerable time in other classrooms. As is the case throughout the country—from failing schools to the prestigious high schools—the teaching of American history, with few exceptions, is cursory, scattered, and superficial.

It's just as bad in most colleges. A recent survey by the American Council of Trustees and Alumni (David Broder's column, *The Washington Post,* July 2) reveals "historical illiteracy" about this country across the board—even among students at Amherst, Williams, Harvard, Duke, and the University of Michigan. Moreover, "none of the 55 elite colleges and universities (as rated by *U.S. News & World Report*) requires a course in American history before graduation." As for high schools, Broder notes, a report by the National Assessment of Educational Progress disclosed that "fully 57 percent of the high school seniors failed to demonstrate a basic level of understanding of American history and institutions—the lowest category in the test."

The foremothers of women's liberation, Susan B. Anthony and Elizabeth Cady Stanton, as well as civil rights leaders like Frederick Douglass and Malcolm X, used the First Amendment as an essential weapon; but how many Americans, including students, know the embattled history of free speech in this nation?

Also neglected in the vast majority of secondary schools and colleges is the history of the American labor movement—its fight against repression in the 19th century and well into this century.

When teaching, I have found interest among a wide array of students in the story of why we have a Fourth Amendment—British officials' random, often savage searches of the colonists' homes and businesses to look for contraband. As Supreme Court Justice William Brennan told me, the resultant fury of those initial Americans was a precipitating cause of the American Revolution. 10

I told that story and others about resistance to discrimination, and worse, throughout American postrevolutionary history to a large group of predominantly black and Hispanic high school students in Miami a couple of years ago.

Before I started, one of their teachers told me, "Don't be upset if they don't pay attention. What they're mostly interested in is clothes and music."

After more than an hour, there was a standing ovation. Not for me, but because they had discovered America—its triumphs and failures. Talking to some of them later, I was told they'd heard none of those stories in school.

Multiculturalism is a welcome development in American education so long as some of its college courses do not exalt one particular culture and history over others. Then, it is indeed ethnocentric. But to understand where you came from, you also have to understand where you are now. You have to know how the society you live in works, and that requires a full-scale knowledge of its history—from its guiding principles to what still has to be done to make them real. For everybody.

Justice William Brennan said: "We do not yet have justice, equal and practical, for the members of minority groups, for the criminally accused, for the displaced persons of the technological revolution, for alienated youth, for the urban masses, for the unrepresented consumer—for all, in short, who do not take part of the abundance of American life. . . . Ugly inequities continue to mar the face of our nation. We are surely nearer the beginning than the end of the struggle." 15

To do something about that, CUNY students should know the strategies, successes, and failures of widely diverse Americans who have been part of that struggle. For insisting on core American history courses, Herman Badillo should be cheered, not scorned.

From the *Village Voice*, July 19–25, 2000

Exercise 7.2 Preview and first reading of an essay

Find an article that interests you in a newspaper or magazine, preview it using the questions in 7b, then read through it in one sitting and record your initial impressions using the questions in 7c.

Exercise 7.3 First reading of a visual

Spend some time looking at the image and text for the ACLU ad on page 146. Record your responses to the following questions:

1. Did you have an emotional response to the ad?
2. What opinion, if any, did you have of the spokesperson (Davis) before you read the ad? What opinion do you have of her now?
3. What opinion, if any, did you have of the ACLU before you read the ad? Has your opinion changed in any way as a result of the ad?
4. What key ideas does the ad attempt to present?

7d Reread using annotation and summary to analyze and interpret.

Once you understand the literal, or surface, meaning of a text, it is time to dig deeper by analyzing and interpreting it. To **analyze** a text is to consider it in detail, in particular by breaking it down into significant parts and examining how those parts relate to each other. We analyze a text to **interpret** it and come to a fuller understanding of its meanings.

1. Questioning the text

Analysis and interpretation require a thorough understanding of the who, what, how, and why of a text:

- **What is the writer's *stance,* or attitude toward the subject?** Does the writer appear to be objective, or does the writer seem to have personal feelings about the subject?

- **What is the writer's *voice*?** Is it that of a reasonable judge, an enthusiastic preacher, a thoughtful teacher, or a reassuring friend? Does the writer seem to be speaking *at, to,* or *with* the audience?

- **What assumptions does the writer seem to be making about the audience?** Does the writer assume an audience of specialists or a general audience? Does the writer assume that the reader agrees with him or her, or does the writer try to build agreement? Does the writer seem to have chosen examples and evidence with a certain audience in mind?

- **What is the author's primary purpose?** Is the purpose to present findings, offer an objective analysis, or argue for a particular action or opinion?
- **How does the author develop ideas?** What kind of support does the author rely on to develop the main point? Does the writer define key terms? Tell relevant stories? Provide logical reasons?
- **Does the text appeal to emotions?** Does the writer use words, phrases, clichés, images, or examples that are emotionally charged?
- **Is the text fair?** Does the author consider opposing ideas, arguments, or evidence? Does he or she deal with them fairly?
- **Is the evidence strong?** Does the author provide sufficient evidence for his or her position? Where is the argument strongest and weakest?
- **Is the text effective?** What are your beliefs on this subject? Has the text changed them?

2. Using annotation and summary

Annotation and **summary** are techniques that can help with analysis and interpretation.

Annotation   Annotation combines reading with analysis. To annotate a text, read through it slowly and carefully while asking yourself the who, what, how, and why questions. As you read, underline or circle words, phrases, and sentences that strike you as significant or puzzling, and write your questions and observations in the margin. If you cannot mark the text, you can make separate notes in a notebook or computer file.

EXAMPLE OF AN ANNOTATED PASSAGE

Introductory paragraphs from "Misguided Multiculturalism" by Nat Hentoff

Both my parents were immigrants from Russia. In my neighborhood, Yiddish was a first and second language. I grew up in the depths of the Great Depression. There were weeks when my father came home with $5 or less. My mother walked blocks to save a few cents on food.

Childhood story—establishes his personal experience of multicultural issues.

I went to public school. Some of my friends were sent to the yeshiva—an Orthodox Jewish religious school—but my parents, having experienced the vicious, pervasive anti-Semitism in the Old Country, wanted me to learn what America was all about. **151**

Essential??

*Supreme Court.
Would they
inspire everyone?*

=introduction

*Smooth transi-
tion to the real
argument.*

At Boston Latin School and Northeastern University—a working-class college—I took classes that taught a great deal about the (fundamental) rights and liberties that had to be fought for during this still "unfinished American revolution," as (Thurgood Marshall) called it. These were required courses, and inspired my lifelong involvement in civil rights and civil liberties.

This is a personal (prelude) to an intense controversy over a proposed four-year master plan for the City University of New York by CUNY's Board of Trustees, which will be voted on by the New York State Board of Regents in September. The leading, and impassioned, advocate of the part of the plan that I'm focusing on here is Herman Badillo, chairman of CUNY's Board of Trustees.

EXAMPLE OF A NOTEBOOK ENTRY

"Misguided Multiculturalism," by Nat Hentoff: Intro paragraphs

Starts by discussing his own background, telling us about his childhood and his education:
—Son of Russian immigrants, grew up poor
—Spoke Yiddish (bilingual upbringing)
—Parents wanted him to "learn what America was all about"
—Took mandatory courses about U.S. rights and liberties in school

Long build-up before he gets to the real subject of his article: a proposal to make American history course mandatory at a university in New York. Is his story really relevant?

Visuals too can be subjected to critical analysis, as the annotations a reader made on the ACLU ad indicate (Figure 7.2).

TEXTCONNEX

Annotating Electronic Text

Unless a copyright notice prohibits it, you can download an electronic file for your own use in order to annotate it. To annotate it, write on a printout of the file, or insert your comments directly in the file using a contrasting typeface or color or the Comments feature of your word-processing program.

Davis is projecting a serious image, and she's dressed very plainly. She looks directly at the camera, directly at the viewer.

She seems to be in a dangerous place, a tunnel entrance with a car whizzing by, at night on a slippery road —but she is unafraid. Does her statement require bravery?

Davis's character "Charlotte" is associated with New York City, and this seems to be a NYC scene. Is there a 9/11 connection?

black and white—like photojournalism— "real," "serious"

Why are these words emphasized?

FIGURE 7.2 An annotated image.

Exercise 7.4   Analyzing an essay

Reread "Misguided Multiculturalism" on pages 147–49. Annotate it or take separate notes as you read, and analyze it to determine how its parts work together. Add your own interpretations of Hentoff's statements.

Exercise 7.5   Analyzing an article

Reread the article you selected for Exercise 7.2, analyzing it with annotations or in separate notes.

Exercise 7.6   Analyzing a visual

1. Add to the annotated analysis of the ACLU ad in Figure 7.2, focusing on the text as well as the photograph.
2. The photograph shown in Figure 7.3 was taken during the January 30, 2005 elections in Iraq. It shows Kurdish women waiting to vote in the city of Kirkuk. First, preview and record your initial impressions of this photograph using the questions in 7b and 7c, then analyze and annotate it, either directly on the page or on a separate sheet of paper.

FIGURE 7.3 **Women voting in Kirkuk, Iraq, January 30, 2005.**

Summary   You cannot analyze or interpret something if you do not understand it. One way to demonstrate that you understand a text is to summarize it. A **summary** conveys the basic content of a text. When you summarize, your goal is to communicate the text's main points in your own words, not to say what you think of it.

An instructor may ask you to write a summary of a reading assignment to determine whether you have understood it, or you may decide to write one yourself in order to clarify a complex text or to record its essential points for use in a paper. A summary typically runs about one paragraph in length. Even when you are writing a fuller summary of a longer work, you should always use the fewest words possible. Clarity and brevity are important. A summary should never be longer than the original work.

Writing a summary requires simplification, but you need to be careful to avoid misrepresenting a writer's points by *oversimplifying* them. Consider, for example, this summary of the main point of the Hentoff essay (*on pp. 147–49*).

OVERSIMPLIFIED SUMMARY

An American history course should be required because college students are ignorant.

Although Hentoff does point to a general lack of knowledge about American history among college students to build his case for a required U.S. history course, a more accurate summary would indicate *why* Hentoff feels an understanding of U.S. history is important.

Here is a summary of Hentoff's essay that Ignacio Sanderson wrote as he was working on the paper that appears at the end of this chapter:

THOUGHTFUL SUMMARY

In his essay "Misguided Multiculturalism," Nat Hentoff defends a proposal to require all students of the City University of New York to take an American history course against opponents who believe the course would be inappropriate for the university's multicultural student body. Hentoff begins by noting that he is the son of immigrants from Russia. He goes on to discuss his upbringing and education, and how the courses he took in American civics inspired his "lifelong involvement in civil rights and civil liberties" (29). In addition to pointing out how valuable the study of American history was to his own career, Hentoff notes that most college students, even at schools like Duke and Harvard, don't know much about U.S. history. Hentoff acknowledges that multiculturalism is a worthwhile value, but stipulates, "You have to know how the society you live in works, and that requires a full-scale knowledge of its history" (30). While multiculturalism is important, a basic knowledge of U.S. history is essential.

TEXTCONNEX

The Pitfalls of "AutoSummarize"

Some word-processing programs include an AutoSummarize feature. Designed to work with very simple reports, AutoSummarize cannot produce a useful summary of the kinds of complex texts that you will most likely encounter in college. Here, for example, is the fractured and confusing summary of Nat Hentoff's "Misguided Multiculturalism" produced by Microsoft Word's Auto-Summarize function:

> I went to public school. Others call the very idea of a required course in American history absurd. As is the case throughout the country—from failing schools to the prestigious high schools—the teaching of American history, with few exceptions, is cursory, scattered, and superficial. Moreover, "none of the 55 elite colleges and universities (as rated by *U.S. News & World Report*) requires a course in American history before graduation." For insisting on core American history courses, Herman Badillo should be cheered, not scorned.

Note: Summaries are especially useful in research as a tool for recording various sources' points of view. A good summary can help you avoid plagiarism as well, because a central characteristic of a summary is that it is expressed in your own words. (*For more on summary, as well as paraphrase and quotation—two other methods of incorporating ideas—see Chapter 21: Working with Sources and Avoiding Plagiarism, pp. 349–56.*)

Exercise 7.7 Summarizing

Evaluate these summaries of passages from the ACLU ad (*p. 146*) and "Misguided Multiculturalism" (*pp. 147–49*). Indicate the problem with each faulty summary, and suggest how it should be revised.

1. In the ACLU ad, Kristin Davis claims that she is not an American.

2. In "Misguided Multiculturalism," Nat Hentoff argues that everyone should have an education like his.

3. In paragraph 7 of "Misguided Multiculturalism," Hentoff argues that American college and high school students have little knowledge about American history.

Exercise 7.8 Summarizing

Identify and describe the problems with the computer-generated summary of Hentoff's article that appears in the TextConnex box on page 156.

Exercise 7.9 Summarizing

1. Summarize the content and message of the ACLU ad (*p. 146*).
2. Summarize the article you selected for Exercise 7.2.
3. Summarize the photograph of Iraqi Kurdish women voting in Figure 7.3.

7e Synthesize your observations in a critical response paper.

To **synthesize** means to bring together, to make something out of different parts. In the last stage of critical reading, you pull your analysis, interpretation, and summary together into a coherent whole. Often this synthesis takes the form of a critical response paper.

A **critical response paper** typically begins with a summary of the text, followed by a thesis. The thesis should encapsulate your response to the text. Here are some possible thesis statements in response to Hentoff's "Misguided Multiculturalism":

POSSIBLE THESIS

Hentoff effectively argues that people need a knowledge of American history to live in America, and that a required U.S. history course is necessary to give people this knowledge.

POSSIBLE THESIS

Hentoff makes valid points about the necessity and importance of learning about American history, but he underestimates the negative impact a required American history course would have on immigrants and first- and second-generation Americans.

The rest of the response paper should elaborate on your thesis, supporting it with evidence from the text, your other reading, and your relevant personal experience.

157

Tips

LEARNING in COLLEGE

Writing a Critical Response Paper

- Summarize the main idea of the text you are responding to in a fair and accurate manner, recognizing its strengths as well as its weaknesses.
- Use your course readings to help formulate an approach to your analysis.
- Narrow your focus to one or two key points rather than responding to every point in the text.
- Use facts as well as personal experience to support your points. Make your points without using phrases such as "I feel" or "In my opinion."
- Avoid derogatory comments and labels such as "stupid" or "sneaky."
- Document the text and any additional sources you refer to using the documentation style required by your instructor. (*See Part 4: Documenting across the Curriculum for guidelines.*)

In the following critical response paper, Ignacio Sanderson synthesizes his reading of Nat Hentoff's "Misguided Multiculturalism" with his own experience.

Ignacio Sanderson

Professor Blackwell

English 99-B

15 March 2005

Critical Response to "Misguided Multiculturalism"

by Nat Hentoff

Multiculturalism is one of the most hotly debated topics in higher education today. As the son of an immigrant to the United States, I take this debate personally. The question of what makes an "American education" strikes a chord in me.

The same is true for Nat Hentoff, as he explains in his article "Misguided Multiculturalism." Hentoff first notes that he is the son of immigrants from Russia. He goes on to discuss his upbringing and education, and how the courses he took in American civics inspired his "lifelong involvement in civil rights and civil liberties" (29).

Hentoff then defends a proposal by the City University of New York's Board of Trustees to introduce a mandatory American history course for all the university's students. In addition to pointing out how valuable the study of American history was to his own career, Hentoff notes that most college students, even at schools like Duke and Harvard, do not know much about U.S. history. He complains that students are ignorant about the history of the Bill of Rights and the American labor movement. Hentoff acknowledges that multiculturalism is a worthwhile value, but stipulates, "You have to know how the society you live in works, and that requires a full-scale knowledge of its history" (30). While multiculturalism is important, a basic knowledge of U.S. history is essential.

Hentoff's argument summarized.

I have experienced the transition from one culture to another firsthand. Although I agree with Hentoff that it is crucial to learn about American history if you want to be an American, requiring an American history course of everyone sends the wrong message to immigrants and first- and second-generation Americans. It tells such people that there is only one important history university students should know: American history.

Thesis statement.

Hentoff is clearly sensitive to the charge of "ethnocentrism," or the placing of one culture or ethnicity above all others. In the article, however, he seems to want to have it both ways: he supports a multicultural, non-ethnocentric curriculum, but also a required American history course. These goals are incompatible, however. Making all students take a course in the history of one society to the exclusion of those of other societies is inevitably ethnocentric.

Objection to Hentoff's argument.

Hentoff tries to answer this objection by pointing out that an American history course might reveal to students the history of discrimination—and the fight against it—in this country. He implies that, even if requiring the course is ethnocentric, the content of the course would not have to be ethnocentric propaganda. That may be true, but Hentoff does not know what the course will cover. He discusses the history he would like students to learn, but offers no evidence that faculty members will teach it. Unless there is a set syllabus for the course, however, there is no guarantee that students will be exposed to a balanced account of U.S. history.

Consideration of Hentoff's response to the objection.

Nat Hentoff's heart is in the right place. It is important for all Americans to know how the United States became the country it is today. This knowledge would be better gained by people acting individually, though, rather than within the context of mandated classes. Each person should have the right to manage for himself or herself the complex task of becoming American.

Conclusion reinforces Sanderson's point.

————————————[new page]————————————

Work Cited

Works-Cited list follows MLA style and begins on a new page.

Hentoff, Nat. "Misguided Multiculturalism." Village Voice 19 July 2000: 29-30.

Exercise 7.10 Writing a critical response to an article

Using the analysis that you prepared in Exercise 7.5 and the summary that you wrote in Exercise 7.9.2, write a critical response to the article you selected for Exercise 7.2.

Exercise 7.11 Writing a critical response to a visual

1. Using the analysis that you prepared in Exercise 7.6 and the summary you wrote in Exercise 7.9.1, write a critical response to the ACLU ad (*p. 146*).

2. Using the analysis that you prepared in Exercise 7.6.2 and the summary you wrote in Exercise 7.9.3, describe your personal reaction to the photograph of Iraqi women voting in Figure 7.3 (*p. 154*).

8 Informative Reports

Imagine what the world would be like if each person had to learn everything from scratch, by trial and error, with no recipes, no encyclopedias, no textbooks, no newspapers—nothing that records what others have learned. Fortunately, we have many sources of information to draw on, including informative reports.

8a Understand the assignment.

An **informative report** passes on what someone has learned about a topic or issue; it teaches. Because a good way for students to reinforce learning is by teaching it to others, college instructors often assign informative reports. When your instructor assigns an informative report, he or she expects you to find out what is currently known about some specific topic and to present what you discover in a clear and unbiased way.

An informative report gives you a chance to do the following:

- Read more about an issue that interests you.
- Make sense of what you have read, heard, and seen.
- Teach others what you have learned.

8b Approach writing an informative report as a process.

www.mhhe.com/nmhh
For an interactive tutorial on writing informative reports, go to
Writing >
Writing Tutors >
Informative Reports

1. Selecting a topic that interests you

An informative report should be clear and accurate but not dull. The major challenge of writing informative reports is engaging the reader's interest. Selecting a topic that interests you makes it more likely that your report will interest your readers.

Consider connecting what you are learning in one course with a topic you are studying in another course or with your personal experience. For example, one student, Joe Smulowitz, worked part-time for a stockbroker and aspired to a career in that field, a field significantly

WRITING beyond COLLEGE

Informative Reports

By writing reports in college, you prepare yourself for future professional and public occasions that will require you to pass on information to others. In many professions, writing informative announcements, manuals, and reports is part of the job. Informative writing is also part of professional writing in the disciplines:

- In a published article, an anthropologist surveys and summarizes a large body of information from archeological, historical, and ethnographic sources relating to warfare among the indigenous peoples of the American Southwest before the arrival of the Spanish conquerors.

- In a report for their colleagues, three physical therapists define what a critical pathway is, trace its development, and summarize the arguments for and against its use in patient care.

- For an encyclopedia of British women writers, a professor of literature briefly recounts the life and works of Eliza Fenwick, a recently rediscovered eighteenth-century author.

- In a journal for research biologists, two biochemists summarize the findings of more than two hundred recently published articles on defense mechanisms in plants.

affected by the Internet. For his topic, he decided to investigate what online stock traders were doing and saying. (*Smulowitz's paper begins on p. 166.*)

2. Considering what your readers know about the topic

Unless the assignment designates a different group, consider your classmates and your instructor as the audience for your report. In other words, assume that your readers have some familiarity with the topic area but that most of them do not have clear, specific knowledge of your particular topic.

3. Developing an objective stance

When writers have an **objective stance,** they do not take sides. Instead, they present differing views fairly, without indicating a preference for one view over another. This commitment to objectivity gives an informative report its authority. Ideas and facts are presented methodically, and the emphasis is on the topic, not the writer. By contrast, when writers are **subjective,** they let readers know their views. Although a subjective stance is appropriate for other types of writing, an informative report should come across as objective rather than subjective.

4. Composing a thesis that summarizes your knowledge of the topic

The thesis of an informative report is usually not controversial, even when the report is about a dispute. Because transmitting knowledge is the primary goal of an informative report, the thesis typically states an accepted generalization or reports the results of the writer's study.

Your thesis should also state the goal of your paper and forecast its content. Before you decide on a thesis, review the information you have collected and divide it into categories, or subtopics. Compose a thesis statement that summarizes—either generally or by category—what the information in your paper shows. (*For more on thesis statements, see Chapter 3: Planning and Shaping the Whole Essay, pp. 45–49.*)

In his paper about online stock trading, Smulowitz's thesis is a generalization that he supports in the body of his paper with information he groups into categories:

> Besides honest investors with various levels of expertise, the Internet grants access to numerous investors who post false information in hopes of making a quick and sometimes large profit. . . . *The one hundred or so postings that I read can be divided into four categories.*

Notice how Smulowitz forecasts the body of his report in the italicized sentence. We expect to learn something about each of the four categories, and the report is structured to give us that information category by category.

5. Providing context in your introduction

Informative reports usually begin with a relatively simple introduction to the topic and a straightforward statement of the thesis. To orient readers, the introduction may provide some relevant context or background, but writers of informative reports generally get to their topic as quickly as possible and keep it in the foreground. (*For more on introductions, see Chapter 4: Drafting Paragraphs and Visuals, pp. 85–86.*)

6. Organizing your paper for clarity by classifying and dividing information

Because you are explaining something in an informative report, clarity matters. Informative writers develop their ideas in an organized

www.mhhe.com/
nmhh
For more help with developing a thesis, go to
Writing >
Paragraph/Essay Development >
Thesis/Central Idea

way, often by classifying and dividing information into categories, subtopics, or the stages of a process. (*For more on developing your ideas, see Chapter 4: Drafting Paragraphs and Visuals, pp. 71–83.*)

www.mhhe.com/
nmhh
For more on using patterns of development, go to

Writing >
Paragraph
Patterns

7. Illustrating key ideas with examples

Because clarity is so important to the success of an informative report, writers of these kinds of papers usually use specific examples to help readers understand their most important ideas. In his paper on online stock trading, Smulowitz devotes a lot of space to examples, including messages posted by various investors and an instance of gender-bending for profit. Examples make his report interesting as well as educational. (*For more on using examples, see Chapter 4: Drafting Paragraphs and Visuals, pp. 76–78.*)

8. Defining specialized terms and spelling out unfamiliar abbreviations

Most informative reports include specialized terms that will probably not be familiar to most readers, or familiar terms that are being used in a specialized or an unfamiliar way. Writers of informative reports usually explain these terms with a synonym or a brief definition. For example, Smulowitz gives a brief definition of the term *online traders* in the first paragraph of his informative report on online stock trading. (*For more on definition, see Chapter 4: Drafting Paragraphs and Visuals, pp. 74–76.*) Unfamiliar abbreviations like CMC (computer-mediated communication) and GDP (gross domestic product) are spelled out the first time they are used, with the abbreviation in parentheses.

www.mhhe.com/
nmhh
For more information on conclusions, go to

Writing >
Paragraph/Essay
Development >
Conclusions

9. Concluding by answering "So what?"

Because informative writers want readers to remember what they have learned, they often conclude their reports with an image that suggests the information's value or a saying that sums it all up. The conclusion reminds readers of the topic and thesis that were first stated in the introduction. It then answers the "So what?" question.

At the end of his report on online stock trading, Smulowitz answers the "So what?" question with a warning:

> Before buying any stock, investors should investigate it thoroughly. When they read what others say about a company, they should remember that if it sounds too good to be true, it probably isn't true.

(*Also see information on conclusions in Chapter 4: Drafting Paragraphs and Visuals, pp. 87–89.*)

8c | Write informative reports on social science research.

www.mhhe.com/
nmhh
For another sample of
informative writing,
go to
Writing >
Writing Samples >
Informative Paper

Informative papers are commonly used in the social sciences to report on research—either the writer's own research or the research of other scholars. In this section, we look at an informative report that would be appropriate for a first- or second-level course. Section 8d considers a more specialized type of informative paper in the social sciences: the review of the literature on a topic. (*For a discussion of the use of case studies in the social sciences, see Chapter 9: Interpretive Reports, pp. 202–6.*)

In the informative paper that follows, Joe Smulowitz reports what he has learned about the people who are talking online about stocks. As you read his report, notice how Smulowitz provides a context for his topic, cites various sources (using the APA documentation style), categorizes the information, and illustrates his ideas with examples, all hallmarks of a clear, carefully developed paper. The annotations in the margin of this paper point out specific aspects of the informative report. (*For details on the proper formatting of a paper in APA style, see Chapter 25 and the sample paper that begins on p. 457.*)

Tips LEARNING in COLLEGE

Informative Reports in the Social Sciences

Informative reports in the social sciences examine a wide range of behavioral and social phenomena, such as consumer spending, courtship rituals, political campaign tactics, and job stress.

Some Types of Informative Reports in the Social Sciences

- *Research reports* describe the process and results of research conducted by the author(s).
- *Reviews of the literature* synthesize the published work on a particular topic.

Documentation Styles

- APA (*see Chapter 25*) and Chicago (*see Chapter 26*)

Sample student informative report

Following APA style, Smulowitz includes a separate title page. He does not include an abstract, however, because his instructor did not require one for this assignment.

Chatting Online about Stocks

Joe Smulowitz

Sociology of Business

Professor Lanahan

November 14, 2005

————————————[new page]————————————

Chatting Online about Stocks

Topic introduced.

The Internet has produced a new kind of investor: the online stock market investor. Until a few years ago, a person who wanted to invest in the stock market had to hire a professional broker, who might charge $300 per trade as well as a substantial commission. Nowadays, an investor can buy and sell stocks over the Internet at costs ranging from only $7.95 to $25 per trade. As a result, more and more lay people have become online traders—investors who use the Internet to buy and sell stocks. Of the 143 million Americans who are currently using the Internet, 39% use it to trade stocks online (National Telecommunications and Information Administration, 2002, chap. 3). *Silicon Investor,* a popular site for chatting about stocks, receives over 12,000 posts a day from online traders (Lucchetti, 1998).

Important term defined.

Source information summarized rather than quoted directly.

Who are these online traders, and what are they talking about in investment-related chats? Besides honest investors with various levels of expertise, the Internet grants access to numerous investors who post false information in hopes of making a quick and sometimes large profit. The Internet is rife with "hundreds of fraudulent and abusive investment schemes, including stock manipulations, pyramid scams, and Ponzi schemes" (Connecticut Department of Banking, 1998, p. 2). State securities agencies and other investment regulators are now looking into cases in which the price of shares in little-known stocks appears to have been manipulated through messages posted on Internet bulletin boards.

Thesis stated.

Direct quotation: page number included in citation.

Many investors find out about online fraud the hard way. Consider the case of Interlock Consolidated Enterprises, Inc. This Canadian company was reported to have landed a major contract to construct housing in the former USSR. When the company became the topic of online hype in early 1994, its stock jumped from 42 cents a share to $1.30 before falling back to 60 cents (Gardner & Gardner, 1994, "The Fairy Tale" section, para. 4). In this type of scam, known as "pump and dump," investors spread unusually positive news about a stock, then sell it when the price gets unrealistically high. This scam is nothing new to the investment world. In fact, pump-and-dump schemes began in the 1700s (Lucchetti, 1998). But now the schemers can reach hundreds of thousands of people with a single posting, and that kind of reach clearly makes a difference.

Unfamiliar term defined.

An example of what is going on in investment-related chats is the online talk about Chico's, a women's clothing company. *Silicon Investor* includes a chat room called "Miscellaneous," where in 1999 one could read a tip about Chico's: the company was about to release good news, which would raise the price of its stock (Vanier, 1999). A savvy investor would have found out more about Chico's from sources such as *Yahoo! Finance* or *Hoover's Online,* Internet-based business information databases. There investors would have found a history of Chico's; a summary of what Chico's produces; the company's location, phone number, number of employees, names of top management; a list of the company's recent press releases; and most importantly, financial data, including stock price and performance over the past year (Yahoo! Finance, 2004, Chico's FAS; Hoover's Online, 2004, Chico's FAS).

Objective stance: first person (I) avoided with APA style.

Having read some facts about Chico's, investors would have been better prepared to understand e-mail messages about the company's stock posted on the *Silicon Investor* bulletin board, messages that fell into four categories. In the first category belonged postings with only positive things to say about Chico's, such as, "CHS [Chico's ticker name] is expected to add 30 stores this year. . . . They are expecting

Information about Smulowitz's classifications.

to grow to over 700 stores in the near future" (mfpcpa, 1999). About 75% of the approximately 100 messages belonged to this positive-only category and appeared to be posted by stockholders trying to spread hype about Chico's so that the stock's price would rise. The few replies to these messages expressed agreement.

In the second category belonged messages that came from investors called "shorts" and "longs." When they think a security's price is going to decrease, shorts borrow the security from a broker or dealer and sell it on the market. The short investor profits if the price goes down because he or she can replace the borrowed security at a lower cost. Longs, on the other hand, purchase a security because they think its price will increase. The long investor profits if the price goes up because he or she can sell the security for more than it cost originally. Because the shorts want the price to decrease and the longs want the price to increase, these two kinds of stock traders often feud in online discussions. For example, in the following exchange about Chico's stock, a short's message entitled "Out of Steam" provoked a reaction entitled "Stay LONG" from cag174, a long:

Categories illustrated with examples and unfamiliar terms defined.

E-mail messages are central to the paper and, thus, are quoted directly, not summarized.

> She can't take it Captain. The stock can't hold its new highs. It keeps closing at the bottom of the range. Shorts will live. We will see 28 again. (Startrader 1975, 1999)

> $38 will come before $28. $43 at year end. (cag174, 1999)

There seemed to be more long investors than short investors on the Chico's bulletin board. Whenever a short posted a negative message aimed at lowering the stock price, several longs retaliated, warning that the short was misleading investors.

In the third category were posts from sneaky investors. For example, the following post appeared to be written by a woman: "Don't know much about stocks, just love the clothes and so do my daughters—31, 35, and 43. Talked hubby into buying in when I read Streisand was buying lots of sweaters . . ." (Katy10121, 1999). Since Chico's is a woman's clothing store, investors are likely to be interested in what women think about the store. But the person who posted this message might not have been female. The poster's online profile listed the poster's sex as "male." This investor could be trying to take advantage of other investors by engaging in gender-bending.

Interpretation provided without biased opinion.

The last category of messages comprised posts from owners of little-known and lightly traded stocks called "penny stocks." Here is an example of such messages:

> CHS has given us a great ride, but now would be a good time to get off, while we're on top, and reinvest profits in a little soon-to-be-rediscovered gem, SNKI (Swank). Low volume right now, but check out the P/E and other stats. . . . (gravytrain2030, 1998)

The price of penny stocks such as SNKI ranges from $0.01 to $5 a share. Enthusiasm from seemingly in-the-know observers like gravytrain2030 can sometimes lead to significant increases in the stock price. For that reason, *Yahoo!* does not offer bulletin boards for such stocks. Nevertheless, people still post their messages on other bulletin boards, just as gravytrain2030 did on the Chico's board.

The Internet gives the average person the opportunity to invest in the stock market without going through a broker. All the information essential to investing is available to *anyone* with access to a computer. But hype, manipulation, and fraud are also on the Internet. Before buying any stock, investors should investigate it thoroughly. When they read what others say about a company, they should remember that if it sounds too good to be true, it probably isn't true.

Point and purpose restated in conclusion.

————————————————[new page]————————————————

References

References list follows APA style and begins on a new page.

cag174. (1999, November 9). Stay LONG. Message posted to Chico's message board, archived at http://finance.yahoo.com/q/mb?s=CHS

Connecticut Department of Banking. (1998). *Investor bulletin: On-line investment schemes.* Hartford: Connecticut Department of Banking.

Gardner, D., & Gardner, T. (1994). Buy Zeigletics! *The Fool's School.* Retrieved December 8, 2004 from http://www.fool.com/School/Zeigletics/ZFairyTale.htm

gravytrain2030. (1998, July 3). Sell CHS, reinvest in SNKI. Message posted to Chico's message board, archived at http://finance .yahoo.com/q/mb?s=CHS

Hoover's Online. (2004, December 6). *Chico's FAS Inc.* Retrieved December 6, 2004, from http://premium.hoovers.com/subscribe/ co/factsheet.xhtml?ID=16010

Katy10121. (1999, June 24). Just love the clothes. Message posted to Chico's message board, archived at http://finance.yahoo.com/ q/mb?s=CHS

Lucchetti, A. (1998, May 28). Some Web sites getting tough on stock chat. *Wall Street Journal,* pp. C1, C12.

mfpcpa. (1999, February 23). Response to Mish's post. Message posted to Chico's message board, archived at http://finance.yahoo .com/q/mb?s=CHS

National Telecommunications and Information Administration. (2002, February). *A nation online: How Americans are expanding their use of the Internet.* (U.S. Department of Commerce Report). Retrieved December 1, 2004 from http://www.ntia.doc.gov/ntiahome/dn/ html/anationonline2.htm

Startrader 1975. (1999, November 5). Out of steam. Message posted to Chico's message board, archived at http://finance.yahoo.com/ q/mb?s=CHS

Vanier, G. (1999, May 1). Time to buy Chico's. Message posted to Chico's message board, archived at http://www.siliconinvestor .com/stocktalk/subject.gsp?subjectid=20636

Yahoo! Finance. (2004, December 6.) *Chico's FAS Inc.* Retrieved December 6, 2004 from http://finance.yahoo.com/q/pr?s=chs

8d Write reviews of the literature to summarize current knowledge in a specific area.

In upper-division courses, instructors sometimes assign a special kind of informative report called a **review of the literature.** Here the term *literature* refers to published research reports, not to poems and novels, and the term *review* means that you need to survey others' ideas, not evaluate them or argue for your opinion. A review presents an organized account of the current state of knowledge in a specific area, an account that you and other researchers can use to figure out new projects and directions for research. A review of the literature may also be a subsection within a research report.

The following paragraph is an excerpt from the review of the literature section in an article by psychologists investigating the motivations for suicide:

> One source of information about suicide motives is suicide notes. International studies of suicide notes suggest that women and men do not differ with regard to love versus achievement motives. For example, in a study of German suicide notes, Linn and Lester (1997) found that women and men did not differ with regard to relationship versus financial or work motives. In a study of Hong Kong suicide notes, Ho, Yip, Chiu, and Halliday (1998) reported no gender or age differences with regard to interpersonal problems or financial/job problems. Similarly, in a UK study, McClelland, Reicher, and Booth (2000) found that men's suicide notes did not differ from women's notes in terms of mentioning career failures. In fact, in the UK study relationship losses were reported more often in men's than in women's suicide notes.

> —CANETTO AND LESTER, *Journal of Psychology,*
> September 2002

8e Write informative papers in the sciences to share discoveries.

Without writing, science would not be possible. Scientists form hypotheses and plan new experiments as they observe, read, and write. When they work in the laboratory, they keep well-organized and detailed notebooks. They also write and publish research reports, using a format that reflects the logic of scientific argument. In this way, they share their discoveries and enable other scientists to use their work.

8f Write lab reports to demonstrate understanding.

As a college student, you may be asked to demonstrate your scientific understanding by showing that you know how to perform and report on an experiment designed to verify some well-established fact or principle. In advanced courses, you may get to design original experiments as well. (*An example of a student lab report can be found on p. 175.*)

> *Note:* When scientists report the results of original experiments designed to provide new insight into issues on the frontiers of scientific knowledge, they go beyond informative reporting to interpretive analysis of the significance of their findings.

Tips

LEARNING in COLLEGE

Informative Reports in the Sciences

Informative reports in the sciences examine a wide range of natural and physical phenomena, such as plant growth, weather patterns, animal behavior, chemical reactions, and magnetic fields.

Some Types of Informative Reports in the Sciences

- *Lab reports* describe experiments, following the steps of the scientific method.
- *Research reports* describe the process and results of research conducted by the author(s). Research reports are more extensive than lab reports.
- *Reviews of the literature* synthesize the published work on a particular topic. (*See 8d, pp. 170–71 for an explanation and example.*)

Documentation Styles

- CSE name-year style and CSE number style (*see Chapter 26*)

Lab reports usually include seven distinctive sections in the following order: Abstract, Introduction, Methods and Materials, Results, Discussion, Acknowledgments, and References. Begin drafting the report, section by section, while your time in the lab is still fresh in your mind.

Follow the scientific conventions for abbreviations, symbols, and numbers. See if your textbook includes a list of accepted abbreviations and symbols, or ask your professor where you might find such a list. Use numerals rather than words for dates, times, pages, figures, tables, and standard units of measurement (for example, g/ml, percentages). Spell out numbers between one and nine that are not part of a series of larger numbers.

1. Abstract

An abstract is a one-paragraph summary of what your lab report covers. Although usually written last, the abstract is the part that others will read first. Scientists often skim professional journals, reading nothing more than the titles and abstracts of articles. Abstracts generally use about 250 words to answer the following questions: What methods were used in the experiment? What variables were measured? What were the findings? What do the findings imply?

2. Introduction

The introduction gives readers the information they need to understand the focus and point of your lab report. State your topic, summarize prior research, and present your hypothesis.

3. Methods and materials

Experiments must be repeatable. The purpose of the methods-and-materials section is to answer the *how* and *what* questions in a way that permits other scientists to replicate your work. Select the details that they will need to know to replicate the experiment. Using the past tense, recount in chronological order what was done with specific materials.

4. Results

In this section, your purpose is to tell your reader about the results that are relevant to your hypothesis, especially those that are statistically significant. Results may be relevant to your hypothesis even if they are different from what you expected. An experiment does not need to confirm your hypothesis to be interesting.

To report what you have learned, you might provide a summarizing table or graph. For example, the graph in Figure 8.1 on page 174, which plots the distance a glider traveled over a period of time, was used to summarize the results of an engineering assignment. In this instance, a paper airplane was launched, and the distance it traveled in a specific period of time was measured. Each point on the graph represents the distance the glider traveled in consecutive tenths of a second from 0.1 second to 1.0 second. By reading the positions of the glider on the XY plot (X equals time; Y equals position in centimeters), we can see that the glider traveled just under 100 centimeters in 1.0 second.

Every table and figure you include in a lab report must be mentioned in the body of your report. Do not repeat all the information in the table or figure, but do point out the relevant patterns it reveals. If you run statistical tests on your findings, be careful not to make the tests themselves the focus of your writing. In this section, you should

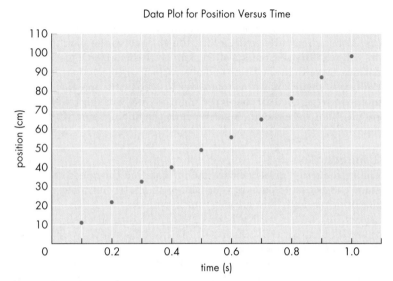

FIGURE 8.1 **The distance traveled by a paper airplane plotted in 0.1 second intervals.**

emphasize the *results* of the tests, not the statistical procedures used to analyze the data. Refrain from interpreting why things happened the way they did. Interpretation belongs in the discussion section.

Note: Choose your words carefully. Refer to an "increase," for example, as "marked" rather than as "significant." Like the terms *correlated* and *random,* the term *significant* has a specific statistical meaning for scientists and should therefore be used in a lab report only in relation to the appropriate statistical tests.

---

5. Discussion

In your discussion section, you need to explain how and why your results do or do not confirm the hypothesis. Lab experiments produce results, not facts or laws. To transform results into accepted facts or laws, the scientific community depends on debate and consensus. In discussing your results, interpret your major findings by explaining how and why each finding does or does not confirm the original hypothesis. Connect your research with prior scientific research. How and why do your findings and interpretations agree or disagree with the prior research summarized in your introduction? Look ahead to future research: where do scientists interested in this area seem to be going?

6. Acknowledgments

You may have reason to include an acknowledgments section. In professional journals, most research papers include a brief statement acknowledging those who assisted the author or authors during the research and writing process.

7. References

This final section of your report should include a listing of all manuals, books, and journal articles you used during your research and writing process. Do not wait until the last minute to prepare this section, or you may find that you do not have time to get some missing piece of information. Use one of the citation formats developed by the Council of Science Editors (CSE style), unless another citation format is favored by those working in the area of your research. If you are uncertain about which format to use, ask your professor for advice.

Sample student lab report

Orientation by Sight in Schooling and Non-schooling Fish

Josephine Hearn

Biology 103

October 5, 2004

Lab partners:

Tracy Luckow

Bryan Mignone

Darcy Langford

Abstract

This experiment examined the tendency of schooling and of non-schooling fish to orient by sight toward conspecifics. Schooling species did orient toward conspecifics by sight and non-schooling species did not show any preference, indicating that schooling fish show a positive phototaxis toward conspecifics.

Experiment
summarized.

Introduction

Vision has been established as the primary method by which many schooling fish maintain a close proximity to one another. Olfaction, sound, and water pressure are secondary factors in schooling.[1] This experiment tested this theory, specifically, to determine whether schooling fish orient by sight toward conspecifics, whether schooling fish orient toward conspecifics more readily in the presence of a non-schooling species than of another schooling species, and whether schooling fish orient toward conspecifics more readily than non-schooling fish do. It was predicted that schooling fish would show a positive phototaxis to conspecifics, and that non-schooling fish would demonstrate no definite taxis movement toward conspecifics; furthermore, schooling fish would orient toward conspecifics more readily in an environment with non-schooling fish than in one with other schooling fish; finally, strongly schooling fish would more readily orient to conspecifics than would less strongly schooling fish.

The hypothesis was tested by placing two species in an aquarium, one species at each end of the tank, with a test fish belonging to one of the two species in the center of the tank allowed to orient by sight toward either species.

Background information provided: earlier study, scope and hypothesis of current experiment.

Methods and materials

Observations were made of 5 species of fish: *Brachydanio* sp. (zebra danios), *Barbus tetrazona* (tiger barbs), *Xiphophorus maculatus* (swordtails), *Hyphessobrycon* sp. (tetras), and *Cichlasoma nigrofasciatum* (juvenile convict cichlids). The species were ranked according to the schooling behavior exhibited, determined by recording the time each species spent schooling. Criteria for ranking were the proximity of conspecifics to one another and the tendency to move together. Barbs were ranked as the species with the strongest schooling tendency, followed closely by tetras, then danios, swordtails, and cichlids. Cichlids were considered a non-schooling species. The top 2 ranking species, barbs and tetras, and the last ranking species, cichlids, were selected for this experiment.

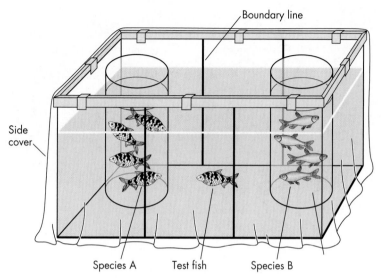

Figure 1 Test tank used to study orientation behavior (from Glase JC; Zimmerman MC, Waldvogel JA[2])

As illustrated in Figure 1, three cylinders were placed inside a filled 10-gallon aquarium surrounded by a dark curtain to prevent the entry of light from the sides.[2] Plexiglas cylinders were used to keep species separated and able to orient to each other by sight alone. The 2 outermost cylinders contained 4 each of two different species. A test fish, belonging to either of those species, was placed in the central cylinder. The water temperature was uniformly 22 °C and remained so throughout the experiment.

When all cylinders were in place, the central cylinder was lifted out of the tank, allowing the test fish to move freely. Over the course of one minute, the time that the test fish spent on the side with conspecifics was recorded. The procedure was repeated with all possible combinations of the 3 species, and 5 replicates of each combination.

Specifics about how the experiment was conducted.

Results

Figure 2 shows the results for each of the three species for all of the trials. As predicted, the mean time out of one minute spent on the

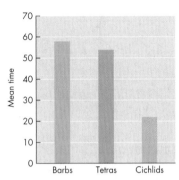

Figure 2 Mean time spent with conspecifics.

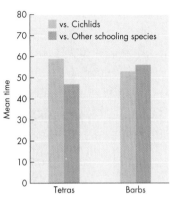

Figure 3 Comparison of mean times.

Outcome of
the experiment
summarized.

conspecifics side is higher for the barbs and tetras than for the cichlids. Figure 3 compares the mean times for each of the schooling species when the test fish were with the other schooling species or with the non-schooling species. The mean times for the schooling species are higher when the test fish was with other schooling species than with the non-schooling species.

Discussion

The hypothesis that schooling fish would orient more readily than non-schooling fish to conspecifics was supported. It was shown that barbs and tetras, both schooling fish, spent nearly the entire time on the side with their own species, whereas the cichlids divided their time almost equally between the 2 sides. This result supports the theory that schooling fish orient to each other visually.[1] Furthermore, the barbs, the species with stronger schooling tendencies, showed more orientation than the tetras, the species with weaker schooling tendencies.

Barbs and tetras did not orient more or less readily to conspecifics depending on whether it was the other schooling species or the non-schooling species present in the tank. This indicates that schooling fish are neither attracted to other species of schooling fish nor repelled by non-schooling fish; however, because of the limited data, this subject deserves more investigation. An experiment should be conducted in which schooling fish are placed in a tank with the choice to orient either toward another schooling species or toward a non-schooling species, neither of which are conspecifics to the test fish.

Other sources of error may have affected the results of this experiment. First, the species of tetra was changed midway through the trials. Second, when test fish were changed, it was not made certain that the new test fish had not already been used. Third, occasionally, test fish were so close to the boundary line dividing the aquarium that it became a subjective decision as to which side the test fish was on. Fourth, during the experiment, fish were continually moved in and out of the water, possibly distressing them and thus affecting their ability to orient.

Results of the experiment interpreted and flaws described.

————————————[new page]————————————

References

1. Burgess JW, Shaw E. Development and ecology of fish schooling. Oceanus 1979 Jul; 22(2):11-17.

2. Glase JC, Zimmerman MC, Waldvogel JA. Investigations in orientation behavior [Internet]. [Cited 2004 Dec 4] Available from: Association for Biology Laboratory Education at http://www.zoo.utoronto.ca/able/volumes/vol-6/1-glase/1-glase.htm

References list follows CSE number style and begins on a new page.

8g Write informative reports on events or findings in the humanities.

In the humanities, informative papers are used primarily to report on an event or finding in one of the humanities disciplines (for example, art, literature, history, philosophy, music, theater, and film). Unlike informative reports in the sciences, informative reports in the humanities may sometimes include subjective responses—your reaction to the event—in addition to specific details that support your points.

LEARNING in COLLEGE

Informative Reports in the Humanities

Informative reports in the humanities describe new and existing knowledge about the ideas, stories, and values of people past and present. Report topics could include archeological discoveries, accounts of musical and dramatic performances, and historical findings about art patronage.

Some Types of Informative Reports in the Humanities

- *Concert, theater, or film reports* describe the elements of a single performance or series of performances.
- *Book reports* describe the plot, characters, setting, and themes of a novel or summarize a nonfiction work.

Documentation Styles

- MLA (*see Chapter 24*), and Chicago (*see Chapter 26*)

In the following example, a journalist explains the recent work of an artist who combines music, video, and readings in live performance.

Sample informative piece

The Sample Life

CARLY BERWICK

Paul D. Miller, a.k.a. DJ Spooky that Subliminal Kid, straddles hip-hop, club culture, and silent film

A young boy danced in the aisle to the DJ's pounding beats until his well-coiffed mother ushered him back to his seat in Lincoln Center's Alice Tully Hall. Behind a series of turntables and computers, Paul D. Miller, a.k.a. DJ Spooky that Subliminal Kid, warmed up his audience for *TransMetropolitan,* a night of music, videos, and readings he likened to a 1960s happening. Later that week, Miller performed *Rebirth of a Nation,* his live remix of D. W. Griffith's 1915 silent film *Birth of a Nation,* which presents the Ku Klux Klan as the saviors of a South overrun by unruly free blacks. Using the computer to edit and project the movie across three

DJ Spooky and Ryuichi Sakamoto during the premiere of *TransMetropolitan.*

screens, Miller cut and grouped scenes from the nearly three-hour film into repeated gestures, as Robert Johnson's blues echoed beneath rhythmic violin chords Miller created on the computer.

For more than ten years, Miller, a 33-year-old writer, artist, and DJ, has been making the case that sampling and remixing—taking existing sounds or images and reconfiguring them into new ones, like collage—are the way we experience the world today. Originally from Washington, D.C., Miller says sampling provides a "seamless consolidation of cultural patterns." His performance of *TransMetropolitan* at Lincoln Center, for example, brought together writers and musicians from Sri Lanka, Pakistan, England, and Brooklyn. Moreover, he says, our invisible networks of

technological communication link us more powerfully than the visible ones. As examples, he lists standard time and wireless Internet networks. "Software," he adds, "has changed all of our cultural patterns."

Films help people respond to certain often-repeated cues. Miller thinks *Birth of a Nation,* one of Hollywood's first blockbusters, "has conditioned people's responses" to race, he says. By reframing the movie, Miller allows contemporary audiences to examine racist gestures established 90 years ago and their persistence in contemporary culture. Miller showed posters and stills from his video, a looped DVD projection, at new York's Paula Cooper Gallery earlier this year, where the prints sold for $1,500 and the edition of five videos was priced at around $10,000.

Miller's music tends to be accessible, with arcane allusions and provocative samples supported by a driving beat. He started working as a DJ to "pay rent," he says, and his desire for people to enjoy the music comes through. "I look at myself as straddling hip-hop, club culture, and the metaphysics of text," says Miller—as he simultaneously scans the paper and answers his cell phone—a relentlessly multitasking interpreter of the wide wired world.

9 Interpretive Analyses and Writing about Literature

Interpretation is one of the key tasks of educated people. As the phrase "That's open to interpretation" suggests, searching for meaning does not involve looking for a single right answer. Instead, it involves figuring out a way of understanding that is meaningful to the writer and convincing to readers.

9a Understand the assignment.

In college, you will frequently get assignments that require you to explore the meaning of written documents, literary works, cultural artifacts, social situations, and natural events. When an assignment asks you to compare, explain, analyze, discuss, or do a reading of something, you are expected to study that subject closely to figure out what it might mean.

Interpretive analyses, including comparative papers, encourage you to move beyond simple description. They call on you to examine or compare particular items for a reason: to enhance your reader's understanding of people's conditions, actions, beliefs, or desires.

9b Approach writing an interpretive analysis as a process.

Writing an interpretive analysis typically begins with critical reading. (*See Chapter 7: Reading, Thinking, Writing: The Critical Connection for a discussion of how to read texts and visuals critically.*)

1. Discovering an aspect of the subject that is meaningful to you
Although you will not include your personal motives in the finished version of your interpretive analysis, your interpretation will be more compelling if you take time to discover why the subject is meaningful to you. Think about your own experience while you read, listen, or observe. Connecting your own thoughts and experience to what you are studying can help you develop fresh interpretations.

www.mhhe.com/
nmhh
For an interactive
tutorial on writing
interpretive analyses,
go to
Writing >
Writing Tutors >
Interpretive
Analysis

Interpretive Analyses

You can find interpretive analyses in professional journals like *PMLA* (*Publications of the Modern Language Association*) as well as popular publications like the *New Yorker* and the *Atlantic Monthly*. Take a look at some of these publications to see how your work connects with that of professional scholars and critics.

- A cultural critic contrasts the way AIDS and cancer are talked about, imagined, and therefore treated.

- Two geologists analyze photos of an arctic coastal plain taken from an airplane and infer that the effects of seismic activity vary according to the type of vegetation in the area.

- A musicologist compares the revised endings of two pieces by Beethoven to figure out what makes a work complete and finished.

- A philosopher reflects on personal identity as a complex and shifting concept by investigating how the ideas of the philosophers Descartes and Hume are alike and different.

- A cultural critic explores Freud's anecdotes, showing how they are used both to control and to dramatize the uncanny.

2. Developing a thoughtful stance

In an interpretive analysis you take your readers with you on an intellectual journey. You are saying, in effect, "Come, think this through with me." Consequently, your stance should be thoughtful, inquisitive, and open-minded. You are exploring the possible meaning of something. Usually it is wise to admit uncertainty and qualify your interpretations with words like *probably, may,* and *perhaps.* Read your writing aloud, and as you listen to your words, ask yourself whether your stance sounds as exploratory as it should.

3. Using an intellectual framework

To interpret your subject effectively, you will have to analyze it using a relevant perspective or intellectual framework. For example, the basic elements of a work of fiction, such as plot, character, and setting, are often used to analyze stories. Sigmund Freud's theory of conscious and unconscious forces in conflict has been applied to various things, including people, poems, and historical periods. In his analysis of Flannery O'Connor's story "Everything That Rises Must Converge," Rajeev

Bector uses sociologist Erving Goffman's ideas about "character contests" to interpret the conflict between a son and his mother. (*Bector's analysis begins on p. 195.*)

No matter what framework you use, analysis often entails taking something apart and then putting it back together by figuring out how the parts make up a cohesive whole. Because the goal of analysis is to create a meaningful interpretation, the writer needs to treat the whole as more than the sum of its parts and recognize that determining meaning is a complex problem with multiple solutions.

4. Listing, comparing, questioning, and classifying to discover your thesis

To figure out a thesis, it is often useful to explore separate aspects of your subject. For example, if you are analyzing literature, you might consider the plot, the characters, the setting, and the tone before deciding to focus your thesis on how a character's personality drives the plot to its conclusion. If you are comparing two subjects, you would look for and list points of likeness and difference. Note that comparing is not just a way of presenting ideas; it is also a way of discovering ideas. What features do the items have—and not have—in common? Can you find subtle differences in aspects that at first seem alike? Subtle similarities in aspects that at first seem very different? Which do you find more interesting, the similarities or the differences? The answers to these questions might help you figure out your thesis.

As you work on discovering your thesis, try one or more of the following strategies:

■ Take notes about what you see or read, and if it helps, write a summary. Look for interesting issues that emerge as you work on your summary and notes.

■ Ask yourself questions about the subject you are analyzing, and write down any interesting answers. Imagine what kinds of questions your professor might ask about the artifact, document, performance, or event you are considering. In answering these questions, try to figure out the thesis you will present and support.

■ Name the class of things to which the item you are analyzing belongs (for example, memoirs). Then identify important parts or aspects of that class (for example, scene, point of view, turning points).

5. Making your thesis focused and purposeful

Because the subject of an interpretative analysis is usually complex, you cannot possibly write about all of its dimensions. Instead, focus your paper on one or two issues or questions that are key to understanding the subject. The goal of an interpretive analysis is to make **185**

www.mhhe.com/
nmhh
For more help with
developing a thesis,
go to
Writing >
Paragraph/Essay
Development >
Thesis/Central
Idea

a point about your subject. Focusing can help you resist the temptation to describe everything you see.

FOCUSED THESIS

In O'Connor's short story, plot, setting, and characterization work together to reinforce the impression that racism is a complex and pervasive problem.

FOCUSED THESIS

In the first section of Shubert's *Der Atlas,* both the tempo and the harmonic progression express the sorrow of the hero's eternal plight.

Although you want your point to be clear, you also want to make sure that your thesis anticipates the "So what?" question and sets up an interesting context for your interpretation. Unless you relate your specific thesis to some more general issue, idea, or problem, your interpretive analysis may seem pointless to readers. (*For more on developing your thesis, see Chapter 3: Planning and Shaping the Whole Essay, pp. 45–47.*)

www.mhhe.com/
nmhh
For more on crafting
introductions, go to

Writing >
Paragraph/Essay
Development >
Introductions

6. Introducing the general issue, a clear thesis or question, and relevant context

In interpretive analyses, it often takes more than one paragraph to do what an introduction needs to do:

- Identify the general issue, concept, or problem at stake. You can also present the intellectual framework that you are applying.
- Provide relevant background information.
- Name the specific item or items you will focus on in your analysis (or the items you will compare).
- State the thesis you will support and develop or the main question(s) your analysis will answer.

You need not do these things in the order listed. Sometimes it is a good idea to introduce the specific focus of your analysis before presenting either the issue or the background information. Just make sure that your introduction does the four things it needs to do, even though you may begin it with a provocative statement or a revealing example designed to capture your readers' attention. (*For more on introductions, see Chapter 4: Drafting Paragraphs and Visuals, p. 85.*)

For example, the following is the introductory paragraph from a paper on the development of Margaret Sanger's and Gloria Steinem's feminism that was written for a history class:

In our male-dominated society, almost every woman has experienced some form of oppression. Being oppressed is like having one end of a rope fastened to a pole and the other end fastened to one's belt: it tends to hold a woman back. But a few tenacious and visionary women have fought oppression and have consequently made the lives of others easier. Two of these visionary women are Margaret Sanger and Gloria Steinem. As their autobiographical texts show, Sanger and Steinem felt compassion for women close to them, and that compassion not only shaped their lives but also empowered them to fight for changes in society.

In one relatively short paragraph, the student identifies her paper's general issue (the feminist struggle against oppression), introduces the items to be compared (two autobiographical texts), and in the last sentence, states her main point or thesis. Although she has made a good beginning, her readers need additional background information about Sanger and Steinem—information that will give them a context for the two texts that are being compared. Therefore, the student must expand on the introduction a bit more before moving on to the points she wants to make to support her thesis.

7. Planning your paper so that each point supports your thesis

As with any paper, an interpretive analysis has three main parts: an introduction, a body, and a conclusion. After you pose a key question or state your thesis in the introduction, you need to work point by point, organizing the points to answer the question and support your interpretive thesis. From beginning to end, readers must be able to follow the train of thought in your interpretive analysis and see how each point you make is related to your thesis. (*For more on developing your ideas, see Chapter 3: Planning and Shaping the Whole Essay, pp. 35–45.*)

9c Write interpretive papers in the humanities.

Writers in the humanities analyze literature, art, film, theater, music, history, and philosophy. In Part 1, we followed a student's analysis of a photograph through several drafts. In this chapter we look at some examples of literary analysis. The following ideas and practices are useful in writing interpretive papers in the humanities:

- **Base your analysis on the work itself.** Works of art affect each of us differently, and any interpretation has a subjective element. Also, every film, musical composition, or other work is open to multiple interpretations because there are numerous critical theories about the significance of art. However,

Tips

LEARNING in COLLEGE

Interpreting in the Visual Arts

Interpreting a painting is similar to interpreting a literary work or any other work of art. For example, your interpretation of this 1965 painting by Andy Warhol, titled *Campbell's Soup Can (Tomato)* would likely reflect your personal reaction to the work as well as what you know about the artist and his times, but it would have to be grounded in a discussion of details of the work itself. What is the subject of the painting? How

has the artist rendered it? How closely does it resemble an actual soup can? Warhol was part of a movement called Pop Art (*Pop* being short for *popular*). What does the painting suggest about the relationship between fine art and popular culture?

the possibility of different interpretations does not mean that all interpretations are equally valid. Your reading of the work needs to be grounded in details from the work itself.

▪ **Consider how the concepts you are learning in your course apply to the work you are analyzing.** If your course focuses on the formal elements of art, for example, you might look at how those elements function in the painting you have chosen to analyze. If your course focuses on the social context of a work, you might look at how the work shares or subverts the belief system and worldview that was common in its time.

■ **Use the present tense when writing about the work and the past tense when writing about its history.** Use the present tense to talk about the events that happen within a work: *In Aristophanes's plays, characters frequently **step** out of the scene and **address** the audience directly.* Use the present tense as well to discuss decisions made by the work's creator: *In his version of the Annunciation, Leonardo **places** the Virgin outside, in an Italian garden.* Use the past tense, however, to relate historical information about the work or creator: *Kant **wrote** about science, history, criminal justice, and politics as well as philosophical ideas.*

9d Write a literary interpretation of a poem.

www.mhhe.com/
nmhh
For another sample of interpretive writing, go to

Writing >
Writing Samples >
Interpretive Paper

The poet Edwin Arlington Robinson defined poetry as "a language that tells us, through a more or less emotional reaction, something that cannot be said." Although literary analysis can never tell us exactly what a poem is saying, it can help us think about it more deeply.

The process of writing an interpretive paper about a poem begins, of course, with reading. First read the complete poem without stopping, and then note your initial thoughts and feelings. What is your first sense of the subject of the poem? What ideas does the poem suggest? What images does it create?

Reread the poem several times, paying close attention to the rhythms of the lines (reading aloud helps) and the poet's choice of words. Look up any unusual words in the dictionary, using the *Oxford English Dictionary* when you are analyzing a poem written in an earlier time. Think about how the poem develops. Do the last lines represent a shift from or fulfillment of the poem's opening? Look for connections among the poem's details, and think about their significance. The questions in the box on page 190 may help guide your analysis.

Use the insights you gain from your close reading to develop a working thesis about the poem. In the student essay that follows, McKenna Doherty develops a thesis about the poem "Testimonial," reprinted on page 191. Doherty's analysis is based on her knowledge of other poems by Rita Dove and her attempt to discover the theme of this particular work. She focuses on how four poetic devices give the theme its emotional impact.

QUESTIONS for ANALYZING POETRY

Speaker and Tone

How would you describe the speaker's voice? Is it that of a parent or a lover, an adult or a child, a man or a woman? What is the speaker's tone—is it stern or playful, melancholy or elated, nostalgic or hopeful?

Connotations

Along with their dictionary meanings, words have connotations—associative meanings. Although both *trudge* and *saunter* mean "walk slowly," their connotations are very different. What feelings or ideas do individual words in the poem connote?

Imagery

Does the poem conjure images that appeal to any of your senses—for example, the shocking feeling of a cold cloth on feverish skin or the sharp smell of a gas station? How do the images shape the mood of the poem? What ideas do they suggest?

Figurative Language

An in-depth study of poetry will acquaint you with the many types of figurative language used by poets, but the two most common are simile and metaphor. Does the poem use **simile** to directly compare two things using *like* or *as* (*his heart is sealed tight like a freezer door*)? Does it use **metaphor** to implicitly link one thing to another (*his ice-hard heart*)? How does the comparison enhance meaning?

Sound, Rhythm, and Meter

What vowel and consonant sounds recur through the poem? Do the lines of the poem resemble the rhythms of ordinary speech, or do they have a more musical quality? Consider how the sounds of the poem create an effect, just as musical notes do.

Structure

Notice how the poem is organized into parts or stanzas, considering spacing, punctuation, capitalization, and rhyme schemes. How do the parts relate to one another?

Theme

What is the subject of the poem? What does the poet's choice of language and imagery suggest about his or her attitude toward that subject?

Testimonial
Rita Dove

Back when the earth was new
and heaven just a whisper,
back when the names of things
hadn't had time to stick;

back when the smallest breezes
melted summer into autumn,
when all the poplars quivered
sweetly in rank and file . . .

the world called, and I answered.
Each glance ignited to a gaze.
I caught my breath and called that life,
swooned between spoonfuls of lemon sorbet.

I was pirouette and flourish,
I was filigree and flame.
How could I count my blessings
when I didn't know their names?

Back when everything was still to come,
luck leaked out everywhere.
I gave my promise to the world,
and the world followed me here.

Sample student analysis of a poem

Rita Dove's "Testimonial": The Music of Childhood

Rita Dove rarely uses obvious, rigid rhyme schemes or strict metrical
patterns in her poetry, and her subtle use of language often obscures
both the subject and themes of her poetry. However, careful analysis of
her work is rewarding, as Dove's poems are dense with ideas and
figurative language. Her poem "Testimonial" is a good example of this
complexity. Although the poem seems ambiguous on first reading,
repeated readings reveal many common and cleverly used poetic
techniques that are employed to express a common literary theme:
the difference between adult knowledge and childhood innocence.

Central
subject of
paper
identified.

191

The first two lines refer to a time when "the earth was new / and heaven just a whisper." At first, these lines appear to refer to the Biblical origins of earth and heaven; however, the title of the poem invites us to take the poem as a personal account of the speaker's experience. The time when "the earth was new" could refer to the speaker's youth. Youth is also the time of life when heaven is "just a whisper," since matters of death and religion are not present in a child's awareness. Thus, Dove's opening lines actually put the reader in the clear, familiar context of childhood.

The lines that follow support this idea. Dove describes the time period of the poem as "when the names of things / hadn't had time to stick" (ll. 3-4). Children often forget the names of things and are constantly asking their parents, "What is this? What is that?" The names of objects do not "stick" in their minds. The second stanza, describing a scene of trees and breezes, seems childlike in its sensitivity to nature, particularly to the change of seasons. The trees swaying "sweetly in rank and file" (l. 8) suggest an innocent, simplistic worldview, in which everything, even the random movement of trees in the wind, occurs in an orderly, nonthreatening fashion.

Notice that Dove does not state "when I was a child" at the beginning of the poem. Instead, she uses poetic language—alliteration, rhyme, uncommon words, and personification—to evoke the experience of childhood. Figurative language may make the poem more difficult to understand on first reading, but it ultimately makes the poem more personally meaningful.

In line 12, "swooned between spoonfuls of lemon sorbet" not only evokes the experience of childhood, a time when ice cream might literally make one swoon, but the alliteration of "swooned," "spoonfuls," and "sorbet" also makes the poem musical. Dove also uses alliteration in lines 14, 15, and 18. This conventional poetic technique is used relatively briefly and not regularly. The alliteration does not call attention to itself—the music is quiet.

Examples provided to illustrate theme.

More examples given and interpreted.

Writer presents four poetic techniques, which she explains in the following paragraphs.

"Testimonial" also uses the best known poetic technique: rhyme. Rhyme is used in many poems—what is unusual about its use in this poem is that, as with alliteration, rhyme appears irregularly. Only a few lines end with rhyming words, and the rhymes are more suggestive than exact: "whisper" and "stick" (ll. 2 and 4), "gaze" and "sorbet" (ll. 10 and 12), "flame" and "names" (ll. 14 and 16), and "everywhere" and "here" (ll. 18 and 20). These rhymes, or consonances, stand out because they are isolated and contrast with the other, unrhymed, lines.

Dove occasionally uses words that children would probably not know, such as "swooned" (l. 12), "sorbet" (l. 12), "pirouette" (l. 13), "flourish" (l. 13), and "filigree" (l. 14). These words suggest the central theme, which is underscored in the final question of the stanza when the narrator of the poem asks, "How could I count my blessings / when I didn't know their names?" The adult words emphasize the contrast between the speaker's past innocence and present knowledge.

The poem ends with the mysterious lines, "I gave my promise to the world / and the world followed me here" (ll. 19-20). The world is personified, given the characteristics of a man or woman capable of accepting a promise and following the speaker. As with the opening lines, these final lines are confusing if they are taken literally, but the lines become clearer when one considers the perspective of the speaker. It is as if the speaker has taken a journey from childhood to adulthood. Just as the speaker has changed during the course of this journey, so too has the world changed. The childhood impressions of the world that make up the poem—the sorbet, the trees swaying in the breeze—do not last into adulthood. The speaker becomes a different person, an adult, and the world also becomes something else. It has "followed" the speaker into adulthood; it has not remained static and unchanging.

In "Testimonial," Dove presents a vision of childhood so beautifully, so musically, that we can experience it with her, if only for the space of a few lines.

Analysis of poem concluded with interpretation of entire poem.

Paper concluded briefly, neatly.

———————————————-[new page]————————————————

Works-Cited
list follows
MLA style and
begins on a
new page.

Work Cited

Dove, Rita. "Testimonial." Literature: Approaches to Fiction,
Poetry, and Drama. Ed. Robert DiYanni. New York: McGraw-
Hill, 2004. 738.

9e Write a literary interpretation of a work of fiction.

When we read a short story or novel, we are often so engaged by the
plot that we may overlook the other literary elements that contribute
to the work's meaning. A literary analysis paper is an opportunity to
look more deeply into the work and develop a better understanding of
it. With a short story, you may want to read it through once for the
plot, the emotional effect, and the theme, and then reread it closely
several times. The questions in the box on this and the next page may
help guide your analysis.

The field of literary criticism offers various perspectives on and
strategies for analyzing fiction. In your studies you may learn about
formalistic theories, reader response theory, and postmodern theories,
for example. However, it is also possible to apply the insights offered by
other disciplines to your literary analysis paper. In the essay that begins on the next page, Rajeev Bector, a sociology major, applies a theory
that he learned in a sociology course to his analysis of a short story.

QUESTIONS for ANALYZING FICTION

Characters

The characters are the people who inhabit the fictional world of
the story. What are the relationships among the characters? What
do the characters' thoughts, actions, and speech reveal about
them? What changes take place among or within the characters?

Point of View

Is the story told by a character speaking as "I" (first-person point
of view)? Is the story, instead, told by a third-person narrator, who
lets the reader know what one or all (or none) of the characters
are thinking? How does point of view affect your understanding
of what happens in the story?

Plot

The plot is the arrangement of episodes in a story. What do these particular episodes in the characters' lives reveal? What did you think and feel at different points in the story? What kinds of changes take place over the course of the story?

Setting

Setting is the time and place of the action—for example, the setting of *The Scarlet Letter* is the Massachusetts Bay Colony of the mid-1600s. Within that setting are symbolically charged contrasting locations—the forest and the marketplace. What is the significance of the story's setting? What associations does the writer make with each location? How does the social context of the setting affect the characters' choices and attitudes?

Language

Fiction writers, like poets, use figurative language and imagery to meaningful effect (*see the box "Questions for Analyzing Poetry" on p. 190*). Are there patterns of imagery and metaphor in the story? What significance can you infer from these patterns?

Theme

What sense of the story's significance can you infer from the elements above? Are there any passages in the work that seem to address the theme directly?

Sample student analysis of a short story

The Character Contest in Flannery O'Connor's

"Everything That Rises Must Converge"

Sociologist Erving Goffman believes that every social interaction establishes our identity and preserves our image, honor, and credibility in the hearts and minds of others. Social interactions, he says, are in essence "character contests" that occur not only in games and sports but also in our everyday dealings with strangers, peers, friends, and even family members. Goffman defines character contests as "disputes [that]

Key idea that provides intellectual framework.

195

are sought out and indulged in (often with glee) as a means of establishing where one's boundaries are" (29). Just such a contest occurs in Flannery O'Connor's short story "Everything That Rises Must Converge."

As they travel from home to the Y, Julian and his mother, Mrs. Chestny, engage in a character contest, a dispute we must understand in order to figure out the story's theme. Julian is so frustrated with his mother that he virtually "declare[s] war on her," "allow[s] no glimmer of sympathy to show on his face," and "imagine[s] various unlikely ways by which he could teach her a lesson" (O'Connor 185, 186). But why would Julian want to hurt his mother, a woman who is already suffering from high blood pressure?

Julian's conflict with Mrs. Chestny results from pent-up hostility and tension. As Goffman explains, character contests are a way of living that often leaves a "residue": "Every day in many ways we can try to score points and every day we can be shot down" (29). For many years, Julian has had to live under his racist mother's authority, and every time he protested her racist views he was probably shot down because of his "radical ideas" and "lack of practical experience" (O'Connor 184). As a result, a residue of defeat and shame has accumulated that fuels a fire of rebellion against his mother. But even though Julian rebels against his mother's racist views, it does not mean that he is not a racist himself. Julian does not realize that in his own way, he is as prejudiced as his mother. He makes it "a point" to sit next to blacks, in contrast to his mother, who purposely sits next to whites (182). They are two extremes, each biased, for if Julian were truly fair to all, he would not care whom he sat next to.

When we look at the situation from Mrs. Chestny's viewpoint, we realize that she must maintain her values and beliefs for two important reasons: to uphold her character as Julian's mother and to act out her prescribed role in society. Even if she finds Julian's arguments on race relations and integration valid and plausible, Mrs. Chestny must still refute them. If she did not, she would lose face as Julian's mother—that image of herself as the one with authority. By preserving her self-image,

---

Annotations (left margin):

Question posed.

Interpretation organized point by point: first point.

"We" indicates thoughtful stance, not Bector's personal feelings.

Mrs. Chestny shows that she has what Goffman sees as key to "character": some quality that seems "essential and unchanging" (28).

    Besides upholding her character as Julian's mother, Mrs. Chestny wants to preserve the honor and dignity of her family tradition. Like an actor performing before an audience, she must play the role prescribed for her—the role of a white supremacist. But her situation is hopeless, for the role she must play fails to acknowledge the racial realities that have transformed her world. According to Goffman, when a "situation" is "hopeless," a character "can gamely give everything . . . and then go down bravely, or proudly, or insolently, or gracefully or with an ironic smile on his lips" (32). For Mrs. Chestny, being game means trying to preserve her honor and dignity as she goes down to physical defeat in the face of hopeless odds.

    Given the differences between Mrs. Chestny's and her son's values, as well as the oppressiveness of Mrs. Chestny's racist views, we can understand why Julian struggles to "teach" his mother "a lesson" (185) throughout the entire bus ride. Goffman would point out that "each individual is engaged in providing evidence to establish a definition of himself at the expense of what can remain for the other" (29). But in the end, neither character wins the contest. Julian's mother loses her sense of self when she is pushed to the ground by a "colored woman" wearing a hat identical to hers (187). Faced with his mother's breakdown, Julian feels his own identity being overwhelmed by "the world of guilt and sorrow" (191).

> Second point.

> Third point.

> Thesis.

> Conclusion: main point about Julian and his mother related to larger issue of racism.

————————————[new page]————————————

Works Cited

Goffman, Erving. "Character Contests." Text Book: An Introduction to Literary Language. Ed. Robert Scholes, Nancy Comley, and Gregory Ulmer. New York: St. Martin's, 1988. 27–33.

O'Connor, Flannery. "Everything That Rises Must Converge." Fiction. Ed. R. S. Gwynn. 2nd ed. New York: Addison, 1998. 179–91.

> Works-Cited list follows MLA style and begins on a new page.

9f Write a literary interpretation of a play.

Every production of a play is an interpretation of that play, a series of decisions on how to bring the words on the page to life in a meaningful way. Similarly, when we interpret a play, we need to imagine the world of the play—the setting and costumes, the delivery of lines of dialogue, and the movement of characters in relation to one another. As our understanding of a play deepens through analysis, we are better able to imagine the action. This means that a play, too, is best read more than once.

Drama shares many elements with poetry and fiction. Like poetry, it is meant to be spoken, and the sound and rhythm of its lines are significant. Like fiction, it is a story that unfolds through characters acting in a plot. As in both genres, imagery and figurative language work to convey emotions and meaning. In addition to reviewing the questions for analyzing poetry and fiction (*see pp. 190 and 194*), you may find it helpful to consider the questions in the box below when analyzing a play.

In the following paper, Sam Chodoff analyzes the theme of honor as it applies to the characters in Shakespeare's *Hamlet,* using dialogue to support his interpretation.

QUESTIONS for ANALYZING DRAMA

Dialogue

What does the dialogue reveal about the characters' thoughts and motivations? How do the characters' words incite other characters to action?

Stage Directions

Do the stage directions include references to any objects that may serve as dramatic symbols? How might costume directions suggest mood or symbolize such concepts as freedom, repression, or chivalry, for example? Do the directions call for any music or sounds to add to the atmosphere of the work? How do directions about gestures and movements affect your interpretation of the dialogue?

Sample student analysis of a play

Honor in Shakespeare's <u>Hamlet</u>

In the world of Shakespeare's <u>Hamlet</u>, actions, not motives, are the measure of a character's honor. Good actions bestow honor; evil actions withdraw it. Not all characters in the play, however, are equally equipped to know one from the other. The main characters receive divine enlightenment about what is right and wrong, but the minor characters have to rely on luck, making choices without divine assistance.

Characters fall into one of three categories of honor determined by where their actions fall on the spectrum between good and evil. Hamlet and Fortinbras represent extreme good; Claudius represents extreme evil. These characters have been enlightened by heaven and their actions are based on this divinely granted knowledge. In the middle of the spectrum are all the other characters, who have chosen a path based on their own, not divine, knowledge, and for whom honor is a matter of luck.

As Hamlet storms into the palace in anger, seeking revenge for the death of his father, Claudius reassures Gertrude, telling her, "Do not fear our person. / There's such divinity doth hedge a king / That treason can but peep to what it would, / Acts little of his will" (4.5.122-25). Claudius knows that by killing his brother and usurping his throne, he has forfeited any chance to be the rightful king, and behind his façade, he struggles with his own guilt, knowing that heaven will remain closed to him while he still holds the "effects for which [he] did the murder" (3.3.54). Meanwhile, unbeknownst to Claudius, heaven has, through the ghost of Hamlet's father, commanded Hamlet to avenge his father's murder and restore a rightful king to the throne, as shown in Fig. 1. This reveals that Claudius is on the lowest end of the honor spectrum, that his honor is false, a mere pretense of honor with nothing but evil underneath. His actions show that an honorable life remains unattainable when the appearance of honor is the only goal, and that, in Hamlet's words, "one may smile, and smile, and be a villain" (1.5.108).

Key term— "honor"— defined.

Points illustrated with quotations from the play.

First of three examples to illustrate the categories of honor.

199

Illustration
of a scene
discussed in
the paper.

Fig. 1. Hamlet confronted by his father's ghost as his mother looks on amazed, engraving from John and Josiah Boydell, <u>Boydell's Shakespeare Prints</u> (Mineola: Dover, 2004) 73.

     Hamlet and Fortinbras, on the other hand, have been shown by heaven the conflict that they must resolve and are left to do that task

Second
example
given.

without any further divine aid. With a clear duty whose virtue is unquestionable, their honor is assured as long as they pursue and complete their objective. The last scene shows that they have achieved

this goal, as Fortinbras gives orders to pay tribute to Hamlet: "Let four captains / Bear Hamlet like a soldier to the stage, / . . . and for his passage / The soldier's music and the rite of war / Speak loudly for him" (5.2.400–01, 403–05). While the bodies of the other characters are ignored, Hamlet's is treated with ceremony. This disparity in how the characters are treated confirms that Hamlet and Fortinbras have been placed at the highest end of the honor spectrum, and it shows that the many grave mistakes they both have made (resulting in the death of many innocent people) will be forgiven because the mistakes were made in pursuit of a divine objective. This idea of honor was acceptable in Shakespeare's day, as illustrated in a treatise by Sir William Segar in 1590: "God . . . would give victory to him that justly adventured his life for truth, honor, and justice. . . . the trial by Arms is not only natural, but also necessary and allowable" (qtd. in Corum 153).

Other characters in <u>Hamlet</u> are not privy to the true nature of the world and are forced to make decisions without heaven's help. The level of honor these characters attain is determined by luck; with their limited knowledge of good and evil, right and wrong, these characters often act dishonorably. When Rosencrantz and Guildenstern are summoned before the king and asked to spy on Hamlet, they respond positively, saying, "[W]e both obey, / And here give up ourselves in the full bent / To lay our service freely at your feet / To be commanded" (2.2.29-32). In their ignorance, they accept Claudius as the rightful king and thus unintentionally align themselves with the evil he represents, losing any honor they might have gained. Other characters are similarly tricked into obeying Claudius.

Third example given.

Luck can go both ways, however, and several characters end up well, even in the absence of a divine messenger. For example, Horatio chooses from the very beginning to follow Hamlet and not only survives but also attains honor. His honor, though, is by no means assured; there are many instances in which he could have acted differently. He could quite easily have gone to Claudius with the news of the ghost, an act which, while perfectly natural, would have left him devoid of honor.

Another example given of the third category of honor, to strengthen claim.

201

We would like to think that, by adhering to virtues, we can control how we will be judged. In Hamlet, we are shown a world in which lives are spent in the struggle between good and evil, often without clear guidance. But those who have lived honorably are rewarded with a place in heaven, the "undiscover'd country" (3.1.79) that every character both fears and desires. Only those characters either chosen by heaven to be honorable or who by luck become honorable reach paradise, while others burn in hell or wait in purgatory (Greenblatt 51). Very few people in Hamlet's world will be granted a place in heaven.

Essay concluded concisely.

————————————————[new page]————————————————

Works Cited

Works-Cited list follows MLA style and begins a new page.

Corum, Richard. Understanding Hamlet: A Student Casebook to Issues, Sources, and Historical Documents. Westport, CT: Greenwood, 1998.

Greenblatt, Stephen. Hamlet in Purgatory. Princeton: Princeton UP, 2001.

Shakespeare, William. Hamlet. Ed. Harold Jenkins. Arden Edition of the Works of William Shakespeare. London: Methuen, 1982.

9g   Write case studies and other interpretive papers in the social sciences.

Social scientists are trained observers and recorders of the behavior of individuals and groups in specific situations and institutions. They use writing not only to see clearly and remember precisely what they observe but also to interpret its meaning, as in this passage from a textbook by anthropologist Conrad Kottak.

Rituals at McDonald's (excerpt)

CONRAD KOTTAK

Each day, on the average, a new McDonald's restaurant opens somewhere in the world. The number of McDonald's outlets today far surpasses the total number of all fast-food restaurants in the United States in 1945. McDonald's has grown from a single hamburger stand in San

Bernardino, California, into today's international web of thousands of outlets. Have factors less obvious to American natives than relatively low cost, fast service, and taste contributed to McDonald's success? Could it be that natives—in consuming the products and propaganda of McDonald's—are not just eating but experiencing something comparable in certain respects to participation in religious rituals? To answer this question, we must briefly review the nature of ritual.

[Religious] [r]ituals . . . are formal—stylized, repetitive, and stereotyped. They are performed in special places at set times. Rituals include liturgical orders—set sequences of words and actions laid down by someone other than the current performers. Rituals also convey information about participants and their cultural traditions. Performed year after year, generation after generation, rituals translate messages, values, and sentiments into action. Rituals are social acts. Inevitably, some participants are more strongly committed than others are to the beliefs on which the rituals are founded. However, just by taking part in a joint public act, people signal that they accept an order that transcends their status as mere individuals.

For many years, like millions of other Americans, I have occasionally eaten at McDonald's. Eventually I began to notice certain ritual-like aspects of Americans' behavior at these fast-food restaurants. Tell your fellow Americans that going to McDonald's is similar in some ways to going to church, and their bias as natives will reveal itself in laughter, denials, or questions about your sanity. Just as football is a game and *Star Trek* is "entertainment," McDonald's, for natives, is just a place to eat. However, an analysis of what natives do at McDonald's will reveal a very high degree of formal, uniform behavior by staff members and customers alike. It is particularly interesting that this invariance in word and deed has developed without any theological doctrine. McDonald's ritual aspect is founded on 20th-century technology, particularly automobiles, television, work away from home, and the short lunch break. It is striking, nevertheless, that one commercial organization should be so much more successful than other businesses, the schools, the military, and even many religions in producing behavioral invariance. Factors other than low cost, fast service, and the taste of the food—all of which are approximated by other chains—have contributed to our acceptance of McDonald's and adherence to its rules. . . .

In this passage, Kottak based many of his conclusions on his observations of the way people behave at McDonald's restaurants. When social scientists conduct a systematic study of people's behavior in groups or institutions, they report on and interpret their observations in **case studies.** Anthropologists, for example, often spend extended periods living among and observing the people of one society or group and then report on their findings in a kind of case study called an *ethnography.*

Accurate observations are essential starting points for a case study, and writing helps researchers make clear and precise observations. Here are some things to consider as you undertake a case study assignment.

1. Choosing a topic that raises a question

In doing a case study, your purpose is to connect what you see and hear with issues and concepts in the social sciences. Choose a topic and turn it into a research question. Before engaging in your field research, write down your hypothesis—a tentative answer to your research question—as well as some categories of behavior or other things to look for.

2. Collecting data

Make a detailed and accurate record of what you observe and when and how you observed it. Whenever you can, count or measure, and take down word for word what is said. Use frequency counts—the number of occurrences of specific, narrowly defined instances of behavior. If you are observing a classroom, for example, you might count the number of teacher-directed questions asked by several children. If you are observing group counseling sessions for female parolees, you might count the number of women who attend. Your research methodologies course will introduce you to many ways to quantify data. Graphs like Figure 9.1 can help you display and summarize frequency data.

3. Assuming an unbiased stance

In case study, you are presenting empirical findings, based on careful observation. Your stance is that of an unbiased observer.

4. Discovering meaning in your data

Your case study is based on the notes you make during your observations. As you review this material, try to uncover connections, identify inconsistencies, and draw inferences. For example, ask yourself why a subject behaved in a specific way, and consider different explanations for the behavior. You will also need to draw upon the techniques for quantitative analysis that you learn in a statistics course.

5. Presenting your findings in an organized way

There are two basic ways to present your findings in the body of a case study. (1) **As stages of a process:** A student studying gang initiation organized her observations chronologically into appropriate stages. If you organize your study this way, be sure to transform the minute-by-minute history of your observations into a pattern with distinctive stages. (2) **In analytic categories:** A student observing the behavior of

Frequency of Behavior x in a Sample of 32 Individuals

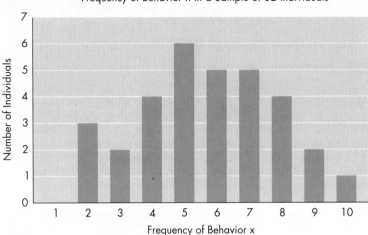

FIGURE 9.1 Graphing frequency data. Column graphs like this one can be useful for summarizing behavioral observations. The numbers on the horizontal axis represent the frequency, or number of occurrences, of a particular behavior. (An example might be the number of teacher-directed questions a student asks during a class). The vertical axis represents the number of individuals at each frequency. In this case, three individuals exhibited the behavior twice, two exhibited it three times, and so forth.

a preschool child used the following categories from the course textbook to present his findings: motor coordination, cognition, and socialization.

> *Note:* You will find it easier to organize the enormous amount of data you gather for a case study if you develop stages or categories while you are making your observations. In your paper, be sure to illustrate your stages or categories with material drawn from your observations—with descriptions of people, places, and behavior, as well as with telling quotations.

6. Including a review of the literature, statement of your hypothesis, and description of your methodology in your introduction
The introduction presents the framework, background, and rationale for your study. Begin with the topic, and review related research, **205**

CHARTING the TERRITORY

Case Studies

You may be asked to write case studies in a number of social science and science disciplines.

- **In sociology:** You may be asked to draw on "insider" knowledge to describe and analyze a small group to which you have belonged or belong now. In this case, your study will address such issues as the group's norms and values, cultural characteristics, stratification and roles, initiation rites, and social control techniques. Your audience will be your professor, who will want to see how your observations reflect current theories on group norms.

- **In nursing:** A case study assignment may be an important part of your practicum in a local hospital. For a nursing class, you will note details of your care of a patient that corroborate or differ from what you have been taught to expect. Your audience is the supervising nurse, who is interested in your interactions with the patient.

- **In education:** As a student teacher in a classroom, you may closely observe and write about one student in the context of his or her socioeconomic and family background. Your audience will be your supervising teacher, who seeks more insight into students' behavior.

working your way to the specific question that your study addresses. Follow that with a statement of your hypothesis, accompanied by a description of your **methodology**—how, when, and where you made your observations and how you recorded them.

7. Discussing your findings in the conclusion

The conclusion of your case study should answer the following three questions: Did you find what you expected? What do your findings show, or what is the bigger picture? Where should researchers working on your topic go now?

9h Write interpretive papers in the sciences.

Many research papers in the sciences, like those in the social sciences, are interpretive as well as informative. As mentioned in Chapter 8, for example, interpretation is a crucial aspect of lab reports describing the results of original experiments designed to create new scientific knowledge.

Scientists, however, may also be called upon to analyze trends and make predictions in papers that do not follow the lab or research report model. In the following example, Carlos Jasperson interprets historical data about hurricanes to see if they reveal trends in weather patterns.

Sample student interpretive paper in the sciences

Keeping an Eye on the Storms

In 2004, Florida was hit by 4 brutal hurricanes. Charley, Frances, Ivan, and Jeanne struck Florida within the space of just 2 months. On the Saffir-Simpson scale, which ranks hurricanes from 1 to 5 based on their wind speeds and destructive power, all but one of the storms (Frances) ranked 3 or higher, making them "major" storms.[1] In all, these 4 hurricanes killed 117 people and cost Florida over $60 billion in damages.[2] When one considers the total number of hurricanes to make landfall in Florida during the 20th century—a total of 57 hurricanes, with 24 of them at category 3 or above[3]—one can imagine the financial and emotional cost.

Interesting details capture readers' attention and use of statistics establishes authority.

Unfortunately, there is reason to believe that the years ahead could bring more of the same. Based on a variety of data, it seems at least possible that the 2005 hurricane season, or one closely following it, could again see multiple storms hitting the U.S. The "hurricane fatigue" that has plagued the state might be in for an encore.

Thesis stated.

Figure 1 shows a graph of the total number of hurricanes to strike the U.S. mainland by decade from 1900 through 1999.[4] A total of 165 hurricanes made landfall, with 65 of them at category 3 or above; however, the graph shows that over the past 30 years there have been relatively few hurricane strikes. The decade of 1970–1979 brought the fewest strikes of any decade this century; the decade of 1990–1999, the second fewest. The number of strikes for 1980–1989 was slightly below the century average. Additionally, in the year 2000, there were no hurricane strikes, a rare occurrence.[3] Thus far this decade, there have been 8 strikes[5]—another 8 hurricanes hitting the U.S. before 2010 would only make for a more or less typical decade. So, even if 16

Topic expanded from Florida to the country as a whole.

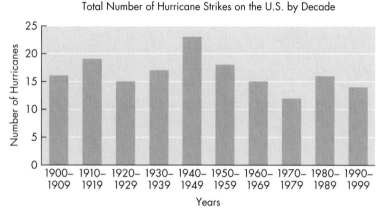

Figure 1 U.S. hurricane strikes by decade (from National Hurricane Center[4])

hurricanes strike the U.S. mainland during the years 2001–2009, this would only put the first decade of 2000 slightly above the average for the previous century.

First warning sign explained.

When compared with the first part of the century in terms of number of hurricanes, the last 30 years of the 20th century can be seen as a grace period from hurricanes. If a higher number of storms strike the U.S. in the first decade of the 21st century, then, it would not represent an aberration but rather a return to the statistical norm, something that hurricane experts see as inevitable. Thus, the relative lull in the number of hurricanes can be seen as a warning sign of sorts.

Another warning sign for the years ahead is the influx of warm water into the Atlantic Basin, where hurricanes begin and strengthen.

Second warning sign explained.

Meteorologists connect this natural, cyclical warming to an increase in the number of hurricanes. The Atlantic Basin was most recently warmed in this way in the 1940s and 1950s.[2] As Figure 1 indicates, this was a time of relatively frequent hurricane hits. One could reasonably expect a similar increase in the coming years as the temperature rises again.

Also frightening is the fact that 4 hurricanes hitting the U.S. in one year, as they did in 2004, is not unprecedented. From 1900 to 2000, there were 4 years in which 4 hurricanes struck.[3] So, there is no reason to expect that enduring 4 hurricanes in one year will guarantee fewer hurricanes in years to come. In fact, in 1906, 4 hurricanes struck, and then just 3 years later, in 1909, another 4 hurricanes struck. And 4 is not even the biggest wallop nature can pack. Twice in the last century, in 1916 and in 1985, 6 hurricanes struck the U.S. in the same year.[3] Clearly, although the cost of the 2004 hurricane season was nearly unbearable for Floridians, it could truly have been much worse, and might be in the seasons ahead.

Point reinforced with grim statistics and prediction.

Ultimately, there is no way to predict exactly where a hurricane will make landfall, despite the great strides that have been made in meteorology in the past few decades. The smartest thing for Floridians and the residents of other coastal states to do is to be prepared every year for a deadly storm. As 2004 taught us, nature's fury can be unforgiving.

Conclusion stated succinctly.

————————————[new page]————————————

References

1. National Geographic News. 2004 hurricane season may be costliest on record [Internet]. Washington: National Geographic; 2004, [Cited 2004 Dec 9]. Available from: http://news.nationalgeographic.com/news/2004/09/0927_040927_jeanne.html

2. Nolin R. Expert sees busy '05 hurricane season. South Florida Sun Sentinel 2004 Dec 4:C6.

3. Jarrell JD, Mayfield M, Rappaport EN, Landsea CW. The deadliest, costliest, and most intense United States hurricanes from 1900 to 2000. Miami (FL): Atlantic Oceanographic and Meteorological Laboratory; 2001 Oct. National Oceanic and Atmospheric Administration [NOAA] Technical Memorandum NWS TPC-1.

4. National Hurricane Center. U.S. hurricane strikes by decade [Internet]. National Weather Service [cited 2004 Dec 12]. Available from: http://www.nhc.noaa.gov/pastdec.shtml

5. National Hurricane Center. Archive of past hurricane seasons [Internet]. National Weather Service [cited 2004 Dec 12]. Available from: http://www.nhc.noaa.gov/pastall.shtml

References list follows CSE number style and begins on a new page.

10 Arguments

The word *argument,* when used in the context of academia, does not mean a shouting match. In the college classroom and in reasoned debate outside the classroom, an **argument** is a path of reasoning aimed at demonstrating the truth or falsehood of an assertion on an issue under debate. In this chapter, we look at how to construct an argument. Arguments often respond to the thinking of others, so we first look at how to evaluate another writer's argument. You can also apply this advice on evaluating arguments as you turn a critical eye to your own argument during the revising phase of the writing process.

10a   Understand the assignment.

In college, reasoned positions matter more than opinions based on personal feelings, and writing arguments is a way to form reasoned positions. Bearing in mind that reasonable people can see things differently, always strive to write well-informed, thoughtful arguments. When you write an argument paper, your purpose is not to win but to take part in a debate by stating and supporting your position on an issue. In addition to position papers, written arguments appear in various forms, including critiques, reviews, and proposals.

- **Critiques:** Critiques focus on answering the question "What is true?" Someone has taken a position on an issue, and the critique fairly summarizes that position before either refuting or defending it. *Refutations* use one of two basic strategies: either the presentation of contradictory evidence to show that the position is false or the exposure of inadequate reasoning to show that the position should not be considered true. In his response to Nat Hentoff's article "Misguided Multiculturalism" in Chapter 7, for example, Ignacio Sanderson attempts to refute Hentoff's claims by identifying weaknesses in Hentoff's reasoning (*pp. 147–49*). *Defenses* make use of three strategies: clarifying a position by explaining in more detail the author's key terms and reasoning, presenting new arguments to support the position, and showing that criticisms of the position are unreasonable or unconvincing.

Arguments

Arguments are central to American democracy and its institutions of higher learning because they help create the common ground that is sometimes called public space. In this space, freedom, justice, and equality—the civic ideals set forth in such documents as the Declaration of Independence and the Constitution—are supposed to rule so that reason may prevail over prejudice. All fields of academic study value reason and welcome arguments such as the following:

- A moral philosopher argues that under certain circumstances people have the right to die and, therefore, that liberal democracies should provide them with the means to exercise their right with dignity.

- The board of a national dietetic association publishes a position statement identifying obesity as a growing health problem that dieticians should be involved in preventing and treating.

- A political scientist critiques the idea that the prospects for Russian democracy depend on the country's economy, not on the quality of its political institutions.

- An art critic praises a museum's special exhibition of modern American paintings for its diversity and thematic coherence.

- A sociologist proposes four policies that he claims will improve the quality of life and socioeconomic prospects of people living in inner-city neighborhoods.

- **Reviews:** Reviews focus on answering the question "What is good?" In a review, the writer evaluates an event, artifact, practice, or institution. Although the evaluation may begin with an everyday gut response—"I like it" or "I don't like it"—such initial opinions must be transformed into judgments. A judge in a court case thinks through a decision in light of legal principles. Likewise, judgments in reviews should be principled; that is, they should not be determined by personal taste or the mood of the moment but by commonly accepted criteria. Dale Jamieson's essay on pages 230–32 is an example of a review.

- **Proposals, or policy papers:** Proposals, sometimes called policy papers, focus on answering the question "What should be done?" They are designed to cause change in the world. Readers are not only asked to see the situation in a specific way, but they are also encouraged to act on that situation in a certain way. Nicholas Buglione's argument about injuries to professional athletes (*see p. 224*) and the Council for Biotechnology's argument about genetically modified foods (*see p. 232*) are examples of proposals.

10b Learn how to evaluate an argument.

There are a number of ways to analyze an argument and evaluate its effectiveness. Two common methods are (1) to concentrate on the type of reasoning the writer is using and (2) to question the logical relation of a writer's claims, grounds, and warrants, using the Toulmin method.

1. Recognizing types of reasoning

Writers may use either inductive or deductive reasoning to make an argument. When writers use **inductive reasoning,** they do not prove that the argument is true; instead they convince reasonable people that it is probable by presenting **evidence** (facts and statistics, anecdotes, and expert opinion). When writers use **deductive reasoning,** on the other hand, they are making the claim that a conclusion follows necessarily from a set of assertions, or **premises**—in other words, that if the premises are true, the conclusion must be true.

To illustrate the two types of reasoning, consider the following scenarios.

Inductive reasoning A journalism student writing for the school paper makes the following claim:

> As Saturday's game shows, the Buckeyes are on their way to winning the Big Ten title.

Reasoning inductively, the student presents a number of facts—her evidence—that support her claim but do not prove it conclusively:

FACT 1 With three games remaining, the Buckeyes have a two-game lead over the second-place Badgers.

FACT 2 The Buckeyes' final three opponents have a combined record of 10 wins and 17 losses.

FACT 3 The Badgers lost their two star players to season-ending injuries last week.

FACT 4 The Buckeyes' last three games will be played at home, where they are undefeated this season, giving them the home-field advantage.

A reader would evaluate this student's argument by judging the quality of her evidence, using the criteria listed in the box below.

Inductive reasoning is a feature of the **scientific method.** Scientists gather data from experiments, surveys, and careful observations to formulate hypotheses that explain the data. Then they test their hypotheses by collecting additional information.

Deductive reasoning Now suppose the journalism student were writing about great baseball teams and made the following argument:

PREMISE	Any baseball team that wins the World Series more than 25 times in 100 years is one of the greatest teams in baseball history.
PREMISE	The New York Yankees have won the World Series more than 25 times in the past 100 years.
CONCLUSION	The New York Yankees are one of the greatest teams in baseball history.

This is a deductive argument because its structure is such that if its premises are true, its conclusion must be true. To challenge the argument, a reader has to evaluate the premises. Do you think, for example, that number of World Series wins is a proper measure of a team's greatness? If not, then you could claim that the first premise is false and does not support the conclusion.

 LEARNING in COLLEGE

Assessing Evidence in an Inductive Argument

- **Is it accurate?** Make sure that any facts presented as evidence are correct.
- **Is it relevant?** Check to see if the evidence is clearly connected to the point being made.
- **Is it representative?** Make sure that the writer's conclusion is supported by evidence gathered from a sample that accurately reflects the larger population (for example, it has the same proportion of men and women, older and younger people, and so on). If the writer is using an example, make sure that the example is typical and not a unique situation.
- **Is it sufficient?** Evaluate whether there is enough evidence to satisfy questioning readers.

In college, deductive reasoning predominates in mathematics and philosophy and some other humanities disciplines. However, you should be alert to both types of reasoning in all your college courses and in your life.

2. Using the Toulmin method to analyze arguments

Philosopher Stephen Toulmin has developed another useful way to understand and implement logical thinking. His analysis of arguments is based on claims (assertions about a topic), grounds (reasons and evidence), and warrants (assumptions or principles that link the grounds to the claims).

Consider the following sentence from an argument by a student:

The death penalty should be abolished because if it is not abolished, innocent people could be executed.

This example, like all logical arguments, has three facets:

1. **The argument makes a claim.** A **claim** is the same thing as a *point* or a *thesis:* it is an assertion about a topic. A strong claim responds to an issue of real interest to its audience (for example, the members of a discipline) in terms that are clear and precise. A weak claim is merely a statement of fact or a statement that few would argue with. Personal feelings are not debatable and thus are not an appropriate claim for an argument.

   WEAK CLAIMS   The death penalty is highly controversial. The death penalty makes me sick.

2. **The argument presents grounds for the claim. Grounds** consist of the reasons and evidence (facts and statistics, anecdotes, and expert opinion) that support the claim. As grounds for the claim in the example, the student would present stories and statistics related to innocent people being executed. The box on page 215 should help you assess the evidence supporting a claim.

3. **The argument depends on assumptions that link the grounds to the claim.** When you analyze an argument, you should be aware of the unstated assumptions, or **warrants,** that underlie both the claim and the grounds that support it. The warrants underlying the example argument against the death penalty include the idea that it is wrong to execute innocent people and that it is not possible to be completely sure of a person's guilt. Warrants differ from discipline to discipline and even from one school of thought to another within

TYPES of EVIDENCE for CLAIMS

- **Facts and statistics:** Facts and statistics can be convincing support for a claim. You should be aware, however, that people on different sides of an issue can interpret the same facts and statistics differently or can cite different facts and statistics to prove their point.
- **Anecdotes:** An anecdote is a brief narrative used as an illustration to support a claim. Stories appeal to the emotions as well as to the intellect and can be very effective in making an argument. Be especially careful to check anecdotes for logical fallacies (*see pp. 216–17*).
- **Expert opinion:** The views of authorities in a given field can also be powerful support for a claim. Check that the expert cited has proper credentials to comment on the issue.

a single discipline. If you were studying the topic of bullfighting and its place in Spanish society in a sociology course, for example, you would probably make different arguments with different warrants than would the writer of a literary analysis of Ernest Hemingway's novel about bullfighting, *Death in the Afternoon.* You might argue that bullfighting serves as a safe outlet for its fans' aggressive feelings. Your warrant would be that sports can have socially useful purposes.

As you read the writing of others and as you write yourself, look for unstated assumptions. What does the reader have to assume—take for granted—to accept the reason and evidence in support of the claim? In particular, hidden assumptions sometimes show **bias,** positive or negative inclinations that can manipulate unwary readers.

3. Avoiding fallacies

Logicians have cataloged some common mistakes that writers commit in their enthusiasm to make a point. These errors are called **fallacies,** or mistakes in logic. Use the box on the next two pages for help identifying fallacies when you read and avoiding them when you write.

10c   Approach writing your own argument as a process.

In every course you take, you will gain practice in addressing issues that are important in the larger community. Selecting a topic that you

(*Text continues on p. 218.*)

www.mhhe.com/
nmhh

For an interactive tutorial on writing arguments, go to

Writing >
Writing Tutors >
Arguments

COMMON LOGICAL FALLACIES

Non sequitur: A conclusion that does not logically follow from the evidence presented or one that is based on irrelevant evidence.

EXAMPLE Students who default on their student loans have no sense of responsibility. [*Students who default on loans could be faced with high medical bills or prolonged unemployment.*]

False cause: An argument that falsely assumes that because one thing happens after another, the first event was a cause of the second event. Also known as *post hoc.*

EXAMPLE I drank green tea and my headache went away; therefore, green tea makes headaches go away. [*How do we know that the headache did not go away for another reason?*]

Self-contradiction: An argument that contradicts itself.

EXAMPLE No absolute statement can be true. [*The statement itself is an absolute.*]

Guilt by association: Discrediting a person because of problems with that person's associates, friends, or family.

EXAMPLE Smith's friend has been convicted of fraud, so Smith cannot be trusted. [*Why should Smith be held responsible for his friend's actions?*]

Stacking the deck/card stacking: Slanting the evidence to support a position.

EXAMPLE Nine out of ten doctors interviewed prefer X. Therefore X is good for you. [*Which doctors were interviewed? Do they all work for the company that produces X? If so, the writer has stacked the deck.*]

False authority: Presenting the testimony of an unqualified person to support a claim.

EXAMPLE As the actor who plays Dr. Fine on *The Emergency Room,* I recommend this weight-loss drug because . . ." [*Is an actor qualified to judge the benefits and dangers of a diet drug?*]

False analogy: A comparison in which a surface similarity masks a significant difference.

EXAMPLE Governments and businesses both work within a budget to accomplish their goals. Just as business must focus on the bottom line, so should government. [*Is the goal of government to make a profit? Does government instead have other, more important goals?*]

Red herring: An argument that diverts attention from the true issue by concentrating on something irrelevant.

EXAMPLE   Hemingway's book *Death in the Afternoon* is unsuccessful because it glorifies the brutal sport of bullfighting. [*Why can't a book about a brutal sport be successful? The statement is irrelevant.*]

Begging the question: A form of circular reasoning that assumes the truth of a questionable opinion.

EXAMPLE   The president's poor relationship with the military has weakened the armed forces. [*Does the president really have a poor relationship with the military?*]

Hasty generalization: A conclusion based on inadequate evidence.

EXAMPLE   Temperatures across the United States last year exceeded the fifty-year average by two degrees, thus proving that global warming is a reality. [*Is this evidence enough to prove this very broad conclusion?*]

Bandwagon: An argument that depends on going along with the crowd, on the false assumption that truth can be determined by a popularity contest.

EXAMPLE   Everybody knows that Hemingway is preoccupied with the theme of death in his novels. [*How do we know that "everybody" agrees with this statement?*]

Ad hominem: A personal attack on someone who disagrees with you rather than on the person's argument.

EXAMPLE   The district attorney is a lazy political hack, so naturally she opposes streamlining the court system. [*Even if the district attorney usually supports her party's position, does that make her wrong about this issue?*]

Circular reasoning: An argument that restates the point rather than supporting it with reasonable evidence.

EXAMPLE   The wealthy should pay more taxes because taxes should be higher for people with higher incomes. [*Why should wealthy people pay more taxes? The rest of the statement does not answer this question; it just restates the position.*]

Either/or fallacy: The idea that a complicated issue can be resolved by resorting to one of only two options when in reality there are additional choices.

EXAMPLE   Either the state legislature will raise taxes or our state's economy will falter. [*Are these really the only two possibilities?*]

care about will give you the energy to think matters through and make cogent arguments. Of course, you will have to go beyond your personal emotions about an issue to make the most convincing case. You will also have to empathize with potential readers who may disagree with you about a subject that is close to your heart.

1. Figuring out what is at issue

People argue about issues, not topics. Before you can take a position on a topic like air pollution or football injuries, you must figure out what is at issue. Try turning your topic into a problem by asking questions about it. Are there indications that all is not as it should be? Have things always been this way, or have they changed for the worse? From what different perspectives—economic, social, political, cultural, medical, geographic—can problems like a wide receiver's recent knee injury or a quarterback's forced retirement be understood? Do people interested in the topic disagree about what is true, what is good, or what should be done?

Based on your answers to such questions, identify the issues your topic raises. Then decide which of those issues you think is most important, interesting, and appropriate for you to write about in response to your assignment.

2. Developing a reasonable stance that negotiates differences

When writing arguments, you want your readers to respect your intelligence and trust your judgment. Conducting research on your issue can make you well informed; reading other people's views and thinking critically about them can enhance your thoughtfulness. Find out what others have to say about the issue, and make it part of your purpose to negotiate the differences between your position and theirs. Pay attention to the places where you disagree with other people's views, but also note what you have in common—topical interests, key questions, or underlying values. (*For more on appeals to your audience, see p. 222.*)

Always remember that two views on an issue can be similar yet not identical, or different yet not completely opposite. It is important to avoid language that may promote prejudice or fear. Also, misrepresentations of other people's ideas are as out of place in a thoughtful argument as are personal attacks on their character. You should write arguments to open minds, not slam doors shut.

Trying out different perspectives can also help you figure out where you stand on an issue. (*Also see the next section on stating your position.*) Argue with yourself. Make a list of the arguments for and against a specific position; then compare the lists and decide where

Tips LEARNING in COLLEGE

Images that Argue

Images can both support arguments and act as arguments themselves. In his paper on the National Football League's treatment of injured players (*see pp. 224–29*), Nicolas Buglione uses a vivid photograph to illustrate his claims about the high potential for injury in professional football. The image here goes further, however, to make an argument, or at least advance a strong claim. Developed by Adbusters—a non-profit advocacy group—it spoofs an alcoholic beverage producer's familiar advertising campaign. Notice how it uses humor to provoke an emotional reaction and convey a specific message. What do you think the message is?

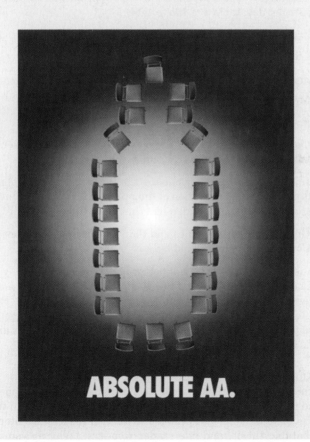

you stand. Does one set of arguments seem stronger than the other? Do you want to change or qualify your initial position to make it more understandable, reasonable, or believable?

3. Making a strong claim

Advancing a strong, debatable thesis (a claim) on a topic of interest to the discipline or the public is key to writing a successful argument. Keep in mind, however, that writing itself is a tool for thinking through your position on a variety of issues. As you think, write, and learn about your topic, you will develop, clarify, and sometimes entirely change your views. Think of yourself as a potter working with soft clay. Your thesis is still forming as you work with the topic.

As noted in the section on the Toulmin model of argument, personal feelings and accepted facts are not appropriate claims because they are not debatable (*see 10b, p. 214*).

PERSONAL FEELING, NOT A DEBATABLE THESIS

I feel that professional football players are treated poorly.

ACCEPTED FACT, NOT A DEBATABLE THESIS

Many players in the NFL are injured each year.

DEBATABLE THESIS

Current NFL regulations are not enough to protect players from suffering the hardships caused by game-related injuries.

In proposals and policy papers, the thesis presents a solution in terms of the writer's definition of the problem. The logic behind a thesis for a proposal can be stated like this:

Given these key variables and their underlying cause, one solution to the problem would be . . .

Because this kind of thesis is both complex and qualified, you will often need more than one sentence to state it clearly. You will also need numerous well-supported arguments to make it creditable. Readers will finally want to know that the proposed solution will not cause worse problems than it solves; they realize that policy papers and proposals call for actions, and actions have consequences.

4. Supporting and developing your claim

A strong, debatable thesis needs to be supported and developed with sound reasoning and carefully documented evidence. You can think of an argument as a dialogue between writer and readers. A writer states a debatable thesis, and one reader wonders, "Why do you believe that?" Another reader wants to know, "But what about this factor?"

A writer needs to anticipate questions such as these and answer them by presenting reasons that are substantiated with evidence and by refuting opposing views.

Usually, a well-developed argument paper includes more than one type of reason and one kind of evidence. Besides generalizations based on empirical data or statistics, it often includes authoritative reasons based on the opinions of experts and ethical reasons based on the application of principle. For example, in his proposal about reducing injuries in professional football, Nicholas Buglione presents facts about the number of injuries in the previous and current seasons to establish the seriousness of the problem. He also includes quotations from an expert in football safety to explain the coach's role in promoting—or failing to promote—team safety (*see p. 227*). As you conduct research for your argument, note evidence—facts, examples, and expert testimony—that can be used to support each argument for or against your position.

In developing your argument, you should also pay attention to **counterarguments,** substantiated claims that do not support your position. Think critically about such claims, and consider using one of the following strategies to take the most important counterarguments into account:

- Qualify your thesis in light of the counterargument by including a word such as *most, some, usually,* or *likely:* "Although many people—fans and nonfans alike—understand that football is a dangerous sport, few realize just how hard *some* NFL players have it."

- Add to the thesis a statement of the conditions for or exceptions to your position: "The NFL pension plan is unfair to players who do not have more than five years in the league."

- Choose one or two counterarguments and plan to refute their truth or their importance in your paper. Buglione, for example, refutes the counterargument that the NFL has a good pension plan for its players.

5. Creating an outline that includes a linked set of reasons
Arguments are most effective when they present a chain—a linked set—of reasons, so it is a good idea to begin drafting by writing down your thesis and outlining the way you will support and develop it. Your outline should include the following parts:

- An introduction to the topic and the debatable issue
- A thesis stating your position on the issue
- A point-by-point account of the reasons for your position, including the evidence (facts, examples, authorities) you will use to substantiate each major reason

www.mhhe.com/
nmhh
For more help with
creating an outline,
go to

Writing >
Paragraph/Essay
Development >
Outlines

- A fair presentation and refutation of one or two key counter-arguments to your thesis
- A response to the "So what?" question. Why does your argument matter?

6. Appealing to your audience

You want your readers to see you as *reasonable, ethical,* and *empathetic*—qualities that promote communication among people who have differences. You display the quality of your thought, character, and feelings—what the ancient Greeks called **logos, ethos,** and **pathos**—by the way that you argue for what you believe.

Giving reasons and supplying evidence for your position and arguing responsibly by avoiding fallacies establish your logos. (*For more on fallacies, see pp. 216–17.*) You also need to show that you are sincere (ethos) and that you care about your readers' feelings (pathos). For example, you might refer to a quality or belief you share with others, even those who disagree with you. Establishing common ground in this way will make readers more open to your argument.

- Do you share an interest in the same issue, topic, or field?
- Do you have overlapping goals or values?

When you read your argument to yourself or to peers, pay attention to how you are coming across. What would readers who have never met you think of you after reading what you have to say?

www.mhhe.com/
nmhh
For more on crafting introductions, go to

Writing >
Paragraph/Essay
Development >
Introductions

7. Emphasizing your commitment to dialogue in the introduction

You want your readers to listen to what you have to say, so make sure that when you present the topic and issue in your introduction, you establish some kind of common ground or shared concern with them. For example, in his essay on the NFL, Buglione begins with a vivid account of a football injury to awaken his readers' concern for injured athletes and make them receptive to his proposal about decreasing the number of injuries in professional football. If possible, you should return to that common ground at the end of your argument.

8. Concluding by restating your position and emphasizing its importance

After presenting your reasoning in detail, conclude by restating your position. Arguments are always thesis driven, so it is appropriate to remind readers of your thesis. The version of your thesis that you present in your conclusion should be more complex and qualified than the thesis statement you included in your introduction, to encourage readers to appreciate both your thoughtfulness and your argument's importance. In the end, readers may not agree with you, but they should know why the issue and your argument matter.

9. Reexamining your reasoning

After you have completed the first draft of your paper, take time to reexamine your reasoning. Checking the logic of your own writing is probably the greatest challenge to your ability to read critically. It is essential to step outside yourself and assess your argument objectively for errors in reasoning. Ask yourself the following questions:

- **Have I given a sufficient number of reasons to support my thesis, or should I add one or two more?**

- **Have I made any mistakes in logic?** Use the box on pages 216–17 to check for logical fallacies.

- **Have I clearly and adequately developed each reason I have presented in support of my thesis?** Is the reason clear? Have I defined its key terms, illustrated its meaning, and explained its implications? Is my supporting evidence sufficient? Have I quoted or paraphrased from sources accurately and documented them properly? (*For more on quoting, paraphrasing, and documenting sources, see Part 3, Researching, and Part 4, Documenting across the Curriculum.*)

Of course, nothing is more helpful than hearing and responding to your classmates' questions. Peer review is one of the best tools for developing critical thinking and writing skills.

For MULTILINGUAL STUDENTS

Learning about Cultural Differences through Peer Review

In some cultures, writing direct and explicit arguments is discouraged, but not so in the United States. When you share your work with peers born and raised in the United States, you may learn that the way in which you have expressed certain ideas and values—the vocabulary or the style of presentation you have used—makes it difficult for them to understand and accept the point you are making. Ask your peers to suggest different words and approaches. Then decide if their suggestions will make your ideas more accessible to others.

www.mhhe.com/
nmhh
For more samples of
argument papers,
go to

Writing >
Writing Samples >
Argument Papers

10d Construct arguments to address issues in the social sciences

In the following position paper, Nicholas Buglione argues that the National Football League can and should do more to protect its players from suffering the physical and economic hardships caused by game-related injuries. As you read Buglione's argument, notice how he tries to get readers to sympathize with the players, how he acknowledges what the league has already done to address the injury problem, and why he insists that more should be done in two areas: safety and pensions. How suitable, complex, and feasible do you think his solutions are?

Sample student argument paper

NFL: Negligent Football League?

Lively open-
ing to hook
reader.

It is fourth down and short on the other team's thirty-five yard line. At this critical point in the game, all eyes are on you, the star running back. The ball is snapped from the center into the quarterback's hands. You sprint up into the pocket, receive the handoff, and race into the hole. At that instant, a rabid 245-pound linebacker drives his massive body into your legs. There is a crunch, followed by excruciating pain: your career in football is over.

Topic
introduced.

Injuries have been a fact of life in the National Football League (NFL) for many years. But in 1995, leg, knee, back, and head injuries piled up, and the NFL decided it was time to take action. Under the auspices of Commissioner Paul Tagliabue, league officials agreed on some basic safety guidelines to solve pro football's woes. These guidelines included the following: (1) making it illegal for players to lead with their heads when they tackle, thereby reducing helmet-to-body contact injuries; (2) allowing the quarterback to ground the ball intentionally in certain situations, thereby lessening the risk of his being injured by a lineman; (3) reducing the size of the helmet's face mask, thereby decreasing its potential as a weapon; and (4) levying a $10,000 to $20,000 fine on any player who hits another player after the play is over (Glauber, 1997).

The NFL expected that these regulations would reduce the number of injuries, but the situation got worse, not better. As an example, the 1996 season began with an unprecedented seven injuries to starting quarterbacks, all within the first week. As the season went on, more leg, rib, head, and shoulder injuries followed, and one quarterback, Chris Miller, was forced to retire after sustaining his fifth head injury in less than two seasons. The epidemic of injuries carried over into the 1997 season. Steve Young of the San Francisco 49ers (Figure 1) suffered three concussions in ten months, and wide receiver Jerry Rice missed much of the season due to a knee injury (Glauber, 1997).

Injuries have an enormous impact on a player's life after football. Retirees tell horror stories about the aftermath of injuries, which

Issue introduced.

Issue illustrated with a photograph.

Figure 1. Jacksonville Jaguars' linebacker Bryce Paup barrels down on San Francisco 49ers quarterback Steve Young (holding the ball) and tackle Jeremy Newberry in a 1999 game. Young suffered three concussions in ten months during the 1997 season.
Note. Copyright Mark Wallheiser/Reuters/Corbis.

too often turn simple, everyday acts like getting out of bed into backbreaking work. Consider the case of Al Toon. Toon, a wide receiver for the New York Jets, enjoyed a career filled with highlights. Unfortunately, his career was also filled with concussions. After the ninth concussion, he called it quits and tried to put the game behind him. Sadly, those nine head injuries continue to punish Toon. On sunny days, he has to wear dark sunglasses because bright light is too much for his damaged head to handle. Even worse, Toon suffers from memory loss and chronic migraine headaches. Fortunately, he has managed his finances well and can afford to live comfortably with his wife and children. Many other retired players are not so fortunate. Those injured at an early age too often find themselves without a job, without a college degree, and without physical health. It is no wonder that a few turn to drugs and alcohol, become homeless, or end up in a morgue long before their time (Glauber, 1997).

A significant problem exists in the NFL. Much more must be done to protect players. However, little progress will be made if the league tries to rectify the problem simply by passing rules and amendments to those rules. Such attempts fail to get at the root of the problem: a coaching tradition that emphasizes aggression over safety and a pension plan that fails to support all retired players adequately.

Perhaps no one is more responsible for a player's physical welfare than the coach. Although it is true that coaches have to win games, which can lead to aggressive methods, and that players readily buy into those methods, a coach needs to balance the need to win with players' safety (SafeUSA, 2002). According to Carl Blyth, an expert on football safety, the head coach's "attitude and leadership" are the most important factors in creating this balance (1971, p. 94). Even though coaches should teach players to value safety, they seldom do so; instead, coaches often encourage feelings and behavior that compromise safety. Tommy Chaikin, a former lineman for South Carolina, has pointed out that his coaches encouraged aggressive feelings and behavior during practice. Fighting was not discouraged, and players were trained to fear being ridiculed for exhibiting any compassion (1988).

Issue explained with an anecdote.

Thesis stated.

Causes of issue identified.

First point—supported by expert testimony.

Point also supported with an anecdote.

226

Because a pugnacious team is more likely to win, it is understandable that coaches want to instill a fighting spirit in their players. What coaches fail to realize, however, is that the aggressive nature of their training programs increases the incidence and severity of injuries. To disregard a player's safety for the purposes of toughening him up is unethical (Lapchick, 2004). It is also foolish because ensuring that players stay healthy is in the best interest of coach and team. When the Rams' quarterback Kurt Warner was sidelined in 2003 after two years of injuries to his head and shoulders, he was immediately relegated to being the backup for the other quarterback and saw very little play during that season (Reilly, 2003). If he had not been pushed so aggressively during those two years, he probably could have continued to play. Clearly, the coaches of the National Football League do not have their players' safety in mind, and this situation must change. Their failure to teach players how to play football safely has made the NFL injury epidemic worse.

Refutes counter-argument that winning is more important than safety.

Injuries often continue to plague players even after they retire. When their football careers are finished, most players still need to work to support themselves and their families; however, about 70 percent of today's current players do not have a college degree (Glauber, 1997). Without a college degree, retired football players have little chance of securing white-collar jobs. The alternative, blue-collar work, is closed to many former players who suffer the lingering effects of injury. Glauber's survey of 1,425 former NFL players found that more than 50% are physically limited by previous injuries. What compensation is there for these retired players, the ones who have essentially destroyed their bodies playing football for the league?

Second point—supported by statistics.

A pension would seem to be the answer. Though the NFL does have a pension plan, it is not adequate or fair. According to Glauber, the NFL's pension plan pays retired players with five or more years of NFL service $300 a month per year of service (1997). The minimum pension is, therefore, $1,500 a month. Although players with permanent injuries certainly deserve more, the bigger problem is that the pension plan only applies to players with five or more years of NFL

Refutes counter-argument that NFL pensions solve the problem.

227

service. Players injured within the first five years of their career receive no pension at all. What would Kurt Warner have done if he had not recovered from his injuries?

Third point—supported by expert testimony.

Why does the NFL treat its players so poorly? One reason may be that professional sports has become big business. The term *corporate athleticism* describes the business-minded attitude that has taken over sports (Hart-Nibbrig & Cottingham, 1986, p. 1). Corporate athleticism means that sports organizations like the NFL are primarily concerned with increasing profits. Winning teams make a larger profit, so coaches try to increase the chance of winning by encouraging anger and aggression in their players. Moreover, it is not in the front office's financial interest to support disabled retirees. When players cease to be lucrative for the league's bottom line, the NFL can simply turn to a younger group of men, all of whom are eager to play pro football. The NFL can then exploit this new crop of players.

Term—*Players' Association*—defined.

Exploitation can be resisted, especially by the Players' Association—the collective bargaining unit of NFL players—even though some observers consider the Association part of the problem (Zimmerman, 2003). To deal with the injury problem, the Players'

Proposed solution.

Association must take three important steps. First, it must make the rest of the sports world aware of the situation. Although many people—fans and non-fans alike—understand that football is a dangerous sport, few realize just how hard some NFL players have it. Second, the Players' Association must pressure NFL coaches to monitor the physical well-being of their players closely and stress the value of staying healthy, not the ill-gotten gains of playing through injuries.

The Players' Association must also work to ease the financial burden on injured retirees. It should demand that the NFL amend its pension plan so that coverage is extended to all players, regardless of how many years they played for the league. In the United States, workers injured on the job are eligible for compensation. Why should NFL players be treated differently just because they have been in the league less than five years? In addition, those players who serve five or more years in the NFL deserve more than $1,500 a month, especially if they suffer from debilitating injuries. Finally, young players should receive financial counseling to make them aware of just how short a football career can be. On average, an "NFL career last[s] only 3.6 years," and as Commissioner Paul Tagliabue admits, what follows that career is likely to be both "painful and tragic" for NFL players who have not been "well-advised and well-served" (Glauber, 1997, p. B6).

———————————————-[new page]————————————————

References

Blyth, C. S. (1971). Tackle football. In C. P. Yost (Ed.), *Sports safety: Accident prevention and injury control in physical education, athletics, and recreation* (pp. 93–96). Washington, DC: Division of Safety Education.

Chaikin, T. (1988, October). The nightmare of steroids. *Sports Illustrated,* 84–102.

Glauber, R. (1997, January 12, 14, 15, 16). Life after football (four-part series). *New York Newsday,* p. B6 (part 1), p. A64 (part 2), p. A66 (part 3), p. A92 (part 4).

Hart-Nibbrig, N., & Cottingham, C. (1986). *The political economy of college sports.* Lexington: Heath.

Lapchik, R. E. (2004). *Dying for the game.* Retrieved April 4, 2004, from Northwestern University, Center for the Study of Sport in Society Web site: http://www.sportinsociety.org/rel-article22.html

Reilly, R. (2003, December 8). Ram shackled. *Sports Illustrated,* 104.

SafeUSA. (2002, July 14). Football safety (American). Retrieved March 9, 2004, from http://www.safeusa.org/sports/football.htm

Zimmerman, P. (2003, October 1). Union job: Safety of its members should be Players' Association top priority. *Sports Illustrated: SI.*com. Retrieved March 9, 2004, from http://www.sportsillustrated.cnn.com/2003/writers/dr_z/10/01/insider/index.html

References list follows APA style and begins on a new page.

www.mhhe.com/
nmhh
For online resources
in various disciplines,
go to

Links across the
Curriculum

10e Construct arguments to address issues in the humanities.

In a sense, most humanities papers, including literary analyses, are arguments in that they make a claim about a text, event, or artwork. Reviews are arguments in the sense that they involve making principled claims about a specific book or performance. The following review essay by philosopher Dale Jamieson evaluates arguments in a book by another philosopher, James Rachels, and then evaluates the merits of the book overall.

Sample review essay

The Morality of Species

DALE JAMIESON

> [A review of] *Created from Animals: The Moral Implications of Darwinism.* By James Rachels. Oxford: Oxford University Press, 1990. 245 pp. $19.95 cloth.

Poor Charles Darwin. For fundamentalists he is the Great Satan, for Social Darwinists the Great Liberator, and for academics, the stuff of dissertations, books, and careers. The sickly gentleman from Downe is roundly loved, hated, reviled, and admired, mostly for bad reasons, by people who never read his books or misread them when they do. Like Matisse, who sometimes claimed forgeries as his own original artworks, Darwin was not always a good judge of what he brought forth: he thought that Spencer was "by far the greatest living philosopher in England: perhaps equal to any that have lived."

In this brilliant but readable book, James Rachels has done much in a few pages to recover the historical Darwin. Although only the first chapter is explicitly about Darwin, his spirit infuses the entire book. Rachels brings out the broadly consequentialist nature of Darwin's moral thinking, and quotes several remarkable passages in which Darwin looks forward to an age in which moral sympathy is "extended to all sentient beings" (p. 165). The Darwin that emerges is not just a biologist cum philosopher. He is also a curious boy, a casual student, an opponent of slavery, and a defender of science. One vignette is especially revealing. Shortly after Darwin's marriage to the devout Emma Wedgewood, who would be his wife for more than forty years, she wrote urging him to reconsider his views about religion. After Darwin's death this letter was found among his papers. Scrawled on the bottom were the words: "When I am dead, know how many times I have kissed and cried over this."

Rachels's first chapter, "Darwin's Discovery," vividly captures the spirit of Darwin's life and work. "How Evolution and Ethics Might Be Related" is a critical but sympathetic discussion of post-Darwinian attempts to connect evolution and ethics. Nodding toward Hume, Rachels rejects deductivist views about what the connection might be but goes on to claim that "Darwinism undermines traditional morality" (p. 97). Chapter three asks, "Must a Darwinian Be Skeptical about Religion?" Yes, is Rachels's answer. Although there is no logical incompatibility between Darwinism and theism, Darwinism "undermines religious belief by removing some of the grounds that previously supported it" (p. 127). "How Different Are Humans from Other Animals?" argues that although some humans are quite different from other animals, the differences are matters of degree rather than kind: "Darwinism leads inevitably to the abandonment of the idea of human dignity and the substitution of a different sort of ethic" (p. 171). The final chapter, "Morality without the Idea That Humans Are Special," outlines that ethic. It is a view that Rachels calls "moral individualism" and it implies the rejection of speciesism in all its forms.

People who make their living fighting over arguments and texts will find much to quarrel with in Rachels's book. No doubt scholars have found other ways of reading Darwin. Not all moral philosophers will be enamored of Rachels's "moral individualism." I myself would have liked to hear more about the relation of "undermining," and I somehow missed the move from the claim that the value of a life is the value that it has to its subject, to the claim that "the more complex their lives are, the greater the objection to destroying them" (p. 209). Nor is it clear how much weight the distinction between differences of degree and differences of kind can bear: contemplate the difference between the bald and the hirsute. In its treatment of texts, claims, and arguments this book is very good, but Rachels's real accomplishment lies elsewhere.

What Rachels has given us is a framework (a "narrative," as a post- 5 modernist might say) that makes sense of much of the debate in recent moral philosophy, especially in such areas as medical and environmental ethics. What we are witnessing, more than a century after the publication of Darwin's *Origin,* is moral change occasioned by the belated impact of the Darwinian perspective.

Rachels describes moral change in the following way. In the first stage a moral outlook "is supported by a world-view in which everyone . . . has confidence" (p. 221). In the second stage the world-view begins to break up. According to Rachels the "old morality" of human uniqueness and dignity was supported by a world-view with the earth at its center, a specially created home for humans who were made in God's image, with animals given to humans to use as they please. Although

COMMON ASSIGNMENTS ■ Arguments

this world-view was under attack long before Darwin, it was he who struck the death blow by showing that humans and animals are both products of purposeless natural processes, and indeed are kin. According to Rachels we are now in the third stage of moral change, in which the old morality is no longer taken for granted. It is widely agreed that it requires defense. The fourth stage is one in which a new morality emerges, one that is at home with our best understandings of ourselves and our relation to the world. If Rachels is right, much of this new morality is implicit in Darwin's own thought.

Rachels has given us an important book that provides a new perspective on what we are doing in moral philosophy. It is well written, well argued, and well-researched. It deserves a very wide readership.

10f Construct arguments to address issues in the sciences.

Scientists are called upon to evaluate the research of others and to argue for changes in policy. In the following essay by the Council for Biotechnology Information, the authors argue that biotech crops offer a solution to a looming crisis in food production.

Sample policy paper

Growing More Food[*]

COUNCIL FOR BIOTECHNOLOGY INFORMATION

The world's population more than doubled in the last half century and topped 6 billion in 1999.[1] Each year, it is adding about 73 million people—a population nearly the size of Vietnam's. By 2030, it is projected to reach around 8 billion, and nearly all of that increase is expected to occur in developing countries,[2] which are also expected to see higher incomes and rapid urbanization.

At the same time, the world's hungry and chronically malnourished remain at about 840 million people, despite global pledges and national efforts to improve food security.

These trends mean the world will have to double its food production and also improve food distribution over the next quarter century.[3]

---

[*]The documentation style used in this paper is that which appeared in the original and does not correspond fully to any of the styles discussed elsewhere in the handbook (see *Part 4: Documenting across the Curriculum*).

These pose staggering challenges for the world's farmers: Much of the world's land suitable for farming is already cultivated and natural resources are under pressure. Soil degradation is widespread, agriculture has already razed 20 to 30 percent of the world's forest areas[4] and water tables in many areas are falling. Agriculture consumes about 70 percent of the fresh water people use every year and, at the current consumption rate, two out of three people will live in water-stressed conditions by 2025.[5]

By 2050, some 4.2 billion people may not have their daily basic needs met.[6]

These projections and complex challenges facing the world's future food supply are prompting international food and agricultural experts and policymakers—including the U.N. Food and Agriculture Organization and the World Health Organization—to call plant biotechnology a critical tool to help feed a growing population in the 21st century.

Governments need to develop policies to ensure greater investment in research and regulatory oversight that's needed to manage the health, environmental and socioeconomic issues associated with biotechnology, according to the Human Development Report 2001, an annual report commissioned by the U.N. Development Programme.[7]

Biotechnology: An eco-efficient option

World crop productivity could increase by as much as 25 percent[8] through the use of biotechnology to grow plants that resist pests and diseases, tolerate harsh growing conditions and delay ripening to reduce spoilage, according to the Consultative Group on International Agricultural Research (CGIAR). All this could be achieved on existing farmland and customized to meet local needs.

Biotechnology also offers the possibility for scientists to design "farming systems that are responsive to local needs and reflect sustainability requirements," said Calestous Juma, director of the Science, Technology and Innovation Program at the Center for International Development and senior research associate at the Belfer Center for Science and International Affairs, both at Harvard University.[9]

Scientists are developing crops that resist diseases, pests, viruses, bacteria and fungi, all of which reduce global production by more than 35 percent at a cost estimated at more than $200 billion a year.[10] For instance, test fields in Kenya are growing sweet potato varieties that are resistant to a complex set of viruses that can wipe out three-fourths of Kenyan farmers' harvest.

In the United States, crops with built-in insect protection and that tolerate a specific herbicide have helped farmers improve yields and reduce costs. In 2000, direct benefit to growers of insect resistant corn, cotton and potatoes exceeded $300 million, according to the Environmental Protection Agency[11]

In a study to be released in 2002, the National Center for Food and Agricultural Policy quantified biotechnology's benefits for U.S. farmers through 44 case studies that covered 30 different crops, including papaya, citrus, soybeans and tomatoes. For instance, it found that herbicide tolerant soybeans helped farmers reduce their annual production costs by $15 an acre, which totals $735 million across 49 million acres. Virus-resistant papaya is credited with saving Hawaii's papaya industry, which produces 53 million pounds of the fruit valued at $17 million a year.[12]

Biotechnology: Getting the most from poor growing conditions

Scientists are developing crops that can tolerate extreme conditions, such as drought, flood and harsh soil. For instance, researchers are working on a rice that can survive long periods under water [13] as well as rice and corn that can tolerate aluminum in soil. [14]

A tomato plant has been developed to grow in salty water that is 50 times higher in salt content than conventional plants can tolerate and nearly half as salty as seawater.[15] About a third of the world's irrigated land has become useless to farmers because of high levels of accumulated salt.

Biotech crops "could significantly reduce malnutrition, which still affects more than 800 million people worldwide, and would be especially valuable for poor farmers working marginal lands in sub-Saharan Africa," the Human Development Report stated.

Technology in a seed

While the Green Revolution kept mass starvation at bay and saw global cereal production double as a result of improved crop varieties, fertilizers, pesticides and irrigation, its benefits bypassed such regions as sub-Saharan Africa. The new hybrids needed irrigation and chemical inputs that farmers there couldn't afford.

In contrast, the benefits of biotechnology are passed on through a seed or plant cutting, so that farmers anywhere around the world can easily adopt the technology. That's why biotechnology is particularly attractive to scientists and rural development experts in poor countries where most of the people farm for a living.

Biotech crops are "tailor-made for Africa's farmers, because the new technology is packaged in the seed, which all farmers know how to handle," said Florence Wambugu, a Kenyan plant scientist who helped develop a virus-resistant sweet potato.[16]

Agreeing with Wambugu, the International Society of African Scientists issued a statement in October 2001 calling plant biotechnology a "major opportunity to enhance the production of food crops."[17]

Notes

[1] United Nations Population Fund (UNFPA), "Population Numbers and Trends," <www.unfpa.org/modules/briefkit/05.htm>.

[2] International Food Policy Research Institute, "World Food Prospects: Critical Issues for the Early Twenty-First Century," October 1999, p. 9.

[3] United Nations Population Fund (UNFPA), "State of World Population 2001 Report," November 7, 2001, <www.unfpa.org/swp/swpmain.htm>.

[4] "New Study Reveals That Environmental Damage Threatens Future World Food Production," World Resources Institute, February 14, 2001, <www.wri.org/press/page_agroecosystems.html>.

[5] Global Environment Outlook, 2000—UN Environment Programme, <www.unep.org/geo2000/>.

[6] "State of World Population 2001 Report," United Nations Population Fund (UNFPA), November 7, 2001, <www.unfpa.org/swp/swpmain.htm>.

[7] "The Human Development Report 2001," United Nations Development Programme, July 2001, <www.undp.org/>.

[8] Prakash, C.S., (October 4, 2001). In a media presentation sponsored by the American Medical Association (AMA), cited Consultative Group on International Agricultural Research (CGIAR) as source. See <www.ama-assn.org> media briefings.

[9] Calestous, Juma, director of the Science, Technology and Innovation Program at the Center for International Development and senior research associate at the Belfer Center for Science and International Affairs, "Appropriate Technology for Sustainable Food Security—Modern Biotechnology," both at Harvard University, *2020 Focus 7,* International Food Policy Research Institute (IFPRI). August 2001.

[10] Krattiger, Anatole, "Food Biotechnology: Promising Havoc or Hope for the Poor?" Proteus, 2000.

[11] "Bt Plant-Pesticides Biopesticides Registration Action Document—Executive Summary," United States Environmental Protection Agency, <www.epa.gov/pesticides/biopesticides/otherdocs/bt_brad2/1 overview.pdf>.

[12] Gianessi, Leonard, (October 4, 2001). "The Potential for Biotechnology to Improve Crop Pest Management in the United States," In a media presentation sponsored by the American Medical Association (AMA). See www.ncfap.org and <www.ama-assn.org> media briefings.

[13] "Food in the 21st Century: From Science to Sustainable Agriculture," CGIAR, p. 36, <www.worldbank.org/html/cgiar/publications/shahbook/shahbook.pdf>.

[14] "Food in the 21st Century: From Science to Sustainable Agriculture," CGIAR, p. 36, <www.worldbank.org/html/cgiar/publications/shahbook/shahbook.pdf>

[15] Owens, Susan, "Genetic engineering may help to reclaim agricultural land lost due to salination," European Molecular Biology Organization (EMBO) Reports 2001, Vol. 2/No. 10, p. 877–879, <www.embo-reports.oupjournals.org/cgi/content/full/2/10/877>.

[16] "Biotech 'Tailor-Made' for Africa, Researcher Tells Tufts Conference," Council for Biotechnology Information, Washington, D.C., November 19, 2001 <index.asp?id=1156&redirect=con1309mid17%2E.html>.

[17] "Position Statement on Agricultural Biotechnology Applications in Africa and the Caribbean," International Society of African Scientists, <www.monsantoafrica.com/reports/ISAS/ISAS.html>.

11 Personal Essays

Personal writing can be found in many places, including diaries and journals, but personal writing is not the same thing as a personal essay. The personal essay is one of the most literary kinds of writing. Like a poem, it should be significant—meaningful to readers and relevant to their lives. Like a play, it should speak to readers in a distinctive voice. Like a good story, it should be both compelling and memorable.

11a Understand the assignment.

When you write a personal essay, you are doing much more than fulfilling an assignment; you are exploring your experiences, clarifying your values, and composing a public self. At one level, your purpose is to reveal something about who you are, how you got where you are

WRITING beyond COLLEGE

Personal Essays

Nowadays it is not uncommon for people from all walks of life to use the personal essay to learn about themselves and explore their experience of the world. Doctors, social workers, nutritionists—as well as novelists—publish memoirs and personal essays based on their life's work.

- Gloria Ladson-Billings, a teacher, reflects on her experience in the classroom to figure out what makes teachers successful.
- Carol Allen, a philosophy professor, uses Plato's allegory of the cave as a metaphor in *Tea with Demons,* her personal account of going mad and finding her way back.
- Oliver Sacks, a neurologist, writes about his experiences with people whose perceptual patterns are impaired and about what it means to be fully human.

now, and what you believe. The focus, however, does not need to be on you. You might write a personal essay about a tree in autumn, a trip to Senegal, an encounter with a stranger, or an athletic event. The real topic, though, is how these objects and experiences have become meaningful to you.

Consider, for example, *The Autobiography of Malcolm X*. After teaching himself to read, the imprisoned Malcolm X wanted to tell others his story. At one level, Malcolm X's *Autobiography* represents his experiences as an individual, as his alone. But at another level, the book has a larger purpose: to suggest that imprisonment is not only a matter of jails but also an issue of social bondage. To realize this larger purpose, the story forges a connection between the individual and the social—between Malcolm X and his readers.

When we read a personal essay, we expect to learn more than the details of the writer's experience; we expect to see the connections between that experience and our own. Depending on your point and what you assume your readers already believe, you may decide to intensify, clarify, or complicate the reader's sense of things. You may even try to change readers' minds. But no matter what you intend your essay to accomplish, your point is likely to be more effective if it is not stated directly. The details you emphasize, the words you choose, and the characters you create all communicate your point implicitly without turning it into "the moral of the story."

1. The personal essay as conversation

Personal essayists usually use the first person (*I* and *we*) to create an interpersonal relationship—a sense that the writer and reader are engaged in the open-ended give-and-take of conversation. The details you include in your essay, as well as the connotations of the words you use, determine how you appear in this conversation—shy, belligerent, or friendly, for example. Consider how Meghan Daum represents herself in relation to both computer-literate and computer-phobic readers in the following excerpt from her personal essay "Virtual Love," which appeared in a 1997 issue of the *New Yorker:*

> The kindness pouring forth from my computer screen was bizarrely exhilarating, and I logged off and thought about it for a few hours before writing back to express how flattered and "touched"—this was probably the first time I had ever used that word in earnest—I was by his message.
>
> I am not what most people would call a computer person. I have no interest in chat rooms, news groups, or most Web sites. I derive a palpable thrill from sticking a letter in the United States mail.

Besides Daum's conversational stance, notice the emotional effect of her remark on the word *touched* and her choice of words connoting excitement: *pouring forth, exhilarating,* and *palpable thrill.*

2. The personal essay as a link between one person's experience and a larger issue

To demonstrate the significance of a personal essay to its readers, writers usually connect their individual experience to a larger issue. Here, for example, are the closing lines of Daum's essay on "Virtual Love":

> The world had proved to be too cluttered and too fast for us, too polluted to allow the thing we'd attempted through technology ever to grow on the earth. PFSlider and I had joined the angry and exhausted living. Even if we met on the street, we wouldn't recognize each other, our particular version of intimacy now obscured by the branches and bodies and falling debris that make up the physical world.

Notice how Daum relates the disappointment of her failed Internet romance with "PFSlider" to a larger social issue: the general contrast between cyberspace and material realities. Her point, however, is quite surprising; most people do not think of cyberspace as more "intimate"—or touching—than their everyday, earthly world of "branches and bodies."

11b Approach writing a personal essay as a process.

Shaping your private personal writing into a personal essay for a public audience can be challenging. The following suggestions should help.

1. Keeping a journal or a writer's notebook where you can practice putting your experience into words

Record your observations about meaningful objects (houses, photographs, personal treasures), memorable incidents and experiences (an encounter with a stranger, coming to America, winning and losing), and distinctive situations (living arrangements, social cliques, neighborhood conflicts) in a journal. These details may provide the germ of a personal essay.

2. Thinking about the broader meaning of your topic when planning the focus of your essay

Stories about winning, losing, or arriving in a new place may have self-evident significance for you, but readers will appreciate that significance only if you connect your individual experience with something

239

more social or general. Try thinking about your focus metaphorically. For example, if you are writing about a turning point in your life, think of your experience as a metaphor for what we gain and what we lose as we grow and change. If you are writing about the clique that teased you in high school, imagine that what is at issue is a power play involving insiders and outsiders.

3. Structuring your essay like a story

Typically, personal essays are centered around either actions or ideas. There are three common ways to narrate events and reflections:

- **Chronological sequence** uses an order determined by clock time; what happened first is presented first, followed by what happened second, then third, and so on.

- **Emphatic sequence** uses an order determined by the point you want to make; for emphasis, events and reflections are arranged either from least to most important or from most to least important.

- **Suspenseful sequence** uses an order determined by the emotional effect the writer wants the essay to have on the reader. To keep the reader hanging, the essay may begin in the middle of things with a puzzling event, then flash back or go forward to clear things up. Some essays may even begin with the end—with the insight achieved—and then flash back to recount how the writer came to that insight.

4. Letting details tell your story

The story of an entire election campaign can be told in one sentence: "He was nominated; he ran; he lost." It is in the details that the story takes shape. No matter what you intend your essay to accomplish, the details you emphasize, the words you choose, and the characters you create all implicitly communicate the point of your essay. Often it is not even necessary to state your thesis.

Consider, for example, the following passage by Gloria Ladson-Billings:

> Mrs. Harris, my third-grade teacher, was quite a sharp dresser. She wore beautiful high-heeled shoes. Sometimes she switched to flats in the afternoon if her feet got tired, but every morning began with the click, click, click of her high heels as she greeted us up and down the rows. I wanted to dress the way Mrs. Harris did. I didn't want to wear old-lady comforters like Mrs. Benn's and I certainly didn't want to wear worn-out loafers

like those of my first-grade teacher, Miss Schwartz. I wanted to wear beautiful, shiny, high-heeled shoes like Mrs. Harris's. That was the way a teacher should look, I thought.

Ladson-Billings uses details to make her idea of a good teacher come alive for the reader. At one level—the literal—the "click, click, click" refers to the sound of Mrs. Harris's shoes. At another level, it represents the glamorous teacher. At the most figurative level, the "click, click, click" evokes the feminine kind of power that the narrator both longs for and admires.

5. Using the present tense strategically

When writers tell stories about themselves, they often use the *past tense,* as if the experience were over and done with ("once upon a time"). This choice makes sense, but the *present tense* has other advantages. It creates a sense of immediacy and helps make an essay vivid and memorable. Notice how the student writer of the following passage puts the reader inside the young girl's head by purposefully changing from the past to the present tense:

> As I was learning the switchboard, I caught my Dad watching me out of the corner of his eye. Hmm, I hope he doesn't think that I'm going to give him the satisfaction of not doing a good job. Yes, he's deprived me of my beach days with Joey. But I am on display here. And the switchboard is so vital to this office!

If they have good reason to do so, writers of personal essays may also sometimes take liberties with certain conventions of grammar and style. Be sure you understand any rules you may be stretching, however, and if you are writing a personal essay for a class assignment, be sure your instructor will accept the results. Some instructors, for example, might object to the shift from past to present tense in the paragraph above (*see Chapter 41: Confusing Shifts*). Some also might object to the last two sentences in the paragraph because they begin with coordinating conjunctions (*but* and *and*).

12 Essay Exams

When you take an essay exam, you probably feel pressed for time and have little interest in examining the process of test taking. Still, if you spend some time thinking about what you are expected to do in an essay exam, you may feel less stress the next time you are faced with one.

12a Prepare to take an essay exam.

Consider the specific course as your writing context and the course's instructor as your audience. As you prepare for the exam, think about how your instructor approached and presented the course material.

- What questions or problems did your instructor explicitly or implicitly address?
- What frameworks did your instructor use to analyze topics?
- What key terms did your instructor repeatedly use during lectures and discussions?

Because essay exams are designed to test your knowledge, not just your memory, working through possible questions is one of the best ways to study. Make up some essay questions that require you to:

- **Explain** what you have learned in a clear, well-organized way. (*See question 1 on the presidency in the box on p. 243.*)
- **Connect** what you know about one topic with what you know about another topic. (*See question 2 on labor supply decisions in the box on p. 243.*)
- **Apply** what you have learned to a new situation. (*See question 3 on a hypothetical particle-scattering experiment in the box on p. 243.*)
- **Interpret** the causes, effects, meanings, value, or potential of something. (*See question 4 on the uses of caesura and enjambment in the box on p. 243.*)
- **Argue** for or against some controversial statement about what you have learned. (*See question 5 on Jefferson in the box on p. 243.*)

CHARTING the TERRITORY

Essay Exam Questions across the Curriculum

During finals week, you may be asked to respond to essay questions like the following:

1. Discuss the power of the contemporary presidency as well as the limits of that power. [*from a political science course*]

2. Compare and contrast the treatment of labor supply decisions in the economic models proposed by Greg Lewis and Gary Becker. [*from an economics course*]

3. Describe the observations that would be made in an alpha-particle scattering experiment if (a) the nucleus of an atom were negatively charged and the protons occupied the empty space outside the nucleus and (b) the electrons were embedded in a positively charged sphere. [*from a chemistry course*]

4. Examine the uses of caesura and enjambment in the following poem, and analyze their effect on the poem's rhythm. [*from a literature course*]

5. In 1800, was Thomas Jefferson a dangerous radical? Be sure to define your key terms and to support your position with evidence from specific events, documents, and so on. [*from an American history course*]

12b Approach essay exams strategically.

1. Planning your time

During the exam period, time management is essential. Quickly look through the whole exam, and determine how much time to spend on each part or question. Your instructor may give the point value for each question or suggest the amount of time that should be spent on each part. You will want to move as quickly as possible through the short-answer questions that have lower point values so that you can spend the bulk of your time responding to the questions that are worth the greatest number of points.

2. Answering identification questions by showing the significance of the information

The most common type of short-answer question is the identification question: Who or what is X? In answering questions of this sort, you need to present just enough information to show that you understand X's significance within the context of the course. For example, if you are

243

asked to identify "Judith Loftus" on an American literature exam, don't just write: "character who knows Huckleberry Finn is a boy." Instead, craft one or two sentences that identify Loftus as a character Huckleberry Finn encounters while he is disguised as a girl; by telling Huck how she knows that he is not a girl, Loftus complicates the reader's understanding of gender.

3. Responding to essay questions tactically

When you are faced with an essay question, you may be inclined to write down everything you remember about the topic. Don't. Be tactical. Keep in mind that essay questions usually ask you to do something specific with a topic. Begin by determining precisely what you are being asked to do.

Before you write anything, read the question—all of it—and circle the key words:

> (Explain) (two) ways in which Picasso's *Guernica* evokes war's terrifying (destructiveness.)

To answer this question, you need to focus on two of the painting's features, such as coloring and composition, not on Picasso's life.

Sometimes you may be uncertain about what you are being asked to do, either because an essay question says too much or because it says too little. If a question includes more information or direction than necessary, try to isolate the kernel of the question—the main topic and tactic. If a question says too little, try to use the context of the course for clues. For example, "Discuss the power of the contemporary presidency as well as the limits of that power" can be made more specific by applying the analytic terms used in class, such as the resources, methods, and conditions of presidential power. You should also consider asking the instructor for clarification.

4. Using the question itself to structure your response

You are unlikely to have time to make a complete outline before you begin writing. Whenever possible, use the question to structure your answer. Usually, you will be able to transform the question itself into the thesis of your answer. If you are asked to agree/disagree with the Federalists' characterization of Thomas Jefferson in the election of 1800, you might begin with the following thesis:

> In the election of 1800, the Federalists characterized Jefferson as a dangerous radical. Although Jefferson's ideas were radical for the times, they were not dangerous to the republic.

Take a minute or two to list evidence for each of your main points, and then write the essay.

5. Checking your work

Leave a few minutes to read quickly through your completed answer, looking for words you might have omitted or key sentences that make no sense. Add the missing words, and rewrite the mixed-up sentences. You can usually cross out incorrect words and sentences and make corrections neatly above the original line of text.

Sample essay test responses

A student's response to an essay question in an art appreciation course appears below. Both the question and the student's notes are provided.

QUESTION

Both of these buildings (Figure 1 and Figure 2) feature dome construction. Identify the buildings, and discuss the differences in the visual effects created by the different dome styles.

STUDENT'S NOTES

Fig 1: Pantheon. Plain outside—concrete, can barely see dome. Dramatic inside—dome opens up huge interior space. Oculus to sky: light, air, rain. Coffered ceiling.

Fig 2: Taj Mahal. Dramatic exterior—dome set high, marble, reflecting pool, exterior lines go up. Inside not meant to be visited.

FIGURE 1

FIGURE 2

STUDENT'S ANSWER

Answers identification question and states thesis.

Key points supported by details.

    The Pantheon (Figure 1) and the Taj Mahal (Figure 2) are famous for their dome construction. The styles of the domes are dramatically different, however, resulting in dramatically different visual effects.
    The Pantheon, which was built by the Romans as a temple to the gods, looks very plain on the exterior. The dome is barely visible from outside, and it is made of a dull grey concrete. Inside the building, however, the dome produces an amazing effect. It opens up a huge space within the building, unobstructed by interior supports. The sides of the dome are coffered, and those recessed rectangles both lessen

the weight of the dome and add to its visual beauty. Most dramatically, the top of the dome is open to the sky, which allows sun or rain to pour into the building. This opening is called the oculus, meaning "eye" (to or of Heaven).

Uses specialized terms from course.

The Taj Mahal, which was built by a Muslim emperor of India as a tomb for his wife, is the complete opposite of the Pantheon—dazzling on the outside and plain on the inside. The large central dome is set up high on the base so that it can be seen from far away. It is made of white marble, which reflects light beautifully. The dome is surrounded by other structures that frame it and draw attention to its exterior— a long reflecting pond and four minarets. Arches and smaller domes on the outside of the building repeat the large dome's shape. Because the Taj Mahal's dome is tall and narrow, however, it does not produce the kind of vast interior space of the shorter, squatter Pantheon dome. Indeed, the inside of the Taj Mahal is not meant to be visited. Unlike the Pantheon, the dome of the Taj Mahal is intended to be admired from the outside.

Sets up comparison.

Key point supported by details.

Overall comparison as a brief conclusion.

13 Oral Presentations

Preparing an oral presentation, like preparing a paper, is a process. As in writing, you need to consider your audience and purpose as you choose the focus and level of your topic. You need to gather information, decide on the main idea of your presentation, think through the organization, and choose visuals that support your points. However, unless you are expected to "present a paper" in class or at a conference, it is usually not advisable to write out your presentation like an essay and simply read it aloud. This chapter will help you deliver a presentation that is appropriate, clear, and memorable.

13a Plan and shape your oral presentation.

1. Considering the interests, background knowledge, and attitudes of your audience

Find out as much as you can about your listeners before you prepare the speech. If your audience is composed of the students in your class, you have the advantage of knowing how much background knowledge you can assume and what their intellectual interests are. What does the audience already think about your topic? What contribution do you most want to make? Do you want to intensify your audience's commitment to what they already think, provide new and clarifying information, provoke more analysis and understanding of the issue, or change what the audience believes about something?

If you are addressing an unfamiliar audience, ask the people who invited you to speak to fill you in on the audience's interests and expectations. It is usually helpful to have a friend listen to your speech from the point of view of your audience. Ask that friend to stop you every time a term, explanation, or example is unclear. It is also possible to adjust your speech once you get in front of your audience, making your language more or less technical, for instance, or adding more examples to illustrate points.

2. Working within the allotted time

When you are narrowing your topic (*see Chapter 2: Understanding Writing Assignments, p. 25*), keep in mind how much time you will have for your presentation. Try gauging how many words you speak a minute by reading a passage aloud at a conversational pace (about 120–150 words a minute is ideal). Be sure to time your presentation when you practice it, but keep in mind that most people speak more quickly when they are nervous.

13b Draft your presentation with the rhetorical situation in mind.

1. Making your opening interesting

Professional speakers stress the importance of a strong opening—both to put the speaker at ease and to gain the audience's attention and confidence. Some suggest that you try out several approaches to your introduction during rehearsal, to see which gets the best reactions from friends. Stories, based on your own experience or drawn from your research, often make for an interesting beginning. Brief quotations, striking statistics, and surprising statements are also attention getters. If one of these devices is not appropriate to your subject, craft an introduction that lets your listeners know what they have to gain from your presentation—for example, new information or new perspectives on a subject of common interest.

www.mhhe.com/
nmhh
For more on crafting introductions, go to

Writing >
Paragraph/Essay
Development >
Introductions

2. Making the focus and organization of your presentation explicit

Just as signs on the highway tell travelers where to go, signs in your presentation set the direction for your audience. Select two or three ideas that you most want your audience to hear—and to remember. Make these ideas the focus of your presentation, and let your audience know what to expect. Preview the content of your presentation, "I intend to make three points about fraternities on campus," and then list the three points.

The phrase "to make three points" in the preceding example signals a topical organization. Of course, there are other common patterns, including chronological organization (*at first, later, in the end*), causal organization (*because of that, then this follows*), and problem-solution organization (*given the situation, then this set of proposals*). A question-answer format also works well, either as an overall strategy or as part of another organizational pattern.

3. Concluding memorably

Your final comments will be the part of your speech that most audience members remember. Try to make your ending truly memorable:

return to that surprising opener, play with the words of your opening quotation, look at the initial image from another angle, or reflect on the story you have told. Make sure your listeners are aware that you are about to end your presentation, using such signal phrases as "in conclusion" or "let me end by saying" if necessary. Keep your conclusion short to maintain the audience's attention.

4. Being direct

What your audience hears and remembers has as much to do with how you say your message as it does with what you say. For clarity, use a direct, simple style.

- Choose basic sentence structures.
- Repeat key terms.
- Pay attention to the rhythm of your speech.
- Don't be afraid to use the pronouns *I, you,* and *we.*

Notice how applying these principles transforms the following written sentence into a group of sentences appropriate for oral presentation:

WRITTEN

Although the claim that writing increases student learning has yet to be substantiated by either an ample body or an exemplary piece of empirical research, advocates of writing across the curriculum persist in pressing the claim.

ORAL

The more students write, the more they learn. So say advocates of writing across the curriculum. But what evidence do we have that writing improves learning? Do we have lots of empirical research or even one really good study? The answer is, "Not yet."

www.mhhe.com/
nmhh
For an interactive
tutorial on using
PowerPoint, go to
Writing >
PowerPoint
Tutorial

5. Using visual aids

One way to make your focus explicit is with visual aids. A computer projection of the points from your outline encourages your audience to make a few notes and discourages you from simply reading from a script. Consider using slides, posters, objects, video clips, and music to emphasize your message.

Presentation software such as PowerPoint can help you stay focused while you are speaking. The twelve PowerPoint slides in Figure 13.1 on pages 252–53 offer advice on how to design effective slides for a presentation. (*For more on using presentation software to incorporate multimedia elements into a presentation, see Chapter 14: Multimedia Writing, pp. 261–65.*)

13c Prepare for your presentation.

1. Deciding whether to use notes or a written script

To be an effective speaker, you need to make eye contact with your listeners to monitor their responses and adjust what you have to say accordingly. A written script can be a barrier between you and your audience. You can relate better to your audience if you speak from an outline. Write out only those parts of your presentation where precise wording counts, such as quotations.

For most occasions, it is inappropriate to write out everything you want to say and then read it word for word. In some scholarly or formal settings, however, precise wording may be necessary, especially if your oral presentation is to be published or if your remarks will be quoted by others, including media representatives. Sometimes the setting for your presentation may be so formal or the audience may be so large that a script feels necessary. In such instances, do the following:

- Triple-space the typescript of your text.
- Avoid carrying sentences over from one page to another.
- Mark your manuscript for pauses, emphasis, and the pronunciation of proper names.

2. Rehearsing, revising, and polishing

Whether you are using an outline or a script, you will need to practice saying your presentation aloud. As you say your speech aloud, you will find transitions that don't quite work, points that need further development, and sections that go on too long. The rehearsal stage is a time to revise the content of your speech.

After you have settled on the content of your speech and can say it comfortably, focus on polishing the style of your delivery. Ask your friends or use a mirror to check that your body posture is straight but relaxed, that your voice is loud and clear, and that you are making eye contact around the room. Time your final rehearsals, adding or cutting as necessary. If you will be speaking in an unfamiliar space, try to practice there before your audience arrives. If an on-site rehearsal is not possible, at least be sure to arrive at your presentation well in advance.

3. Accepting nervousness as normal

Many people dread giving oral presentations and worry that their stage fright will sabotage their delivery. Key to dealing with stage fright is recognizing that the adrenaline surge you feel before a presentation can invest your talk with positive energy and knowing that

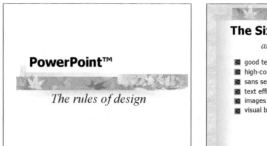

PowerPoint™

The rules of design

The Six Rules of Design
are a matter of using ...

- ☒ good templates
- ☒ high-contrast colors
- ☒ sans serif fonts
- ☒ text efficiently
- ☒ images wisely
- ☒ visual balance to arrange slide elements

1 Choose the right template.

- You can also make your own template.
  - Begin with a blank presentation.
  - Place objects, shapes, etc. on **slide master.**
  - Change fonts, colors, other elements as needed.

Click to edit Master title style
- Click to edit Master text styles
  - Second level
    - Third level
      - Fourth level
        - Fifth level

2 Use high-contrast colors.

- Dark text on a light field
- Light text on a dark field

Alas, poor Yorick!
I knew him, Horatio:
**a fellow of
infinite jest**

Alas, poor Yorick!
I knew him, Horatio:
a fellow of
infinite jest

3 Use *sans* serif fonts.

- Sans serif:
  Tahoma, 24-pt
- Serif:
  Bookman, 24-pt

O for a Muse of fire,
that would ascend
the brightest heaven
of invention;
A kingdom for a stage

O for a Muse of fire,
that would ascend
the brightest heaven
of invention;
A kingdom for a stage

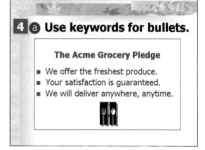

4 ⓐ Use keywords for bullets.

The Acme Grocery Pledge

- We offer the freshest produce.
- Your satisfaction is guaranteed.
- We will deliver anywhere, anytime.

FIGURE 13.1 A sample PowerPoint presentation with advice on designing effective presentation slides.

other people usually cannot tell that you are nervous. Practice and revise your presentation until it flows smoothly, and make sure that you have a strong opener to get you through the first, most difficult moments of a speech. If your phobia is extreme, look for a course on overcoming stage fright.

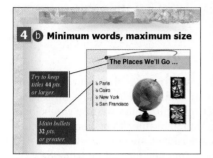

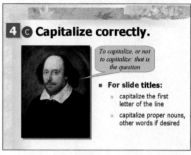

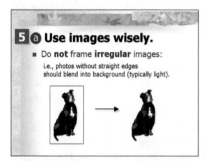

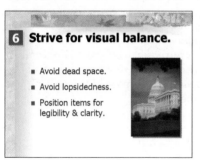

14 Multimedia Writing

Multimedia writing combines words with images, video, or audio into a single composition. The products of multimedia writing can be both dynamic and memorable. To be done well, they require considerable time and effort.

The most common form of multimedia writing—discussed in many chapters of this book—is a combination of words and still visuals such as photographs, maps, charts, or graphs. Another form is an oral presentation with any kind of visual support, from a diagram on a blackboard to a PowerPoint slide show (*see Chapter 13: Oral Presentations*). In addition to these forms, digital technology now makes it possible to combine written words with sound, video, and animation. Of course, you cannot include audio or video on a piece of paper the way you can words and still images. Just as you need a computer to create multimedia presentations with audio and video, you also need a computer or other display technology to deliver or read them.

Although multimedia writing requires technology, it is not *about* technology. Like any writing, it allows you to convey a message to a particular audience for a particular purpose: to inform, to interpret, or to persuade with argument. A video or audio segment—like a photograph, map, or chart—must support the purpose of the writing in a way that is appropriate to the audience.

14a Learn about the tools for creating multimedia texts.

Multimedia writing can take a variety of forms and can be created with a variety of software tools. Here are a few options:

- Most word processors allow you to integrate still visuals with text in a single document, but many also make it possible to write a paper that permits readers, with the click of the mouse, to connect to various files—including audio, image, and video. (*See sections 14b and 14c.*)

- Most presentation software packages similarly allow you to accompany a presentation with audio and video files as well as still visuals. (*See section 14d.*)

TEXTCONNEX

Some Key Concepts in Multimedia Writing

File: A collection of information in computer-readable form. Text files store words, image files store pictures, audio files store sounds, and video files store moving images.

Link: A connection from one file to another, or from one place to another in the same file. You can link to files stored on your own computer or, through the Internet and World Wide Web, to files stored on other computers.

Hypertext: Text with links. (In a sense, the Web is one vast hypertext document with countless paths to a nearly endless variety of files.)

- A variety of programs and Web-based tools allow you to create your own **Web pages** and **Web sites,** which can include a wide range of multimedia features. (*See section 14e.*)
- You can create a **weblog** (**blog** for short), on which, in addition to your written entries, you can post your own multimedia files and links to files on other blogs and Web sites. (*See section 14f.*)

14b Combine text and images with a word-processing program to analyze images.

Texts that combine words and images are, as already noted, the most common form of multimedia writing. Two types of papers you might be called on to write are image interpretations and photographic stories.

1. Composing image interpretations

You may be called on to analyze a single image along the lines described in Chapter 7: Reading, Thinking, Writing. Such a paper might combine an image—say, a reproduction of a painting from a museum—with the writer's interpretation of the image. The writer of such an **image interpretation** has two tasks. The first is to describe the picture as fully as possible, using adjectives, comparisons, and words that help the reader look at the picture. The second is to analyze the *argument* the picture seems to be making.

Exercise 14.1   Image interpretations

1. In a local museum or on a museum Web site, find a painting created by an artist whose work is new to you. (Some examples of
museum Web sites include http://www.moma.org/collection/ for
the Museum of Modern Art, http://www.artic.edu/aic/ for the Art
Institute of Chicago, and http://www.louvre.fr/louvrea.htm for the
Louvre in Paris, France.)

    Take notes on your response to the painting, and write an ini-
tial analysis of it. As you do, consider the following:

    ▪ Who or what is in the painting?

    ▪ If there are people in the painting, are they active or passive?
    Rich or poor? Old or young?

    ▪ Are the people central to the painting, or are they peripheral?
    If peripheral, what is the painting's central focus?

    ▪ How does the artist represent the subjects of the painting—
    in other words, what does the artist's presentation of people,
    objects, buildings, or landscapes say about his or her attitude
    toward them?

    ▪ What in your own experience may be affecting your response?
    What personal associations do you feel with the subject of the
    painting? How might your own position—for example, as a stu-
    dent, daughter or son, member of a political party—influence
    the way you interpret the painting?

    Now read a short biography of the artist in a book or on the Web,
and add that information to your analysis. Point out whether and
how the biographical information either reinforces your interpretation or leads you to alter it.

2. Find an image in a current newspaper or magazine. First outline two possible arguments that the picture might be making.
Then decide which is the more likely of the two arguments, and
explain why.

---

2. Telling photographic stories

In another basic paper that combines words and images—a photographic story—the writer tries to imagine the story behind an evocative photograph. Often as we look at a photograph, we automatically
create a story about it. That story is as much an expression of ourselves as it is a statement about the photograph. In other words, the
story we read into a photograph is as heavily influenced by the context
we bring to it as by the photographer's intent.

During the Great Depression of the 1930s, for example, the photographer Walker Evans and the writer James Agee traveled to Alabama to take pictures of poor farmers and sharecroppers. These pictures—such as the one in Figure 14.1—invite storytelling. One story this picture might tell is of a hard-pressed farmer worried about his family and his unpayable debts. Or you might see this one farmer as

FIGURE 14.1 **A Walker Evans photograph.**

a symbol of all the hardship brought on by the Depression. Remove him from his Depression-era context, however, and you might see a father suspiciously eyeing the young man bringing his daughter home late from her first date. Is there anything in particular that ties this farmer to a specific time and place? What makes you think so?

Exercise 14.2 Photographic stories

1. Find one photograph in a magazine or book from at least fifty years ago. For the photograph, create two short, specific stories and one more general story. Explain the "logic" of each story using evidence from the photograph. As you look for stories, ask yourself these questions:

   ■ Who or what is in the photograph?

   ■ How is the photograph composed? What first draws your attention?

   ■ If you think of the photograph as having a center, where would it be, and what would be in it?

   ■ If you think of the photograph as being divided into quadrants, what is in each one?

   ■ What emotional reaction do you have to the photograph?

   ■ If the photograph is in color, how is color used? What does the use of color contribute to the photograph, both in terms of depicting people and objects and in terms of evoking a mood? If the photograph is in black and white, what effect does that have on you?

   ■ What details in the picture evoke a mood?

   ■ What is left out of the photograph and why? Can you imagine other items or people who, if included, would help tell a different story?

   ■ Is the photograph about a short, specific story, a longer story, or both kinds of stories?

   ■ How might your own position—for example, as a student, daughter or son, member of a political party—influence your view of the photo?

2. Take several photographs that allow for rich interpretations. Choose two of the photos and interpret them. Bring them to

class, and ask two classmates to provide you with a story for each. Do their stories match yours? Do their stories seem more interesting than yours? Why or why not?

14c Use a word-processing program to create a hypertext essay.

Most word processors allow writers to create multimedia **hypertext essays** by inserting **links** in a document that take the reader to other **files,** including text, image, audio, and video files (*see the TextConnex box on p. 255*). Links can take several forms:

- **Internal links** connect from one place to another in the same document, or to other files stored on the writer's computer.

- **External links** connect to Web sites on the Internet and any text, image, audio, or video files stored on them.

This ability to link to multimedia files provides writers with a new kind of evidence to use in their work. As with any evidence, however, it must be relevant to the audience and purpose of the essay. It can either complement the essay's verbal claims or, like a good chart or graph, support the claims directly. For example, in a political science project on inaugural addresses, you might include links to video files of several presidents delivering their inaugural addresses. These links might simply complement your thesis, or they might provide direct evidence for an important point about, say, a particular president's style of delivery. However, unless your assignment includes specific directions to emphasize linked material as evidence, you should probably think of it as supplemental to your written claims.

If you have never created a hypertext essay, start small, with a limited set of links that all clearly serve your audience and purpose. Here are some suggestions:

- Create an internal link from a work you cite in your essay to the full information about the work on your works-cited page.

- Create an internal link to other papers you have written that are related to your current topic.

- Create an internal link to material you collected while working on the essay that is related only indirectly to the essay's point and that would diminish the essay's coherence if included.

- Create an internal link to a file in which you raise additional questions you might want to pursue in another essay or in which you talk back to your own essay.

- Create an external link taking readers to works on the topic written by your classmates.
- Create an external link taking readers to background material on the Web.

Caution: When you revise your hypertext essay, be sure to check all links to make sure they are relevant and function correctly. Also, if your essay includes internal links to files on your computer, be sure to include those files with the essay file when you submit it to your instructor.

Tips

LEARNING in COLLEGE

Using Hypertext as a Writing Process Tool

Some students insert a variety of links in their essays to help them during the writing process. For example, they might include a link to additional research, to a source that refutes an argument, or to interesting information that is not directly relevant to the primary subject. These links can help writers refer to supplemental material without undermining the coherence of their text. If a reader of an early draft—an instructor or a colleague—thinks the linked material should be in the essay itself, the writer can include it in the next draft.

Exercise 14.3 Hypertext essays

1. Have fun! Construct a hypertext essay in which you use links to create puns or jokes. In other words, compose the text; then insert links that let you talk back to your own points, as well as link to puns, jokes, and visuals on the Web.

2. Create a hypertext essay in which you use five links to connect your piece with some personal experience relevant to it or to connect it with relevant information about another assignment you are working on. For example, if you are writing about changes in agricultural societies, you might include links to your own experience with agriculture, from growing up on a farm to buying groceries in a store. You might also link to material you are studying in an economics class or an ancient history class.

14d Use presentation software to create multimedia presentations.

www.mhhe.com/
nmhh
For an interactive
tutorial on using
PowerPoint, go to

Writing >
PowerPoint
Tutorial

Originally intended as an electronic replacement for the traditional kinds of visual aids that speakers have used to accompany their oral presentations, **presentation software** makes it possible to incorporate audio, video, and animation into a talk as well. Presentation software can also be used to create multimedia compositions that viewers can go through on their own.

1. Using presentation software for an oral presentation

Presentation slides that accompany a talk should accomplish two tasks:

1. Identify major points
2. Display information in a visually effective way

As you prepare your slides, remember that they support your talk, they do not replace it. The quickest way to lose your audience is to read to them slides they can read themselves. In general, limit the amount of information on each slide, and plan to show each slide for about one minute.

For a talk in a science course you might want to include only a single image and a set of key terms on each slide. For a talk about the writers Langston Hughes and Ralph Ellison you might use a slide like

Tips LEARNING in COLLEGE

Using Presentation Software as a Writing Process Tool

Many students have discovered that presentation-software slides provide a useful tool for exploring and organizing their ideas before they start drafting. The slides also give you another way to get feedback from peer reviewers and others. Here are the steps to follow:

- Well before a paper is due, create a very brief, three- to five-slide presentation—with visuals if appropriate—that previews the key points you intend to make in the paper.
- Present the preview to an audience—friends, other students in the class, perhaps even the course instructor—and ask for reactions and suggestions for improvement.

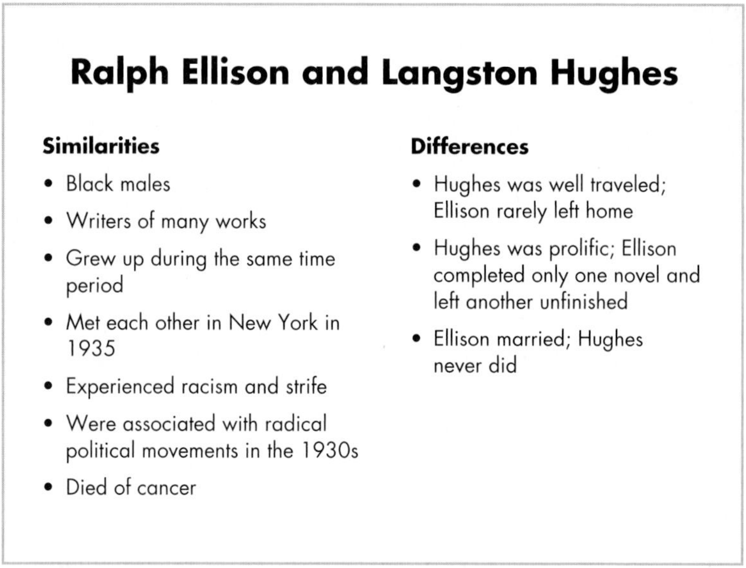

Ralph Ellison and Langston Hughes

Similarities

- Black males
- Writers of many works
- Grew up during the same time period
- Met each other in New York in 1935
- Experienced racism and strife
- Were associated with radical political movements in the 1930s
- Died of cancer

Differences

- Hughes was well traveled; Ellison rarely left home
- Hughes was prolific; Ellison completed only one novel and left another unfinished
- Ellison married; Hughes never did

FIGURE 14.2 **A slide for a presentation on Ralph Ellison and Langston Hughes.**

the one in Figure 14.2 briefly to summarize their similarities and differences. Notice also that the creator of this presentation chose a stark, black-and-white format for the slide, which hints symbolically at the themes of race and racism that preoccupied both authors.

(For more on preparing and presenting oral presentations, see Chapter 13: Oral Presentations, pp. 248–53.)

2. Using presentation software to create an independent composition

With presentation software, you can also create compositions that run on their own or at the prompting of the viewer. This capability is especially useful in distance learning settings, in which students attend class and share information electronically. For example, a student might deliver a presentation to the class in the form of an independent composition. The text of the presentation might appear on slides, or the student might record portions of it, such as the introduction, and incorporate them as audio files.

3. Preparing a slide presentation

Whether you are preparing slides for an oral presentation or an independent composition, the following guidelines apply.

Decide on a slide format   You should begin thinking about slides while you plan what you are going to say. The two processes work together: as you decide on the words for your talk or independent composition, you will think of visuals that support your points, and as you work out the visuals, you are likely to see additional points you can make—and adjust your presentation as a result.

Before you create your slides, you need to establish their basic appearance. What background color will they have? What typeface or typefaces? What design elements, such as borders and rules? You can use the templates provided by the software, although they may force you into a kind of organization that does not fit your talk or that may be overly familiar to your audience. A better approach might be to begin with a template and modify it to suit your needs. Keep in mind that the format you establish will be the canvas for all your slides—it needs to complement, not distract from, the images and text you intend to display.

Incorporate images into your presentation   Because presentation slides are a visual medium, you will want to include images when appropriate. To summarize quantitative information, you might use a chart or graph. To show geographical relationships, you would likely use a map. You can also add photographs that illustrate your points or help your audience follow your discussion. In all cases, use only images that support your purpose.

www.mhhe.com/
nmhh
For more on designing
documents, go to

Writing >
Writing Web
Links > Document
and Web Design

Incorporate audio, video, and animation   Slides can also include audio files. This means that you can, for example, record a narrative accompaniment or background information for each slide in an independent composition, or for a presentation on music you can insert audio files to show how a type of music has developed over time.

Slides can also include video files and animated drawings and diagrams. A video clip of the collapse of the Tacoma Narrows Bridge in violently high winds on November 7, 1940, for example (*see Figure 14.3*), might help illustrate a presentation on bridge construction. A presentation on advertising techniques might include examples of televised automobile ads. Similarly, an animated diagram of the process of cell division could help illustrate a presentation on cellular biology, or an animated map of changing population densities over time might accompany an American history presentation. As you would for any other material you did not create yourself, if you are using audio, video, or animation files that belong to others, you need to cite the source.

Incorporate hypertext links   Presentation slides, like hypertext essays, can include both internal and external links. A presenter might use an internal link within a slide sequence to jump to another slide

FIGURE 14.3 The collapse of the Tacoma Narrows Bridge. The dramatic collapse of the bridge was captured on film, and some of the footage is available in video files.

that illustrates or explains a particular point or issue. For instance, for a presentation on insects, you might include a hyperlink to a slide about insects specific to the part of the country in which you live, complete with an image of one of them, as an illustration. Such a local connection might enliven the presentation and help the audience remember important information. You can also create external links to files on the Web. The value of this kind of link is that it allows you to showcase resources for your audience. You should be careful not to rely too much on external links, however, because they can undermine the coherence of a presentation. External links can also take a long time to load.

> *Caution:* If you plan to make external links part of your presentation, make sure that you have a functioning Web browser on your computer and that a fast connection to the Internet is available where you will be giving the presentation.

4. Reviewing a slide presentation

Once you have the text of your presentation in final form and the multimedia elements in place, you should carefully review your slides to make sure they work together coherently.

- Look at the slides in your software's slide sorter window, and see how they move one to the next. Do you have an introductory slide? Do you need to add transitional effects that reveal the content of a slide gradually or point by point? Some transitions permit audio: do you want that? Do you have a concluding slide? Are the slides consistent with the script of the talk you plan to deliver? If the slides are to function as an independent document, do they include enough introduction, an adequate explanation, and a clear conclusion?

- Check the arrangement of your slides. You might try printing them out as paper handouts and spreading them out over a large surface or printing out and cutting apart the thumbnail version of the slides for sorting. You can then rearrange the slides physically, if need be, before implementing your changes on the computer.

- Be sure the slides have a unified look. For example, do all the slides have the same background? Do all use the same typefaces in the same way?

Exercise 14.4 Presentation slides

1. Choose three key terms related to multimedia, and define them in a three- to five-slide presentation for your class. In doing so, use any two of the features of presentation slides discussed in this section, and write a one-page reflection about why you chose those terms and those presentation features.

2. Draft a preview of a paper you are working on in an eight-slide presentation. Share this preview with your colleagues in an eight-minute talk. Then ask them to tell you (a) what they think your main purpose is, (b) what worked well in the presentation, and (c) what you should consider changing when you write the paper.

14e Create a Web site.

Thanks to Web editing software, it is now almost as easy to create a Web site and post it on the Internet as it is to write a paper using word-processing software. Many Web-based businesses like Yahoo!

www.mhhe.com/
nmhh
For more on designing
Web sites, go to

Writing >
Writing Web
Links > Document
and Web Design

provide free server space for hosting sites and offer tools for creating Web pages. Many schools also make server space available for student Web sites.

As is true of the other multimedia texts discussed in this chapter, a Web site, to be effective, must be well designed, and it must serve a well-defined purpose for its audience. In creating a Web site, you need to plan the site, draft its content and select its visuals, and then revise and edit as you would for any other composition. (*See Chapters 3–5 in Part 1: Writing and Designing Papers, for more on these stages.*) When you create a Web site, however, the composing process involves decisions and requirements that are unique to this medium. The following sections offer guidelines for making some of these decisions.

1. Planning a structure for your site

Like most paper documents, a Web site can have a linear structure, where one page leads to the next, and so on. Because of the hyperlinked nature of this medium, however, a site can also be organized in a hierarchy or with a number of pages that connect to a central page, or hub, like the spokes of a wheel. The diagrams in Figure 14.4, one showing the structure of a Web site about a county's historic buildings and the other the structure of a site for caregivers, illustrate these two possible structures.

To choose the structure that will work best for your site, consider how you expect visitors to use it. Visitors intrigued by the topic of Tyler County's historic buildings will probably want to explore, following different paths of interest to see where they lead. Visitors to a caregiver resources site will probably be looking for specific information. The structure of a site should accommodate its users' needs.

2. Gathering content for your site

The content for a Web site usually consists of written work along with links and graphics. Depending on your topic and purpose, you might also provide audio files, video files, and even animations.

As with any writing you do, your writing for a Web site should be clear, well developed, and free of errors. However, there are some special requirements for written content that appears on a Web site:

- Usually readers neither expect nor want lengthy text explanations on the home page. Instead, they want to find the link or button they are looking for within a few seconds.

- In general, readers prefer short paragraphs, and the text for each topic or point should fit on one page if possible. Avoid long passages that require readers to use the scroll bar.

Hierarchical Structure

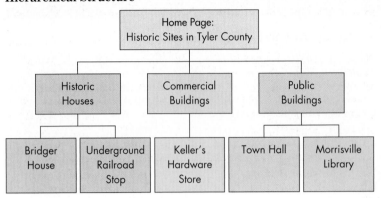

Hub Structure

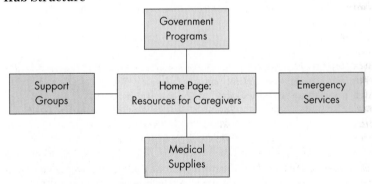

FIGURE 14.4 **Hub and hierarchical structures compared.**

- Use links to connect your interests with those of others and to provide extra sources of information. Avoid using the command "Click Here" on your Web site. Instead, make links part of your text. As with any evidence that you use in your writing, your links should lead readers to content that is relevant to your point and credible.

As you prepare your written text, you should also gather any graphics, photographs, and audio and video files that you plan to include. Some sites, such as http://gallery.yahoo.com, allow you to download images; and some images, including many of the historical photographs available through the Library of Congress, are in the public domain. Be sure to give proper credit for any material that you do not generate yourself and, if necessary, request permission for its use.

TEXTCONNEX

Understanding Web Jargon

Browser: Software that allows you to view material on the World Wide Web. When you identify a site you want to see on the Web by typing in a URL (*see below*), your browser (Netscape Navigator or Microsoft Internet Explorer, for example) tells a distant computer (a **server**) to send that site to you.

JPEG and **GIF:** Formats for photographs and other visuals that are recognized by browsers. Photographs that appear on a Web site should be saved in JPEG (pronounced "*jay-peg*") format, which stands for Joint Photographic Experts Group. The file extension is .jpg or .jpeg. Clip art should be saved as GIF files (Graphics Interchange Format, pronounced like *gift* without the *t*.)

Home page: The opening page of a Web site. A home page typically includes general information about the site as well as links to various parts of it.

HTML/XML: Hypertext markup language/extensible markup language. These languages tag or code text so that your browser can rebuild a document from the compressed files that travel through the Internet. When your browser retrieves a page, you end up with an "original copy" of the document, usually in a matter of seconds. It is no longer necessary to learn HTML or XML to publish on the Web. Programs such as FrontPage, PageMill, Dreamweaver, and Netscape Composer now provide a **WYSIWYG** (what you see is what you get) interface for creating Web pages.

Protocol: A set of rules controlling data exchange between computers. **HTTP** (hypertext transfer protocol) is a way of breaking down and then reconstructing a document when it is sent over the Internet.

URL: Uniform resource locator or Web address. When you type or paste a URL into your Web browser, you are sending a request through your browser to another computer, asking it to transfer data to your computer.

3. Designing Web pages to capture and hold interest

Whatever leads them to a Web page, visitors to a site usually decide in ten to twenty seconds whether to stay. An inviting or interesting photograph or other visual can often grab even a casual Web surfer's

FIGURE 14.5 The home page of the National Museum of the American Indian.

attention. On good Web sites, you will also find such easy-to-follow links as "what you'll find here," FAQs (frequently asked questions), or "list of those involved." Notice how easy it is for readers to find what they need on the home page of the National Museum of the American Indian (*see Figure 14.5*).

4. Designing a readable site with a unified look

As you gather your material, you also need to think about the overall design for your site. Because the Web is a visual medium, readers appreciate a site with a unified look. "Sets" or "themes" are readily available at free graphics sites offering banners, navigation buttons, and other design elements. Design your home page to complement your other pages, or your readers may lose track of where they are in the site—as well as their interest in staying.

- Consider including a site map, a Web page that serves as a table of contents for your entire site.

- Select elements such as buttons, signs, animations, sounds, and backgrounds with a consistent design.

- Use colors that provide adequate contrast, white space, and sans serif fonts that make text easy to read. Pages that are too busy are not visually compelling. (*For more on design, see Chapter 6: Designing Academic Papers and Preparing Port-folios, pp. 125–33.*)

- Limit the width of your text; readers find wide lines of text difficult to process.

The two Web pages shown in Figure 14.6 illustrate some of these design considerations.

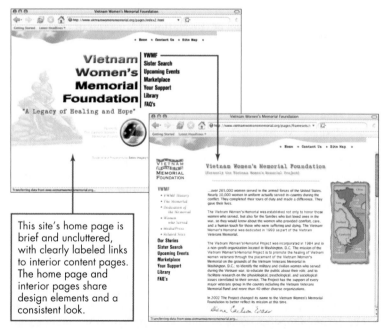

FIGURE 14.6 The home page and an interior page from the Web site of the Vietnam Women's Memorial Foundation.

Web Resources for Site Design and Construction

- *www.teach.science's Surf and Master the Web: Writing Web Pages*
  <http://www2.ncsu.edu/ncsu/pams/science_house/workshops/web/writing.html>
- *Web Guide: Designing a Web Page*
  <http://people.depauw.edu/djp/webguide/designwebpage.html>
- *Designing Accessible Web Pages*—information about creating Web pages for people with disabilities
  <http://nadc.ucla.edu/dawpi.htm>

5. Designing a Web site that is easy to access and navigate

Because most Web sites are not linear, writers need to take special care to help readers find their way to the areas of the site that they want to visit. Writers also need to make it easy for readers to take interesting side trips if they would like to without wasting their time or losing their way.

- **Identify your Web site on each page, and provide a link to the home page.** Remember that people will not always enter your Web site through the home page. Therefore, you should usually give the title of the site on each page. Provide an easy-to-spot link to your home page as well.
- **Provide a navigation bar on each page.** A navigation **bar** can be a simple line of links that you copy and paste at the top or bottom of each page. A navigation bar on each page makes it easy for visitors to move from the site's home page to other pages and back again. For example, on the Web page from University of Alaska Anchorage shown in Figure 14.7, visitors can choose from five links in the navigation bar under the title.
- **Use graphics that load quickly.** Be considerate of viewers who have older computers that cannot handle huge graphics files. Limit the size of your images to no more than 40 kilobytes, so that they will load quickly.
- **Use graphics judiciously.** Even though a picture may be worth a thousand words, your Web site should not depend on graphics alone to make its message clear and interesting. Graphics should be used to reinforce your message. For

This navigation bar appears on every page of the Web site for the University of Alaska Anchorage.

FIGURE 14.7 A page from the Web site of the University of Alaska Anchorage.

example, the designers of the Library of Congress Web site (*see Figure 14.8*) use graphics to help visitors navigate the site.

■ **Be aware of the needs of visitors with disabilities.** Bear in mind that visitors to your site may have impaired vision or hearing. Provide alternate ways of accessing visual or auditory information such as audio descriptions of visual texts and transcriptions of audio files.

6. Using peer feedback to revise your Web site

Before publishing your site on the Web, proofread your text carefully, and ask a couple of friends to look at your site and share their responses with you. When you publish on the Web, you offer your work to be read by anyone in the world. Make sure your site reflects favorably on your abilities.

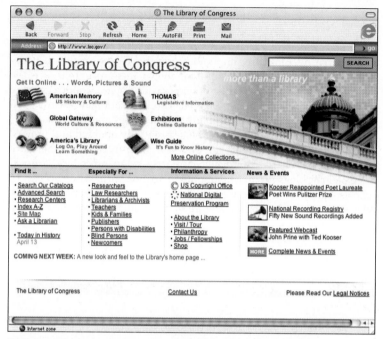

FIGURE 14.8 The home page of the Web site of the Library of Congress.

For MULTILINGUAL STUDENTS

Designing a Web Site Collaboratively

If you are asked to create a Web site as part of a class assignment, try to arrange to work with a partner or a small group. The kind of interaction involved in writing the content and designing the site will provide you with beneficial language support. Periodically, you can invite peers to check over the writing you contribute and make suggestions. At the same time, you will be able to provide the project with the benefit of your multicultural viewpoint.

Exercise 14.5 | Web page creation

Take the two hypertext essays you created for Exercise 14.3. Use Web editing software to add visual elements and convert them into Web pages.

14f Create and interact with weblogs.

Weblogs—called **blogs** for short—provide another opportunity for multimedia writing. Blogs are simply Web sites that can be continuously updated. Some blogs, such as the one shown in Figure 14.9, are the exclusive creations of one writer; others provide a space where a group of writers can share ideas and discuss each other's work and research. You can include images in a blog and link to other blogs and Web pages.

Unlike standard Web pages, blogs are easily updated and provide a format for compiling material and searching it. Because there are several free servers for creating blogs, and the set-up procedures are outlined clearly, blogs are also available to anyone with online access. In schools, classes have used blogs to discuss issues, organize work, compile portfolios, and gather and store material and commentary.

FIGURE 14.9 A personal blog. Musician Scott August's blog, hosted on blogger.com, contains posts about his music and travels.

In general, blogs are developing more as vehicles for public discussion and commentary than as private online journals. Several bloggers, for example, played a prominent role in reporting on the 2004 presidential campaign. Others covered the tsunami disaster later in the same year. To begin blogging, you need to set up a blog site with a server such as www.blogger.com. You may at first want to confine yourself to a very specific purpose before launching into wide-ranging commentary. When you begin your blog, consider these questions:

- What is your purpose?
- To whom will you give access? Should the blog be public for all to see? Should it instead be limited by password protection to a specific group of viewers?
- Do you want to allow others to post on your blog, or is it only for you?
- Do you want to set up a schedule of postings or a series of events that will cue you to post?
- Do you know others with blogs? Do you want to link to their sites?

Caution: Remember that all blogs are more or less public, depending on how much access they allow. Do not post anything you would not want everybody to know about.

Exercise 14.6 Weblogs

1. Examine a variety of blogs, and identify their purpose and audience. Do you find enough consistency among the blogs to conclude that bloggers form a distinct world, or community?
2. Create your own blog with three of your class colleagues, and use it as a peer-review forum for your next paper assignment. How does this kind of peer review compare with a face-to-face review?

Interplanetary probes help astronomers research the far reaches of the solar system. Voyager 2 sent this image of Saturn's rings to Earth.

PART

3

For all knowledge and wonder (which is the seed of knowledge) is an impression of pleasure in itself.

—FRANCIS BACON

Researching

15 Understanding Research

You do research all the time. When you shop for a car, you talk with friends about their cars, read *Consumer Reports,* interview car dealers, and take a number of test drives. When your doctor says that you have a particular medical condition, you find out as much as possible about the condition and the conventional and latest treatments for it.

Your campus or neighborhood library provides valuable resources for almost any kind of research. These include not just books, magazines, and journals but access to specialized online databases and the expert guidance of a research librarian.

Doing research in the twenty-first century is hardly limited to the library. The Internet now provides direct access in seconds to an abundance of information unimaginable to earlier generations of students. This ease of access, however, can be treacherous. The results of Internet searches can sometimes provide an overwhelming flood of sources, many of them of questionable legitimacy.

The goal of Part 3 of this book is to help you learn about the research process. Chapters 15–23 provide tips for skillfully navigating today's research landscape, managing the information you discover within it, and using that information to write research papers.

15a Understand the purpose of primary and secondary research.

Academic inquiry calls for both primary and secondary research. **Primary research** involves working in a laboratory, in the field, or with an archive of raw data, original documents, or authentic artifacts to make firsthand discoveries. **Secondary research** involves looking to see what other people have learned and written about a field or topic.

College faculty in all fields are researchers. They may search out existing information about a particular subject in their specialty, which involves secondary research, or they may seek to create new knowledge about that topic, which often requires primary research. When they report on primary research, faculty usually *contextualize* their findings by comparing them with what is already known about their subject, a process that requires secondary research.

As you begin exploring a field of study, you will be engaging mostly in secondary research. As you move deeper into the field, you will probably spend more time conducting primary research. Depending on the academic discipline, your research writing as a student might require primary research, secondary research, or some combination of the two. For example, a research project for an education course might ask you to observe and document the behavior of children in a classroom, and then to analyze your findings based on the work of child development specialists.

Knowing how to identify facts, interpretations, and evaluations is key to good secondary research:

- **Facts** are objective. Like your body weight, facts can be measured, observed, or independently verified in some way.

- **Interpretations** spell out the implications of facts. Are you as thin as you are because of your genes—or because you exercise every day? The answer to this question is an interpretation.

- **Evaluations** are debatable judgments about a set of facts or a situation. Attributing a person's thinness to genes is an interpretation, but the assertion that "one can never be too rich or too thin" is an evaluation.

Once you are up-to-date on the facts, interpretations, and evaluations in a particular area, you will be able to design a research project that adds to this knowledge. Usually, what you will add is your *perspective* on the sources you found and read:

- Given all that you have learned about the topic, what strikes you as important or interesting?

- What patterns do you see, or what connections can you make between one person's work and another's?

- Where is the research going, and what problems still need to be explored?

15b Recognize the connection between research and college writing.

In one way or another, research informs all college writing. To get material for a personal essay, you have to search through your memory; reflect on events that have happened to you; and select a person, event, place, or other topic to write about. When you write essay exams, you rely on what you have read in college textbooks and learned from lectures.

CHARTING the TERRITORY

Classic and Current Sources

Classic sources are well-known and respected older works that have made such an important contribution to a discipline or a particular area of research that contemporary researchers use them as touchstones for further research in that area. Current research is up to date but has not yet met the test of time. In many fields, sources published within the past five years are considered current.

Many disciplines also have key reference texts—discipline-specific encyclopedias and dictionaries, for example. These are not usually considered classic sources themselves, but they can direct you to classic sources. Many departments require majors to take a course in the history of the discipline that introduces students to its classic sources.

But some assignments require more rigorous and systematic research than others. These **research project** assignments offer you a chance to go beyond your course texts—to find and read both classic and current material on a specific issue.

A paper based on research is not just a step-by-step account of your "search-and-find" mission. It is not a string of quotations from other writers or a set of summaries of your sources. A research paper constitutes your contribution to the ongoing conversation about a specific issue.

When you are assigned to write a research paper for any of your college courses, the project may seem overwhelming at first. If you break the project into phases, however, and allow enough time for each phase, you should be able to manage your work and write a paper that contributes to the academic conversation.

www.mhhe.com/
nmhh
For more on
narrowing your
topic, go to

Writing >
Paragraph/Essay
Development >
Thesis/Central
Idea

15c   Choose an interesting research question for critical inquiry.

Approach your assignment in a spirit of critical inquiry. *Critical* in this sense does not mean "skeptical," "cynical," or even "urgent." Rather it refers to a receptive but reasonable and discerning frame of mind. Choosing a topic that interests you will help make the results of your inquiry meaningful to you and your readers.

1. Choosing a question with personal significance

Even though you are writing for a college assignment, you can still get personally involved in your work. Begin with the wording of the assignment, analyzing the project's required scope, purpose, and audience (*see Chapter 2: Understanding Writing Assignments, pp. 21–23*). Then browse through the course texts and your class notes, looking for a match between your interests and topics, issues, or problems in the subject area.

For example, suppose you have been assigned to write a seven- to ten-page report on some country's global economic prospects, for a business course. If you have recently visited Mexico, you might find it interesting to explore that country's prospects.

2. Making your question specific

The more specific your question, the more your research will have direction and focus. To make a question more specific, use the "five *w*'s and an *h*" strategy by asking about the *who, what, why, when, where,* and *how* of a topic (*see Chapter 3: Planning and Shaping the Whole Essay, pp. 39–41*).

After you have compiled a list of possible research questions, choose one that is relatively specific, or rewrite a broad one to make it more specific and therefore answerable. For example, as Audrey Galeano worked to develop a topic for a research paper on the impact

---

CHARTING the TERRITORY

Typical Lines of Inquiry in Different Disciplines

Research topics and questions—even when related to a single broad issue—differ from one discipline to another. The following examples show the distinctions:

History: How did India's experience of British imperialism affect its response to globalization?

Marketing: How do corporations develop strategies for marketing their products to an international consumer audience?

Political Science: Why did many nations of Europe agree to unite, creating a common currency and an essentially "borderless" state called the European Union, or E.U.?

Anthropology: What is the impact of globalization on the world's indigenous cultures?

of globalization for an anthropology course, she rewrote the following broad question to make it answerable:

TOO BROAD	How has globalization affected the Amazon River Basin?
ANSWERABLE	How has large-scale agriculture in the Amazon Basin affected the region's indigenous peoples?

(*Galeano's finished paper appears at the end of Chapter 25: APA Documentation Style, pp. 455–65.*)

One quick strategy for moving from an overly broad question to an answerable question is to rephrase the broad question as a statement, then add the word *because* or *by* at the end, and fill in the blank with possible answers. For example, if your broad question is "How has globalization affected the Amazon Basin?" restate it as "Globalization has affected the Amazon Basin by _____" and fill in the blank with a few precise reasons that will guide you toward a more specific topic. Here are some examples Audrey Galeano considered:

> *Globalization has affected the Amazon Basin* by _____
>
> . . . overwhelming traditional forms of music, dress, and expression with global pop culture.
>
> . . . introducing large-scale mechanized agriculture to grow food for export, which displaces the region's indigenous people.
>
> . . . encouraging the construction of roads that make the region more accessible.

3. Finding a challenging question

If it is to interest you and your readers, a research question must be challenging. If a question can be answered with a simple yes or no, a dictionary-like definition, or a textbook presentation of information, you should choose another question or rework the simple one to make it more challenging.

NOT CHALLENGING	Has economic globalization contributed to the destruction of the Amazon rain forest?
CHALLENGING	How can agricultural interests and indigenous peoples in the Amazon region work together to preserve the environment while creating a sustainable economy?

4. Speculating about answers

Sometimes it can be useful to speculate on the answer to your research
question so that you have a **hypothesis** to work with during the

research process. Do not forget, however, that a hypothesis is a tentative answer that must be tested and revised against the evidence you turn up in your research. Be aware of the assumptions embedded in your hypothesis or research question. Do not assume your hypothesis is true and blind yourself to other possible answers. Consider, for example, the following hypothesis:

HYPOTHESIS   The global market for agricultural products will destroy the Amazon rain forest.

This hypothesis assumes that destructive farming practices are the only possible response in the Amazon to global demand. But assumptions are always open to question. Researchers must be willing to adjust their ideas as they learn more about a topic.

Exercise 15.1   Answerable, challenging questions

For each of the following broad topics, create at least three answerable, challenging questions.

1. Internet access is becoming as important as literacy in determining the livelihood of a nation's people.
2. Genetically modified organisms (GMOs) and biotechnology are controversial approaches to addressing the world's food problems.
3. The problem of terrorism requires a multilateral solution.

15d   Understand the research assignment.

Once you have chosen a topic and a tentative research question, spend some time considering your audience and your purpose. Although your *audience* will most likely include only your instructor and perhaps your fellow students, thinking critically about their needs and expectations will help you plan a research strategy and create a schedule for writing your paper.

Your *purpose* for writing a research paper depends both on the specifics of the assignment as set by your instructor and your own engagement with, and interest in, your topic. Your purpose might be *informative*—to educate your audience about an unfamiliar subject or point of view (*see Chapter 8: Informative Reports, p. 161*). Your purpose might be *interpretive*—to reveal the meaning or significance of a work of art, a historic document, or a scientific study (*see Chapter 9: Interpretive Analyses, p. 183*). Your purpose might instead be *persuasive*—that is, to convince your audience, with logic and evidence, to accept your point of view on a contentious issue or to act on the information in your paper (*see Chapter 10: Arguments, p. 210*).   **283**

Audience in Research Writing

Ask yourself the following questions about your audience. If your instructor approves, use your imagination to think about alternative audiences for your research—for example, a local school board for a paper about an education issue, the members of a state legislature for a paper about an environmental issue, or the readers of a newspaper's editorial page for a paper on a political issue.

- What does my audience already know about my topic? How much background information and context will I need to provide? (Your research should include *facts.*)

- Is my topic controversial or challenging? How should I accommodate and acknowledge different perspectives and viewpoints? (Your research should include *interpretations,* and you will need to be careful to balance interpretations that might be opposed to each other.)

- Do I expect my audience to take action based on the results of my research? (Your research should include *evaluations,* carefully supported by facts and interpretations, that demonstrate clearly to your audience why they should adopt a particular course of action or point of view.)

www.mhhe.com/
nmhh
For resources to start
your research, go to

Research >
Discipline Specific
Resources

15e Create a research plan.

Your research will be more productive if you create both a general plan and a detailed schedule immediately after you receive your assignment. A general plan will ensure that you understand the full scope of your assignment. A detailed schedule will help you set priorities and meet your deadlines.

To develop a general plan of research, answer the following questions:

- Do I understand exactly what my instructor expects?

- Is the purpose of my paper fundamentally informative, interpretive, or persuasive? Do I have a choice?

- If the topic is assigned: What do I already know about this topic?

- If the specific topic is open: What idea-generation techniques can I use to help me discover a topic?

LEARNING in COLLEGE

Keywords Indicating Purpose in Research Assignments

Review your original assignment for keywords that signal its purpose. Note, however, that some terms can signal more than one type of assignment, depending on the context. Here are some examples.

- **Informative research assignment:** *explain, describe, compare, review*
- **Interpretive research assignment:** *analyze, compare, explain, interpret*
- **Persuasive research assignment:** *assess, justify, defend, refute, determine*

Sample Informative Research Assignments

- **History:** Describe the relationship between abolitionism and the women's suffrage movement in the period before the Civil War.
- **Biology:** Explain the impact of zebra mussels on native fauna in a lake.
- **Education:** Describe and compare the phonics and whole-language approaches to the teaching of reading.

Sample Interpretive Research Assignments

- **History:** Interpret the *Declaration of Sentiments*—issued at the first women's rights convention in 1848—as a response to the *Declaration of Independence*.
- **Biology:** Analyze the results of recent studies of lakes infested with zebra mussels.
- **Education:** Explain the selections and exercises in a reading textbook in terms of its approach to the teaching of reading.

Sample Persuasive Research Assignments

- **History:** Defend or refute this statement: "The women's movement and the civil rights movement have long cooperated based on a historically rooted shared agenda."
- **Biology:** Determine the least invasive way to remove zebra mussels from a local ecosystem, and create an implementation plan for doing so.
- **Education:** Justify the use of a phonics-only approach to reading in a remedial classroom.

- Will collaboration be allowed, or am I required to work independently?
- Will I need to conduct primary as well as secondary research? If so, what general arrangements do I anticipate needing to make?
- How many and what kinds of sources am I expected to consult? (*See Chapters 16–18 for information on finding and evaluating sources.*)
- What citation style does my instructor want me to use? What are the expectations for the final presentation format of my research? (*See Part 4: Documenting across the Curriculum.*)

Exercise 15.2   Research schedule

Adapt this worksheet to create a research schedule whenever you have a research assignment. This worksheet assumes you will have four weeks between the time you receive your assignment and the time the final draft is due. If you use a PDA, type in this schedule and set reminders or alarms for key dates (such as completing library research, completing a first draft, or conferring with the campus Writing Center).

Task	Date

Phase I: Five days

Complete a general plan for research.   _____

Decide on a topic and a research question.   _____

Consult reference works and reference librarians.   _____

List relevant **keywords** for online searching
(*see Chapter 16: Finding and Managing Print
and Online Sources, p. 294*).   _____

Compile a **working bibliography**
(*see Chapter 21, Working with Sources: p. 347*).   _____

Sample some of the items in the bibliography.   _____

Make arrangements for primary research
(if necessary).   _____

Phase II: Twelve days

Locate, read, and evaluate selected sources.   _____

Take notes.   _____

Cross-check notes with working bibliography.   _____

Conduct primary research (if necessary).   _____

Confer with instructor or Writing Center
(optional).   _____

Outline or plan organization of paper. _____

Phase III: Ten days

Write first draft. _____

Decide which primary and secondary resource
materials to include. _____

Peer review (optional). _____

Revise draft. _____

Conference with instructor or Writing Center
(optional). _____

Perform final revision and editing. _____

Create Works-Cited or References page. _____

Due Date _____

16 Finding and Managing Print and Online Sources

Your research process will take place both in the library and on the Internet. The amount of information available in the library and on the Internet is vast. Usually, a search for useful sources entails three activities:

- Collecting keywords from reference works
- Using library databases
- Finding material in the library and on the World Wide Web

16a Use the library in person and online.

Consider your college librarians as consultants in your research. They know what is available at your library and how to get material on loan from other libraries. They can also show you how to access the library's computerized book catalog, periodical databases, and electronic resources or how to use the Internet to find information relevant to your research project. Most college libraries list their reference works, books, and periodical holdings online. Your library's Web site may also have links to important reference works available on the Internet, as shown in Figure 16.1.

In addition, **help sheets** can be found at most college libraries. These documents provide information about the location of both general and discipline-specific periodicals and noncirculating reference books, along with information about special databases, indexes, and sources of information on the Internet. You may be able to access your library's help sheets online from the library's Web site or its online catalog.

www.mhhe.com/
nmhh
For more information on and links to library resources, go to

Research >
Using the Library

16b Consult various kinds of sources.

The number and kinds of sources you will need to consult will vary from one research project to another. You should always review more than one source, however, and usually more than one kind of source. Chances are, you will consult more sources during your research than you will cite in your final project. Your assignment may specify how many print and electronic sources you are expected to look at and cite.

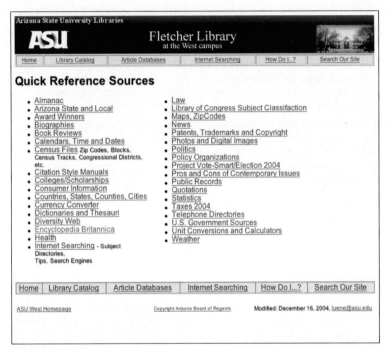

FIGURE 16.1 Linking to online resources from a college library's Web site. This page from the Web site of the Arizona State University West Library provides links to a variety of Web-based reference sources, ranging from encyclopedias and dictionaries to telephone books and government statistics.

If you are uncertain, talk to your instructor early in the research process—when you have decided on a working thesis statement or question, for example—to determine the range of sources you should consult. Some of the kinds of sources available to you are summarized in the following sections.

1. General reference works

General reference works provide overview information about a variety of topics. General encyclopedias, for example, include entries for anything from the history of the alphabet to the science of zoology. Other general reference works include dictionaries, annuals, almanacs, biographical encyclopedias, and world atlases. General reference works can introduce you to the basic concepts and vocabulary of a subject,

289

Tips

LEARNING in COLLEGE

Touring Your Library

Make it a point to tour your library when you begin college. If the library offers an orientation tour to incoming students, be sure to take advantage of it. Here is a checklist for your tour:

- Locate the reference desk and note its hours. (Reference books cannot be checked out, so you will need to schedule time to consult them while the library is open.) Collect any help sheets.
- Locate the terminals that provide access to the library's online catalog. If you need to set up an account or a password to use the catalog, do so. Find out how to link to the catalog from a computer in your dorm or home.
- Locate the library's card catalog if it has one. (Although almost all libraries are converting entirely to online catalogs, some still maintain information about their holdings in card catalogs.)
- Locate the library's **stacks** (the shelves where it stores its collections of books). Find out if any parts of the stacks are closed. (To get books from closed stacks, you have to request them and have them brought to you by a library employee.)
- Learn your library's interlibrary loan policies in case you need to procure books from another library.
- Learn about the library's **reserve service,** which lets professors set aside books and articles for students to consult for limited times, ensuring their availability to everyone in the class. At many schools, professors can also make excerpts of books and articles available on electronic reserve through the library's home page.
- Locate your library's photocopying machines, computer terminals, printers, and other helpful devices.
- Many libraries have decades-old back issues of newspapers and other publications stored on microfilm or microfiche that can be viewed only with special readers and printers. Be sure to learn the location of these devices as well as any other multimedia resources.

giving you a source of **keywords** to use in online searches for more specialized sources. (*The basics of keyword searches are covered in section 16c.*)

2. Specialized reference works

Specialized reference works provide specific information relevant to particular disciplines. A discipline-specific encyclopedia of philosophy, for example, would have entries on important philosophers, major approaches to philosophy, and the meaning of significant philosophical terms. Other specialized reference works include discipline-specific biographical encyclopedias and discipline-specific almanacs, dictionaries, and bibliographies.

3. Books

Nonfiction books usually provide an in-depth look at a specific topic. Books of fiction or literature range from novels to collections of stories or poetry. Most of the books you use will be in the library in printed form. Some books, however, are now available online, including, for example, reports by think tanks, government agencies, and research groups. Some Web sites (such as Project Gutenberg (http://www.gutenberg.org/) provide the complete texts of classic works of literature that are no longer under copyright (*see Chapter 20: Plagiarism, Copyright, and Intellectual Property, pp. 341–46*).

4. Periodical articles

Periodicals are publications that appear at regular intervals (periodically). They include newspapers and magazines from around the world (most available in both print and online versions), scholarly and technical journals (some of which may be available through online databases as well as in print), and Web-only publications.

5. Web sites

Many special-interest groups, government and academic organizations, and businesses maintain Web sites that provide information about policies, products, or particular points of view.

6. Other online sources

Online discussion groups, bulletin boards, news groups, chat rooms, and blogs (Web-based online personal journals) can sometimes provide access to people knowledgeable about a particular subject who can help guide your research. (Be careful, though; you can also encounter many unqualified people with suspect views in these environments.)

7. Primary print sources

Primary print resources include government documents (the text of a law, for example); census data; pamphlets; maps; the original text of literary works; and the original manuscripts (or facsimiles) of literary works, letters, and personal journals, among many others. You can find these in your library, in special collections at other libraries, and in government offices, among other places. Many Web sites also provide access to primary sources.

8. Primary nonprint sources

In addition to written works, primary sources also include such nonprint items as works of art, video and audio recordings, sound archives, photographs, and the artifacts of everyday life.

9. Other primary sources

Other primary sources include a researcher's records from experiments or field research. These may include interviews, field notes, surveys, and the results of observation and laboratory experiments.

Exercise 16.1   Finding information at your library

Choose anyone born between 1900 and 1950 whose life and accomplishments interest you. You could select a politician, a film director, a rock star, a Nobel Prize–winning economist—*anyone*. At your library, find at least one of each of the following resources with information about or relevant to this person:

- A directory of biographies
- An article in a pre-1990 newspaper
- An article in a scholarly journal
- An audio or video recording, a photograph, or a work of art
- A printout of the search results of your library's electronic catalog

- An obituary (if your subject has died)
- A list of your subject's accomplishments, including, for example, prizes received, books published, albums released, or movies made

 LEARNING in COLLEGE

Popular or Scholarly?

The audience for and purpose of a source, especially a publication, determine whether it should be considered *scholarly* or *popular.* You may begin your inquiry into a research topic with popular sources, but to become fully informed about the topic of your research, you need to delve into scholarly sources as well. Some newsstand periodicals (such as the *Atlantic Monthly* or *Psychology Today*) include writing and reporting of a thoroughness comparable to that of academic sources. Other popular sources may be appropriate for the early stages of inquiry but cannot by themselves provide the basis of your research.

Popular sources:

- Are widely available on newsstands and in retail stores.
- Accept advertising for a wide range of popular consumer goods.
- Are themselves advertised (in the case of books).
- Are printed on magazine paper with a color cover.
- Are published by a commercial publishing house or media company (such as Time Warner, Inc.).
- Include a wide range of topics in each issue, from international affairs to popular entertainment.

Scholarly sources:

- Are usually found in libraries, not on newsstands.
- Include articles with extensive citations and bibliographies.
- Are **refereed** (which means, in the case of a scholarly journal, that each article has been reviewed, commented on, and accepted for publication by other scholars who are expert in the field the article is about).
- List article titles and authors on the cover.
- Include articles mostly by authors who are affiliated with a college, museum, or some other scholarly institution.
- Are published by scholarly or nonprofit organizations, often in association with a university press.
- Focus on discipline-specific topics.

16c Understand keywords and keyword searches.

Most online research—whether in your library's catalog, in a specialized database, or on the entire World Wide Web—requires an understanding of **keyword searches.** In the context of online searching, a **keyword** is a term (or terms) you enter into a **search engine** (searching software) to find sources—books, journal articles, Web sites—that have information about a particular subject.

A successful keyword search is one that returns a manageable number of relevant sources—sources that relate to your subject. For this to happen, your keyword should be a term that occurs in the sources you need but not in an even greater number of sources that you do not need. If you were to enter the keyword "Armstrong" in a search engine, for example, you would get information about Louis Armstrong the musician, but you would also get information about Neil Armstrong the astronaut; Lance Armstrong the cyclist; and many other individuals, companies, or institutions with "Armstrong" as part of their names.

To hone in on your subject, you often need to refine your initial search term. The Learning in College box on the next page describes a variety of techniques for doing so that work in most search engines. Many search engines also have an advanced search feature that can help with the refining process.

16d Use printed and online reference works for general information.

Reference works provide an overview of a subject area. The information contained in general encyclopedias like *Encyclopædia Britannica, Collier's Encyclopedia,* and *Encyclopedia Americana* is less authoritative than the specialized knowledge found in discipline-specific encyclopedias, academic journals, and scholarly books. There is nothing wrong with starting your research by consulting a general encyclopedia, but for college research you will need to explore your topic in scholarly resources as well. Often, the list of references at the end of an encyclopedia article can lead you to useful sources on your topic.

Reference books do not circulate, so plan to take notes or make photocopies of pages you may need to consult later. Many college libraries subscribe to services that provide access to online encyclopedias. Check your college library's home page for appropriate links to the resources.

LEARNING in COLLEGE

Refining Keyword Searches

Although search engines vary, the following advice should work for many of the search engines you will use.

Group words together. Put quotation marks or parentheses around the phrase you are looking for—for example, "Dixieland Jazz." This tells the search engine to find only sites with those two words in sequence.

Use Boolean operators.

AND (+)   Use AND or + when you need sites with both of two or more words: **Armstrong + Glaser.**

OR   Use OR if you want sites with either of two or more terms: **jazz OR "musical improvisation."**

NOT (–)   Use NOT or – in front of words that you do not want to appear together in your results: **Armstrong NOT Neil.**

Use truncation plus a "wildcard." To find sites that include all the variations on a single root word, combine part of a keyword with an asterisk (*) used as a wildcard: **music*** (for "music," "musician," "musical," and so forth).

Search the fields. Some search engines permit you to search within fields, such as the title field of Web pages or the author field of a library catalog. Thus **TITLE + "Louis Armstrong"** will give you all items that have "Louis Armstrong" in their title.

Here is a list of some other kinds of reference materials available in print, on the Internet, or both:

ALMANACS

- *Almanac of American Politics*
- *Information Please Almanac*
- *World Almanac*

BIBLIOGRAPHIES

- *Bibliographic Index*
- *Bibliography of Asian Studies*
- *MLA International Bibliography*

BIOGRAPHIES

- *African American Biographical Database*
- *American Men and Women of Science*
- *Dictionary of American Biography*
- *Dictionary of Literary Biography: Chicano Writers*
- *Dictionary of National Biography*
- *Webster's New Biographical Dictionary*
- *Who's Who*

DICTIONARIES

- *American Heritage Dictionary of the English Language*
- *Concise Oxford Dictionary of Literary Terms*
- *Dictionary of American History*
- *Dictionary of Philosophy*
- *Dictionary of the Social Sciences*
- *Oxford English Dictionary (OED)*

www.mhhe.com/
nmhh
For access to an online database through *Catalyst*, go to

Research >
Factiva
PowerSearch

16e Use print indexes and online databases to find articles in journals and other periodicals.

1. Periodicals

Newspapers, magazines, and scholarly journals that are published at regular intervals, be it daily, weekly, monthly, or quarterly, are classified as **periodicals.** The articles in scholarly and technical journals, written by experts and based on up-to-date research and information, are generally more reliable than articles in popular newspapers and magazines. Although newspapers and magazines can provide useful background information, the journalists who write for them are often not specialists in the field they are writing about, and they sometimes oversimplify complex issues. If you do not know which periodicals are considered important in a discipline, ask your instructor or librarian.

2. Indexes and Databases

Articles published in periodicals are cataloged in general and specialized **indexes.** Indexes are available on subscription-only **databases,** on CD-ROMs your library owns, and as print volumes. If you are searching for articles that are more than twenty years old, you should use print indexes, which can be found in the reference section of your library. Print indexes can be searched by author, subject, or title. Electronic databases can be searched by date and keyword and will provide you with a list of articles that meet your search criteria. Each entry in the list will include the information you need to find and cite the article. Depending on the database, you may also be able to see an abstract of each article, or even its full text. (*See the box "Learning in College: Formats for Database Information," on p. 301.*)

The TextConnex box on page 300 lists some of the major online databases, and Figures 16.2, 16.3, and 16.4 illustrate a search on one of them, ProQuest. Keep in mind that not all libraries subscribe to all databases.

> *Caution:* When you refer to the full text of an article that you retrieved from a subscription database service, your citation needs to include information about the service (including its name and the date on which you retrieved the article) as well as information about the publication in which the article appeared.

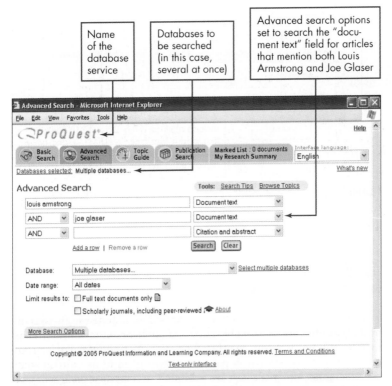

Name of the database service

Databases to be searched (in this case, several at once)

Advanced search options set to search the "document text" field for articles that mention both Louis Armstrong and Joe Glaser

FIGURE 16.2 ProQuest's Advanced Search page. Image published with permission of ProQuest Information and Learning Company. Further reproduction is prohibited without permission.

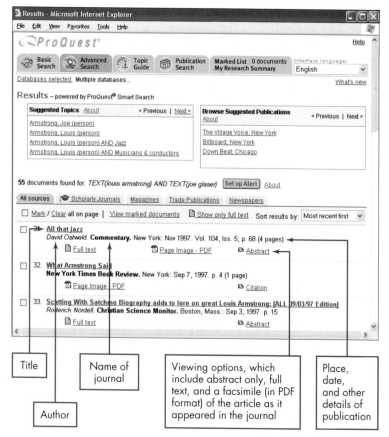

FIGURE 16.3 Partial results of the search started in Figure 16.2.
Image published with permission of ProQuest Information and Learning Company. Further reproduction is prohibited without permission.

www.mhhe.com/
nmhh
For more information
on and links to
Internet resources,
go to
Research >
Using the Internet

16f Use search engines and subject directories to find sources on the Internet.

Searches of subscription-only databases available through your library will link you to reliable sources of published information. They usually will not link you to other Web sites. To find information that has been published in Web pages, you will need to use an Internet search engine. Many of these are available, and because each searches the Web in its own way, you will probably use more than one.

Each search engine's home page provides a link to advice on using the search engine efficiently as well as help with refining a search.

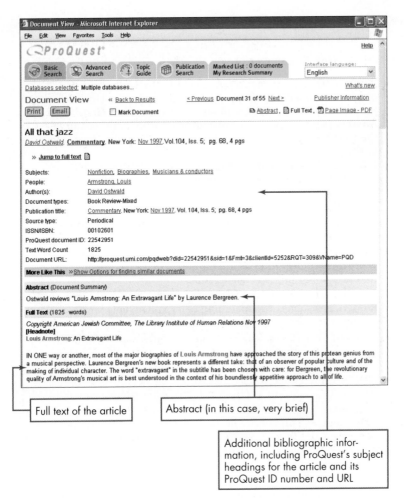

Full text of the article

Abstract (in this case, very brief)

Additional bibliographic information, including ProQuest's subject headings for the article and its ProQuest ID number and URL

FIGURE 16.4 The abstract and the beginning of the full text of an article selected from results in Figure 16.3. Image published with permission of ProQuest Information and Learning Company. Further reproduction is prohibited without permission.

Look for a link labeled "search help," "about us," or something similar, and click on it to learn about that specific search engine.

Some Internet search engines provide for specialized searches—for images, for example (*see Chapter 17*). *Google* offers a service called Google Scholar that functions similarly to a database, locating only scholarly sources in response to a search term. Many of the links, however, are to subscription-based online journals that charge a fee for access to full-text articles. (*Text continues on p. 302.*) **299**

TEXTCONNEX

Some Online Databases

- **ABC-CLIO:** This service offers access to two history-related databases. *America: History and Life* covers the United States and Canada from prehistory to the present. *Historical Abstracts* provides similar resources relating to the history of the world (excluding the United States and Canada) from 1450 to the present.

- **Lexis-Nexis Academic:** Updated daily, this online service provides full-text access to around 6,000 newspapers, professional publications, legal references, and congressional sources.

- **EBSCOhost:** The *Academic Search Premier* service provides full-text coverage for more than 8,000 scholarly publications and indexes articles in all academic subject areas.

- **ERIC:** This database lists publications in the area of education. It provides information on 1.1 million articles to 1966 and access to 107,000 full-text documents.

- **Factiva:** This database offers access to the Dow Jones and Reuters news agencies, including newspapers, magazines, journals, and Web sites.

- **General Science Index:** This index is general and therefore most appropriate for beginning science students. It lists articles by biologists, chemists, and other scientists.

- **GDCS:** Updated monthly, the *Government Documents Catalog Service (GDCS)* contains records of all publications printed by the United States Government Printing Office since 1976.

- **GPO Access:** This service of the U.S. Government Printing Office provides free electronic access to government documents.

- **Humanities Index:** This index lists articles from journals in language and literature, history, philosophy, and similar areas.

- **InfoTrac Web:** This Web-based service searches bibliographic and other databases such as the *General Reference Center Gold, General Business File ASAP,* and *Health Reference Center.*

- **JSTOR:** This archive provides full-text access to journals in the humanities, social sciences, and natural sciences.

- **MLA Bibliography:** Covering from 1963 to the present, the *MLA Bibliography* indexes more than 4,000 journals, dissertations, and serials published worldwide in the fields of modern languages, literature, literary criticism, linguistics, and folklore. Coverage includes all modern national literatures.

- **PAIS International:** Produced by the Public Affairs Information Service, this database indexes literature on public policy, social policy, and the general social sciences from 1972 to the present.

- *Periodical Abstracts:* This database indexes more than 2,000 general and academic journals covering business, current affairs, economics, literature, religion, psychology, and women's studies from 1987 to the present.

- *ProQuest:* This database provides access to dissertations; many newspapers and journals, including many full-text articles back to 1996; information on sources in business, general reference, the social sciences, and humanities back to 1986; and a wealth of historical sources back to the nineteenth century.

- *PsycInfo:* Sponsored by the American Psychological Association (APA), this database indexes and abstracts books, scholarly articles, technical reports, and dissertations in the area of psychology and related disciplines.

- *Social Science Index:* This index lists articles from such fields as economics, psychology, political science, and sociology.

- *WorldCat:* This is a catalog of books and other resources available in libraries worldwide.

LEARNING in COLLEGE

Formats for Database Information

When searching a database, you may encounter both abstracts and the full texts of articles. Full-text articles may be available in either .pdf or .html format.

- **Abstract:** An **abstract** is a brief summary of a full-text article. Abstracts appear at the beginning of articles in some scholarly journals and are used in databases to summarize complete articles. Do not mistake an abstract for a full article. If what you read in an abstract sounds useful, consult the full article.

- **Full text:** In a database search an article listed as "full text" comes with a link to the complete text of the article. Note, however, that full-text articles accessed through databases do not always include accompanying photographs or other illustrations.

- **.pdf** and **.html:** Articles in databases and other online sources may be in either .pdf or .html format (or both). Documents in .html (Hypertext Markup Language) have been formatted to read as Web pages. Documents in .pdf format (Portable Document Format) duplicate the original print source and appear as a facsimile of the original page. To read a .pdf document, you need a program like Adobe Acrobat Reader.

FIGURE 16.5 A keyword search in *Google*. An initial search using the keywords *louis armstrong* yields more than three million hits.

Many Internet search engines also include sponsored links—links that a commercial enterprise has paid to have appear in response to specific search terms. These are usually clearly identified.

Internet keyword searches usually need to be carefully worded to provide relevant results. For example, a search of *Google* using the keywords *louis armstrong* (Figure 16.5) yields a list of more than 3,810,000 Web sites, a staggering number of links, or **hits.**

Altering the keywords to make them more specific narrows the results significantly (Figures 16.6 and 16.7).

In addition to keyword searches, many Internet search engines offer a **subject directory,** a listing of broad categories (Figure 16.8). Clicking through this hierarchy of choices eventually brings you to a list of sites related to a specific topic.

Just as with online databases and print indexes, some Web sites provide content-specific subject directories designed for research in a particular field. These sites are often reviewed or screened and are excellent starting points for academic research.

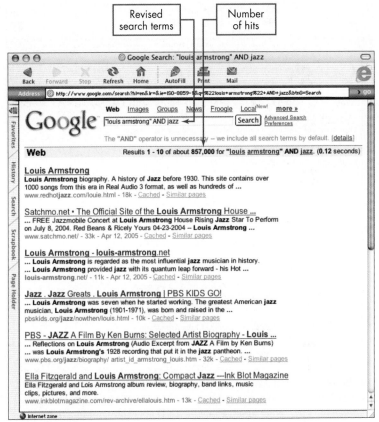

FIGURE 16.6 **Refining the search.** Putting quotes around *louis armstrong* and linking that term to the term *jazz* with the Boolean operator AND reduces the number of hits to a still unmanageable 857,000. (Note that the AND operator could have been omitted in this search because *Google* treats terms by default as if they were joined by AND.)

Exercise 16.2 Finding information online

Look at the sample research topics listed in the Charting the Territory box on page 281, and conduct a keyword search for each on at least three search engines. Experiment with the phrasing of each keyword search, and compare your results with those of other classmates.

EXAMPLE **What is the impact of globalization on the world's indigenous cultures?**

"indigenous culture" AND globalization

303

FIGURE 16.7 Further refining the search. Adding *joe glaser* (Armstrong's longtime manager) reduces the number of hits to an almost manageable 698. (Note again that the AND operator could have been omitted.)

16g Use your library's online catalog or card catalog to find books.

Books in most libraries are shelved by **call numbers** based on the Library of Congress classification system. In this system, books on the same topic have similar call numbers and are shelved together. Some libraries use the Dewey Decimal system of call numbering, which classifies knowledge in divisions of 10 from 000 to 990. Whichever system your library uses, you will need the call number to locate the book on the library's shelves. When consulting an online library catalog, be sure to jot down (or print out) the call numbers of books you want to consult.

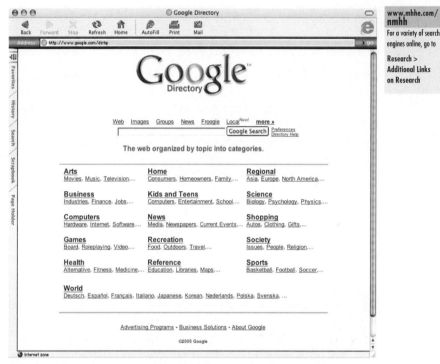

www.mhhe.com/
nmhh

For a variety of search
engines online, go to

Research >
Additional Links
on Research

FIGURE 16.8 The opening page of *Google*'s subject directory.

Tips LEARNING in COLLEGE

Cautions for Researching Online

Internet search engines can swamp you with irrelevant or inaccurate information. In Chapter 18, we will consider ways to evaluate the usefulness and credibility of information you find on the Web. Here are some general cautions:

- The URL ("uniform resource locator," or Web address) is always subject to change. What you find today may be gone tomorrow.
- Topics are not usually covered in depth online. For depth and context, consult library sources such as books and databases.
- Searching for relevant information can often feel like looking for a needle in a haystack. For example, a search of the phrase "textile industry" can call up 538,000 sites, varying from equipment for sale to human rights organizations. Learn how to structure a keyword search to retrieve information relevant to you.

You can conduct a keyword search of most online library catalogs by author, by title, or by subject (Figure 16.9). A search of the term *Louis Armstrong* by author would produce a list of works by Louis Armstrong; a search by title would produce a list of works with Louis Armstrong in the title; and a search by subject would produce a list of works that are all or partly about Louis Armstrong.

The results of a keyword search of a library's online catalog will provide a list composed mostly of books. In the examples that follow of a search of the City University of New York Library's online catalog, notice that under the column "Format" other kinds of media that match a keyword subject search are also listed; you can alter the terms of a search to restrict the formats to a specific medium.

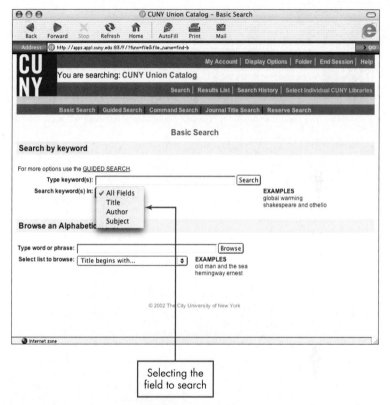

FIGURE 16.9 The opening search page of the online library system of the City University of New York (CUNY).

As with any keyword search, whether you get what you really need—a reasonable number of relevant sources—depends on your choice of keywords. When searching by subject, if your search terms are too broad, you will get too many hits; if they are too narrow, you will get few or none.

Figures 16.10 and 16.11 show the results of experimenting with different keywords on the topic of jazz in general and Louis Armstrong in particular. Figure 16.10, a subject search using only the keyword *jazz,* resulted in too many hits to be practical. Figure 16.11, a subject search using the key term *Louis Armstrong,* produced a workable number.

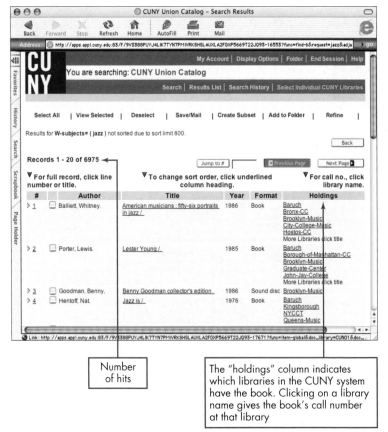

Number of hits

The "holdings" column indicates which libraries in the CUNY system have the book. Clicking on a library name gives the book's call number at that library

FIGURE 16.10 Searching an online catalog. Using the word *jazz* as a keyword in a subject search produces an unmanageable 6975 sources.

16h Take advantage of printed and online government documents.

The U.S. government publishes an enormous amount of information and research every year, most of which is available online. At your library's reference desk, ask for the *Monthly Catalog of U.S. Government Publications* and the *U.S. Government Periodicals Index* (both of which are available as online databases). The Government Printing Office's own Web site, *GPO Access* <http://www.gpoaccess.gov/>, is an excellent resource for identifying federal government publications and where to find them. Other online government resources include:

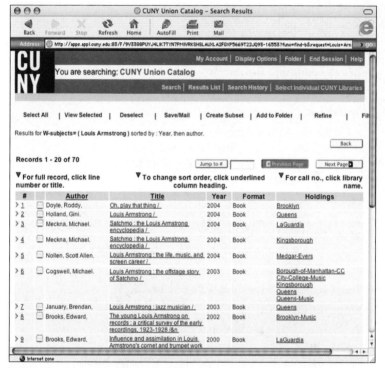

FIGURE 16.11 Changing a search term. A keyword search using the search term *Louis Armstrong* produces 70 results, a manageable number.

- *FedWorld Information Network* (maintained by the National Technical Information Service) <http://www.fedworld.gov/>
- *FirstGov* (the "U.S. Government's Official Web Portal") <http://firstgov.gov/>
- *The National Institutes of Health* <http://www.nih.gov>
- *U.S. Census Bureau* <http://www.census.gov>

16i Explore online communication.

In addition to providing information, the Internet also provides access to communities with common interests and varying levels of expertise on different subjects. Among the online forums for these communities

TEXTCONNEX

Starting Points for Research in the Disciplines

General Academic Research:

■ *WWW Virtual Library* <http://vlib.org/>

Humanities:

■ *Artcyclopedia* <http://artcyclopedia.com/>
■ *Arts and Letters Daily* <http://www.aldaily.com>
■ *Project Gutenberg* <http://www.promo.net/pg/>
■ *Voice of the Shuttle* <http://vos.ucsb.edu/>

Social Sciences:

■ *New York Times "Politics Navigator"* <http://www.nytimes.com/ref/politics/POLI_NAVI.html>
■ *Social Science Information Gateway* <http://sosig.esrc.bris.ac.uk/>

Current Events:

■ *NewsLink* <http://newslink.org/menu.html>

Science and Health:

■ *HealthWeb* <http://healthweb.org/>
■ *Scirus* <http://www.scirus.com/srsapp/>
■ *Virtual Library: Science* <http://vlib.org/Science.html>

are discussion lists (electronic mailing lists) and Usenet news groups, as well as various forms of synchronous communication in which people interact in real time. Online forums can help you with research in the following ways:

■ You can get an idea for a paper by finding out what topics interest and concern people.

■ You can learn what people think about almost any topic, from food to pop culture to sports to science.

■ You can zero in on a very specific topic, such as sushi, a comic book character, a vintage TV show, a singer, or a scientific theory.

■ You can query an expert in the field about your topic.

Caution: The level of expertise among the people who participate in online forums and the scholarly seriousness of the forums themselves vary widely. You can find solid information and advice, but you can also find fringe ideas from people with questionable qualifications.

Discussion lists (electronic mailing lists) are networked e-mail conversations on particular topics that may be relevant to your research topic. Lists can be open (anyone can join) or closed (only certain people, such as members of a particular class or group, can join). If the list is open, you can subscribe by sending a message to a computer that has list-processing software installed on it.

Usenet news groups are one of the oldest features of the Internet. Like lists, news groups may exist on topics relevant to your research. You must subscribe to read postings. Unlike lists, news groups are posted to a *news server,* a computer that hosts the news group and distributes postings to participating servers. Postings are not automatically distributed by e-mail.

Interactively structured Web sites provide another medium for online communication. **Blogs,** for example (*see Chapter 14*), can be designed to allow readers to post their own comments and queries. **Wikis,** sites designed for online collaboration, go further, allowing people both to comment on and modify one another's contributions.

Synchronous communication involves various types of real-time electronic exchanges between individuals. **Chat rooms** are sites

---

 TEXTCONNEX

Discussion Lists

Check the following Web sites for more information about discussion lists:

- *Harness E-mail: Mailing Lists* <http://www.learnthenet.com/english/html/24mlists.htm>: Explains how discussion lists work.
- *Topica* <http://www.topica.com>: Contains a searchable directory of 90,095 discussion lists.
- *Tile.net: The Reference to Internet Discussion and Information Lists* <http://tile.net/lists>: Allows you to search for discussion lists by name, description, or domain.

TextConnex

News Groups

For more information about news groups, refer to these resources online:

- *Newsreaders.com* <http://www.newsreaders.com/guide/news.html>: Explains why you would want a newsreader and how to use one.
- *Tile.net.news* <http://tile.net/news>: A complete index to Internet Usenet news groups. Browse by subject, hierarchy, or search. Provides links to news group FAQs and use statistics.
- *Harley Hahn's Master List of Usenet Newsgroups* <http://www.harley.com/usenet>: A master list of Usenet news groups with descriptions. Search by category or keyword.

on the Internet where people can carry on real-time discussions. Chat rooms are usually organized by topic, so the people who use a room are likely to share an interest in its topic. **Instant messaging (IM)** is another medium for real-time communication, but it involves only people who have agreed to form a conversing group. Other, less common formats for synchronous communication include multiuser dimensions and object-oriented multiuser dimensions (MUDs and MOOs), both of which are used for role-playing simulations and can be adapted for scholarly interaction.

17 Finding and Creating Effective Visuals

Visuals are often included as support for a writer's thesis. Sometimes, they are included principally to enhance an argument. For example, a bar graph comparing the number of violent scenes in several episodes of two television series can help you make a point about media violence. Other visuals, such as those used in many advertisements, make their own argument. In some cases, visuals may constitute the complete argument. A relief organization, for example, might post a series of compelling visuals on its Web site to persuade potential donors to contribute money following a catastrophic event.

For some writing situations, you will be able to prepare or provide your own visuals. You may, for example, provide your own sketch of an experiment, or, as the authors of the lab report in Chapter 8 have done, create bar graphs from data that you have collected (*see section 8g, p. 178*). In other situations, however, you may decide to create a visual from data that you have found in a print or an online source, you may decide to include a visual that you have found during your research, or you may search in your library or on the Internet for a visual to use.

Caution: Whether you are using data from a source to create an image or incorporating an image created by someone else into your paper, your use of data or images created by others is a kind of quoting. You must give credit to the source of the data or image, just as you do when you paraphrase or quote the writing of others. Furthermore, if you plan to publish a visual you have selected from a source on a Web site or in another medium, you must obtain permission to use it from the copyright holder. If the copyright holder refuses permission, you must remove the image before you publish.

17a Find quantitative data and display the data visually.

www.mhhe.com/nmhh

For resources to begin your search, go to

Research >
Discipline Specific
Resources

Research writing in many disciplines—especially in the sciences, social sciences, business, math, engineering, and other technical fields—often requires reference to quantitative information. That information

LEARNING in COLLEGE

Deciding When to Use an Image in Your Paper

Regardless of the kind of images you use, there are several questions to consider as you look for visuals:

- How many images will you need?
- Where will each image appear in the text?
- What contribution will each image make to the text?
- What contribution will the set of images make to the text?
- Does the audience have enough background information to interpret the image in the way you intend?
- If not, what additional information should you include in the text or a caption?
- If no additional information is needed, does the image nonetheless need a caption?
- Have you reviewed your own text (and perhaps asked a colleague to review it, as well) to see how well the image is "working"—in terms of appropriateness, location, and context?

generally has more impact when it is displayed visually in a chart, graph, or map than as raw numbers alone. Pie charts, for instance, are often used to show percentages of a whole; businesses use them to show allocation of effort toward a goal, or kinds of resources designated for a project. Bar graphs are often used to compare one group to another over time. Line graphs can similarly show trends over time. A historian, for example, might choose a line graph to plot rates of immigration over time, relating the patterns the graph reveals to historical events—wars, for example, or an economic depression—to make a point about the effect of such events on population movements. In other words, in addition to documenting patterns and events, these ways of showing information are also tools of analysis. (*For examples of graphs and charts and situations in which to use them, see pp. 71–85 in Chapter 4: Drafting Paragraphs and Visuals.*)

1. Finding existing graphs, charts, and maps

www.mhhe.com/
nmhh
For an interactive
tutorial, go to

Writing >
Visual Rhetoric

As you search for print and online sources for your research project (*see Chapter 16*), take notes on useful graphs, charts, or maps that you can incorporate (with proper acknowledgment) into your paper. Some you may find in online sources. A *Google* search, for example, turned up a site affiliated with Columbia University that displayed the map

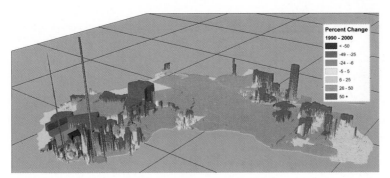

FIGURE 17.1 Africa population change, 1990–95.

shown in Figure 17.1, which might be useful for a paper on population trends in Africa. (Note, however, that you would need to have access to a color printer to use this map effectively; when printed in black and white—or grayscale—it is difficult to interpret.)

If an image is available in print only, you may be able to use a scanner to capture and digitize it. No matter how you incorporate an existing visual showing data, however, be sure that you do so within fair use guidelines (*see Chapters 20 and 21*).

2. Creating visuals from quantitative data
Sometimes you may find data presented in writing or in tables that would be effective in your paper as a chart or graph. You can use the data to create a visual using spreadsheet or other software.

For example, suppose you were writing a paper on population trends in the United States in the nineteenth century and wanted to illustrate the country's population growth during that period with a line graph. For population data, you might go to the Web site of the U.S. Census Bureau, which provides a wealth of quantitative historical information about the United States, all of it in the public domain. Most Census data, however, appears in tables like the one at the top of Figure 17.2 on the next page. As the figure shows, if you transfer data from such a table to a spreadsheet program like Microsoft Excel, you can use the program to create a graph that you can insert into a paper.

3. Displaying the right data
Make sure that you display data in a way that is consistent with your purpose and that what you display does not deceptively leave out information that could undermine your claims. Consider, for example, the

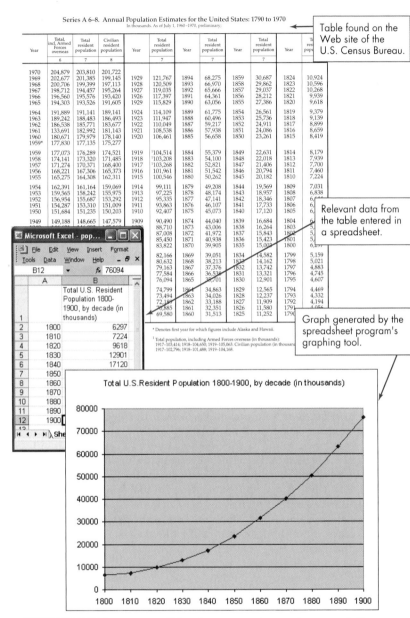

Table found on the Web site of the U.S. Census Bureau.

Series A 6–8. Annual Population Estimates for the United States: 1790 to 1970
In thousands. As of July 1, 1960–1970, preliminary;

Year	Total, incl. Armed Forces overseas (6)	Total resident population (7)	Civilian resident population (8)
1970	204,879	203,810	201,722
1969	202,677	201,385	199,145
1968	200,706	199,399	197,113
1967	198,712	194,457	195,264
1966	196,560	195,576	193,420
1965	194,303	193,526	191,605
1964	191,889	191,141	189,141
1963	189,242	188,483	186,493
1962	186,538	185,771	183,677
1961	133,691	182,992	181,143
1960	180,671	179,979	178,140
1959*	177,830	177,135	175,277
1959	177,073	176,289	174,521
1958	174,141	173,320	171,485
1957	171,274	170,371	168,400
1956	168,221	167,306	165,373
1955	165,275	164,308	162,311
1954	162,391	161,164	159,069
1953	159,565	158,242	155,975
1952	156,954	155,687	153,292
1951	154,287	153,310	151,009
1950	151,684	151,235	150,203
1949	149,188	148,665	147,579

Year	Total resident population (7)
1929	121,767
1928	120,509
1927	119,035
1926	117,397
1929	115,829
1924	114,109
1923	111,947
1922	110,049
1921	108,538
1920	106,461
1919	¹104,514
1918	¹103,208
1917	¹103,268
1916	101,961
1915	100,546
1914	99,111
1913	97,225
1912	95,335
1911	93,863
1910	92,407
1909	90,490
1908	88,710
1907	87,008
1906	85,450
1905	83,822
1904	82,166
1903	80,632
1902	79,163
1901	77,584
1900	76,094
1899	74,799
1898	73,494
1897	72,189
1896	70,885
1895	69,580

Year	Total resident population (7)
1894	68,275
1893	66,970
1892	65,666
1891	64,361
1890	63,056
1889	61,775
1888	60,496
1887	59,217
1886	57,938
1885	56,658
1884	55,379
1883	54,100
1882	52,821
1881	51,542
1880	50,262
1879	49,208
1878	48,174
1877	47,141
1876	46,107
1875	45,073
1874	44,040
1873	43,006
1872	41,972
1871	40,938
1870	39,905
1869	39,051
1868	38,213
1867	37,376
1866	36,538
1865	35,701
1864	34,863
1863	34,026
1862	33,188
1861	32,351
1860	31,513

Year	Total resident population (7)
1859	30,687
1858	29,862
1857	29,037
1856	28,212
1855	27,386
1854	26,561
1853	25,736
1852	24,911
1851	24,086
1850	23,261
1849	22,631
1848	22,018
1847	21,406
1846	20,794
1845	20,182
1844	19,569
1843	18,957
1842	18,346
1841	17,733
1840	17,120
1839	16,684
1838	16,264
1837	15,843
1836	15,423
1835	15,003
1834	14,582
1833	14,162
1832	13,742
1831	13,321
1830	12,901
1829	12,565
1828	12,237
1827	11,909
1826	11,580
1825	11,252

Year	Total resident population (7)
1824	10,924
1823	10,596
1822	10,268
1821	9,939
1820	9,618
1819	9,379
1818	9,139
1817	8,899
1816	8,659
1815	8,419
1814	8,179
1813	7,939
1812	7,700
1811	7,460
1810	7,224
1809	7,031
1808	6,838
1807	6,
1806	6,
1805	6,
1804	5,
1803	5,
1801	5,
1800	5,
1799	5,159
1798	5,021
1797	4,883
1796	4,745
1795	4,607
1794	4,469
1793	4,332
1792	4,194
1791	
1790	

* Denotes first year for which figures include Alaska and Hawaii.

¹ Total population, including Armed Forces overseas (in thousands): 1917–103,414; 1918–104,650; 1919–105,063. Civilian population (in thousands): 1917–102,796; 1918–101,488; 1919–104,168.

Relevant data from the table entered in a spreadsheet.

Microsoft Excel - pop...
File Edit View Insert Format
Tools Data Window Help
B12 ▾ fx 76094

	A	B
1		Total U.S. Resident Population 1800-1900, by decade (in thousands)
2	1800	6297
3	1810	7224
4	1820	9618
5	1830	12901
6	1840	17120
7	1850	
8	1860	
9	1870	
10	1880	
11	1890	
12	1900	

Graph generated by the spreadsheet program's graphing tool.

Total U.S. Resident Population 1800-1900, by decade (in thousands)

FIGURE 17.2 **Using a spreadsheet program to create a graph from data in a table.**

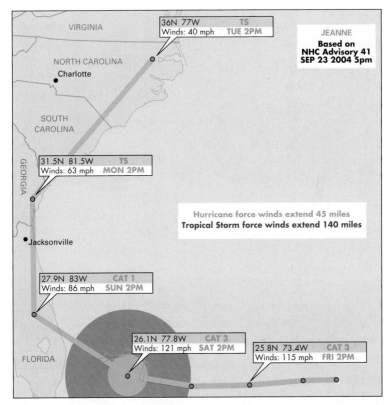

FIGURE 17.3 A map showing the projected path and intensity of Hurricane Jeanne.

two maps shown here of the paths of hurricanes in 2004. The first, Figure 17.3, is a predictive map: it shows the position of Hurricane Jeanne early on the evening of Thursday, September 23, 2004, and Jeanne's predicted path for the next five days. Note how it also incorporates a variety of quantitative data—the storm's predicted wind speed and its classification on a scale of storm intensity—in addition to Jeanne's position. The purpose of the map is to help people in the predicted path understand the risk they face from the storm.

The second map, Figure 17.4 on page 318, is comparative, showing the paths of two hurricanes—Ivan and Jeanne—that were both active at the same time. This map conveys both how active the 2004 hurricane season was and how erratic storm paths can be. It does not, however, provide information about the intensity of either storm, making both appear equal at all times. Were the intent to deceive—to support the erroneous claim, say, that coastal Texas suffered as badly

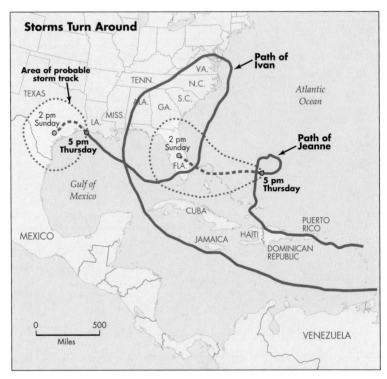

Storms Turn Around

Area of probable
storm track

TEXAS

2 pm
Sunday

5 pm
Thursday

LA.

MISS.

TENN.

ALA.

GA.

MISS.

N.C.

S.C.

VA.

Path of
Ivan

Atlantic
Ocean

2 pm
Sunday

FLA.

Path of
Jeanne

5 pm
Thursday

Gulf of
Mexico

MEXICO

CUBA

JAMAICA

HAITI

DOMINICAN
REPUBLIC

PUERTO
RICO

0   500
Miles

VENEZUELA

**FIGURE 17.4 A map showing the paths of Hurricanes Ivan
and Jeanne.**

from Ivan as coastal Alabama—this seeming equivalence would be a
problem. In sum, you should always consider what a visual leaves out
as well as what it displays.

Although each map emphasizes a different aspect of a single phenomenon—hurricanes—both show in a single unit the information the
writers want their readers to have. In addition, these maps illustrate
another general principle: it is better to use more visuals, each with
less information, than to try to squeeze too much information into a
single visual.

17b Search for appropriate images in online
collections; with an Internet search engine; or
in books, journals, and other print sources.

Photographs, pictures of artwork, drawings, diagrams, and maps can
318 provide visual support for many kinds of papers, particularly in the hu-

What Kind of Chart or Graph Should I Use?

In deciding on the kind of chart or graph to use, you will want to consider the following questions:

- What information do you want to show, and why?
- What options do you have for displaying the information?
- How much context do you want to include, and why?
- How many charts or graphs might you need?
- How detailed should each one be, and why?
- Will your visual serve to analyze the future, or will it report on the past?
- How dynamic does the chart or graph need to be?
- What information will you leave out or minimize, and how important is that loss?
- What other information—an introduction, an explanation, a summary, an interpretation—will your readers need to make sense of the chart or graph?

manities (English and other languages, philosophy, music, theater, and other performing arts). As with a display of quantitative data, you might choose an image from a source to use in your paper, or you might create one. If you were preparing a report comparing the way corporations are organized, for example, you might use organization charts that appear in corporate reports. Alternatively, you might use your word processor's drawing features to create your own organization charts based on information you find in the corporate reports.

Similarly, when appropriate, you could include photographs you have taken yourself in your work. You might use a picture you took of a geological formation during a class field trip for a geology paper, for example, or a picture of an interesting sculpture on your campus for an art appreciation course.

1. Search online image collections

Several libraries and other archival institutions maintain collections of images online. The Library of Congress, for example, is a rich source of images (most in the public domain) relating to American history and American culture. The Schomburg Center for Research in Black Culture, part of the New York Public Library, is an excellent source for images and other resources relating to African American studies. (*See the TextConnex box on page 320 for the URLs of these and other collections.*)

www.mhhe.com/
nmhh
For a wide range of
visual and text
sources, go to
Research > Factiva
PowerSearch

TEXTCONNEX

Some Online Image Collections

Art Institute of Chicago <http://www.artic.edu/aic/index.html>: Selected works from the museum's collection

Library of Congress <http://www.loc.gov/>

National Archives Digital Classroom <http://www.archives.gov/digital_classroom/index.html>: Documents and photographs from American history

National Aeronautics and Space Administration <http://www.nasa.gov/vision/universe/features/index.html>: Images and multimedia features on space exploration

National Park Service Digital Image Archive <http://photo.itc.nps.gov/storage/images/index.html>: Thousands of public domain photographs of U.S. national parks

New York Public Library <www.nypl.org/digital/>

Schomburg Center for Research in Black Culture <www.nypl.org/research/sc/sc.html>

VRoma: A Virtual Community for Teaching and Learning Classics <http://www.vroma.org/>: Images and other resources related to ancient Rome

www.mhhe.com/
nmhh
For a selection of
search engines, go to

Research >
Additional Links
on Research

2. Using a search engine to conduct a keyword search for images on the Internet

Many search engines have the ability to search the Web for images alone. Suppose you were writing a paper on the northern frontier of Roman Britain. You might include a map of England separated from Scotland by Hadrian's Wall to show the two territories—one occupied by Rome to the south, and the one to the north, what we now know as Scotland. Such an image would help the reader understand the relationship between these different territories. Alternatively, if the focus of the text were on the relationship between borders and structures, then a picture of Hadrian's Wall itself—rather than the map—might better make the point visually.

To find either kind of image—a map or a photograph—you could conduct an image search on *Google* by clicking on the Images option, entering the key word *Hadrian's Wall,* and then clicking on Search. The results of such a search include more than four thousand hits, the first of which are shown.

FIGURE 17.5 An image search on *Google*. A search using the term
Hadrian's Wall brings up pictures of the wall itself, as well as maps of its
location and other images, some relevant and some not.

Caution: The results of Internet image searches, like those of
any Internet search, need to be carefully evaluated for relevance
and reliability. (*See Chapter 18: Evaluating Sources, pp. 323–25.*)
Make sure you record proper source information for any pictures
you use that you find in this way.

---

3. Scanning images from a book or journal

You can use a scanner to scan some images from books and journals
into a paper for a class assignment, but as always, only if you are sure
your use is within fair use guidelines. Also, be sure to credit the source
of the image as well as the publication in which you found it.

18 Evaluating Sources

New technologies may grant fast access to a tremendous variety of sources, but they cannot by themselves help you decide which of those sources to use for your research. It is up to you to evaluate each potential source to determine whether it is both *relevant* and *reliable*. A source is relevant if it pertains to your research topic. A source is reliable if it provides trustworthy information.

Evaluating sources requires you to think critically and make judgments about which sources will be useful for answering your research question. This process helps you manage your research and focus your time on those sources that deserve close scrutiny.

www.mhhe.com/
nmhh
For an interactive tutorial on using the CARS checklist, go to
Research > CARS Source Evaluation Tutor

18a Question print sources.

Just because something is in print does not make it true or relevant. How can you determine if a print source is likely to be both reliable and useful? Here are some questions to ask about any source you are considering.

1. Judging reliability

- **What information can you find about the writer's credentials?** Consult biographical information about the writer in the source itself, in a biographical dictionary, or with an Internet search of the writer's name. Is the writer affiliated with a research institution dedicated to contributing to knowledge about an issue? Is the writer an expert on the topic? Is the writer cited frequently in other sources about the topic?

- **Who is the publisher?** University presses and academic publishers are considered more reliable than the popular press because they usually publish only work that is based on research and subjected to rigorous peer review.

- **Does the work include a bibliography of works consulted or cited?** Reliable research is always part of a conversation among specialists. To show familiarity with what other researchers have said about a topic, trustworthy writers cite a variety of sources and document their citations properly. Does this source do so? Does the source include a variety of citations?

- **Is the work balanced in tone, or does the writer appear biased?** What kind of tone does the author use? Is the work objective or subjective? Are the writer's arguments clear and logical? What is the author's point of view? Does he or she present opposing views fairly? (*For more on evaluating arguments, see Chapter 10: Arguments, pp. 212–15.*)

2. Judging relevance

- **Do the source's title and subtitle indicate that it addresses your specific research question?**

- **What is the publication date?** Is the material up-to-date (published within the past five years)? If you have a reason for working with older sources, is the publication date appropriate for your research?

- **If the source is a book, does the table of contents indicate that it contains useful information?**

- **If the source is a book, does it have an index?** Scan the index for keywords related to your topic to see how useful the book might be.

- **If the source is an article, does it have an abstract at the beginning or a summary at the end?** An abstract or a summary presents the main points made in an article and can help you decide if a source is likely to be useful.

- **Does the work contain subheadings?** Skim the headings to see if they indicate that the source covers useful information.

In college research, relevance can be a tricky matter. Your sociology instructor will expect you to give special preference to sociological sources in a project on the organization of the workplace. Your business management instructor will expect you to use material from that field in a project on the same topic. Be prepared to find that some promising sources turn out to be less relevant than you first thought.

18b Question Internet sources.

With print sources, you can have at least some confidence that the material has been filtered through editors and publishers. The Internet,

Evaluating Sources

"Primary or Secondary? Popular or Scholarly?" <http://www.sport.ussa.edu/library/primary.asp>: This page from the United States Sports Academy site discusses the difference between primary and secondary research sources, as well as the difference between popular and scholarly periodicals.

"Evaluating Sources of Information" <http://owl.english.purdue.edu/handouts/research/r_evalsource.html>: From the Purdue Online Writing Lab, this page provides guidelines for evaluating print and online sources.

however, is unfiltered. Anyone can design a Web page that looks authoritative but contains utter nonsense. The Internet is a free-for-all. You may find up-to-the-minute material there, but you must question every source.

When you use sources from the Internet, analyze their reliability carefully and critically. Here are some points to keep in mind and guidelines to follow.

1. Assessing authority and credibility

Look for information about the author of a site and the individual or organization that sponsors and produces it. This information can be an important indication of the site's reliability. Are the author and producer of the Web site identifiable? Is the author's biographical information included? Is there any indication that the author has relevant expertise on the subject? The following extensions in the Web address, or uniform resource locator (URL), can help you determine the type of site (which often tells you something about its purpose):

.com commercial (business)	**.edu** educational	**.mil** military
.org nonprofit organization	**.gov** U.S. government	**.net** network

A tilde (~) followed by a name in a URL usually means the site is a personal home page not affiliated with any organization.

2. Evaluating audience and purpose

To evaluate the intended audience of a Web site, apply the same criteria that you would use for a print source. You should also consider additional factors: Does the site assume special technical knowledge, capabilities, and access? (A site that uses Flash technology and streaming video, for example, is likely aiming for an audience with access to high-speed Internet connections and state-of-the-art hardware.) How does the appearance of the site work with the tone of any written material to suggest an audience? (For example, a commercial site such as *nike.com* uses music, graphics, and streaming technology to appeal to a certain kind of consumer.)

As Figures 18.1 and 18.2 on the next pages suggest, a site's purpose influences the way it presents information and the reliability of that information. Is the site's main purpose to advocate a cause, raise money, advertise a product or service, provide factual information, present research results, provide news, share personal information, or offer entertainment?

Remember that search engines return specific pages, sometimes buried deep within a Web site. If you access a page through a search engine, always try to view the site's home page so that you can best evaluate its audience and purpose.

3. Judging objectivity or bias

Do not take the information that a site presents at face value. Look carefully at the purpose and tone of the text. Is there evidence of obvious bias? Clues that indicate a lack of reasonableness or bias include an intemperate tone, broad claims, exaggerated statements of significance, conflicts of interest, no recognition of opposing views, and strident attacks on opposing views. (*For more on evaluating arguments, see Chapter 10: Arguments, pp. 212–15.*)

4. Weighing relevance and timeliness

Keep your topic and thesis in mind as you browse online. In what ways does the information from the online source specifically address your topic or thesis? Are the site's intended audience and purpose similar to yours? Does the site name its authors and sponsors, give additional links and resources, and make its purposes clear? Does the site indicate how recently it was updated, and are most of its links still working? (If many of its links lead to dead, or "ghost," sites, the site probably has not been updated for some time.)

18c Evaluate a source's arguments.

As you read the sources you have selected, you should continue to assess their reliability. Does the writer of a piece appeal to your emotions, to your reason, or to both in a balanced way? Regardless of

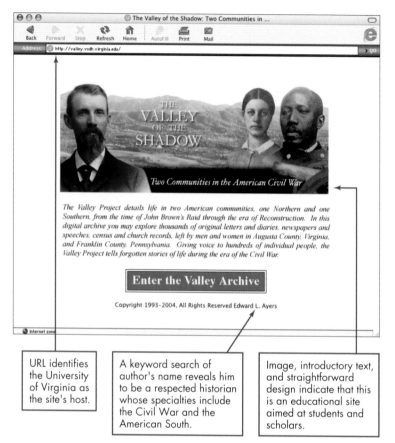

FIGURE 18.1 **The home page of the Valley Project.** This site provides a collection of primary source documents related to two communities in the years before, during, and after the American Civil War.

where a source comes from, always ask yourself whether a particular writer is objective and fair-minded. Look for arguments that are qualified, supported with evidence, and well documented. Avoid relying on biased sources that appeal to emotions instead of rational thought or that promote one-sided political or religious agendas instead of inquiry and discussion.

The debate surrounding the use of stem cells for research on neurological diseases is an excellent example of the need to evaluate arguments for possible bias. Web sites and print publications that support the use of cells taken from frozen embryos stored in fertility clinics and slated to be discarded are likely to cite facts and arguments favorable to

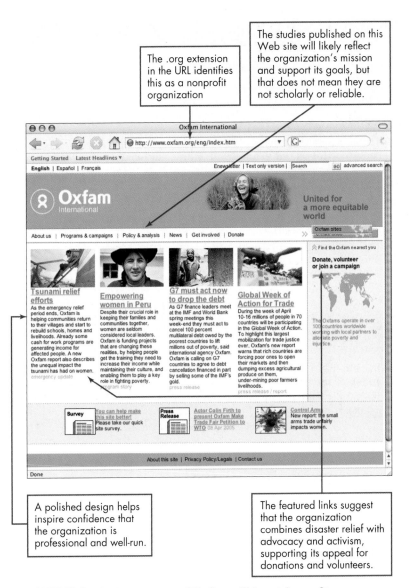

The .org extension in the URL identifies this as a nonprofit organization

The studies published on this Web site will likely reflect the organization's mission and support its goals, but that does not mean they are not scholarly or reliable.

A polished design helps inspire confidence that the organization is professional and well-run.

The featured links suggest that the organization combines disaster relief with advocacy and activism, supporting its appeal for donations and volunteers.

FIGURE 18.2 **The home page of Oxfam.** This not-for-profit organization provides disaster relief and seeks to alleviate poverty.

their position. Web sites and print publications opposed to this research, however, are more likely to challenge the credibility of claims about its potential benefits and to cite arguments about the sanctity of all life. **327**

TEXTCONNEX

Using the CARS Checklist to Evaluate Web Sites

A Web site that is **c**redible, **a**ccurate, **r**easonable, and **s**upported (CARS) should meet the following criteria.

Credibility

- The source is trustworthy; you would consider a print version to be authoritative (for example, an online edition of a respected newspaper or major news magazine).
- The argument and use of evidence are clear and logical.
- The author's or sponsor's credentials are available.
- Quality control is evident (spelling and grammar are correct; links are functional).
- The source is a known or respected authority; it has organizational support (such as a university, a research institution, a major news publication).
- The source appears at or near the top of a *Google* search. (*Google.com* ranks sites according to their popularity; sites near the top of a list of hits are the most frequently accessed by people looking for the same information you seek.)

Accuracy

- The site is updated frequently, if not daily (and includes "last-updated" information).
- The site is factual, not speculative, and provides evidence for its assertions.

A fair-minded researcher needs to read and evaluate sources on both sides of this and other issues. Doing so includes consulting relevant primary sources if they exist.

Exercise 18.1   Web site evaluation

Working alone or in groups, choose one of the following topics:

1. The cost of prescription drugs in the United States
2. Drilling for oil in the Arctic National Wildlife Refuge
3. The reintroduction of wolves in Yellowstone National Park
4. The legalization of marijuana
5. Global warming
6. Second Amendment rights/gun control

- The site is detailed; text appears in full paragraphs.
- The site is comprehensive, including archives, links, and additional resources. A search feature and table of contents or tabs allow users to quickly find the information they need.
- The site's purpose includes completeness and accuracy.

Reasonableness

- The site is fair, balanced, and objective.
- The site makes its purpose clear (is it selling something? prompting site visitors to sign a petition? promoting a new film?).
- The site contains no conflicts of interest.
- The site content does not include fallacies or a slanted tone (*for more on fallacies, see Chapter 10: Arguments, pp. 216–17*).

Support

- The site lists sources for its information, providing links where appropriate.
- The site clarifies which content it is responsible for and which links are created by unrelated authors or sponsors.
- The site provides contact information for its authors and/or sponsors.
- If the site is an academic resource, it follows the conventions of a specific citation style (for example, MLA, APA).

For your topic, find at least three Web sites that clearly demonstrate at least one of the following characteristics:

Bias	Conflict of interest
Objectivity	Timeliness
Authority	Quality control (or lack thereof)
Fallacy	Obvious audience and purpose

Be prepared to share example Web pages with your class (either print them out, or use a projection screen) and to point out how they demonstrate the characteristics you have identified.

19 Doing Research in the Archive, Field, and Lab

Research involves using both primary and secondary sources of information. When you consult books, journal articles, and other print and online resources, you are doing **secondary research;** you are gathering information from sources that have already been created by another writer or researcher. Primary research, in contrast, takes you out into the world. When you conduct **primary research**—looking up old maps, consulting census records, polling community members about a current issue, interviewing participants in a campus protest, observing the social and natural world—you participate in the discovery of knowledge.

The Internet has transformed primary research. For example, meteorological databases housed in Colorado are now available on the Internet in a format that students as well as specialists can use. Laboratory research is being transformed by the development of dry labs—computer-based experimental arenas in which research is conducted through simulations. Also, researchers can now use e-mail to carry out surveys and interviews.

The three kinds of primary research discussed in this chapter are archival research, field research, and laboratory research:

- **Archival research:** An **archive** is a cataloged collection of documents, manuscripts, or other materials, possibly including receipts, wills, photographs, sound recordings, or other kinds of media. Archives are found in campus libraries, museums, performing arts centers, and municipal buildings, among other places. Usually, an archive is organized around one key person, movement, circumstance, or phenomenon. For example, the Louis Armstrong House and Archives, a National Historic Site and New York City landmark, is a freestanding museum whose archives are managed by Queens College. The archives include everything from Louis Armstrong's handwritten scores to several of his trumpets and mouthpieces. Esther Hoffman, a student researcher, consulted the Louis Armstrong archives for her research paper on the jazz great and his manager (see p. 416).

- **Field research:** You may have taken field trips when you were in primary or middle school. The purpose of those trips was to expose you to something you could not experience in the classroom—for example, a boat going through a lock and dam, a working farm, a musical rehearsal, or an automotive repair shop. Field research similarly takes you out into the world to gather and record information not available in a library, laboratory, or classroom.

■ **Laboratory research:** Every science course you take will most likely involve a laboratory component. In the laboratory, you work individually or as a team carefully to record each step of an experiment. You strive for accuracy as you follow the process and describe the results. Eventually, you will begin to create your own experiments to try out an idea, or hypothesis, based on what you have learned from prior experiments.

CHARTING the TERRITORY

Research in the Disciplines

Different disciplines engage in characteristically different forms of primary research. Here are some examples:

■ **Archival research:** Languages and literature; education; music and the performing arts; visual arts; media and popular culture; social sciences

■ **Field research:** Social sciences; marketing and advertising; media and communication

■ **Laboratory research:** Life sciences; physical sciences; computer science; engineering

19a Adhere to ethical principles when doing primary research.

In the archive, field, or lab, you work directly with something precious and immediate: an original record, a group of people, or special materials. Sometimes you will be the first person to see the significance of a document, to observe a particular pattern of behavior, or to perform a new test in the lab. An ethical researcher shows respect for materials, experimental subjects, fellow researchers, and readers.

Ethics also require you to accurately and completely describe what your primary research reveals—even if it means revising your thesis or reconsidering your entire argument. An ethical researcher does not overlook or conceal data that do not support a hypothesis; and of course, an ethical researcher never fabricates supporting data.

Here are some guidelines for ethical research:

- Handle original documents and materials with great care, always leaving sources and data available for other researchers.
- Report your sources and results accurately.
- Follow the procedures mandated by your college and your field when working with human participants.

Research with human participants that you do as an undergraduate should also adhere to the following basic principles:

- **Confidentiality:** People who fill out surveys, participate in focus groups, or respond to interviews should be assured that their names will not be used without their permission.
- **Informed consent:** Before participating in an experiment, all participants must sign a statement affirming that they understand the general purpose of the research. Researchers agree that observations of crowds in a shopping mall or children in a classroom do not require informed consent, unless the observations intrude on the lives of the people being observed.
- **Minimal risk:** Researchers must design experiments so that participants do not incur any risks greater than they do in everyday life.
- **Protection of vulnerable groups:** Researchers must be held strictly accountable for research done with participants in the following categories: the physically disabled, prisoners, those who are mentally incompetent, minors, the elderly, and pregnant women.

Be fair when you refute the primary research or the views of others. Even if your purpose is to prove fellow researchers wrong, review their work and state their viewpoints in words that they themselves would recognize as accurate.

19b Prepare yourself before beginning archival research.

Archives are found in libraries, museums, other institutions, private collections, and on video- and audiotape. Your own attic may contain family archives—letters, diaries, and photograph collections that could have value to a researcher.

The more you know about your area of study, the more likely you will be to see the significance of an item in an archival collection. Reading about your topic in books, journals, and Internet documents provides a framework for discovery and leads you to questions that can be answered only by consulting original materials in an archive.

Archives generally require that you telephone or e-mail to arrange a time for your visit. Some archives may be restricted; if you find an archive on the Internet that you would like to visit, call or e-mail well in advance to find out if you will need references, a letter of introduction, or other qualifying papers. If the archive is not open to the general public, politely inquire how you might gain access; if your request is denied, be gracious about it.

Archives generally require you to present a photo identification and to leave bags, coats, cameras, and even ink pens and notebooks at a locker or coat check. Some archives provide users with special gloves for handling materials, as well as pencils and paper for taking notes. Archives also have strict policies about photocopying or otherwise reproducing materials and rarely if ever allow anything to leave the premises. The more you know about the archive's policies and procedures before you visit, the more productive your visit will be.

The home page for the Louis Armstrong Archives at Queens College, illustrated in Figure 19.1 on the next page, includes links to specific holdings in the archive. It also provides information about how to arrange a visit.

19c Plan your field research carefully.

Field research involves making and recording observations, as well as eliciting information with interviews and surveys. An archeologist excavating a site is conducting field research, as is a primatologist observing chimpanzees in the wild or a sociologist interviewing commuters at a train station. Effective field research requires a strong research design and a plan for keeping accurate records.

Plan and arrange your field visit considerately. If your research plans include visiting a place of business, a house of worship, a school or hospital, or nearly any other building, call first and ask to speak with the public relations or media relations department. (If the place you wish to visit has no such office, explain to the receptionist the purpose of your visit and ask to whom you should speak to request permission.) Explain to this person the nature of your project, the date and time you would like to visit, how much time you think you will need, and exactly what it is you will be doing (just observing? interviewing people? taking photographs?). When you have secured permission, ask your contact to send you a confirming letter or e-mail (and be sure that

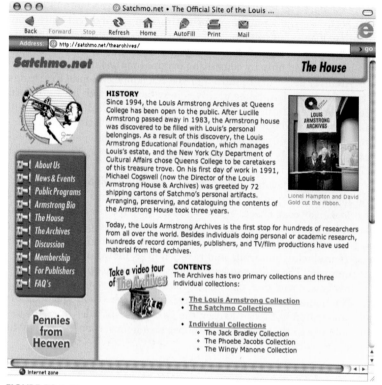

FIGURE 19.1 **Part of the home page for the Louis Armstrong archives.**

you write down this person's name and direct telephone number). This way you will have confirmation that you have permission to do your primary research at this site. If you need to cancel or reschedule your visit, be sure to give this person ample notice. Always write a thank-you note after you have concluded your research.

If you are denied permission to do your field research at a particular place, do not take it personally. Security procedures are much tighter in many places than they were just a few years ago. *Do not* attempt to conduct your research without first obtaining permission. To do so is unethical.

1. Observing, and writing field notes

When you use direct observation, you need to keep careful records (*see Figure 19.2 on page 336*). Here are some guidelines to follow:

TextConnex

Online Information about Archives

Here are some Internet sites that will help you find and understand a wide range of archival sources:

- **American Memory** <http://memory.loc.gov/ammem>: This site offers access to more than 9 million digital items from over 100 collections of material on U.S. history and culture.

- **ArchivesUSA** <http://archives.chadwyck.com>: This subscription service is available through ProQuest. It provides information about 150,000 collections of primary source material and more than 5,000 other manuscript repositories.

- **Radio Program Archive** <http://umdrive.memphis.edu/mbensman/public>: This site lists radio archives available from the University of Memphis and explains how to obtain audio cassettes of significant radio programs.

- **Repositories of Primary Sources** <www.uidaho.edu/special-collections/OtherRepositories.html>: This site lists more than 5,000 Web sites internationally, including holdings of manuscripts, rare books, historical photographs, and other archival materials.

- **Television News Archive** <http://tvnews.vanderbilt.edu>: This site provides summaries of television news broadcasts and information on how to order videocassettes.

- **U.S. National Archives and Record Administration** (NARA) <http://www.nara.gov>: Learn how to use the National Archives in this site's research room, and then search the site for the documents you want.

- **Virtual Library Museums Page** <http://www.icom.org/vlmp>: This site lists online museums throughout the world.

- **Women Writers Project** <http://www.wwp.brown.edu/texts/wwoentry.html>: This site lists archived texts—by pre-Victorian women writers—that are available through the project.

- Be systematic and purposeful in your observations, but be alert to unexpected behavior.
- Record what you see and hear as objectively as possible.
- Take more notes than you think you will ever need.
- When appropriate, categorize the types of behavior you are looking for, and devise a system for counting instances of each type.

FIGURE 19.2 Observing and taking notes. Systematic, purposeful observation and careful note taking are crucial to the success of all field work. Above, archeologist Anna Roosevelt takes notes during the excavation of a site in the Amazon region of South America. Below, biologists record observations for a study of foxes on Catalina Island, California.

■ When you have recorded data over a significant period of time, group your observations into categories for more careful study and discussion.

(For advice on conducting direct observations for a case study, see Chapter 9: Interpretive Analyses, pp. 204–6.)

2. Conducting interviews

Asking relevant questions of experts or people who are members of a population you are studying is a powerful research tool. Group interviews, called *focus groups,* are used in a number of fields, including marketing, education, and psychology. Interviews should be conducted in a relaxed atmosphere, but they are not simply conversations. To be useful as research tools, interviews require systematic preparation and implementation.

■ Identify appropriate people for your interviews.

■ Do background research, and plan your questions.

■ Take careful notes, and if possible make a recording of the interview (but only if you have obtained your subject's permission beforehand).

■ Follow up on vague responses with questions that ask for specific information.

■ Politely probe inconsistencies and contradictions.

■ Write thank-you notes to interviewees, and later send them copies of your report.

If you are conducting interviews to gather the opinions of experts on a particular topic, you might identify appropriate subjects on your campus through a relevant academic department. For example, if your research paper is on the effects of globalization on manufacturing jobs in the United States, you might visit the home pages of your campus business and political science departments to see if anyone on the faculty is studying that issue.

To find subjects for a focus group, consider posting flyers around campus. You might even place a small ad in your campus newspaper describing your project and asking interested people to e-mail you for further information.

3. Taking surveys

Surveys collect the responses of a group of subjects to a **questionnaire,** a series of structured questions. The researcher might read from the questionnaire like a script and record the subjects' responses, or the subjects might read and respond to the questionnaire on their own. Survey research is much more complex than it looks. In fact, students in advanced social science courses spend a great deal of time studying the design and analysis of surveys.

The surveys and polls used by political campaigns and the news media are designed with the help of statisticians and tabulated according to complex mathematical equations. For many college research projects, an informal survey (one not designed to be statistically accurate) may be adequate.

The following suggestions will help you prepare informal surveys:

- **Define your purpose.** Are you trying to gauge attitudes, learn about typical behaviors, or both?

- **Write clear directions and questions.** For example, if you are asking multiple-choice questions, make sure that you cover all possible options and that none of your options overlap.

- **Use neutral language.** Make sure your questions do not suggest a preference for one answer over another.

- **Make the survey brief and easy to complete.** Most informal surveys should be no longer than one page (front and back).

19d Keep a notebook when doing lab research.

All experimenters, from undergraduates to professional scientists, are required to keep careful records of their laboratory work in a notebook. The purpose of this research notebook is to provide a complete and accurate account of the testing of a hypothesis in the controlled environment of the laboratory. In many courses, you will be required to use a lab manual for your notes. Whether or not you are using such a manual, the following guidelines will help you take accurate notes on your research:

1. **Record immediate, on-the-spot, accurate notes on what happens in the lab.** Write down as much detail as possible. Measure precisely; do not estimate. Identify major pieces of apparatus, unusual chemicals, and laboratory animals in enough detail that a reader can determine, for example, the size or type of equipment you used (instead of "physiograph," write "physiograph, Grass model 7B"). Use drawings, when appropriate, to illustrate complicated equipment setups. Include tables, when useful, to present results.

2. **Follow a basic format.** If you are working without a lab manual or if no standard format is provided, you will be expected to present your results in a format that allows you to communicate all the major features of an experiment. The

LEARNING in COLLEGE

Conducting a Survey

Survey questionnaires can be printed with space for respondents to write in their responses. Alternately, the researcher can read the questions to respondents and carefully record their responses.

The following questionnaire was designed by student Lara Delforest for a research project about creating new parking spaces on campus. Lara wanted to know if students would support a plan to provide more shuttle-bus service from existing parking garages as an alternative to creating more on-campus parking.

First, she asked a few questions to be sure that a potential respondent was appropriate for the topic:

1. Are you a student on this campus?
2. Do you currently drive to campus?
3. If you do drive, where do you park?
4. If you don't drive, how do you get to campus?

Lara thanked but did not ask further questions of respondents who were not regularly on campus or who did not drive or take public transportation. She asked these additional questions of the rest:

5. Is the availability of parking on or near campus a factor in your decision to drive or not to drive?
6. If you drive to campus, are you aware of other options? If so, what are those options?
7. For each of the options you just mentioned, explain what would make you consider or reject each one.
8. Are you in favor of creating more parking spaces on campus? Why or why not?
9. Would you be in favor of adding additional campus shuttle buses from existing off-campus parking? Why or why not?

Lara kept notes as people spoke. She asked the respondents their full name (but accepted just a first name from those who did not want to give their full names) so that she could accurately identify them later in her research. To keep her notes organized, Lara turned to a new page of her notebook for each respondent. She used numbers (rather than writing out the entire question over and over) to identify which question the respondent was answering.

five basic sections that must be included are title, purpose, materials and methods, results, and conclusions. (*For more advice on preparing a lab report, see Chapter 8: Informative Reports, pp. 171–79.*)

3. **Write in complete sentences.** Even if you are filling in answers to questions in a lab manual, resist using shorthand to record your notes. Writing in complete sentences helps ensure that you understand the concepts in the experiment. Later, when you study your lab notebook, the complete sentences will provide a clear, unambiguous record of your procedures and results. Notice the difference between the following two responses to a typical question in a lab manual:

QUESTION   *Why is water easily polluted?*

INCOMPLETE ANSWER   universal solvent

COMPLETE ANSWER   Water is a universal solvent. Consequently, many compounds, including pollutants, dissolve in water.

Highlight connections within and between sentences by using the following transitions: *then, next, consequently, because,* and *therefore.* Cause-effect relationships are important to working scientists. Give them similar importance in your lab notebook.

4. **Revise and correct your laboratory notebook in visible ways when necessary.** If you make mistakes in recording laboratory results, correct them as clearly as possible, either by erasing or by crossing out and rewriting on the original sheet. If you make an uncorrectable mistake in your lab notebook, do not tear out the sheet. Simply fold the sheet lengthwise and mark "omit" on the face side.

If you need to add sheets to your notebook, paste them permanently to the appropriate pages. No matter how much preparation you do, unanticipated results often occur in the lab, and you may find yourself jotting down notes on a convenient piece of scrap paper or even a paper towel. Attach these notes to your laboratory notebook.

20 Plagiarism, Copyright, and Intellectual Property

Knowledge develops socially in a give-and-take process akin to conversation. In this environment, integrity and honesty require us to acknowledge others, especially when we use their words or ideas. Researchers who fail to acknowledge their sources—either intentionally or unintentionally—commit plagiarism. Buying a term paper from an online paper mill or "borrowing" a friend's completed assignment are obvious forms of plagiarism. But plagiarism also includes paraphrasing others' material without properly citing the source of the idea or information. (*See Chapter 21: Working with Sources and Avoiding Plagiarism, pp. 353–55, for more on paraphrasing.*)

www.mhhe.com/nmhh
For more information, go to

Research >
Avoiding
Plagiarism > What
Is Plagiarism?

Professional writers who are caught plagiarizing are publicly exposed and often fired by the publishers they write for. Those publications must then work hard to repair their credibility.

The costs of plagiarism are similarly high in the academic world. Scholars who steal the words and ideas of others lose their professional credibility, and often their jobs. Students who plagiarize may receive a failing grade for the assignment or course and face other disciplinary action—including expulsion. Your campus probably has a written policy regarding plagiarism and its consequences.

20a Understand how plagiarism relates to copyright and intellectual property.

Understood broadly, plagiarism is a kind of theft. Thinking of it as such shows how it relates to the concepts of copyright and intellectual property. **Copyright** is the legal right to control the reproduction of any original work—a piece of writing, a musical composition, a play, a movie, a computer program, a photograph, a work of art. A copyrighted work is the **intellectual property** of the copyright holder, whether that is a publisher, a record company, an entertainment conglomerate, or the individual who created the work. When you plagiarize a copyrighted work, you are stealing intellectual property.

LEARNING in COLLEGE

Determining What Is "Common Knowledge"

Information that an audience could be expected to know about from a wide range of sources is considered common knowledge. For example, the structure of DNA and the process of photosynthesis are considered common knowledge among biologists. However, a recent scientific discovery about genetics would not be common knowledge, and so you would need to cite the source of this information. To political scientists, the structure and role of the Electoral College in American presidential elections is common knowledge, but a particular writer's interpretation of the impact of the Electoral College on the 2004 presidential election between George W. Bush and John Kerry would need to be cited.

Maps, charts, graphs, and other visual displays of information are not considered common knowledge. Even though everyone knows that Paris is the capital of France, if you reproduce a map of France in your paper, you must credit the map's creator.

1. Copyright

A copyrighted text—such as a novel, a short story in a magazine, or an article in an academic journal—cannot be reprinted without the written permission of the copyright holder. The copyright protects the right of authors and publishers to make money from their productions. The recent legal efforts of musicians and recording companies to stop the free downloading of music from the Internet are based on copyright law. The musicians and companies claim—and the courts have so far agreed—that downloaders are stealing their intellectual property.

www.mhhe.com/
nmhh
For information on
material that does not
need citing, go to

Research >
Avoiding
Plagiarism >
Common
Knowledge

2. Fair use

Most academic uses of copyrighted sources are protected under the **fair use** provision of copyright law. Under this provision, you can legally quote a brief passage from a copyrighted text in a paper without infringing on the copyright. Of course, to avoid plagiarism, you must identify the passage as a quotation and cite it properly.

3. Intellectual property

In addition to works protected by copyright, intellectual property includes patented inventions, trademarks, industrial designs, and similar intellectual creations that are protected by other laws.

20b Avoid plagiarism.

Under pressure, we tend to make poor choices. Inadvertent plagiarism occurs when busy students take notes carelessly, forgetting to jot down the source of a paraphrase. Deliberate plagiarism occurs when students wait until the last minute and then "borrow" a paper from a friend or cut-and-paste large portions of an online article into their own work. No matter how tired or pressured you may be, nothing can justify plagiarism.

Aside from managing your time and planning your research and writing carefully, here are some suggestions for avoiding plagiarism:

- Do not rely too much on one source, or you may easily slip into using that person's thoughts as your own.

 TEXTCONNEX

Learning More about Plagiarism,
Copyright and Fair Use, and Intellectual Property

Plagiarism

- For the Council of Writing Program Administrators' "Defining and Avoiding Plagiarism: The WPA Statement on Best Practices," see <www.wpacouncil.org/positions/index.html>.
- Educators at Indiana University offer tips on avoiding plagiarism at <www.Indiana.edu/~wts/wts/pamphlets.html>.
- Georgetown University's Honor Council offers an example of a campus honor code pertaining to plagiarism and academic ethics at <www.georgetown.edu/honor/plagiarism.html>.

Copyright and Fair Use

- For information on and a discussion of fair use, see *Copyright and Fair Use* at <fairuse.stanford.edu>, and the U.S. Copyright Office at <www.copyright.gov>.

Intellectual Property

- For information about what constitutes intellectual property and related issues, see the World Intellectual Property Organization Web site at <www.wipo.int>.
- For a legal perspective, the American Intellectual Property Law Association offers information and overviews of recent cases at <www.aipla.org>.

Tips

LEARNING in COLLEGE

Avoiding Inadvertent Plagiarism: Questions to Ask Yourself

- Is my thesis my own idea, or did I find it in one of my sources?
- Have I relied extensively on only one or two sources, instead of a variety of sources?
- Have I used uncommon terms, distinctive phrases, or quotations from a source but failed to enclose them in quotation marks?
- Have I included any words, phrases, or ideas that I don't really understand or explain?
- Have I indicated my source for all quotations, paraphrases, and summaries, either within the text or in a parenthetical citation?
- Have I included page numbers as required for all quotations, paraphrases, and summaries?
- Does every in-text citation have a corresponding entry in the list of works cited or references?

- Keep accurate records while doing research and taking notes, or you may lose track of where an idea came from. If you do not know where you got an idea or a piece of information, do not use it in your paper until you find out.

- When you take notes, be sure to put quotation marks around words, phrases, or sentences taken verbatim from a source. If you use any of those words, phrases, or sentences when summarizing or paraphrasing the source, make sure to put them in quotation marks. Keep in mind that changing a word here and there while keeping a source's sentence structure or phrasing constitutes plagiarism, even if you credit the source for the ideas. (*For more on paraphrase and quotation, see Chapter 21: Working with Sources and Avoiding Plagiarism, pp. 353–54 and 356–57.*)

- Cite the sources of all ideas, opinions, facts, and statistics that are not common knowledge.

- Choose an appropriate documentation style, and use it consistently and properly. (*See Part 4: Documenting across the Curriculum for information about the most common documentation styles for academic writing.*)

- Print out any online source you consult, note the date on which you viewed it, and be sure to keep the complete URL of the site for correct citation. (*See Chapter 21: Working with Sources and Avoiding Plagiarism, pp. 347–51.*)

For MULTILINGUAL STUDENTS

Cultural Assumptions and Misunderstandings about Plagiarism

Respect for ownership of ideas is a core value of Western society. Your culture may consider the knowledge in classic texts a national heritage and, therefore, common property. As a result, you may have been encouraged to incorporate words and information from those texts into your writing without citing their source. American academic culture, however, requires you to identify any use you make of someone else's original work and to cite the work properly in an appropriate documentation style (*see Part 4: Documenting across the Curriculum, which begins on p. 373*). You must similarly credit the source of ideas that are not considered common knowledge. You should accept these rules as nonnegotiable and apply them conscientiously to avoid plagiarism and its serious consequences. When in doubt about citation rules, ask your instructor.

- If you cut-and-paste material from a Web site into a word-processing file, use a different font to identify that material. Also copy the URL for the material, and note the date on which you visited the site. (*See Chapter 21: Working with Sources and Avoiding Plagiarism, pp. 347–51.*)

20c Use copyrighted materials fairly.

www.mhhe.com/
nmhh
For more information
and interactive
exercises, go to

Research >
Avoiding
Plagiarism > Using
Copyrighted
Materials

All written materials, including student papers, letters, and e-mail, are covered by copyright, even if they do not bear an official copyright symbol. A copyright grants its owner exclusive rights to the use of a protected work, including reproducing, distributing, and displaying the work. The popularity of the World Wide Web has led to increased concerns about the fair use of copyrighted material. Before you post your paper on the Web or produce a multimedia presentation that includes audio, video, and graphic elements copied from a Web site, make sure that you have used copyrighted material fairly.

The following four criteria determine if copyrighted material has been used fairly:

- **What is the purpose of the use?** Educational, nonprofit, and personal uses are more likely to be considered fair than commercial use.

345

- **What is the nature of the work being used?** In most cases, imaginative and unpublished materials can be used only if you have the permission of the copyright holder.

- **How much of the copyrighted work is being used?** If a writer uses a small portion of a text for academic purposes, this use is more likely to be considered fair than if he or she uses a whole work for commercial purposes.

- **What effect would this use have on the market for the original?** The use of a work is usually considered unfair if it would hurt sales of the original.

TEXTCONNEX

Plagiarism and Online Sources

The ability of the Internet to make everyone a publisher and broadcaster does not necessarily mean that everything published and broadcast online has been appropriately credited, cited, and documented—or that it is there with the knowledge and permission of the person who created it. When you use material from a Web site, you cannot always be sure that the material you are quoting originated with that site. That is, you might inadvertently be quoting material that has itself been plagiarized from another source.

How can you be certain that material in an online source is being used fairly? Follow the guidelines in Chapter 18: Evaluating Sources to evaluate a Web site's reliability. You can also employ the same strategies that teachers use to investigate possible plagiarism: choose a sentence from the suspect material, and type it between quotation marks into the search box of *Google* or *Yahoo!* If you get a hit, investigate further to see if one site is copying from the other—or both are copying from some other source. Ask your instructor for further advice.

21 Working with Sources and Avoiding Plagiarism

Once you have a research question to answer, an idea about what the library and Internet have to offer, and some sense of the kinds of materials you need, you are ready to begin selecting and using sources. Attention to detail and keeping careful records at this stage will help you avoid plagiarism later.

21a Maintain a working bibliography.

www.mhhe.com/nmhh
For help with creating a bibliography, go to

Research >
Bibliomaker

As you research, compile a **working bibliography**—a list of those books, articles, pamphlets, Web sites, and other sources that seem most likely to help you answer your research question. It is essential to maintain an accurate and complete record of all sources you consult.

For each source, record the following bibliographic information:

- Call number of book, reference work, or other print source; URL of each Web site
- All authors, editors, and translators
- Title of chapter, article, or Web page
- Title of book, periodical, or Web site in which the chapter, article, or page appears
- For books—place, publisher, and date of publication, as well as edition or volume numbers if applicable (*see pp. 378 and 431 for illustrations showing where to find this information*)
- For periodical articles—the date and volume number, issue, and page numbers if applicable (*see pp. 379 and 432 for illustrations showing where to find this information*)
- For a Web source—the date you consulted it and the date that the Web site was last updated, if available

You can record bibliographic information on note cards or in a word-processing file, you can print out bibliographic information from the results of online searches in databases and library catalogs, or you can record bibliographic information directly on photocopies or printouts of source material. You can also save most Web pages and other online sources to your computer.

347

Note: Many professional researchers use bibliographic software that can help them keep track of sources and format bibliographic information in a variety of documentation styles. Examples include *Endnote, ProCite,* and *Reference Manager.* The *Catalyst* Web site that accompanies this handbook includes *Bibliomaker,* a program that can automatically format citations in the most common documentation styles: MLA, APA, Chicago, and CSE (*see Chapters 24–26*).

1. Using note cards or a word processor

Before computers became widely available, most researchers used 3-by-5-inch or 4-by-6-inch note cards to compile the working bibliography, with each potential source getting a separate card as in Figure 21.1. This method is still useful. Besides including all the information you need to document the source, you can also use the cards to record brief quotations from or comments on those sources you decide to read and use.

Instead of handwriting on cards, you can record bibliographic information in a word-processor file. You can also combine the two methods, recording bibliographic information in a word-processing file then printing it, cutting it out, and taping it on a note card.

BMCC Library ML419.A75 B47 1997

Bergreen, Laurence. Louis Armstrong:
An Extravagant Life. New York:
Broadway, 1997.

Ostwald, David. "All That Jazz." Rev. of
Louis Armstrong: An Extravagant Life,
by Laurence Bergreen.
Commentary Nov. 1997: 68–72.

"Satchmo!" New Orleans Online. 1998.
New Orleans Tourism Marketing
Corporation. 26 Feb. 2004
<http://www.neworleansonline.com/
neworleans/music/satchmobio.html>

FIGURE 21.1 **Three sample bibliography note cards—one for a book (*top*), one for a journal article (*middle*), and one for a Web site (*bottom*).**

2. Printing the results of online searches in databases and library catalogs

Search results in online indexes and databases usually include complete bibliographic information about the sources they list. (*See Figure 16.3, p. 298, as well as pp. 380 and 433 for illustrations showing where to find this information.*) You can print these results directly from your browser or, in some cases, save them on disk and transfer them to a word-processing file. Be sure to record also the name and URL of the database and the date of your search. (If you download the full text of an article from a database and refer to it in your paper, your citation must include information about the database as well as bibliographic information about the article itself.) If you rely on search-result printouts to compile your working bibliography, you may want to use a highlighter to indicate those sources you plan to consult.

You can similarly print out or save bibliographic information from the results of searches of online library catalogs. Some college libraries make it possible to compile a list of sources and e-mail it to yourself as in Figure 21.2.

3. Using photocopies and printouts from Web sites

If you photocopy articles, essays, or pages of reference works from a print or microfilm source, take time to note the bibliographic information on the photocopy. Spending a few extra minutes to do so can save you lots of time later. Similarly, if you print out a source you find on a Web site or copy it to your computer, be sure to note the site's complete URL and the date you visited it.

21b Take notes on your sources.

Taking notes helps you think through your research question. As you work, you can take notes on the information you find in sources by annotating photocopies of the source material or by noting useful ideas and quotations on paper, on cards, or in a computer file.

1. Annotating

One way to take notes is to annotate photocopied articles and printouts from online information services or Web sites, as in Figure 21.3. As you read, write the following notes directly on the page:

- On the first page, write down complete bibliographic information for the source.

- As you read, record your questions, reactions, and ideas in the margins.

www.mhhe.com/
nmhh
For more information
and interactive
exercises, go to

Research >
Research
Techniques

349

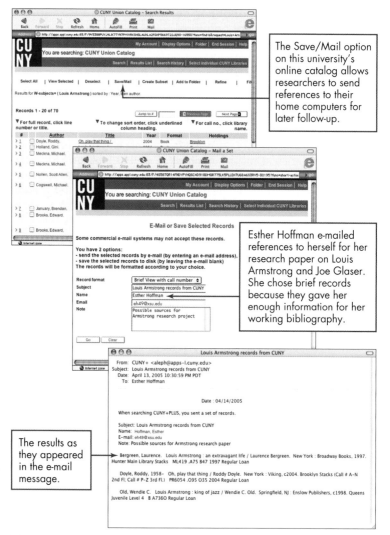

FIGURE 21.2 E-mailing the results of an online library catalog search.

- Comment in the margins on ideas that agree with or differ from those you have already learned about.
- Put important and difficult passages into your own words by paraphrasing or summarizing them in the margins. (*For help with paraphrasing and summarizing, see pp. 353–57.*)

FIGURE 21.3 **An annotated Web page printout.**

■ Use a highlighter to mark statements that you may want to quote because they are key to your readers' understanding of the issue or are especially well expressed.

2. Taking notes in a research journal or log

A **research journal** or **research log** is a tool for keeping track of your research. It can be a spiral or loose-leaf notebook, a box of note cards, or a word processing document on a laptop computer—whatever you are most comfortable with. Use the journal to write down leads for sources to consult and to record ideas and observations about your topic as they occur to you.

When you have finished annotating a photocopy or printout of an article, use your research journal to explore some of the comments, connections, and questions you recorded in the margins. If you do not have photocopies or printouts to annotate, take notes directly in your journal. Writing down each idea on a separate card, notebook page, or word processing page will make it easier to organize the material later. Whatever method you use, be sure to record the source's bibliographic information as well as the specific page number for each idea.

It is important to enclose in quotation marks any exact words from a source. If you think you may forget that the phrasing, as well as the idea, came from someone else, label the passage a "quote," as Esther Hoffman did in the following excerpt from her research journal:

Notes on Dan Morgenstern. "Louis Armstrong and the Development and Diffusion of Jazz." *Louis Armstrong: A Cultural Legacy.* Ed. Marc H. Miller. Seattle: U of Washington P and Queens Museum of Art, 1994. 94-145

• Armstrong having trouble with managers. Fires Johnny Collins in London, 1933. Collins blocks Armstrong from playing with Chick Webb's band (pp. 124-5).

• Armstrong turns to Glaser, an old Chicago acquaintance. Quote: "Joe Glaser . . . proved to be the right man at the right time" (p.128).

Unless you think you might use a quotation in your paper, it is usually better to express the author's ideas in your own words in your notes. To do this you need to understand paraphrasing and summarizing.

3. Paraphrasing

www.mhhe.com/
nmhh
For more information
and interactive
exercises, go to

Research >
Avoiding
Plagiarism >
Summarize/
Paraphrase

When you **paraphrase,** you put someone else's statements into other words. Keep in mind that a paraphrase is not a word-for-word translation. Instead, you need to express the source's ideas *in your own way,* a way that will usually be shorter and less detailed than the original. Even though the sentences are yours, you must still credit the original writer for the ideas by citing his or her work properly. If your paraphrase includes any exact phrasing from the source, put quotation marks around those words.

In the first, unacceptable paraphrase that follows, the writer has done a word-for-word translation, using synonyms for some terms but retaining the phrases from the original (highlighted) and failing to enclose them in quotation marks ("nonsense syllables," "free invention of rhythm, melody, and syllables"). Notice also how close the sentence structures in the faulty paraphrase are to the original. The acceptable paraphrase, by contrast, is more concise than the original. Although it quotes a few words from the source, the writer has expressed the definition in a new and different way.

SOURCE

Scat singing. A technique of jazz singing in which onomatopoeic or nonsense syllables are sung to improvised melodies. Some writers have traced scat singing back to the practice, common in West African musics, of translating percussion patterns into vocal lines by assigning syllables to characteristic rhythms. However, since this allows little scope for melodic improvisation and the earliest recorded examples of jazz scat singing involved the

 LEARNING in COLLEGE

Using Sources to Establish Your Credibility

As noted in Chapter 10, effective writers appeal to their audience by demonstrating that they are *reasonable, ethical,* and *empathetic (see p. 222).* When you present relevant evidence from reliable sources, you demonstrate that you are reasonable. When you take care to put other writers' ideas into your own words and indicate the sources of all ideas and quotations that are not your own and that are not common knowledge, you demonstrate that you are ethical, and therefore trustworthy. When you carefully follow the citation formats required by the discipline that you are writing in, you demonstrate your consideration, or empathy, for your readers by making it easier for them to consult your sources if they wish to.

free invention of rhythm, melody, and syllables, it is more likely that the technique began in the USA as singers imitated the sounds of jazz instrumentalists.

—J. BRADFORD ROBINSON, *The New Grove Dictionary of Jazz*

UNACCEPTABLE PARAPHRASE: PLAGIARISM

Scat is a way of singing that uses nonsense syllables and extemporaneous melodies. Some people think that scat goes back to the custom in West African music of turning drum rhythms into vocal lines. But that does not explain the free invention of rhythm, melody, and syllables of the first recorded instances of scat singing. It is more likely that scat was started in the U.S. by singers imitating the way instrumental jazz sounded (Robinson 425).

ACCEPTABLE PARAPHRASE

Scat, a highly inventive type of jazz singing, combines "nonsense syllables [with] improvised melodies." Although syllabic singing of drum rhythms occurs in West Africa, scat probably owes more to the early attempts of American singers to mimic both the sound and the inventive musical style of instrumental jazz (Robinson 425).

Exercise 21.1 Paraphrase

Read the following passage, annotating as necessary. Write a paraphrase of the passage, and then compare your paraphrase with those of your classmates. What are the similarities and differences among your paraphrases? How can you tell if a paraphrase is acceptable or unacceptable?

SOURCE

The origins of jazz, an urban music, stemmed from the countryside of the South as well as the streets of America's cities. It resulted from two distinct musical traditions, those of West Africa and Europe. West Africa gave jazz its incessant rhythmic drive, the need to move and the emotional urgency that has served the music so well. The European ingredients had more to do with classical qualities pertaining to harmony and melody.

The blending of these two traditions resulted in a music that played around with meter and reinterpreted the use of notes in new combinations, creating blue notes that expressed feelings both sad and joyous. The field hollers of Southern sharecropping slaves combined with the more urban, stylized sounds of musicians from New Orleans, creating a new music. Gospel music from the church melded with what became known in the 20th century as the blues offered a vocal ingredient that translated well to instruments.

—JOHN EPHLAND, "Down Beat's Jazz 101: The Very Beginning"

4. Summarizing

When you **summarize,** you state the main point of a piece, condensing a few paragraphs into one sentence or a few pages into one paragraph. Here are some suggestions for approaching the task:

- **Write down the text's main point.** Compose a sentence that identifies the text, the writer, what the writer does (reports, explores, analyzes, argues), and the most important point the writer makes about the topic. If you are unsure of the meaning of any words in the reading, look them up in a dictionary before you attempt the summary.

- **Divide the text into sections.** To develop their main point, writers move from one subtopic to another or from the statement of an idea to the reasons, evidence, and examples that support it. If you own the text, annotate it to indicate where sections begin and end.

- **In one or two sentences, sum up what each of the text's sections says.** When you summarize, you in effect compose your own topic sentence for each major section of the text. If you own the text, highlight key sentences in each section to help focus your summary.

- **Combine your sentence stating the writer's main point with your sentences summarizing each of the text's major sections.** Now you have a first draft of a summary. Read the draft to see if it makes sense. Add, remove, or change parts as needed.

Here are two summaries of the passage by John Ephland in Exercise 21.1. The unacceptable summary is simply a restatement of Ephland's thesis using much of his phrasing (highlighted). The acceptable summary states Ephland's main point in the writer's own words.

www.mhhe.com/
nmhh
For more information
and interactive
exercises, go to

Research >
Avoiding
Plagiarism >
Summarize/
Paraphrase

355

UNACCEPTABLE SUMMARY: PLAGIARISM

The origins of jazz are two distinct musical traditions, those of West Africa and Europe. New meters and new note combinations capable of expressing both sad and joyous feelings resulted from the blending of these two traditions.

ACCEPTABLE SUMMARY

Jazz has its roots in the musical traditions of both West Africa and Europe. It combines rhythmic, harmonic, and melodic features of both traditions in new and emotionally expressive ways.

(For a summary of a longer passage, see Chapter 7: Reading, Thinking, Writing: The Critical Connection, p. 155.)

Exercise 21.2 Summary

Read the following passage and write a summary of it. Compare your summary with those of your classmates. What are the similarities and differences among your summaries? How does writing a paraphrase compare with writing a summary? Which task was more difficult, and why?

SOURCE

Male musicians dominated the jazz scene when the music first surfaced, making it difficult for women to enter their ranks. The fraternity of jazzmen also frowned upon women wind instrumentalists. However, some African American women, in the late 19th century, played the instruments that were barred from the "opposite sex". . . . Many of their names have been lost in history, but, a few have survived. For example, Mattie Simpson, a cornetist, performed 'on principal and prominent streets of each city.' (10) in Indianapolis, in 1895; Nettie Goff, a trombonist, was a member of The Mahara Minstrels, and Mrs. Laurie Johnson, a trumpeter, had a career that spanned 30 years. They all broke instrumental taboos.

—MARIO A. CHARLES, "The Age of a Jazzwoman:
Valaida Snow, 1900–1956"

---

5. Quoting directly

Sometimes the writer of a source will say something so eloquently and perceptively that you will want to include that writer's words as a **direct quotation** in your paper. In general, you will want to quote directly from writers who are themselves primary sources—for example, in a research paper about Louis Armstrong, a direct quotation from Armstrong himself (or a direct quotation from someone who worked with him) would add nuance and texture to the paper. To avoid inadvertent plagiarism, be careful to indicate that the content is a direct quotation when you copy it into your note cards or your research notebook. Place quotation marks around the direct quotation. You might also use a special ink color to indicate direct quotations.

www.mhhe.com/
nmhh
For more information
and interactive
exercises, go to

Research >
Avoiding
Plagiarism >
Using Quotations

Note: Beware of writing a paper that consists of a string of quotations or paraphrases, one after another. If you notice that you have used more than one quotation or substantial paraphrase every paragraph or two, revise your work to include more of your own reflections on the topic.

21c Synthesize: Take stock of what you have learned.

When you take stock, you assess the research you have done. You also synthesize what you have learned from the sources you have consulted. It is also important to think about how the sources you have read relate to one another. Ask yourself when, how, and why your sources agree or disagree, and consider where you stand on the issues they raise. Did anything you read surprise or disturb you? Writing down your responses to such questions can help you clarify what you have learned from working with sources.

In college writing, the credibility of your work depends on the relevance and reliability of your sources as well as the scope and depth of your reading and observation. A paper on Louis Armstrong, for example, is unlikely to be credible if it relies on only one source of information. For lab reports, detailed observations are likely to be most important because they are the main kind of source that experimenters use when writing up their work.

As the context and kind of writing change, so too do the requirements for types and numbers of sources. As a general rule, however, you should consult more than two sources and use only sources that are both reliable and respected by people working in the field. Ask yourself the following questions about the sources you have consulted:

■ Are your sources trustworthy? (*See Chapter 18: Evaluating Sources, for more on evaluating sources.*)

■ If you have started to develop a tentative answer to your research question, have your sources provided you with a sufficient number of facts, examples, and ideas to support that answer?

■ Have you used sources that examine the issue from several different perspectives?

**www.mhhe.com/
nmhh**
For more information
and interactive
exercises, go to

Research >
Avoiding
Plagiarism >
Using Sources
Accurately

21d Integrate quotations, paraphrases, and summaries properly and effectively.

Ultimately you will use some of the paraphrases, summaries, and quotations you have collected during the course of your research to support and develop the ideas you present in your research paper. Here are some guidelines for integrating them properly and effectively.

1. Integrating quotations

Use quotations when a source's exact words are important to your point and make your writing more memorable, fair, or authoritative. Quotes should be short, enclosed in quotation marks, and well integrated into your sentence structure, as in the following example from Esther Hoffman's paper on Louis Armstrong and Joe Glaser:

> In his dedication to the unpublished manuscript "Louis Armstrong and the Jewish Family in New Orleans," Armstrong calls Glaser "the best friend that I ever had," while in a letter to Max Jones, he writes, "I did not get really happy until I got with my man—my dearest friend—Joe Glaser" (qtd. in Jones and Chilton 16).

When you are integrating someone else's words into your writing, use a **signal phrase** that indicates whom you are quoting. The signal phrases "Armstrong calls Glaser," and "he writes" identify Armstrong as the source of the two quotations in the passage above.

Brackets within quotations Sentences that include quotations must make sense grammatically. Sometimes you may have to adjust a quotation to make it fit properly into your sentence. Use brackets to indicate any minor adjustments you have made. For example, *my* has been changed to *his* to make the quotation fit in the following sentence:

> Armstrong confided to a friend that Glaser's death "broke [his] heart" (Bergreen 490).

Ellipses within quotations Use ellipses to indicate that words have been omitted from the body of a quotation, but be sure that what you omit does not significantly alter the source's meaning. (*For more on using ellipses, see Chapter 54: Quotation Marks.*)

> As Morgenstern put it, "Joe Glaser . . . proved to be the right man at the right time" (128).

Quotations in block format   Quotations longer than four lines should be used rarely. When they are used too frequently, long quotations tend to break up your text and make your reader impatient. If you include a longer quotation, put it in block format (*see Chapter 54: Quotation Marks*) and be especially careful to integrate it into your paper. Tell your readers why you want them to read the block quotation, and afterwards, comment on it.

2. Integrating paraphrases and summaries

The principles for integrating paraphrases and summaries into your text are similar to those for including direct quotations. You want a smooth transition between a source's point and your own voice, and

---

Tips   LEARNING in COLLEGE

Varying Signal Phrases

When a writer relies on the same signal phrase throughout a paper, readers quickly become bored. To keep things interesting, vary your signal phrases. Instead of using the verbs *says* and *writes* again and again, consider including some of the following:

acknowledges	concedes	holds	refutes
adds	concludes	implies	rejects
admits	considers	insists	remarks
argues	contends	interprets	reports
asks	denies	maintains	responds
asserts	describes	notes	shows
charges	emphasizes	observes	speculates
claims	explains	points out	states
comments	expresses	proposes	suggests
complains	finds	proves	warns

   Signal phrases can be livelier in some kinds of researched writing and in some disciplines, but in general you should avoid ascribing emotion or tone to a written source unless that emotion is very clear. For example, you should avoid verbs like *smirks, huffs, retorts,* and *cries,* as well as adverbs such as *angrily, knowingly,* and *coyly.*

you want to accurately attribute the information to its source. Although you do not need to use ellipses or the block format for paraphrases and summaries (because they are in your own words), you will want to use signal phrases.

Besides crediting others for their work, signal phrases can make ideas more interesting by giving them a human face. Here are some examples:

> *As Bergreen points out,* Armstrong easily reached difficult high notes, the F's and G's that stymied other trumpeters (248).

In this passage, Esther Hoffman uses the signal phrase "As Bergreen points out" to identify Bergreen as the source of the paraphrased information about Louis Armstrong's extraordinary technical abilities.

> A 1960 letter from Glaser to Lucille Armstrong corroborates Gold's account; it shows that Glaser assumed responsibility for buying the musician and his wife a new car as well as for filing the paperwork needed to retain the old license plate number.

In this passage, Hoffman uses the word *corroborates* to signal her paraphrase of an original letter she found in the Louis Armstrong archives. She directly names the source (the author of the letter), so she does not need additional parenthetical documentation.

22 Writing the Paper

You have chosen a challenging research question and have located, read, and evaluated a variety of relevant sources. Now you need to come up with a thesis that will allow you to share what you have learned as well as your perspective on the issue.

22a Plan and draft your paper.

Begin planning by recalling the context and purpose of your paper. If you have an assignment sheet, review it to see if the paper is supposed to be primarily informative, interpretive, or argumentative. Keep your purpose and context in mind as you decide on a thesis to support and develop.

1. Deciding on a thesis

Consider the question that guided your research as well as others provoked by what you have learned during your research. Revise the wording of your question to make it intriguing as well as suitable (*see Chapter 15: Understanding Research, pp. 280–83*). After you write down this question, compose an answer that you can use as your working thesis, as Esther Hoffman does in the following example:

HOFFMAN'S FOCAL QUESTION

What kind of relationship did Louis Armstrong and Joe Glaser have?

HOFFMAN'S WORKING THESIS

Armstrong and Glaser enjoyed not only a successful business partnership but also a complex friendship based on mutual respect and caring.

(*For more on devising a thesis, see Chapter 3: Planning and Shaping the Whole Essay, pp. 45–48.*)

www.mhhe.com/nmhh
For help with developing a thesis, go to
Writing > Paragraph/Essay Development > Thesis/Central Idea

www.mhhe.com/
nmhh
For interactive help
with outlines, go to

Writing >
Outlining Tutor

2. Outlining a plan for supporting and developing your thesis

Guided by your tentative thesis, outline a plan that uses your sources in a purposeful way. Decide on the organization you will use to support your thesis—chronological, problem-solution, or thematic—and develop your support by choosing facts, examples, and ideas drawn from a variety of sources. (*See Chapter 3: Planning and Shaping the Whole Essay, p. 50, for more on these organizational structures.*)

For her interpretive paper on Armstrong and Glaser, Hoffman decided on a thematic organization, an approach structured around raising and answering a central question:

- Introduce Armstrong as a great musician who was once a poor waif.

- Introduce Glaser, Armstrong's manager for thirty-four years.

- State the question: what kind of relationship did these two have? Did Glaser dominate Armstrong?

- Discuss Glaser as Armstrong's business manager and his role in making Armstrong a star.

- Discuss Armstrong's resistance to being controlled by Glaser.

- Conclude: Armstrong and Glaser worked well together as friends who respected and cared for each other.

To develop this outline, Hoffman would need to list supporting facts, examples, or ideas for each point. (*For more on developing an outline, see Chapter 3: Planning and Shaping the Whole Essay, pp. 49–54.*)

3. Organizing and evaluating your information

Your note-taking strategies will determine how you collect and organize your information. If you have taken notes on index cards, group them according to topic and subtopic, using your paper's formal or informal outline as a guide. For example, Esther Hoffman could have used the following categories based on her outline for her paper on Louis Armstrong:

Biography – Armstrong
Biography – Glaser
Glaser as manager
Conflict – A & G
Armstrong – media image
Jazz – general info

Sorting index cards into stacks corresponding to topics and subtopics allows you to see what you have gathered. A small stack of cards for a particular topic might mean that the topic is not as important to your thesis as you had originally thought—or that you may need to do additional research on that specific subtopic.

If your notes are primarily on your computer, you can create a new folder or page for each topic and subtopic, and then cut and paste to move information to the appropriate category.

4. Writing a draft that you can revise, share, and edit

When you have a tentative thesis and a plan, you are ready to write a draft. As her outline shows, Hoffman planned to use a few pages to set up the context for her issue, but many writers find that they can present their thesis or focal question at the end of an introductory paragraph or two.

As you write beyond the introduction, be prepared to reexamine and refine your thesis. Discovering interesting connections as well as new ways to express your ideas makes writing exciting. Such discoveries often occur when writers use what they have read in various sources to support and develop their ideas. When you draw on ideas from your sources, be sure to quote and paraphrase effectively and properly. (*For advice on quoting and paraphrasing, see Chapter 21: Working with Sources and Avoiding Plagiarism, pp. 347–60, and section 22c of this chapter.*)

Make your conclusion as memorable as possible. In the final version of Hoffman's paper, on pages 423–24, note how she uses a visual and a play on words—"more than meets the eye"—to end her paper. In doing so, she enhances her concluding point—that Armstrong and Glaser were different, yet complementary, and that their relationship was complex. Hoffman did not come up with the last line of her paper until she revised and edited her first draft. It is not uncommon for writers to come up with fresh ideas for their introduction, body paragraphs, or conclusion at this stage—one reason why it is important to spend time revising and editing your paper. (*For more on revising, see Chapter 5: Revising and Editing, pp. 91–124.*)

5. Integrating visuals

Well-chosen visuals like photographs, drawings, charts, graphs, and maps can sometimes help illustrate your argument. In some cases, a visual might itself be a subject of your analysis. Esther Hoffman found two paintings in her archival research about Louis Armstrong. She describes both of them in her paper and was able to include a reproduction of one in her work.

There are two additional things to consider when integrating visuals into your paper: figure numbers and captions.

■ **Figure numbers:** Both MLA and APA styles require writers to number each image in a research paper. In MLA style, the word *figure* is abbreviated to *Fig.* In APA style, the full word *Figure* is written out.

www.mhhe.com/
nmhh
For more information and interactive exercises, go to
Writing >
Paragraph/Essay Development >
Drafting and Revising

Tips

Guidelines for Revising Your Research Paper

Consider these questions as you read your draft and gather feedback from your instructor and peers:

- Is my thesis clear and engaging? Where in my draft do I most clearly state my thesis?
- Does each paragraph include a topic sentence? Are the transitions between paragraphs clear and logical?
- Have I provided adequate in-text citation for each source?
- Do I have enough evidence to support each point I make? Where should I include additional research?
- Does my introduction give a specific and interesting overview of my topic and thesis? Does my conclusion provide a compelling synthesis of my research and clearly sum up the support for my thesis?
- Have I integrated quotations, summaries, and paraphrases smoothly and used a variety of signal phrases?
- Do all of my illustrations have complete and accurate captions?
- Do all of my in-text citations match my works-cited or references page? Is there anything on my works-cited or references page that is not referred to in the text of my paper?

- **Captions:** Each visual that you include in your paper must be followed by a caption that includes the title of the visual (if it has one; otherwise, a brief description will do) and its source. In MLA style, each caption begins with the figure number and a period after the number (Fig. 1.); in APA style, use italics for the figure number (*Figure 1*) and no period.

22b Revise your draft.

After you have completed a draft of your research paper, you will probably be asked to share it with other members of your class for peer review and feedback. This is how research is prepared for circulation and publication in the academic and professional worlds. Academic researchers often present their papers at conferences to get feedback from others working in their field; journalists work closely with their editors to develop a story and contact appropriate sources; sales professionals work as teams on quarterly reports to show management how a business is doing.

You may prefer to revise a hard copy of your draft by hand, or you might find it easier to use the Track Changes feature in your word-processing program. Either way, be sure to keep previous versions of your essay drafts. Even if your instructor does not require you to hand in preliminary drafts, it is useful to have a record of how your paper evolved—especially if you need to track down a particular source or want to reincorporate something that you had removed earlier in the process.

22c Document your sources.

www.mhhe.com/ nmhh
For help with documenting sources, go to
Research > Avoiding Plagiarism > Citing Sources

Whenever you use information, ideas, or words from someone else's work, you must acknowledge that person. As noted in the box on page 342, the only exception to this principle is when you use information that is common knowledge, such as the chemical composition of water or the names of the thirteen original states. When you tell readers what sources you have consulted, they can more readily understand your paper as well as the conversation you are participating in by writing it.

CHARTING the TERRITORY

Documentation Styles Explained in This Text

TYPE OF COURSE	DOCUMENTATION STYLE MOST COMMONLY USED	WHERE TO FIND THIS STYLE IN THE HANDBOOK
Humanities (English, religion, music, art, philosophy)	MLA (Modern Language Association) or Chicago (*Chicago Manual of Style*)	MLA: *pp. 374–426* Chicago: *pp. 466–85*
Social sciences (anthropology, psychology, sociology. education, and business)	APA (American Psychological Association)	APA: *pp. 427–65*
Sciences (mathematics, natural sciences, engineering, physical therapy, computer science)	CSE (Council of Science Editors)	CSE: *pp. 486–95*

How sources are documented varies by field and discipline. Choose a documentation style that is appropriate for the particular course you are taking, and use it properly and consistently.

If you are not sure which of the styles covered in this handbook to use, ask your instructor. If you are required to use an alternative, discipline-specific documentation style, consult the list of manuals on page 367.

For her paper on Louis Armstrong and Joe Glaser, Esther Hoffman used the MLA documentation style. (*The final draft of the paper appears at the end of Chapter 24: MLA Documentation Style, on pp. 416–26.*)

22d Present and publish your work.

There are many ways to share the results of your research. New technologies make it possible to create sophisticated audio and video presentations and Web sites. In both your academic and your professional career, you will likely be called upon to present your ideas, information, and research using prsentation software such as PowerPoint or through visual tools such as iDVD. You might use desktop publishing software to prepare a research manuscript for interoffice or interdepartmental publication, or for publication in a newspaper or journal. Make the presentation of your research suit your audience and your purpose.

(For more information on oral presentations, see Chapter 13: Oral Presentations, pp. 248–53. To learn more about presentation software and other multimedia tools, see Chapter 14: Multimedia Writing, pp. 254–75. For a discussion of document design, see Chapter 6: Designing Academic Papers, pp. 125–39.)

CHARTING the TERRITORY

Style Manuals for Specific Disciplines

SPECIFIC DISCIPLINE	POSSIBLE STYLE MANUAL
Chemistry	Dodd, Janet S., ed. *The ACS Style Guide: A Manual for Authors and Editors.* 2nd ed. Washington: American Chemical Society, 1997.
Geology	Bates, Robert L., Rex Buchanan, and Marla Adkins-Heljeson, eds. *Geowriting: A Guide to Writing, Editing, and Printing in Earth Science.* 5th ed. Alexandria: American Geological Institute, 1995.
Government and Law	Garner, Diane L., and Diane H. Smith, eds. *The Complete Guide to Citing Government Information Resources: A Manual for Writers and Librarians.* Rev. ed. Bethesda: Congressional Information Service, 1993.
	Harvard Law Review et al. *The Bluebook: A Uniform System of Citation.* 17th ed. Cambridge: Harvard Law Review Assn., 2000.
Journalism	Goldstein, Norm, ed. *Associated Press Stylebook and Briefing on Media Law.* Rev. and upd. ed. New York: Associated Press, 2002.
Linguistics	Linguistic Society of America. "LSA Style Sheet." *LSA Bulletin.* Published annually in the December issue.
Mathematics	American Mathematical Society. *AMS Author Handbook: General Instructions for Preparing Manuscripts.* Providence: AMS, 1997.
Medicine	Iverson, Cheryl, ed. *American Medical Association Manual of Style: A Guide for Authors and Editors.* 9th ed. Baltimore: Williams and Wilkins, 1998.
Physics	American Institute of Physics. *Style Manual for Guidance in the Preparation of Papers.* 5th ed. New York: AIP, 1995.
Political Science	American Political Science Association. *Style Manual for Political Science.* Rev. ed. Washington: APSA, 2001.

23 — Discipline-Specific Resources in the Library and on the Internet

The list that follows will help you get started doing research in specific disciplines. Both print and electronic resources are listed because you should use both types in your research. (Print entries precede electronic entries.) Most major academic disciplines have computerized bibliographies, databases, and indexes that you can access through your college's library. (*For a list of online databases, see pp. 300–1.*)

www.mhhe.com/ nmhh
For an updated listing of resources, go to

Research >
Discipline Specific
Resources

> *Note:* Remember that Web addresses change frequently. If you get the 4040 (File not found) message, try doing a search for the page using a search engine, or look for the URL on this handbook's Web site, which is updated frequently.

Anthropology
Abstracts in Anthropology
Annual Review of Anthropology
Dictionary of Anthropology
Encyclopedia of World Cultures
American Anthropological Association
<http://www.aaanet.org>

National Anthropology Archives
<http://www.nmnh.si.edu/index.htm>

WWW Virtual Library: Anthropology
<http://vlib.anthrotech.com>

Art and Architecture
Art Abstracts
Art Index
BHA: Bibliography of the History of Art
Encyclopedia of World Art
McGraw-Hill Dictionary of Art

Artcyclopedia
<http://www.artcyclopedia.com>

The Louvre
<http://www.louvre.fr/louvrea.htm>

The Metropolitan Museum of Art (New York)
<http://www.metmuseum.org>

The National Gallery of Art (Washington, D.C.)
<http://www.nga.gov>

Voice of the Shuttle Art History and Architecture
<http://vos.ucsb.edu/index.asp>

Biology
Biological Abstracts
Biological and Agricultural Index
Encyclopedia of the Biological Sciences

368

*Henderson's Dictionary of
   Biological Terms*
Zoological Record
Biology Online
   <http://www.biology-online.org/>

Harvard University Biology Links
   <http://mcb.harvard.edu/
   BioLinks.html>

*National Science Foundation:
   Biology*
   <http://www.nsf.gov/news/
   overviews/biology/index.jsp>

Business

Accounting and Tax Index
*Encyclopedia of Business
   Information Sources*
ABI / Inform
Business Periodicals
Business and Industry
Newslink Business Newspapers
   <http://newslink.org/
   biznews.html>

Chemistry

Chemical Abstracts (CASEARCH)
*McGraw-Hill Dictionary of
   Chemistry*
*Van Nostrand Reinhold
   Encyclopedia of Chemistry*
American Chemical Society
   <http://www.chemistry.org>

Sheffield ChemDex
   <http://www.chemdex.org>

WWW Virtual Library: Chemistry
   <http://www.liv.ac.uk/chemistry/
   links/links.html>

Classics

Oxford Classical Dictionary
*Princeton Encyclopedia of Classical
   Sites*
Perseus Digital Library
   <http://www.perseus.tufts.edu>

Communications and Journalism

Mass Media Bibliography

Communication Abstracts
*International Encyclopedia of
   Communications*
Journalism Abstracts
*American Communication
   Association*
   <http://www.americancomm.org>

*Journalism and Mass
   Communications Abstracts*
   <http://www.aejmc.org/abstracts/>

The Poynter Institute
   <http://poynter.org>

Computer Science and Technology

Computer Abstracts
Dictionary of Computing
Encyclopedia of Computer Science
*McGraw-Hill Encyclopedia of
   Science and Technology*
*FOLDOC (Free Online Dictionary
   of Computing)*
   <http://wombat.doc.ic.ac.uk/
   foldoc/>

*MIT Laboratory Computer Science
   and Artificial Intelligence
   Laboratory*
   <http://www.csail.mit.edu/
   index.php>

Cultural Studies, American and Ethnic Studies

Encyclopedia of World Cultures
*Dictionary of American Negro
   Biography*
*Gale Encyclopedia of Multicultural
   America*
Mexican American Biographies
American Studies Association
   <http://lumen.georgetown.edu/
   projects/asw>

*National Museum of the American
   Indian*
   <http://www.nmai.si.edu>

*Schomburg Center for Research in
   Black Culture*
   <http://www.nypl.org/research/
   sc/sc.html>

Smithsonian Center for Folklife and Cultural Heritage
<http://www.folklife.si.edu/index.html>

Economics

EconLit

PAIS: Public Affairs Information Service

American Economic Association
<http://www.aeaweb.org>

Internet Resources for Economists
<http://www.oswego.edu/~economic/econweb.htm>

Resources for Economists on the Internet
<http://rfe.wustl.edu>

Education

Dictionary of Education

Education Index

Encyclopedia of Educational Research

International Encyclopedia of Education

Resources in Education

The Educator's Reference Desk
<http://www.eduref.org>

EdWeb
<http://edwebproject.org>

U.S. Department of Education
<http://www.ed.gov>

Engineering

Applied Science and Technology Index

Engineering Index

McGraw-Hill Encyclopedia of Engineering

IEEE Spectrum
<http://www.spectrum.ieee.org>

WWW Virtual Library: Engineering
<http://www.eevl.ac.uk/wwwvl.html>

Environmental Sciences

Dictionary of the Environment

Encyclopedia of Energy, Technology, and the Environment

Encyclopedia of the Environment

Environment Abstracts

Environment Index

Envirolink
<http://envirolink.org>

U.S. Environmental Protection Agency
<http://www.epa.gov>

Film

Dictionary of Film Terms

The Film Encyclopedia

Film Index International

Film Literature Index

Internet Movie Database
<http://www.imdb.com>

Geography

Geographical Abstracts

Longman Dictionary of Geography

Modern Geography: An Encyclopedic Survey

CIA World Factbook
<http://www.cia.gov/cia/publications/factbook/index.html>

Resources for Geographers
<http://www.Colorado.edu/geography/virtdept/resources/contents.htm>

Geology

Bibliography and Index of Geology

Challinor's Dictionary of Geology

The Encyclopedia of Field and General Geology

American Geological Institute
<http://www.agiweb.org>

U.S. Geological Survey
<http://www.usgs.gov>

Health and Medicine

American Medical Association Encyclopedia of Medicine

Cumulated Index Medicus

Medical and Health Information Directory

Nutrition Abstracts and Reviews
PubMed Central
   <http://www.pubmedcentral.
   nih.gov>

U.S. National Library of Medicine
   <http://www.nlm.nih.gov>

World Health Organization
   <http://www.who.int>

History

America: History and Life
Dictionary of Historical Terms
Encyclopedia of American History
An Encyclopedia of World History
Historical Abstracts
Electronic Documents in History
   <http://www.tntech.edu/history/
   edocs.html>

History Cooperative
   <http://historycooperative.
   press.uiuc.edu>

HistoryWorld
   <http://www.historyworld.net/>

NARA Archival Research Catalog
   <www.archives.gov/
   research_room/arc/index.htm>

Languages and Linguistics

*Cambridge Encyclopedia of
   Language*
*An Encyclopedic Dictionary of
   Language and Languages*
*International Encyclopedia of
   Linguistics*
*LLBA: Linguistics and Language
   Behavior Abstracts*
MLA International Bibliography
Center for Applied Linguistics
   <http://www.cal.org>

SIL International Linguistics
   <http://www.sil.org/linguistics>

Literature

*Concise Oxford Dictionary of
   Literary Terms*
MLA International Bibliography

*The New Princeton Encyclopedia of
   Poetry and Poetics*
*Electronic Text Center at the
   University of Virginia Library*
   <http://etext.lib.virginia.edu>

Project Gutenberg
   <http://www.gutenberg.org>

Voice of the Shuttle
   <http://vos.ucsb.edu/index.asp>

Mathematics

American Statistics Index
*Facts on File Dictionary of
   Mathematics*
*International Dictionary of Applied
   Mathematics*
Mathematical Reviews (MathSciNet)
American Mathematical Society
   <http://www.ams.org>

Math Forum
   <http://mathforum.com>

Music

Music Index
*New Grove Dictionary of Music and
   Musicians*
New Oxford Companion to Music
New Oxford Dictionary of Music
RILM Abstracts of Music Literature
AllMusic
   <http://allmusic.com>

Philosophy

Dictionary of Philosophy
Philosopher's Index
*Routledge Encyclopedia of
   Philosophy*
American Philosophical Association
   <http://www.apa.udel.edu/apa/
   index.html>

EpistemeLinks.com
   <http://www.epistemelinks.com>

Physics

Dictionary of Physics
*McGraw-Hill Encyclopedia of
   Physics*

Physics Abstracts
American Institute of Physics
<http://aip.org>

American Physical Society
<http://www.aps.org>

Institute of Physics
<http://ioppublishing.com>

PhysicsWeb
<http://physicsweb.org/>

Political Science

Almanac of American Politics
Congressional Quarterly Almanac
Encyclopedia of Government and Politics
International Political Science Abstracts
Political Resources on the Web
<http://www.politicalresources.net>

Public Affairs Information Service (PAIS)
Non-Western Sources on Contemporary Political Issues
<http://library.lib.binghamton.edu/subjects/polsci/home.html>

Thomas: Legislative Information on the Internet
<http://thomas.loc.gov>

United Nations
<http://www.un.org>

Psychology

International Dictionary of Psychology
International Encyclopedia of Psychiatry, Psychology, Psychoanalysis, and Neurology
Psychological Abstracts
American Psychological Association
<http://www.apa.org>

American Psychological Society
<http://www.psychologicalscience.org>

Encyclopedia of Psychology
<http://www.psychology.org/>

PsychWeb
<http://www.psywww.com>

Religion

ATLA Religion
Dictionary of Bible and Religion
Encyclopedia of Religion
Religions and Scriptures
<http://www.wam.umd.edu/~stwright/rel>

Sociology

Annual Review of Sociology
Encyclopedia of Social Work
Encyclopedia of Sociology
Sociological Abstracts
Academic Info Sociology: Databases and Centers
<http://www.academicinfo.net/socdata.html>

American Sociological Association
<http://asanet.org>

The SocioWeb
<http://www.socioweb.com/~markbl/socioweb/indexes>

Theater and Dance

International Encyclopedia of the Dance
McGraw-Hill Encyclopedia of World Drama
American Theater Web
<http://www.americantheaterweb.com/>

The WWW Virtual Library: Theatre and Drama
<http://vl-theatre.com>

Women's Studies

Women Studies Abstracts
Women's Studies: A Guide to Information Sources
Women's Studies Encyclopedia
Feminist Majority Foundation Online
<http://www.feminist.org>

National Women's History Project
<http://www.nwhp.org>

The Library of Congress houses the largest collection of books and documents in the world, and all U.S. libraries use its cataloguing systems. The Library's architectural design suggests the Italian Renaissance; its interior features work by American artists.

PART 4

Nothing gives an author so much pleasure as to find his works respectfully quoted by other learned authors.
—BENJAMIN FRANKLIN

Documenting
across the
Curriculum

24 MLA Documentation Style

The documentation style developed by the Modern Language Association (MLA) is used by many researchers in the arts and humanities, especially by those who write about language and literature. The guidelines presented here are based on the sixth edition of Joseph Gibaldi's *MLA Handbook for Writers of Research Papers* (New York: MLA, 2003).

Tips

LEARNING in COLLEGE

What Kind of Source Am I Citing?

MLA style requires writers to list their sources in a works-cited list at the end of a paper. To format works-cited entries correctly, you need to know first of all what kind of source you are citing. The directory on pages 391–92 will help you find the appropriate sample to use as your model. As an alternative, you can use the charts on the pages that follow to help you locate the right example. Answering the questions provided in the charts will usually lead you to the sample entry you need. If you cannot find what you are looking for after consulting the appropriate directory or chart, ask your instructor for help. (*To learn where to find the information you need to complete a citation, see the examples on pp. 378–80.*)

www.mhhe.com/
nmhh
For links to Web sites
for documentation
styles used in various
disciplines, go to

Research > Links
to Documentation
Sites

374

Entries in a Works-Cited List: BOOKS

❓ *Is your source a complete book?*

No   Yes
   ↓

Go to this entry

Is it a complete book with one named author?
   Is it the only book by this author that you are citing? | 1
   Are you citing more than one book by this author? | 2
   Does it also have an editor or translator? | 6,15
   Is it a published doctoral dissertation? | 36

Is it a complete book with more than one named author? | 3

Is it a complete book without a named author?
   Is the author an organization? | 4
   Is the author anonymous or unknown? | 22

Is it a complete book with an editor or a translator?
   Is there an editor instead of an author? | 5
   Does it have both an editor and an author? | 6
   Is it an anthology? | 12
   Is it a translation? | 15
   Is it the published proceedings of an academic conference? | 35

Is it a complete book with a volume or an edition number?
   Is it part of a multivolume work (e.g., Volume 3)? | 18
   Is it one in a series? | 19
   Does it have an edition number (e.g., Second Edition)? | 16

Is it a complete book but not the only version?
   Is your book a republished work (e.g., a classic novel)? | 20
   Is your book a religious text (e.g., the Bible)? | 17

Is the book from a publisher's imprint? | 13

Does the book's title include the title of another book? | 21

❓ *Is your source part of a book?*

No   Yes
   ↓

Go to this entry

Is it from an edited book?
   Is it a work in an anthology? | 7
   Is it a chapter in an edited book? | 7
   Are you citing two or more items from the same anthology? | 8
   Is it an article from a collection of reprinted articles? | 11
   Is it a published letter (e.g., part of a published collection)? | 43

Is it from a reference work (e.g., an encyclopedia)?
   Is it an article with an author? | 9
   Is it an article without a named author? | 10

Is it a preface, an introduction, a foreword, or an afterword? | 14

Check the next page or the directory on pages 391–92 or consult your instructor.

Entries in a Works-Cited List: PRINT PERIODICALS
OR OTHER PRINT SOURCES

? *Is your source from a journal, a magazine, or a newspaper?*

No   **Yes**
        ↓

	Go to this entry
Is it from an academic journal?	
Are the page numbers continued from one issue to the next?	23
Do the page numbers in each issue start with 1?	24
Is your source an abstract (a brief summary) of an article?	31
Is it from a magazine?	
Is the magazine published monthly?	25
Is the magazine published weekly?	26
Is your source a letter to the editor?	32
Is it a review (e.g., a review of a book or film)?	29
Is it an interview?	39
Is it stored on microfiche, microform, or microfilm?	47
Is it from a newspaper?	
Is it an article?	27
Is it an interview?	39
Is it an editorial?	30
Is it a letter to the editor?	32
Is it a review (e.g., a review of a book or film)?	29
Is it stored on microfiche, microform, or microfilm?	47
Is the author unknown?	28

? *Is it a print source but not a book, a part of a book, or an article
in an academic journal, a magazine, or a newspaper?*

No   **Yes**
        ↓

	Go to this entry
Is it published by the government or a nongovernment organization?	
Is it a pamphlet or other type of document?	33, 34
Is it a court case or other legal document?	46
Is it from the *Congressional Record*?	62
Is it an academic work?	
Is it an unpublished dissertation or essay?	37
Is it an abstract of a dissertation?	38
Is it a personal letter or a letter from an archive?	44, 45
Is it a visual text or an advertisement?	
Is it a map or chart?	40
Is it a cartoon?	41
Is it an advertisement?	42
Is it stored in an archive?	45
Is it published in more than one medium (e.g., a book and a CD-ROM)?	48

Check the directory on pages 391–92 or consult your instructor.

Entries in a Works-Cited List: ELECTRONIC
OR OTHER NONPRINT SOURCES

❓ *Did you find your nonprint source online?*

No Yes
↓

Go to this entry

Is it a Web site?
Is it a professional or personal Web site? 50
Is it a home page for a course? 51
Is it authored by a person using a pseudonym? 52
Is it an entry from a Weblog (blog)? 64

Is it an article from an online scholarly journal?
Is it an article from a journal that is available only online? ... 54
Is it an article from a journal that is also available in print? ... 55

Is it an article you found through a subscription database
service (e.g., EBSCO or ProQuest)? 68

Is it from an online magazine or newspaper?
Is it an article from an online version of a print periodical? ... 56
Is it an article from a periodical that is only available online? ... 57
Is it an article from an online newspaper? 58
Is it an editorial? 59
Is it a letter to the editor? 60
Is it a review? 63

Is it an online book or scholarly project?
Is it an online book? 53
Is it an online scholarly project? 49

Is it sponsored by or related to the government? 61, 62

Is it an online communication?
Is it a posting to a news group or other type of online forum? ... 69, 70
Is it an e-mail communication? 71
Is it an e-mail interview? 83

Is your source an online graphic, audio, or video file? 72–75

❓ *Is your source a nonprint source that is not published online?*

No Yes
↓

Go to this entry

Is your source stored on a CD-ROM or DVD?
Is it a CD-ROM or DVD with or without a print version? ... 65–67
Is it computer software on a CD-ROM or DVD? 76

Is it a film, DVD, or videotape? 77
Is it a television or radio program? 78
Is it a broadcast interview? 79
Is it a personal or telephone interview? 83
Is it a sound recording, musical composition, or work of art? ... 80–82
Is it a lecture, speech, or performance? 84, 85

Check the directory on pages 391–92 or consult your instructor.

The Elements of an MLA Works-Cited Entry: Books

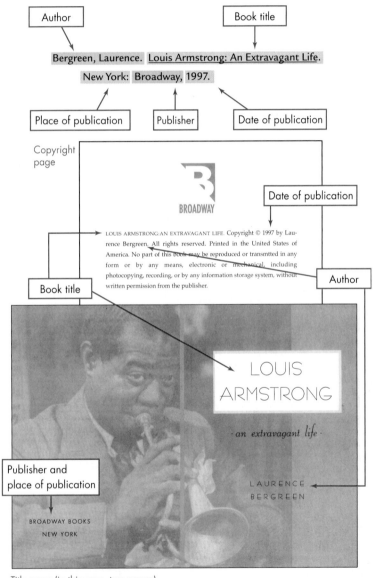

Author

Book title

Bergreen, Laurence. Louis Armstrong: An Extravagant Life.
New York: Broadway, 1997.

Place of publication

Publisher

Date of publication

Copyright page

Date of publication

LOUIS ARMSTRONG:AN EXTRAVAGANT LIFE. Copyright © 1997 by Laurence Bergreen. All rights reserved. Printed in the United States of America. No part of this book may be reproduced or transmitted in any form or by any means, electronic or mechanical, including photocopying, recording, or by any information storage system, without written permission from the publisher.

Book title

Author

LOUIS ARMSTRONG

an extravagant life

LAURENCE BERGREEN

Publisher and place of publication

BROADWAY BOOKS
NEW YORK

Title page (in this case, two pages)

Information for a book citation can be found on the book's title and copyright pages.

MLA MLA MLA MLA MLA MLA MLA MLA MLA MLA MLA MLA MLA MLA MLA MLA ML

The Elements of an MLA Works-Cited Entry: Journal Articles

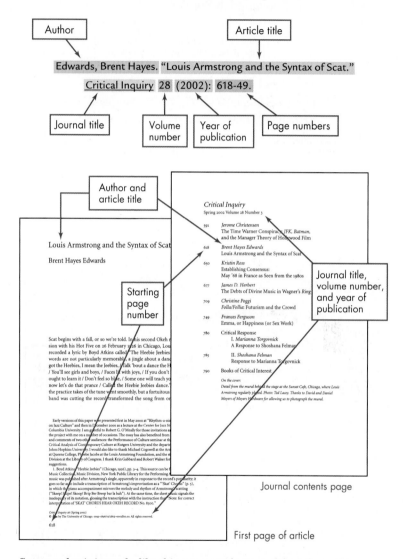

Author

Article title

Edwards, Brent Hayes. "Louis Armstrong and the Syntax of Scat."
Critical Inquiry 28 (2002): 618-49.

Journal title

Volume number

Year of publication

Page numbers

Author and article title

Louis Armstrong and the Syntax of Scat

Brent Hayes Edwards

Starting page number

Critical Inquiry
Spring 2002 Volume 28 Number 3

591 Jerome Christensen
The Time Warner Conspiracy: JFK, Batman, and the Manager Theory of Hollywood Film

618 Brent Hayes Edwards
Louis Armstrong and the Syntax of Scat

650 Kristin Ross
Establishing Consensus: May '68 in France as Seen from the 1980s

677 James D. Herbert
The Debts of Divine Music in Wagner's Ring

709 Christine Poggi
Folla/Follia: Futurism and the Crowd

749 Frances Ferguson
Emma, or Happiness (or Sex Work)

780 Critical Response
I. Marianna Torgovnick
A Response to Shoshana Felman

785 II. Shoshana Felman
Response to Marianna Torgovnick

790 Books of Critical Interest

On the cover:
Detail from the mural behind the stage at the Sunset Cafe, Chicago, where Louis Armstrong regularly played. Photo: Ted Lacey. Thanks to David and Daniel Meyers of Meyers Hardware for allowing us to photograph the mural.

Journal title, volume number, and year of publication

Scat begins with a fall, or so we're told. In his second Okeh session with his Hot Five on 26 February 1926 in Chicago, Lou recorded a lyric by Boyd Atkins called "The Heebie Jeebies words are not particularly memorable, a jingle about a danc got the the Heebies, I mean the Jeebies, /Talk 'bout a dance the H / You'll see girls and boys, / Faces lit with joys, / If you don't ought to learn it / Don't feel so blue, / Some one will teach yo now let's do that prance / Called the Heebie Jeebies dance." the practice takes of the tune went smoothly, but a fortuitous band was cutting the record transformed the song from on

Early versions of this paper were presented first in May 2000 at "Rhythm-a-ni on Jazz Culture" and then in December 2000 as a lecture at the Center for Jazz St Columbia University. I am grateful to Robert G. O'Meally for those invitations a the project with me on a number of occasions. The essay has also benefited from and comments of two other audiences: the Performance of Culture seminar at th Critical Analysis of Contemporary Culture at Rutgers University and the departm Johns Hopkins University. I would also like to thank Michael Cogswell at the Arm at Queens College, Phoebe Jacobs at the Louis Armstrong Foundation, and the m Division at the Library of Congress. I thank Krin Gabbard and Robert Walser for suggestions.
1. Boyd Atkins, "Heebie Jeebies" (Chicago, 1926), pp. 3–4. This source can be f Music Collection, Music Division, New York Public Library for the Performing A music was published after Armstrong's single, apparently in response to the record's popularity; it goes so far as to include a transcription of Armstrong's improvisation as a "Skat" Cho in which the piano accompaniment mirrors the melody and rhythm of Armstrong ("Skeep! Skipe! Skoop! Brip Ber Breep bar la bah"). At the same time, the sheet music signals the inadequacy of its notation, glossing the transcription with the instruction that "Note: for correct interpretation of 'SKAT' CHORUS HEAR OKEH RECORD No. 8300."

Critical Inquiry 28 (Spring 2002)
© by The University of Chicago. 0093-1896/02/2803-0001$10.00. All rights reserved.
618

Journal contents page

First page of article

Some academic journals, like this one, provide most of the information needed for a citation on the first page of an article as well as, like others, on the cover or contents page. You will need to look at the article's last page for the last page number. This journal is paged continuously throughout each yearly volume, so only the volume number is needed in the works-cited entry.

The Elements of an MLA Works-Cited Entry: Journal Articles from an Online Subscription Service

Author, title, and other information about the print version of the article

Edwards, Brent Hayes. "Louis Armstrong and the Syntax of
Scat." <u>Critical Inquiry</u> 28 (2002): 618-49. ProQuest.
Columbia U. Libraries. 5 May 2005 <http://proquest.com/
proquest/>.

Subscribing library system

Date of access

Subscription service home page

Name of subscription service

Link to home page for subscription service (home page URL)

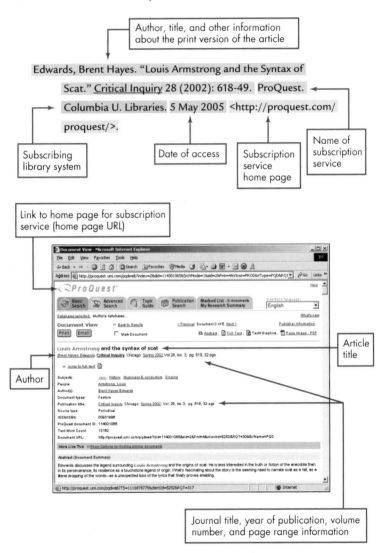

Article title

Author

Journal title, year of publication, volume number, and page range information

A citation for an article obtained from an online subscription database service like ProQuest includes information about the service, the subscribing library, and the date of access in addition to information about the print version of the article. Information about the library and the date of access comes from the researcher's notes.

24a The elements of MLA documentation style

College papers include information, ideas, and quotations from sources that must be accurately documented. Documentation allows others to see the path you have taken in researching and writing your paper, be it informative, interpretive, or argumentative. *(For more on what to document, see Chapter 22: Writing the Paper, pp. 361–67.)*

The MLA documentation style has three parts:

- In-text citations
- List of works cited
- Explanatory notes and acknowledgments

In-text citations and a list of works cited are mandatory; explanatory notes are optional.

24b MLA style: In-text citations

In-text citations let readers know that they can find full information about the source of a quotation or an idea you have paraphrased or summarized in the list of works cited at the end of your paper.

1. Author named in sentence: You can use the last name only, unless two or more of your sources have the same last name.

signal phrase
As Hennessey explains, record deals were usually negotiated by "white

middlemen" (127).

Note that the parenthetical page citation comes after the closing quotation mark but before the period.

2. Author named in parentheses: If you do not name the source's author in your sentence, then you must provide the name in the parentheses.

Armstrong easily reached difficult high notes, the F's and G's that
no punctuation within parentheses
stymied other trumpeters (Bergreen 248).

Note that there is no comma between the author's name and the page number. If you cite two or more distinct pages, however, separate the numbers with a comma: (Bergreen 450, 457).

3. Two or more works by the same author: If you use two or more works by the same author, you must identify which work you are citing, either in your sentence or in an abbreviated form in parentheses. **381**

MLA
MLA

MLA MLA MLA

title is underlined

In <u>Louis Armstrong, an American Genius</u>, Collier reports that Glaser paid Armstrong's mortgage, taxes, and basic living expenses (330).

During those years, Glaser paid Armstrong's mortgage, taxes, and basic living expenses (Collier, <u>Louis Armstrong</u> 330).

MLA MLA MLA MLA

4. Two or three authors of the same work:

If a source has up to three authors, you should name them all either in your text, as shown below, or in parentheses: (Jones and Chilton 160, 220).

According to Jones and Chilton, Glaser's responsibilities included booking appearances, making travel arrangements, and paying the band members' salaries (160, 220).

GENERAL GUIDELINES
for MLA IN-TEXT CITATIONS

- Name the author, either in a signal phrase such as "Bergreen maintains" or in a parenthetical citation.
- Include a page reference in parentheses. No "p." precedes the page number, and if the author is named in the parentheses, there is no punctuation between the author's name and the page number.
- Place the citation as close to the material being cited as possible and before any punctuation marks that divide or end the sentence, such as commas, semicolons, or periods—except in a block quotation, where the citation comes one space after the period or final punctuation mark.
- Underline the titles of books and magazines, and place quotation marks around the titles of articles, poems, and plays. Do not use italics.
- For Internet sources, follow the same general guidelines as for print sources. Keep the parenthetical citation as simple as possible, providing enough information for your reader to find the full citation in your works-cited list. (Do not, for example, provide a long URL within a parenthetical citation; instead, cite either the author's name or the title of the site or article.)

5. More than three authors: If a source has more than three authors, either list all the authors or give the first author's last name followed by "et al.," the abbreviation for the Latin phrase meaning "and others."

> Changes in social regulations are bound to produce new forms of subjectivity (Henriques et al. 275).

6. Authors with the same last name: If the authors of two or more of your sources have the same last name, include the first initial of the author you are citing; if the first initial is also shared, use the full first name, as shown below.

> In the late nineteenth century, the sale of sheet music spread rapidly in a Manhattan area along Broadway known as Tin Pan Alley (Richard Campbell 63).

LEARNING in COLLEGE

What Is the Modern Language Association?

The Modern Language Association (MLA) is a professional organization of language teachers that was founded in the United States in 1883. Its purpose is to support the study and teaching of languages. The MLA published its first handbook in 1977, and since then the book has become a widely accepted guide to rules for writing research papers. The *MLA Handbook* focuses on the mechanics of academic writing, including punctuation, quotation, and documentation of sources. In addition, the MLA guidelines are used by academic journals, newsletters, magazines, and university presses in both the United States and Canada. Recently, translated versions have also appeared in Japan and China. Following the MLA guidelines will help you document your research and write a clear and credible research paper.

7. Organization as author: To cite works by organized groups, government agencies, associations, or corporations, treat the organization as the author. If the name is long, either put it in a signal phrase or use an abbreviated version in the parentheses.

> The Centre for Contemporary Cultural Studies claims that "there is nothing inherently concrete about historiography" (10).

> Historiography deals with abstract issues (Centre 10).

8. Unknown author: When no author is given, cite a work by its title, using either the full title in a signal phrase or an abbreviated version in the parentheses. Be sure to abbreviate in a way that points clearly to the corresponding entry in your list of works cited.

> title of article
> "Squaresville, U.S.A. vs. Beatsville" makes the Midwestern small-town home seem boring compared with the West Coast artist's "pad" (31).

> The Midwestern small-town home seems boring compared with the West Coast artist's "pad" ("Squaresville" 31).

9. Entire work: When you want to acknowledge an entire work, such as a film or a book, you should do so in your text, not in a parenthetical citation. Be sure to include the work in your list of works cited.

Sidney J. Furie's film <u>Lady Sings the Blues</u> presents Billie Holiday as a beautiful woman in pain rather than as the great jazz artist she was.

10. Paraphrased or summarized source: If you include the author's name in your paraphrase or summary, include only the page number or numbers in your parenthetical citation. Signal phrases clarify that you are paraphrasing or summarizing.

signal phrase
Bergreen recounts how in southern states, where blacks were prohibited from entering many stores, Glaser sometimes had to shop for the band's food and other supplies (378, 381).

11. Source of a long quotation: For a quotation of four or more typed lines, do not use quotation marks. Instead, indent the material you are quoting by one inch (most word-processing programs will automatically set the correct indention if you use the "Increase Indent" command or button). Allow one space before the parenthetical information following the final punctuation mark of the quotation.

Glaser managed the Sunset Café, a club where Armstrong often performed:

> There was a pronounced gangster element at the Sunset, but Louis, accustomed to being employed and protected by mobsters, didn't think twice about that. Mr. Capone's men ensured the flow of alcohol, and their presence reassured many whites. (Bergreen 279)

12. Source of a short quotation: Close the quotation before the parenthetical citation. If the quotation concludes with an exclamation point or a question mark, place the closing quotation mark after that punctuation mark and insert a period after the parenthetical citation.

His innovative singing style also featured "scat," a technique that
brackets enclose a word that substitutes for omitted text
combines "nonsense syllables [with] improvised melodies"

(Robinson 515).

13. One-page source: You need not include a page number in the parenthetical citation for a one-page printed source, but doing so is never wrong.

NO PAGE NUMBER

Knittle notes that a benefit of deep breathing and relaxation is the "circulation of lymph throughout the body, a process that removes toxins from tissues and organs."

PAGE NUMBER

Knittle notes that a benefit of deep breathing and relaxation is the "circulation of lymph throughout the body, a process that removes toxins from the tissues and organs" (34).

14. Government publication: To avoid an overly long parenthetical citation, give the name of the government agency that published the source within your text.

According to a report issued by the Bureau of National Affairs, many employers in 1964 needed guidance to apply new workplace rules that ensured fairness and complied with the Civil Rights Act of 1964 (32).

The President's Council on Bioethics documents the disturbing trend toward using genetic engineering to "enhance" lifestyles rather than cure disease (Beyond Therapy).

15. Photograph, map, graph, chart, or other visual:

VISUAL APPEARS IN YOUR PAPER

An aerial photograph of Manhattan (Fig. 3), taken by the United States Geographical Survey, demonstrates how creative city planning can introduce parks and green spaces within even the most densely populated urban areas.

The caption you write for the image should include citation information.

VISUAL DOES NOT APPEAR IN YOUR PAPER

An aerial photograph of Manhattan taken by the United States Geographical Survey demonstrates how creative city planning can introduce parks and green spaces within even the most densely populated urban areas (TerraServer-USA).

Because you are not including the image, you need to provide a parenthetical citation that directs your reader to information about the source of the image in your works-cited list. Do not put the full URL of the site here, but do put it in the works-cited list.

16. Web site or other online electronic source: For online sources such as Web sites, the MLA recommends using the guidelines established for print sources. If you cannot find the author of an online source, then identify the source by title, either in your text or in a parenthetical citation. Because most online sources do not have set page, section, or paragraph numbers, they must usually be cited as entire works.

> In the 1920s, many young black musicians from New Orleans migrated
>
> north to Chicago, hoping for a chance to perform with the best
>
> ("Chicago").

17. Work with numbered paragraphs or screens instead of pages: Give the paragraph or screen number(s) after the author's name and a comma. To distinguish them from page numbers, use the abbreviation *par(s).* or the word *screen(s).*

> Goodman understood how to balance the public's demand for pop
>
> with his own desire to push his players (Edgers, screen 1).

18. Work with no page or paragraph numbers: When citing an online or print source without page, paragraph, or other reference numbers, try to work the author's name into your text instead of putting it in a parenthetical citation.

> author's name
> Crouch argues that Armstrong remains a driving force in present-day
>
> music, from country and western music to the chanted doggerel of rap.

19. Multivolume work: When citing more than one volume, include the volume number, followed by a colon, a space, and the page number.

> Schuller argues that even though jazz's traditional framework appears
>
> European, its musical essence is African (1: 62).

If you consult only one volume of a multivolume work, it is unnecessary to cite the volume number in the parenthetical reference. You should include it as part of the works-cited entry (*see p. 396*).

20. Literary work:

Novels and literary nonfiction books: Include the relevant page number, followed by a semicolon, a space, and the chapter number.

> Louis Armstrong figures throughout Ellison's Invisible Man, including
> in the narrator's penultimate decision to become a "yes" man who
> "undermine[s] them with grins" (384; ch. 23).

If the author is not named in your sentence, add the name in front of the page number: (Ellison 384; ch. 23).

Poems: Use line numbers, not page numbers.

> In "Trumpet Player," Hughes says that the music "Is honey / Mixed with
> liquid fire" (lines 19-20). This image returns at the end of the poem, when
> Hughes concludes that "Trouble / Mellows to a golden note" (43-44).

Note that the word *lines* (not *l.* or *ll.*) is used in the first citation to establish what the numbers in parentheses refer to; subsequent citations need not use the word *lines.*

Plays and long, multisection poems: Use division (act, scene, canto, book, part) and lines, not page numbers. In the following example, notice that arabic numerals are used for act and scene divisions as well as for line numbers: (*Hamlet* 2.3.22–27). The same is true for canto, verse, and lines in the following citation of Byron's *Don Juan:* (*DJ* 1.37.4–8).

21. Religious text: Cite material in the Bible, Upanishads, or Koran by book, chapter, and verse, using an appropriate abbreviation when the name of the book is in the parentheses rather than in your sentence. Name the edition from which you are citing.

> As the Bible says, "The wise man knows there will be a time of
> judgment" (Holy Bible, Revised Standard Version, Eccles. 8.5).

Note that titles of biblical books are not underlined.

22. Historical document: Cite familiar documents such as the Constitution and the Declaration of Independence in your text, providing the document's name and the numbers of the parts you are citing; it is not necessary to include a familiar document in your list of works cited.

> Judges are allowed to remain in office "during good behavior," a vague
>
> standard that has had various interpretations (US Const., art. 3, sec. 1).

23. Indirect source: When you quote or paraphrase a quotation you found in someone else's work, put *qtd. in* (meaning "quoted in") before the name of your source.

> Armstrong confided to a friend that Glaser's death "broke [his] heart"
>
> (qtd. in Bergreen 490).

In your list of works cited, list only the work you consulted, in this case the indirect source by Bergreen.

24. Two or more sources in one citation: When you credit two or more sources, use a semicolon to separate the citations.

> Giving up his other business ventures, Glaser now became Armstrong's
>
> exclusive agent (Bergreen 376-78; Collier 273-76; Morgenstern 124-28).

25. Two or more sources in one sentence: Include a parenthetical reference after each idea or quotation you have borrowed.

> Ironically, Americans lavish more money each year on their pets than
>
> they spend on children's toys (Merkins 21), but the feral cat
>
> population—consisting of abandoned pets and their offspring—is
>
> at an estimated 70 million and growing (Mott).

26. Work in an anthology: When citing a work in a collection, give the name of the specific work's author, not the name of the editor of the whole collection.

> When Dexter Gordon threatened to quit, Armstrong offered him a
>
> raise—without consulting with Glaser (Morgenstern 132).

Here, Morgenstern is cited as the source even though his work appears in a collection edited by Marc Miller. Note that the list of works cited must include an entry for Morgenstern (*see p. 425*).

27. E-mail, letter, or personal interview: Cite by name the person you communicated with, using either a signal phrase or parentheses.

> Much to Glaser's surprise, both "Hello, Dolly" and "What a Wonderful World" became big hits after the rights had been sold (Jacobs).

In the works-cited list, you will need to identify the kind of communication and its date (*see pp. 401, 409, and 412*).

www.mhhe.com/
nmhh
To download
Bibliomaker software
for MLA, go to
Research >
Bibliomaker

24c MLA style: List of works cited

Besides in-text citations, MLA documentation style requires a works-cited page, where readers can find full bibliographic information about the sources you have used. The list of works cited should appear at the end of your paper, beginning on a new page entitled "Works Cited." Include only those sources you cite in your paper, unless your instructor tells you to prepare a "Works Consulted" list.

Books

1. Book with one author: Underline the book's title. Only the city, not the state, is included in the publication data. Notice that in the example the publisher's name, *Wayne State University Press,* is abbreviated to *Wayne State UP.*

> Hennessey, Thomas J. From Jazz to Swing: African-Americans and Their
>
> Music 1890-1935. Detroit: Wayne State UP, 1984.

2. Two or more works by the same author(s): When you list more than one work by the same author, give the author's name in the first entry only. For subsequent works authored by that person, replace the name with three hyphens and a period. Multiple works by one author are alphabetized by title.

> Collier, James Lincoln. Jazz: The American Theme Song. New York:
>
> Oxford UP, 1993.
>
> ---. Louis Armstrong, an American Genius. New York: Oxford UP, 1983.

3. Book with two or more authors: Name the two or three authors in the order in which they appear on the title page, putting the last name first for the first author only. When a work has more than three authors, you may use the abbreviation *et al.* (meaning "and others") to replace the names of all authors except the first.

MLA WORKS-CITED ENTRIES: DIRECTORY to SAMPLE TYPES

(continued)

MLA WORKS-CITED ENTRIES: DIRECTORY to SAMPLE TYPES *(continued)*

Davis, Miles, and Quincy Troupe. Miles: The Autobiography. New York: Simon, 1989.

Henriques, Julian, et al. Changing the Subject: Psychology, Social Regulation, and Subjectivity. New York: Methuen, 1984.

4. Organization as author: Consider as an organization any group, commission, association, or corporation whose members are not identified on the title page.

Centre for Contemporary Cultural Studies. Making Histories: Studies in History Writing and Politics. London: Hutchinson, 1982.

GENERAL GUIDELINES for the LIST of WORKS CITED in MLA STYLE

- Begin on a new page.
- Begin with the centered title "Works Cited."
- Include an entry for every in-text citation.
- Include author, title, and publication data for each entry, if available. Use a period to set off each of these elements from the others. Leave one space after the periods.
- Do not number the entries.
- Put entries in alphabetical order by author's or editor's last name. Do not add academic titles (such as PhD) to the author's name. If the work has more than one author, see item 3 (*p. 390*). (If the author is unknown, use the first word of the title, excluding the articles a, an, or the).
- Underline titles of books and periodicals. Put quotation marks around titles of articles and poems. Do not use italics. Give all titles, including titles of works in a foreign language, exactly as they appear on the title page.
- Capitalize the first and last and all important words in all titles and subtitles. Do not capitalize articles, prepositions, coordinating conjunctions, and the to in infinitives.
- In the publication data, abbreviate publishers' names and months (Dec. rather than December; Oxford UP instead of Oxford University Press), and include the name of the city in which the publisher is located but not the state: Danbury: Grolier. If the date of publication is not given, provide the approximate date, enclosed in brackets: [c. 1975]. If you cannot approximate the date, write n.d. for "no date."
- Do not use p., pp., or page(s). Numbers alone will do. When page spans over 100 have the same first digit, use only the last two digits of the second number: 243–47.
- Abbreviate all months (for newspaper, magazine, and some online sources) except May, June, and July.
- For articles and other print sources that skip pages, provide the page number for the beginning of the article followed by a plus (+) sign.
- Use a hanging indent: Start the first line of each entry at the left margin, and indent all subsequent lines of the entry five spaces (or one-half inch on the computer).
- Double-space within entries and between them.

5. Book by an editor or editors: If the title page lists an editor instead of an author, treat the editor as an author but put the abbreviation *ed.* after the name. Use *eds.* when more than one editor is listed. Only the first editor's name should appear in reverse order.

> Miller, Paul Eduard, ed. Esquire's Jazz Book. New York: Smith, 1944.

6. Book with an author and an editor: Put the author and title first, followed by *Ed.* (meaning "edited by") and the name of the editor. However, if you cited something written by the editor rather than the author, see item 14.

> editor's name not in reverse order
> Armstrong, Louis. Louis Armstrong--A Self-Portrait. Ed. Richard
>
> Meryman. New York: Eakins, 1971.

7. Work in an anthology or chapter in an edited book: List the author and title of the selection, followed by the title of the anthology, the abbreviation *Ed.* for "edited by," the editor's name, publication data, and page numbers of the selection.

> Smith, Hale. "Here I Stand." Readings in Black American Music.
>
> Ed. Eileen Southern. New York: Norton, 1971. 286-89.

8. Two or more items from one anthology: Include a complete entry for the anthology beginning with the name of the editor(s). Each selection from the anthology that you are citing should have its own entry in the alphabetical list that includes only the author, title of the selection, editor, and page numbers.

> entry for a selection from the anthology
> Johnson, Hall. "Notes on the Negro Spiritual." Southern 268-75.
>
> entry for the anthology
> Southern, Eileen, ed. Readings in Black American Music. New York:
>
> Norton, 1971.
>
> entry for a selection from the anthology
> Still, William Grant. "The Structure of Music." Southern 276-79.

9. Signed article in a reference work: Cite the author's name, title of the entry (in quotation marks), title of the reference work (underlined), and publication information.

Robinson, J. Bradford. "Scat Singing." The New Grove Dictionary of
Jazz. Ed. Barry Kernfeld. Vol. 3. London: Macmillan, 2002. 515-16.

10. Unsigned entry in a reference work: Start the entry with
the title. For well-known reference works such as general-interest encyclopedias and dictionaries, the place and publisher can be omitted.

"Scat." Merriam-Webster's Collegiate Dictionary. 11th ed. 2003.

11. Article from a collection of reprinted articles:

Prager, Joshua Harris. "The Longest Replay." Wall Street Journal July
  abbreviation for "reprinted"
  1998. Rpt. in Floating Off the Page: The Best Stories from The

Wall Street Journal's "Middle Column." Ed. Ken Wells. New York:

Wall Street Journal-Simon, 2002. 149-53.

12. Anthology:

Eggers, Dave, ed. The Best American Nonrequired Reading 2003.

Boston: Houghton, 2003.

13. Publisher's imprint: For books published by a division within
a publishing company, known as an "imprint," put a hyphen between
the imprint and publisher.

Wells, Ken, ed. Floating Off the Page: The Best Stories from The Wall

Street Journal's "Middle Column." New York: Wall Street Journal-

Simon, 2002.

14. Preface, foreword, introduction, or afterword: When the
writer of the part is different from the author of the book, use the word
By after the book's title and cite the author's full name. If the book's
author wrote the part, use only the author's last name after *By*.

  name of part of book
Crawford, Richard. Foreword. The Jazz Tradition. By Martin Williams.

New York: Oxford UP, 1993. v-xiii.

Fowles, John. Preface. Islands. By Fowles. Boston: Little, 1978. 1-2.

15. Translation: Cite the work under the author's name, not the translator's. The translator's name goes after the title, with the abbreviation *Trans.* (meaning "translated by").

> Goffin, Robert. Horn of Plenty: The Story of Louis Armstrong.
>
> Trans. James F. Bezov. New York: Da Capo, 1977.

16. Edition other than the first: Include the number of the edition: *2nd ed., 3rd ed.,* and so on. Place the number after the title, or if there is an editor, after that person's name.

> Panassie, Hugues. Louis Armstrong. 2nd ed. New York: Da Capo, 1980.

17. Religious text: Give the version, underlined; the editor's or translator's name (if any); and the publication information.

> New American Standard Bible. La Habra: Lockman Foundation, 1995.
>
> The Upanishads. Trans. Eknath Easwaran. Tomales: Nilgiri, 1987.

18. Multivolume work: Your citation should indicate whether you used more than one volume of a multivolume work. The first example indicates that the researcher used all three volumes; the second shows that only the second volume of the work was used.

> Lissauer, Robert. Lissauer's Encyclopedia of Popular Music in America.
>
> 3 vols. New York: Facts on File, 1996.
>
> Lissauer, Robert. Lissauer's Encyclopedia of Popular Music in America.
>
> Vol. 2. New York: Facts on File, 1996.

19. Book in a series: After the title of the book, put the name of the series and, if available on the title page, the number of the work.

> Floyd, Samuel A., Jr., ed. Black Music in the Harlem Renaissance.
> Name of series not underlined
> Contributions in Afro-American and African Studies 128. New
>
> York: Greenwood, 1990.

20. Republished book: Put the original date of publication, followed by a period, before the current publication data. In the following example, the writer cites a 1974 republication of a book that originally appeared in 1936.

> Cuney-Hare, Maud. <u>Negro Musicians and Their Music</u>. 1936. New York:
>
> Da Capo, 1974.

21. Title in a title: When a book's title contains the title of another book, do not underline the second title. In the following example, the novel *Invisible Man* is not underlined.

> O'Meally, Robert, ed. <u>New Essays on</u> Invisible Man. Cambridge:
>
> Cambridge UP, 1988.

22. Unknown author: The citation begins with the title. In the list of works cited, alphabetize the citation by the first important word, excluding the articles *A, An,* and *The.*

> <u>Webster's College Dictionary</u>. New York: Random; New York: McGraw,
>
> 1991.

Note that this entry includes both of the publishers listed on the dictionary's title page; they are separated by a semicolon.

Periodicals

Periodicals are published at set intervals, usually four times a year for scholarly journals, monthly or weekly for magazines, and daily or weekly for newspapers. Between the author and the publication data are two titles: the title of the article, in quotation marks, and the title of the periodical, underlined. (*For online versions of print periodicals and periodicals published only online, see the box on p. 406.*)

23. Article in a journal paginated by volume: Many scholarly journals are published a handful of times each year and are then bound together by libraries into yearly volumes. For journals paginated by yearly volume, not individual issue, put the volume number after the title. Give the year of publication in parentheses, followed by a colon, a space, and the page numbers of the article.

> Tirro, Frank. "Constructive Elements in Jazz Improvisation." <u>Journal of</u>
>
> <u>the American Musicological Society</u> 27 (1974): 285-305.

24. Article in a journal paginated by issue: For scholarly journals paginated by issue, not volume, you must also give the issue number.

Place a period after the volume number, and follow it with the issue number. In the example, the volume is 25 and the issue is 4.

> Aguiar, Sarah Appleton. " 'Everywhere and Nowhere': Beloved's 'Wild'
>
> Legacy in Toni Morrison's Jazz." Notes on Contemporary
>
> Literature 25.4 (1995): 11-12.

25. Article in a monthly magazine: Provide the month and year, abbreviating the names of all months except May, June, and July.

> Walker, Malcolm. "Discography: Bill Evans." Jazz Monthly June 1965:
>
> 20-22.

26. Article in a weekly magazine: Include the complete date of publication: day, month, and year.

> Taylor, J. R. "Jazz History: The Incompleted Past." Village Voice 3 July
>
> 1978: 65-67.

27. Article in a newspaper: Provide the day, month, and year. If an edition is named on the masthead (the top of the first page, which includes the name of the newspaper), specify the edition (*natl. ed.* or *late ed.*, for example) after the date and use a comma between the date and the edition. Whenever possible, give a section designation (*E* in the example) along with the page number. If the article appears on nonconsecutive pages, put a plus (+) sign after the first page number.

> Blumenthal, Ralph. "Satchmo with His Tape Recorder Running."
>
> New York Times 3 Aug. 1999: E1+.

28. Unsigned article: The citation begins with the title and is alphabetized by the first word other than an article like *A, An,* or *The.*

> "Squaresville, U.S.A. vs. Beatsville." Life 21 Sept. 1959: 31.

29. Review: Begin with the name of the reviewer and, if there is one, the title of the review. Add *Rev. of* (meaning "review of") and the title plus the author or performer of the work being reviewed. Notice that the word *by* precedes the author's name.

> Ostwald, David. "All That Jazz." Rev. of Louis Armstrong: An
>
> Extravagant Life, by Laurence Bergreen. Commentary Nov. 1997:
>
> 68-72.

30. Editorial: Treat editorials as articles, but add the word *Editorial* after the title. If the editorial is unsigned, begin with the title.

> Shaw, Theodore M. "The Debate over Race Needs Minority Students'
>
> Voices." Editorial. Chronicle of Higher Education 25 Feb.
>
> 2000: A72.

31. Abstract of a journal article: Collections of abstracts from journals in specific disciplines can be found in the reference section of your library. Include the publication information for the original article, followed by the title of the publication that provides the abstract, the volume, the year in parentheses, and the item or page number.

> Theiler, Anne M. and Louise G. Lippman. "Effects of Mental Practice
>
> and Modeling on Guitar and Vocal Performance." Journal of
>
> General Psychology 122.4 (1995): 329-43. Psychological Abstracts
>
> 83 (1996): item 30039.

32. Letter to the editor:

> Tyler, Steve. Letter. National Geographic Adventure Apr. 2004: 11.

Other Print Sources

33. Government document: Either the name of the government and agency or the name of the document's author comes first. If the government and agency name come first, follow the title of the document with the word *By* for a writer, *Ed.* for an editor, or *Comp.* for a compiler. Publication information, abbreviated, comes last.

> United States. Bureau of National Affairs. The Civil Rights Act of 1964:
>
> Text, Analysis, Legislative History; What It Means to Employers,
>
> Businessmen, Unions, Employees, Minority Groups. Washington:
>
> BNA, 1964.

For the format to use when citing the *Congressional Record,* whether in print or online, see item 62.

34. Pamphlet: Treat as you would a book. If the pamphlet has an author, list his or her name first; otherwise, begin with the title.

> All Music Guide to Jazz. 2nd ed. San Francisco: Miller Freeman, 1996.   **399**

35. Conference proceedings: Cite as you would a book, but include information about the conference if it is not in the title.

> Mendel, Arthur, Gustave Reese, and Gilbert Chase, eds. Papers Read
>
> at the International Congress of Musicology Held at New York
>
> September 11th to 16th, 1939. New York: Music Educators'
>
> National Conference for the American Musicological Society, 1944.

36. Published dissertation: Cite as you would a book. After the title, add *Diss.* for "dissertation," the name of the institution, and the year the dissertation was written.

> Fraser, Wilmot Alfred. Jazzology: A Study of the Tradition in Which
>
> Jazz Musicians Learn to Improvise. Diss. U of Pennsylvania, 1983.
>
> Ann Arbor: UMI, 1987.

37. Unpublished dissertation or essay: For dissertations, begin with the author's name, followed by the title in quotation marks, the abbreviation *Diss.*, the name of the institution, and the year the dissertation was written.

> Reyes-Schramm, Adelaida. "The Role of Music in the Interaction of
>
> Black Americans and Hispanos in New York City's East Harlem."
>
> Diss. Columbia U, 1975.

For an unpublished essay, include the phrase *Unpublished essay* after the title.

> Pollack, Bracha. "A Man ahead of His Time." Unpublished essay, 1997.

38. Abstract of a dissertation: Use the format for an unpublished dissertation. After the dissertation date, give the abbreviation *DA* or *DAI* (for *Dissertation Abstracts* or *Dissertation Abstracts International*), then the volume number, the date of publication, and the page number.

> Quinn, Richard Allen. "Playing Together: Improvisation in Postwar
>
> American Literature and Culture." Diss. U of Iowa, 2000. DAI 61
>
> (2001): 2305A.

39. Published interview: Name the person interviewed and give the title of the interview or the descriptive term *Interview,* the name of the interviewer (if known and relevant), and the publication information.

Armstrong, Louis. "Authentic American Genius." Interview with Richard

Meryman. Life 15 Apr. 1966: 92-102.

40. Map or chart: Cite as you would a book with an unknown author. Underline the title of the map or chart, and add the word *Map* or *Chart* following the title.

Let's Go Map Guide to New Orleans. Map. New York: St. Martin's,

1997.

41. Cartoon: Include the cartoonist's name, the title of the cartoon (if any) in quotation marks, the word *Cartoon,* and the publication information.

Myller, Jorgen. "Louis Armstrong's First Lesson." Cartoon. Melody

Maker Mar. 1931: 12.

42. Advertisement: Name the item or organization being advertised, include the word *Advertisement,* and indicate where the ad appeared.

Hartwick College Summer Music Festival and Institute. Advertisement.

New York Times Magazine 3 Jan. 1999: 54.

43. Published letter: Treat like a work in an anthology, but include the date. Include the number, if one was assigned by the editor. If you use more than one letter from a published collection, follow the instructions for cross-referencing in item 8.

Hughes, Langston. "To Arna Bontemps." 17 Jan. 1938. Arna

Bontemps--Langston Hughes Letters 1925-1967. Ed. Charles H.

Nichols. New York: Dodd, 1980. 27-28.

44. Personal letter: To cite a letter you received, start with the writer's name, followed by the descriptive phrase *Letter to the author* and then the date.

Cogswell, Michael. Letter to the author. 15 Mar. 1998.

To cite someone else's unpublished personal letter, see the guidelines in item 45.

45. Manuscripts, typescripts, and material in archives: Give the author, a title or description of the material (*Letter, Notebook*), the form (*ms.* if manuscript, *ts.* if typescript), any identifying number, and the name and location of the institution housing the material.

> Glaser, Joe. Letter to Lucille Armstrong. 28 Sept. 1960. Box 3.
>
> Armstrong Archives. Queens College CUNY, Flushing, NY.

46. Legal source: Cite familiar government documents such as the Constitution within the body of your text only (*see item 22 on p. 389*). To cite a specific act, give its name, Public Law number, the date it was enacted, and its Statutes at Large number.

> Microenterprise Results and Accountability Act of 2004. Pub. L.
>
> 108-484. 23 Dec. 2004. Stat. 3922.

To cite a law case, provide the name of the plaintiff and defendant, the case number, the court that decided the case, and the date of the decision.

> Hamdi v. Rumsfeld. No. 03-6696. Supreme Ct. of the US.
>
> 28 June 2004.

For more information about citing legal documents or from case law, MLA recommends consulting *The Blue Book: A Uniform System of Citation,* published by the Harvard Law Review Association and available in the reference section of your library.

47. Microfiche/microform/microfilm: Sources that have been photographed, greatly reduced, and stored on microfilm, which you view with the help of a projector, are cited exactly as you would the print version.

48. Publication in more than one medium: If you are citing a publication that consists of several different media (for example, a book accompanied by a CD-ROM and a Web site), list all of the media included.

> Kamien, Roger. Music: An Appreciation. 8th ed. Book, CD-ROM,
>
> interactive online site. New York: McGraw, 2000.

Electronic Sources

The examples that follow are based on guidelines for the citation of electronic sources in the sixth edition of the *MLA Handbook for Writers of Research Papers* (2003).

Note: The Internet address for an electronic source is its uniform resource locator, or URL. If you need to divide a URL between lines, divide it after a slash. Do not insert a hyphen. If the URL is too long and complex to enter, give the URL of the site's search page.

 TEXTCONNEX

URL Addresses

Some popular word-processing programs automatically turn all URLs into hyperlinks. The MLA recommends disabling this automatic hyperlinking before you print your document. To turn off automatic hyperlinking, go to "AutoFormat As You Type" in the "AutoCorrect" part of the "Tools" menu and remove the check mark next to "Internet and network paths with hyperlinks."

49. Online scholarly project:

Entire Web site: Begin with the title (underlined) of the source, followed by the name of the editor (if any) and the electronic publication data, which includes, if relevant, the version number, the date of publication or update, and the name of the sponsoring institution (if any). End with the date you used the source and, in angle brackets (< >), the source's complete URL.

William Ransom Hogan Archive of New Orleans Jazz. Ed. Bruce Boyd

Raeburn. 30 Oct. 2004. Tulane U. 3 May 2005 <http://   *URL divided after a slash*

www.tulane.edu/~lmiller/jazzHome.html>.

Part of a scholarly Web site: When citing one part, document, or page of a source, add the author (if known) and the title of the part in quotation marks. If the author is unknown, start with the title of the part in quotation marks.

Raeburn, Bruce Boyd. "An Introduction to New Orleans Jazz." William

Ransom Hogan Archive of New Orleans Jazz. Ed. Bruce Boyd

Raeburn. 30 Oct. 2004. Tulane U. 3 May 2005 <http://

www.tulane.edu/~lmiller/BeginnersIntro.html>. **403**

"Armstrong Biography." Satchmo.Net: The Official Site for the Louis

Armstrong House and Archives. 2003. Queens College CUNY.

3 May 2005 <http://www.satchmo.net/bio/>.

50. Professional or personal Web site: Name the person responsible for the site, the title of the site (underlined), the name of the associated institution or organization (if any), date of access, and URL. If no title is available, use a descriptive term such as "Home page" (without underlining or quotation marks).

Henson, Keith. The Keith Henson Jazzpage. 3 May 2005

<http://www.home.earthlink.net/~keithhenson>.

Wildman, Joan. The World of Jazz Improvisation. U of Wisconsin,

Madison. 3 May 2005 <http://hum.lss.wisc.edu/jazz>.

51. Home page for a course: After the instructor's name, list the course title; if there is no course title on the home page, use the title from the school's course catalog, if available, or the course number. Add the inclusive dates of the course, then the department and school names.

Marshall, S. A. Insects in Relation to Wildlife. Course home page.

Jan. 2005-May 2005. Dept. of Environmental Biology, U of

Guelph. 18 Apr. 2005 <http://www.uoguelph.ca/OAC/env/

co_3090.shtml>.

52. Site authored by a person using a pseudonym: Provide the name given on the Web site, even if it is obviously not the author's real name. If the author's real name is known, you may add it in brackets. (*See also item 64.*)

Instapundit [Glenn Reynolds]. Weblog posting. Instapundit.com.

3 Sept. 2005. 20 Sept. 2005 <http://instapundit.com/archives/

week_2005_08_28.php>.

53. Online book:

Entire book: Cite as for a print book, including author; title (underlined); editor, translator, or compiler (if any); and publication data for the print version. Add, if available, the name of the database or project, date of electronic publication, sponsoring organization, date of access, and URL.

> database underlined
>
> Sandburg, Carl. <u>Chicago Poems</u>. New York: Holt, 1916. <u>Bartleby.com</u>.
>
> Aug. 1999. 3 May 2005 <http://www.bartleby.com/165>.

Work in an online book: If you use part of an online book, add the title of the part after the author and put it in quotation marks, unless the part cited is an introduction, foreword, preface, or afterword.

> Sandburg, Carl. "Chicago." <u>Chicago Poems</u>. New York: Holt, 1916.
>
> <u>Bartleby.com</u>. Aug. 1999. 3 May 2005. <http://
>
> www.bartleby.com/165>.

54. Article in an online scholarly journal, published only online: Most legitimate online journals have volume and possibly issue numbers, just as print journals do (*see items 23 and 24*). Include these numbers after the journal name, with the year of publication in parentheses. Follow this information with access information, as you would do with any online source. Online scholarly periodicals often number paragraphs or sections of their articles. When this is the case, indicate the number of sections or paragraphs in your citation.

> Schmalfeldt, Janet. "On Keeping the Score." <u>Music Theory Online</u> 4.2
>
> (1998). 20 pars. 3 May 2005 <http://www.societymusictheory.org>.

55. Article in an online scholarly journal, previously published in print: List information about the print source, including volume number, issue number, publication year, and page numbers, before listing information about the online source.

> Tsal, Yehoshua, Lilach Shalev, and Carmel Mevorach. "The Diversity
>
> of Attention Deficits in ADHD: The Prevalence of Four Cognitive
>
> Factors in ADHD Versus Controls." <u>Journal of Learning Disabilities</u>
>
> 38.2 (2005): 142-57. <u>IngentaConnect</u>. 5 Aug. 2005 <http://
>
> www.ingentaconnect.com/content/proedcw/jld/2005/>.

56. Article in an online version of a print magazine or periodical: Provide the publication date—day, month, and year, or month and year—rather than the volume and issue number.

GENERAL GUIDELINES for CITING ONLINE PERIODICALS

- Begin with the author's name.
- Put the title of the article in quotation marks.
- If there is no title, use a descriptive term such as *Editorial* or *Comment*.
- Add the name of the publication and underline it. Note that the online versions of some print magazines and newspapers have slightly different titles than the print versions; be sure to cite the online version (*see items 55, 56, and 61*).
- Cite the volume, issue, or other identifying number, if relevant, just as you would for a print version.
- Cite the publication date of the original print version of an article or the "posted" date for an article that appeared only in the online version of the publication.
- If the article is divided into pages, numbered paragraphs, or sections, indicate the total number of pages, paragraphs, or sections (*see item 55*).
- If the article is not divided into sections or pages, do not impose an artificial division (for example, "on the second screen"). Just leave out that part of the citation.
- Include the date you first accessed the specific article (not the site itself), even if you return to the site several times in the course of your research.
- Conclude the citation with a reasonable URL. If the URL for a specific article is too long (if it takes up much more than one full line of your citation), just give the search page or, if the site does not have a search page, the home page for the site. If readers can access the document through a series of links from the home page, include them after the word *Path* and a colon. Separate the links with semicolons.
- If you need to break a URL, do so after a slash (/) mark. Do not include extra spaces or hyphens.
- Do not create a hyperlink for the URL. See page 403 for instructions on how to turn off automatic hyperlinking in most word-processing programs.

name of the *Atlantic Monthly* magazine's Web site

Davis, Francis. "Jazz--Religious and Circus." <u>Atlantic Online</u> Feb. 2000.

3 Apr. 2004 <http://www.theatlantic.com/issues/2000/ 002davis.html>.

57. Article in a periodical published only online:

Ross, Michael E. "The New Sultans of Swing." Salon 18 Apr. 1996.

3 May 2005 <http://www.salon.com/weekly/music1.html>.

58. Article in an online newspaper: Follow the format for an article in an online magazine.

overly long URL abbreviated

"Bulletin Board: Louis Armstrong Centenary." New York Times

on the Web 7 Nov. 2001. 3 May 2005. <http://www.nytimes.com>.

59. Editorial in an online newspaper: Include the word *Editorial* after the published title of the editorial.

"A New Pope's Old Message." Editorial. San Francisco Chronicle

20 Apr. 2005. 20 Apr. 2005 <http://www.sfgate.com>.

60. Letter to the editor in an online newspaper: Include the name of the letter writer, as well as the word *Letter.*

Hughan, Wade C. Letter. San Francisco Chronicle 20 Apr. 2005.

20 Apr. 2005 <http://www.sfgate.com>.

61. Online government publication except the *Congressional Record:* Begin with the name of the country, followed by the name of the sponsoring department, the title of the document, and the names (if listed) of the authors.

United States. National Commission on Terrorist Attacks upon the United

States. The 9/11 Commission Report. By Thomas H. Kean et al.

5 Aug. 2004. 30 Mar. 2005 <http://www.gpoaccess.gov/911/

index.html>.

62. Online *Congressional Record:* Abbreviate the title, and include the date and page numbers.

Cong. Rec. 28 Apr. 2005: D419-D428.

63. Online review:

Kot, Greg. "The Mekons Find Renewal in Their Loud, Punky Past."

Rev of Punk Rock, CD, the Mekons. Chicago Tribune Online Edition

26 Mar. 2004. 2 Apr. 2004 <http://www.chicagotribune.com>.

64. Weblog (blog) posting: A weblog, or blog, is an online diary. (*For more on blogs, see Chapter 14: Multimedia Writing, pp. 274–75.*) Citing a blog entry is similar to citing other online postings.

Sullivan, Andrew. "The Grim Task in Iraq." Web log posting.

Andrewsullivan.com: The Daily Dish. 25 Nov. 2003. 24 Feb. 2004

<http://www.andrewsullivan.com/index.php?dish_inc=archives>.

65. CD-ROM or DVD: Works on CD-ROM are usually cited like books or parts of books, but the term *CD-ROM* and the name of the vendor, if different from the publisher, are added before the publication data.

"Armstrong, (Daniel) Louis 'Satchmo.' " Microsoft Encarta Multimedia

Encyclopedia. CD-ROM. Redmond: Microsoft, 1994.

66. CD-ROM or DVD: Material with no print version:

"Aristotle." Encarta 2000. CD-ROM. Redmond: Microsoft, 1999.

67. CD-ROM or DVD: Entire book:

Jones, Owen. The Grammar of Ornament. CD-ROM. Palo Alto:

Octavo, 1998.

68. Work from a library or personal subscription service: For material that you accessed through a library subscription service such as *EBSCO, InfoTrac,* and *Lexis-Nexis,* add the following to your citation: the name of the online service used; the library's name; the date of access; and, if known, the URL of the site's home page.

Hardack, Richard. " 'A Music Seeking Its Words': Double-Timing and

Double Consciousness in Toni Morrison's Jazz." Callaloo 18

(1995): 451-72. Expanded Academic ASAP. InfoTrac. Rosenthal

Lib., Queens College CUNY. 3 May 2005 <http://

web7.infotrac.galegroup.com>.

If you used a personal subscription service such as America Online, and you retrieved information by using a keyword or a topic path, identify the online service, the date accessed, and either the keyword used or the path taken. Use a colon after the capitalized word *Keyword* or *Path,* and use semicolons to separate topics.

> "Jazz." World Book Online Reference Center. 2005. America Online.
>
> 3 May 2005. Path: Research and Learn; References; Encyclopedia;
>
> Site Contents; Jazz.

69. Posting to a news group: Begin with the author and (in quotation marks) the title or subject line; the words *Online posting,* without quotation marks or underlining, follow. End with the posting date, the list or group name, the date of access, and the URL of the list or the e-mail address of the moderator if no URL is available.

> Mopsick, Don. "Favorite Jazz Quotes." Online posting. 17 Mar. 2000. Big
>
> Band-Music Fans. 17 June 2000 <http://www.remarq.com/list>.

70. Synchronous communication: Include a description and the date of the event, the title of the forum, the date of access, and the URL. If relevant, the speaker's name can begin the citation.

> Curran, Stuart, and Harry Rusche. Discussion: Plenary Log 6. Third
>
> Annual Graduate Student Conference in Romanticism. 20 Apr.
>
> 1996. Prometheus Unplugged: Emory MOO. 4 Jan. 1999
>
> <http://prometheus.cc.emory.edu/plen/plenary6.txt>.

71. E-mail: Include the author; the subject line (if any), in quotation marks; the descriptive term *E-mail* plus the name of the recipient; and the date of the message.

> Hoffman, Esther. "Re: My Louis Armstrong Paper." E-mail to J. Peritz.
>
> 14 Mar. 2005.

72. Online graphic: Base the form of your citation on the most closely related print or nonprint model. When possible, include the creator's name, the title or description of the source, the title of the larger work in which the source appears (underlined), the publication data, the date of access, and the URL.

Hirschfeld, Al. Louis "Satchmo" Armstrong. Margo Feiden Galleries.

5 May 2005 <http:// www.alhirschfeld.com/cgi-bin/

cat_alpha?CAT=A2#L>.

73. Online audio or video file: Follow the guidelines in item 72.

Adderley, Nat. Interview with Jimmy Owens. Video clip. Louis Armstrong

Jazz Oral History Project. 2 Apr. 1993. Schomburg Center for

Research in Black Culture. 3 May 2005 <http://www.nypl.org/

research/sc/scl/MULTIMED/JAZZHIST/jazzhist.html>.

74. Online cartoon:

Toles, Tom. "The Rubik's Food Pyramid." Cartoon.

Washingtonpost.com. 21 Apr. 2005. 29 Apr. 2005 <http://

www.washingtonpost.com/wp-srv/opinion/toles_archive.html>.

75. Online map:

New Orleans. Map. Lonely Planet. 2 May 2005 <http://

www.lonelyplanet.com/mapshells/north_america/

new_orleans/new_orleans.htm>.

76. Computer software: Provide the author's or editor's name, if

available; the title (underlined); the medium; the version number; and
the publication information, including place of publication, publisher,
and date. If you downloaded the software from the Internet, replace
the publication information with the date of access and the URL.

AllWrite! 2.1 with Online Handbook. CD-ROM. Vers. 2.1. New York:

McGraw, 2003.

Audiovisual and Other Nonprint Sources

77. Film, videotape, or DVD: Begin with the title (underlined). For

a film, cite the director and the lead actors or narrator (*Perf.* or *Narr.*),
followed by the distributor and year. For a videotape or DVD, add the
medium (*Videocassette* or *DVD*) before the name of the distributor.

Artists and Models. Dir. Raoul Walsh. Perf. Louis Armstrong, Martha

Raye, and Connee Boswell. Paramount Pictures, 1937.

78. TV or radio program: Give the episode title (in quotation marks), the program title (underlined), the name of the series (if any), the name of the network, the city, and the broadcast date.

"The Music of Charlie Parker." Jazz Set. WBGO-FM, New York.

2 Dec. 1998.

79. Broadcast interview: Give the name of the person interviewed, followed by the word *Interview* and the name of the interviewer if you know it. End with information about the broadcast.

Knox, Shelby. Interview with David Brancaccio. NOW. PBS. WNET,

New York. 17 June 2005.

80. Sound recording: The entry starts with the composer, conductor, or performer, depending on your focus. Include the following information: the work's title (underlined); the medium (*LP* below), unless it is a compact disc; the artist(s), if not already mentioned; the manufacturer; and the date of release.

Armstrong, Louis. Town Hall Concert Plus. LP. RCA Victor, 1957.

81. Musical composition: Include only the composer and title, unless you are referring to a published score. Published scores are treated like books except that the date of composition appears after the title. Note that the titles of instrumental pieces are underlined only when they are known by name, not just by form and number, or when the reference is to a published score.

Ellington, Duke. Satin Doll.

Haydn, Franz Josef. Symphony No. 94 in G Major.

reference to a published score
Haydn, Franz Josef. Symphony No. 94 in G Major. 1791. Ed. H. C.

Robbins Landon. Salzburg: Haydn-Mozart, 1965.

82. Artwork: Provide the artist's name, the title of the artwork (underlined), and the institution or private collection and city in which the artwork can be found.

Leonard, Herman. Louis Armstrong: Birdland. Barbara Gillman Gallery,

Miami.

If you used a photograph of a work of art from a book, treat it like a work in an anthology (*item 7*), but underline the titles of both the work and the book and include the institution or collection and city where the work can be found.

83. Personal, telephone, or e-mail interview: Begin with the person interviewed, followed by *Personal interview, Telephone interview,* or *E-mail interview* and the date of the interview. (*See item 39 for a published interview.*)

> Jacobs, Phoebe. Personal interview. 5 May 2005.

84. Lecture or speech: To cite an oral presentation, give the speaker's name, the title (in quotation marks) or a descriptive label such as *Address* or *Lecture,* the name of the forum or sponsor, the location, and the date.

> Taylor, Billy. "What Is Jazz?" John F. Kennedy Center for the Performing
>
> Arts, Washington. 14 Feb. 1995.

85. Performance: To cite a play, opera, ballet, or concert, begin with the title; followed by the authors (*By*); pertinent information about the live performance, such as the director (*Dir.*) and major performers; the site; the city; and the performance date.

> Ragtime. By Terrence McNally, Lynn Athrens, and Stephen Flaherty.
>
> Dir. Frank Galati. Ford Performing Arts Center, New York.
>
> 11 Nov. 1998.

24d   MLA style: Explanatory notes and acknowledgments

Explanatory notes are used to cite multiple sources for borrowed material or to give readers supplemental information. Their purpose is to avoid distracting readers with an overly long parenthetical citation or an interesting but not directly relevant idea. You can also use explanatory notes to acknowledge people who helped you with research and writing. Acknowledgments are a courteous gesture in academic as well as workplace writing, even if you do not intend your paper for publication. If you acknowledge someone's assistance in your explanatory notes, be sure to send that person a copy of your paper. Because they contributed in some way to your work, they are likely to be very interested in your final product.

TEXT

One answer to these questions is suggested by a large (24-by-36-inch) painting discovered in Armstrong's house.[2]

NOTE

[2]I want to thank George Arevalo of the Louis Armstrong Archives for his help on this project. When I was low on inspiration and in search of some direction, George showed me the two pictures I describe in this paper. Seeing those pictures helped me figure out what I wanted to say—and why I wanted to say it. For introducing me to archival research and to the art of Louis Armstrong, I also want to thank the head of the Louis Armstrong Archives, Michael Cogswell, and my English teacher, Professor Amy Tucker.

24e MLA style: Paper format

The following guidelines will help you prepare your research paper in the format recommended by the sixth edition of the *MLA Handbook for Writers of Research Papers.* For an example of a research paper that has been prepared using MLA style, see pages 416–26.

Materials. Before printing your paper, make sure that you have stored your final draft on a backup disk. Use a high-quality printer and high-quality, white 8½-by-11-inch paper. Put the printed pages together with a paper clip, not a staple, and do not use a binder unless you have been told to do so by your instructor.

Heading and title. No separate title page is needed. In the upper left-hand corner of the first page, one inch from the top and side, type on separate, double-spaced lines your name, your instructor's name, the course number, and the date. Double-space between the date and the paper's title and the title and the first line of text, as well as throughout your paper. The title should be centered and properly capitalized (*see p. 416*). Do not underline the title or put it in quotation marks or bold type.

TEXTCONNEX

Electronic Submission of Papers

Some instructors may request that you submit your paper electronically. (You may also need to submit documents electronically in other situations, such as job or internship applications or business correspondence.) Keep the following tips in mind:

- Confirm your instructor's e-mail address before submitting the paper.
- Find out in advance what format your instructor prefers for submission of documents. Some instructors prefer that short documents be cut and pasted into the body of an e-mail message. Others might prefer that you submit documents as attachments to e-mail messages. However, very long documents or documents that contain visuals can inconvenience those with dial-up modems. *Always ask permission before sending an attached document to anyone.*
- If you are asked to send a document as an attachment, confirm that the format of your document is compatible with the receiver's software. Documents with a great deal of formatting tend to become garbled, or filled with strange characters, when "translated" from one program to another. Save your document as a "rich text format" (.rtf) file or in ASCII format, which simplifies the formatting of your document and makes it easier to share.
- As a courtesy, run a virus scan on any file you intend to submit electronically before sending it. You should also scan for viruses if you are submitting the document on a disk or CD-ROM.

Margins and spacing.   Use one-inch margins all around, except for the top right-hand corner, where the page number goes. Your right margin should be ragged (not "justified," or even).

Double-space lines throughout the paper, including in quotations, notes, and works-cited list. Indent the first word of each paragraph one-half inch (or five spaces) from the left margin. For block quotations, indent one inch (or ten spaces) from the left.

Page numbers.   Put your last name and the page number in the upper right-hand corner of the page, one-half inch from the top and flush with the right margin.

Visuals.   Place visuals (tables, charts, graphs, and images) close to the place in your text where you refer to them. Label and number tables consecutively (*Table 1, Table 2*) and give each one an explanatory caption; put this information above the table. The term *Figure* (abbreviated *Fig.*) is used to label all other kinds of visuals, except for musical illustrations, which are labeled *Example* (abbreviated *Ex.*). Place figure or example captions below the visual. Below all visuals, cite the source of the material and provide explanatory notes as needed. *(For more on using visuals effectively, see Part 1: Writing and Designing Papers.)*

24f   Student Paper in MLA Style

As a first-year college student, Esther Hoffman wrote the following paper for her composition course. She knew little about Louis Armstrong and jazz before her instructor took the class to visit the Louis Armstrong Archives. Esther did archival research based on what she learned from consulting online and print sources.

www.mhhe.com/
nmhh
For another sample of
a paper in MLA style,
go to

Research > Sample
Research Papers >
MLA Style

½"

1"

1"

Esther Hoffman

Professor Tucker

English 120

10 May 2005

Louis Armstrong and Joe Glaser:

More Than Meets the Eye

In the 1920s, jazz music was at its height in creativity and popularity. Chicago had become one of the jazz capitals of America, and its clubs showcased the premier talents of the time, performers like Jelly Roll Morton and Joe Oliver. It has always been difficult to break into the music business, and the jazz scene of the twenties was no exception. Eager for fame and fortune, though, many young black musicians who had honed their craft in New Orleans migrated north to Chicago, hoping for a chance to perform with the best ("Chicago").

Among these émigres was Louis Armstrong, a gifted musician who developed into the "first true virtuoso soloist of jazz" ("Armstrong"). Armstrong played the trumpet and sang with unusual improvisational ability as well as technical mastery. As Bergreen points out, Armstrong easily reached difficult high notes, the F's and G's that stymied other trumpeters (248). His innovative singing style also featured "scat," a technique that combines "nonsense syllables [with] improvised melodies" (Robinson 515). According to one popular anecdote, Armstrong invented scat during a recording session; mid-song, he dropped his lyrics sheet and--not wanting to disrupt a great take--began to improvise (Edwards 619). Eventually Armstrong's innovations became the standard, as more and more jazz musicians took their cue from his style.

Armstrong's beginnings give no hint of the greatness that he would achieve. In New Orleans, he was born into poverty and

1"

Hoffman 2

received little formal education. As a youngster, Armstrong had
to take odd jobs like delivering coal and selling newspapers so
that he could earn money to help his family. At the age of twelve,
Armstrong was placed in the Colored Waifs' Home to serve an
eighteen-month sentence for firing a gun in a public place. There
"Captain" Peter Davis gave him "basic musical training on the
cornet" ("Satchmo!"). Older, more established musicians soon
noticed Armstrong's talent and offered him opportunities to play
with them. In 1922, Joe Oliver invited Armstrong to join his band
in Chicago, and the twenty-one-year-old trumpeter headed north.

It was in Chicago that Armstrong met Joe Glaser, the man
who eventually became his longtime manager. According to
Bergreen, Glaser had a reputation for being a tough but
trustworthy guy who could handle any situation. He was raised in
a middle-class home by parents who were Jewish immigrants from
Russia. As a young man, Glaser got caught up in the Chicago
underworld and soon had a rap sheet that included indictments
for running a brothel as well as for statutory rape.[1] Glaser's mob
connections also led to his involvement in Chicago's club scene, a
business almost completely controlled by gangsters like Al Capone.
During the era of Prohibition, Glaser managed the Sunset Cafe,
a club where Armstrong often performed:

> There was a pronounced gangster element at the
> Sunset, but Louis, accustomed to being employed and
> protected by mobsters, didn't think twice about that.
> Mr. Capone's men ensured the flow of alcohol, and their
> presence reassured many whites. (Bergreen 279)

By the early thirties, Armstrong had become one of the most
popular musicians in the world. He attracted thousands of fans

Development by narration (see p. 71).

Focus introduced.

Superscript number indicating an explanatory note.

Block quotation indented 10 spaces or 1".

417

Hoffman 3

during his 1930 European tour, and his "Hot Five" and "Hot Seven" recordings were considered some of the best jazz ever played. Financially, Armstrong should have been doing very well, but instead he was having business difficulties. He owed money to Johnny Collins, his former manager, and Lil' Hardin, his ex-wife, was suing him for a share of the royalties on the song "Struttin' with Some Barbecue." At this point, Armstrong asked Glaser to be his business manager. Glaser quickly paid off Collins and settled with Lil' Hardin. Giving up his other business ventures, Glaser now became Armstrong's exclusive agent (Morgenstern 124-28; Collier 273-76; Bergreen 376-78). For the next thirty-four years, his responsibilities included booking appearances, organizing the bands, making travel arrangements, and paying the band members' salaries (Jones and Chilton 160, 220).

Under Glaser's management, Armstrong reached the pinnacle of his fame, an achievement for which he was profoundly grateful. Once, while discussing the creation of the All-Star bands, Armstrong even credited his musical accomplishments to Glaser, saying, "Anything that I have done musically since I signed up with Joe Glaser at the Sunset, it was his suggestions" (qtd. in Jones and Chilton 175). Was Glaser really as central to Armstrong's work and life as this comment makes him seem? To what extent did Glaser create and control the star known nowadays as a "King of Jazz"? What kind of relationship did Joe Glaser and Louis Armstrong actually have?

One answer to these questions is suggested by a large (24-by-36-inch) oil painting discovered in Armstrong's house.[2] Joe Glaser is pictured in the middle of the canvas. Four black-and-white quadrants surround the central image of Glaser. One quadrant

Annotations (left margin):

Summary of material from a number of sources.

Citation of multiple sources.

Use of information from two separate pages in one source.

Indirect source.

Poses key questions that thesis will answer.

418

depicts a city scene, the scene in which Glaser thrived. The bottom
two quadrants picture dogs, a reminder that Glaser raised show
dogs. The remaining quadrant presents an image of Louis
Armstrong. By placing Glaser in the center and Armstrong off
in a corner, the unknown artist seems to suggest that even though
Armstrong was the star, it was Glaser who made him one.

In fact, Glaser did advance Armstrong's career in numerous
important ways. In 1935, he negotiated the lucrative record
contract with Decca that led to the production of hits like "I'm in
the Mood for Love" and "You Are My Lucky Star" (Bergreen 380).
Glaser also decided when to sell the rights to Armstrong's songs.
Determined to make as much money as possible, he sometimes
sold the rights to a song as soon as it was released, especially
when he thought the song might not turn out to be a big hit.
However, in at least two instances, this money-making strategy
backfired: much to Glaser's surprise, both "Hello, Dolly" and
"What a Wonderful World" became big hits after the rights had
been sold (Jacobs).

To expand Armstrong's popularity, Glaser increased his
exposure to white audiences in the United States. In 1935, articles
on Armstrong appeared in Vanity Fair and Esquire, two magazines
with a predominantly white readership (Bergreen 385). Glaser also
promoted Armstrong's movie career. At a time when only a
handful of black performers were accepted in Hollywood,
Armstrong had roles in a number of films, including Pennies from
Heaven (1936) with Bing Crosby. Moreover, "Jeepers Creepers," a
song Armstrong sang in Going Places (1938), received an Academy
Award nomination (Bogle 149, 157). Of course, more exposure
sometimes meant more discomfort, if not danger, especially when

Development
by description
(*see pp.
72–74*).

Presents a
claim plus
supporting
evidence.

Development
by illustration
(*see pp.
76–78*).

Note use of
transitional
expressions
(*see pp.
103–4*).

Armstrong and his band members were touring in the South. Bergreen recounts how in southern states, where blacks were prohibited from entering many stores, Glaser sometimes had to shop for the band's food and other supplies (378, 381).

As Armstrong's manager, Glaser also exerted some control over the musician's personal finances and habits. According to Dave Gold, an accountant who worked for Associated Booking, it was Glaser who paid Armstrong's mortgage, taxes, and basic living expenses (Collier 330). A 1960 letter from Glaser to Lucille Armstrong corroborates Gold's account; it shows that Glaser assumed responsibility for buying the musician and his wife a new car as well as for filing the paperwork needed to retain the old license plate number. More personal were Glaser's attempts to control Armstrong's habitual use of marijuana. In 1931, Armstrong received a suspended sentence after his arrest for marijuana possession. He continued to use the drug, however, especially during performances, and told Glaser that he wanted to write a book about marijuana's positive effects. Glaser flatly rejected the book idea and, fearful of a scandal, also forbade Armstrong's smoking any marijuana while on tour in Europe (Pollack).

Clearly, Glaser was in a position to affect powerfully Armstrong's career and his life. Armstrong acknowledged Glaser's importance, at one point referring to him as "the man who has guided me all through my career" (qtd. in Jones and Chilton 175). However, there is little evidence that the musician submitted to whatever his business manager wanted or demanded. In fact, Armstrong seemed to recognize that he gave Glaser whatever power over him the manager enjoyed. When he wanted to, Armstrong could and did resist Glaser's control, and

Support by expert opinion (see p. 215).

Support by key fact (see p. 215).

Support by anecdote (see p. 215).

Thesis paragraph.

420

Hoffman 6

that may be one reason why he liked and trusted Glaser as much as he did.

After Glaser became his manager, Armstrong no longer had to worry about the behind-the-scenes details of his career. He was free to concentrate on creating music and making the most of the opportunities his manager worked out for him. Glaser booked Armstrong into engagements with legendary performers like Benny Goodman, Ella Fitzgerald, and Duke Ellington. He also worked with the record companies to ensure that Armstrong would make the best and most profitable recordings possible (Bergreen 457). During the thirty-four years they worked together, both Armstrong and Glaser made lots of money. More important, their relationship freed Armstrong to make extraordinary music.

If Armstrong acquiesced to most of Glaser's business decisions, it may have been because he had no reason to resist them. However, when he deemed it necessary, Armstrong acted on his own. For example, in 1944 a talented band member named Dexter Gordon threatened to quit, so Armstrong offered him a raise--without consulting first with Glaser (Morgenstern 132). In 1957, when Armstrong wanted to put a stop to backstage crowding, he not only directed Glaser to make a sign prohibiting guests from going backstage but also told him exactly what to say on the sign (Armstrong, Backstage Instructions). As these incidents suggest, when Armstrong was displeased with the way his career was being handled, he acted to amend the situation.

Armstrong also knew how to resist Glaser's attempts to control the more personal aspects of his life. In a recent interview, Phoebe Jacobs, formerly one of Glaser's employees, sheds new light on the relationship between the manager and the musician.

Source cited: archival material.

Source cited: personal interview.

421

Armstrong's legendary generosity was tough on his pocketbook.
It was well known that if someone needed money, Armstrong
would readily hand over some bills. At one point, Glaser asked
Jacobs to give Armstrong smaller denominations so that he would
not give away so much money. The trumpeter soon figured out
what was going on and admonished Jacobs for following Glaser's
orders about money that belonged to him, not Glaser. On another
occasion, Armstrong declined an invitation to join Glaser for
dinner at a Chinese restaurant, saying, "I want to eat what I want
to eat" (qtd. by Jacobs).

Even though he sometimes pushed Glaser away, Armstrong
obviously loved and trusted his manager. In all the years of their
association, the two men signed only one contract and, in the
musician's words, "after that we didn't bother" (qtd. in Jones and
Chilton 240). A picture of Joe Glaser in one of Armstrong's
scrapbooks bears the following label in the star's handwriting:
"the greatest." In his dedication to the unpublished manuscript
"Louis Armstrong and the Jewish Family in New Orleans,"
Armstrong calls Glaser "the best friend that I ever had," while in a
letter to Max Jones, he writes, "I did not get really happy until I got
with my man--my dearest friend--Joe Glaser" (qtd. in Jones and
Chilton 16). In 1969, Joe Glaser died. Referring to him again as
"the greatest," Armstrong confided to a friend that Glaser's death
"broke [his] heart" (qtd. in Bergreen 490).

Although there are hints of a struggle for the upper hand, the
relationship between Louis Armstrong and Joe Glaser seems to
have been genuinely friendly and trusting. Armstrong gave Glaser
a good deal of authority over his career, and Glaser used that
authority to make Armstrong a musical and monetary success.

Authoritative
quotation
(*see pp.
220–21*).

Memorable
quotation
(*see pp.
358–60*).

Wording
of quotation
adjusted (*see
pp. 358–59*).

Concludes
with qualified
version of
thesis.

Hoffman 8

Fig. 1 An anonymous watercolor caricature of Armstrong with his manager, Joe Glaser, c. 1950. Louis Armstrong Archives, Queens College, City University of New York, Flushing.

Armstrong was happy to take the opportunities that Glaser provided for him, but he was not submissive. This equitable and friendly relationship is depicted by another picture found in Armstrong's house. The 25-by-21-inch picture, shown in Fig. 1,

Effective visual.

Memorable illustration.

423

Hoffman 9

is a caricature of Armstrong and Glaser. The pair stand side by side, and Glaser has his hand on Armstrong's shoulder. Armstrong, who is dressed for a performance, looks and smiles at us as if he were facing an audience. But Glaser looks only at Armstrong, the musician who was his main concern from 1935 to the day he died. In appearance alone, the men are clearly different. But seen in their longstanding partnership, the two make up a whole--one picture that offers us more than meets the eye.

Hoffman 10

Notes

[1]Bergreen 372-76. Even though Ostwald points out a few mistakes in Bergreen's Louis Armstrong: An Extravagant Life, I think the book's new information about Glaser is useful and trustworthy.

[2]I want to thank George Arevalo of the Louis Armstrong Archives for his help on this project. When I was low on inspiration and in search of some direction, George showed me the two pictures I describe in this paper. Seeing those pictures helped me figure out what I wanted to say--and why I wanted to say it. For introducing me to archival research and to the art of Louis Armstrong, I also want to thank the head of the Louis Armstrong Archives, Michael Cogswell, and my English teacher, Professor Amy Tucker.

New page, title centered.

Gives supplemental information about key source.

Indent first line 5 spaces or ½".

Acknowledges others who helped.

Hoffman 11

Works Cited

"Armstrong, (Daniel) Louis 'Satchmo.' " Microsoft Encarta
    Multimedia Encyclopedia. CD-ROM. Redmond: Microsoft,
    1994.

Armstrong, Louis. Backstage instructions to Glaser. April 1957.
    Accessions 1997-26. Louis Armstrong Archives. Queens
    College CUNY, Flushing, NY.

---. "Louis Armstrong and the Jewish Family in New Orleans."
    Unpublished ms. 31 March 1969. Louis Armstrong Archives.
    Queens College CUNY, Flushing, NY.

Bergreen, Laurence. Louis Armstrong: An Extravagant Life. New
    York: Broadway, 1997.

Bogle, Donald. "Louis Armstrong: The Films." Louis Armstrong: A
    Cultural Legacy. Ed. Marc H. Miller. Seattle: U of Washington
    P and Queens Museum of Art, 1994. 147-79.

"Chicago: Early 1920s." Wolverine Antique Music Society. Ed.
    R. D. Frederick. 1998. 3 May 2005 <http://www.shellac.org/
    wams/wchicag1.html>.

Collier, James Lincoln. Louis Armstrong, an American Genius. New
    York: Oxford UP, 1983.

Edwards, Brent Hayes. "Louis Armstrong and the Syntax of Scat."
    Critical Inquiry 28 (2002): 618-49.

Glaser, Joe. Letter to Lucille Armstrong. 28 Sept. 1960. Box 3.
    Armstrong Archives. Queens College CUNY, Flushing, NY.

Jacobs, Phoebe. Personal interview. 5 May 2005.

Jones, Max, and John Chilton. Louis: The Louis Armstrong Story,
    1900-1971. Boston: Little, 1971.

Morgenstern, Dan. "Louis Armstrong and the Development and
    Diffusion of Jazz." Louis Armstrong: A Cultural Legacy. Ed.

New page,
title centered.

Entries in
alphabetical
order.

Source:
archival
material.

3 hyphens
used instead
of repeating
author's name.

Source:
whole book.

Hanging
indent
5 spaces
or ½".

Source:
Web site
document.

Source:
journal
paginated
by volume.

Source:
personal
interview.

Source:
selection in
an edited
book.

Hoffman 12

Marc H. Miller. Seattle: U of Washington P and Queens
Museum of Art, 1994. 95-145.

Ostwald, David. "All That Jazz." Rev. of <u>Louis Armstrong:</u>
<u>An Extravagant Life</u>, by Laurence Bergreen. <u>Commentary</u>
Nov. 1997: 68-72.

Pollack, Bracha. "A Man ahead of His Time." Unpublished essay,
1997.

Robinson, J. Bradford. "Scat Singing." <u>The New Grove Dictionary</u>
<u>of Jazz</u>. Ed. Barry Kernfeld. Vol. 3. London: Macmillan, 2002.
515-16.

"Satchmo!" New Orleans Online. 2005. New Orleans Tourism
Marketing Corporation. 5 Apr. 2005 <http://
www.neworleansonline.com/neworleans/music/
satchmobio.html>.

Source: review
in a monthly
magazine.

Source: a
classmate's
paper.

25 APA Documentation Style

Many researchers in behavioral and social sciences like psychology, sociology, and political science as well as in communications, education, and business use the documentation style developed by the American Psychological Association (APA). The guidelines presented here are based on the fifth edition of its *Publication Manual* (Washington: APA, 2001). For updates to the APA documentation system, check the APA-sponsored Web site at <http://www.apastyle.org>.

Tips   LEARNING in COLLEGE

What Kind of Source Am I Citing?

APA style requires writers to provide bibliographic information about their sources in a references list at the end of a paper. To format reference entries correctly, you need to know first of all what kind of source you are citing. The directory on page 434 will help you find the appropriate sample to use as your model. As an alternative, you can use the charts on the pages that follow to help you locate the right example. Answering the questions provided in the charts will usually lead you to the sample entry you need. If you cannot find what you are looking for after consulting the appropriate directory or chart, ask your instructor for help. (*To learn where to find the information you need to complete a citation, see the examples on pp. 431–33.*)

www.mhhe.com/
nmhh
For links to Web sites
for documentation
styles used in various
disciplines, go to
Research > Links
to Documentation
Sites

Entries in a List of References: BOOKS

❓ *Is your source a complete book?*

No   Yes
         ↓

	Go to this entry
Is it a complete book with one named author?	
Is it the only book by this author that you are citing?	1
Are you citing more than one book by this author?	4
Does it also have an editor or translator?	5, 7
Is it a complete book with more than one named author?	2
Is it a complete book without a named author or editor?	
Is the author an organization?	3
Is the author anonymous or unknown?	10
Is it a complete book with an editor or translator?	
Is there an editor instead of an author?	5
Is it a translation?	7
Is it an entire reference work?	9
Is it a complete book with a volume or an edition number?	
Is it part of a multivolume work (e.g., Volume 3)?	12
Does it have an edition number (e.g., Second Edition)?	11
Is it a republished work (e.g., a classic study)?	13

❓ *Is your source part of a book?*

No   Yes
         ↓

	Go to this entry
Is it a work from an anthology or a chapter in an edited book?	6
Is it an article in a reference work (e.g., an encyclopedia)?	8
Is it a published presentation from a conference?	27

↓

Check the next page or the directory on page 440 or consult your instructor.

Entries in a List of References: PRINT PERIODICALS OR OTHER PRINT SOURCES

❷ *Is your source from an academic journal, a magazine, or a newspaper?*

No   Yes
↓

	Go to this entry
Is it from an academic journal?	
Are the page numbers continued from one issue of the journal to the next?	14
Do the page numbers in each issue of the journal start with 1?	15
Is the article from a journal supplement?	16
Is it an abstract (a brief summary) of a journal article?	17
Is it a review (e.g., a review of a book)?	24
Is it a published presentation from a conference?	27
Is it from a monthly or weekly magazine?	
Is it an article?	19
Is it a letter to the editor?	21
Is it a review (e.g., a review of a book)?	24
Is it from a newspaper?	
Is it an article?	20
Is it an editorial or a letter to the editor?	21
Is it a review (e.g., a review of a book)?	24
Is it from a newsletter?	23
Is the author unknown?	22
Are you citing two or more articles published in the same year by the same author?	18

❷ *Is it a print source but not a book, a part of a book, or an article in an academic journal, a magazine, or a newspaper?*

No   Yes
↓

	Go to this entry
Is it published by the government or a nongovernment organization?	
Is it a government document?	25
Is it a report or a working paper?	26
Is it a brochure, pamphlet, or fact sheet?	29
Is it from the *Congressional Record*?	42
Is it an unpublished work?	
Is it an unpublished conference presentation?	27
Is it an unpublished dissertation or a dissertation abstract?	28

Check the directory on page 440 or consult your instructor.

Entries in a List of References: ELECTRONIC OR OTHER NONPRINT SOURCES

❓ Did you find your nonprint source online?

No   Yes
       ↓

	Go to this entry
Is it an article you found through a subscription database service (e.g., EBSCO or ProQuest)?	32
Is it from an online scholarly journal?	
Is it an article from a journal that is available only online?	33
Is it an article from a journal that is also available in print?	34
Is it from an online publication?	
Is it an article from an online newspaper?	35
Is it an article from an online newsletter?	40
Is it from a personal or organizational Web site?	
Is it a document or visual from a Web site?	36
Is it produced by one organization but posted on another organization's Web site?	37
Is it part of a long online document?	38
Is it a document on a university's Web site?	39
Is it an entry from a Weblog (blog)?	45
Is it a government publication?	
Is it a government document available online?	41
Is it from the *Congressional Record*?	42
Is it an online document without a date or an author?	43
Is it a posting to a news group or other online forum?	44

❓ Is your source a nonprint source that is not published online?

No   Yes
       ↓

	Go to this entry
Is it a film, a DVD, a videotape, a CD-ROM, or an audio recording?	30
Is it a television program?	31
Is it computer software?	46

Check the directory on page 440 or consult your instructor.

The Elements of an APA References Entry: Books

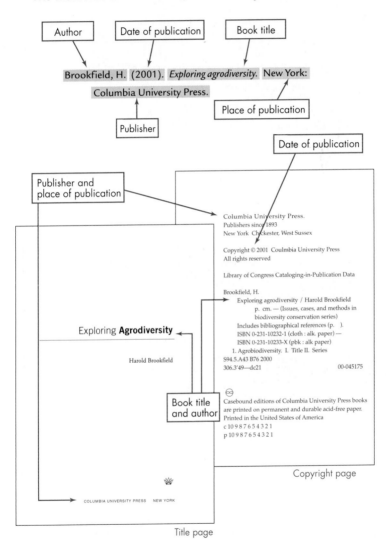

Title page

Copyright page

Information for a book citation can be found on the book's title and copyright pages.

The Elements of an APA References Entry: Journal Articles

Author | Year of publication | Article title | Journal title

Epstein, J. (2002). A voice in the wilderness. *Latin Trade,*
10(12), 26.

Volume | Issue number | Page number

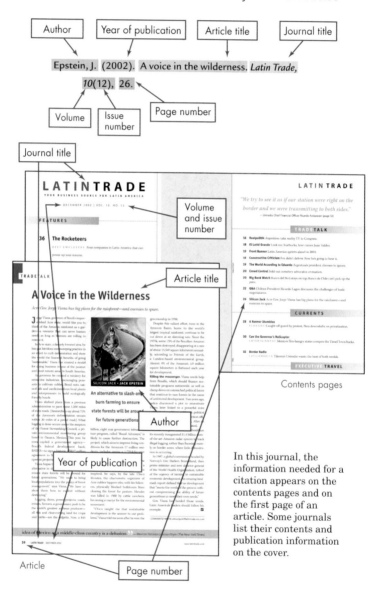

Journal title

Volume and issue number

Article title

Author

Year of publication

Page number

Contents pages

Article

In this journal, the information needed for a citation appears on the contents pages and on the first page of an article. Some journals list their contents and publication information on the cover.

The Elements of an APA References Entry: Journal Articles from an Online Subscription Service

Author, title, and other information about the print version of the article

Epstein, J. (2002). A voice in the wilderness. *Latin Trade,*
10(12), 26. Retrieved March 15, 2004, from EbscoHost
Research Databases.

Date of access

Subscription database service

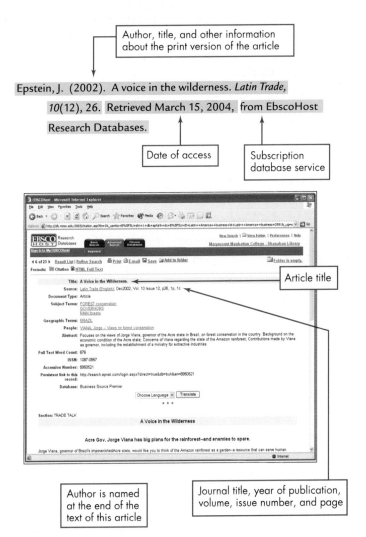

Article title

Author is named at the end of the text of this article

Journal title, year of publication, volume, issue number, and page

A citation for an article obtained from an online subscription database service like EBSCO includes the name of the service and the date of access in addition to information about the print version of the article. In this database listing, the author's name appears at the end of the full text of the article; usually you can also find the author's name in the listing.

25a The elements of APA documentation style

A documentation style that emphasizes the author and year of publication makes it easy for readers to tell if the sources cited are current. The APA's widely used version of the author-year style has two mandatory parts:

- In-text citations
- List of references

25b APA style: In-text citations

In-text citations let readers know that they can find full information about an idea you have paraphrased or summarized or the source of a quotation in the list of references at the end of your paper.

1. Author named in sentence: Follow the author's name with the year of publication (in parentheses).

signal phrase
According to Brookfield (2001), nearly 12 percent of the Amazonian

rain forest in Brazil has been shaped or influenced by thousands of

years of indigenous human culture.

APA IN-TEXT CITATIONS: DIRECTORY to SAMPLE TYPES

(See pp. 439–52 for examples of references entries.)

GENERAL GUIDELINES for APA IN-TEXT CITATIONS

- Identify the author(s) of the source, either in the sentence or in a parenthetical citation. Use only the last name of an author or author(s).

- Indicate the year of publication of the source following the author's name, either in parentheses if the author's name is part of the sentence or, if the author is not named in the sentence, after the author's name and a comma in the parenthetical citation.

- Include a page reference for a quotation or specific piece of information. Put a "p." before the page number. If the author is named in the text, the page number appears in the parenthetical citation following the borrowed material. Page numbers are not necessary when you are summarizing the source as a whole or paraphrasing an idea found throughout a work. (*For more on summary, paraphrase, and quotation, see Chapter 21: Working with Sources, pp. 353–57.*)

- If the source does not have page numbers (as with many online sources), do your best to direct readers toward the specific part of the text you are citing (for example, by citing the section title of an online source). If the source has no page or paragraph numbering or easily identifiable headings, just use the name and date.

2. Author named in parentheses: If you do not name the source's author in your sentence, then you must include the name in the parentheses, followed by the date and, if you are giving a quotation or a specific piece of information, the page number. Separate the name, date, and page number with commas.

> The Organization of Indigenous Peoples of the Colombian Amazon
>
> attempted in 2001 to take legal action to ban such fumigation over
>
> indigenous lands. Their efforts were not supported by the Colombian
>
> *ampersand used within parentheses*
> government (Lloyd & Soltani, 2001, p. 5).

3. Two to five authors: If a source has five or fewer authors, name all of them the first time you cite the source.

> As Kaimowitz, Mertens, Wunder, and Pacheco (2004) report in
>
> "Hamburger Connection Fuels Amazon Destruction," there are three

435

LEARNING in COLLEGE

What Is the American Psychological Association?

The American Psychological Association (APA) is the largest psychological organization in the world. It has more than 155,000 members and supports advances in psychological research and the practice of psychology. Now in its fifth edition, the *Publication Manual of the American Psychological Association* has become an accepted guide for writers in many areas of science, not just psychology. Like the *MLA Handbook* (*see p. 384*), the *Publication Manual* is concerned with the mechanics of academic writing. The manual is especially useful in helping students prepare and present scientific facts and figures, and it contains special sections on how to construct tables, present statistics, and cite scientific references.

> key factors behind the burgeoning demand for Brazilian beef and the
>
> resulting burning of the Amazon rain forest for pasture.

If you put the names of the authors in parentheses, use an ampersand (&) instead of *and.*

> There are three key factors behind the burgeoning demand for Brazilian
>
> beef and the resulting burning of the Amazon rain forest for
>
> pastureland (Kaimowitz, Mertens, Wunder, & Pacheco, 2004, p. 3).

After the first time you cite a work by three or more authors, use the first author's name plus *et al.* Always use both names when citing a work by two authors.

> Another key factor is concern over livestock diseases in other countries
>
> (Kaimowitz et al., 2004, p. 4).

4. Six or more authors: For in-text citations of a work by six or more authors, always give the first author's name plus *et al.* In the reference list, however, list the first six authors' names, followed by *et al.*

> As Barbre et al. (1989) have argued, using personal narratives enables
>
> researchers to connect the individual and the social.

5. Organization as author: Treat the organization as the author, and spell out its name the first time the source is cited. If the organization is well known, you may use an abbreviation thereafter.

According to a report issued by the Inter-American Association for
Environmental Defense (2004), a significant proportion of Colombia's
indigenous peoples live within these protected parklands.

Public service announcements were used to inform parents of these
findings (National Institute of Mental Health [NIMH], 1991).

In subsequent citations, only the abbreviation and the date need to
be given: (*NIMH, 1991*).

6. Unknown author: When no author or editor is given, use the
first one or two important words of the title. Use quotation marks for
titles of articles or chapters and italics for titles of books or reports.

The transformation of women's lives has been hailed as "the single
most important change of the past 1,000 years" ("Reflections," 1999,
p. 77).

7. Two or more authors with the same last name: If the authors of two or more sources have the same last name, always include
their first initial, even if the year of publication differs.

M. Smith (1988) showed how globalization has restructured both cities
and states.

8. Two or more sources cited at one time: When you are in-
debted to two or more sources, cite the authors in the order in which
they appear in the list of references, separated by a semicolon.

Other years see greater destruction from large-scale economic and
industrial initiatives, such as logging (Geographical, 2000; Kaimowitz
et al., 2004, p. 2).

9. E-mail, letters, conversations: To cite information received
from unpublished forms of personal communication, such as conversations, letters, notes, and e-mail messages, give the source's initials
and last name, and provide as precise a date as possible.

According to ethnobotanist Dr. Gordon Freid (personal communication,
May 4, 2004), the work of research scientists in the Brazilian Amazon
has been greatly impeded within the past ten years because of the
destruction of potentially unrecorded plant species.

Note: Because readers do not have access to them, you should not include personal communications—e-mail, notes, and letters—in your reference list.

---

10. Indirect source: When referring to a source that you know only from reading another source, use the phrase *as cited in,* followed by the author of the source you actually read and its year of publication.

> According to the Center for International Forestry Research, an
>
> Indonesia-based NGO (as cited in Prugh, 2004), an area of land the
>
> size of Uruguay was deforested in the years 2002 and 2003 alone.

The work by Prugh would be included in the references list, but the work by the Center for International Forestry Research would not.

11. Electronic source: Cite an electronic source the same way you would a print source, with the author's last name and the publication date. If the document is a .pdf (portable document format) file with stable page numbers, cite the page number as you would a print source. If the source has paragraph numbers instead of page numbers, use *para.* or ¶ instead of *p.* when citing a specific part of the source (*see item 12*).

> Applications of herbicides have caused widespread damage to biodiversity,
>
> livestock, and crops and have caused "thousands" of peasants and
>
> indigenous peoples to flee these lands (Amazon Alliance, 2004).

Note: If the specific part lacks any kind of page or paragraph numbering, cite the heading and the number of the paragraph under that heading where the information can be found. If you cannot find the name of the author, or if the author is an organization, follow the appropriate guidelines for print sources (*see items 5 and 6*). If you cannot determine the date, use the abbreviation "n.d." in its place: (*Wilson, n.d.*).

---

12. Two or more sources in one sentence: Include a parenthetical reference after each fact, idea, or quotation you have borrowed and put it after the fact, idea, or quotation:

By one estimate, nearly 12 percent of the Amazonian rain forest in
Brazil has been shaped or influenced by thousands of years of
indigenous human culture (Brookfield, 2001); the evidence is as basic
as the *terra preta do Indio,* or "Indian black soil," for which the Brazilian
region of Santarem is known (Rough Guides, 2003, para. 2).

13. Sacred or classical text: Cite these sources within your text
only, and include the version you consulted as well as any book, part,
or section numbers that are standard for all versions.

The famous song sets forth a series of opposites, culminating in
"a time to love, and a time to hate; a time of war, and a time of peace"
(Eccles. 3:8, King James Bible).

25c APA style: References

APA documentation style requires a list of references where readers
can find complete bibliographical information about the sources referred to in your paper. The list of references should appear at the end
of your paper, beginning on a new page entitled "References."

www.mhhe.com/
nmhh
To download
Bibliomaker software
for APA, go to
Research >
Bibliomaker

Books

1. Book with one author:

Brookfield, H. (2001). *Exploring agrodiversity.* New York: Columbia
University Press.

2. Book with two or more authors:

Goulding, M., Mahar, D., & Smith, N. (1996). *Floods of fortune: Ecology
and economy along the Amazon.* New York: Columbia University Press.

3. Organization as author:

To credit a subdivision like "Econom-
ics Department," put its name after the name of the parent organization. When the publisher is the same as the author, use *Author* instead
of repeating the organization's name as the publisher.

Deutsche Bank, Economics Department. (1991). *Rebuilding eastern
Europe.* Frankfurt, Germany: Author.

4. Two or more works by the same author: List the works in
publication order, with the earliest one first.

> Wilson, S. (Ed.). (1997). *The indigenous people of the Caribbean.*
> Gainesville: University Press of Florida.

> Wilson, S. (1999). *The emperor's giraffe and other stories of cultures in*
> *contact.* Boulder, CO: Westview Press.

If the works were published in the same year, put them in alphabetical order by title and add a letter (*a, b, c*) to the year to distinguish
each entry in your in-text citations; see item 18 for an example.

GENERAL GUIDELINES for
APA LIST of REFERENCES

- Begin on a new page.
- Begin with the centered title "References."
- Include a reference for every in-text citation except personal
  communications (*see item 9 on pp. 437–38*).
- Put references in alphabetical order by author's last name.
- Give the last name and first or both initials for each author.
  If the work has more than one author, see item 2 (*p. 439*).
  Do not add academic titles (such as PhD) to the author's name.
- Put the publication year in parentheses following the author or
  authors' names.
- Capitalize only the first word and proper nouns in titles. Also
  capitalize the first word in a subtitle following the colon.
- Use italics for titles of books but not articles. Do not enclose
  titles of articles in quotation marks.
- Include the city and publisher for books. If the city is not well
  known, include the state, using its two-letter postal abbreviation.
- Include the periodical name and volume number (both in
  italics) as well as the page numbers for a periodical article.
- Separate the author's or authors' names, date (in parentheses),
  title, and publication information with periods.
- Use a hanging indent: Begin the first line of each entry flush
  left, and indent all subsequent lines of an entry one-half inch
  (five spaces).
- Double-space within and between entries.

5. Book with editor(s): Add (*Ed.*) or (*Eds.*) after the name. If a book lists an author and an editor, treat the editor like a translator (*see item 7*).

> Lifton, K. (Ed.). (1998). *The greening of sovereignty in world politics.*
>
> Cambridge, MA: MIT Press.

6. Selection in an edited book or anthology: The selection's author, year of publication, and title come first, followed by the word *In* and information about the edited book. Note that the page numbers of the selection go in parentheses after the book's title.

> Wilmer, F. (1998). Taking indigenous critiques seriously: The enemy
>
> 'r' us. In K. Lifton (Ed.), *The greening of sovereignty in world politics*
>
> (pp. 55-60). Cambridge, MA: MIT Press.

7. Translation: After the title of the translation, put the name(s) of the translator(s) in parentheses, followed by the abbreviation *Trans.*

> Jarausch, K. H., & Gransow, V. (1994). *Uniting Germany: Documents and*
>
> *debates, 1944-1993* (A. Brown & B. Cooper, Trans.). Providence,
>
> RI: Berg.

8. Article in a reference work: Some encyclopedias and similar reference works name the authors of individual selections. Begin with the author's name, if given. If no author is given, begin with the title.

> title of the selection
> Arawak. (2000). In *The Columbia encyclopedia* (p. 2533). New York:
>
> Columbia University Press.

9. Entire dictionary or reference work: Unless an author is indicated on the title page, list dictionaries by title, with the edition number in parentheses, followed by the date and publication information. (The in-text citation should include the title or a portion of the title.) (*See item 8 for information on citing an article in a reference book and item 10 on alphabetizing a work listed by title.*)

> *The American Heritage dictionary of the English language* (4th ed.). (2000).
>
> Boston: Houghton Mifflin.

> Hinson, M. (2004). *The pianist's dictionary.* Bloomington: Indiana
>
> University Press.

10. Unknown author or editor: Start with the title. When alphabetizing, use the first important word of the title (excluding articles such as *The, A,* or *An*).

> *Give me liberty.* (1969). New York: World.

11. Edition other than the first: After the title, put the edition number in parentheses, followed by a period.

> Smyser, W. R. (1993). *The German economy: Colossus at crossroads*
>
> (2nd ed.). New York: St. Martin's Press.

12. One volume of a multivolume work: If the volume has its own title, put it before the title of the whole work. No period separates the title and parenthetical volume number.

> Handl, G. (1990). The Mesoamerican Biodiversity Legal Project. In
>
> *Yearbook of international environmental law* (Vol. 4). London: Graham
>
> & Trotman.

13. Republished book:

> Le Bon, G. (1960). *The crowd: A study of the popular mind.* New York:
>
> Viking. (Original work published 1895).

In-text citations should give both years: "As Le Bon (1895/1960) pointed out . . ."

Periodicals

14. Article in a journal paginated by volume: Do not put the article title in quotation marks, and do not use *pp.* before the page numbers. Italicize the title of the periodical and the volume number.

> da Cunha, M. C., & de Almeida, M. (2000). Indigenous people, traditional
>
> people and conservation in the Amazon. *Daedalus, 129,* 315.

15. Article in a journal paginated by issue: Include the issue number (in parentheses). Notice that the issue number is not italicized as part of the journal's title.

> Epstein, J. (2002). A voice in the wilderness. *Latin Trade, 10*(12), 26.

16. Journal supplement: Begin with the names of the authors or editors followed by the date and supplement title, the journal name and volume number, and—if needed—the issue number and the word *Suppl.* with supplement number, if there is one, in parentheses.

> Barnsteener, J. H., Burke, K. G., & Rich, V. (Eds.). (2005, March). State
>
> of the science on safe medication administration. *American Journal*
>
> *of Nursing 2005, 105*(3)(Suppl.), 1-56.

17. Abstract: For an abstract that appears in the original source, add the word *Abstract* in brackets after the title. If the abstract appears in a printed source that is different from the original publication, first give the original publication information for the article, followed by the publication information for the source of the abstract.

> Burnby, J. G. L. (1985, June). Pharmaceutical connections: The Maw's
>
> family [Abstract]. *Pharmaceutical Historian, 15*(2), 9-11.

> Murphy, M. (2003). Getting carbon out of thin air. *Chemistry and*
>
> *Industry, 6,* 14-16. Abstract obtained from *Fuel and Energy Abstracts,*
>
> 2004, *45*(6), 389.

If the dates of the publications differ, cite them both, with a slash between them, in the in-text citation: *Murphy (2003/2004).*

18. Two or more works in one year by the same author: Alphabetize by title, and attach a letter to each entry's year of publication, beginning with *a.* In-text citations must use the letter as well as the year so that readers know exactly which work is being cited.

> Agarwal, J. P. (1996a). *Does foreign direct investment contribute to*
>
> *unemployment in home countries?—An empirical survey* (Discussion
>
> Paper No. 765). Kiel, Germany: Institute of World Economics.

> Agarwal, J. P. (1996b). Impact of Europe agreements on FDI in
>
> developing countries. *International Journal of Social Economics,*
>
> *23*(10/11), 150-163.

19. Article in a magazine: After the year, add the month for magazines published monthly or the month and day for magazines published weekly. Note that the volume number is also included.

> Gross, P. (2001, February). Exorcising sociobiology. *New Criterion, 19,* 24.

20. Article in a newspaper: Use *p.* or *pp.* with the section and page number. List all page numbers, separated by commas, if the article appears on discontinuous pages: *pp. C1, C4, C6.* If there is no identified author, begin with the title of the article.

> Smith, T. (2003, October 8). Grass is green for Amazon farmers.
>
> *The New York Times,* p. W1.

21. Editorial or letter to the editor:

> Krugman, P. (2000, July 16). Who's acquiring whom? [Editorial].
>
> *The New York Times,* Sec. 4, p. 15.

> Deren, C. (2005, May 5). The last days of LI potatoes? [Letter to the
>
> editor]. *Newsday,* p. A49.

22. Unsigned article: Begin the entry with the title, and alphabetize it by the first important word (excluding articles such as *The, A,* or *An*).

> Reflection on a thousand years: Introduction. (1999, April 18). *The New*
>
> *York Times Magazine,* p. 77.

23. Newsletter article: Add the season or month of the newsletter after the year in parentheses. If the article has no author, begin the listing with the title. If the pages are discontinuous, separate the page numbers with a comma.

> Gardiner, P. (2005, April). Can you say cold turkey? California's prisons
>
> set to go smoke-free. *Burning Issues, 7*(2), 1-4, 9-10.

> Largest ever study of osteoarthritis of the knee is seeking volunteers.
>
> (2004, Winter). *Johns Hopkins Arthritis Center Newsletter, 2*(2), 3.

24. Review:

> Kaimowitz, D. (2002). Amazon deforestation revisited. [Review of
>
> the book *Brazil, forests in the balance: Challenges of conservation with*
>
> *development*]. *Latin American Research Review, 37,* 221-236.

> Scott, A. O. (2002, May 10). Kicking up cosmic dust. [Review of the
>
> motion picture *Star wars*]. *The New York Times,* p. B1. **445**

If the review is untitled, use the bracketed description in place of a title.

Other Print and Audiovisual Sources

25. Government document: When no author is listed, use the government agency as the author.

> U.S. Bureau of the Census. (1976) *Historical statistics of the United States: Colonial times to 1970.* Washington, DC: U.S. Government Printing Office.

For the format to use when citing an enacted resolution or piece of legislation, see item 42.

26. Report or working paper: If the issuing agency numbered the report, include that number in parentheses after the title.

> Agarwal, J. P. (1996a). *Does foreign direct investment contribute to unemployment in home countries?—An empirical survey* (Discussion Paper No. 765). Kiel, Germany: Institute of World Economics.

For reports from a deposit service like the Educational Resources Information Center (ERIC), put the document number in parentheses at the end of the entry.

27. Conference presentation: Treat published conference presentations as a selection in a book (*item 6*), as a periodical article (*item 14 or item 15*), or as a report (*item 26*), whichever applies. For unpublished conference presentations, including poster sessions, provide the author, the year and month of the conference, the title of the presentation, and information on the presentation's form, forum, and place.

> Markusen, J. (1998, June). *The role of multinationals in global economic analysis.* Paper presented at the First Annual Conference in Global Economic Analysis, West Lafayette, IN.

> Desantis, R. (1998, June). *Optimal export taxes, welfare, industry concentration and firm size: A general equilibrium analysis.* Poster session presented at the First Annual Conference in Global Economic Analysis, West Lafayette, IN.

28. Unpublished dissertation or dissertation abstract:

Weinbaum, A. E. (1998). Genealogies of "race" and reproduction in
transatlantic modern thought (Doctoral dissertation, Columbia
University, 1998). *Dissertation Abstracts International, 58,* 229.

If you used the abstract but not the actual dissertation, treat the
entry like a periodical article, with *Dissertation Abstracts International* as the periodical.

Weinbaum, A. E. (1998). Genealogies of "race" and reproduction
in transatlantic modern thought. *Dissertation Abstracts International,
58,* 229.

29. Brochure, pamphlet, fact sheet: Identify the type of publi-
cation in brackets. If there is no date of publication, put *n.d.* in place of
the date. If the publisher is an organization, list it first, and name the
publisher as *Author.*

United States Postal Service. (1995, January). *A consumer's guide to postal
services and products* [Brochure]. Washington, DC: Author.

Union College. (n.d.) *The Nott Memorial: A national historic landmark at
Union College* [Pamphlet]. Schenectady, NY: Author.

Department of Health and Human Services, Centers for Disease
Control and Prevention. (2003, July 31). *Anthrax: What you need to
know* [Fact sheet]. Washington, DC: Author.

30. Film, DVD, videotape, CD-ROM, recording: Begin with the
cited person's name and, if appropriate, a parenthetical notation of his
or her role. After the title, identify the medium in brackets, followed by
the country and name of the distributor.

Towner, R. (1989). *City of eyes* [Record]. Munich: ECM.

Wenders, W. (Director). (1989). *Wings of desire* [Videotape]. Germany:
Orion Home Video.

For films and videotapes that might be hard to find, add the name
and address of the distributor in parentheses after the bracketed
medium information. For audio recordings for which an identification
number is needed, add the number immediately following the medium

description, and use parentheses instead of brackets; add the name and address of the distributor.

> National Geographic Society (Producer). (1993). *Killer whales: Wolves of the sea* [Videotape]. (Available from the National Geographic Society, 3400 Riverside Drive, Burbank, CA 91505-4627).

> Bolles, R. N. (Speaker/Author). (2000). *What color is your parachute? 2000: A practical manual for job-hunters and career changers* [Cassette recording]. San Bruno, CA: Audio Literature.

31. Television program: When citing a single episode, treat the writer as the author and the producer as the editor of the series.

> Weissman, G. (Writer). (2000). Mississippi: River out of control [Television series episode]. In J. Towers (Producer), *Wrath of God*. New York: The History Channel.

When citing a whole series or a specific news broadcast, name the producer as author.

> Towers, J. (Producer). (2000). *Wrath of God*. New York: The History Channel.

> Crystal, L. (Executive Producer). (2000, July 18).*The NewsHour with Jim Lehrer* [Television broadcast]. Washington, DC: Public Broadcasting Service.

Electronic Sources

32. Online article or abstract from a database: When you use material from databases such as *PsycInfo, Sociological Abstracts, General BusinessFile ASAP,* and *Lexis-Nexis,* include a retrieval date and the name of the database in addition to the standard information about author, year, title, and publisher.

> Epstein, J. (2002). A voice in the wilderness. *Latin Trade, 10*(12), 26. Retrieved March 15, 2004, from EbscoHost Research Databases.

> Haas, R. (1994). Eastern Europe: A subsidy strategy for ecological recovery. *Global Energy Issues 6*(3), 133-138. Abstract retrieved April 22, 2001, from Lexis-Nexis database.

When citing an abstract instead of the article, add the word *abstract* to the retrieval statement.

33. Online article from a journal published only online: Include a retrieval date and the URL.

Amazon Alliance. (2004). Colombia: US acknowledges funding for

fumigations in national parks and protected areas. *Amazon Update*

98 (2004). Retrieved April 7, 2004, from http://

www.amazonalliance.org/upd_jan04_en.html

34. Online article from a journal previously published in print: To cite an electronic version of an article from a print journal, use the standard format for a periodical article (*see item 14*) and add "[Electronic version]" after the article title. If the article appears not to have been altered from the print version, you need not include the URL. If the article has been altered from the print version, include a retrieval date and URL as for online-only articles (*see item 33*)

Cook, B. G., & Cook, L. (2004). Bringing science into the classroom by

basing craft on research [Electronic version]. *Journal of Learning*

Disabilities, 37, 240-247.

35. Article in an online newspaper:

Feller, B. (2005, May 6). GM, Ford get "junk" rating. *The Detroit News*

Online. Retrieved May 6, 2005, from http://www.detnews.com/

2005/autoinsider/0505/06/A01-173553.htm

36. Document on a Web site: If the document is an entire article or report, include the basic information for an online document. If you have used a graph, chart, map, or image, give the source information following the figure caption (*for an example, see p. 458*).

Lloyd, J., & Soltani, A. (2001, December). *Report on: Plan Colombia*

and indigenous peoples. Retrieved April 2, 2004, from http://

www.amazonwatch.org/amazon/CO/uwa/reports/

plancol_march02.pdf

37. Article or report from a secondary source's Web site: Include information about the host organization's Web site after the retrieval date.

> World Health Organization. (1992). *ICD-10 criteria for borderline personality disorder.* Retrieved March 28, 2005, from the Mental Health Sanctuary Web site: http://www.mhsanctuary.com/ borderline/icd10.htm

38. Chapter or section in a long online document: Include the chapter title, if there is one, before the title of the work.

> Fielding, H. (1749). Book XV: In which the history advances about two days. In *The history of Tom Jones, a foundling* (chap. 15). Retrieved September 18, 2005, from http://www. bartleby.com/302/1501.html

> Woolf, V. (1920). In *Night and day* (chap. 3). Retrieved October 3, 2005, from http://www.netlibrary.com/Reader/Woolf/

39. Document on a university's Web site: Include relevant information about the university and department after the retrieval date.

> Tugal, C. (2002, February). *Islamism in Turkey: Beyond instrument and meaning.* Retrieved August 16, 2005, from University of California–Berkeley, Department of Sociology Web site: http://sociology.berkeley.edu/public%5Fsociology/

40. Article in an online newsletter:

> Shenandoah Chapter, Virginia Native Plant Society. (2005, April). Conservation. *Shenandoah Chapter Newsletter.* Retrieved May 6, 2005, from http://www.vnps.org/shenan.htm

> Lekwa, S. (2003, October-November). Cougars in Iowa pose little threat to people and animals. *Acreage Living: A Bi-monthly Newsletter for Rural Residents Highlighting Timely Topics on Country Living.* Retrieved May 6, 2005, from http://www.extension.iastate.edu/ acreage/AL2003/aloctnovt03.html

41. Online government document except the *Congressional Record:*

> National Commission on Terrorist Attacks upon the United States.
> (2004, August 5). *The 9/11 Commission report.* Retrieved March 30,
> 2005, from http://www.gpoaccess.gov/911/index.html

> Centers for Disease Control and Prevention. (2003, July 31). *Anthrax:*
> *What you need to know.* Retrieved March 30, 2005, from http://
> www.bt.cdc.gov/agent/anthrax/needtoknow.asp

42. *Congressional Record* (online or in print):
To cite enacted resolutions or legislation, give the number of the congress after the number of the resolution or legislation, the *Congressional Record* volume number, the page number(s), and year, followed by "(enacted)."

> H. Res. 2408, 108th Cong., 150 Cong. Rec. 1331-1332
> (2004)(enacted).

Give the full name of the resolution or legislation when citing it within your sentence, but abbreviate the name when it appears in a parenthetical in-text citation: *(H. Res. 2408, 2004).*

43. Online document without a date or author:
Use the abbreviation *n.d.* (no date) for any undated document. Begin the entry with the document's title if no author is given.

> Center for Science in the Public Interest. (n.d.). *Food additives to avoid.*
> Retrieved July 10, 2005, from http://www.mindfully.org/Food/
> Food-Additives-Avoid.htm

> *Raw food vegans thin, but healthy.* (2005, March 28). Retrieved April 23,
> 2005, from CNN.com: http://www.cnn.com/2005/HEALTH/
> diet.fitness/03/28/raw.vegans.reut/index.html

44. Online posting to news group, discussion forum, or mailing list:
Messages posted to archived online electronic mailing lists, discussion forums, or news groups can be retrieved and should therefore be included in the reference list when you use them as sources. Provide the message's author, its date, and the subject line as the title. After the phrase *Message posted to,* give the name of the discussion forum or news group, followed by the address of the message.

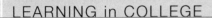

Red Wave. (2000, April 8). Pareto/allocative efficiency of gift economy.

    Message posted to alt.society.economic-dev message board, archived

    at http://www.remarq.com/read/9755/qAyjNymZ61SoC-vwH#LR

45. Weblog (blog) posting:

Sullivan, A. (2003, November 23). The grim task in Iraq.

    Andrewsullivan.com: The Daily Dish. Retrieved February 24, 2004,

    from http://www.andrewsullivan.com/index.php?dish_inc=archives

46. Computer software:

AllWrite! 2.1 with Online Handbook. (2003). [Computer software].

    New York: McGraw-Hill.

25d APA style: Paper format

The following guidelines will help you prepare your research paper in the format recommended by the *Publication Manual of the American Psychological Association,* fifth edition. For an example of a research paper that has been prepared using APA style, see pages 455–65.

Materials. Before printing your paper, make sure that you have stored your final draft on a backup disk. Use a high-quality printer and high-quality white 8½-by-11-inch paper. Choose a standard 10- or

12-point font such as Courier, Times, or Bookman. Do not justify your text or hyphenate words at the right margin; it should be ragged.

Title page.   The first page of your paper should be a title page. Center the title between the left and right margins in the upper half of the page, and put your name a few lines below the title. Most instructors will also want you to include the course number and title, the instructor's name, and the date. (*See p. 455 for an example.*)

Margins and spacing.   Use one-inch margins all around, except for the right-hand top corner, where the page number goes.

Double-space lines throughout the paper, including in the abstract, within any notes, and in the list of references. Indent the first word of each paragraph one-half inch (or five spaces).

For quotations of more than forty words, use block format and indent five spaces from the left margin. Double-space the quoted lines.

Page numbers and abbreviated titles.   All pages, including the title page, should have a number preceded by a short version of your title. Put this information in the upper right-hand corner of each page, about one-half inch from the top.

Abstract.   Instructors sometimes require an abstract—a 75- to 100-word summary of your paper's thesis, major points or lines of development, and conclusions. The abstract appears on its own numbered page, entitled "Abstract," and is placed right after the title page.

Headings.   Although headings are not required, most instructors welcome them. The primary headings should be centered, and all key words in the heading should be capitalized.

You can also use secondary headings if you need them; they should be italicized and should appear flush against the left-hand margin. Do not use a heading for your introduction, however. (*For more on headings, see Chapter 6: Designing Academic Papers and Portfolios, pp. 131–33.*)

Visuals.   Place visuals (tables, charts, graphs, and images) close to the place in your text where you refer to them. Label each visual as a table or a figure, and number each kind consecutively (Table 1, Table 2). You will also need to provide an informative caption for each visual. Cite the source of the material, preceded by the word *Note* and a period, and provide explanatory notes as needed. (*For more on using visuals effectively, see Chapter 4: Drafting Paragraphs and Visuals, pp. 71–84.*)

**www.mhhe.com/
nmhh**
For another sample
of a paper in
APA style, go to

Research > Sample
Research Papers >
APA Style

25e Student paper in APA style

Audrey Galeano researched and wrote the following report on the impact of globalization on the indigenous peoples of the Amazon for a course entitled Indigenous Peoples and Globalization. Her sources included books, journals, articles, and Web sites.

Saving the Amazon 1

Saving the Amazon:

Globalization and Deforestation

Audrey Galeano

Anthropology 314: Indigenous Peoples and Globalization

Professor Mura

May 3, 2005

Title appears on separate page, centered, with student's name, course information, and date.

Saving the Amazon   2

Abstract

The impact of globalization on fragile ecosystems is a complex problem. In the Amazon River basin, globalization has led to massive deforestation as multinational corporations exploit the rain forest's natural resources. In particular, large-scale industrial agriculture has caused significant damage to the local environment. In an effort to resist the loss of this ecosystem, indigenous peoples in the Amazon basin are reaching out to each other, to nongovernmental organizations (NGOs), and to other interest groups to combat industrial agriculture and promote sustainable regional agriculture. Although these efforts have had mixed success, it is hoped that the native peoples of this region can continue to live on their homelands without feeling intense pressure to acquiesce to industrialization or to relocate.

Abstract appears on a new page after the title page. First line is not indented.

Essay concisely and objectively summarized —key points included, but not details or statistics.

Paragraph should be no longer than 120 words.

1"

½"

Saving the Amazon:

Globalization and Deforestation

For thousands of years, the indigenous peoples of the Amazon
River basin have practiced forms of sustainable agriculture. These
peoples developed ways of farming and hunting that enabled them
to provide food and trade goods for their communities with
minimal impact on the environment. These methods have endured
despite colonization and industrialization. Today, the greatest
threat to indigenous peoples in the Amazon River basin is posed by
the massive deforestation caused by industrial-scale farming and
ranching, as revealed in satellite images taken since 1988 by
Brazil's National Institute of Space Research. (See Figure 1.)
Because of the injury to ecosystems and native ways of life,
indigenous peoples and antiglobalization activists have joined
forces to promote sustainable agriculture and the rights of native
peoples throughout the Amazon River basin.

Sustainable Lifeways, Endangered Lives

Recent work in historical ecology has altered our understanding
of how humans have shaped what is romantically called "virgin
forest." As anthropologist Anna Roosevelt (as cited in Society for
California Archaeology, 2000) observes, "People adapt to
environments but they also change them. There are no virgin
environments on earth in areas where people lived." By one
estimate, nearly 12 percent of the Amazonian rain forest in Brazil
has been shaped or influenced by thousands of years of indigenous
human culture (Brookfield, 2001); the evidence is as basic as the
terra preta do Indio, or "Indian black soil," for which the Brazilian
region of Santarem is known (Rough Guides, 2003, para. 2).

1"

Full title
repeated on
first page
only.

Figure
introduced
and com-
mented on.

Thesis
statement.

Primary
heading,
centered,
subtly reveals
writer's
stance.

Parenthetical
citation of
source with
organization
as author.

Information
from two
sources com-
bined in one
sentence.

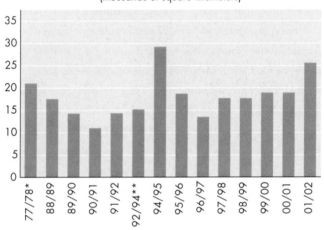

Graph in
introduction
presents
statistics in
visual form
for readers.

Saving the Amazon   4

Annual Deforestation Rates in Brazilian Amazon
(thousands of square kilometers)

Figure 1 Annual deforestation rates in the Brazilian Amazon,
1988-2002 (square kilometers). *Note.* From National Institute of
Space Research. (2002). In D. Kaimowitz, B. Mertens, S. Wunder,
& P. Pacheco, *Hamburger connection fuels Amazon destruction: Cattle
ranching and deforestation in Brazil's Amazon.* Retrieved July 16, 2004
from http://www.cifor.cgiar.org/publications/pdf_files/media/
Amazon.pdf

Informative
caption and
source note
appear below
the figure.

The human influence on the Amazon of the previous
thousands of years is slight, however, compared with the modern-
day destruction of rain forests around the globe, and in the
Amazon River basin in particular. The sources of this destruction
vary from country to country and year to year, with climate change

Support by
key facts
(*see p. 251*).

Saving the Amazon   5

producing more impact in certain years and human initiatives, such
as logging, causing greater destruction in other years (Walker,
Moran, & Anselin, 2000). According to the Center for International
Forestry Research, an Indonesia-based nongovernmental
organization (NGO) (as cited in Prugh, 2004), an area of land the
size of Uruguay was deforested in the years 2002 and 2003 alone.
Nearly all of this land was cleared for industrial agriculture and
cattle ranching.

Paragraphs expand on introductory paragraph.

Globalization and Agricultural Destruction

Large-scale industrial agriculture seeks out the least expensive
ways to produce the highest number of crops. Perhaps the largest
cash crop of the late 20th century is soy, which has numerous uses
and is among the least expensive crops to produce. According to
Roberto Smeraldi, director of the environmental action group
Friends of the Earth, "soybeans are the single biggest driver for
deforestation" in the Brazilian Amazon; in the 12 months ending in
August 2003, 9,169 square miles of rain forest had been cleared by
soy farmers, ranchers, and loggers in Brazil (as cited in Stewart,
2004, paras. 4–5). Although Brazilian officials have attempted to
regulate depredations of the rain forest by multinational soy
producers, Stewart notes that, in 2003, soybean production
brought nearly $8 billion to the Brazilian economy, forcing
indigenous and small-scale farmers off their lands and damaging
local climate.

Details introduced and linked to broader issue of globalization.

An Associated Press (AP) report reprinted on the Organic
Consumer's Association Web site describes the impact of soy
production on Brazil's Xingu National Park, a protected rain forest

Abbreviation given at first mention of organization.

reserve that is home to 14 indigenous tribes. "The soy is arriving

First main
cause of
deforestation
discussed.

very fast. Every time I leave the reservation I don't recognize
anything anymore because the forest keeps disappearing," a
director of the Xingu Indian Land Association is quoted as

Abbreviation
for organiza-
tion used in
parenthetical
citation.

observing (AP, 2003, para. 11). Although the industrial soy farms
have not crossed the borders of the Xingu National Park, they
surround the protected lands and have raised fears that chemical
pesticides and deforestation will dry up rivers and kill fish. "Our
Xingu is not just what's here. It's a very long thread, and when it
rains the soy brings venom down the same river that passes by our
door," says Capivara chief Jywapan Kayabi (para. 24).

Second main
cause of
deforestation
discussed.

Cattle ranching has also led to the deforestation of the
Amazon. The cattle population of the Amazon nations increased
from 26 million in 1990 to 57 million in 2002 (Prugh, 2004).
Attention to the destruction caused by industrial cattle ranching
began in the late 1980s. Barrett (2001) points out that ranchers
followed onto land already depleted of fertility and biodiversity by
logging, road building, and colonization of the Brazilian Amazon in
the 1960s and 1970s. Ranching, Barrett observes, "doesn't require
nutrient-rich soil" and therefore "took the place vacated by other
activities, along with the blame for soil erosion and loss of

Page number
given for
quotation.

biodiversity" (p. 1).

Indigenous Peoples and Regional Activism

Depopulation of these lands as a result of colonization meant

A contributing
factor in the
problem of
deforestation
shows the
complexity of
the situation.

that traditional agricultural practices were no longer sustained. In
recent years, antiglobalization NGOs, the international movement
for indigenous peoples' rights, and increased understanding of the
consequences of deforestation are helping native peoples reclaim

lands and reestablish traditional agricultural practices. However, some kinds of alliances and interventions are not as productive as others.

Anthropologists da Cunha and de Almeida ask a provocative question: "Can traditional peoples be described as 'cultural conservationists'?" (2000, p. 315). Although as many as 50 indigenous groups in Amazonia still have no contact with the outside world, other indigenous peoples have secured their land rights through international efforts over the past 20 years. Some of these efforts, da Cunha and de Almeida argue, are influenced by romantic ideas about "noble savages" and fail to acknowledge the ways in which indigenous peoples in contemporary Brazil make a living from rain forest resources.

Barham and Coomes (1997) also note that a better understanding of how indigenous peoples live is necessary if the efforts of international groups such as Amazon Alliance are to succeed. Indigenous peoples need to see some material benefit from conservationist practices. After all, as da Cunha and de Almeida write, "traditional peoples are neither outside the central economy nor any longer simply in the periphery of the world system" (2000).

Franke Wilmer (1998) suggests that "human action and its impact in the world are directed by a view that is dangerously out of touch with natural laws which, according to indigenous peoples, govern all life on this planet." For instance, although the Kayapo people of south-central Amazonia have been devastated by colonization, they still "used their knowledge to manipulate ecosystems in remarkable ways . . . to maximize biological diversity" (Brookfield, 2001, p. 141). Among the Kayapo's

> Local culture, history, and economics are linked to global systems.

> Ellipses indicate omission in quotation.

Saving the Amazon   8

sustainable practices are crop rotation, the use of ash to fertilize fields, and the transition of older fields back to secondary forest (Brookfield, 2001).

Some socially conscious global corporations have attempted to help indigenous Amazonian farmers develop sustainable, profitable crops. Two of the best-known efforts, described in a 2003 *New York Times* article by Tony Smith, provide a cautionary tale. In the 1990s, the British multinational "green" cosmetics company The Body Shop and American ice cream manufacturer Ben and Jerry's both developed "eco-friendly" products from the Amazon. Ben and Jerry's Rainforest Crunch ice cream used Brazil nuts that were harvested in a sustainable fashion by an Amazonian cooperative, and The Body Shop used the oils from Brazil nuts in some of its cosmetics. But Rainforest Crunch proved so popular that the cooperative could not meet the demand, and Ben and Jerry's had to turn to other suppliers, "some notorious for their antilabor practices" (Smith, 2003, p. W1). The Body Shop wound up being sued by a chief of the Kayapo tribe, whose image was used in Body Shop advertising without permission (Smith).

The best solution might be for Brazilian business, developers, government officials, and indigenous peoples to work together. One new initiative described in the *Times* article is the cultivation of the sweet-scented native Amazon grass called priprioca, on which the Sao Paulo cosmetics company Natura is basing a new fragrance. Farmer Jose Mateus, who has grown watermelons and manioc on his small farm near the Amazon city of Belem, has agreed to grow priprioca instead—and he expects to get twice the price for the grass that he would for his usual crop (Smith, 2003).

Problems caused by one of the solutions discussed.

Solutions described, backed up with quotations from experts, which come from a secondary source.

Saving the Amazon   9

Eduardo Luppi, director of innovation for Natura, comments, "We do have the advantage that we are Brazilian and we are in Brazil. If you are in England or America and want to manage something like this in the Amazon by remote control, you can forget it" (as cited in Smith, 2003, p. W1).

Although indigenous peoples face extraordinary obstacles in their quest for environmental justice, some political officials support their struggles. In the Acre state of Brazil, Governor Jorge Viana was inspired by the example of martyred environmental activist Chico Mendes to secure financing from Brazil's federal development bank for sustainable development in his impoverished Amazonian state (Epstein, 2002). Viana, who holds a degree in forest engineering, told the journal *Latin Trade* that "we want to bring local populations into the policy of forest management. . . . We have to show them how to exploit without destroying" (as cited in Epstein, p. 26).

Conclusion

The social, economic, climate-related, and political pressures on the Amazonian ecosystem may prove insurmountable; report after report describes the enormous annual loss of rain forest habitat. The best hope for saving the rain forest is public pressure on multinational agricultural corporations to practice accountable, safe, and sustainable methods. In addition, it is important to encourage indigenous peoples to practice their age-old sustainable agriculture and land-management strategies while guaranteeing their rights and safety. Much in the Amazon has been ruined, but cooperative efforts like those discussed in this paper can nurture and sustain what remains for future generations.

Essay concludes on a concerned but hopeful note.

Saving the Amazon   10

References

Associated Press. (2003, December 18). *Soybeans: The new threat to Brazilian rainforest.* Retrieved April 8, 2004, from http://www.organicconsumers.org/corp/soy121903.cfm

Barham, B. L., & Coomes, O. T. (1997). Rain forest extraction and conservation in Amazonia. *The Geographical Journal, 163*(2), 180+.

Barrett, J. R. (2001). Livestock farming: Eating up the environment? *Environmental Health Perspectives, 109*(7), 1.

Brookfield, H. (2001). *Exploring agrodiversity.* New York: Columbia University Press.

da Cunha, M. C., & de Almeida, M. (2000). Indigenous people, traditional people and conservation in the Amazon. *Daedalus, 129,* 315.

Epstein, J. (2002). A voice in the wilderness. *Latin Trade, 10*(12), 26. Retrieved March 15, 2004, from EbscoHost Research Databases.

Prugh, T. (2004). Ranching accelerates Amazon deforestation. *World Watch, 17*(4), 8.

Rough Guides. (2003). *Santarem.* Retrieved July 25, 2004, from http://www.travelingo.org/south-america/brazil/amazon/eastern-amazonia/santarem/

Smith, T. (2003, October 8). Grass is green for Amazon farmers. *The New York Times,* p. W1.

Society for California Archaeology. (2000). *Interview with Dr. Anna Roosevelt.* Retrieved July 20, 2004, from http://www.scahome.org/educational_resources/2000_ Roosevelt. html

New page,
heading
centered.

Entries in
alphabetical
order and
double-spaced.

Hanging indent
5 spaces or ½″.

Saving the Amazon   11

Stewart, A. (2004, July 14). Brazil's soy success brings environmental challenges. *Dow Jones*. Retrieved July 15, 2004, from http://www.amazonia.org.br/English/noticias/noticia.cfm?id=116059

Walker, R., E. Moran, & L. Anselin. (2000). Deforestation and cattle ranching in the Brazilian Amazon: External capital and household processes. *World Development 28*(4), 683-699.

Wilmer, F. (1998). Taking indigenous critiques seriously: The enemy 'r' us. In K. Lifton (Ed.), *The greening of sovereignty in world politics* (pp. 55-60). Cambridge: MIT Press.

26 Chicago and CSE Documentation Styles

There are many documentation styles besides those developed by the Modern Language Association (*see Chapter 24*) and the American Psychological Association (*see Chapter 25*). In this chapter, we cover three additional documentation styles: the *Chicago Manual* style and the two styles developed by the Council of Science Editors. To find out where you can learn about other style types, consult the list of style manuals on page 367. If you are not sure which style to use, ask your instructor.

For MULTILINGUAL STUDENTS

Deciding Which Documentation Style to Use

Always check with your instructor if you are not sure which documentation style you should use for a particular paper. Each of the styles presented in this book is academically sound, and it is possible that any one of several styles could provide the guidance you need to format and document your paper. The choice of which style to use is often guided by the personal preference of the professor.

www.mhhe.com/
nmhh
For links to Web sites
for documentation
styles in various
disciplines, go to
Research > Links
to Documentation
Sites

CHICAGO DOCUMENTATION STYLE

The note and bibliography style presented in the fifteenth edition of *The Chicago Manual of Style* (Chicago: University of Chicago Press, 2003) is used in many disciplines, including history, art, philosophy, business, and communications. This style has three parts:

- Numbered in-text citations
- Numbered footnotes or endnotes
- A bibliography of works consulted

The first two parts are necessary; the third is optional, unless your instructor requires it. (Chicago also has an alternative author-date system that is similar to APA style.) For more information on this style, consult the *Chicago Manual of Style*. For updates and answers to frequently asked questions about this style, go to the *Chicago Manual*'s Web site at <http://www.Press.uchicago.edu> and click on *Chicago Manual of Style* Web site.

26a Use numbered in-text citations and notes.

Whenever you use information or ideas from a source, you need to indicate what you have borrowed by putting a superscript number in the text (^{1}) at the end of the borrowed material. These superscript numbers are placed after all punctuation marks except for the dash.

> As Bergreen points out, Armstrong easily reached difficult high notes, the F's and G's that stymied other trumpeters.[3] His innovative singing style also featured "scat," a technique that combines "nonsense syllables [with] improvised melodies."[4]

If a quotation is fairly long, you can set it off as a block quotation. Indent it five spaces or one-half inch from the left margin, and single-space the quotation, leaving an extra space above and below it. Place the superscript number after the period that ends the quotation. (*See p. 483 for an example.*)

Each in-text superscript number must have a corresponding note either at the foot of the page or at the end of the text. Indent the first line of each footnote like a paragraph. Footnotes begin with the number and are single-spaced, with a double space between notes.

If you are using endnotes instead of footnotes, they should begin after the last page of your text on a new numbered page entitled "Notes." Single-space within and double-space between endnotes.

The first time a source is cited in either a footnote or an endnote, include a full citation. Subsequent citations require less information.

FIRST REFERENCE TO SOURCE

3. Laurence Bergreen, *Louis Armstrong: An Extravagant Life* (New York: Broadway Books, 1997), 248.

ENTRY FOR SOURCE ALREADY CITED

6. Bergreen, 370.

If several pages pass between references to the same title, include a brief version of the title to clarify the reference.

ENTRY FOR A SOURCE ALREADY CITED IN A LONGER PAPER

7. Bergreen, *Louis Armstrong,* 370.

If you quote from the same work immediately after providing a full footnote, use the abbreviation *Ibid.* (Latin for "in the same place"), followed by the page number.

> 8. Ibid., 370.

TEXTCONNEX

Superscript Numbers

To find the superscript option in your computer's word-processing program, click on Format on your tool bar and then choose Font. Superscript is one of many font options.

www.mhhe.com/
nmhh
To download
Bibliomaker software
for Chicago style,
go to

Research >
Bibliomaker

26b Prepare a separate bibliography if your instructor requires one.

Some instructors require a separate list of works cited or of works consulted. If you are asked to provide a works-cited list, then do so on a separate, numbered page that has the title "Works Cited." If the list should include all works you consulted, then title it "Bibliography."

> Bergreen, Laurence. *Louis Armstrong: An Extravagant Life.* New York: Broadway Books, 1997.

GENERAL GUIDELINES for a BIBLIOGRAPHY or a WORKS-CITED LIST in CHICAGO STYLE

- Begin on a new page.
- Begin with the centered title "Works Cited" if you are including only works referred to in your paper. Use the title "Bibliography" if you are including every work you consulted.
- List sources alphabetically by author's (or editor's) last name.
- Capitalize the first and last words in titles as well as all important words and words that follow colons.
- Indent all lines except the first of each entry five spaces using your word processor's hanging indent feature.
- Use periods between author and title as well as between title and publication data.
- Single-space each entry; double-space between entries.

26c Use the correct Chicago style for notes and bibliography entries.

Books

1. Book with one author:

NOTE

1. James Lincoln Collier, *Louis Armstrong: An American Genius* (New York: Oxford University Press, 1983), 82.

BIBLIOGRAPHY ENTRY

Collier, James Lincoln. *Louis Armstrong: An American Genius.* New York: Oxford University Press, 1983.

2. Multiple works by the same author: After providing complete information in the first footnote, include only a shortened version of the title with the author's last name and the page number in any subsequent footnotes. In the bibliography, list entries either in alphabetical order by title or in chronological order from earliest to latest. After the first listing, replace the author's name with a "3-em" dash (type three dashes in a row).

NOTES

> 7. Collier, *Jazz*, 154.

> 12. Collier, *Louis Armstrong*, 32.

BIBLIOGRAPHY ENTRIES

Collier, James Lincoln. *Jazz: The American Theme Song.* New York: Oxford University Press, 1993.

———. *Louis Armstrong, An American Genius.* New York: Oxford University Press, 1983.

3. Book with two or more authors: In notes, you can name up to three authors. When there are three authors, put a comma after the first name and a comma plus *and* after the second.

NOTE

> 2. Miles Davis and Quincy Troupe, *Miles: The Autobiography* (New York: Simon & Schuster, 1989), 15.

BIBLIOGRAPHY ENTRY

Davis, Miles, and Quincy Troupe. *Miles: The Autobiography.* New York: Simon & Schuster, 1989.

When more than three authors are listed on the title page, use *and others* or *et al.* after the first author's name in the note.

NOTE

> 3. Julian Henriques and others, *Changing the Subject: Psychology, Social Regulation and Subjectivity* (New York: Methuen, 1984), 275.

BIBLIOGRAPHY ENTRY

Henriques, Julian, Wendy Holloway, Cathy Urwin, Couze Venn, and Valerie Walkerdine. *Changing the Subject: Psychology, Social Regulation and Subjectivity.* New York: Methuen, 1984.

Notice that *and others* or *et al.* is not used in bibliography entries, even when a book has more than three authors.

4. Book with an author and an editor or a translator: Put the author's name first and add the editor's (*ed.*) or translator's (*trans.*) name after the title. Spell out *Edited* or *Translated* in the bibliography entry.

NOTE

4. Louis Armstrong, *Louis Armstrong--A Self-Portrait,* ed. Richard Meryman (New York: Eakins Press, 1971), 54.

BIBLIOGRAPHY ENTRIES

Armstrong, Louis. *Louis Armstrong--A Self-Portrait.* Edited by Richard Meryman. New York: Eakins Press, 1971.

Goffin, Robert. *Horn of Plenty: The Story of Louis Armstrong.* Translated by James F. Bezov. New York: Da Capo Press, 1977.

5. Book with editor(s):

NOTE

5. Paul Eduard Miller, ed., *Esquire's Jazz Book* (New York: Smith & Durrell, 1944), 31.

BIBLIOGRAPHY ENTRY

Miller, Paul Eduard, ed. *Esquire's Jazz Book.* New York: Smith & Durrell, 1944.

6. Organization as author:

NOTE

6. Centre for Contemporary Cultural Studies, *Making Histories: Studies in History Writing and Politics* (London: Hutchinson, 1982), 10.

BIBLIOGRAPHY ENTRY

Centre for Contemporary Cultural Studies. *Making Histories: Studies in History Writing and Politics.* London: Hutchinson, 1982.

7. Work in an anthology or part of an edited book: Begin with the author and title of the specific work or part.

NOTES

    7. Hale Smith, "Here I Stand," in *Readings in Black American Music,* ed. Eileen Southern (New York: Norton, 1971), 287.

    8. Richard Crawford, foreword to *The Jazz Tradition,* by Martin Williams (New York: Oxford University Press, 1993).

BIBLIOGRAPHY ENTRIES

Crawford, Richard. Foreword to *The Jazz Tradition,* by Martin Williams. New York: Oxford University Press, 1993.

Smith, Hale. "Here I Stand." In *Readings in Black American Music,* edited by Eileen Southern, 286-89. New York: W. W. Norton, 1971.

In notes, descriptive terms such as *foreword* are not capitalized. In bibliography entries, these descriptive terms are capitalized.

8. Article in an encyclopedia or a dictionary: For well-known reference works, publication data can be omitted from a note, but the edition or copyright date should be included. There is no need to include page numbers for entries in reference works that are arranged alphabetically; the abbreviation *s.v.* (meaning "under the word") plus the entry's title can be used instead.

NOTES

    9. J. Bradford Robinson, "Scat Singing," in *The New Grove Dictionary of Jazz* (2002).

    10. *Encyclopedia Britannica,* 15th ed., s.v. "Jazz."

Reference works are not listed in the bibliography unless they are unusual or crucial to your paper.

BIBLIOGRAPHY ENTRY

Robinson, J. Bradford. "Scat Singing." In *The New Grove Dictionary of Jazz.* Edited by Barry Kernfeld. Vol. 3. London: Macmillan, 2002.

9. The Bible: Abbreviate the name of the book, and use arabic numbers for chapter and verse separated by a colon. Name the version of the Bible cited only if it matters, and do not include the Bible in your bibliography.

NOTE

    11. Eccles. 8:5 (Jerusalem Bible).

10. Edition other than the first: Include the number of the edition after the title or, if there is an editor, after that person's name.

NOTE

12. Hugues Panassie, *Louis Armstrong,* 2d ed. (New York: Da Capo Press, 1980), 12.

BIBLIOGRAPHY ENTRY

Panassie, Hugues. *Louis Armstrong.* 2d ed. New York: Da Capo Press, 1980.

11. Multivolume work: Put the volume number in arabic numerals (even if the volume number is spelled out or in roman numerals in the original), followed by a colon, before the page number.

NOTE

13. Robert Lissauer, *Lissauer's Encyclopedia of Popular Music in America* (New York: Facts on File, 1996), 2:33-34.

BIBLIOGRAPHY ENTRY

Lissauer, Robert. *Lissauer's Encyclopedia of Popular Music in America.* Vol. 2. New York: Facts on File, 1996.

12. Work in a series: Include the name of the series as well as the book's series number. The series name should not be italicized or underlined.

NOTE

14. Samuel A. Floyd, ed., *Black Music in the Harlem Renaissance,* Contributions in Afro-American and African Studies, no. 128 (New York: Greenwood Press, 1990), 2.

BIBLIOGRAPHY ENTRY

Floyd, Samuel A., ed. *Black Music in the Harlem Renaissance.* Contributions in Afro-American and African Studies, no. 128. New York: Greenwood Press, 1990.

13. Unknown author: Cite anonymous works by title, and alphabetize them by the first word, ignoring *A, An,* or *The.*

NOTE

15. *The British Album* (London: John Bell, 1790), 2:43-47.

BIBLIOGRAPHY ENTRY

The British Album. Vol. 2. London: John Bell, 1790.

Periodicals

14. Article in a journal paginated by volume: When journals are paginated by yearly volume, your citation should include the following: author, title of article in quotation marks, title of journal, volume number and year, and page number(s).

NOTE

16. Frank Tirro, "Constructive Elements in Jazz Improvisation," *Journal of the American Musicological Society* 27 (1974): 300.

BIBLIOGRAPHY ENTRY

Tirro, Frank. "Constructive Elements in Jazz Improvisation." *Journal of the American Musicological Society* 27 (1974): 285-305.

15. Article in a journal paginated by issue: If the periodical is paginated by issue rather than by volume, add the issue number, preceded by the abbreviation *no.*

NOTE

17. Sarah Appleton Aguiar, "'Everywhere and Nowhere': *Beloved*'s 'Wild' Legacy in Toni Morrison's *Jazz*," *Notes on Contemporary Literature* 25, no. 4 (1995): 11.

BIBLIOGRAPHY ENTRY

Aguiar, Sarah Appleton. "'Everywhere and Nowhere': *Beloved*'s 'Wild' Legacy in Toni Morrison's *Jazz*." *Notes on Contemporary Literature* 25, no. 4 (1995): 11-12.

16. Article in a magazine: Identify magazines by week (if available) and month of publication. In the note, give only the specific page cited; in the bibliography, give the full range of pages.

NOTE

18. Malcolm Walker, "Discography: Bill Evans," *Jazz Monthly,* June 1965, 22.

BIBLIOGRAPHY ENTRY

Walker, Malcolm. "Discography: Bill Evans." *Jazz Monthly,* June 1965, 20-22.

If the article cited does not appear on consecutive pages, do not put any page numbers in the bibliography entry. You can, however, give specific pages in the note. In Chicago style, the month precedes the day, and months are not abbreviated.

NOTE

19. J. R. Taylor, "Jazz History: The Incompleted Past," *Village Voice,* July 3, 1978, 65.

BIBLIOGRAPHY ENTRY

Taylor, J. R. "Jazz History: The Incompleted Past." *Village Voice,* July 3, 1978.

17. Article in a newspaper: Citations for newspaper articles in Chicago format provide four pieces of information: the author's name (if known), the title of the article, the name of the newspaper, and the date of publication. Because newspapers publish in multiple editions, do not give a page number. Instead, give the section number or title if it is indicated. If applicable, indicate the edition (for example, *national edition*) before the section number.

NOTE

20. Ralph Blumenthal, "Satchmo with His Tape Recorder Running," *New York Times,* August 3, 1999, sec. E.

Newspaper articles that you have cited in the text of your paper do not need to be included in a bibliography or works-cited list. However, if you are asked to include newspaper articles in the bibliography or works-cited list, or if you did not provide full citation information in the essay or the note, format the entry as follows.

BIBLIOGRAPHY ENTRY

Blumenthal, Ralph. "Satchmo with His Tape Recorder Running," *New York Times,* August 3, 1999, sec. E.

18. Unsigned article or editorial in a newspaper: Begin the note and the bibliography or works-cited entry with the name of the newspaper.

NOTE

21. *New York Times,* "A Promising Cloning Proposal," October 15, 2004.

BIBLIOGRAPHY ENTRY

New York Times, "A Promising Cloning Proposal," October 15, 2004.

Other Sources

19. Review: If the review is untitled, start with *review of* for a note or *Review of* for a bibliography entry.

NOTE

22. David Ostwald, "All That Jazz," review of *Louis Armstrong: An Extravagant Life,* by Laurence Bergreen, *Commentary,* November 1997, 72.

BIBLIOGRAPHY ENTRY

Ostwald, David. "All That Jazz." Review of *Louis Armstrong: An Extravagant Life,* by Laurence Bergreen. *Commentary,* November 1997, 68-72.

20. Interview: Start with the name of the person interviewed, and note the nonprint medium (tape recording, video). Only interviews accessible to your readers are listed in the bibliography.

NOTES

23. Louis Armstrong, "Authentic American Genius," interview by Richard Meryman, *Life,* April 15, 1966, 92.

24. Michael Cogswell, interview by author, tape recording, Louis Armstrong Archives, Queens College CUNY, Flushing, NY, May 3, 2005.

BIBLIOGRAPHY ENTRY

Armstrong, Louis. "Authentic American Genius." Interview by Richard Meryman. *Life,* April 15, 1966, 92-102.

21. Government document: If it is not already obvious in your text, name the country first.

NOTE

25. Bureau of National Affairs, *The Civil Rights Act of 1964: Text, Analysis, Legislative History; What It Means to Employers, Businessmen, Unions, Employees, Minority Groups* (Washington, DC: BNA, 1964), 22-23.

BIBLIOGRAPHY ENTRY

U.S. Bureau of National Affairs. *The Civil Rights Act of 1964: Text, Analysis, Legislative History; What It Means to Employers, Businessmen, Unions, Employees, Minority Groups.* Washington, DC: BNA, 1964.

22. Unpublished dissertation or document: Include a description of the document as well as information about where it is available. If more than one item from an archive is cited, include only one entry for the archive in your bibliography (*see p. 485*).

NOTES

26. Adelaida Reyes-Schramm, "The Role of Music in the Interaction of Black Americans and Hispanos in New York City's East Harlem" (Ph.D. diss., Columbia University, 1975), 34-37.

27. Joe Glaser to Lucille Armstrong, 28 September 1960, Louis Armstrong Archives, Rosenthal Library, Queens College CUNY, Flushing, NY.

BIBLIOGRAPHY ENTRIES

Glaser, Joe. Letter to Lucille Armstrong, September 28, 1960. Louis Armstrong Archives, Rosenthal Library, Queens College CUNY, Flushing, NY.

Reyes-Schramm, Adelaida. "The Role of Music in the Interaction of Black Americans and Hispanos in New York City's East Harlem." Ph.D. diss., Columbia University, 1975.

23. Musical score or composition: Treat a published score as a book, and include it in the bibliography.

NOTE

28. Franz Josef Haydn, *Symphony No. 94 in G Major,* ed. H. C. Robbins Landon (Salzburg: Haydn-Mozart Press, 1965), 22.

BIBLIOGRAPHY ENTRY

Haydn, Franz Josef. *Symphony No. 94 in G Major.* Edited by H. C. Robbins Landon. Salzburg: Haydn-Mozart Press, 1965.

For a musical composition, give the composer's name, followed by the title of the work. Put the title in italics unless it names an instrumental work known only by its form, number, and key.

NOTES

29. Duke Ellington, *Satin Doll.*

30. Franz Josef Haydn, Symphony no. 94 in G Major.

24. DVD or videocassette: Include the original release date before the publication information if it differs from the release date for the DVD or videocassette.

NOTE

31. *Wit,* DVD, directed by Mike Nichols (New York: HBO Home Video, 2001).

BIBLIOGRAPHY ENTRY

Wit. DVD. Directed by Mike Nichols. New York: HBO Home Video, 2001.

25. Sound recording: Begin with the composer or other person responsible for the content.

NOTE

32. Louis Armstrong, *Town Hall Concert Plus,* RCA INTS 5070.

BIBLIOGRAPHY ENTRY

Armstrong, Louis. *Town Hall Concert Plus.* RCA INTS 5070.

26. Artwork: Begin with the artist's name, and include both the name and location of the institution holding the work. Works of art are usually not included in the bibliography.

NOTE

33. Herman Leonard, *Louis Armstrong: Birdland,* black-and-white photograph, 1956, Barbara Gillman Gallery, Miami.

27. Performance: Begin with the author, director, or performer—whoever is most relevant to your study.

NOTE

34. Terrence McNally, Lynn Athrens, and Stephen Flaherty, *Ragtime,* dir. Frank Galati, Ford Performing Arts Center, New York, November 11, 1998.

BIBLIOGRAPHY ENTRY

McNally, Terrence, Lynn Athrens, and Stephen Flaherty. *Ragtime.* Directed by Frank Galati. Ford Performing Arts Center, New York, November 11, 1998.

28. CD-ROM or other electronic non-Internet source: Indicate the format after the publication information.

NOTE

> 35. *Microsoft Encarta Multimedia Encyclopedia,* s.v. "Armstrong, (Daniel) Louis 'Satchmo' " (Redmond, WA: Microsoft, 1994), CD-ROM.

BIBLIOGRAPHY ENTRY

Microsoft Encarta Multimedia Encyclopedia. "Armstrong, (Daniel) Louis 'Satchmo.' " Redmond, WA: Microsoft, 1994. CD-ROM.

Online Sources

The fifteenth edition of *The Chicago Manual of Style* specifically addresses the documentation of electronic and online sources. In general, electronic citations include all of the information required for print sources, with the addition of a URL and, in some cases, the date of access. There are three key differences between Chicago- and MLA-style online citations:

- Chicago does not require that URLs be enclosed in angle brackets.

- Names of months are not abbreviated, and the date is usually given in the following order: month, day, year (September 13, 2004).

- Dates of access are necessary only for sites that are frequently updated (such as news media sites or blogs) and for books.

29. Online book: Include the date of access in parentheses.

NOTE

> 36. Carl Sandburg, *Chicago Poems* (New York: Henry Holt, 1916), http://www.bartleby.com/165/index.html (accessed May 3, 2005).

BIBLIOGRAPHY ENTRY

Sandburg, Carl. *Chicago Poems.* New York: Henry Holt, 1916. http://www.bartleby.com/165/index.html (accessed May 3, 2005).

30. Online journal:

NOTE

> 37. Janet Schmalfeldt, "On Keeping the Score," *Music Theory Online* 4, no. 2 (1998), http://smt.ucsb.edu/mto/issues/ mto.98.4.2.schmalfeldt.html.

BIBLIOGRAPHY ENTRY

Schmalfeldt, Janet. "On Keeping the Score." *Music Theory Online* 4,
    no. 2 (1998). http://smt.ucsb.edu/mto/issues/
    mto.98.4.2.schmalfeldt.html.

31. Online database, Web site, or discussion group: Identify
as many of the following items as you can: author, title, kind of source
(in brackets), publication data, and URL. It is not necessary to include
bibliography entries for postings to a dicussion group.

NOTES

    38. Bruce Boyd Raeburn, "An Introduction to New Orleans
Jazz," in *William Ransom Hogan Archive of New Orleans Jazz* (Tulane
University, October 30, 2004), http://www.tulane.edu/~lmiller/
BeginnersIntro.html.

    39. Don Mopsick, "Favorite Jazz Quotes," in Big Band
Music Fans, March 17, 2000, http://www.remarq.com/list/
4755?nav+FIRST&rf+1&si+grou.

BIBLIOGRAPHY ENTRY

Raeburn, Bruce Boyd. "An Introduction to New Orleans Jazz."
    In *William Ransom Hogan Archive of New Orleans Jazz*. Tulane
    University, October 30, 2004. http://www.tulane.edu/~.lmiller/
    BeginnersIntro.html.

32. Article from an online magazine or newspaper:

NOTES

    40. Michael E. Ross, "The New Sultans of Swing," *Salon,*
April 18, 1996, http://www.salon.com/weekly/music1.html.

    41. Don Heckman, "Jazz, Pop in Spirited Harmony," *Los Angeles
Times,* August 10, 2005, http://www.calendarlive.com/music/jazz/
cl-et-hancock10aug10,0,7414710.story?coll=cl-home-more-channels.

BIBLIOGRAPHY ENTRIES

Ross, Michael E. "The New Sultans of Swing." *Salon,* April 18, 1996.
    http://www.salon.com/weekly/music1.html.

Heckman, Don. "Jazz, Pop in Spirited Harmony." *Los Angeles Times,*
    August 10, 2005. http://www.calendarlive.com/music/jazz/
    cl-et-hancock10aug10,0,7414710.story?
    coll=cl-home-more-channels.

26d Sample from a student paper in Chicago style

The following excerpt from Esther Hoffman's paper on Louis Armstrong has been put into Chicago style so that you can see how citation numbers, endnotes, and bibliography work together. (*Esther's entire paper, in MLA style, can be found on pp. 416–26.*)

Chicago style allows you the option of including a title page. If you do provide a title page, count it as page 1, but do not include the number on the page. Put page numbers in the upper right-hand corner of the remaining pages, except for the pages with the titles "Notes" and "Bibliography" or "Works Cited"; on these pages, the number should be centered at the bottom of the page.

www.mhhe.com/
nmhh
For a complete sample
paper in Chicago style,
go to
Research > Sample
Research Papers >
CMS Style

2

In the 1920s, jazz music was at its height in creativity and popularity. Chicago had become one of the jazz capitals of America, and its clubs showcased the premier talents of the time, performers like Jelly Roll Morton and Joe Oliver. It has always been difficult to break into the music business, and the jazz scene of the twenties was no exception. Eager for fame and fortune, though, many young black musicians who had honed their craft in New Orleans migrated north to Chicago, hoping for a chance to perform with the best.[1]

Among these emigres was Louis Armstrong, a gifted musician who developed into the "first true virtuoso soloist of jazz."[2] Armstrong played the trumpet and sang with unusual improvisational ability as well as technical mastery. As Bergreen points out, he easily reached difficult high notes, the F's and G's that stymied other trumpeters.[3] His innovative singing style also featured "scat," a technique that combines "nonsense syllables [with] improvised melodies."[4] According to one popular anecdote, Armstrong invented scat during a recording session; mid-song, he dropped his lyrics sheet and—not wanting to disrupt a great take—began to improvise.[5] Eventually, Armstrong's innovations became the standard, as more and more jazz musicians took their cue from his style.

Armstrong's beginnings give no hint of the greatness that he would achieve. In New Orleans, he was born into poverty and received little formal education. As a youngster, Armstrong had to take odd jobs like delivering coal and selling newspapers so that he could earn money to help his family. At the age of twelve, Armstrong was placed in the Colored Waifs' Home to serve an eighteen-month sentence for firing a gun in a public place. There

3

"Captain" Peter Davis gave him "basic musical training on the cornet."[6] Older, more established musicians soon noticed Armstrong's talent and offered him opportunities to play with them. In 1922, Joe Oliver invited Armstrong to join his band in Chicago, and the twenty-one-year-old trumpeter headed north.

It was in Chicago that Armstrong met Joe Glaser, the man who eventually became his longtime manager. According to Bergreen, Glaser had a reputation for being a tough but trustworthy guy who could handle any situation. He was raised in a middle-class home by parents who were Jewish immigrants from Russia. As a young man, Glaser got caught up in the Chicago underworld and soon had a rap sheet that included indictments for running a brothel as well as for statutory rape.[7] Glaser's mob connections also led to his involvement in Chicago's club scene, a business almost completely controlled by gangsters like Al Capone. During the era of Prohibition, Glaser managed the Sunset Café, a club where Armstrong often performed:

> There was a pronounced gangster element at the Sunset, but Louis, accustomed to being employed and protected by mobsters, didn't think twice about that. Mr. Capone's men ensured the flow of alcohol, and their presence reassured many whites.[8]

Notes

1. R. D. Frederick, ed., "Chicago: Early 1920s," Wolverine Antique Music Society, http://www.shellac.org/wams/wchicag1.html.

2. *Microsoft Encarta Multimedia Encyclopedia,* s.v. "Armstrong, (Daniel) Louis 'Satchmo'" (Redmond, WA: Microsoft, 1994), CD-ROM.

3. Laurence Bergreen, *Louis Armstrong: An Extravagant Life* (New York: Broadway Books, 1997), 248.

4. J. Bradford Robinson, "Scat Singing," in *The New Grove Dictionary of Jazz* (2002).

5. Brent Hayes Edwards, "Louis Armstrong and the Syntax of Scat." *Critical Inquiry* 28 (2002): 619.

6. "Satchmo!" *New Orleans Online* (New Orleans Tourism Marketing Corporation, 2005), http://www.neworleansonline.com/neworleans/music/satchmobio.html.

7. Bergreen, 372-76.

8. Ibid., 279.

Bibliography

Armstrong, Louis. "Authentic American Genius." Interview by
Richard Meryman. *Life,* April 15, 1966, 92-102.

———. Louis Armstrong Archives. Rosenthal Library, Queens College
CUNY, Flushing, NY.

———. *Town Hall Concert Plus.* RCA INTS 5070.

Bergreen, Laurence. *Louis Armstrong: An Extravagant Life.* New York:
Broadway Books, 1997.

Bogle, Donald. "Louis Armstrong: The Films." In *Louis Armstrong:
A Cultural Legacy.* Edited by Marc H. Miller, 147-79. Seattle:
University of Washington Press and Queens Museum of Art,
1994.

Collier, James Lincoln. *Jazz: The American Theme Song.* New York:
Oxford University Press, 1993.

———. *Louis Armstrong: An American Genius.* New York: Oxford
University Press, 1983.

Crawford, Richard. Foreword to *The Jazz Tradition,* by Martin
Williams. New York: Oxford University Press, 1993.

Davis, Miles, and Quincy Troupe. *Miles: The Autobiography.*
New York: Simon & Schuster, 1989.

Edwards, Brent Hayes. "Louis Armstrong and the Syntax of Scat."
Critical Inquiry 28 (2002): 618-49.

Frederick, R. D., ed. "Chicago; Early 1920s." Wolverine Antique
Music Society. http://www.shellac.org/wams/
wchicag1.html.

Jones, Max and John Chilton. *Louis: The Armstrong Story,* 1900-1971.
Boston: Little, Brown, 1971.

Morgenstern, Dan. "Louis Armstrong and the Development and
Diffusion of Jazz." In *Louis Armstrong: A Cultural Legacy.* Edited
by Marc H. Miller, 95-145. Seattle: University of Washington
Press and Queens Museum of Art, 1994.

Writer
includes *all*
sources she
consulted,
not just those
she cited in
the body of
her paper.

12

CSE DOCUMENTATION STYLE

The Council of Science Editors (CSE), formerly known as the Council of Biology Editors (CBE), endorses two documentation styles in the sixth edition of *Scientific Style and Format: The CBE Manual for Authors, Editors, and Publishers* (New York: Cambridge University Press, 1994):

- **A name-year style** that includes the last name of the author and year of publication in the text. (*This system resembles APA style; for APA style, see pp. 427–65.*)

- **A number style** that includes a superscript number ([1]) in the text and a list of references in citation sequence. (This system is distinctive to the natural and applied sciences.)

These two styles cannot be mixed within a paper. Consult your instructor for the preferred style, and use it consistently.

A major new edition of *The CSE Manual* is being prepared. This new edition will specifically address online and electronic citations. For more information, go to the Council of Science Editors' Web site at <http://www.councilscienceeditors.org/publications/ssf_7th.cfm>.

www.mhhe.com/
nmhh
For links to Web sites for documentation styles used in various disciplines, go to

Research > Links to Documentation Sites

26e CSE name-year style: In-text citations

Include the source's author, the publication date, and, if you are citing a particular passage, the page number(s).

According to Gleason (1993), a woman loses 35% of cortical bone and 50% of trabecular bone during her lifetime.

Osteoporosis has been defined as "a disease characterized by low bone mass, micro-architectural deterioration of bone tissue, leading to enhanced bone fragility and a consequent increase in fracture risk" (Johnston 1996, p 30S).

Note: When a page number is cited, no period follows the *p.*

www.mhhe.com/
nmhh
To download
Bibliomaker software
for CSE style, go to
Research >
Bibliomaker

26f CSE name-year style: List of references

Every source cited in your paper must correspond to an entry in your list of references, which should be prepared according to the guidelines in the box on page 488.

CSE NAME-YEAR STYLE: DIRECTORY to SAMPLE TYPES

Books
1. One author *487*
2. Two or more authors *487*
3. Selection in an edited book *487*
4. Technical report or government document *488*
5. Organization as author *488*
6. Book with editor(s) *488*

Periodicals
7. Article in a journal paginated by volume *489*

8. Article in a journal paginated by issue *489*
9. Article in a supplement to a journal *489*
10. Article in a magazine *489*

Online Sources
11. Online journal article *489*
12. Online book (monograph) *489*
13. Online database or Web site *489*

Books

Include the author(s), last name first; publication year; title; place and publisher; and number of pages.

1. One author:

Bailey C. 1991. The new fit or fat. Boston: Houghton Mifflin. 167 p.

2. Two or more authors:

Begon M, Harper JL, Townsend CR. 1990. Ecology: Individuals, populations, and communities. 2nd ed. Boston: Blackwell. 945 p.

3. Selection in an edited book:

Bohus B, Koolhaas JM. 1993. Psychoimmunology of social factors in rodents and other subprimate vertebrates. In: Ader R, Felten DL, Cohen N, editors. Psychoneuroimmunology. San Diego (CA): Academic Pr. p 807-30.

487

GUIDELINES for the CSE LIST of REFERENCES: NAME-YEAR STYLE

- Begin the list on a new page after your text but before any appendixes, tables, and figures.
- Use the centered title "References."
- Include only references that are cited in your paper.
- Indent all lines except the first in each entry.
- Arrange the entries alphabetically by author's last name.
- Single-space within each entry, and double-space between entries.
- Do not underline or italicize titles.
- Capitalize only the first word and proper nouns in titles.

4. Technical report or government document:

Gleeson P. 1993. Osteoporosis. Rockville (MD): Public Health Service of the US Dept. of Health and Human Services; Agency for Health Care Policy Research [AHCPR] Publication nr 92-0038. 27 p.

5. Organization as author:

[NIH] National Institutes of Health. 1993. Clinical trials supported by the National Eye Institute: celebrating vision research. Bethesda (MD): US Dept. of Health and Human Services. 112 p.

6. Book with editor(s):

Wilder E, editor. 1988. Obstetric and gynecologic physical therapy. New York: Churchill Livingstone. 225 p.

Periodicals

When listing periodical articles, include the following information: author(s); year; title of article; title of journal; number of the volume and, if needed, of the issue; and page numbers.

> *Note:* Up to ten authors can be listed by name; periodical titles are abbreviated; an issue number is needed only when a journal is not paginated by volume; year, month, and day are listed for magazines.

7. Article in a journal paginated by volume:

Devine A, Prince RL, Bell R. 1996. Nutritional effect of calcium supplementation by skim milk powder or calcium tablets on total nutrient intake in postmenopausal women. Am J Clin Nutr 64:731-7.

8. Article in a journal paginated by issue:

Hummel-Berry K. 1990. Obstetric low back pain, a comprehensive review, part 2: evaluation and treatment. J Ob Gyn PT 14(2):9-11.

9. Article in a supplement to a journal:

Seeman E, Tsalamandris C, Bass S, Pearce G. 1995. Present and future of osteoporosis therapy. Bone 17(2 Suppl):23S-29S.

10. Article in a magazine:

Sternfeld P. 1997 Jan 1. Physical activity and pregnancy outcome review and recommendations. Sports Med:33-47.

Online Sources
11. Online journal article:

Krieger D, Onodipe S, Charles PJ, Sclabassi RJ. Real time signal processing in the clinical setting. Ann Biomed Engn [Internet] 1998 [cited 2000 Jul 6]; 26(3); 462-7. Available from: http://www.kluweronline.com/issn/0090-6964

12. Online book (monograph):

Kohn LT, Corrigan JM, Donaldson MS. To err is human: building a safer health system [online monograph]. Washington: National Academy Press: 2000 [cited 2000 Jul 6]. 312 p. Available from http://www.nap.edu/books/0309068371/html

13. Online database or Web site:

National Osteoporosis Foundation. 2000. Osteoporosis and related bone disease—national resource center [Internet]. Bethesda (MD): National Institutes of Health [NIH] [cited 2000 Jul 6]. Available from: http://www.osteo.org/osteo.html

www.mhhe.com/
nmhh
For a complete sample
paper in CSE style,
go to

Research > Sample
Research Papers >
CSE Style

26g Sample reference list: CSE name-year style

References

American Association of Clinical Endocrinologists. 1991. Clinical
practice guidelines for the prevention and treatment of
postmenopausal osteoporosis. J Fla Med Assoc 83:552-66.

Caldwell JR. 1996. Epidemiologic and economic considerations
of osteoporosis. J Fla Med Assoc 83:548-51.

Gleeson P. 1993. Osteoporosis. Rockville (MD): Public Health
Service of the US Dept. of Health and Human Services.
AHCPR Publication nr 92-0038. 27 p.

Johnson CC. 1996. Development of clinical practice guidelines
for prevention and treatment of osteoporosis. Calci Tiss Int
59(1 Suppl):30S-33S.

Roberts MM. 1997. Osteoporosis: update on prevention and
treatment [lecture handout]. Pennsylvania Physical Therapy
Assn [PPTA] Conference. Harrisburg.

Seeman E, Tsalamandris C, Bass S, Pearce G. 1995. Present and
future of osteoporosis therapy. Bone 17(2 Suppl):23S-29S.

26h CSE number style: In-text citations

To cite a source, insert a superscript number immediately after the
relevant name, word, or phrase.

As a group, American women over 45 years of age sustain approximately
1 million fractures each year, 70% of which are due to osteoporosis.[1]

That number now belongs to that source, and it should be used if you
refer to that source again later in your paper.

A BMD value more than 1 SD but less than 2.5 SD below the young adult mean is considered as osteopenia,[4] while osteoporosis is defined as a BMD 2.5 SD below the young adult mean.[1]

Credit more than one source at a time by referring to each source's number. Separate the numbers with a comma.

According to studies by Yomo,[2] Paleg,[3] and others,[1,4] barley seed embryos produce a substance that stimulates the release of hydrolytic enzymes.

If the numbers are in sequence, however, separate them with a hyphen.

As several others[1-4] have documented, GA has an RNA-enhancing effect.

26i CSE number style: List of references

www.mhhe.com/
nmhh
To download
Bibliomaker software
for CSE style, go to
Research >
Bibliomaker

Every source cited in your paper must correspond to an entry in your list of references, which should be prepared according to the guidelines in the box on page 493.

Books and Reports

1. One author:

> 1. Bailey C. The new fit or fat. Boston: Houghton Mifflin; 1991. 167 p.

2. Two or more authors: List up to ten authors; if there are more than ten, use the first author's name with the phrase *and others.*

> 2. Begon M, Harper JL, Townsend CR. Ecology: individuals, populations, and communities. 2nd ed. Boston: Blackwell; 1990. 945 p.

3. Organization as author:

> 3. National Institutes of Health. Clinical trials supported by the National Eye Institute: celebrating vision research. Bethesda (MD): US Dept. of Health and Human Services; 1993. 112 p.

4. Chapter in a book: Note that the author of the chapter and the book are the same. Consult item 6 below when the authors are not the same person.

> 4. Castro J. The American way of health: how medicine is changing and what it means to you. Boston: Little, Brown; 1994. Chapter 9, Why doctors, hospitals, and drugs cost so much; p 131-53.

5. Book with editor(s):

> 5. Ader R, Felten DL, Cohen N, editors. Psychoneuroimmunology. San Diego (CA): Academic Pr; 1993. 1218 p.

6. Selection in an edited book:

> 6. Bohus B, Koolhaas JM. Psychoimmunology of social factors in rodents and other subprimate vertebrates. In: Ader R, Felten DL, Cohen N, editors. Psychoneuroimmunology. San Diego (CA): Academic Pr; 1993. p 807-30.

7. Technical report or government document: Include the name of the sponsoring organization or agency as well as any report or contract number.

> 7. Gleeson P. Osteoporosis. Rockville (MD): Public Health Service of US Dept. of Health and Human Services; 1993 Mar. Agency for Health Care Policy Research [AHCPR] Publication nr 92-0038. 27 p.

Periodicals

8. Article in a journal paginated by volume: There is no need to designate issue number and month for journals paginated by yearly volume rather than issue. Note that titles of journals are abbreviated.

GUIDELINES for the CSE LIST of REFERENCES: NUMBER STYLE

- Assign numbers to the sources cited in your paper, in the order in which you cite them.
- In the list of references (titled "References"), list sources in the numerical order of their citation, not in alphabetical order.
- Align the second and subsequent lines of the entry with the first word of the first line, not with the number.
- Single-space within each entry, and double-space between entries.
- Do not underline or italicize titles.
- Capitalize only the first word and proper nouns in titles.
- Give the names of up to ten authors, last name first, followed by the first initial or initials.
- Do not place a period at the end of a URL.

8. Devine A, Prince RL, Bell R. Nutritional effect of calcium supplementation by skim milk powder or calcium tablets on total nutrient intake in postmenopausal women. Am J Clin Nutr 1996; 64:731-7.

9. Article in a journal or supplement paginated by issue: Include the year, the month, the volume number, and the issue number (in parentheses). Be sure to indicate when the article is in a supplement rather than in the issue itself. Note that semicolons separate the month from the volume number.

9. Hummel-Berry K. Obstetric low back pain, a comprehensive review, part 2: evaluation and treatment. J Ob Gyn PT 1990 Jun;14(2):9-11.

10. Seeman E, Tsalamandris C, Bass S, Pearce G. Present and future of osteoporosis therapy. Bone 1995 Aug;17(2 Suppl):23S-29S.

10. Article in a magazine or newspaper: Indicate the year, month, and day of publication. For newspapers, identify the section before the page number: *NY Times 2000 Jul 9;Sect C:2.*

11. Sternfeld P. Physical activity and pregnancy outcome review and recommendations. Sports Med 1997 Jan 1:33-47.

Online Sources

In addition to the information that is normally included, CSE requires the following data: type of document, availability information, and date of access.

11. Online journal article:

12. Krieger D, Onodipe S, Charles PJ, Sclabassi RJ. Real time signal processing in the clinical setting. Ann Biomed Engn [Internet] 1998 [cited 2000 Jul 6];26(3):462-72. Available from: http://www.kluweronline.com/issn/0090-6964

12. Online book (monograph):

13. Kohn LT, Corrigan JM, Donaldson MS. To err is human: building a safer health system [online monograph]. Washington: National Academy Press; 2000. Available from: National Academy Press at http://www.nap.edu/books/0309068371/html

13. Online database or Web site:

14. National Osteoporosis Foundation. Osteoporosis and related bone diseases—national resource center [Internet]. Bethesda (MD): National Institutes of Health (NIH) [cited 2000 Jul 6,]. Available from: http://www.osteo.org/osteo.html

26j Sample reference list: CSE number style

www.mhhe.com/
nmhh
For a complete sample
paper in CSE style,
go to
Research > Sample
Research Papers >
CSE Style

References

1. American Association of Clinical Endocrinologists. Clinical practice guidelines for the prevention and treatment of postmenopausal osteoporosis. J Fla Med Assoc 1991; 83:552-66.

2. Johnston CC. Development of clinical practice guidelines for prevention and treatment of osteoporosis. Calci Tiss Int 1996;59(1 Suppl):30S-33S.

3. Caldwell JR. Epidemiologic and economic considerations of osteoporosis. J Fla Med Assoc 1996;83:548-51.

4. Seeman E, Tsalamandris C, Bass S, Pearce G. Present and future of osteoporosis therapy. Bone 1995 Aug; 17(2 Suppl):23S-29S.

5. Roberts MM. Osteoporosis: update on prevention and treatment [lecture handout]. Pennsylvania Physical Therapy Assn [PPTA] Conference. 1997 Oct. Harrisburg.

6. Gleeson P. Osteoporosis. Rockville (MD): Public Health Service of US Dept. of Health and Human Services; 1993 Mar. AHCPR Publication nr 92-0038. 27 p.

A National Audubon Society employee wrote and designed this page from one of the Society's annual reports to show donors how their money helps this environmental organization—and why its cause matters.

PART 5

The aim of education must be the training of independently acting and thinking individuals, who, however, see in the service of the community their highest life problem.
—ALBERT EINSTEIN

Writing
beyond College

Birds
Wild
life &
Habitat

27 Service Learning and Community-Service Writing

Although college may be unfamiliar territory to the newcomer, it is part of the larger world. Like an access road, writing is a way of connecting classroom, workplace, and community.

27a Address the community on behalf of your organization.

Your ability to research and write can be of great value to organizations that serve the community. Courses at every level of the university, as well as extracurricular activities, offer opportunities to work with organizations such as homeless shelters, tutoring centers, and environmental groups. Your work with groups like these may involve writing newsletters, press releases, or funding proposals. When you are writing for a community group, ask yourself these questions:

- What do community members talk about?
- How do they talk about these issues, and why?
- Who is an outsider (member of the community), and who is an insider (member of the organization)?
- How can I best write from the inside to the outside?

Your answers will help you shape your writing so that it reaches its intended audience and moves the members of that audience to action.

Writing on behalf of a community organization almost always involves negotiation and collaboration. Writing on behalf of others often requires relinquishing individual authorship. A community organization may revise your draft to fit its needs, and you will have to live with those revisions. In these situations, having a cooperative attitude is as important as having strong writing skills.

Even if you are not writing on behalf of a group, you can still do community-service writing. You can write in your own name to raise an issue of concern to the community in a public forum; for example, you might write a newspaper editorial or a letter to a public official (*see Chapter 28: Letters to Raise Awareness and Share Concern*).

WRITING beyond COLLEGE

A Writer at Work

When Laura Amabisca entered Glendale Community College, she volunteered to be a tutor in the writing center. Upon transferring to Arizona State University West, she joined the Writing Tutors' Club, continuing her service to the campus community. In addition, she became a mentor for other Glendale Community College students who were trying to build the confidence to transfer to the university.

In a course in advanced expository writing, she was able to draw on these experiences for an essay on the special needs of community-college transfer students. She also wrote a letter on the same theme to the student newspaper.

The satisfaction and sense of involvement Amabisca felt about her on-campus service motivated her to visit the ASU West Volunteer Office for ideas about off-campus service. She then became a volunteer for America Reads, joining students from ASU West and from various community colleges who tutor in this national literacy project. The Phoenix office of America Reads asked Amabisca to help design a public relations campaign to explain the value of the project. After writing reflectively in her journal, Laura volunteered to draft a brochure to convince other college students to join the project. In this way, she moved from involvement in her own campus to service in the wider community.

27b Design brochures, newsletters, and posters with an eye to purpose and audience.

www.mhhe.com/
nmhh
For interactive help
with document design,
go to

Writing >
Visual Rhetoric >
Document Design

If you are participating in a service learning program or an internship, you may have opportunities to design brochures and newsletters for wide distribution and posters to create awareness and promote events. To create an effective brochure, newsletter, or poster, you will need to integrate your skills in document design with what you have learned about purpose and audience.

Here are a few tips that will help you create effective brochures, newsletters, and posters, whatever your audience and purpose may be:

1. Before you begin, consider how your reader will gain access to and review the pages of the brochure or newsletter. Will it be

distributed by mail? By hand? Electronically? What are the implications for the overall design?

2. Sketch the design in pencil before you start using the high-tech capabilities of the computer. Use the computer to solve design problems, not to create them.

3. In making decisions about photographs, illustrations, type faces, and the design in general, think about the overall image you want to convey about the organization sponsoring the brochure, newsletter, or poster.

4. If the organization has a logo, include it; if not, suggest designing one. A logo is a small visual symbol, like the Nike "swoosh" or the distinctive font used for Coca-Cola.

5. Set up a template for a brochure or newsletter so that you can create future editions easily. In word-processing and document-design programs, a template is a blank document that includes all of the formatting and codes a specific document requires. When you use a template, you just "plug in" new content and visuals—the format and design are already done.

For example, notice how the brochure for the PSFS Building in Philadelphia, Pennsylvania, shown in Figure 27.1, purposefully connects the history and importance of an architectural landmark with the prestige of Loews Hotel, into which "the world's first Modernist skyscraper" has been renovated. The brochure has an informative and also a subtly persuasive purpose. Its intent is to make readers feel that by staying at the Loews Philadelphia Hotel, they will be participating in a great tradition. The front cover is divided in half, with a striking photo of the building on the left side and an account of its history on the right. The name of the hotel appears in white letters near the bottom of the page. The interior page places a vintage photo of the revered banking establishment next to an image of hotel comfort. On both pages, quotations running vertically beside the photographs reinforce the building's architectural significance.

The Harvard Medical School newsletter entitled "Women's Health Watch," shown in Figure 27.2 on page 502, has a simple, clear design. The designer keeps in mind the newsletter's purpose and audience, which are explicitly stated in the title and the headline below it. The shaded area on the right lists the topics that are covered on the interior pages so that readers can get to the information they need quickly and easily. The Web address is prominently displayed in blue so that readers can find more information. The lead article, "Does Excess Vitamin A Cause Hip Fracture?" is designed simply in two columns, with the headline in bold type, subheadings in blue, a readable typeface, and a graphic strategically placed to break up the text and add visual interest.

FIGURE 27.1 Example of a brochure.

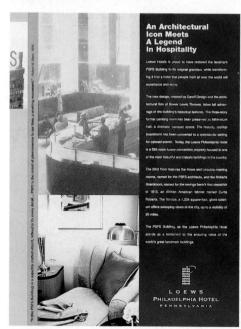

In all of these ways, the design supports the Harvard Medical School's purpose of helping the general public get reliable information about the latest advances in medical research. (*For more information on document design, see Chapter 6, Designing Academic Papers, pp. 125–33.*)

H A R V A R D

Women's Health Watch

INFORMATION FOR ENLIGHTENED CHOICES FROM HARVARD MEDICAL SCHOOL

Does Excess Vitamin A Cause Hip Fracture?

Hip fracture is one of the most dreaded risks of aging. More than 350,000 hip fractures occur annually in the United States, mostly in women over 65. Half of these women never regain the ability to live independently. About 20% die within a year. Many others suffer chronic pain, anxiety, and depression. The consequences are so grim that many older women contacted in surveys on this subject say they'd rather die than suffer a hip fracture that would send them to a nursing home.

Current recommendations on reducing fracture risk advise women to exercise, make sure they get enough calcium and vitamin D, and, if necessary, take medications that help preserve bone strength. Some women also learn strategies for preventing falls or take classes such as tai chi to improve their balance. Now, a new study suggests that we should also pay attention to vitamin A. At high levels, this essential nutrient may actually increase our risk for hip fracture.

NEW STUDY FINDS LINK

Researchers at Harvard Medical School reported in the Jan. 2, 2002, *Journal of the American Medical Association* on the relationship between postmenopausal hip fracture and vitamin A intake. The data came from 72,337 women enrolled in the Nurses' Health Study. The women were divided into five groups according to their average daily consumption, over an 18-year period, of vitamin A from food and supplements.

Researchers then correlated vitamin A intake with hip fracture incidence. They found that women with the highest intake—3,000 micrograms (mcg) or more per day—had a 48% greater risk for hip fractures, compared to women with the lowest intake (1,250 mcg or less per day).

The increased risk was mainly due to *retinol*, a particular form of vitamin A. In fact, women consuming 2,000 mcg of retinol or more daily had a hip fracture risk almost *double* that of women whose daily intake was under 500 mcg. In contrast, consuming high levels of *beta-carotene*, also a source of vitamin A, had a negligible impact on hip fracture risk. Participants taking hormone replacement therapy (HRT) were somewhat protected from the effects of too much retinol.

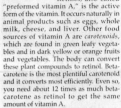

15% of women age 50 will suffer a hip fracture before age 80.

ABOUT VITAMIN A

Vitamin A is important for vision, the immune system, and the growth of bone, hair, and skin cells. Retinol, also called "preformed vitamin A," is the active form of the vitamin. It occurs naturally in animal products such as eggs, whole milk, cheese, and liver. Other food sources of vitamin A are *carotenoids*, which are found in green leafy vegetables and in dark yellow or orange fruits and vegetables. The body can convert these plant compounds to retinol. Beta-carotene is the most plentiful carotenoid and it converts most efficiently. Even so, you need about 12 times as much beta-carotene as retinol to get the same amount of vitamin A.

Because vitamin A is lost in the process of removing fat, many fat-free dairy products are fortified with retinol. So are some margarines and ready-to-eat cereals. The vitamin A in supplements and multivitamins may come from retinol, beta-carotene, or both. Beta-carotene is preferable because it's also an antioxidant.

Although vitamin A deficiency is a leading cause of blindness in developing countries, it's not a major problem in the United States. The main concern here is excess vitamin A, which can produce birth defects, liver damage, and reduced bone mineral density (BMD).

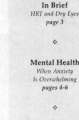

Volume IX Number 7
March 2002

In Brief
HRT and Dry Eyes
page 3

❖

Mental Health
When Anxiety
Is Overwhelming
pages 4-6

❖

Research Brief
The Genetics of
Lactose Intolerance
page 6

❖

Massage
Massage Is More Than
an Indulgence
page 7

❖

By the Way, Doctor
Should I Still Get
Mammograms?
page 8

www.health.harvard.edu

FIGURE 27.2 Example of a well-designed newsletter.

Birds
Wild
life&
Habitat

28 Letters to Raise Awareness and Share Concern

Any time you address readers as fellow citizens with the purpose of educating them or making a change for the better, you are doing community-service writing. Your ability to write and your willingness to share your opinions and insights can influence local, community, and even national events and decisions. A letter that is clearly argued, concisely phrased, and appropriately directed can accomplish a great deal, whether you are writing to a local politician or to a corporation's board of directors. Your task in writing such a letter is to present yourself as a polite, engaged, and reasonable person who is invested in a particular issue and who can present a compelling and persuasive case for a particular course of action.

Here are some guidelines for writing a letter to raise awareness and share concern:

- **Address the letter appropriately.** If you are writing to a newspaper or magazine's editorial pages, see how published letters are addressed ("To the editors," for example) and if the publication supplies guidelines for letters to the editor. If you are writing to a community or nonprofit organization or a private corporation, consult the organization's Web site or call its main number. You will probably be referred to a department called "consumer relations" or "public relations." It is always best to address your letter to a specific person, or at least to a specific department within an organization.

- **Use the format for a business letter.** (*See the example of a business letter in block format on pp. 521–22.*)

- **Consider using the Internet.** Some publications, corporations, and nonprofit organizations include links on their Web sites for correspondence or for submitting letters to the editor. If the recipient's Web site includes such a link, use that instead of writing a print letter. The Web site will either provide an e-mail address or a box in which to type your letter. Do not send your document as an attachment to an e-mail. Many corporate and organization Web servers are protected by firewalls that screen out e-mails with attachments. Concisely state your area of concern in the Subject line of the e-mail.

- **Construct a strong opening paragraph.** In the first paragraph of your letter, clearly state the area of interest or concern you wish to address and why the issue is important to you. For example, if you are writing to your local school board about proposed budget changes, you would state in your first paragraph that you are the parent of a child who attends a local school.

- **Support your position.** In your second and subsequent paragraphs, provide clear and compelling evidence for your concern. If relevant, propose a solution.

- **Keep it brief.** Community organizations and corporations receive hundreds, even thousands, of letters each week. Letters to the editor that are selected for publication tend to be no more than three or four paragraphs.

- **Conclude effectively.** In your conclusion, thank the reader for taking the time to consider your thoughts. If you are writing to request a specific action—for example, that an item be added to the agenda of the next school board meeting—repeat that request. If you would like a specific response to your concern, politely request a letter or telephone call. If you intend to follow up on your letter, note that you will be calling or writing again within a week (or however long is appropriate).

On the following pages (505–7) are letters by two different writers addressing a community issue. One writer sent his letter to the local newspaper's editorial page editor. The other writer wrote to the principal of her local school. Although both writers address the same concern, notice how they tailor their letters for their specific audience and purpose.

TEXTCONNEX

Making Yourself Heard

The Web sites of most major daily newspapers provide access to their opinion pages and an e-mail address readers can use to send letters to the editor. The Web site *Opinion-Pages* (http://www.opinion-pages.org) provides links to the editorial and opinion pages of more than six hundred mainstream and alternative English language publications worldwide, as well as to more than two hundred letters-to-the-editor pages.

34 Terrace Lane
Maple Crest, NJ 07405
May 12, 2005

Letters to the Editor
Maple Crest *Herald*
126 Essex Turnpike
Maple Crest, NJ 07400

To the Editors:

Yesterday's article ("Local Parents Protest Sudden Budget Cuts," May 11) did not accurately convey the full extent of inconsistent funding in Maple Crest public schools. Although the parents of students at Middle Park Elementary are concerned about losing part of their music program, students at John Dewey High School have been without any music program at all for the past three years. I am a senior at John Dewey, and when I first came to the school, I joined both the orchestra and the marching band as a trumpet player. Both programs, which provided an after-school activity for at least one hundred students, gave me a sense of discipline and school pride.

I know from personal experience that studying music and practicing an instrument consistently can teach a young person patience and discipline as well as instill a lifelong understanding of and appreciation for music. If the proposed budget cuts are allowed to take effect, however, no school in our district will offer a substantive music program. I am fortunate to have received a terrific education in our local public schools, and I know I am well prepared for college. I urge the Maple Crest School Board and local taxpayers to find ways to support more fully their most important community resource—the school system—so that future students will be able to say the same.

Joshua Morton

Joshua Morton

1324 Owen Drive
Maple Crest, NJ 07405
May 3, 2005

Dr. Joann Malvern
Principal
Middle Park Elementary School
47 Valley Street
Maple Crest, NJ 07405

Dear Dr. Malvern:

I am a parent of two children who attend Middle Park Elementary
School. My son is in the third grade, and my daughter is in the sixth
grade. We have lived in Maple Crest for ten years, and my children
have always attended local schools. We have been delighted with
the attention and opportunities that both children have received
in their classrooms. However, the School Board's proposed new
budget cuts would, I believe, significantly reduce both that
attention and the opportunities all children currently enjoy.

In a letter to all Middle Park parents that was sent home with
children during the last week of April, you outlined changes for
the upcoming school year. The area of greatest concern to me
is the termination of three classroom assistant positions and the
reduction of the music teacher's position from full- to part-time.
In the letter, you stated that the reason for these reductions was a
call from the Board of Education to cut operating costs for the
next school year.

As our community has grown and more children have enrolled
in Middle Park, the presence of classroom assistants has helped
teachers to maintain discipline in the classroom as well as offer
additional adult support and attention to every child in the
classroom. The school's music teacher, Mr. Jack Delvarez, has
inspired both of my children to take up musical instruments,
and all parents look forward to the Fall and Spring concerts.

I know from my conversations with other Middle Park parents
that we would appreciate the opportunity to suggest alternative
ways to save money and preserve the high quality of education

Dr. Joann Malvern
Page 2
May 3, 2005

that Middle Park currently offers. I would like to request that a special Parent-Teacher Association meeting be held within the next two weeks in order to discuss the sudden nature of these staffing changes as well as other options.

Thank you for your consideration. I hope to hear from you soon, and I will be telephoning your office next week to explore times and places for the special meeting.

Sincerely,

Norma David

Norma David

For MULTILINGUAL STUDENTS

Writing Letters

In formal correspondence, as in most forms of academic writing, American culture favors directness, clarity, and simplicity, regardless of the writer's purpose or audience. If you come from a culture that instead favors a subtle, indirect approach to a topic or one that values rich embellishment and digression, it may be a challenge to adopt the more linear American style.

When you want to persuade, start by identifying your goals and your audience's expectations, and then tailor the format of your writing to both. Regardless of the purpose of your letter, some general rules apply:

- Practice a confident, direct style in all professional communication.
- Minimize introductory remarks, make the topic explicit, address the issues point by point, and end on a cordial note.
- Familiarize yourself with the customary format for the document you are creating. Its layout makes the first impression on its recipient.

Birds Wild life & Habitat

29 Writing to Get and Keep a Job

Like many students, you may already have a job on or off campus, or you may be doing an internship or volunteering for a community-based organization. Writing is one way to connect your work, your other activities, and your studies. Strong writing skills will also help you find a good job once you leave college and advance in your chosen career.

www.mhhe.com/
nmhh
For more information
on professional
writing, go to

College to Career

29a Explore internship possibilities, and keep a portfolio of career-related writing.

An internship, in which you do actual work in your chosen field, is a vital connection between the classroom and the workplace. You gain academic credit, not for the hours you spend on the job, but for what you learn from the job. Writing and learning go together. During your internship, keep a journal to record and analyze your experiences, as well as a file of any writing you do on the job. Your final project for the internship credit may require you to analyze the file of writing that you have produced.

Files of writing from internships, clippings of articles and editorials you have written for the student newspaper, writing you have done for a community organization—these and other documents demonstrate your ability to apply intellectual concepts to real-world demands. Organized into a portfolio, this material displays your marketable skills. Use a tabbed loose-leaf notebook or an actual portfolio with compartments for different categories of work. Arrange your writing samples by project or by kind of writing. Within each category, use reverse chronological order so that your most recent work appears first.

Your campus career resource center may offer assistance in compiling a portfolio. The center may also keep your portfolio on file for you and send it to future employers or graduate schools.

To begin your search for a suitable internship, visit your campus career counseling center. There, usually for no fee, you can meet with a career guidance counselor who can help you assess your skills and determine what kind of internship would best suit your career goals. Many local nonprofit organizations, television and radio stations, newspapers, and both small and large companies offer internship op-

Although your internship might pay only a modest amount (or nothing at all), your employer will nonetheless have high expectations of you. If this is your first time working in an office or a professional environment, be sure that you understand, not only what is expected of you in terms of work, but also how to fit in with the workplace culture.

- **Always be on time.** Your employer is making an investment in you. Even if you are not being paid, you are learning about a possible career field and picking up invaluable business skills.

- **Dress appropriately.** You need not invest in an expensive new wardrobe, but dress in a way that is appropriate to the culture of your employer's office. If, as is likely, you meet with a representative of your employer's human resources division when you begin work, ask about any dress codes. Even if you are interning in an organization that permits informal or creative attire, it is probably best to dress conservatively.

- **Understand what is expected.** Be sure you clearly understand your specific assignments and duties. The first few weeks of an internship might involve nothing more than filing and word processing. Once you have demonstrated your responsibility and efficiency, you might be assigned to work on more complex and interesting projects. Remember, at the end of your internship you want to have a strong reference for future positions.

- **Ask questions.** If you discover that you want to pursue a career in the field in which you are interning, be sure to ask lots of questions of your coworkers. Find out, for example, what additional coursework you should take to prepare. What is an entry-level position like in this field? How do people distinguish themselves in the field and rise to greater levels of responsibility in it? What are the field's key issues and challenges?

- **Request a recommendation.** Ask—politely, and with plenty of advance notice—if your employer would provide you with a letter of recommendation to show potential employers in the future. (Your campus career center will probably keep such letters on file for you and will assist you with your job search after graduation.) Also ask if you may list your supervisor as a reference for future job applications.

29b Keep your résumé up-to-date and available on a computer disk.

A **résumé** is an informative piece of writing, a brief summary of your education and work experience that you send to prospective employ- **509** ers. It is never finished. As you continue to learn, work, and write, you should be rethinking and reorganizing your résumé. You will want to emphasize different accomplishments and talents for different employers. Some employers—for example, banks and accounting firms—expect a résumé from a college student or recent graduate to be no longer than one page. Some public relations firms and other organizations with more informal cultures want to see more detail, especially about a future employee's special skills and interests. Saving your résumé as a computer file allows you to tailor it to the needs and requirements of its readers.

Your résumé should be designed for quick reading. Expect the person reviewing it to give it no more than sixty seconds at first glance. Make that first impression count. Design a document that is easy to read, attractively formatted, and flawlessly spelled. Few things will lose you a job quicker than a messy résumé with misspelled words.

Guidelines for writing a résumé

Always include the following *necessary* categories in a résumé:

- Heading (name, address, telephone number, e-mail address)
- Education (in reverse chronological order; do not include high school)
- Work experience (in reverse chronological order)
- References (often placed on a separate sheet; for many situations, you can add the line "References available on request" instead)

Include the following *optional* categories in your résumé as appropriate:

- Honors and awards
- Internships
- Activities and service
- Special skills

Laura Amabisca has organized the information in her résumé (*see p. 512*) by time and by categories. Within each category, she has listed items from most to least recent. This reverse chronological order gives appropriate emphasis to what she is doing now and has just done.

Because Amabisca is applying for jobs in public relations, she has highlighted her internship in that field by giving it its own category. People who have been working for a while often divide their work experience into separate categories, emphasizing experience pertinent to their career goal and listing other jobs separately. For example, Amabisca

Electronic Technology and Your Résumé

Many employers now request résumés by e-mail and electronically scan print résumés. Both of these innovations require you to take special care with your résumé. (For more information and step-by-step advice on tailoring résumés for specific industries, see the Web site at *Monster.com* http://resume.monster.com/.)

Scanning allows a human resources department to compile print résumés in keyword-searchable electronic databases. Contact the human resources department of a potential employer and ask if your résumé should be scannable. If so, be sure to use a clear, common typeface in an easy-to-read size. Do not include any unusual symbols or characters. Print your résumé on white paper.

Sending your résumé by e-mail allows your potential employer to enter it into a searchable database. Be sure, before you apply by e-mail, that the employer accepts electronically submitted résumés. Also find out whether you should include the résumé in the body of an e-mail message or send it as an attached document. If the employer expects the résumé as an attached document, be sure to save it in a widely readable form like rich text format (RTF) or ASCII. Use minimal formatting and no colors, unusual fonts, or other decorative flourishes. Be aware, too, that many companies have secure firewalls around their servers that screen out all attachments or attachments that include certain words. You can configure your e-mail program to send you an automatic reply when your e-mail has been successfully received.

Because employers use specific keywords to search scanned or electronically submitted résumés, you will want to be sure to include those words in your résumé. The résumé section of *Monster.com* contains industry-specific advice on appropriate words.

might have used the categories "Public Relations Experience" and "Other Work Experience" instead of "Work Experience" and "Internship."

Sometimes career counselors recommend that you list a career objective directly under the heading of your résumé. There is a delicate balance, however, between presenting yourself as someone with clear goals and as someone who can be flexible. Unless you have done enough research to know exactly what a particular company is looking for, it is usually best to leave your career objective out of your résumé. Deal with this issue in your application letter instead.

Laura's entire résumé is just one page. A brief, well-organized résumé is more attractive to potential employers than a rambling, multipaged résumé. Laura uses a simple font and no bold or italic type, to ensure that her résumé is scannable.

Laura was sure to include keywords (highlighted here) that will be most likely to catch the eye of a potential employer. Laura knows that a position in public relations requires computer skills, communication skills, and experience working with diverse groups of people. Keywords such as "sales," "bilingual," HTML," and "public relations" are critical to her résumé.

Laura Amabisca
20650 North 58th Avenue, Apt. 15A
Glendale, AZ 85308
(623) 555-7310
lamabisca@peoplelink.com

EDUCATION
B.A., Arizona State University West, Phoenix (May 2005)
    Major: History
    Minor: Global Management
    Senior Thesis: Picturing the Hopi, 1920–1940: A Historical Analysis
Glendale Community College, Glendale, AZ (2001–2003)

HONORS AND AWARDS
Westmarc Writing Prize (2005)
Arizona Regents' Scholarship (2002–2005)

WORK EXPERIENCE
Sears, Bell Road, Phoenix, AZ
    Assistant Manager, Sporting Goods Department (2003–present)
    Sales Associate, Sporting Goods Department (2001–2003)
    Stock Clerk, Sporting Goods Department (1997–2001)

INTERNSHIP
Public Relations Office, Arizona State University West (Summer 2004)

ACTIVITIES AND SERVICE
Tutor, Public-Relations Consultant, America Reads (2005)
Student Coordinator, Multicultural Festival, ASU West (2004)
Tutor, Writing Center, Glendale Community College (2002–2005)

SPECIAL SKILLS
Bilingual: Spanish/English
Skill and experience with Windows, WordPerfect, Word (IBM and Mac), and
HTML authoring

REFERENCES
Ms. Carol Martinez
Director, Public Relations
Arizona State University West
PO Box 371000
Phoenix, AZ 85069-7100

Mr. James Corrothers
Sales Manager
Sporting Goods Department
Sears
302 N. Central Avenue
Phoenix, AZ 85043-6011

As Laura's work experience grows, she can make more space on her résumé by not including the names of references and instead adding the notation "References available upon request."

A file of confidential references is available upon request to Career Services,
Arizona State University West.

29c Write an application letter that highlights the information on your résumé and demonstrates that your skills match the job you are seeking.

A clear and concise **application letter** should always accompany a résumé. Before drafting a job application letter, do some research about the organization you are writing to. For example, even though Laura Amabisca was already familiar with the Heard Museum when she applied for a position there, she took time to find out the name of the director of public relations instead of mailing her letter and résumé to an unnamed recipient. (*Amabisca's application letter appears on p. 515.*) If the want ad you are answering does not include a name, call the organization and find out the name of the person responsible for your area of interest. If you are unable to identify an appropriate name, it is better to direct the letter to "Dear Director of Public Relations" than to "Dear Sir or Madam."

Here are additional guidelines for composing a letter of application:

- **Use business style.** Use the block form shown on pages 521–22. Type your address flush at the top of the page, starting each line at the left margin. Follow it with the date at the left margin two lines above the recipient's name and address. Use a colon (:) after the greeting. Double-space between single-spaced paragraphs. Use a traditional closing (*Sincerely, Sincerely yours, Yours truly*). Make sure that the inside address and the address on the envelope match exactly.

- **Limit your letter to three or four paragraphs.** Many prospective employers will not bother to turn to page two of an application letter. Focus clearly and concisely on what the employer needs to know. In the first paragraph, identify the position you are applying for, mention how you heard about it, and briefly state that you are qualified. In the following one or two paragraphs, explain your qualifications, elaborating on the most pertinent items in your résumé. Because Amabisca was applying for a public relations job at a museum of Native American culture, she chose to highlight her internship and her thesis. In another application letter, however, this time for a management position at American Express, she made different choices. In that letter, she emphasized her work experience at Sears, including the fact that she had moved up in the organization through positions of increasing responsibility.

- **State your expectation for future contact.** Conclude with a one- or two-sentence paragraph informing the reader that you are anticipating a follow-up to your letter.

513

■ **Use *Enc.* if you are enclosing additional materials.** Decide whether it is appropriate to enclose supporting materials other than your résumé, such as samples of your writing. Amabisca decided to do so because she was applying for her ideal job and had highly relevant materials to send. If you have been instructed to send a cover letter and résumé by e-mail as attachments, include the word "Attachments" after your e-mail "signature."

For MULTILINGUAL STUDENTS

Applying for a Job

Different cultures approach the job application process differently. Whatever your experiences may have been, keep the following guidelines in mind as you search for a job in the United States:

■ A form letter accompanied by a generic résumé is not an effective way of getting a job interview. Before writing an application letter or preparing a résumé, you need to have a sense of exactly what the employer is looking for. You can then tailor your documents to those exact requirements.

■ The main purpose of the application letter is to motivate the employer to read your résumé carefully and to arrange for an interview. It is a brief introduction, not the place to list all your qualifications and work experience. Your cover letter should be crisp and to the point. Avoid personal details, and present your qualifications objectively. Use a courteous, dignified tone and approach.

■ Your résumé should contain only education- and work-related information. It is better not to include the kind of personal information (ethnicity, age, marital status) that may be expected in other countries.

■ Time is of the essence when sending in application materials and when arriving at the interview. American culture is notoriously time conscious; a last-minute application or a late appearance at an interview can count heavily against you.

■ Before applying for an internship or a job in the United States, be sure that you have the appropriate visa or work permit. American employers are required by law to confirm such documentation before they hire anyone. (American citizens must prove their citizenship as well.) For more information, visit your campus international student center as well as the campus career resource center.

20650 North 58th Avenue, Apt. 15A
Glendale, AZ 85308
August 17, 2005

Ms. Jaclyn Abel
Director of Public Relations
Heard Museum
2301 North Central Avenue
Phoenix, AZ 85004

Dear Ms. Abel:

I am writing to apply for the position of Public Relations Assistant that you recently advertised in the *Arizona Republic*. I believe that my experience and qualifications fit well with your needs at the Heard, a museum that I have visited and loved all my life.

As the enclosed résumé indicates, I have experience in the public relations field. While at Arizona State University West, I worked as an intern in the Public Relations Office, where I was responsible for analyzing and reporting on the image projected by the university's external publications. I also had a hand in creating the brochure for the University-College Center and participated in planning ASU West's "Dream Big" campaign. In addition I assisted in organizing an opening convocation attended by 800 people. This work in the not-for-profit sector has prepared me well for employment at the Heard.

Additionally, my undergraduate major in American history has helped me understand the rich heritage of Native Americans. In my senior thesis, which received the Westmarc Writing Award, I studied the history of the relationship between the Hopis and the Anglo population as reflected in photographs taken from 1920 to 1940. Although my thesis focuses on a specific tribe, I have been interested for many years in Native-American culture and have often made use of resources in the Heard. I think that I would do a superior job of presenting the Heard as the premier museum of Native American culture.

Confidential reference letters are available from ASU West Career Services. I sincerely hope that we will have an opportunity to talk further about the Heard Museum and its outstanding cultural contributions to the Phoenix metropolitan area. Please contact me at 623-555-7310.

Sincerely,

Laura Amabisca

Laura Amabisca

Enc.

Laura writes to a specific person and uses the correct salutation (*Mr., Ms., Dr.,* etc.). Never use someone's first name in an application letter, even if you are already acquainted.

Laura briefly sums up her work experience. This information is also available on her résumé, but she makes evident in her cover letter why she is applying for the job. Without this explanation, a potential employer might not even look at her résumé.

Laura demonstrates her familiarity with the museum to which she is applying. This shows her genuine interest in joining the organization.

29d Prepare in advance for the job interview.

An interview with a potential employer is like an oral presentation. You should prepare in advance, rehearse before an audience, and be prepared to answer unexpected questions. Many campus career resource centers offer free seminars on interviewing skills and can also arrange for you to role-play an interview with a career guidance counselor. Some career resource centers also record you in a mock interview situation and then review the recording with you to determine your strengths and weaknesses.

- Call to confirm your interview the day before it is scheduled. If you are unsure of the location of the interview, make a scouting trip at least a day in advance to determine how much time you will need to get there.

- Dress modestly and formally, even if you are interviewing for an unpaid internship or with a company with a relaxed dress code.

- Bring an extra copy of your résumé and cover letter to refer to during your interview.

- Expect to speak with several people—perhaps someone from human resources as well as the person for whom you would work and other people in his or her department. Understand that questions about salary and benefits should be brought up with human resources, not with your immediate supervisor.

- *Always* send an e-mail or handwritten thank-you note to everyone who took the time to meet you. Send a separate message to each person, reiterating a particularly interesting point the indivdual made and your interest in working with him or her. Thank each one for showing interest in you. Send these notes within twenty-four hours of your interview.

29e Apply what you learn in college to your on-the-job writing.

Once you get a job, writing is a way to establish and maintain lines of communication with your colleagues and other contacts. You will probably be writing much of the time, to internal and external audiences, both on- and off-line. Much of what you have learned in college about writing for different purposes, occasions, and audiences will come in handy. When you write in the workplace, you should imagine a reader who is pressed for time and wants you to get to the point immediately.

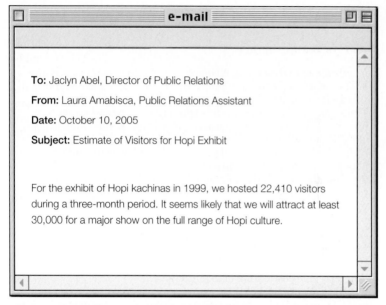

FIGURE 29.1 Sample workplace e-mail.

1. Writing e-mail and memos in the workplace

In the workplace you will do much of your writing online, in the form of e-mail. Most e-mail programs set up messages in memo format, with To, From, Date, and Subject lines, as in Figure 29.1.

Whether you are writing an e-mail message or a conventional memo, you need to consider not only what your workplace document says but also the way it looks. Various strategies can make your document easier to read. For example, presenting your information as a numbered or bulleted list surrounded by white space aids readability. It also allows you to highlight important points and emphasize crucial ideas.

2. Writing other business genres

Readers have built-in expectations for conventional forms of business communication and know what to look for when they read them. Besides the memo, there are a number of common business genres:

- **Business letters:** Use business letters to communicate formally with people outside an organization. Typically, letters in business format have single-spaced block paragraphs with double spacing between the paragraphs. (*See the example on pp. 521–22.*)

TEXTCONNEX

E-mail in the Workplace

- Anything you write using a company's or organization's computers is considered company property. Many people have found themselves in situations—some funny, some embarrassing, and some grounds for termination—when their personal e-mail was broadcast to an entire corporation or beyond. If you want to gossip with a coworker or share a funny joke, do so over a cup of coffee. If you want to e-mail your best friend or your mother about your personal life, do so from your home computer. Never use the office's computer, fax machine, or photocopy machine to prepare and send your résumé to another company.

- When you are replying to an e-mail that has been sent to several people (the term *cc* means "carbon copy," a twentieth-century form of duplicating documents), determine whether your response needs to go to all of the original recipients or just to the original sender. Avoid cluttering other people's inboxes.

- When responding to an e-mail, either begin an entirely new e-mail or delete most of the original message. Avoid long e-mails with strings of Re:Re:Re: in the subject box; these become increasingly cumbersome as they pass from one sender to the next.

- File your e-mail as carefully as you would paper documents. Create a separate folder in your e-mail program for each client, project, or coworker. One tremendous advantage of e-mail is that these electronic "paper trails" of correspondence can be easily searched, organized, and accessed.

- Corporations and organizations have a legal right to trace all Internet activity on any computer that they own. Although it is probably acceptable for you to browse news and shopping sites during your breaks and lunch time, do not visit any sites in the workplace that would embarrass you if a colleague or your supervisor suddenly looked over your shoulder.

- **Business reports and proposals:** Like college research papers, business reports and proposals can be used to inform, analyze, and interpret. An abstract, sometimes called an *executive summary,* is almost always required, as are tables and graphs. (*For more on these visual elements, see Chapter 6: Designing Papers and Preparing Portfolios, pp. 126–33.*)

- **Evaluations and recommendations:** You might need to evaluate a person, or you might be called on to evaluate a product or a procedure and recommend whether the company should buy or use it. Like the reviews and critiques that college writers compose, workplace evaluations are supposed to be reasonable as well as convincing. It is important to be fair, so you should always support your account of both strengths and weaknesses with specific illustrations or examples.

■ **Presentations**: In many professions, information is presented in ways both formal and informal to groups of people. You might suddenly be asked to offer an opinion in a group meeting; or you might be given a week to prepare a formal presentation, with visuals, on an ongoing project. (*For more information on oral presentations, see Chapter 13, pp. 248–53. To learn more about PowerPoint and other presentation tools, see Chapter 14, pp. 261–65.*)

www.mhhe.com/
nmhh
For more information
on PowerPoint, go to
Writing >
PowerPoint
Tutorial

TEXTCONNEX

Writing Connections

Job Central <http://jobstar.org/tools/resume/samples.cfm>: This site provides samples of résumés for many different situations, as well as sample cover letters.

Career Collection: Write a Résumé <http://college.library.wisc.edu/collections/career/careerresume.html>: This site provides help with preparing cover letters and writing résumés.

29f Write as a consumer.

Your ability to write can influence how you are treated as a client or a customer by large and seemingly faceless organizations. A carefully constructed letter can convey a legitimate grievance or it can express your pleasure.

1. Writing a letter of protest
Suppose, for example, that an airline's staff bumped you from a flight without offering you any consideration or compensation, leaving you angry and frustrated. You want action. Compose yourself, and then compose a letter of complaint. Your task is to present yourself as a polite and reasonable person who has experienced rude and unfair treatment by representatives of the company. If you are writing a letter of

complaint on behalf of your company or as a representative of your company (if, for example, you are the travel agent for the person who was treated rudely by the airline), your goal would be the same: to compose a letter that states the complaint clearly but calmly and proposes a resolution.

- Address the letter to the person in charge by name. (If you do not know the correct name and title to use, call the corporate headquarters.)

- Use the format for a business letter. (*See the example on pp. 521–22.*)

- In the first paragraph, concisely state the problem and the action you request.

- In the following paragraphs, narrate clearly and objectively what happened. Refer to details such as the date and time of the incident so that the person you are writing to can follow up.

- Recognize those who tried to help you as well as those who did not.

- Mention previous positive experiences with the organization, if you can. Your protest will have more credibility if you come across as a person who does not usually complain but is forced to do so in this instance.

- Increase your credibility by proposing reasonable compensation and providing receipts, if appropriate. Enclose photocopies of the receipts and documentation with your letter; keep the originals.

- Conclude by thanking the person you are writing to for his or her time and expressing the hope that you will be able to continue as a customer.

- Send copies to the people whom you mention.

- Keep copies of all correspondence for your records.

Consider, for example, the letter on pages 521–22 written by Jonathan Corrigan. Notice how Corrigan's letter adheres to the guidelines just presented.

↑ 1"
↓

10653 North 53rd Drive
Glendale, AZ 85308-9100
August 12, 2005

Mr. Thomas Stern
Chief Executive Officer
Europe Atlantic Airways
PO Box 43
London, England

Dear Mr. Stern:

Because Europe Atlantic Airways (EA) strives to provide the best
international service possible, my fiancée and I chose to fly EA
on our recent trip to Berlin. The service for most of the trip was
excellent, but unfortunately, on the final leg of our journey, EA failed
to transfer our luggage, leaving us stranded without our clothing for
several days. When we finally did receive our luggage, it was damaged
and items were missing. I am writing to request compensation for
the expenses we incurred because of this problem.

Service was excellent on our flights from Phoenix to Berlin. On
Wednesday, August 2, we flew EA 642 from Berlin to London and
EA 2146 from London to Phoenix. The crew of flight 2146 from
London to Phoenix, in particular, was exceptional.

After arriving in Phoenix, we were told that our luggage had not
been transferred from Heathrow Airport to flight 2146 at Gatwick
Airport. When we requested that our luggage be sent to Denver
once it arrived in Phoenix, EA representative Jane Franklin
informed us, rather impolitely, that EA would not transfer our
luggage because we were flying on a different carrier from
Phoenix to Denver. Upon arrival in Denver, we had to purchase
items (clothing and toiletries) necessary for the two-day stay.
Enclosed are receipts for the purchases we made, which total
$377.45.

Upon our return to Phoenix from Denver, we retrieved our luggage
and found that (1) one side of the large suitcase was ripped, (2)
our large duffle bag was missing, and (3) clothing and purchases

1"
←→

	Return address and date.
	Double space.
	Inside address.
	Double space.
	Salutation.
	Double space.
	Body— paragraphs single-spaced, double space between paragraphs.

↑ 1"
↓

Mr. Thomas Stern
Page 2
August 12, 2005

2 to 5 spaces
↑ depending on
↕ the length of
↓ the second
page.

we had made in Berlin were missing. While the sentimental value of these items cannot be quantified, I have enclosed receipts showing the replacement cost for the duffle bag: $125.

I suggest EA reimburse us $502.45 (please see enclosures). Your doing so would go a long way toward restoring our confidence in EA. Review of this matter would be greatly appreciated.

I look forward to hearing from you.

Sincerely,

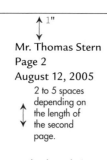

Jonathan Corrigan

cc: Ms. Jane Franklin

Close.

Signature.

Name of
person to
whom copy
will be sent.

2. Writing a letter of praise

On the other hand, suppose that an airline employee was exceptionally helpful to you when you missed a connecting flight, and you are grateful. Express your gratitude by writing a letter of praise. Like letters of protest, letters of praise are intended to shape future action. In the workplace, you might write a letter of praise to a colleague who worked long hours to complete a project, or to congratulate a team for bringing in new clients. The writing techniques are similar for both praise and protest letters. Always send copies of praise letters to the human resources department for your colleagues' files.

- Address the letter to the person in charge by name. (If you do not know the correct name and title to use, call the corporate headquarters.)
- Use the format for a business letter.
- In the first paragraph, concisely state the situation and the help that was provided.
- In the following paragraphs, narrate what happened, referring to details such as the date and time of the incident so that the person you are writing to can follow up with the person who helped you.
- Conclude by thanking the person you are writing to for his or her time and expressing your intention to continue doing business with the company.
- Send copies to the people whom you mention (and to the human resources department if you are writing to a coworker).

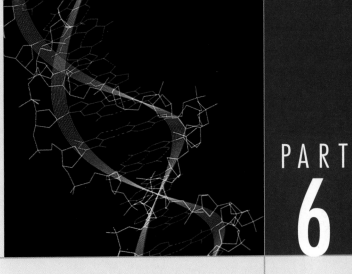

Like DNA, which provides a chemical blueprint for the construction of living organisms, grammar and syntax provide a blueprint for transforming words into intelligible sentences.

Grammar and rhetoric are complementary.... Grammar maps out the possible; rhetoric narrows the possible down to the desirable or effective.

—FRANCIS CHRISTENSEN

Grammar
Basics

Grammar Basics

Answer these questions to test your knowledge of basic grammatical terms. Check your work against the answer sheet at the back of the book. As you read Chapters 30 and 31, pay particular attention to the sections that correspond to the questions you answer incorrectly.

1. People often confuse a vegan diet with vegetarianism.

   The main verb in this sentence is

   a. often

   b. confuse

   c. a

   d. with

2. Author Toni Morrison has received such notable literary awards as the Pulitzer Prize and the Nobel Prize for Literature.

   The helping verb in this sentence is

   a. has

   b. received

   c. such

   d. as

3. Students who take a world religion class may be asked to read such sacred texts as the Bhagavad-Gita.

   The proper noun in this sentence is

   a. Students

   b. religion

   c. sacred

   d. Bhagavad-Gita

4. Americans often watch daytime talk shows for marital advice.

   The noncount noun in this sentence is

   a. Americans

   b. shows

   c. marital

   d. advice

5. Henry David Thoreau wrote his famous essay "Civil Disobedience" after spending only one night in a Massachusetts jail.

   The personal pronoun in this sentence is

   a. Thoreau

   b. his

   c. only

   d. one

6. The polar ice caps may melt as a result of global warming, and in that case, the sea level will rise.

The demonstrative pronoun in this sentence is

   a. The

   b. as

   c. a

   d. that

7. Smokers often do not heed prominent warnings about the dangers of cigarettes.

The adjective in this sentence is

   a. Smokers

   b. not

   c. prominent

   d. warnings

8. The Antarctic ice shelf is rapidly melting.

The adverb in this sentence is

   a. Antarctic

   b. ice

   c. rapidly

   d. melting

9. During the 1916 presidential election, Democrat Woodrow Wilson received only twenty-three more electoral votes than Republican Charles R. Hughes.

The prepositional phrase in this sentence is

   a. During the 1916 presidential election

   b. Democrat Woodrow Wilson

   c. received only twenty-three more electoral votes

   d. than Republican Charles R. Hughes

10. *Hamlet* and *Othello* are two of Shakespeare's most famous tragedies.

The coordinating conjunction in this sentence is

   a. and

   b. are

   c. two

   d. Shakespeare's

11. Even though Hamlet knows Claudius killed his father, he hesitates to take his revenge.

The subordinating phrase in this sentence is

a. Even though

b. Hamlet knows

c. killed his

d. to take

12. Do remember that greenhouse gases such as carbon dioxide and methane can affect our environment.

This sentence is

a. declarative

b. interrogative

c. imperative

d. exclamatory

13. Do Americans understand what it means that less than half the electorate votes in most presidential elections?

This sentence is

a. declarative

b. interrogative

c. imperative

d. exclamatory

14. *Cats* and *The Phantom of the Opera* are among the longest running Broadway plays.

The compound subject in this sentence is

a. *The Phantom of the Opera*

b. *Cats* and *The Phantom of the Opera*

c. Broadway plays

d. longest running Broadway plays

15. Recent archeological studies <u>confirm</u> the presence of humans in South America much earlier than previously thought.

The underlined verb in this sentence is a(n)

a. linking verb

b. transitive verb

c. intransitive verb

16. The Labrador Retriever <u>is</u> the most popular dog breed in the United States.

The underlined verb in this sentence is a(n)

a. linking verb

b. transitive verb

c. intransitive verb

17. The Alumni Association offers scholarships to qualified students.

The direct object in this sentence is

a. Alumni

b. scholarships

c. students

d. offers

18. Drivers need <u>to buckle their seat belts</u>.

The underlined words form a

a. noun phrase

b. infinitive phrase

c. participial phrase

d. gerund phrase

e. appositive phrase

f. absolute phrase

19. <u>After World War II ended</u>, Japan abolished State Shinto, which had been the country's official religion since the Meiji Restoration of the late nineteenth century.

The underlined words form a(n)

a. adjective clause

b. adverb clause

c. noun clause

20. Although most people know that smoking is bad for their health, many do not know that lying on a tanning bed can be, too.

This sentence is a

a. simple sentence

b. compound sentence

c. complex sentence

d. compound-complex sentence

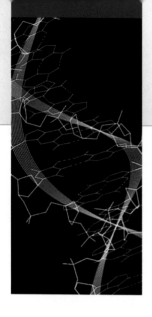

30 Parts of Speech

When we speak in our native language, we usually do not worry too much about grammar. The order and endings of our words seem to come naturally. Written language, although based on the grammar of spoken language, has a logic and rules of its own. This chapter and the next (*Chapter 31: Sentence Basics*) explain the basic rules of standard written English.

Grammar gives us a way of talking about how sentences are put together to make sense. Take, for example, this group of words, adapted from Lewis Carroll's poem "Jabberwocky":

The toves gimbled in the wabe.

Most of these are nonsense words: Carroll made them up. What makes a sentence meaningful, however, is not just its individual words.

CHARTING the TERRITORY

Grammar, Human Thought, and the Origins of Language

The study of grammar—or, more broadly, **syntax,** the rules for forming grammatical sentences in a language—is not confined to English or other language departments. On the contrary, grammar and syntax are defining features of human language, making them of great interest in the social sciences and humanities. They are among the features of language that make it so powerful compared with other forms of animal communication. Grammar and syntax allow us to talk about the past and the future as well as the here and now, to describe something we have seen to someone who has not seen it, and even to describe imaginary places and events—in other words, to tell stories. Psychologists, linguists, and philosophers study grammar and syntax for clues to the nature of the human mind. Anthropologists and psychologists study the limited language abilities of chimpanzees and other primates for evidence of syntax and clues to the origin of language. Similarly, paleontologists, archeologists, and art historians study the first appearance of another uniquely human form of symbolic communication—art—for clues to the emergence of our capacity for syntax and language.

Because of the form of the words in this sentence and the way they relate to each other, we can answer questions about them:

www.mhhe.com/
nmhh
For information and
exercises on parts of
speech, go to

Editing >
Parts of Speech

> What gimbled in the wabe? *The toves did.*
> What did the toves do in the wabe? *They gimbled.*
> Where did the toves gimble? *They gimbled in the wabe.*

We can answer these questions because we can tell from the form and relationship of the words what grammatical role each one plays in the sentence.

English has eight primary grammatical categories, or **parts of speech:** *verbs, nouns, pronouns, adjectives, adverbs, prepositions, conjunctions,* and *interjections.* All English words belong to one or more of these categories. Particular words can belong in different categories, depending on the role they play in a sentence. For example, the word *button* can be a noun:

➤ The *button* is on the coat.

or a verb:

➤ He will *button* his jacket now.

The Eight Parts of Speech in English

- **Verbs** report action (*run, write*), condition (*bloom, sit*), or state of being (*be, seem*).
- **Nouns** name people (*Shakespeare, actors, Englishman*), places (*Manhattan, city, island*), things (*Kleenex, handkerchief, sneeze, cats*), and ideas (*Marxism, justice, democracy, clarity*).
- **Pronouns** (*she, her, herself, who, that, all*) take the place of nouns.
- **Adjectives** (*green, smaller, perfect*) modify nouns and pronouns by answering questions like *Which one? What kind? How many? What size? What condition?*
- **Adverbs** (*quietly, better, never*) modify verbs, other adverbs, adjectives, and whole clauses. They usually answer such questions as *When? Where? How? How often? How much? To what degree?* and *Why?*
- **Prepositions** (*on, in, at, by, as well as*) usually appear as part of a **prepositional phrase.** Their main function is to allow the noun or pronoun in the phrase to modify another word in the sentence.
- **Conjunctions** (*and, but, both . . . and, neither . . . nor, after*) join words, phrases, or clauses and indicate their relation to each other.
- **Interjections** (*alas, oh no*) are forceful expressions, usually written with an exclamation point.

531

www.mhhe.com/
nmhh
For information and
exercises on verbs,
go to

Editing >
Verbs and Verbals

30a Verbs

Verbs carry a lot of information. They report action (*run, write*), condition (*bloom, sit*), or state of being (*be, seem*). Verbs also change form to indicate person, number, tense, voice, and mood (*see Chapters 34: Subject-Verb Agreement, and 35: Problems with Verbs*). To do all this, a **main verb** is sometimes accompanied by one or more **helping verbs,** thereby becoming a **verb phrase.** Helping verbs precede the main verb in a verb phrase.

➤ The play *begins* at eight.
　　　　　　　mv

➤ I *may change* seats after the play *has begun.*
　 hv　mv　　　　　　　　　　hv　mv

1. Main verbs

Main verbs change form to indicate when something occurs (**tense)** and to whom it occurs (**person** and **number**). If a word does not indicate tense, it is not a main verb. All main verbs have five forms, except for *be,* which has eight.

BASE FORM	(*talk, sing*)
PAST TENSE	Yesterday I (*talked, sang*).
PAST PARTICIPLE	In the past, I have (*talked, sung*).
PRESENT PARTICIPLE	Right now I am (*talking, singing*).
-S FORM	Usually he/she/it (*talks, sings*).

Whether or not English is your first language, verb forms—especially irregular verb forms—can be troublesome. (*For more on subject-verb agreement and verb tense, see Chapter 34: Subject-Verb Agreement, pp. 597–612, Chapter 35: Problems with Verbs, pp. 613–37, and the list of common irregular verbs on pp. 615–16.*)

2. Helping verbs that show time

Some helping verbs—mostly forms of *be, have,* and *do*—function to signify time (*will have been playing, has played*) or emphasis (*does play*). Forms of *do* are also used to ask questions (*Do you play?*). Here is a fuller list of such helping (or **auxiliary**) verbs:

be, am, is	being, been	do, does, did
are, was, were	have, has, had	

3. Modals: Helping verbs that show manner

Other helping verbs, called **modals,** signify the manner, or mode, of an action. Modals fall into two categories:

- one-word
- phrasal

One-word modals Unlike the auxiliaries *be, have,* and *do,* one-word modals such as *may, must,* and *will* are almost never used alone as main verbs, nor do they change form to show person or number. One-word modals do not add *-s* endings, two of them are never used together (such as *might could*), and each is always followed by the base form of the verb without *to* (*He could be nicer*).

➤   hv   mv
  Contrary to press reports, she *will* not *run* for political

office.

Note that a negative word such as *not* may come between the helping and the main verb.

The one-word modals are as follows:

can	might	shall
could	will	should
may	would	must

Phrasal modals Phrasal modals do change form to show time, person, and number.

➤   hv   mv
  Yesterday, I *was going to* study for three hours.

➤   hv   mv
  Next week, I *am going to* study three hours a day.

Here are some phrasal modals:

have to	be supposed to	be able to
have got to	be going to	
used to	be allowed to	

For MULTILINGUAL STUDENTS

For more on the form and meaning of modal verbs, see Chapter 64: English Basics (*pp. 957–63*).

Exercise 30.1 Identifying verbs

Underline the main verb in each sentence. If there is a helping verb or verbs, circle them.

> **EXAMPLE** **Government of the people, by the people, for the people (shall) not <u>perish</u> from the earth.**

1. An increasing number of Americans, both men and women, undergo cosmetic surgery for aesthetic rather than medical reasons.
2. A decade ago, the average American believed that only Hollywood celebrities underwent facelifts and tummy tucks.
3. Do you think that you need to improve your physical appearance?
4. Men, often in their mid-forties, are choosing a variety of surgical procedures, including hair replacement and chin augmentation.
5. For a lean, flat abdomen, a cosmetic surgeon may suggest both abdominoplasty and liposuction.
6. People are now able to achieve their ideal body image, not through exercise and diet, but through elective cosmetic surgery.

30b Nouns

Nouns name people (*Shakespeare, actors, Englishman*), places (*Manhattan, city, island*), things (*Kleenex, handkerchief, sneeze, cats*), and ideas (*Marxism, justice, democracy, clarity*).

➤ **Shakespeare** lived in **England** and wrote **plays** about the human **condition.**

1. Proper nouns and common nouns

Proper nouns name specific people, places, and things and are always capitalized: *Aretha Franklin, Hinduism, Albany, Microsoft.* All other nouns are **common nouns:** *singer, religion, capital, corporation.*

2. Count nouns and noncount nouns

A common noun that refers to something specific that can be counted is a **count noun.** Count nouns can be singular or plural, like *cup* or *suggestion* (*four cups, several suggestions*). **Noncount nouns** are nonspecific; these common nouns refer to categories of people, places, or things and cannot be counted. They do not have a plural form. (*The <u>pottery</u> is beautiful. His <u>advice</u> was useful.*)

SOME COUNT and NONCOUNT NOUNS

COUNT NOUNS	NONCOUNT NOUNS
cars	transportation
computers	Internet
facts	information
clouds	rain
stars	sunshine
tools	equipment
machines	machinery
suggestions	advice
earrings	jewelry
tables	furniture
smiles	happiness

 For MULTILINGUAL STUDENTS

For help using quantifiers with count and noncount nouns, see Chapter 64: English Basics (*pp. 948–55*).

3. Concrete nouns and abstract nouns

Nouns that name things that can be perceived by the senses are called **concrete nouns:** *boy, wind, book, song.* **Abstract nouns** name qualities and concepts that do not have physical properties: *charity, patience, beauty, hope.* (*For more on using concrete and abstract nouns, see Chapter 49: Exact Language, pp. 781–82.*)

4. Singular nouns and plural nouns

Most nouns name things that can be counted and are **singular** or **plural.** Singular nouns typically become plural by adding -*s* or -*es:* *boy / boys, ocean / oceans, church / churches, agency / agencies.* Some count nouns have irregular plurals, such as *man / men, child / children,* and *tooth / teeth.* Noncount nouns like *intelligence* and *electricity* do not form plurals.

5. Collective nouns

Nouns such as *team, family, herd,* and *orchestra*—called **collective nouns**—are treated as singular. They are not noncount nouns, however, because collective nouns can be counted and can be made plural: *teams, families. (Also see Chapter 34: Subject-Verb Agreement, pp. 605–7, and Chapter 36: Problems with Pronouns, pp. 649–55.)*

6. Possessive nouns

Nouns change their form to indicate possession, or ownership. To form a singular **possessive noun,** add apostrophe plus *s* ('s); for plural nouns ending in *s,* just add an apostrophe ('). (*Also see Chapter 61: Apostrophes, pp. 921–27.*)

SINGULAR	insect	insect's sting
PLURAL	neighbors	neighbors' car

www.mhhe.com/
nmhh
For information
and exercises on
pronouns, go to
Editing > Pronouns

30c Pronouns

A pronoun takes the place of a noun. The noun that the pronoun replaces is called its **antecedent.** (*For more on pronoun-antecedent agreement, see Chapter 36: Problems with Pronouns, pp. 649–55.*)

➤ The *snow* fell all day long, and by nightfall *it* was three

feet deep.

The box on pages 538–39 summarizes the various kinds of pronouns. Each type is explained below.

1. Personal pronouns

The **personal pronouns** *I, me, you, he, his, she, her, it, we, us, they,* and *them* refer to specific people or things and vary in form to indicate person, number, gender, and case. (*For more on pronoun referents and case, such as distinguishing between* I *and* me, *see Chapter 36: Problems with Pronouns, pp. 638–43.*)

➤ *You* told *us* that *he* gave Jane a lock of *his* hair.

2. Possessive pronouns

Like possessive nouns, **possessive pronouns** indicate ownership. However, unlike possessive nouns, possessive pronouns do not add apostrophes: *my/mine, your/yours, her/hers, his, its, our/ours, their/theirs.*

➤ Brunch is at *her* place this Saturday.

➤ *Hers* was the best performance of the evening.

3. Reflexive pronouns and intensive pronouns

Pronouns ending in *-self* or *-selves* are either reflexive or intensive. **Reflexive pronouns** refer back to the subject and are necessary for sentence sense.

➤ Many of the women blamed *themselves* for the problem.

Intensive pronouns add emphasis to the nouns or pronouns they follow and are grammatically optional.

➤ President Harding *himself* drank whiskey during Prohibition.

4. Relative pronouns

Who, whom, whose, that, and *which* are relative pronouns. A **relative pronoun** relates a dependent clause—a word group containing a subject and verb and a subordinating word—to an antecedent noun or pronoun in the sentence.

dependent clause

➤ In Kipling's story, Dravot is the man *who* would be king.

The form of a relative pronoun varies according to its **case**—the grammatical role it plays in the sentence. (*For more on pronoun case, particularly distinguishing between* who *and* whom, *see Chapter 36: Problems with Pronouns, pp. 647–49.*)

5. Demonstrative pronouns

The **demonstrative pronouns** *this, that, these,* and *those* point out nouns and pronouns that come later.

➤ *This* is the book literary critics have been waiting for.

Sometimes these pronouns function as adjectives: *This book won the Pulitzer.* Sometimes they are noun equivalents: *This is my book.*

6. Interrogative pronouns

Interrogative pronouns such as *who, whatever,* and *whom* are used to ask questions.

➤ *Whatever* happened to you?

PRONOUNS

PERSONAL (INCLUDING POSSESSIVE)

SINGULAR	PLURAL
I, me, my, mine	we, us, our, ours
you, your, yours	you, your, yours
he, him, his	they, them, their, theirs
she, her, hers	
it, its	

REFLEXIVE AND INTENSIVE

SINGULAR	PLURAL
myself	ourselves
yourself	yourselves
himself, herself, itself	themselves
oneself	

RELATIVE

who	whoever	what	whatever	that
whom	whomever	whose	whichever	which

DEMONSTRATIVE
this, that, these, those

The form of the interrogative pronouns *who, whom, whoever,* and *whomever* indicates the grammatical role they play in a sentence. (*See Chapter 36: Problems with Pronouns, pp. 647–49.*)

7. Indefinite pronouns
Indefinite pronouns such as *someone, anybody, nothing,* and *few* refer to a nonspecific person or thing and do not change form to indicate person, number, or gender.

➤   ***Anybody*** **who cares enough to come and help may take** ***some*** **home.**

INTERROGATIVE

who	what	which
whoever	whatever	whichever
whom	whomever	whose

INDEFINITE

SINGULAR		PLURAL	SINGULAR/PLURAL
anybody	nobody	both	all
anyone	no one	few	any
anything	none	many	either
each	nothing	several	more
everybody	one		most
everyone	somebody		some
everything	someone		
much	something		
neither			

RECIPROCAL

each other

any other

Most indefinite pronouns are always singular (*anybody, everyone*). Some are always plural (*many, few*). A handful can be singular or plural (*any, most*). (*See Chapter 34: Subject-Verb Agreement, pp. 597–612.*)

8. Reciprocal pronouns

Reciprocal pronouns such as *each other* and *one another* refer to the separate parts of their plural antecedent.

➤ **My sister and I are close because we live near *each other*.**   **539**

Exercise 30.2   Identifying nouns and pronouns

Underline the nouns and circle the pronouns in each sentence.

    EXAMPLE   (We) have (nothing) to fear but <u>fear</u> (itself.)

1. Following World War I, the nation witnessed an unprecedented explosion of African-American fiction, poetry, drama, music, art, social commentary, and political activism.
2. Many African-American intellectuals, artists, cultural critics, and political leaders during the 1920s and 1930s were drawn to Harlem, a vibrant section of upper Manhattan in New York City.
3. Sociologist and intellectual Alain Locke, author of *The New Negro,* is best known as the New Negro Movement's founder.
4. W.E.B. DuBois was the author of *The Souls of Black Folk,* and he was also a cofounder of the National Association for the Advancement of Colored People (NAACP), a preeminent civil rights organization.
5. These intellectuals of the Harlem Renaissance profoundly influenced each other.
6. They spoke about the effect of marginality and alienation on themselves and on the shaping of their consciousness as African Americans.
7. Zora Neal Hurston was herself a cultural anthropologist who studied the folklore of the rural South, which is reflected in her novel *Their Eyes Were Watching God.*
8. Nella Larson, author of *Quicksand* and *Passing,* was awarded a Guggenheim fellowship for her creative writing in 1929.
9. Who among the visual artists during the Harlem Renaissance did not use Africa as a source of inspiration?

Exercise 30.3   Identifying types of nouns and pronouns

On a separate sheet of paper, list each noun and pronoun that you identified in Exercise 30.2. For each noun, label it proper or common, count or noncount, concrete or abstract, and singular or plural. Also identify the one collective noun and the one possessive noun. For each pronoun, label it personal, possessive, reflexive, intensive, relative, demonstrative, interrogative, indefinite, or reciprocal. Note if the pronoun is singular or plural.

30d Adjectives

Adjectives modify nouns and pronouns by answering questions like *Which one? What kind? How many? What size? What color? What condition?* and *Whose?* Adjectives can:

- describe (*red* car, *dangerous* mission)
- enumerate (*tenth* floor, *seventy-six* trombones)
- identify (*British* parliament, *American* constitution)
- define (*democratic* constitution, *capitalist* economy)
- limit (*one* person, *that* person).

When **articles** (*a, an,* and *the*) identify nouns, they function as adjectives.

www.mhhe.com/
nmhh
For information
and exercises on
adjectives, go to
Editing >
Adjectives
and Adverbs

For MULTILINGUAL STUDENTS

For help with using articles appropriately, see Chapter 64: English Basics (*pp. 948–54*).

Some proper nouns have an adjective form. Like the nouns from which they derive, these **proper adjectives** are capitalized: *Britain / British.* Pronouns and nouns can also function as adjectives (*his green car, the car door*), and adjectives often have forms that allow you to make comparisons (*great, greater, greatest*).

➤ The *decisive* and *diligent* **king regularly attended meetings of the council.** [What kind of king?]

➤ *These four artistic* **qualities affect how an advertisement is received.** [Which, how many, what kind of qualities?]

➤ *My little blue* **Volkswagen died** *one icy winter* **morning.** [Whose, what size, what color car? Which, what kind of morning?]

➤ **Lincoln was one of the country's** *greatest* **presidents.** [The adjective compares Lincoln with other presidents.]

Like all modifiers, adjectives should be close to the words they modify. Most often, adjectives appear before the noun they modify. However, **descriptive adjectives**—adjectives that designate qualities or attributes—may come before or after the noun or pronoun they modify, depending on the stylistic effect a writer wishes to achieve. Adjectives that describe the subject and follow linking verbs (*be, am, is, are, was, being, been, appear, become, feel, grow, look, make, prove, smell, sound, seem, taste*) are called **subject complements.**

BEFORE THE SUBJECT

The *sick* and *destitute* poet no longer believed that love would save him.

AFTER THE SUBJECT

The poet, *sick* and *destitute,* no longer believed that love would save him.

AFTER A LINKING VERB

No longer believing that love would save him, the poet was *sick* and *destitute.*

For MULTILINGUAL STUDENTS

For information on the order of adjectives in English, see Chapter 64: English Basics (*pp. 954–55*).

www.mhhe.com/
nmhh
For information and exercises on adverbs, go to

Editing >
Adjectives
and Adverbs

30e   Adverbs

Adverbs modify verbs, other adverbs, and adjectives, answering such questions as *When? Where? How? How often? How much? To what degree?* and *Why?* They often end in *-ly* (*beautifully, gracefully, quietly*).

➤   **The authenticity of the document is *hotly* contested.**
[How is it contested?]

Like adjectives, adverbs can be used to compare (*less, lesser, least*). In addition to modifying individual words, they can be used to modify whole clauses. Adverbs can be placed at the beginning or end of a sentence or before the verb they modify, but they should not be placed between the verb and its direct object.

➤ **The water was *brilliant* blue and *icy* cold.** [The adverbs intensify the adjectives *blue* and *cold*.]

➤ **Dickens mixed humor and pathos *better* than any other English writer after Shakespeare.** [The adverb compares Dickens with other writers.]

➤ ***Consequently,* he is still read by millions.**

Consequently is a conjunctive adverb that modifies the independent clause that follows it and shows how the sentence is related to the preceding sentence. (*For more on conjunctive adverbs, see pp. 545–47 in section 30g, on conjunctions.*)

The negators *no, not,* and *never* are among the most common adverbs.

SAY *NO* ONLY ONCE

In English, it takes only one negator (*no / not / never*) to change the meaning of a sentence from positive to negative. When two negatives are used together, they may seem to cancel each other out.

any

➤ **They don't have ~~no~~ reason to go there.**
^

Exercise 30.4 Identifying adjectives and adverbs

Underline the adjectives and circle the adverbs in each sentence.

   EXAMPLE   **Peter Piper (patiently) picked a peck of <u>pickled</u> peppers.**

1. A growing number of Americans are overweight or clinically obese.
2. Obesity increases a person's risk for type 2 diabetes, heart disease, high blood pressure, stroke, liver damage, cancer, and premature death.
3. Fad diets promise Americans rapid but temporary weight loss, not weight management.
4. Robert C. Atkins, M.D., author of *Dr. Atkins' New Diet Revolution,* best explains a low-carbohydrate, high-protein diet.

5. Other fad diets, such as the Sugar Busters diet, work on the premise that high glycemic carbohydrates are primarily responsible for weight gain.
6. In the best seller *Eat Right for Your Type,* naturopath Peter J. D'Adamo argues that certain foods should be avoided based on a person's blood type.
7. Many other fad diets, such as the grapefruit diet and the cabbage diet, promise quick weight loss.
8. Many fad diets inevitably drive dieters to carbohydrate cravings and binge eating.
9. Few fad diets emphasize the need for dieters to increase their metabolic rate significantly with regular aerobic exercise.

30f Prepositions

Prepositions (*on, in, at, by*) usually appear as part of a **prepositional phrase.** Their main function is to allow the noun or pronoun

COMMON PREPOSITIONS

about	by	near
above	by means of	of
according to	by way of	on
across	down	on account of
after	during	over
against	except	since
along	except for	through
along with	excluding	to
among	following	toward
apart from	from	under
as	in	underneath
as to	in addition to	until
as well as	in case of	up
at	in front of	up to
because of	in place of	upon
before	in regard to	via
behind	including	with
below	inside	with reference to
beside	instead of	with respect to
between	into	within
beyond	like	without

For MULTILINGUAL STUDENTS

For more on using prepositions, see Chapter 66: Identifying and Editing Common Errors (*pp. 974–75*).

in the phrase to modify another word in the sentence. Prepositional phrases always begin with a preposition and end with a noun, pronoun, or other word group that functions as the **object of the preposition** (in *time,* on the *table*).

A preposition can be one word (*about, despite, on*) or a word group (*according to, as well as, in spite of*). Place prepositional phrases as close as possible to the words they modify. Adjectival prepositional phrases usually appear immediately after the noun or pronoun they modify and answer questions like *Which one?* and *What kind of?* Adverbial phrases can appear anywhere in a sentence; they answer questions like *When? Where? How?* and *Why?*

AS ADJECTIVE	Many species *of birds* nest there.
AS ADVERB	The younger children stared *out the window.*

30g Conjunctions

Conjunctions join words, phrases, or clauses and indicate their relation to each other.

1. Coordinating conjunctions

The common **coordinating conjunctions** (or **coordinators**) are *and, but, or, for, nor, yet,* and *so.* Coordinating conjunctions join elements of equal weight or function.

➤ She was strong *and* healthy.

➤ The war was short *but* devastating.

➤ They must have been tired, *for* they had been climbing all day long.

COMMON SUBORDINATING CONJUNCTIONS

SUBORDINATING WORDS

after	once	until
although	since	when
as	that	whenever
because	though	where
before	till	wherever
if	unless	while

SUBORDINATING PHRASES

as if	even though	in that
as soon as	even when	rather than
as though	for as much as	so that
even after	in order that	sooner than
even if	in order to	

2. Correlative conjunctions

The **correlative conjunctions** also link sentence elements of equal value, but they always come in pairs: *both . . . and, either . . . or, neither . . . nor,* and *not only . . . but also.*

➤ *Neither* **the doctor** *nor* **the social worker believes his story.**

3. Subordinating conjunctions

Common **subordinating conjunctions** (or **subordinators**) link sentence elements that are not of equal importance. Because subordinating conjunctions join unequal sentence parts, they are used to introduce dependent, or subordinate, clauses in a sentence.

➤ **The software will not run properly** *if* **the computer lacks sufficient memory.**

(*For help in punctuating sentences with conjunctions, see Chapter 51: Commas, pp. 806–9 and 844.*)

For MULTILINGUAL STUDENTS

For information on using coordination and subordination appropriately, see Chapter 65, English Sentence Structure (*pp. 968–69*).

COMMON CONJUNCTIVE ADVERBS

accordingly	however	now
also	incidentally	otherwise
anyway	indeed	similarly
as a result	instead	specifically
besides	likewise	still
certainly	meanwhile	subsequently
consequently	moreover	suddenly
finally	nevertheless	then
furthermore	next	therefore
hence	nonetheless	thus

4. Conjunctive adverbs

Conjunctive adverbs indicate the relation between one clause and another, but unlike conjunctions (*and, but*), they are not grammatically strong enough on their own to hold the two clauses together. A period or semicolon is also needed.

➤ **Swimming is an excellent exercise for the heart and for the muscles; *however,* swimming is not as effective a weight control measure as jogging is.**

30h Interjections

Interjections are forceful expressions, usually written with an exclamation point. They are not often used in academic writing except in quotations of dialogue.

➤ ***"Wow!"* Davis said. "Are you telling me that there's a former presidential adviser who hasn't written a book?"**

➤ **Tell-all books are, *alas,* the biggest sellers.**

Exercise 30.5   Chapter review: Parts of speech

In the following sentences, label each word according to its part of speech: verb (v), noun (n), pronoun (pn), adjective (adj), adverb (adv), preposition (prep), conjunction (conj), or interjection (interj).

adj   n   v   interj   adj   adj   n

EXAMPLE   **Tell-all books are, alas, the biggest sellers.**

1. Cancer begins when your body's cells divide abnormally and form a malignant growth or tumor.
2. Many types of cancer can, alas, attack parts of your body imperceptibly, including your body's skin, organs, and blood.
3. One of the most commonly diagnosed types of cancer in the United States, however, is skin cancer.
4. People who are fair-skinned and freckled are more prone to develop skin cancer if they are exposed often to ultraviolet radiation.
5. Many people are relieved to discover that skin cancer can usually be treated successfully if it is detected early.

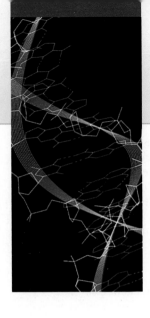

31 | Sentence Basics

Every complete **sentence** contains at least one **subject** (a noun and its modifiers) and one **predicate** (a verb and its objects, complements, and modifiers) that fit together to make a statement, ask a question, give a command, or express an emotion.

subject	predicate

➤ The *children* *solved* the puzzle.

subject	predicate

➤ *Whatever she decides* *is* fine with me.

31a Sentence purpose

When you write, your purpose helps you decide which sentence type—declarative, interrogative, imperative, or exclamatory—to use.

Sentence Types and Their Purposes

1. **Declarative sentences** provide information (*declare*) something about their subjects.

   ➤ He watches *Sex and the City* reruns.

2. **Interrogative sentences** pose questions about their subjects.

   ➤ Does he watch *Sex and the City* reruns?

3. **Imperative sentences** demand something of their subjects.

   ➤ Do not watch reruns of *Sex and the City*.

4. **Exclamatory sentences** emphasize a point or express strong emotion.

   ➤ I'm really looking forward to watching *Sex and the City* reruns with you!

31b Subjects

1. Simple subjects and complete subjects

The **simple subject** of a sentence is the noun or pronoun that names the topic of the sentence. The **complete subject** is the simple subject plus its modifiers. To find the complete subject, ask who or what the sentence is about. Then, to find the simple subject, identify the noun or pronoun within the complete subject. (If the simple subject has no modifiers, then it is also the complete subject.)

complete subject

simple subject

➤ ***Three six-year-old children* solved the puzzle in less than**

five minutes.

The subject answers the question "Who solved the puzzle?"

To identify the subject of a question, it sometimes helps to rephrase the question as a declarative sentence.

➤ **Did Claudius murder Hamlet's father?** [Question]

simp subj

➤ **Claudius murdered Hamlet's father.** [Question rephrased]

The subject answers the question "Who murdered Hamlet's father?"

It is useful to know how to isolate the simple subject of a sentence when you have a question about subject-verb agreement. (*See Chapter 34, pp. 597–612.*)

2. Compound subjects

A **compound subject** contains two or more simple subjects connected with a conjunction such as *and, but, or,* or *neither . . . nor.*

compound

simple   simple

➤ **Original *thinking* and bold *design* are characteristics of**

her work.

3. Implied subjects

In **imperative sentences,** which give directions or commands, the **subject** *you* is usually **implied,** not stated. A helping verb is needed

to transform an imperative sentence into a question.

impl
subj
➤ [*You*] **Keep this advice in mind.**

hv
➤ ***Would*** **you keep this advice in mind?**

4. Subject position

In English declarative sentences, the subject usually precedes the verb. In sentences beginning with *there* or *here* followed by some form of *be*, the subject comes after the verb.

simple subject
➤ **Here are the *remnants* of an infamous empire.**

31c Predicates: Verbs and their objects or complements

1. Simple predicates and complete predicates

In a sentence, the **predicate** says something about the subject. The verb (including any helping verbs) constitutes the **simple predicate.** The verb and any **modifiers, objects,** or **complements** make up the **complete predicate.**

complete predicate
⌐simple pred ⌐
➤ **The Fugitive Slave Act of 1850 *dismayed many Northerners.***

2. Compound predicates

A **compound predicate** contains two or more predicates connected with a conjunction such as *and, but, or,* or *neither . . . nor.*

compound
➤ **The Fugitive Slave Act of 1850 *dismayed many Northerners* and**
predicate
contributed to the outbreak of the Civil War ten years later.

Exercise 31.1   Identifying the subject and predicate

Place one line under the complete subject and two lines under the complete predicate in each sentence. Circle the simple subject and simple predicate. If the subject is implied, write "implied subject" instead.

EXAMPLE   **Little Jack Horner sat in a corner.**

1. Did Gene Roddenberry, the creator and producer of *Star Trek,* anticipate that his science fiction television series would be watched by people of all ages for more than thirty years?
2. Both Captain James T. Kirk from *Star Trek: The Original Series* and Captain Jean-Luc Picard from *Star Trek: The Next Generation* command a ship called the *Enterprise.*
3. Do not forget that the captain in *Star Trek: Voyager* is a woman, Kathryn Janeway.
4. There are six *Star Trek* series: *The Original Series, The Next Generation, Deep Space Nine, Voyager, Enterprise,* and *The Animated Adventures.*
5. Captain Benjamin Sisko commanded Starfleet's Deep Space Nine station and served as the emissary for the Bajoran people.

---

3. Verb types and sentence patterns

Verbs fall into one of three categories—*linking, transitive,* or *intransitive*—depending on how they function in a sentence. The kind of verb determines what elements the complete predicate must include. Most meaningful English sentences follow one of the five basic patterns summarized in the box on page 554. These patterns are the subjects of the remainder of this section.

1. Linking verbs and subject complements A **linking verb** joins a subject to more information about it that is located on the other side of the verb. That information is called the **subject complement.** The subject complement may be a noun, an adjective, or a pronoun.

	subject	predicate	
		linking verb	subject complement
NOUN	Ann Yearsley	was	*a milkmaid.*
ADJECTIVE	Hamlet	is	*indecisive.*
PRONOUN	His enemy	was	*himself.*

The most frequently used linking verb is the *be* verb (*am, is, are, was, were*). Verbs such as *seem, look, appear, feel, become, smell, sound,* and *taste* can also function as links between a sentence's subject and its complement.

➤ **That new hairstyle *looks* beautiful.**

➤ **The music *sounds* chaotic.**

➤ **The decision *seems* unfair.**

For MULTILINGUAL STUDENTS

English Word Order: A Brief Overview

The English sentence consists of a subject and a predicate, but English has a fairly fixed word order compared with many other languages. As a result, multilingual writers often make mistakes when they transfer word order patterns that might be acceptable in their native languages into English.

The basic word order of an English sentence is subject (S), verb (V), object (O):

  S   V   O
➤ **The child threw the ball.** [correct English word order]

French, Spanish, and Cantonese Chinese share this word order.

Other languages, in contrast, follow an S-O-V pattern:

  S   O   V
➤ **The child the ball threw.** [unacceptable in English]

These include Japanese, Korean, Turkish, and Farsi.

Still other languages, such as Hebrew and Arabic, follow a V-S-O pattern:

  V   S   O
➤ **Threw the child the ball.** [unacceptable in English]

Some variation is possible in the basic S-V-O order in English. There must however, be a special reason for moving a sentence constituent into an unusual position.

English requires that a subject appear in all but imperative sentences (unlike Spanish). It does not allow verb omission (unlike Arabic).

Language differences in word order at the level of the phrase may also cause problems for multilingual writers. For example, in English, auxiliary verbs normally precede main verbs and prepositions precede their objects.When constructing a sentence, also keep in mind that English does not allow double negation; the negative meaning is conveyed either by the form of the verb or by another word in the sentence. Thus, *I don't have no homework during vacation* needs to be corrected to either *I don't have any homework during vacation* or *I have no homework during vacation.*

(*For more on word order in English, see Chapter 65: English Sentence Structure, pp. 964–68.*)

BASIC SENTENCE PATTERNS

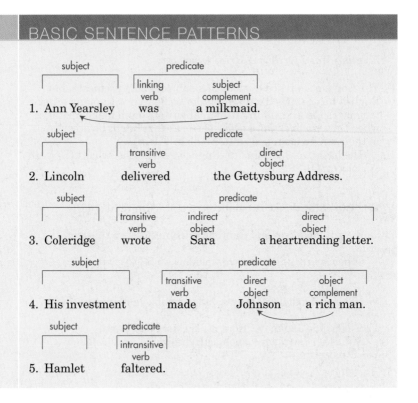

2. *Transitive verbs and direct objects*   A **transitive verb** identifies an action that the subject performs or does to somebody or something else—the receiver of the action, or **direct object.** To complete its meaning, a transitive verb needs a direct object in the predicate. Direct objects are usually nouns, pronouns, or word groups that act like nouns or pronouns.

	subject	predicate	
		trans verb	direct object
NOUN	Lincoln	delivered	*the address.*
PRONOUN	He	delivered	*it.*
WORD GROUP	He	said	*no more than was needed.*

Transitive verbs, unlike linking verbs or intransitive verbs, have two voices: active and passive. In a sentence with a transitive verb in the **active voice,** the subject is doing the action and the direct object is being acted upon.

	subj	trans verb	dir obj
ACTIVE	Parents sometimes consider their *children* unreasonable.		

When this sentence is rewritten in the **passive voice,** the direct object (*children*) becomes the subject, and the original subject (*parents*) becomes part of a phrase introduced with the preposition *by.*

PASSIVE   Children are sometimes considered unreasonable by their parents.

(*For more on voice in verbs, see Chapter 35: Problems with Verbs, pp. 613–32.*)

Exercise 31.2   Using active and passive voice

Rewrite each sentence, changing the verb from the passive to the active voice.

EXAMPLE

A new nation was brought forth on this continent by our fathers four score and seven years ago.

Four score and seven years ago our fathers brought forth on this continent a new nation.

1. The first national convention on women's rights was organized by Lucretia Mott and Elizabeth Cady Stanton.
2. The convention was held by them in 1848 at Seneca Falls, a town in upstate New York.
3. The Declaration of Sentiments, which included a demand that women be granted the right to vote, was issued by the convention.
4. The Declaration of Sentiments was modeled by the leaders who drafted it on the Declaration of Independence.

---

3. Transitive verbs, indirect objects, and direct objects   **Indirect objects** name to whom an action was done or for whom it was completed. They are most commonly used with verbs such as *give, ask, tell, send, sing,* and *write.*

subject		predicate	
	trans verb	ind obj	dir obj
Coleridge	wrote	*Sara*	a heartrending letter.
Maria	told	*the child*	a story.
The general	gave	*the army*	new orders.

Note that indirect objects appear after the verb but before the direct object.

For MULTILINGUAL STUDENTS

Word Order of Direct and Indirect Objects

In a typical English predicate both the direct and indirect objects follow the verb. Unless the indirect object (IO) is preceded by a preposition (such as *to, for, of*), the IO is placed before the direct object (DO):

          IO   DO
➤ **The student wrote his teacher a note.**

          IO   DO
➤ **The student wrote a note to his teacher.**

but not:

          IO   DO
➤ **The student wrote to his teacher a note.** [unacceptable in English]

Note, however, that in standard English, the indirect object cannot follow the verb if the direct object is a pronoun (a frequent source of errors among multilingual writers):

          IO DO
➤ **The student wrote his teacher it.** [unacceptable in English]

4. Transitive verbs, direct objects, and object complements In addition to a direct object and an indirect object, a transitive verb can take another element in its predicate: an **object complement.** An object complement describes or renames the direct object it follows.

subject	predicate		
	trans verb	dir obj	object complement
His investment	made	Johnson	*a rich man.*
The judge	declared	the plaintiff	*the winner.*
The decision	left	the company	*bankrupt.*

5. Intransitive verbs An **intransitive verb** describes an action by a subject, but it is not an action that is done directly to anything or anyone else. Therefore, an intransitive verb cannot take an object or a complement.

subject	predicate
	intrans verb
Hamlet	*faltered.*
The empire	*collapsed.*
The runners	*tired.*

However, adverbs and adverb phrases often appear in predicates built around intransitive verbs. In the sentence that follows, the complete predicate is in italics and the intransitive verb is underlined.

➤ Hamlet *faltered in his resolve to avenge his father's murder.*

Some verbs, such as *cooperate, assent, disappear,* and *insist,* are always intransitive. Others, such as *increase, grow, roll,* and *work,* can be either transitive or intransitive.

TRANSITIVE
trans verb
I *grow* carrots and celery in my victory garden.

INTRANSITIVE
intrans verb
My son *grows* taller every week.

LEARNING in COLLEGE

***Using the Dictionary to Select Prepositions,
and to Identify Transitive and Intransitive Verbs***

Your dictionary tells you whether a verb is *v.i.* (intransitive), *v.t.* (transitive), or both. It also tells you—or shows by example—the appropriate preposition to use when you are modifying an intransitive verb with an adverbial phrase. For example, we may *accede to* a rule, but if and when we *comply,* it has to be *with* something or someone.

For MULTILINGUAL STUDENTS

Including Only One Direct Object

In English, a sentence with a transitive verb must include an explicit direct object. For example, *Take it* is a complete sentence, but *Take!* is not, even if *it* is clearly implied. Be careful not to repeat the object, especially if the object includes a relative adverb (*where, when, how*) or a relative pronoun (*which, who, what*), even if the relative pronoun does not appear in the sentence but is only implied.

➤ Our dog guards the house *where* we live ~~there~~.

Exercise 31.3 Identifying objects and complements of verbs

Underline the verb in each sentence, and label it transitive (trans), intransitive (intrans), or linking (link). If the verb is transitive, circle and label the direct object (DO) and label any indirect object (IO) or object complement (OC). If the verb is linking, circle and label the subject complement (SC).

EXAMPLE

> trans   DO
> The ancient Mayas <u>deserve</u> a (place) in the history
>
> of mathematics.

1. Hybrid cars produce low tailpipe emissions.
2. Automakers promise consumers affordable gasoline-electric cars.
3. Hybrid cars are desirable alternatives to gasoline-powered vehicles.
4. Their two sources of power make hybrid cars fuel efficient.
5. Consumers agree that automakers should design and manufacture more hybrid models.

www.mhhe.com/
nmhh
For information and
exercises on phrases
and clauses, go to

Editing > Phrases
and Clauses

31d Phrases and clauses

A **phrase** is a group of related words that lacks a subject, a predicate, or both. Phrases function within sentences but not on their own. A **clause** is a group of related words that includes a subject and a predicate. Some clauses are independent; others are dependent, or subordinate. **Independent clauses** can stand on their own as complete sentences. **Dependent,** or **subordinate, clauses** cannot stand alone; they function in sentences as adjectives, adverbs, or nouns.

31e Noun phrases and verb phrases

A **noun phrase** consists of a noun or noun substitute plus all of its modifiers. Noun phrases can function as a sentence's subject, object, or subject complement.

SUBJECT	*The old, dark, ramshackle house* collapsed.
OBJECT	Greg cooked *an authentic, delicious haggis* for the Robert Burns dinner.
SUBJECT COMPLEMENT	Tom became *an accomplished and well-known cook.*

A **verb phrase** is a verb plus its helping verbs.

➤ Mary *should have photographed* me.

www.mhhe.com/
nmhh
For information and
exercises on verbs
and verbals, go to
Editing > Verbs
and Verbals

31f Verbals and verbal phrases

Verbals are words derived from verbs. They function as nouns, adjectives, or adverbs, not as verbs.

VERBAL AS NOUN	*Crawling* comes before walking.
VERBAL AS ADJECTIVE	Chris tripped over the *crawling* child.
VERBAL AS ADVERB	The child went *crawling* across the floor.

Verbals may take modifiers, objects, and complements to form **verbal phrases.** There are three kinds of verbal phrases:

- participial
- gerund
- infinitive

1. Participial phrases
A **participial phrase** begins with either a present participle (the *-ing* form of a verb) or a past participle (the *–ed* or *-en* form of a verb). Participial phrases always function as adjectives.

➤ *Working in groups,* **the children solved the problem.**

➤ *Insulted by his remark,* **Elizabeth refused to dance.**

➤ **His pitching arm,** *broken in two places by the fall,* **would never be the same again.**

2. Gerund phrases
A **gerund phrase** uses the *-ing* form of the verb, just as some participial phrases do. But gerund phrases always function as nouns, not adjectives.

subj
➤ *Walking one hour a day* **will keep you fit.**

dir obj
➤ **The instructor praised** *my acting in both scenes.*

3. Infinitive phrases
An **infinitive phrase** is formed using the infinitive, or *to* form, of a verb: *to be, to do, to live.* It can function as an adverb, an adjective, or a noun and can be the subject, subject or object complement, or direct object in a sentence. **559**

> noun/subj
> *To finish his novel* was his greatest ambition.

> adj/obj comp
> He made many efforts *to finish his novel* for his publisher.

> adv/dir obj
> He needed *to finish his novel.*

31g Appositive phrases

Appositives rename nouns or pronouns and appear right after the word they rename.

> noun   appositive
> One researcher, *the widely respected R. S. Smith,* has

> shown that a child's performance on such tests can be

> very consistent.

31h Absolute phrases

Absolute phrases modify an entire sentence. They include a noun or pronoun; a participle; and their related modifiers, objects, or complements.

> The sheriff strode into the bar, *his hands hovering over his pistols.*

> The actors took their bows, *their spirits lifted by the rousing applause.*

Exercise 31.4   Identifying phrases

For the underlined words in the sentences below, identify the kind of phrase each is and how it functions in the sentence.

> EXAMPLE   **Raking leaves is a seasonal chore for many American teenagers.** [*verbal phrase, gerund, functioning as the subject of the sentence*]

1. The earliest of the little-known ancient civilizations of the Andes emerged more than four thousand years ago.

2. The Chavin culture, the earliest Andean culture with widespread influence, dates to between 800 and 200 BCE.

3. The distinctive art style of the Chavin culture probably reflects a compelling and influential religious movement.

4. The Paracas and Nazca cultures appear to have been the regional successors to the Chavin culture on Peru's south coast.

5. The Moche culture, encompassing most of Peru's north coast, flourished from about CE 200 to 700.

6. The primary function of Moche warfare was probably to secure captives for sacrifice.

7. Interpreting the silent remnants of past cultures is the archeologist's challenge.

8. To see the magnificent objects buried with the Moche lord at Sipan is an awe-inspiring experience.

9. Hiram Bingham, an American archeologist, set out for Peru in 1911.

10. Bingham discovered the spectacular ruins of the Inca city of Machu Picchu, securing for himself an enduring place in the history of Andean archeology.

31i Dependent clauses

Although **dependent clauses** (also known as **subordinate clauses**) have a subject and a predicate, they cannot stand alone as complete sentences. They are introduced by subordinators—either by a subordinating conjunction such as *after, in order to, since* (*for a more complete listing, see the box on p. 546*), or by a relative pronoun such as *who, which,* or *that* (*for more, see the box on p. 538*). Dependent clauses function in sentences as adjectives, adverbs, or nouns.

1. Adjective clauses

An **adjective clause** (also called a **relative clause**) modifies a noun or pronoun. Relative pronouns (*who, whom, whose, which,* or *that*) or relative adverbs (*where, when*) are used to connect adjective clauses to the nouns or pronouns they modify. The relative pronoun usually follows the word that is being modified and also serves to point back to the noun or pronoun. (*For help with punctuating restrictive and nonrestrictive clauses, see Chapter 51: Commas, pp. 816–24.*)

➤ Odysseus's journey, *which can be traced on modern maps,*

has inspired many works of literature.

In adjective clauses, the direct object sometimes comes before rather than after the verb.

dir obj   subj   verb
➤ **The contestant *whom he most admired* was his father.**

2. Adverb clauses

An **adverb clause** modifies a verb, an adjective, or an adverb and answers the questions adverbs answer: *When? Where? What? Why?* and *How?* Adverb clauses are often introduced by subordinators (*after, when, before, because, although, if, though, whenever, where, wherever*).

➤ *After we had talked for an hour,* he began to get nervous.

➤ He reacted *as if he already knew.*

3. Noun clauses

A **noun clause** is a dependent clause that functions as a noun. Often the noun clause is so important that without it, the independent clause would be incomplete. A noun clause may serve as the subject, object, or complement of a sentence. It is usually introduced by a relative pronoun (*who, which, that*) or a relative adverb (*how, what, where, when, why*).

SUBJECT   *What he saw* shocked him.

OBJECT   The instructor found out *who had skipped class.*

COMPLEMENT   The book was *where I had left it.*

As in an adjective clause, in a noun clause the direct object or subject complement can come first, violating the typical sentence order.

dir obj subj   verb
➤ **The doctor wondered *whom he* should bill for the consultation.**

4. Elliptical clauses

In an **elliptical clause** one or more grammatically necessary words are omitted because their meaning and function are clear from the surrounding context.

➤ **This is the house [that] Jack built.**

➤ **After Antietam, Lincoln decided [that] it was time to issue the Emancipation Proclamation.**

➤ **Two are better than one [is].**

| **Exercise 31.5** | Identifying dependent clauses |

Underline any dependent clauses in the sentences below. Identify each one as an adjective, adverb, or noun clause.

EXAMPLE **Because they were among the first to develop the concept of zero, the ancient Mayas deserve a prominent place in the history of mathematics.**
[*adverb clause*]

1. During the 1970s and 1980s, Asian-American writers, who often drew upon their immigrant experiences, gained a wide readership.
2. Because these writers wrote about their struggles and the struggles of their ancestors, readers were able to learn about the Chinese Exclusion Act of 1892 and the internment of Japanese Americans during World War II.
3. Many readers know Amy Tan as the Chinese-American novelist who wrote *The Joy Luck Club,* which was adapted into a feature film, but are unfamiliar with most of her other novels, such as *The Kitchen God's Wife, The Hundred Secret Senses,* and *The Bonesetter's Daughter.*
4. During the 1990s, Asian-American novelists, poets, and playwrights wrote about how their experiences related to those of other immigrant groups.

31j Sentence structures

Sentences can be classified by the number of clauses they contain and how those clauses are joined. This method of classification results in four types of sentences:

- simple
- compound
- complex
- compound-complex

1. Simple sentences

A **simple sentence** is composed of only one independent clause. Simple does not necessarily mean short, however. Although a simple sentence does not include any dependent clauses, it may have several embedded phrases, a compound subject, and a compound predicate.

No matter how long it is, however, a sentence that has only one independent clause is, grammatically speaking, a simple sentence.

INDEPENDENT CLAUSE

The bloodhound is the oldest known breed of dog.

INDEPENDENT CLAUSE: COMPOUND SUBJ + COMPOUND PRED

Historians, novelists, short-story writers, and playwrights write about characters, design plots, and usually seek the dramatic resolution of a problem.

2. Compound sentences

A **compound sentence** contains two or more coordinated independent clauses but no dependent clause. The independent clauses may be joined by a comma and a coordinating conjunction or by a semicolon with or without a conjunctive adverb.

➤ **The police arrested him for drunk driving, *so* he lost his car.**

➤ **The sun blasted the earth; *therefore*, the plants withered and died.**

3. Complex sentences

A **complex sentence** contains one independent clause and one or more dependent clauses.

independent clause	dependent clause

➤ **He consulted the dictionary** *because he did not know how to pronounce the word.*

4. Compound-complex sentences

A **compound-complex sentence** contains two or more coordinated independent clauses and at least one dependent clause (italicized in the example).

➤ **She discovered a new world of international finance, but she worked so hard investing other people's money *that she had no time to invest any of her own.***

Exercise 31.6 Classifying sentences

Identify each sentence as simple, compound, complex, or compound-complex.

EXAMPLE   **Biotechnology promises great benefits for humanity, but it also raises many difficult ethical issues.** [*compound*]

1. Rock and roll originated in the 1950s.
2. Chuck Berry, Jerry Lee Lewis, and Elvis Presley were early rock-and-roll greats.
3. Teenagers loved the new music, but it disturbed many parents.
4. As much as the music itself, it was the sexually suggestive body language of the performers that worried the older generation.
5. The social turmoil that marked the 1960s influenced many performers, and some began to use their music as a vehicle for protest.

Exercise 31.7   Chapter review: Sentence basics

Circle the simple subjects and verbs in the following passage. Place one line under each independent clause and two lines under each dependent clause. (Recall that an independent clause can stand on its own as a complete sentence.)

Many argue that the blues and jazz are the first truly American musical forms. With its origins in slave narratives, the blues took root during the 1920s and 1930s as African-American composers, musicians, and singers performed in the cabarets and clubs of Harlem. Jazz, however, has its origins in New Orleans. Today, we can still appreciate the music of Bessie Smith, Duke Ellington, and B. B. King.

Rock and roll is also a distinctively American form of music. Our country's first "rock star" was without a doubt Elvis Presley, who emerged on the nation's airwaves in the mid-1950s with such hits as *Heartbreak Hotel, Don't Be Cruel,* and *All Shook Up.* A decade later, Americans were expressing themselves musically through rhythm and blues, pop, folk rock, and protest music. Today, thanks to recording technology, we have easy access to our country's rich musical history.

This detail from a first century CE wall painting in the ancient Roman city of Pompeii shows a woman writing on a wax covered tablet. Working on tablets like this, Roman writers could smooth over words and make corrections with ease.

There is a core simplicity to the English language and its American variant, but it's a slippery core.

—STEPHEN KING

Editing
for Grammar
Conventions

Answer these questions to test your familiarity with the topics covered in Chapters 32–37. For each example, select the choice that best replaces the highlighted words. If the example is correct as is, select "no change." Check your work against the answer sheet at the back of the book. As you read Chapters 32–37, pay particular attention to the sections that correspond to the questions you answer incorrectly.

1. There are several political parties in the **United States. Although most Americans** are familiar only with the two dominant parties, the Democratic and Republican.

   a. United States; although most Americans

   b. United States: although most Americans

   c. no change

   d. United States, although most Americans

2. Martin Luther King, Jr. delivered his famous "I have a dream" **speech. During the March on Washington** on August 28, 1963.

   a. speech, during the March on Washington

   b. no change

   c. speech during the March on Washington.

   d. during; the March on Washington.

3. U.S. military personnel are stationed on many atolls in the **Pacific. Such as Wake Island and Johnston Atoll.**

   a. no change

   b. Pacific, such as; Wake Island and Johnston Atoll.

   c. Pacific, such as Wake Island and Johnston Atoll.

   d. Pacific; such as Wake Island and Johnston Atoll.

4. Celebrities often undergo cosmetic dentistry to improve their **appearance. Hoping to straighten their teeth** and whiten their smiles.

   a. appearance, hoping to straighten their teeth

   b. appearance; hoping to straighten their teeth

   c. appearance: hoping to straighten their teeth

   d. no change

5. The Great Wall of China extends more than a thousand **miles, it was built during the reign** of Emperor Ch'in Shih Huang Ti.

   a. no change

   b. miles however it was built during the reign

   c. miles. It was built during the reign

   d. miles it was built during the reign

6. Dinosaurs and birds first appeared during the Mesozoic **Era. This era dates to more than 245 million years ago.**

   a. Era, this era dates to more than 245 million years ago.

   b. no change

   c. Era this era dates to more 245 million years ago.

   d. Era; and this dates to more over 245 million years ago.

7. Students who rely on credit cards risk ruining their **credit rating, however, they can build a strong credit rating** if they pay their balances on time.

   a. credit rating, however; they can build a strong credit rating

   b. credit rating however, they can build a strong credit rating

   c. no change

   d. credit rating; however, they can build a strong credit rating

8. People often confuse the words "principal" and **"principle" in addition they also confuse** "effect" and "affect."

   a. "principle," in addition, they also confuse

   b. "principle" in addition, they also confuse

   c. "principle." In addition, they also confuse

   d. no change

9. **The most popular color for luxury cars are metallic white.**

   a. no change

   b. The most popular colors for luxury cars are metallic white.

   c. The most popular colors for a luxury car is metallic white.

   d. The most popular color for luxury cars is metallic white.

10. The Pregnancy Discrimination Act of 1978 **is among the laws that protects women** from inequity in the workplace.

    a. is among the laws that protect women

    b. is among the law that protects women

    c. no change

    d. are among the laws that protect women

11. **Everyone are encouraged to eat leafy vegetables** such as spinach and collard greens, which are rich in vitamins A and C.

    a. Everyone is encouraged to eat leafy vegetables

    b. no change

    c. Everybody are encourage to eat leafy vegetables

12. An injured person **should remain laying down until emergency medical technicians arrive to administer** first aid.

    a. should remain laying down until emergency medical technicians arrive to have administered

    b. no change

    c. should remain lying down until emergency medical technicians arrive to have administered

    d. should remain lying down until emergency medical technicians arrive to administer

13. The narrator in the novel *The House on Mango Street* by Sandra Cisneros **was a young Latina girl living in poverty.**

    a. no change

    b. was a young Latina girl who lived in poverty.

    c. is a young Latina girl who was living in poverty.

    d. is a young Latina girl living in poverty.

14. Some people believe that many of the nation's domestic and foreign problems **could be solved if the U.S. President was allowed to serve** more than two terms in office.

    a. can be solved if the U.S. President was allowed to serve

    b. can be solved if the U.S. President were allowed to serve

    c. could be solved if the U.S. President were allowed to serve

    d. no change

15. Frederick Douglass, **whom wrote *The Narrative of the Life of Frederick Douglass, an American Slave,*** remains an inspiration to civil rights activists.

    a. no change

    b. whom he wrote *The Narrative of the Life of Frederick Douglass, an American Slave,*

    c. who wrote *The Narrative of the Life of Frederick Douglass, an American Slave,*

    d. who he wrote *The Narrative of the Life of Frederick Douglass, an American Slave,*

16. A person with a family history of cardiovascular disease **should monitor his blood pressure** on a regular basis.

    a. no change

    b. should monitor her blood pressure

    c. should monitor his or her blood pressure

    d. should monitor their blood pressure

17. According to the Federal Election Campaign Act, **you must disclose** election contributions and expenditures.

   a. no change

   b. I must disclose

   c. we must disclose

   d. candidates must disclose

18. Most educators and child psychologists agree **that young children sure watch too much television.**

   a. no change

   b. that surely young children watch too much television.

   c. that young children certainly watch too much television.

   d. that young children definite watch too much television.

19. A person suffering from food poisoning **will feel worser than a person** suffering from mere indigestion.

   a. no change

   b. will feel worse than a person

   c. will feel badder than a person

   d. will feel more bad than a person

20. Most college students **do not realize that they won't hardly be able to juggle** working and going to school full time.

   a. do not realize that they will not hardly be able to juggle

   b. do not realize that they will hardly be able to juggle

   c. do realize that they will not hardly be able to juggle

   d. no change

32 Sentence Fragments

A **sentence fragment** is an incomplete sentence treated as if it were complete. It may begin with a capital letter and end with a period, question mark, or exclamation point, but it lacks one or more of the following:

- a complete verb
- a subject
- an independent clause

Although writers sometimes use them intentionally (*see the box "Charting the Territory: Intentional Fragments" on p. 577*), fragments are rarely appropriate in college assignments.

www.mhhe.com/
nmhh
For more information on and practice avoiding sentence fragments, go to

Editing > Sentence Fragments

32a Learn how to identify sentence fragments.

You can identify fragments in your work by asking yourself three questions as you edit:

Three Questions for Identifying Fragments

1. Do you see a complete verb?
2. Do you see a subject?
3. Do you see *only* a dependent clause?

---

1. Do you see a complete verb?

A **complete verb** consists of a main verb and any helping verbs needed to indicate tense, person, and number (*see Chapter 35: Problems with Verbs, p. 622*). A group of related words without a complete verb is a phrase fragment, not a sentence.

FRAGMENT	The ancient Mayas were among the first to develop many mathematical concepts. *For example, the concept of zero.* [no verb]
SENTENCE	The ancient Mayas were among the first to develop many mathematical concepts. *For example, they developed the concept of zero.*

Caution: **Don't be fooled by verbals.** **Verbals** are words derived from verbs that function as nouns, adjectives, or adverbs, but not as verbs. The present participle or *-ing* form of a verb (as in *working*), the past participle or *-ed* form (as in *worked*), or the infinitive or *to* form (as in *to work*) may all function as verbals (*see Chapter 31: Sentence Basics, pp. 559–60.*)

FRAGMENT	Pool hustlers deceive their opponents in many ways. *For example, deliberately putting so much spin on the ball that it jumps out of the intended pocket.* [*Putting* is a verbal, not a verb.]
SENTENCE	Pool hustlers deceive their opponents in many ways. *For example, they will deliberately put so much spin on the ball that it jumps out of the intended pocket.*

2. Do you see a subject?

A subject is the *who* or *what* that a sentence is about (*see Chapter 31: Sentence Basics, pp. 550–57*). A group of related words without a subject or a complete verb is a phrase fragment, not a sentence.

FRAGMENT	The ancient Mayas were accomplished mathematicians. *Developed the concept of zero, for example.* [no subject]
SENTENCE	The ancient Mayas were accomplished mathematicians. *They developed the concept of zero, for example.*

3. Do you see *only* a dependent clause?

An independent clause has a subject and a complete verb and can stand on its own as a sentence. A **dependent,** or subordinate, **clause** also has a subject and a complete verb, but it begins with a subordinating word such as *although, because, since, that, unless, which,* or *while.* Dependent clauses function within sentences as modifiers or nouns, but they cannot stand as sentences on their own (*see Chapter 31: Sentence Basics, pp. 561–62*).

FRAGMENT	The ancient Mayas deserve a place in the history of mathematics. *Because they were among the earliest people to develop the concept of zero.*
SENTENCE	The ancient Mayas deserve a place in the history of mathematics *because they were among the earliest people to develop the concept of zero.*

573

IDENTIFY AND EDIT
Fragments

frag

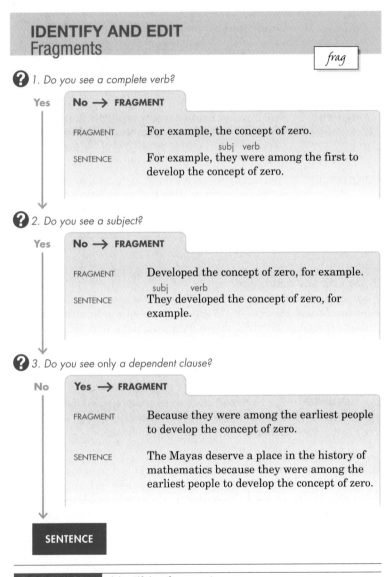

❓ 1. Do you see a complete verb?

Yes   **No → FRAGMENT**

FRAGMENT   For example, the concept of zero.

                    subj   verb
SENTENCE   For example, they were among the first to develop the concept of zero.

❓ 2. Do you see a subject?

Yes   **No → FRAGMENT**

FRAGMENT   Developed the concept of zero, for example.

              subj   verb
SENTENCE   They developed the concept of zero, for example.

❓ 3. Do you see only a dependent clause?

No   **Yes → FRAGMENT**

FRAGMENT   Because they were among the earliest people to develop the concept of zero.

SENTENCE   The Mayas deserve a place in the history of mathematics because they were among the earliest people to develop the concept of zero.

SENTENCE

Exercise 32.1   Identifying fragments

Underline the fragments in the following passage, and identify each as either a phrase (without a subject or verb) or a dependent clause.

     EXAMPLE   **I am headed to the library tonight.**

                          dependent clause

          Because I have a paper due.

Pool hustlers deceive their opponents in many ways. Sometimes appearing unfamiliar with the rules of the game. They may try acting as if they are drunk. Or pretend to be inept. For example, they will put so much spin on the ball that it jumps out of the intended pocket. So their opponents will be tricked into betting. Some other ways to cheat. When their opponents are not looking, pool hustlers may remove their own balls from the table. Then change the position of the balls on the table. Because today's pool balls have metallic cores. Hustlers can use electromagnets to affect the path of the balls. Be aware of these tricks!

Fragments and Grammar Checkers

Grammar checkers identify some fragments, but they will not tell you what a fragment is missing or how to edit it. Grammar checkers can also miss fragments without subjects that could be interpreted as commands. In commands, the subject—*you*—is implied. A grammar checker might, for example, fail to tag this fragment—*Develop the concept of zero, for example*—because it has the form of a command (*see Chapter 31, Sentence Basics, pp. 550–51*).

32b Edit sentence fragments.

You can repair sentence fragments by editing them in one of two ways:

1. Transform them into sentences.

➤ **Pool hustlers deceive their opponents in many ways.**

         they
For example,˄ deliberately putting ~~put~~ so much spin on

the ball that it jumps out of the intended pocket.

➤ **Many people feel threatened by globalization. ~~Because~~**

  They
~~they~~ think it will undermine their cultural traditions.
˄

2. Attach them to a nearby independent clause.

➤ **Pool hustlers deceive their opponents in many ways,̷ For**

for example, by

~~example,~~ **deliberately putting so much spin on the ball**

that it jumps out of the intended pocket.

because

➤ **Many people feel threatened by globalization,̷ ~~Because~~**

they think it will undermine their cultural traditions.

Two Ways to Correct Sentence Fragments

1. Transform them into sentences.
2. Attach them to a nearby independent clause.

The approach to take in any particular case is a stylistic decision. Sometimes one approach may produce better results than the other, and in other instances the results may seem equally effective.

You may, for example, choose to rewrite a fragment as a sentence for emphasis.

➤ **The ambulance crew gave us tips on handling**

They stressed

emergencies. ~~Stressing~~ the importance of staying calm.

Rewriting long fragments as separate sentences can help keep your writing direct and concise.

➤ **Students with good time management habits start**

Others

studying right away in the evening. ~~Whereas others,~~ the

procrastinators, may go running first, or make phone calls,

or clean their rooms, or surf the Internet, or watch

television—anything to avoid getting to work.

Attaching a fragment to a related sentence, on the other hand, can highlight the relationship between ideas.

even

➤ **The Mayas built great cities,̷ ~~Even~~ though they lacked**

   metal tools.

CHARTING the TERRITORY

Intentional Fragments

Advertisers often use attention-getting fragments: "Hot deal. Big savings. Best wireless." "Nothing but net." "Because you're worth it." In everyday life we often speak in fragments, like this, for example:

"What time did you get home?"
"In time to watch the evening news."

As a result, people who write fiction and drama use fragments to create realistic dialogue. Writers also sometimes use fragments deliberately in other contexts for stylistic effect. You, too, may occasionally want to use a sentence fragment for stylistic reasons. Keep in mind, however, that advertising, literary writing, and college writing have different contexts and purposes. In formal writing, use intentional sentence fragments sparingly if at all.

32c Connect a phrase fragment to another sentence, or add the missing elements.

1. Watching for verbals

Phrase fragments frequently begin with verbals. Here is an example of a phrase fragment that begins with an *-ing* verbal.

FRAGMENT   That summer, we had the time of our lives. *Fishing in the early morning hours, splashing in the lake after lunch, exploring the woods before dinner, and playing Scrabble until it was time for bed.*

One way to fix this fragment is to transform it into an independent clause with its own subject and verb:

➤ **That summer, we had the time of our lives. ~~Fishing~~ in the** *We fished*

early morning hours, ~~splashing~~ in the lake after lunch, *splashed*

~~exploring~~ the woods before dinner, and ~~playing~~ Scrabble *explored* *played*

until it was time for bed.

Notice that all of the *-ing* verbals in the fragment need to be changed to keep the phrases in the new sentence parallel. (*For more on parallelism, see Chapter 42: Faulty Parallelism, pp. 710–19.*)

Another way to fix the problem is to attach the fragment to the part of the previous sentence that it modifies (in this case, *the time of our lives*):

➤ **That summer, we had the time of our lives.~~,~~** *fishing* **~~Fishing~~ in the**
  early morning hours, splashing in the lake after lunch,
  exploring the woods before dinner, and playing Scrabble
  until it was time for bed.

For MULTILINGUAL STUDENTS

Avoiding Fragments

A fragment is a group of words punctuated as a sentence but missing some components of a sentence. Fragments are almost never acceptable in formal writing in standard American English. Many languages other than English, however, permit constructions that, translated literally into English, would be fragments. Multilingual students need to be aware of these potential pitfalls.

Missing verb: Some languages—Russian and Chinese, for example—permit omission of the auxiliary or linking verb *be*. Transferred directly into English, this pattern can result in fragments like *He very happy with the news,* instead of the correct *He is very happy with the news.*

Missing subject: Spanish and Portuguese permit the dropping of a subject when it is a pronoun that is otherwise indicated by a verb ending. Transferred into English, this pattern can result in fragments like *Always takes pleasure in reading,* instead of the correct *He (or she) always takes pleasure in reading.*

Subordinate clause used on its own: Some languages permit a dependent clause to stand alone when it follows a main clause. Transfer of the Japanese *because* clause, for example, can result in fragments like *Because he had problems with sentence structure.* To be correct in English, a subordinate clause must be attached to an independent clause, as in *He had to work with a tutor because he had problems with sentence structure.*

2. Watching for prepositional fragments

Phrase fragments can also begin with one-word prepositions such as *as, at, by, for, from, in, of, on,* or *to.* To correct these types of fragments, it is usually easiest to attach them to a nearby sentence.

➤ **Impressionist painters often depicted their subjects in**

                           at
   everyday situations./ At a restaurant, perhaps, or by

   the seashore.

3. Watching for transitional phrases

Some fragments start with two- or three-word prepositions that function as transitions. Such transitional phrases include *as well as, as compared with, except for, in addition to, in contrast with, in spite of,* and *instead of.*

➤ **For the past sixty-five years, the growth in consumer**

                                  as
   spending has been both steep and steady./ As compared

   with the growth in gross domestic product (GDP), which

   fluctuated significantly between 1929 and 1950.

4. Watching for words and phrases that introduce examples

Check word groups beginning with expressions that introduce examples—such as *for example, like, specifically,* or *such as*—to make sure they are complete sentences. If they are fragments, edit to make them into sentences or attach them to an independent clause.

➤ **Elizabeth I of England faced many dangers as a princess.**

                she fell
   For example, ~~falling~~ out of favor with her sister, Queen Mary,

       was
   and ~~being~~ imprisoned in the Tower of London.

                                 such
➤ **The experiment did not account for other variables./ Such as**

   light, water, and air temperature.

5. Watching for appositives

An **appositive** is a noun or noun phrase that renames a noun or pronoun.

➤ **In 1965, Lyndon Johnson increased the number of troops**

                         a

   in Vietnam⁄, A̶ former French colony in Southeast Asia.

6. Watching for fragments that consist of lists

Usually, you can connect a list to the preceding sentence using a colon. If you want to emphasize the list, consider using a dash instead.

➤ **In the 1930s, three great band leaders helped popularize**

   jazz⁄: Louis Armstrong, Benny Goodman, and Duke

   Ellington.

7. Watching for fragments that are parts of compound predicates

A **compound predicate** is made up of at least two verbs as well as their objects and modifiers, connected by a coordinating conjunction such as *and, but,* or *or.* The parts of a compound predicate have the same subject and should be together in one sentence.

➤ **The group gathered at dawn at the base of the mountain⁄**

      and

   A̶n̶d̶ assembled their gear in preparation for the morning's

   climb.

Exercise 32.2 Editing to repair phrase fragments

Repair the phrase fragments in the items that follow by attaching them to a sentence or adding words to turn them into sentences.

EXAMPLE

                           such

Film music can create a mood⁄ S̶u̶c̶h̶ as romantic,

lighthearted, or mysterious.

1. The ominous music prepares us for a shocking scene. And confuses us when the shock does not come.
2. Filmmakers may try to evoke nostalgic feelings. By choosing songs from a particular era.
3. The musical producer used a mix of traditional songs and new compositions. In the Civil War drama *Cold Mountain*.
4. Usually filmmakers edit the images first and add music later. To be sure that the music supports the visual elements.
5. Music can provide transitions between scenes. Marking the passage of time, signaling a change of place, or foreshadowing a shift in mood.
6. Exactly matching the rhythms of the music to the movement on screen is known as "Mickey Mousing." After the animated classic.
7. To create atmosphere, filmmakers sometimes use sounds from nature. Such as crashing waves, bird calls, and moaning winds.
8. Do not underestimate the effect of a short "dead track," the complete absence of sound. Forcing us to look intently at the image.

32d Connect a dependent-clause fragment to another sentence, or make it into a sentence by eliminating or changing the subordinating word.

Dependent-clause fragments begin with a subordinating word. Subordinating words include subordinating conjunctions such as *because, although, since,* or *while* (*see Chapter 30: Parts of Speech, p. 546*) and relative pronouns such as *who* or *which* (*see Chapter 30, p. 538*). A fragment that begins with a subordinating word can usually be attached to a nearby independent clause.

➤ On the questionnaire, none of the thirty-three subjects

indicated concern about the amount or kind of fruit the

institution served/, ~~Even~~ *even* though all identified diet as an

important issue for those with diabetes.

➤ Hubble discovered that the universe is expanding/, ~~Which~~ *which*

means it must have originated in what astronomers call the

Big Bang.

> *Punctuation tip:* A comma usually follows a dependent clause that begins a sentence.

As the next example shows, however, it is sometimes better to transform such a fragment into a complete sentence by deleting the subordinating word.

➤ **The solidarity of our group was undermined in two ways.**
   Participants
   ~~When participants~~ either disagreed about priorities or
   ^

   advocated significantly different political strategies.

For MULTILINGUAL STUDENTS

Adding a Subject Pronoun to a Dependent Clause

In English, a dependent clause needs a subject, even if it repeats the subject of the main clause. *The tire lost air because was punctured* should be changed to *The tire lost air because it was punctured.* In a dependent clause that begins with a relative pronoun, however, the pronoun is the subject. For example, *that* is the subject of the dependent clause in this sentence: *We replaced the tire that was punctured.*

Exercise 32.3   Editing to repair dependent-clause fragments

Correct the dependent-clause fragments in the following items by attaching them to a sentence or by eliminating or replacing the subordinating word.

EXAMPLE

The most commonly traded stone in Mesopotamia was
       which
obsidian./, ~~Which~~ is black, volcanic, and glasslike.
    ^   ^

1. Ancient people traded salt. Which is an important nutrient.
2. Some groups resorted to war and conquest. Because they
   wanted to gain control over valuable goods and resources.

3. When they could, people transported large stones by river. Since doing so required less effort than other means of moving them.
4. Obsidian is hard and makes a sharp edge. Even though it is brittle.
5. After a while, a type of currency developed. When traders began exchanging silver bars or rings.
6. The earliest writing appeared in Mesopotamia. After people there began living in cities.
7. Agriculture thrived in Egypt. Because the Nile flooded regularly.
8. Although the Egyptians had abundant crops and large supplies of limestone. They imported many goods.
9. Egypt added gold objects to its lengthy list of exports. After its artisans began to work the precious metal in about 4000 BCE.
10. Egypt's first king was Menes. Who united the country by conquest in about 3150 BCE.

Exercise 32.4   Chapter review: Sentence fragments

Return to Exercise 32.1 (*pp. 574–75*), and edit the passage to repair sentence fragments using what you have learned in this chapter.

Exercise 32.5   Chapter review: Sentence fragments

Edit the following passage to repair fragments.

According to the United States Constitution, which was ratified in 1788, the president and vice president of the United States were not to be elected directly by the people in a popular election. But elected indirectly by an "electoral college," made up of "electors." Who were at first often chosen by the state legislatures. In the early nineteenth century, the population of the United States grew rapidly and electors were increasingly chosen by statewide popular vote. Gradually making the electoral college system more democratic. Nonetheless, in the elections of 1824, 1876, 1888, and 2000, the elected candidate won the vote in the electoral college. But not a majority of the popular vote.

33 Comma Splices and Run-on Sentences

Comma splices and run-on sentences are sentences with improperly joined independent clauses. An **independent clause** is a clause that can stand on its own as a sentence (*see Chapter 31: Sentence Basics, p. 558*). Comma splices and run-ons confuse readers, leaving them unsure how one clause relates to the other or where one ends and the next begins.

www.mhhe.com/
nmhh
For information
and exercises on
comma splices, go to

Editing >
Comma Splices

33a Learn how to identify comma splices and run-on sentences.

A **comma splice** is a sentence containing two independent clauses joined only by a comma.

                                      independent clause

COMMA SPLICE   **Dogs that compete in the annual Westminster Dog Show are already champions, they have**

                              independent clause

each won at least one show before arriving at

Madison Square Garden.

www.mhhe.com/
nmhh
For information
and exercises on
run-on sentences,
go to

Editing > Fused
Sentences

A **run-on sentence,** sometimes called a **fused sentence,** does not even have a comma between the independent clauses.

                            independent clause

RUN-ON   **From time to time, new breeds enter the ring the**

                            independent clause

Border collie is a recent addition to the show.

1. Recognizing situations in which comma splices and run-ons often occur

Writers may mistakenly join independent clauses in a comma splice or a run-on sentence in three situations:

> **Situations in Which Writers May Mistakenly Join Two Independent Clauses in a Comma Splice or Run-on**
>
> 1. When a transitional expression or conjunctive adverb links the second clause to the first
> 2. When the second clause specifies or explains the first
> 3. When the second clause begins with a pronoun

1. Comma splices and run-ons often occur when clauses are linked with a transitional expression or a conjunctive adverb. Transitional expressions are phrases such as *as a result, for example, in addition, in other words,* and *on the contrary.* **Conjunctive adverbs** are words such as *however, consequently, moreover,* and *nevertheless. (See p. 592 for a list of familiar conjunctive adverbs and transitional expressions.)*

independent clause

COMMA SPLICE **Rare books can be extremely valuable, for**

independent clause

example, an original edition of Audubon's *Birds*

of *America* is worth thousands of dollars.

For example is a transitional expression.

independent clause

RUN-ON **Most students complied with the new policy**

independent clause

however a few refused to do so.

However is a conjunctive adverb.

(For help punctuating a sentence in which a transitional expression or conjunctive adverb links the clauses, see Chapter 52: Semicolons, p. 838.)

2. Comma splices and run-ons may also occur when the second clause of a sentence either specifies or explains the first clause.

independent clause

RUN-ON **The economy changed in 1991 corporate**

independent clause

bankruptcies increased by 40 percent.

585

3. Comma splices and run-ons may also occur when one independent clause is followed by another that begins with a pronoun.

independent clause

COMMA SPLICE **President Garfield was assassinated, he served**

independent clause

only six months in office.

2. Finding comma splices and run-ons

To find comma splices and run-ons, begin by checking those sentences that include transitional expressions or conjunctive adverbs. If a comma precedes one of these words or phrases, you may have found a comma splice. If no punctuation precedes one of them, you may have found a run-on sentence. Check the word groups that precede and follow the conjunctive adverb or transitional expression. Can they both stand alone as sentences? If so, you have found a comma splice or a run-on sentence.

A second method for locating comma splices is to check sentences that contain commas. Can the word groups that appear on both sides of the comma stand alone as sentences? If so, you have found a comma splice. Similarly, if you see two word groups that can stand alone as sentences with *no* punctuation between them, you have found a run-on.

Comma Splices, Run-on Sentences, and Grammar Checkers

Computer grammar checkers are unreliable at distinguishing properly from improperly joined independent clauses. One grammar checker, for example, correctly flagged this sentence for incorrect comma usage:

Many history textbooks are clear, some are hard to follow.

It failed, however, to flag this longer alternative:

Many history textbooks are clear and easy to read, some are dense and hard to follow.

It also failed to flag this run-on:

The best history books are clear they are also compelling.

IDENTIFY AND EDIT
Comma Splices and Run-ons

| *c s* | *run-on* |

These questions can help you spot comma splices and run-on sentences:

? *1. Does the sentence contain only one independent clause?*

No   **Yes → Not a run-on or comma splice**
↓

? *2. Does it contain two independent clauses joined by a comma and a coordinating conjunction such as and, but, or, not, for, so, or yet?*

No   **Yes → Not a run-on or comma splice**
↓

? *3. Does it contain two independent clauses joined by a semicolon or a semicolon and a transitional expression?*

No   **Yes → Not a run-on or comma splice**
↓

	├———————— independent clause ————————┤
RUN-ON	Football and most other team sports have a time limit
	├—— independent clause ——┤
	baseball has no time limit.
COMMA SPLICE	Football and most other team sports have a time limit, baseball has no time limit.
REVISED: COMMA AND COORDINATING CONJUNCTION	Football and most other team sports have a time limit, but baseball has no time limit. [See 33c.]
REVISED: SEMICOLON	Football and most other team sports have a time limit; baseball has no time limit. [See 33d.]
REVISED: TWO SENTENCES	Football and most other team sports have a time limit. Baseball has no time limit. [See 33e.]
REVISED: SUBORDINATION	Although football and most other team sports have a time limit, baseball has no time limit. [See 33f.]
REVISED: ONE INDEPENDENT CLAUSE	Baseball, unlike football and most other team sports, has no time limit. [See 33g.]

Exercise 33.1 Identifying comma splices and run-on sentences

Bracket the comma splices and run-on sentences in the following passage. For each error, note if it is a comma splice (CS) or a run-on sentence (RO).

> EXAMPLE *[The Gutenberg Bible is one of the first printed
> *CS*
> books, copies are extremely rare.]*

Rare books can be extremely valuable. Most books have to be in good shape to fetch high prices nevertheless some remain valuable no matter what. A first edition of Audubon's *Birds of America* can be worth more than a million dollars however it must be in good condition. On the other hand, even without a cover, an early edition of Cotton Mather's *An Ecclesiastical History of New England* will be worth at least three thousand dollars. Generally speaking, the newer a book is the more important its condition, even a book from the 1940s will have to be in excellent condition to be worth three figures. There are other factors that determine a book's value, certainly whether the author has signed it is important. Even students can collect books for instance they can search for bargains and great "finds" at yard and garage sales. In addition, used-book and author sites on the Internet offer opportunities for beginning collectors.

33b Edit comma splices and run-on sentences in one of five ways.

Comma splices and run-ons can be edited in five ways:

Five Ways to Edit Comma Splices and Run-on Sentences

1. Join the clauses with a comma and a coordinating conjunction.
2. Join the clauses with a semicolon.
3. Separate the clauses into two sentences.
4. Turn one of the independent clauses into a dependent clause.
5. Transform the clauses into a single independent clause.

Base your choice on both sense and style. That is, join (or separate) clauses in a way that reflects their meaning and their relationship to one another. Also think about the length and rhythm of the surrounding sentences. Breaking a comma splice into two sentences, for example, may help you avoid an overly long sentence. Transforming two independent clauses into one may make your sentence more concise.

1. Join the clauses with a comma and a coordinating conjunction (*and, but, or, nor, for, so, yet*).

> **Many history textbooks are dense and hard to follow,**
> *but*
> **the good ones are clear and easy to read.**
> ^

2. Join the clauses with a semicolon.

> **From time to time, new breeds enter the ring; the**
> ^
>
> **Border collie is a recent addition to the show.**

You can also add an appropriate conjunctive adverb or transitional expression, followed by a comma.

>   *; for instance,*
> **From time to time, new breeds enter the ring the**
> ^
>
> **Border collie is a recent addition to the show.**

3. Separate the clauses into two sentences.

>   *. Therefore,*
> **Salt air corrodes metal easily ~~therefore~~ automobiles**
> ^
>
> **in coastal regions require frequent washing.**

4. Turn one of the independent clauses into a dependent clause.

> **Treasure hunters shopping at garage sales should be**
>   *because*
> **realistic, valuable finds are extremely rare.**
>   ^

5. Transform the two clauses into a single independent clause.

>   *and*
> **The best history books are clear, ~~they also~~ tell a**
>   ^
>
> **compelling story.**

589

LEARNING in COLLEGE

When (If Ever) Is a Comma Splice Not a Comma Splice?

Many writers believe that it is acceptable, and stylistically effective, to combine short independent clauses with a comma. They make this choice especially, but not exclusively, when one of the clauses is negative, and the other, positive.

> *That's not a book, it's a doorstop.*

> *Don't worry, be happy.*

> *Float like a butterfly, sting like a bee.*

Many readers, however, including many college professors, accept no exceptions. To them, these are comma splices and should be revised accordingly. As a result, in college writing, it is best to replace the comma in sentences like these with a semicolon.

33c Join the two clauses with a comma and a coordinating conjunction such as *and, but, or, nor, for, so,* or *yet.*

If you decide to correct a comma splice or a run-on by joining the two clauses, be sure to choose the coordinating conjunction that most clearly expresses the logical relationship between the clauses. In the following example, the logical coordinating conjunction is *so.*

> ➤ John is a very stubborn person, ^*so* I had a hard time convincing
>
> him to let me take the wheel.

33d Join the two clauses with a semicolon.

Like a coordinating conjunction, a semicolon tells your reader that two clauses are logically connected. However, a semicolon alone does not spell out the logic of the connection.

> ➤ Most students complied with the new policy./; a few refused
>
> to do so.

To make the logic of the connection clear, you can add an appropriate conjunctive adverb or transitional expression.

➤ **Most students complied with the new policy,/ a few refused**
; however,

to do so.

> ***Punctuation tip:*** A conjunctive adverb or transitional expression is usually followed by a comma when it appears at the beginning of the second clause of a sentence. It can also appear in the middle of a clause, set off by two commas, or at the end, preceded by a comma.
>
> ➤ **Most students complied with the new policy,/ a few**
> _; however,_
>
> **refused to do so.**
>
> ➤ **Most students complied with the new policy,/; a few**
> _, however,_
>
> **refused to do so.**
>
> ➤ **Most students complied with the new policy,/; a few**
>
> **refused to do so./**
> _, however._
>
> Often the first independent clause introduces the second one. In this situation, you can add a colon instead of a semicolon. A colon is also appropriate if the second clause expands on the first one in some way. (*See Chapter 53: Colons, p. 845.*)
>
> ➤ **Professor Johnson then revealed his most important**
>
> **point: the paper would count for half of my grade.**

Exercise 33.2   Editing to repair comma splices and run-on sentences

Some of the sentences below contain comma splices, and some are run-ons. Circle the number of each sentence that is correct. Edit those that are not correct using either (1) a semicolon and, if appropriate, a conjunctive adverb or transitional expression or (2) a comma with a coordinating conjunction.

FAMILIAR CONJUNCTIVE ADVERBS and TRANSITIONAL EXPRESSIONS

also	in the meantime	nonetheless
as a result	in fact	now
besides	in other words	of course
certainly	incidentally	on the contrary
consequently	indeed	otherwise
finally	instead	similarly
for example	likewise	still
for instance	meanwhile	then
furthermore	moreover	therefore
however	nevertheless	thus
in addition	next	undoubtedly

EXAMPLE **Slavery has always been an oppressive**

but

institution, its severity has varied from society

to society throughout history.

1. The earliest large societies probably did not depend on slave labor, but that does not mean the people in them were free to work where and how they pleased.
2. All early civilizations were autocratic in a sense all people in them were slaves.
3. No one knows when slavery began, it was common in many ancient agricultural civilizations.
4. The ancient Egyptians enslaved thousands of people from Nubia and other parts of Africa, some of these people were then sent to Mesopotamia.
5. Egypt's kings also used slaves to build some of the country's most famous monuments, for example, the pyramids were almost entirely the work of slaves.
6. Some stones in the Great Pyramid at Giza weigh nearly one hundred tons they could never have been set in place without the effort of thousands of workers.
7. In ancient Mesopotamia slavery was not necessarily a lifelong condition, in fact slaves could sometimes work their way to freedom.
8. In both Egypt and Mesopotamia, slaves could sometimes own property.

33e Separate the clauses into two sentences.

The simplest way to correct comma splices and run-on sentences is to turn the clauses into separate sentences. The simplest solution is not always the best solution, however, especially if the result is one short, simple sentence followed by another. The simplest solution works well in this example because the second sentence is a compound sentence.

➤ **I realized that it was time to choose,/ either I had to learn**
. Either

how to drive, or I had to move back to the city.

When the two independent clauses are part of a quoted passage, with a phrase such as *he said* or *she noted* between them, each clause should be a separate sentence.

➤ **"Physical force is wrongly considered to be used to protect**

the weak," Gandhi said,/ "it makes them dependent upon
It

their so-called defenders or protectors."

33f Turn one of the independent clauses into a dependent clause.

Turning one of the clauses in a comma splice or a run-on sentence into a dependent clause can clarify the relationship between the clauses by indicating which carries the main point and which conveys a subordinate idea. In editing the following sentence, for example, the writer chose to make the clause about *a few* her main point and the clause about *most students* a subordinate idea. Because she made this choice, readers will expect subsequent sentences to tell them more about those few students who refused to comply.

➤ **Most students complied with the new policy, however a few**
Although most

refused to do so.

33g Transform the two clauses into one independent clause.

It is sometimes possible to transform the two clauses into one clear and correct independent clause, particularly when both clauses have the same subject. This kind of transformation, although often challenging, **593** can reward you with a clearer, more concise sentence than the other solutions might produce.

➤ **I realized that it was time ~~to choose,~~ either ~~I had~~ to learn to drive or ~~I had~~ to move back to the city.**

Often you can change one of the clauses to a phrase and place it next to the word it modifies.

➤ **Baseball cards** *, first printed in the nineteenth century,* **are an obsession among some collectors/. ~~the cards were first printed in the nineteenth century.~~**

Exercise 33.3 | Editing to repair comma splices and run-on sentences

Some of the sentences below contain comma splices, and some are run-ons. Circle the number of each sentence that is correct. Edit those that are not correct by (1) separating the clauses into two sentences, (2) changing one clause into a dependent clause introduced by a subordinating word, or (3) combining the clauses into one independent clause.

> **EXAMPLE** **The human population of the world, ~~was~~ no more than about 10 million at the beginning of the agricultural revolution 10,000 years ago, ~~it~~ had increased to about 800 million by the beginning of the industrial revolution in the eighteenth century.**

1. Globally, population has increased steadily particular regions have suffered sometimes drastic declines.
2. For example, Europe lost about one-third of its population when the bubonic plague struck for the first time in the fourteenth century.
3. The plague was not the only catastrophe to strike Europe in the fourteenth century, a devastating famine also slowed population growth at the beginning of the century.
4. Images of death and destruction pervade the art of the time these images reflect the demoralizing effect of the plague.
5. The native population of Mexico collapsed in the wake of European conquest and colonization in the sixteenth century, it

FIGURE 33.1 The plague in art. This painting from a fifteenth-century manuscript shows the plague, in the form of an army of death, advancing on a city.

dropped from perhaps as many as 25 million in 1500 to little more than 1 million by 1600.

6. Hernando Cortés used diplomacy and superior military technology—horses and cannons—to conquer the Aztecs, whose forces vastly outnumbered his.

7. These were not the only reasons for Spanish success, however, at least as important was the impact of a smallpox epidemic on Aztec population and morale.

8. The population decline had many causes, these included the conquerors' efforts to destroy native culture and exploit native labor as well as the devastating effect of disease.

595

Exercise 33.4 Chapter review: Comma splices and run-ons

Turn back to Exercise 33.1 (*p. 588*). Edit the paragraph to eliminate comma splices and run-ons using the methods described in this chapter.

Exercise 33.5 Chapter review: Comma splices and run-ons

Edit the passage that follows to eliminate comma splices and run-on sentences.

The economy of the United States has always been turbulent. Many people think that the Great Depression of the 1930s was the only economic cataclysm this country has suffered the United States has had a long history of financial panics and upheavals. The early years of the nation were no exception.

Before the revolution, the American economy was closely linked with Britain's, during the war and for many years after it Britain barred the import of American goods. Americans, however, continued to import British goods with the loss of British markets the new country's trade deficit ballooned. Eventually this deficit triggered a severe depression social unrest followed. The economy began to recover at the end of the 1780s with the establishment of a stable government, the opening of new markets to American shipping, and the adoption of new forms of industry. Exports grew steadily throughout the 1790s, indeed the United States soon found itself in direct competition with both England and France.

The American economy suffered a new setback beginning in 1803 England declared war on France. France and England each threatened to impound any American ships engaged in trade with the other. President Thomas Jefferson sought to change the policies of France and England with the Embargo Act of 1807, it prohibited all trade between the United States and the warring countries. Jefferson hoped to bring France and England to the negotiating table, the ploy failed. The economies of France and England suffered little from the loss of trade with the United States, meanwhile the United States' shipping industry came almost to a halt.

34 Subject-Verb Agreement

The relationship between the subject of a sentence (or clause) and the form of its corresponding verb is termed **subject-verb agreement.** In English, subjects vary in two ways: number and person.

- **Number** refers to whether a subject is singular (only one) or plural (more than one).
- **Person** refers to the identity of the subject:

Identity of Subject

First person	The speaker or writer of the sentence	The pronouns *I* (singular) and *we* (plural)
Second person	The person or people the sentence addresses	The pronoun *you* (singular and plural)
Third person	The people or things the sentence is about	Can include all nouns and noun phrases as well as the pronouns *he, she,* and *it* (singular) and *they* (plural)

Verbs have different forms depending on the number and person of the subject. The subject and verb agree when the form of the verb corresponds with the subject in number and person.

➤ A *bear lives* in the woods near my home.

> *Bear* is a third-person singular noun, and *lives* is the third-person singular form of the verb.

➤ **Many North American *mammals hibernate* in the winter.**

> *Mammals* is a third-person plural noun, and *hibernate* is the third-person plural form of the verb.

597

➤ *We hold* **these truths to be self-evident.**

We is the subject form (or subjective case, *see p. 638*) of the first-person plural personal pronoun, and *hold* is the first-person plural form of the verb.

➤ *You study* **harder than your roommate.**

You is the subject form of the second-person personal pronoun (singular in this sentence), and *study* is the second-person singular form of the verb.

www.mhhe.com/
nmhh
For information
and exercises on
subject-verb
agreement, go to

Editing >
Subject-Verb
Agreement

34a Identify problems with subject-verb agreement.

1. Knowing the standard subject-verb combinations

To form the present tense third-person singular in regular verbs, add the ending *-s* or *-es*. The other forms have no ending.

Present Tense Forms of the Regular Verb *Read*

	SINGULAR	PLURAL
First person	I *read.*	We *read.*
Second person	You *read.*	You *read.*
Third person	He, she, it *reads.*	They *read.*

Tips LEARNING in COLLEGE

Subject-Verb Agreement

When writers make mistakes in subject-verb agreement, those mistakes often involve the proper use of the *-s* (or *-es*) ending with nouns and verbs.

- Adding *-s* to most nouns makes them *plural.*
- Adding *-s* (or *-es*) to regular present tense verbs makes them *singular.*

In other words, for proper agreement in the present tense, if a noun that is the subject of a sentence ends with an *s*, the verb should not; if the noun does not end with an *s*, the verb should.

SINGULAR	PLURAL
The team play**s** five games.	The team**s** play five games.
The school teach**es** good behavior.	The school**s** teach good behavior.

Several important verbs, however, have irregular forms in both the present and the past tense. These include the verbs *be, have,* and *do.*

Present Tense and Past Tense Forms of the Irregular Verb *Be*

	SINGULAR	PLURAL
First person	I *am/was* here.	We *are/were* here.
Second person	You *are/were* here.	You *are/were* here.
Third person	He, she, it *is/was* here.	They *are/were* here.

Present Tense Forms of the Verb *Have*

	SINGULAR	PLURAL
First person	I *have.*	We *have.*
Second person	You *have.*	You *have.*
Third person	He, she, it *has.*	They *have.*

Present Tense Forms of the Verb *Do* and Its Negative *Don't*

	SINGULAR	PLURAL
First person	I *do/don't.*	We *do/don't.*
Second person	You *do/don't.*	You *do/don't.*
Third person	He, she, it *does/doesn't.*	They *do/don't.*

2. Recognizing situations in which problems with subject-verb agreement often occur

Several situations can lead to subject-verb agreement errors:

Situations in Which Writers May Make Errors in Subject-Verb Agreement

1. When words come between the subject and the verb
2. When the subject is compound, collective, or indefinite
3. When the subject follows the verb
4. When there is a subject complement as well as a subject
5. When a relative pronoun is the subject of a dependent clause
6. When the subject is a gerund phrase (a phrase beginning with an *-ing* verb treated as a noun)

599

1. Avoid mistaking a word that comes between the subject and the verb for the subject:

   ➤ **The candidate's position on foreign policy issues**

   troubles
   ~~trouble~~ some voters.
       ^

   The subject is *position,* not *issues.*

2. Avoid being confused by compound, collective, or indefinite subjects:

   is
   ➤ **The chorus ~~are~~ singing Beethoven's Ninth Symphony**
                ^

   in Carnegie Hall.

   Chorus is a collective noun, a unit made up of many persons or things but treated as a single entity.

3. Avoid being confused when the subject follows the verb:

   follow
   ➤ **Often in the wake of a natural catastrophe ~~follows~~**
                                                       ^

   financial disasters.

   The subject is the plural noun *disasters.*

4. Avoid confusing the subject complement for the subject:

   is
   ➤ **The goal of the new law ~~are~~ improvements in air and**
                              ^

   water quality.

   The subject is the singular noun *goal;* the subject complement is *improvements.*

5. Avoid being confused when a relative pronoun is the subject of a dependent clause:

   ➤ ***Anorexia nervosa* is among the eating disorders that**

   afflict
   ~~afflicts~~ teenagers.
       ^

   The relative pronoun *that* refers to the plural noun *disorders,* so it takes the plural form of the verb.

6. Avoid being confused when the subject is a gerund phrase (a phrase beginning with an *-ing* verb treated as a noun):

➤ **Reducing emissions of greenhouse gases a̶r̶e̶ a goal of** *is*

 the Kyoto Treaty.

 The subject is the gerund phrase *reducing emissions of greenhouse gases.*

Exercise 34.1 Identifying subject-verb agreement

In each sentence, underline the subject, and circle the verb that goes with it.

EXAMPLE **Graphic design studios (require/requires) their**

 designers to be trained in the use of design

 software.

1. Nowadays computers (gives/give) graphic designers a great deal of freedom.
2. Before computers, a design (was/were) produced mostly by hand.
3. Alternative designs (is/are) produced much faster on the computer than by hand.
4. With computers, a designer (is/are) able to reduce or enlarge text in seconds.
5. Page layout programs (takes/take) some of the drudgery out of combining images with text.
6. Designers (has/have) the option of removing blemishes and other imperfections from photographs.
7. They (doesn't/don't) have to make special prints to show their work to others.
8. Designs (is/are) e-mailed as attachments all the time.
9. Still, the design professional (doesn't/don't) feel that the computer is anything more than just another tool.
10. Nonetheless, to be a graphic designer today you (needs/need) to be ready to spend a lot of time staring at a screen.

IDENTIFY AND EDIT
Problems with Subject-Verb Agreement

agr

★ 1. Find the verb.

> verb
> PROBLEM SENTENCE   Hamlet and Claudius *brings* down the Danish royal family.
>
> Verbs are words that specify action, condition, or state of being.

★ 2. Ask the who or what question to identify the subject.

> |—————— subject ——————| |–verb–|
> PROBLEM SENTENCE   *Hamlet and Claudius brings* down the Danish royal family.
>
> The answer to the question "What brings" is *Hamlet and Claudius.*

★ 3. Determine the person (first, second, or third) and number (singular or plural) of the subject.

> |—————— subject ——————|
> PROBLEM SENTENCE   *Hamlet and Claudius* brings down the Danish royal family.
>
> The subject of the sentence—*Hamlet and Claudius*—is a compound joined by *and,* and is third-person plural.

★ 4. If necessary, change the verb to agree with the subject.

> bring
> EDITED PROBLEM SENTENCE   Hamlet and Claudius ~~brings~~ down the Danish royal family.
>   ^
>
> *Bring* is the third-person plural form of the verb.

Subject-Verb Agreement and Grammar Checkers

Computer grammar checkers are unreliable guides to subject-verb agreement, often stumbling in the very situations that writers find troublesome. One grammar checker, for example, failed to flag this sentence for correction:

> *The candidate's position on foreign policy issues trouble some voters.*

The subject is the singular noun *position,* and the verb should be *troubles.* Apparently, however, the grammar checker interpreted a word that follows the subject—the plural noun *issues*—as the subject and let the sentence pass with the incorrect verb form.

34b Learn to edit errors in subject-verb agreement.

When you are checking for subject-verb agreement, begin by finding the subject. To locate the subject, find the verb (for example, *is*), and then ask the *who* or *what* question about it ("Who is?" "What is?"). Does that subject match the verb in person and number? If it does not, then you have to bring subject and verb into agreement. Changing the verb to agree with the subject usually solves the problem.

>   *bring*
> ➤ **Hamlet and Claudius ~~brings~~ down the Danish royal family.**

Sometimes, however, you may want to reword your sentence to avoid awkwardness or confusion even after you have corrected for subject-verb agreement.

CORRECT BUT AWKWARD	Either three French hens, two turtledoves, or a partridge in a pear tree is what I want.
REVISED	I want either three French hens, two turtle-doves, or a partridge in a pear tree.

34c Do not lose sight of the subject when other words separate it from the verb.

It is easy to lose sight of the subject when other words intervene between it and the verb. If you are confused, remember to ask the *who* or *what* question about the verb.

➤ The leaders of the trade union ~~opposes~~ *oppose* the new law.

The answer to the question "Who opposes?" is *leaders,* a plural noun, so the verb should be in the plural form: *oppose.*

Note: If a word group beginning with *as well as, along with,* or *in addition to* follows a singular subject, the subject does not become plural.

➤ My teacher, as well as other faculty members, ~~oppose~~ *opposes* the

new school policy.

34d Distinguish plural from singular compound subjects.

Compound subjects are made up of two or more parts. The two parts are joined by either a coordinating conjunction (*and, or, nor*) or a correlative conjunction (*both . . . and, either . . . or, neither . . . nor*).

1. Treating most compound subjects joined by and as plural
Most subjects that are joined by *and* should be treated as plural.

PLURAL   *The king and his advisers were* shocked by this turn of events.

PLURAL   This poem's *first line and last word have* a powerful effect on the reader.

2. Treating some compound subjects joined by *and* as singular
There are exceptions to the rule that subjects joined by *and* are plural. Compound subjects should be treated as singular in the following circumstances:

1. When they refer to the same entity:

   ➤ *My best girlfriend and most dependable adviser is*

   my mother.

2. When they are considered a single unit:

   ➤ In some ways, *forty acres and a mule continues* to be

what is needed.

3. When they are preceded by the word *each* or *every:*

➤ **Each man, woman, and child *deserves* respect.**

3. Treating subjects joined by *or, nor, either . . . or,* or *neither . . . nor* as either plural or singular depending on context

Compound subjects connected by *or, nor, either . . . or,* or *neither . . . nor* can take either a singular or a plural verb, depending on the subject that is closest to the verb.

SINGULAR   **Either the children or *their mother is* to blame.**

PLURAL   **Neither the experimenter nor *her subjects were* aware of the takeover.**

34e Treat most collective nouns—nouns like *audience, family,* and *committee*—as singular subjects.

A **collective noun** names a unit made up of many people or things, treating it as an entity. Some familiar examples are *audience, family, group,* and *committee.*

1. Treating most collective nouns as singular

When a collective noun is the subject of a sentence, it is usually singular.

➤ **The *audience fills* the theater.**

➤ **The *committee votes* on the budget tomorrow.**

Units of measurement—amounts, fractions, and percentages—take a singular verb when they are used collectively.

➤ **One-fourth of the liquid *was* poured into the test tube.**

➤ **One hundred thirty feet *is* the maximum safe depth for recreational scuba diving.**

➤ **Three hundred dollars *is* a high price to pay.**   **605**

The collective noun *number* is always treated as singular when it is preceded by *the*.

➤ The *number* of casualties *was* underreported.

2. Using a singular verb with nouns that are plural in form but singular in meaning

Some nouns are plural in form—that is, they end in *s*—but singular in meaning. Examples include the names of fields of study like *physics, mathematics,* and *statistics* and the word *news*.

➤ That *news leaves* me speechless.

➤ Advanced *physics requires* years of study to master.

➤ *Statistics is* important in most social sciences.

Note, however, that a word like *statistics* takes a plural verb when it designates specific results rather than a subject of study.

➤ The *statistics confirm* that smoking is dangerous.

3. Treating the titles of works; the names of companies, institutions, or countries; and words as words as singular

➤ Ernest Hemingway's *For Whom the Bell Tolls is* arguably his darkest work.

➤ *The Misfits features* Monroe and Gable in their last film.

➤ *Simon and Schuster* no longer *publishes* college textbooks.

➤ The *United States was* a charter member of the United Nations.

➤ *Mice is* an example of an irregular plural noun in English.

4. Recognizing when some collective nouns should be considered plural

When the members of a group are acting as individuals, the collective subject can be considered plural.

➤ The *committee were discussing* the issue among themselves.

You may want to revise the subject of such a sentence with a clarifying plural noun to avoid awkwardness.

➤ The *members of the committee were discussing* the issue

among themselves.

Units of measurement take a plural verb when they refer to a collection of individual people or things.

➤ *One-fourth* of the students in the class *are* failing the course.

➤ *Seventy-five percent* of the applicants *are* unemployed.

The collective noun *number* takes a plural verb when preceded by *a*.

➤ A *number* of cases *do* not fit the predicted pattern.

Exercise 34.2 Editing for subject-verb agreement

Underline the simple subject and verb in each of the following sentences, and then check for subject-verb agreement. Circle the number of each correct sentence. Repair the other sentences by changing the verb form.

EXAMPLE   The <u>audience</u> for new productions of

                   appears
Shakespeare's plays ~~appear~~ to be growing.

1. Designers since the invention of printing has sought to create attractive, readable type.
2. A layout shows the general design of a book or magazine.
3. Half of all ad pages contains lots of white space.
4. The size of the page, width of the margins, and style of type is some of the things that concern a designer.
5. China and Japan were centers for the development of the art of calligraphy.

6. Neither a standard style of lettering nor a uniform alphabet were prevalent in the early days of the printing press.
7. A pioneering type designer and graphic artist were Albrecht Dürer.
8. A number of contemporary typefaces show the influence of Dürer's designs.
9. A design committee approve any changes to the look of a publication.
10. Each letter and punctuation mark are designed for maximum readability.

34f Treat most indefinite subjects—subjects like *everybody, no one, each, all,* and *none*—as singular.

Indefinite pronouns such as *everybody* and *no one* do not refer to a specific person or item.

1. Recognizing that most indefinite pronouns are singular
The following indefinite pronouns are always singular:

anybody	everybody	nothing
anyone	everyone	one
anything	everything	somebody
each	no one	someone
either	nobody	something

➤ *Everyone* in my hiking club *is* an experienced climber.

None and *neither* are singular when they appear by themselves.

➤ In the movie, five men set out on an expedition, but *none returns.*

➤ *Neither sees* a way out of this predicament.

2. Recognizing that some indefinite pronouns are always plural
A handful of indefinite pronouns (*both, few, many, several*) are always plural because they mean "more than one" by definition. *Both,* for example, always indicates two.

➤ *Both* of us *want* to go to the rally for the environment.

LEARNING in COLLEGE

Are **None** *and* **Neither** *Ever Plural?*

If a prepositional phrase that includes a plural noun or pronoun follows *none* or *neither,* the indefinite pronoun seems to have a plural meaning. Although some writers treat *none* or *neither* as plural in such situations, other authorities on language maintain that these two pronouns are always singular. It is a safe bet to consider them singular.

SINGULAR   **In the movie, five men set out on an expedition,**

but *none* **of them** *returns.*

SINGULAR   *Neither* **of the hikers** *sees* **a way out of this**

predicament.

➤   *Several* **of my friends** *were* **very happy about the outcome of**

the election.

3. Recognizing that some indefinite pronouns can be either plural or singular

Some indefinite pronouns (*some, any, all, most*) may be either plural or singular. To decide, consider the context of the sentence, especially noting any noun or pronoun that the indefinite pronoun refers to.

➤   *Some* **of the** *book* *is* **missing, but** *all* **of the** *papers* *are* **here.**

34g   Make sure the subject and verb agree when the subject comes after the verb.

In most English sentences, the verb comes after the subject. Sometimes, however, a writer may invert the order for emphasis. To check for agreement, first locate the verb, and then ask the *who* or *what* question to find the subject.

609

➤ **In the courtyard *stand a leafless tree and a rusted arbor.***

What *stand in the courtyard?* The compound subject—*tree* and *arbor*—requires the plural verb *stand.*

In sentences that begin with *there is* or *there are,* the subject always follows the verb.

➤ **There *is* a worn wooden *bench* in the shade of the two trees.**

34h Make sure the verb agrees with its subject, not the subject complement.

A **subject complement** renames and specifies the sentence's subject. It follows a **linking verb**—a verb, often a form of *be,* that joins the subject to its description or definition: *Children are innocent.* In the sentence that follows, the singular noun *gift* is the subject. *Books* is the subject complement. Therefore, *are* has been changed to *is* to agree in number with *gift.*

➤ **One gift that gives her pleasure ~~are~~ ^is^ books.**

34i *Who, which,* and *that* (relative pronouns) take verbs that agree with the subject they replace.

When a relative pronoun such as *who, which,* or *that* is the subject of a dependent clause, the pronoun is taking the place of a noun that appears earlier in the sentence—its **antecedent.** Therefore, the verb that goes with *who, which,* or *that* needs to agree with this antecedent. In the following sentence, the relative pronoun *that* is the subject of the dependent clause *that has dangerous side effects. Disease,* a singular noun, is the antecedent of *that;* therefore, the verb in the dependent clause is singular.

➤ **Measles is a childhood *disease that has* dangerous**

   side effects.

When *one of the* or *only one of the* precedes the antecedent in a sentence, writers can become confused about which form of the verb to use. The phrase *one of the* implies "more than one" and is, therefore, plural. *Only one of the* implies "just one," however, and is singular. Generally, use the plural form of the verb when the phrase *one of the* comes before the antecedent. Use the singular form of the verb when *only one of the* comes before the antecedent.

PLURAL   Tuberculosis is *one of the* diseases *that have*

long, tragic histories in many parts of the world.

SINGULAR   Barbara is the *only one of the* managers *who has*

a degree in physics.

34j   Gerund phrases (phrases beginning with an *-ing* verb treated as a noun) take the singular form of the verb when they are subjects.

A **gerund phrase** is an *-ing* verb form followed by objects, complements, or modifiers. When a gerund phrase is the subject in a sentence, it is singular.

➤   *Experimenting with drugs is* a dangerous rave practice.

Exercise 34.3   Editing for subject-verb agreement problems

In some of the sentences below, the verb does not agree with the subject. Circle the number of each sentence in which subject and verb agree. In the others, change verbs as needed to bring subjects and verbs into agreement.

EXAMPLE   The best part of the play ~~are~~ her soliloquies.
                                              is

1. The Guerilla Girls are a group of women who acts on behalf of female artists.
2. One of their main concerns are to combat the underrepresentation of women artists in museum shows.
3. No one knows how many Guerilla Girls there are, and none of them have ever revealed her true identity.
4. The Guerilla Girls maintain their anonymity by appearing only in gorilla masks.

5. Some people claim that a few famous artists is members of the Guerilla Girls.
6. Their story begin in 1985, when the Museum of Modern Art in New York exhibited a major survey of contemporary art.
7. Fewer than ten percent of the artists represented was women.
8. Not everyone is amused by the protests of the Guerilla Girls.
9. They often shows up in costume at exhibits dominated by the work of male artists.
10. Several of the Guerilla Girls have coauthored a book.

Exercise 34.4   Chapter review: Subject-verb agreement

Edit the passage to correct subject-verb agreement errors.

The end of the nineteenth century saw the rise of a new kind of architecture. Originating in response to the development of new building materials, this so-called modern architecture characterizes most of the buildings we sees around us today.

Iron and reinforced concrete makes the modern building possible. Previously, the structural characteristics of wood and stone limited the dimensions of a building. Wood-frame structures becomes unstable above a certain height. Stone can bear great weight, but architects building in stone confronts severe limits on the height of a structure in relation to the width of its base. The principal advantage of iron and steel are that they reduce those limits, permitting much greater height than stone.

At first the new materials was used for decoration. However, architects like Hermann Muthesius and Walter Gropius began to use iron and steel as structural elements within their buildings. The designs of Frank Lloyd Wright also shows how the development of iron and steel technology revolutionized building interiors. When every wall do not have to bear weight from the floors above, open floor plans is possible.

35 Problems with Verbs

Verbs provide a great deal of information. They report action (*run, write*) and show time (*going, gone*). They change form to indicate person (first, second, or third—*I, we; you; he, she, it, they*) and number (singular or plural). They also change to indicate mood and voice.

VERB FORMS

35a Learn the principal forms of regular and irregular verbs.

www.mhhe.com/nmhh
For information and exercises on verbs, go to
Editing >
Verbs and Verbals

All English verbs except the verb *be* have five principal forms:

- base form
- *-s* form
- past tense form
- past participle
- present participle

Regular verbs all form the past tense and the past participle in the same way, by adding *-d* or *-ed* to the base form. Here are the five principal forms of the regular verb *walk* with an example of each in a sentence:

BASE	*walk*	The students *walk* to school.
-S	*walks*	The student *walks* to school.
PAST TENSE	*walked*	The student *walked* to school.
PAST PARTICIPLE	*walked*	The student had *walked* to school.
PRESENT PARTICIPLE	*walking*	The student is *walking* to school.

Irregular verbs, in contrast, do not form the past tense or past participle in a consistent way. Here are the five principal forms of the irregular verb *begin* with an example of each in a sentence:

613

BASE FORM
- The form you find if you look up the verb in a dictionary. (For irregular verbs, dictionaries give other forms as well.)
- Used to indicate an action occurring at the moment or habitually (**present tense**) when the subject is *I* or *you* (first- and second-person singular) or a plural noun or pronoun (first-, second-, and third-person plural). (*See Chapter 34: Subject-Verb Agreement, pp. 597–603.*)

-S FORM
- Used to indicate an action occurring at the moment or habitually (present tense) when the subject is a singular noun, a singular pronoun like *anyone,* or the personal pronouns *he, she,* and *it.* (*See Chapter 34: Subject-Verb Agreement, pp. 597–603.*)

PAST TENSE FORM
- Used to indicate an action completed at a specific time in the past.

PAST PARTICIPLE
- Used with *have, has,* or *had* to form the perfect tenses. (*See 35g, pp. 623–27.*)
- Used with a form of the verb *be* to form the passive voice. (*See 35l, pp. 635–36.*)
- Used sometimes as an adjective (the *polished* silver).

PRESENT PARTICIPLE
- Used with a form of the verb *be* to form the progressive tenses. (*See 35g, pp. 625–27.*)
- Used sometimes as a noun (the *writing* is finished) or an adjective (the *smiling* man).

BASE	*begin*	The concerts *begin* at nine.
-S	*begins*	The concert *begins* at nine.
PAST TENSE	*began*	The concert *began* at nine.
PAST PARTICIPLE	*begun*	The concert had *begun* at nine.
PRESENT PARTICIPLE	*beginning*	The concert is *beginning* at nine.

The irregular verb *be,* unlike any other English verb, has eight principal forms:

BASE	*be*
THREE PRESENT TENSE FORMS	I *am.* He, she, it *is.* We, you, they *are.*
TWO PAST TENSE FORMS	I, he, she, it *was.* We, you, they *were*
PAST PARTICIPLE	*been*
PRESENT PARTICIPLE	*being*

35b Identify and edit problems with common irregular verbs.

If you are not sure which form of an irregular verb is called for in a sentence, consult the list of common irregular verbs on this and the next page. You can also find the past tense and past participle forms of irregular verbs by looking up the base form in a standard dictionary.

wove
➤ In *A Midsummer Night's Dream,* Shakespeare ~~weaved~~
  ^
  together two complementary plots.

FORMS of COMMON IRREGULAR VERBS

BASE	PAST TENSE	PAST PARTICIPLE
arise	arose	arisen
awake	awoke	awoke/awakened
be	was/were	been
beat	beat	beaten
become	became	become
begin	began	begun
blow	blew	blown
break	broke	broken
bring	brought	brought
buy	bought	bought
catch	caught	caught
choose	chose	chosen
cling	clung	clung
come	came	come
do	did	done
draw	drew	drawn
drink	drank	drunk

(continued) **615**

IRREGULAR VERBS *(continued)*

BASE	PAST TENSE	PAST PARTICIPLE
drive	drove	driven
eat	ate	eaten
fall	fell	fallen
fight	fought	fought
flee	fled	fled
fly	flew	flown
forget	forgot	forgotten/forgot
forgive	forgave	forgiven
freeze	froze	frozen
get	got	gotten/got
give	gave	given
go	went	gone
grow	grew	grown
hang	hung	hung (for things)
hang	hanged	hanged (for people)
have	had	had
hear	heard	heard
hit	hit	hit
know	knew	known
lose	lost	lost
pay	paid	paid
raise	raised	raised
ride	rode	ridden
ring	rang	rung
rise	rose	risen
say	said	said
see	saw	seen
set	set	set
shake	shook	shaken
sit	sat	sat
spend	spent	spent
spin	spun	spun
steal	stole	stolen
strive	strove/strived	striven/strived
swear	swore	sworn
swim	swam	swum
swing	swung	swung
take	took	taken
tear	tore	torn
tread	trod	trod/trodden
wear	wore	worn
weave	wove	woven
wring	wrung	wrung
write	wrote	written

LEARNING in COLLEGE

Finding a Verb's Principal Forms

If you are unsure of a verb's principal forms, check a dictionary. If the verb is regular, the dictionary will list only the base form, and you will know that you should form the verb's past tense and past participle by adding -ed or -d. If the verb is irregular, the dictionary will give its principal forms.

Dictionary entry for an irregular verb:

Preferred past tense form given first

sing (sing) *v.,* sang or, often, sung; sung; singing

part of speech (v, verb)   past participle   present participle

1. Using the correct forms of irregular verbs such as *ride* (*rode / ridden*)

The forms of irregular verbs with past tenses that end in -*e* and past participles that end in -*n* or -*en,* such as *ate / eaten, rode / ridden, wore / worn, stole / stolen,* and *swore / sworn,* are sometimes confused.

➤ He had ~~ate~~ the apple.
   eaten

➤ They had ~~rode~~ the whole way on the bus.
   ridden

➤ I could have ~~swore~~ the necklace was here.
   sworn

2. Using the correct forms of *went* and *gone, saw* and *seen*

Went and *saw* are the past tense forms of the irregular verbs *go* and *see. Gone* and *seen* are the past participle forms. These verb forms are commonly confused. Check carefully to make sure that you are using the correct form as you edit your writing.

➤ I had ~~went~~ there yesterday.
   gone

➤ We ~~seen~~ the rabid dog and called for help.
   saw

3. Using the correct forms of irregular verbs such as *drink* (*drank / drunk*)

For a few irregular verbs, such as *swim* (*swam / swum*), *drink* (*drank / drunk*), and *ring* (*rang / rung*), the difference between the past tense

617

form and the past participle is only one letter. Be careful not to mix
up these forms in your writing.

> *drunk*
> I had ~~drank~~ more than eight bottles of water that day.
>   ^

> *swam*
> On August 6, Gertrude Caroline Ederle ~~swum~~ the English
>   ^

Channel, becoming the first woman to do so.

For MULTILINGUAL STUDENTS

Nonstandard Irregular Verb Forms

In many dialects of English, the forms of some irregular verbs
vary from those of standard English. In academic writing, however, always use the standard forms. When in doubt, consult the
list of irregular verbs on pages 615–16, and if necessary, edit your
work accordingly.

> *grew*
> The neighborhood gardeners ~~growed~~ their own vegetables
>   ^
>
> in the empty lot.

> *were*
> The Sistine Chapel frescoes ~~be~~ cleaned over a twenty
>   ^
>
> year period.

> *dragged*
> Achilles ~~drug~~ Hector's body three times around the walls
>   ^
>
> of Troy.

Exercise 35.1   Using irregular verb forms

Use the past participle or past tense form of the verb in parentheses,
whichever is apropriate, to fill in the blanks in the following sentences.

> **EXAMPLE**   Today, a woman's right to vote is _taken_ for
>   granted. (take)

1. Elizabeth Cady Stanton and Lucretia Mott _____ two of the
   founders of the women's rights movement in the United States. (be)
2. The movement had _____ out of the abolitionist movement. (grow)

3. Stanton and Mott hoped to address the inequalities between men and women that they _____ in American society. (see)
4. In 1848, hundreds of people, both men and women, _____ to Seneca Falls in upstate New York for the first convention on women's rights. (go)
5. Many of the words in the convention's Declaration of Sentiments were _____ directly from the Declaration of Independence. (draw)
6. With the Declaration of Sentiments' demand for a woman's right to vote, the women's suffrage movement had _____ . (begin)

35c Distinguish between *lie* and *lay, sit* and *set,* and *rise* and *raise.*

Even the most experienced writers commonly confuse the verbs *lie* and *lay, sit* and *set,* and *rise* and *raise.* The correct forms are given below.

Often-Confused Verb Pairs and Their Principal Forms

BASE	PAST TENSE	PAST PARTICIPLE	PRESENT PARTICIPLE
lie (to recline)	lay	lain	lying
lay (to place)	laid	laid	laying
sit (to be seated)	sat	sat	sitting
set (to put on a surface)	set	set	setting
rise (to go/get up)	rose	risen	rising
raise (to lift up)	raised	raised	raising

One verb in each of these pairs (*lay, set, raise*) is **transitive,** which means that an object receives the action of the verb. The other verb (*lie, sit, rise*) is **intransitive** and cannot take an object. You should use a form of *lay, set,* or *raise* if you can replace the verb with *place* or *put.* (*See Chapter 31: Sentence Basics, pp. 552–57, for more on transitive and intransitive verbs.*)

➤ **The dog *lies* down on the floor and closes his eyes.**

dir obj
➤ **The dog *lays a bone* at your feet.**

619

➤ The technician *sits* down at the table.

dir obj
➤ She *sets* the samples in front of her.

➤ The flames *rise* from the fire.

dir obj
➤ The heat *raises* the temperature of the room.

Tips

LEARNING in COLLEGE

Using Lie *and* Lay *Correctly*

Lie (to recline) and *lay* (to place) are also confusing because the past tense of the irregular verb *lie* is *lay* (*lie, lay, lain*). To avoid using the wrong form, always double-check the verb *lay* when it appears in your writing.

laid
➤ He washed the dishes carefully, and then ~~lay~~ them on
                                                    ^

a clean towel.

Exercise 35.2 Distinguishing commonly confused verbs

Some of the sentences that follow have the wrong choice of verb. Edit the incorrect sentences, and circle the number next to each sentence that is already correct.

lying
EXAMPLE   She was ~~laying~~ down after nearly fainting.
                      ^

1. Humans, like many other animals, usually lay down to sleep.
2. We found the manuscript lying on the desk where he left it.
3. The restless students had been setting at their desks all morning.
4. The actor sat the prop on the wrong table.
5. The archeologists rose the lid of the tomb.
6. The Wright Brothers' contraption rose above the sands of Kitty Hawk.

35d Do not forget to add an -*s* or -*es* ending to the verb when it is necessary.

In the present tense, almost all verbs add an -*s* or -*es* ending if the subject is third-person singular. (*See Chapter 34: Subject-Verb Agreement, pp. 598–99, for more on standard subject-verb combinations.*) Third-person singular subjects can be nouns (*woman, Benjamin, desk*), pronouns (*he, she, it*), or indefinite pronouns (*everyone*).

rises
➤ The stock market ~~rise~~ when the economic news is good.

If the subject is in the first person (*I* or *we*), the second person (*you*), or the third-person plural (*people, they*), the verb does *not* add an -*s* or -*es* ending.

➤ You invest$ your money wisely.

➤ People need$ to learn about a company before buying

its stock.

35e Do not forget to add a -*d* or an -*ed* ending to the verb when it is necessary.

When they are speaking, people sometimes leave the -*d* or -*ed* ending off certain verbs such as *asked, fixed, mixed, supposed to,* and *used to.* In writing, however, the endings should be included on all regular verbs in the past tense and all past participles of regular verbs.

asked
➤ The driving instructor ~~ask~~ the student driver to pull over to

the curb.

mixed
➤ After we had ~~mix~~ the formula, we let it cool.

Also check for missing -*d* or -*ed* endings on past participles used as adjectives.

concerned
➤ The ~~concern~~ parents met with the school board.

Exercise 35.3   Editing for verb form

Underline the verbs in each sentence. Then check to ensure that the correct verb forms are used, using the advice in sections 35a–e. Circle the number of each correct sentence. Edit the remaining sentences.

forgiven
EXAMPLE   The dentist has ~~forgave~~ Maya for biting his finger.

621

1. Humans are tremendously adaptable creatures.
2. Desert peoples have learn that loose, light garments protects them from the heat.
3. They have long drank from deep wells that they digged for water.
4. Arctic peoples have developed cultural practices that keeps them alive in a region where the temperature rarely rise above zero for months at a time.
5. Many people in mountainous areas have long builded terraces on steep slopes to create more land for farming.
6. Anthropologists and archeologists have argued about whether all cultural practices have an adaptive purpose.
7. Some practices may have went from adaptive to destructive.
8. For example, in ancient times irrigation canals increased food production in arid areas.
9. After many centuries passed, however, the canals had deposit so much salt on the irrigated fields that the fields had became unfarmable.
10. By then, much of the population had fleed.

35f Make sure your verbs are complete.

With only a few exceptions, all English sentences must contain complete verbs. A **complete verb** consists of the main verb along with any helping verbs that are needed to express the tense (*see pp. 623–32*) or voice (*see pp. 635–36*). **Helping verbs** include forms of *be, have,* and *do* and the modal verbs *can, could, may, might, shall, should,* and *will.*

		helping verb	main verb	
➤	The economy	*was*	growing	at a fast rate.
➤	The author	*has*	written	a first-rate thriller.
➤	They	*should*	reach	their destination soon.
➤	The campaign	*might*	begin	early this year.

Helping verbs can be part of contractions (*He's running, we'd better go*), but they cannot be left out of the sentence entirely.

　　　　will
➤ **They͜ be going on a field trip next week.**

Linking verbs are another type of verb that writers sometimes accidentally omit. A **linking verb,** often a form of *be,* connects the subject to a description or definition of it.

➤ **Mountains *are* beautiful.**

Like helping verbs, linking verbs can be part of contractions (*She's a student*), but they should not be left out entirely.

➤ **Montreal** is **a major Canadian city.**
^

VERB TENSE

35g Use verb tenses accurately.

Tenses show the time of a verb's action. English has three basic time frames: present, past, and future. Each tense has simple, perfect, and progressive verb forms to indicate the time span of the actions that are taking place. The verbs in the clauses and phrases of a sentence must follow a **sequence of tenses** that logically reflects the relationships in time among the actions each expresses. (*For a review of the present tense forms of a typical verb and of the verbs* be, have, *and* do, *see the material on standard subject-verb combinations in 34a, pp. 598–99; for a review of the principal forms of regular and irregular verbs, which are used to form tenses, see 35a and 35b, pp. 613–19.*)

1. The simple present and past tenses use only the verb itself (the base form or the -*s* form), without a helping verb or verbs.

The **simple present tense** is used for actions occurring at the moment or habitually. The **simple past tense** is used for actions completed at a specific time in the past.

SIMPLE PRESENT

Every May, she *plans* next year's marketing strategy.

623

SIMPLE PAST

In the early morning hours before the office opened, she *planned* her marketing strategy.

2. The simple future tense takes *will* plus the verb.

The **simple future tense** is used for actions that have not yet begun.

SIMPLE FUTURE

In May, I *will plan* next year's marketing strategy.

3. Perfect tenses take a form of *have* (*has, had*) plus the past participle.

The **perfect tenses** are used to indicate actions that were or will be completed by the time of another action or a specific time.

PRESENT PERFECT

She *has* already *planned* next year's marketing strategy.

PAST PERFECT

By the time she resigned, Mary *had* already *planned* next year's marketing strategy.

FUTURE PERFECT

By the end of May, she *will have planned* next year's marketing strategy.

When the verb in the past perfect is irregular, be sure to use the proper form of the past participle.

➤ **By the time the week was over, both plants had ~~grew~~ grown**

   five inches.

4. Progressive tenses take a form of *be* (*am, are, were*) plus the present participle.

The **progressive forms** of the simple and perfect tenses are used to indicate ongoing action.

PRESENT PROGRESSIVE

She *is planning* next year's marketing strategy now.

PAST PROGRESSIVE

She *was planning* next year's marketing strategy when she started to look for another job.

FUTURE PROGRESSIVE

During the month of May, she *will be planning* next year's marketing strategy.

For MULTILINGUAL STUDENTS

When Not to Use the Progressive Tenses

Some verbs are not used in the progressive tenses, even when they describe a continuous state or action. Typically, these verbs relate to thoughts, preferences, and ownership.

        understood
➤ I ~~was understanding~~ the lecture until the last ten minutes.

         wants
➤ The manager ~~is wanting~~ the report by the end of the day.

     own
➤ They ~~are owning~~ the house they are renovating.

5. Perfect progressive tenses take *have* plus *be* plus the verb.

Perfect progressive tenses indicate an action that takes place over a specific period of time. The **present perfect progressive tense** is used for actions that start in the past and continue to the present; the **past** and **future perfect progressive tenses** are used for actions that ended or will end at a specified time or before another action.

PRESENT PERFECT PROGRESSIVE

She *has been planning* next year's marketing strategy since the beginning of May.

PAST PERFECT PROGRESSIVE

She *had been planning* next year's marketing strategy when she was offered another job.

FUTURE PERFECT PROGRESSIVE

By May 18, she *will have been planning* next year's marketing strategy for more than two weeks.

LEARNING in COLLEGE

Checking Verb Tenses

Is the time frame of your paper predominantly present, past, or future? Keep this time frame in mind as you edit, and you will be better able to see and solve problems with the accuracy and consistency of your verb tenses. (*For more on keeping verb tenses consistent, see Chapter 41: Confusing Shifts, pp. 704–5.*)

A SUMMARY of ENGLISH TENSES and HOW to FORM THEM

Present Tenses

Simple present	base form/-s form	They *study* in the library. She *studies* in the library.
Present perfect	*has/have* + past participle	She *has studied* all day. They *have studied* all day.
Present progressive	*am/is/are* + present participle	I *am studying* for an exam. Juan *is studying* for an exam. We *are studying* for an exam.
Present perfect progressive	*have/has been* + present participle	They *have been studying* since noon. She *has been studying* since noon.

Past Tenses

Simple past	past tense	The students *visited* Peru last summer.
Past perfect	*had* + past participle	They *had planned* a trip to Peru the summer before.
Past Progressive	*was/were* + present participle	They *were planning* a trip to Peru to see the Andes Mountains.
Past perfect progressive	*had been* + present participle	They *had been planning* a trip to Peru for many years.

(continued)

A SUMMARY of ENGLISH TENSES and HOW to FORM THEM *(continued)*

Future Tenses

Simple future	*will* + base form	We *will study* the Incas before we return next summer.
Future perfect	*will have* + past participle	They *will have studied* the Incas by the time they return.
Future progressive	*will be* + present participle	They *will be studying* the Incas to prepare for their return.
Future perfect progressive	*will have been* + present participle	They *will have been studying* the Incas for a full year by the time they return.

35h Use the past perfect tense to indicate an action completed at a specific time or before another event.

When a past event was ongoing but ended before a particular time or another past event, use the past perfect rather than the simple past to describe it.

➤ **Before the Johnstown Flood occurred in 1889, people in the**

    had

  area expressed their concern about the safety of the dam on
      ^

  the Conemaugh River.

People expressed their concern before the flood occurred.

If two past events happened simultaneously, however, use the simple past, not the past perfect, to describe them.

➤ **When the Conemaugh flooded, many people in the area ~~had~~**

  lost their lives.

35i Use the present tense for literary events, scientific facts, and introductions to quotations.

If the conventions of a discipline require you to state what your paper does, do so in the present, not the future, tense.

➤ In this paper, I *describe* the effects of increasing NaCl

concentrations on the germination of radish seeds.

Here are some other special uses of the present tense:

■ By convention, events in a novel, short story, poem, or other literary work are described in the present tense.

➤ Even though Huck's journey down the river ~~was~~ *is* an escape

from society, his relationship with Jim ~~was~~ *is* a form of

community.

■ Artworks and musical compositions are also conventionally described in the present tense.

➤ Brueghel's paintings ~~captured~~ *capture* the social conditions

of his time.

■ Like events in a literary work, scientific facts are considered to be perpetually present, even though they were discovered in the past.

➤ Mendel discovered that genes ~~had~~ *have* different forms, or

alleles.

■ The present tense is also used to introduce a quotation, paraphrase, or summary of someone else's writing.

➤ William Julius Wilson ~~wrote~~ *writes* that "the disappearance of

work has become a characteristic feature of the inner-city

ghetto" (31).

CHARTING the TERRITORY

Reporting Research Findings

Although a written work can be seen as always present, research findings are thought of as having been collected at one time in the past. Use the past or present perfect tense to report the results of research:

responded
➤ **Three of the compounds (nos. 2, 3, and 6) ~~respond~~**
                                              ^

positively by turning purple.

has reviewed
➤ **Clegg (1990) ~~reviews~~ studies of workplace organization**
                  ^

focused on struggles for control of the labor process.

Exercise 35.4 | Using verb tenses

Underline the verb that best fits the sentence.

> **EXAMPLE** **Marlowe (<u>encounters</u>/encountered) Kurtz in the climax of Conrad's *Heart of Darkness*.**

1. Newton showed that planetary motion (followed/follows) mathematical laws.
2. In *Principia Mathematica,* Newton (states/stated), "To every action there is always opposed an equal reaction."
3. Newton (publishes/published) the *Principia* in 1675.
4. With the *Principia,* Newton (had changed/changed) the course of science.
5. By the time of his death, Newton (had become/became) internationally famous.
6. Scientists and philosophers (were absorbing/absorbed) the implications of Newton's discoveries long after his death.

Exercise 35.5 | Editing for verb tense

Edit the following passage, replacing or deleting verb parts so that the tenses reflect the context of the passage.

> **EXAMPLE** **Returning to the area, the survivors ~~had~~ found massive destruction.**

For some time, anthropologists are being puzzled by the lack of a written language among the ancient Incas of South America. The Incas, who had conquered most of Andean South America by about 1500, had sophisticated architecture, advanced knowledge of engineering and astronomy, and sophisticated social and political structures. Why aren't they having a written language as well?

Ancient Egypt, Iraq, and China, as well as early Mexican civilizations such as the Aztec and Maya, had all been having written language. It is seeming strange that only the Incas will have lacked a written language.

Anthropologists now think that the Incas have possessed a kind of written language after all. Scholars will believe that the Incas used knots in multicolored strings as the medium for their "writing." The researchers call these strings *khipu.*

FIGURE 35.1 An Inca official with a *khipu.*

35j Make sure infinitives and participles fit with the tense of the main verb.

Infinitives and participles are **verbals,** words formed from verbs that have various functions within a sentence. Because they are derived from verbs and can express time, verbals need to fit with the main verb in a sentence. Verbals can also form phrases by taking objects, modifiers, or complements.

1. Using the correct tense for infinitives

An **infinitive** is *to* plus the base verb (*to breathe, to sing, to dance*). The perfect form of the infinitive is *to have* plus the past participle (*to have breathed, to have sung, to have danced*).

The tense of an infinitive needs to fit with the tense of the main verb. If the action of the infinitive happens at the same time as or after the action of the main verb, use the present tense (*to* plus the base form).

➤ **I hope *to sing and dance* on Broadway next summer.**

> The infinitive expresses an action (*to sing and dance*) that will occur later than the action of the sentence (*hope*), so the infinitive needs to be in the present tense.

If the action of the infinitive happened before the action of the main verb, use the perfect form.

➤ **My talented mother would like *to have sung and danced* on Broadway as a young woman, but she never had the chance.**

> The action of the main verb (*would like*) is in the present, but the missed opportunity is in the past, so the infinitive needs to be in the perfect tense.

2. Using the correct tense for participles that are part of phrases

Participial phrases can begin with the present participle (*breathing, dancing, singing*), the present perfect participle (*having breathed, having danced, having sung*), or the past participle (*breathed, danced, sung*). If the action of the participle happens simultaneously with the action of the sentence's verb, use the present participle.

➤ *Singing one hour a day together,* **the chorus developed perfect harmony.**

The chorus developed harmony as they sang together, so the present participle (*singing*) is appropriate.

If the action of the participle happened before the action of the main verb, use the present perfect or past participle form.

➤ *Having breathed* **the air of New York, I exulted in the possibilities for my life in the city.**

The breathing took place before the exulting, so the present perfect (*having breathed*) is appropriate.

➤ *Tinted* **with a strange green light, the western sky looked threatening.**

The green light had to appear before the sky started to look threatening, so the past participle (*tinted*) is the right choice.

Exercise 35.6 Choosing tense sequence

Underline the form of the infinitive or participle that fits the main verb in each sentence.

EXAMPLE **We hope (<u>to complete</u>/to have completed) the project by next week.**

1. Magellan's expedition was the first (to circle/to have circled) the globe.
2. They expected the tide (to free/to have freed) the ship from the sandbar.
3. They expected the tide (to free/to have freed) the ship by the time the storm arrived.
4. (To grasp/Grasping) the tiller, the sailor turned the ship into the wind.
5. (Completing/Having completed) the voyage, the crew returned to port.
6. (Covered/Having covered) with phosphorus, Ahab's harpoon glowed eerily.

MOOD

The **mood** of a verb indicates the writer's attitude. English verbs have three moods: indicative, imperative, and subjunctive.

- Use the **indicative mood** to state or question facts, acts, and opinions.

  Our collection is on display.
  Did you see it?

- Use the **imperative mood** for commands, directions, and entreaties. The subject of an imperative sentence is always *you,* but the *you* is usually understood, not written out.

  Shut the door!

- Use the **subjunctive mood** to express a wish or a demand or to make a statement contrary to fact.

  I wish I were a millionaire.

35k Use the subjunctive mood for wishes, requests, and conjecture.

The mood that writers have the most trouble with is the subjunctive.

Verbs in the subjunctive mood may be in the present tense, the past tense, or the perfect tense. The form of the present tense subjunctive is the same as the base form of the verb, but with no change to signal person or number: *accompany* or *be,* not *accompanies* or *am, are, is.* Also, the verb *be* has only one past tense form in the subjunctive mood: *were.*

1. Using the subjunctive mood to express a wish

WISHES

If only I *were* more prepared for this test.

We wish we *were* on vacation.

The candidates wish the election *were* over.

Note: In everyday conversation, most speakers use the indicative rather than the subjunctive when expressing wishes (*If only I was more prepared for this test*).

2. Using the subjunctive mood for requests, recommendations, and demands

Because requests, recommendations, and demands have not yet happened, they—like wishes—are expressed in the subjunctive mood. Words such as *ask, insist, recommend, request,* and *suggest* indicate the subjunctive mood; the verb in the *that* clause that follows should be in the subjunctive.

DEMANDS AND RECOMMENDATIONS

I insist that all applicants *find* their seats by 8:00 AM.

They suggest that we *be* [not *are*] on our way early to avoid traffic.

The doctor recommended that he *stop* [not *stops*] smoking.

3. Using the subjunctive in statements that are contrary to fact

Often, contrary-to-fact statements contain a subordinate clause that begins with *if.* The verb in the *if* clause should be in the subjunctive mood.

CONTRARY-TO-FACT STATEMENTS

He would not be so irresponsible if his father *were* [not *was*] still alive.

If the election *were* today, our candidate would win.

If Hamlet *were* more decisive, the play would be less interesting.

Note: Some common expressions of conjecture are in the subjunctive mood, including *as it were, come rain or shine, far be it from me,* and *be that as it may.*

Exercise 35.7   Using the subjunctive

Fill in each blank with the correct form of the base verb in parentheses. Some of the sentences are in the subjunctive; others are in the indicative or imperative mood.

EXAMPLE   **We ask that everyone __*bring*__ pencils to the exam. (bring)**

1. The stockholders wish the company _____ run more profitably. (be)
2. The board demanded that the CEO _____. (resign)
3. "If I _____ you," said the board chairperson, "I would take a long vacation." (be)

4. Judging from the stock's recent rise, the management change
_____ investors. (please)

5. _____ share value or face the consequences! (increase)

VOICE

The term **voice** in verbs refers to the relation of the subject of a sentence to the action of the verb. A verb is in the **active voice** when the subject of the sentence does the acting; it is in the **passive voice** when the subject is acted upon by an agent that is implied or by one that is expressed in a prepositional phrase. Only transitive verbs—verbs that take objects—can be passive.

To make a verb passive, use the appropriate form of the *be* verb plus the past participle. To transform a sentence from active to passive, make the direct object the subject, and make the subject part of a phrase introduced by the preposition *by*.

	original subject	active verb	direct object
ACTIVE	Professor Jones	*solved*	the problem.
	old dir obj/ new subject	passive verb	old subject
PASSIVE	The problem	*was solved*	by Professor Jones.

In a passive sentence, you can also leave the doer of the action—the subject of the active sentence—unidentified.

PASSIVE   The problem *was solved.*

351   Choose the active voice unless a special situation calls for the passive.

Whenever possible, choose the active voice. The passive voice emphasizes the recipient rather than the doer of the action. In general, you should use it only when the doer of the action is not known or is less important than the recipient of the action.

PASSIVE   My car *was stolen* last night. [The identity of the thief is unknown.]

ACTIVE   James Wyatt invented the steam engine in 1769. [The emphasis is on the inventor.]

PASSIVE   The steam engine was invented in 1769, a hundred years before the internal combustion engine. [The emphasis is on the invention, not the inventor.]

CHARTING the TERRITORY

Passive Voice in Scientific Writing

To keep the focus on objects and actions, scientists writing about the results of their research regularly use the passive voice in their laboratory reports.

PASSIVE   A sample of 20 radish seeds *was germinated* on filter paper soaked in a 10% sodium chloride solution.

Exercise 35.8   Changing active to passive and passive to active

Rewrite each active-voice sentence in the passive voice and each passive-voice sentence in the active voice, paying attention to the effectiveness of the result in each case. If a passive-voice sentence has no identified agent, you may need to supply one to convert it to active voice.

EXAMPLES   **Roberto handled the request.**
The request was handled by Roberto.

My car was stolen last night.
Someone [Somebody, A thief] stole my car last night.

1. Fourscore and seven years ago, our fathers brought forth on this continent a new nation.
2. Humpty Dumpty could not be put together again.
3. The impressive sales of the new product raised the company's stock price.
4. The Great Depression was caused by many factors.
5. The economy is sustained by consumer spending.
6. Economic developments affect the outcome of many presidential elections.

Exercise 35.9   Chapter review: Problems with verbs

Underline the correct verb or verb phrase within the parentheses.

1. Anthropologists are forced (to have confronted/to confront) certain ethical issues in the course of their work.
2. In the field, they (be careful/must be careful) that their work (not harms, does not harm) the people they are studying by (having introduced/introducing) diseases or disruptive goods and customs.

3. Anthropologists (should aware/should be aware) that their mere presence (changes/has changed) the behavior of their subjects.
4. Although anthropologists may wish (to be/to have been) invisible, they cannot help (to affect/affecting) their surroundings.
5. When anthropologists (write/will write), they face other ethical considerations.
6. As Michael F. Brown (asks/asked), "Who owns native culture?"
7. In other words, what can anthropologists (do/have done) with the information they gather?
8. Many insist that a researcher (get/gets) permission to reveal details of religious ceremonies.

Exercise 35.10 Chapter review: Problems with verbs

Edit the following passage, adding, deleting, and changing verbs and verb phrases as needed to reflect the tense, mood, and voice suggested by the sentence and the overall passage.

The *American Heritage Dictionary* defined a state as "the supreme public power within a sovereign political entity." We typically thought of "the state" as the apparatus of government: the elected officials, appointed bureaucrats, and their employees, as well as the rules, traditions, buildings, weapons, and tools that the state controls. How the phenomenon of the state arise?

Anthropologists not agreed on the answer to this question. Many will be surmising a correlation between the development of the state and the rise of large-scale agriculture. One group of researchers believes that states tend to develop where trade routes intersected. Another group of researchers believed that several factors, such as population density, war, and environmental circumscription, interacted to produce states.

In the 1950s, anthropologists believe that the need to administering large-scale irrigation systems gave rise to the first states. The first function of the state was to be controlling water. Researchers later founded that some states developed without hydraulic systems, whereas other areas with hydraulic systems never will develop into states.

36 Problems with Pronouns

Pronouns are words that take the place of nouns. (*For a complete list of pronouns, see Chapter 30: Parts of Speech, pp. 538–39.*)

Three aspects of pronoun usage are the most likely to be troublesome to writers: pronoun case, pronoun-antecedent agreement, and pronoun reference:

- Editing for **pronoun case** involves making sure that a pronoun's form correctly reflects its function—as subject, as object, or to indicate possession.

- Editing for **pronoun-antecedent agreement** involves making sure a pronoun agrees grammatically with the word or words it replaces.

- Editing for **pronoun reference** involves making sure the relationship between a pronoun and the word or words it replaces is clear and unambiguous.

PRONOUN CASE

www.mhhe.com/
nmhh
For information and
exercises on pronouns,
go to
Editing > Pronouns

The term **case** refers to the function of a noun or pronoun in a sentence. There are three main cases in English:

- subjective
- objective
- possessive

Nouns and indefinite pronouns (such as *everybody, somebody,* and *everything*) have the same form in the subjective and objective case. They form the possessive case with an apostrophe or an apostrophe and an -s. (*For more on using apostrophes to indicate possession, see Chapter 61: Apostrophes, pp. 921–24.*)

Most personal pronouns and some relative and interrogative pronouns, however, have different forms for each case. It is these pronouns that are the source of most case-related confusion for writers.

		SUBJECTIVE	OBJECTIVE	POSSESSIVE
Personal pronouns	**Singular**	I	me	my, mine
		you	you	yours
		he/she/it	him/her/it	his, hers, its
	Plural	we	us	ours
		you	you	yours
		they	them	their, theirs
Case-sensitive relative and interrogative pronouns		who, whoever	whom, whomever	whose

subjective		possessive	objective
The community	supports	the mayor's	program
The program	benefits	the town's	children.
The children	deserve	everyone's	support.
Everyone	contributes		time and money.
We	support	his	program.
It	benefits		us.
They	deserve	our	support.

36a Identify problems with pronoun case.

When a pronoun's case does not match its function in a sentence, readers feel that something is wrong. Case errors are usually easy to spot in simple sentences in which a pronoun stands alone as subject or object.

➤ ~~Me~~ *I* hit the ball.

➤ The ball hit ~~I~~ *me*.

Problems arise in more complicated situations that obscure a pronoun's function. These include the following:

639

Situations That Give Rise to Pronoun Case Errors

1. Pronouns in compound structures
2. Pronouns in subject complements
3. Pronouns in appositives
4. *We* or *us* before a noun
5. Pronouns in comparisons with *than* or *as*
6. Pronouns are subjects or objects of infinitives
7. Pronouns preceding a gerund
8. Use of *who/whom* and *whoever/whomever* in dependent clauses and questions

---

36b   Learn to edit for pronoun case.

Editing for case always involves identifying the function of a pronoun—is it part of a subject, a subject complement, a direct object, or the object of a preposition?—and matching the pronoun's form to its function. Often, stripping away words to isolate the pronoun reveals errors clearly.

➤   **[The author and] me share many interests.**

> Isolating *me* shows that it is clearly wrong and should be replaced with *I*. (*See section 36c on the correct use of pronouns in compound structures.*)

In other cases, especially when formal and informal usage conflict, your ear alone cannot guide you reliably, and you may need to consult the rules in sections 36c–36g. In everyday speech, for example, when you knock on a door and someone asks "Who's there?" you are probably more likely to answer "It's me" than the formally correct "It is I." (*See section 36d on p. 642 for more on the correct use of pronouns in subject complements.*)

36c   Use the correct pronoun in compound structures.

Compound structures (words or phrases joined by *and, or,* or *nor*) can appear as subjects or objects. If you are not sure which form of a pronoun to use in a compound structure, treat the pronoun as the only subject or object, and note how the sentence sounds.

IDENTIFY AND EDIT
Problems with Pronoun Case

case

Follow these steps to decide on the proper form of pronouns in compound structures:

★ 1. *Identify the compound structure (a pronoun and a noun or other pronoun joined by and, but, or, or nor) in the problem sentence.*

> compound structure
>
> PROBLEM SENTENCE [Her or her roommate] should call the campus technical support office and sign up for broadband Internet service.
>
> compound structure
>
> PROBLEM SENTENCE The director gave the leading roles to [my brother and I].

★ 2. *Isolate the pronoun that you are unsure about, then read the sentence to yourself without the rest of the compound structure. If the result sounds wrong, change the case of the pronoun (subjective to objective, or vice versa), and read the sentence again.*

> PROBLEM SENTENCE [Her ~~or her roommate~~] should call the campus technical support office and sign up for broadband Internet service.
>
> *Her should call the campus technical support* sounds wrong. The pronoun should be in the subjective case: *she.*
>
> PROBLEM SENTENCE The director gave the leading roles to [~~my brother and~~ I]
>
> *The director gave the leading roles to I* sounds wrong. The pronoun should be in the objective case: *me.*

★ 3. *If necessary, correct the original sentence.*

> *She*
> ◆ ~~Her~~ or her roommate should call the campus technical
> support office and sign up for broadband Internet service.
>
> *me*
> ◆ The director gave the leading roles to my brother and ~~I~~.

SUBJECT   **Angela and ~~me~~ were cleaning up the kitchen.**

I

If you treat the pronoun as the only subject, the sentence is clearly wrong: *Me [was] cleaning up the kitchen.* The correct form is the subjective pronoun *I.*

OBJECT   **My parents waited for an explanation from**

John and ~~I~~.

me

If you treat the pronoun as the only object, the sentence is clearly wrong: *My parents waited for an explanation from I.* The correct form is the objective pronoun *me.*

Pronoun Case and Grammar Checkers

Some computer grammar checkers reliably flag many, but by no means all, errors in pronoun case. One grammar checker, for example, missed the case error in the following sentence:

Ford's son Edsel, *who* the auto magnate treated cruelly, was a brilliant automobile designer. [should be *whom*]

(*See section 36j, pp. 647–49, for a discussion of the proper use of* who *and* whom.)

36d   Use the correct pronoun in subject complements.

A **subject complement** renames and specifies the sentence's subject. It follows a **linking verb,** which is a verb, often a form of *be,* that links the subject to its description or definition: *Alaska is beautiful.*

SUBJECT
COMPLEMENT   **Mark's best friends are Jane and ~~me~~.**

I

If you think editing like this results in sentences that sound too awkward or formal, try switching the order to turn the pronoun into the subject.

SUBJECT   **Jane and I are Mark's best friends.**

Exercise 36.1 Choosing pronoun case

Underline the pronoun in parentheses that is appropriate to the sentence.

    EXAMPLE   **Michael and (I/me) grew up in Philadelphia.**

1. The first person to receive a diploma was (I/me). Matt and Lara followed behind me.
2. Throughout the ceremony I joked with Lara and (he/him), enjoying my last official college event with them.
3. Lara joked that the people least likely to succeed after college were Matt and (her/she).
4. That outcome is highly unlikely, however, because Lara and (he/him) were tied for valedictorian.
5. Graduation was a bittersweet day for my friends and (I/me).

36e Use the correct pronoun in appositives.

Appositives are nouns or noun phrases that rename nouns or pronouns. They appear right after the word or words they rename and have the same function in the sentence as the renamed word or words do.

➤ **The two weary travelers, Ramon and ~~me~~ *I*, found shelter in an**

    old cabin.

    The appositive renames the subject, *two weary travelers,* so the pronoun should be in the subjective case: *I.*

➤ **The police arrested two protesters, Jane and ~~I~~ *me*.**

    The appositive renames the direct object, *protesters,* so the pronoun should be in the objective case: *me.*

36f Use either *we* or *us* before a noun, depending on the noun's function.

When *we* or *us* comes before a noun, it has the same function in the sentence as the noun it precedes.

➤ **~~Us~~ *We* students never get to decide such things.**

    We renames the subject: *students.*

> *us*
> **Things were looking desperate for ~~we~~ campers.**
> ^

Us renames the object of the preposition *for: campers.*

Exercise 36.2 Choosing pronoun case with appositives

Underline the pronoun in parentheses that is appropriate to the sentence.

EXAMPLE (<u>We</u>/Us) **players are ready to hit the field.**

1. (We/Us) Americans live in a cultural melting pot.
2. My parents, for example, have passed on Finnish and Spanish cultural traditions to their children, my two brothers and (I/me).
3. Our grandparents have told fascinating stories about our ancestors to (we/us) grandchildren.
4. On New Year's Eve, the younger family members, my brothers and (I/me), tell fortunes according to a Finnish custom, and then, following a Spanish tradition, the whole family eats grapes.
5. My grandmother gave her oldest grandchild, (I/me), a journal with her observations of our family's varied cultural traditions— our own melting pot.

36g Use the correct pronoun in comparisons with *than* or *as*.

In comparisons, words are often left out of a sentence because the reader knows what they would be. When a pronoun follows *than* or *as,* make sure you are using the correct form by mentally adding the missing word or words.

> **The tuition hikes affect them as much as [the hikes affect]** *us.*

> **Meg is quicker than** *she* **[is].**

If a sentence with a comparison sounds too awkward or formal, add the missing words: *Meg is quicker than she is.*

Note also that some sentences can be correct with either a subjective or an objective pronoun—depending on the sense of the omitted words—but with a very different meaning in each case.

➤ **My brother likes our dog more than *I* [do].**

➤ **My brother likes our dog more than [he likes] *me*.**

36h Use the correct form when the pronoun is the subject or the object of an infinitive.

An **infinitive** is *to* plus the base verb (*to breathe, to sing, to dance*). Whether a pronoun functions as the subject or the object of an infinitive, it should be in the objective case.

subject   object

➤ **We wanted our lawyer and *her* to defend *us* against this**

unfair charge.

Both the subject of the infinitive (*her*) and its object (*us*) are in the objective case.

36i Use the possessive case in front of a gerund.

When a noun or pronoun appears before a **gerund** (an *-ing* verb form functioning as a noun), it should usually be treated as a possessive. Possessive nouns are formed by adding *'s* to singular nouns (*the teacher's desk*) or an apostrophe only (*'*) to plural nouns (*three teachers' rooms*). (*See Chapter 61: Apostrophes, pp. 921–23.*)

animals'
➤ **The ~~animals~~ fighting disturbed the entire neighborhood.**
   ^

their
➤ **Because of ~~them~~ screeching, no one could get any sleep.**
     ^

When the *-ing* word is functioning as a modifier, not a noun, use the subjective or objective case for the pronoun that precedes it. Compare these two sentences, for example.

➤ **The teacher punished *their* cheating.**

➤ **The teacher saw *them* cheating.**

In the first sentence, *cheating* is the object of the sentence, modified by the possessive pronoun *their*. In the second, the pronoun *them* is the object of the sentence, modified by *cheating*.

Exercise 36.3   Choosing pronoun case with comparisons, infinitives, and gerunds

Underline the pronoun in parentheses that is appropriate to the sentence.

> **EXAMPLE**   **Troy is a better driver than (<u>she</u>/her).**

1. Robert Browning, an admirer of Elizabeth Barrett, started to court (she/her) in 1844, thus beginning one of the most famous romances in history.
2. Elizabeth Barrett's parents did not want Robert Browning and (she/her) to marry, but the couple wed secretly in 1846.
3. (Their/Them) moving to Italy from England helped Elizabeth improve her poor health.
4. Even though Robert Browning also had great talent, Elizabeth was recognized as a poet earlier than (he/him).
5. Today, however, he is considered as prominent a poet as (she/her).

   FIGURE 36.1 **Elizabeth Barrett Browning.**

Exercise 36.4   Editing for pronoun case

Edit the following passage, substituting the correct form of the pronoun for any pronoun in the wrong case.

me
EXAMPLE   **The winning points were scored by Hatcher and I.**
                                                                     ^

Sociolinguists investigate the relationship between linguistic variations and culture. They spend a lot of time in the field to gather data for analysis. For instance, them might compare the speech patterns of people who live in a city with those of people who reside in the suburbs. Sociolinguists might discover differences in pronunciation or word choice. Their researching helps us understand both language and culture.

Us laypeople might confuse sociolinguistics with sociology. Sociolinguists do a more specialized type of research than do most sociologists, who study broad patterns within societies. Being concerned with such particulars as the pronunciation of a single vowel, sociolinguists work at a finer level of detail than them.

36j   Distinguish between *who* and *whom*.

The relative pronouns *who, whom, whoever,* and *whomever* are used to introduce dependent clauses and in questions. Their case depends on their function in the dependent clause or question.

SUBJECTIVE   who, whoever

Who wrote Hamlet?

Shakespeare is the playwright *who* wrote Hamlet.

Whoever wrote Hamlet had remarkable insight into human nature.

OBJECTIVE   whom, whomever

The playwright *whom* audiences most admire is Shakespeare.

Of *whom* was Shakespeare thinking when he invented such a complex character?

Whomever Shakespeare imagines, he imagines in rich psychological detail.

Although the distinction between the subjective and objective forms is fading from informal speech, readers expect to see it maintained in formal writing. Here are some suggestions for deciding which form to use.   **647**

1. **Determine how the pronoun functions in a dependent clause.** If the pronoun is functioning as a subject and is performing an action, use *who* or *whoever.* If the pronoun is the object of a verb or preposition, use *whom* or *whomever.*

> **Henry Ford, *who* started the Ford Motor Company, was autocratic and stubborn.**

> **Ford was the industrialist *who* introduced assembly-line techniques to automobile manufacture.**

In both sentences, *who* refers to Henry Ford, the person performing the action in a dependent clause—starting a company in the first sentence, introducing assembly-line techniques in the second.

> **It is he *whom* we should credit with making automobiles widely affordable.**

Whom refers to Ford and is the object of the verb *credit.* You can check the pronoun for case by rephrasing the clause and substituting an appropriate personal pronoun: *We should credit whom [him] for making automobiles widely affordable.*

> **Ford's son Edsel, *whom* the auto magnate treated cruelly, was a brilliant automobile designer.**

Whom, which refers to *Edsel,* is the object of the verb *treated.* Again, you can check the pronoun for case by rephrasing the clause: *The auto magnate treated whom [him] cruelly.*

Be on the lookout for expressions like *they say* or *people think,* which can obscure the function of a relative pronoun when they come between it and a verb.

> **It was Ford *who* [not *whom*] historians think revolutionized the American workplace.**

The pronoun is the subject of *revolutionized,* not the object of *think.*

2. **Determine how the pronoun functions in a question.** To choose the correct form for the pronoun, answer the question with a personal pronoun.

> ***Who* founded the General Motors Corporation?**

The answer could be *He founded it. He* is in the subjective case, so *who* is correct.

➤ ***Whom* did the Chrysler Corporation turn to for leadership in the 1980s?**

The answer could be *It turned to him. Him* is in the objective case, so *whom* is correct.

Exercise 36.5 | Choosing between *who* and *whom*

Underline the pronoun that is appropriate to the sentence.

EXAMPLE **Arlia is the one (<u>who</u>/whom) people say will have the top sales results.**

1. (Who/Whom) invented the light bulb? Thomas Edison did.
2. He was a scientist and inventor (who/whom) also discovered the phonograph and improved the telegraph, telephone, and motion picture technology.
3. Edison, (who/whom) patented 1,093 inventions in his lifetime, was nicknamed The "Wizard of Menlo Park."
4. The hardworking Edison, (who/whom) everyone greatly admired, believed that "genius is one percent inspiration and ninety-nine percent perspiration."
5. (Who/Whom) should we remember the next time we switch on the light? Thomas Edison.

PRONOUN-ANTECEDENT AGREEMENT

A pronoun's **antecedent** is the word or words—nouns or other pronouns—to which the pronoun refers. A pronoun must match its antecedent in person (first, second, or third), number (plural or singular), and gender (masculine: *he / him / his;* feminine: *she / her / hers;* or neuter: *it / its*).

antecedent
➤ **The *snow* fell all day long, and by nightfall *it* was three**

feet deep.

The antecedent, *snow,* is neuter third-person singular.

antecedent
➤ ***Margo and I* discussed *our* relationship over dinner.**

The antecedent, *Margo and I,* is first-person plural.

www.mhhe.com/nmhh
For information and exercises on pronoun-antecedent agreement, go to

Editing >
Pronoun-Antecedent Agreement

649

antecedent

➤ *Jake* and I discussed *his* problems with Margo.

The antecedent, *Jake,* is masculine third-person singular.

For MULTILINGUAL STUDENTS

In English, most nouns are neuter in gender. The exceptions are nouns that specifically name females or males, such as *woman, girl, sister, mother, man, boy, brother, father,* and names like *Louis* and *Anna.*

The gender of a pronoun should match its antecedent, not the word it modifies.

➤ Penelope waited twenty years for *her* [not *his*] husband

Odysseus to return from Troy.

36k Identify and edit problems with pronoun-antecedent agreement.

Problems with pronoun-antecedent agreement tend to occur in these situations:

- When a pronoun's antecedent is an indefinite pronoun, a collective noun, or a compound noun.
- When writers are trying to avoid the generic use of *he.*

In both cases, editing requires clearly identifying the person, number, and gender of the antecedent and making sure the pronoun agrees with it.

The use of a singular masculine pronoun to refer generically to both male and female individuals was once common practice but is now considered sexist and unacceptable. Editing to avoid this usage often requires rewording a sentence—changing a singular antecedent to a plural one, for example—to avoid awkwardness.

36l Choose the right pronoun to agree with an indefinite-pronoun antecedent.

Indefinite pronouns, such as *someone, anybody,* and *nothing,* refer to nonspecific people or things. They sometimes function as antecedents for other pronouns.

Most indefinite pronouns are singular (*anybody, anyone, anything, each, either, everybody, everyone, everything, much, neither, no one, nobody, none, nothing, one, somebody, someone, something*).

ALWAYS SINGULAR Did *either* of the boys lose *his* bicycle?

A few indefinite pronouns—*both, few, many,* and *several*—are plural.

ALWAYS PLURAL *Both* of the boys lost *their* bicycles.

The indefinite pronouns *all, any, more, most,* and *some* can be either singular or plural depending on the noun to which the pronoun refers.

PLURAL The students debated, *some* arguing that *their* assumptions about the issue were more credible than the teacher's.

SINGULAR The bread is on the counter, but *some* of *it* has already been eaten.

36m Avoid gender bias with indefinite-pronoun and generic-noun antecedents.

Writers often mismatch the plural pronouns *they* and *their* with singular indefinite pronoun antecedents.

singular   plural
antecedent   pronoun

INCORRECT *Everybody* took *their* turn.

This error often occurs when writers are trying to avoid gender bias. In the sentence above, for example, changing *their* to *his* would correct the pronoun-antecedent problem. Presumably, however, *everybody* includes both men and women, and using *his* generically to represent both genders is unacceptable.

Notice how the writer edited the following sentence to avoid gender bias while remedying the agreement problem.

➤ ~~None~~ *All* of the great Romantic writers believed that their
        ^
             fell short of
achievements ~~equaled~~ their aspirations.
        ^

Replacing *their* in the original sentence with *his* would have made the sentence probably untrue and certainly biased: many women were writing and publishing during the Romantic Age. The writer could have changed *their* to *his or her* to avoid bias but thought *his or her* sounded awkward. To solve the problem the writer chose an indefinite pronoun that can have a plural meaning (*all*) and revised the sentence. An alternative would be to eliminate the indefinite pronoun altogether:

➤ **The great Romantic writers believed that their achievements fell short of their aspirations.**

Generic nouns present a similar challenge. A **generic noun** represents anyone and everyone in a group—a typical doctor, the average voter. As with a singular indefinite pronoun, it is incorrect to use a singular generic noun as the antecedent for a plural pronoun.

INCORRECT

The responsible citizen decides their vote based on issues, not personality.

However, because most groups consist of both males and females, to correct such a sentence by changing *their* to the generic *his* would usually be sexist. Strategies for avoiding gender bias with generic nouns are the same as those just described for indefinite pronouns and are summarized in the Identify and Edit box on the facing page.

Note: The use of *their* to avoid gender bias when referring to a singular antecedent or generic noun is becoming increasingly common in everyday speech, and some writers consider it acceptable. In academic writing, however, this usage is rarely acceptable.

Pronoun-Antecedent Agreement and Grammar Checkers

Do not rely on computer grammar checkers to alert you to problems in pronoun-antecedent agreement. Computer grammar checkers are not yet fully capable of detecting these problems.

agr

IDENTIFY AND EDIT
Gender Bias and Pronoun-Antecedent Agreement

Try these three strategies for avoiding gender bias when an indefinite pronoun or generic noun is the antecedent in a sentence:

✱ 1. *If possible, change the antecedent to a plural indefinite pronoun or a plural noun.*

> ◆ ~~Each~~ of us should decide ~~their~~ vote on issues, not
>   personality. *(All / our)*
>
> ◆ ~~The responsible citizen decides~~ their vote on issues, not
>   personality. *(Responsible citizens decide)*

✱ 2. *Reword the sentence to eliminate the pronoun.*

> ◆ Each of us should ~~decide their~~ vote on issues, not
>   personality.
>
> ◆ The responsible citizen ~~decides their vote~~ on issues, not
>   personality. *(votes)*

✱ 3. *Substitute* he or she *or* his or her *(but never his/her) for the singular pronoun to maintain pronoun-antecedent agreement.*

> ◆ Each of us should decide ~~their~~ vote on issues, not
>   personality. *(his or her)*
>
> ◆ The responsible citizen decides ~~their~~ vote on issues, not
>   personality. *(his or her)*
>
> **Caution:** Use this strategy sparingly. Using *he or she* or *his and her* several times in quick succession makes for tedious reading.

36n Treat most collective nouns as singular.

Collective nouns such as *team, family, jury, committee,* and *crowd* are treated as singular unless the people in the group are acting as individuals.

➤ **All together, the crowd surged through the palace gates,**

its
trampling over everything in ~~their~~ path.
 ^

The phrase *all together* indicates that this writer does not see—and does not want readers to see—the crowd as a collection of distinct individuals. Therefore, the plural *their* has been changed to the singular *its*.

➤ **The committee left the conference room and returned**

their
to ~~its~~ offices.
 ^

In this case, the writer sees—and wants readers to see—the members of the committee as individuals returning to separate offices.

If you are using a collective noun that has a plural meaning, consider adding a plural noun to clarify the meaning.

➤ **The *committee members* left the conference room and returned to *their* offices.**

36o Choose the right pronoun for a compound antecedent.

Compound antecedents joined by *and* are almost always plural.

➤ **To remove all traces of the crime, James put the book and**

their
the magnifying glass back in ~~its~~ place.
 ^

When a compound antecedent is joined by *or* or *nor,* the pronoun should agree with the closest part of the compound antecedent. If one part is singular and the other is plural, the sentence will be smoother and more effective if the plural antecedent is closest to the pronoun.

PLURAL **Neither *the child nor the parents* shared *their***

food.

Note: When the two parts of the compound antecedent refer to the same person, or when the word *each* or *every* precedes the compound antecedent, use a singular pronoun.

SINGULAR **Being *a teacher and a mother* keeps *her* busy.**

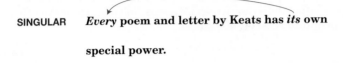

SINGULAR　　*Every* poem and letter by Keats has *its* own

　　　　　　special power.

Exercise 36.6　Editing for pronoun-antecedent agreement

Some of the sentences that follow contain errors in pronoun-antecedent agreement. Circle the number of each correct sentence, and edit the others so that the pronouns agree with their antecedents. Rewrite sentences as necessary to avoid gender bias; you may eliminate pronouns or change words. There will be several possible answers for rewritten sentences.

EXAMPLE　　Neither the dog nor the cats ate ~~its~~ *their* chow.

1. Everybody at the displaced-persons camp had to submit his medical records before boarding the ships to the United States.
2. Many were forbidden to board because they had histories of tuberculosis and other illnesses.
3. This was always devastating news because no one wanted to be separated from their family.
4. Some immigrants resorted to forging his medical records.
5. After all, a mother could not be separated from their children, and the family had to get to America.
6. Immigrants had heard that a doctor in America takes good care of their patients and felt they had a chance for a better life there.
7. Even so, was it fair to expose others to illness just to bring parents and a child to its new surroundings?
8. Every difficulty and ethical dilemma presented its own challenge for displaced persons trying to find a home with a future after World War II.

PRONOUN REFERENCE

A pronoun must refer clearly to a specific antecedent if its meaning or the meaning of the sentence it appears in is to be clear. Consider this sentence:

➤　**Near the end of Homer's *Odyssey*, Odysseus and Telemachus take their revenge on the suitors harassing his wife, Penelope.**

www.mhhe.com/
nmhh
For information and
exercises on pronoun
reference, go to

Editing >
Pronoun Reference

To whose wife does the pronoun *his* refer? We can not tell from the sentence whether the antecedent is Odysseus, Telemachus, or even Homer. The **pronoun reference** is vague.

36p Identify and edit problems with pronoun reference.

Problems with pronoun reference take two common forms:

- **Ambiguous reference:** The pronoun has two or more equally plausible antecedents.
- **Implied reference:** The antecedent is implied but not explicitly stated.

Editing for pronoun reference requires writers to be alert to potential vagueness and ambiguity and, especially, to think of their readers. Whose wife are the suitors harassing? The writer of the sentence above knows, but readers, even those familiar with the *Odyssey,* are left scratching their heads. One solution for clearing the confusion is to replace the pronoun with the correct name.

➤ **Near the end of Homer's *Odyssey*, Odysseus and Telemachus**

take their revenge on the suitors harassing ~~his~~ wife, *Odysseus's*

Penelope.

36q Avoid ambiguous pronoun references.

If a pronoun can refer to more than one noun in a sentence, the reference is ambiguous. In the following unedited sentence, who is the antecedent of *him* and *his*—Hamlet or Horatio?

> **VAGUE**   The friendly banter between Hamlet and Horatio eventually provokes him to declare that his world view has changed.

To clear up the ambiguity, the writer decided to eliminate the pronoun and use the appropriate noun.

> **BETTER**   The friendly banter between Hamlet and Horatio eventually provokes Hamlet to declare that his world view has changed.

The reader now knows that Hamlet is doing the declaring but may still be uncertain whose world view, Hamlet's or Horatio's, Hamlet thinks has changed. Eliminating this additional ambiguity without awkwardly repeating Hamlet's name a third time requires rewriting.

CLEAR   The friendly banter between Hamlet and Horatio eventually provokes Hamlet to admit to a changed view of the world.

Here is another example in which rewriting clarifies an ambiguous reference.

VAGUE   Jane Austen and Cassandra corresponded regularly when she was in London.

CLEAR   When Jane Austen was in London, she corresponded regularly with Cassandra.

36r Watch out for implied pronoun references.

A pronoun must refer to an explicitly stated noun or pronoun antecedent. Problems arise when writers rely on other words—verbs or possessives—to imply an unstated antecedent.

➤ **Every weekday afternoon, my brothers cycle home**
                                                        their bikes
   from school, and then they leave ~~them~~ in the driveway.
                                       ^

In the original sentence, the writer relied confusingly on the verb *cycle* to imply the antecedent—*their bikes*—of the pronoun *them*.

                 his   *Wilson*
➤ **In ~~Wilson's~~ essay "When Work Disappears," ~~he~~ proposes**
         ^   ^

   a four-point plan for the revitalization of blighted inner-city

   communities.

In the original sentence, the antecedent for *he* is unclear but implied by the possessive noun *Wilson's*. In the edited sentence, which clarifies who is proposing the plan, the antecedent of *his* is the explicitly stated noun *Wilson*.

1. Using clear references for *this, that,* and *which*

Writers often use the pronouns *this, that,* and *which* to refer loosely—and vaguely—to ideas expressed in preceding sentences. To make sentences containing one of these pronouns clearer, either change the pronoun to a specific noun or add a specific antecedent or clarifying noun.

657

VAGUE	As government funding for higher education de- creases, tuition increases. Are we students sup- posed to accept *this* without protest?
CLEAR	As government funding for higher education de- creases, tuition increases. Are we students sup- posed to accept *these higher costs* without protest?
CLEAR	As government funding for higher education de- creases, tuition increases. Are we students sup- posed to accept *this situation* without protest?

2. Using clear references for *they* and *it*

The pronouns *they* and *it* should refer to definite, explicitly stated an- tecedents. If the antecedent is unclear, replace the pronoun with a noun, or rewrite the sentence to eliminate the pronoun.

➤ **In some countries such as Canada, ~~they pay~~ for such medical**

    the government pays

    ^

procedures.

➤ **~~In the~~ textbook, ~~it~~ states that borrowing to fund the purchase**

    The

    ^

of financial assets results in a double-counting of debt.

3. Reserving *you* for directly addressing the reader

In formal writing, you should reserve the pronoun *you* (as this sen- tence itself illustrates) for directly addressing the reader—that is, you should use it to mean "you, the reader." Avoid using *you* as a synonym for words that refer to individual people, like *one* or *a person*.

INAPPROPRIATE	You could be executed for heresy during the Spanish Inquisition.
REVISED	One could be executed for heresy during the Spanish Inquisition.
REVISED	Accused heretics faced execution during the Spanish Inquisition.

36s Keep track of pronoun reference in paragraphs.

When the same noun is the antecedent for pronouns in a sequence of related sentences, as in a paragraph, a pronoun's antecedent does not have to be stated in every sentence as long as it is stated at the beginning. To maintain clarity and variety, alternate between pronouns and the antecedent noun.

➤ **Berlioz's unconventional music irritated the opera and**

  concert establishment. To get a hearing for his works,

  he had to arrange concerts at his own expense. Although

  he had a following of about twelve hundred who faithfully

  Berlioz
  bought tickets to his concerts, ~~he~~ needed supplementary
  ^

  income to finance the performances. He turned to music

  journalism, becoming a witty critic who tried to convince

  Parisians that music was more than mere entertainment.

36t Use *who, whom,* and *whose,* not *that* or *which,* to refer to people.

In everyday speech, people often use *that* and *which* interchangeably with *who, whom,* and *whose* to refer to people. In formal writing, however, only *who, whom,* or *whose* should be used to refer to people. *That* and *which* refer to animals or things.

  who
➤ **FDR was the president ~~that~~ led the country during World**
  ^
  War II.

  that
➤ **Animal shelters take in dogs ~~who~~ have been abandoned.**
  ^

  Who and *whom* may, however, be used to refer to animals with names.

  who
➤ **Ferdinand is the bull ~~that~~ wanted only to sit and smell the**
  ^
  flowers, not to snort and romp about like the other bulls.

659

Exercise 36.7 Editing to clarify pronoun reference

Rewrite each sentence to eliminate unclear pronoun references. Some sentences have several possible correct answers.

> EXAMPLE **You are not allowed to drive if you are a woman in Saudi Arabia.**
> *Women in Saudi Arabia are not allowed to drive.*

1. The tight race between presidential candidates John Kerry and George W. Bush in 2004 compelled him to campaign intensively in many states.
2. The candidates debated three times, answering them thoughtfully.
3. During one debate, Kerry told Bush that he had an inadequate plan of action.
4. After Bush's election, he promised to return money to some taxpayers.
5. When Kerry challenged the numbers behind Bush's proposed tax cuts, Bush accused Kerry of being "wishy-washy." This stuck throughout the campaign.
6. With Kerry as president, they would work on strengthening the economy with more jobs and higher incomes.
7. Even after all the campaigning, debating, and polling, you were still left wondering who would win the election on Tuesday, November 2, 2004.

Exercise 36.8 Chapter review: Problems with pronouns

Edit the passage below so that all pronouns have clear antecedents, agree with their antecedents, and are in the appropriate case.

> Margaret Mead was probably the best-known anthropologist of the twentieth century. It was she whom wrote *Coming of Age in Samoa,* a book well known in the 1930s and still in print today. It was her who gave us the idea that Melanesian natives grow up free of the strictures and repressions that can characterize adolescence in our society. Her writings found an audience just as the work of Sigmund Freud was becoming widely known in the United States.
>
> In his work, he argued for "an incomparably freer sexual life," saying that rigid attitudes toward sexuality contributed to mental illness among we Westerners. Her accessible and gracefully written account of life among the Samoans showed them to be both relatively free of pathology and relaxed about sexual matters. Their work both provoked and contributed to a debate over theories about the best way to raise children.

37 Problems with Adjectives and Adverbs

Adjectives and **adverbs** are words that describe. Because they qualify the meanings of other words—for example, telling which, how many, what kind, where, or how—we say that they *modify* them. Adjectives modify nouns and pronouns. Adverbs modify verbs, adjectives, and other adverbs. Adverbs can also modify entire phrases and clauses.

www.mhhe.com/
nmhh
For information and exercises on adjectives and adverbs, go to

Editing >
Adjectives and Adverbs

What Adjectives and Adverbs Do

Adjectives modify:

NOUNS
The stock price took a **sudden** *plunge.*
(adjective) (noun)

PRONOUNS
It was **low.**
(pron) (adj)

Adverbs modify:

VERBS
The price *plunged* **suddenly.**
(verb) (adverb)

ADJECTIVES
The **abnormally** *low* price attracted bargain hunters.
(adverb) (adj)

ADVERBS
The price recovered **unusually** *quickly.*
(adverb) (adverb)

PHRASES
It fell **nearly** *to its twelve-month low.*
(adverb) (phrase)

CLAUSES
It ended the day **almost** *where it began.*
(adverb) (clause)

37a Identify and edit problems with adjectives and adverbs.

When they are used with care, adjectives and adverbs add flavor and precision to writing. The problems writers have with adjectives and adverbs fall mostly into two categories:

Common Problems with Adjectives and Adverbs

1. Improperly using an adverb as an adjective
2. Using incorrectly formed comparative and superlative adjectives and adverbs

---

To identify and correct errors of the first type, writers need first to identify the kind of word or words being modified. If they are nouns or pronouns, the modifier should be an adjective; if not, it should probably be an adverb.

> ➤ **The price plunged ~~sudden~~.** *suddenly*

The adverb *suddenly* replaces the adjective *sudden* in this sentence because it modifies the verb *plunged,* not the noun *price.*

To identify and edit problems with comparatives and superlatives, consult the rules and guidelines in section 37g (*pp. 668–70*).

Adjectives, Adverbs, and Grammar Checkers

Computer grammar checkers are sensitive to some problems with adjectives and adverbs, but they miss far more than they catch. A grammar checker failed to flag the error in each of the following sentences (and, indeed, in most of the problem sentences throughout this chapter):

> The price took a *suddenly* plunge. [should be *sudden*]
> The price plunged *sudden*. [should be *suddenly*]

37b Use adjectives to modify nouns or pronouns.

Adjectives modify nouns and pronouns; they do not modify any other kind of word. Adjectives tell what kind or how many and may come before or after the noun or pronoun they modify.

➤ *Ominous gray* clouds loomed over the lake.

➤ The *looming* clouds, *ominous* and *gray,* frightened the

children.

➤ The dealer stocks more *white* cars than *red* ones.

Some proper nouns have adjective forms. Proper adjectives, like the proper nouns they are derived from, are capitalized: *Victoria/Victorian, Britain/British, America/American, Shakespeare/Shakespearean.*
Occasionally, descriptive adjectives function as nouns:

➤ The *unemployed* should not be equated with the *lazy.*

➤ F. Scott Fitzgerald wrote that the *rich* "are different from you and me."

For MULTILINGUAL STUDENTS

Using Adjectives

In English, adjectives do not change form to agree with plural nouns or pronouns.

➤ The recipe calls for one green pepper and two ~~reds~~ peppers.
          red

For more about adjectives in English, including rules for ordering adjectives when several act together to modify the same word, see Chapter 64: English Basics, pages 954–55.

37c Use nouns as adjectives sparingly.

In some cases, a noun is used as an adjective without a change in form:

➤ *Cigarette* smoking harms the lungs and is banned in offices.

Long strings of noun modifiers, however, are confusing and tedious to read. Consider revising sentences with more than one or two noun modifiers in a row.

> **CONFUSING**   The customer service improvement plan manager explained the new procedures.

> **BETTER**   The manager responsible for planning improvements in customer service explained the new procedures.

37d Use adverbs to modify verbs, adjectives, and other adverbs.

Adverbs modify verbs, adjectives, other adverbs, and even whole phrases and clauses. They tell where, when, why, how, how often, how much, or to what degree.

➤ **Dickens mixed humor and pathos *better* than any other**

   English writer after Shakespeare.

   The adverb *better* modifies the verb *mixed*.

➤ **The *notoriously* quick-tempered batter *hotly* contested**

   the umpire's call.

   The adverb *notoriously* modifies the adjective *quick-tempered* (which, in turn, modifies the noun *batter*); the adverb *hotly* modifies the verb *contested*.

➤ **The jurors came to a verdict *ominously swiftly*.**

   The adverb *ominously* modifies the adverb *swiftly*, which modifies the verb *came*.

➤ ***Afterward*, the defendants thanked their lawyers.**

   The adverb *afterward* modifies the entire independent clause that follows it.

37e Do not use an adjective when an adverb is needed.

In conversation, we sometimes treat adjectives as adverbs. In writing, this informal usage should be avoided.

LEARNING in COLLEGE

Recognizing Adverbs and Adjectives

Many adverbs in English end in *-ly,* but not all words that end in *-ly* are adverbs. Some, like *lovely,* are adjectives (*the lovely painting*). Other adverbs—*almost, now, often,* for example—do not end in *-ly.*

Adjectives, likewise, have no single form. Common endings for adjectives include *-al (comical), -an (vegetarian), - ful (wonderful), -ish (fiendish),* and *-ous (famous),* but some adjectives—*bad, large, red, short, small, tall,* for example—have no ending.

Finally, some words—including *fast, only, hard,* and *straight*—are both adjectives and adverbs. Their function depends on the context in which they appear.

When you are in doubt, consult a dictionary.

NONSTANDARD	The crowd yelled *loud* after the game-winning home run.
REVISED	The crowd yelled *loudly* after the game-winning home run.

The adjective *loud* tries to do the work of its adverb counterpart, *loudly,* to modify the verb *yelled.*

NONSTANDARD	She *sure* made me work hard for my grade.
REVISED	She *certainly* made me work hard for my grade.

The adjective *sure* tries to do the work of an adverb modifying the verb *made.*

37f Use adjectives after linking verbs to describe the subject.

A **linking verb** connects the subject of a sentence to its description. The most common linking verb is *be.* A descriptive adjective that modifies a sentence's subject but appears after a linking verb is called a **subject complement.**

➤ During the winter, both Emily and Anne *were sick.*

➤ The road *is long, winding,* and *dangerous.*

Other linking verbs are related to states of being and the five senses: *appear, become, feel, grow, look, smell, sound,* and *taste.* Verbs related to the senses can be either linking or action verbs, depending on the meaning of the sentence.

➤ The actor's *gesture looks awkward.*

Here *look* is a linking verb and *awkward* is a subject complement modifying *gesture.*

➤ The actor *looks awkwardly* over his shoulder.

Here *looks* is an action verb modified by the adverb *awkwardly.*

Pay particular attention to the distinction between *bad* and *badly, good* and *well* when these words follow verbs of this kind.

➤ The crop *grows badly* in wet regions.

➤ The weather *grew bad* as the hurricane approached.

➤ The crop *looks good* compared with last year's.

In some cases, otherwise identical sentences can have very different meanings depending on which form of these words—adjective or adverb—a writer chooses.

ADJECTIVE   The dog smelled *bad.*

The dog smelled *good.*

In both sentences, the adjectives modify the noun *dog,* which is connected to the adjectives by the linking verb *smelled.* The first sentence indicates that the dog needed a bath; the second, that the dog had probably recently had one.

ADVERB   The dog smelled *well.*

The dog smelled *badly.*

The adverbs modify the verb *smelled,* an action verb in these sentences. The dog in the first sentence might be good at tracking; the dog in the second probably would not be.

Note, however, that *well* can function as an adjective and subject complement with a linking verb to describe a person's health.

➤ After the treatment, the patient felt *well* again.

Exercise 37.1 | Identifying adjectives and adverbs

In the sentences that follow, underline and label all adjectives (adj), nouns used as adjectives (n), and adverbs (adv). Then draw an arrow from each modifier to the word or words it modifies.

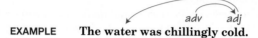

EXAMPLE   The water was <u>chillingly</u> <u>cold</u>.

1. The spread of destructive viruses to computers around the world is a serious problem with potentially deadly consequences.
2. Carried by infected e-mails, the viruses spread fast, moving from computer to computer at the click of a mouse.
3. Viruses have hit businesses badly in the past, disrupting railroads, delaying flights, and closing stores and offices.
4. Because viruses are so harmful, computer users should install antivirus software and update it regularly.
5. Other precautions include maintaining a good firewall and screening e-mail well to avoid opening suspicious messages.

Exercise 37.2 | Editing adjectives and adverbs

Edit the sentences that follow so that adjectives are not used where adverbs belong and adverbs are not used where adjectives belong. Circle the number of any sentence that is already correct.

EXAMPLE   She hid the money so ~~good~~ *well* that she could not

find it when she needed it.

1. Sociology, the scholarly study of human society, is well and thriving today.
2. The discipline's intellectual roots reach real far back, to the eighteenth century.
3. Auguste Comte (1798–1857) invented the word *sociology,* and mostly sociologists would probable agree that he founded the discipline.
4. According to Comte, scientific laws control human social behavior as sure as they control the motion of planets around the sun.
5. Comte believed his scientific approach was good because it would further human progress.
6. Emile Durkheim (1858–1917) helped place modern sociology on a well foundation.

667

7. Durkheim argued that societies can be good understood only if analyzed on their own terms, apart from the individuals who constitute them.
8. He proposed that society shapes the individual more than the other way around, and that the individual fares bad without a sense of social belonging.
9. Noting that the less cohesive a society, the higher its suicide rate, Durkheim argued that it is well for individuals to feel strongly social bonds with others.

37g Use positive, comparative, and superlative adjectives and adverbs correctly.

Most adjectives and adverbs have three forms, or **degrees,** that indicate comparison:

- the positive degree
- the comparative degree
- the superlative degree

The **positive degree** is the simple form of the adjective or adverb, the one found in the dictionary. It applies to the modified word or words alone.

POSITIVE ADJECTIVE

Pennsylvania is a *large* state.

We are tackling a *difficult* problem.

They drive an *expensive* car.

POSITIVE ADVERB

The first batter hit the ball *far.*

The company performs the play *confidently.*

The **comparative degree** of an adjective or adverb compares two things.

COMPARATIVE ADJECTIVE

New York is *larger* than Pennsylvania.

This problem is *more difficult* than the last one.

You drive a *less expensive* car than theirs.

COMPARATIVE ADVERB

The second batter hit the ball *farther* than the first.

The company performs *more confidently* now than last season but *less confidently* than the season before.

The **superlative degree** of an adjective or adverb compares three or more things, indicating which is the greatest or least.

SUPERLATIVE ADJECTIVE

Texas is the *largest* state in the Southwest.

This problem is the *most difficult* we have encountered so far.

We drive the *least expensive* car we can find.

SUPERLATIVE ADVERB

The third batter hit the ball *farthest* of all.

The company performs *most confidently* on Friday nights and *least confidently* on Tuesday nights.

1. Forming comparatives and superlatives

For most one-syllable adjectives, add *-er* to form the comparative and *-est* to form the superlative.

➤ Mercury is the ~~most near~~ planet to the sun.
   nearest

For one- or two-syllable adjectives ending in the letter *y*, change the *y* to *i* and then add the *er* or *est* ending.

➤ The ~~most lovely~~ sunsets come after volcanic eruptions.
   loveliest

For most other adjectives of two or more syllables, use *more* and *most*.

A few short adverbs take *-er* and *-est* endings to form the comparative and superlative (*harder/hardest*). Most adverbs, however, including all adverbs that end in *-ly,* form the comparative with *more* and *most* (*more loudly/most loudly*).

➤ She sings *more loudly* than we expected.

Several common adjectives and adverbs—*good* and *well,* for example—have irregular comparative and superlative forms.

➤ He felt ~~gooder~~ as his fever broke.
   better

Some of these irregular adjectives and adverbs are listed in the box on page 671. When in doubt, consult a dictionary.

> *Note:* For all adjectives and adverbs, form negative comparisons and superlatives with *less* and *least*.
>
> ➤ **The grass may seem *greener* on the other side of the fence, but you may find it *less green* when you get there.**

2. Watching out for double comparatives and superlatives

Use either an *-er* or an *-est* ending or *more/most* to form the comparative or superlative, as appropriate. Do not use both.

➤ **Since World War II, Britain has been the ~~most~~ closest ally of the United States.**

3. Being aware of concepts that cannot be compared

Do not use comparative or superlative forms with adjectives such as *unique, infinite, impossible, perfect, round, square,* and *destroyed*. These concepts are *absolutes*. If something is unique, for example, it is the only one of its kind, making comparison impossible.

> another   like
➤ **You will never find ~~a more unique~~ restaurant ~~than~~ this one.**
>   ^   ^

37h Avoid double negatives.

The words *no, not,* and *never* can modify the meaning of nouns and pronouns as well as other sentence elements.

NOUN	You are *no* friend of mine.
ADJECTIVE	The red house was *not* large.
VERB	He *never* ran in a marathon.

However, it takes only one negative word to change the meaning of a sentence from positive to negative. When two negatives are used together, they cancel each other out, resulting in a positive meaning. Unless you want your sentence to have a positive meaning (*I am not unaware of your feelings in this matter*), edit by changing or eliminating one of the negative words.

> any
➤ **They do not have ~~no~~ reason to go there.**
>   ^

> can
➤ **He ~~cannot~~ hardly do that assignment.**
>   ^

Note that *hardly* has a negative meaning and cannot be used with *no, not,* or *never*.

COMPARISON in ADJECTIVES and ADVERBS: EXAMPLES of REGULAR and IRREGULAR FORMS

Regular Adjectives

	POSITIVE	COMPARATIVE	SUPERLATIVE
One-syllable adjectives	red	redder less red	reddest least red
Two-syllable adjectives ending in *y*	lonely	lonelier less lonely	loneliest least lonely
Other adjectives of two or more syllables	famous	more/less famous	most/least famous

Regular Adverbs

	POSITIVE	COMPARATIVE	SUPERLATIVE
One-syllable adverbs	hard	harder less hard	hardest least hard
Most other adverbs	truthfully	more/less truthfully	most/least truthfully

Irregular Adjectives

	POSITIVE	COMPARATIVE	SUPERLATIVE
	good	better	best
	bad	worse	worst
	little	less, littler	least, littlest
	many	more	most
	much	more	most
	some	more	most

Irregular Adverbs

	POSITIVE	COMPARATIVE	SUPERLATIVE
	badly	worse	worst
	well	better	best

Exercise 37.3 Editing comparisons

Edit the sentences that follow so that adjectives and adverbs are used correctly in comparisons. Some of the sentences are already correct; circle their numbers.

                              worse
EXAMPLE   **He felt ~~badder~~ as his illness progressed.**
                          ^

1. Biotechnology, perhaps the controversialest application of science in recent decades, is the basis of genetic engineering, cloning, and gene therapy.
2. Some of these fields are more popular than others.
3. Ethicists find it more easy to defend the genetic engineering of plants than the cloning of animals.
4. Gene therapy is often a last resort for people suffering from the worser types of cancer.
5. Gene therapy, one of the more newer forms of biotechnology, involves introducing cells containing specialized genetic material into the patient's body.
6. Cloning, a way of creating an exact duplicate of an organism, is probably more hard to justify than any other biotechnological procedure.
7. A female lamb cloned in Scotland in 1997 seemed no different than others of her breed.
8. Despite the successes that have been achieved with animal cloning, most people do not want no humans to be cloned.
9. The Raelians, a fringe group, claimed they had cloned a human infant.
10. Many people cannot hardly believe that the Raelians really cloned an infant.

Exercise 37.4 Chapter review: Problems with adjectives and adverbs

Edit the following passage to correct any problems with adjectives and adverbs.

   Although there are many approaches to sociology, the two most commonest ones are functionalism and conflict theory. The functionalist view, usual associated with Harvard sociologist Talcott Parsons, sees society as a whole that tries to maintain equilibrium, or stasis. No ancestor of conflict theory is most famous than Karl Marx, who invented the concept of class warfare. Promoted here in the United States by the African-American sociologist W.E.B. Dubois, conflict theory sees society as made up of groups that cannot hardly avoid being in conflict or competition with one another.

For a functionalist like Parsons, societies are best understood according to how good they maintain stability. On the other hand, for a conflict theorist like Dubois, a society is more better analyzed in terms of how its parts compete for power.

Other sociological theories, such as interactionist and feminist theory, have sure made major contributions to the field. However, each of these can be seen most best as examples of functionalist or conflict theory. Relating small-scale behavior such as gestures and facial expressions to the larger context of a group or society, interactionist theory is really a development of the functionalist view. Similarly, feminist sociological theory understands society in terms of gender inequality—a view most perfectly recognizable as a subtype of conflict theory.

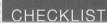

CHECKLIST

Editing for Grammar Conventions

How can you tell if one of your sentences has a grammatical problem that needs to be fixed? Focusing on each sentence in turn, look for problems that may confuse or distract readers. Ask yourself the following questions:

☐ Is each sentence grammatically complete, or is some necessary part missing? Does each sentence include a subject, a complete verb, and an independent clause? (*See Chapter 32, Sentence Fragments, pp. 572–83.*)

☐ Does any sentence seem like two or more sentences jammed together without a break? If a sentence has more than one independent clause, are those clauses joined in an acceptable way? (*See Chapter 33, Comma Splices and Run-on Sentences, pp. 584–96.*)

☐ Do the key parts of each sentence fit together well, or are the subjects and verbs mismatched in person and number? (*See Chapter 34, Subject-Verb Agreement, pp. 597–612.*)

☐ Is the time frame of events represented accurately, conventionally, and consistently, or are there problems with verb form, tense, and sequence? (*See Chapter 35, Problems with Verbs, pp. 613–37.*)

☐ Do the pronouns in every sentence clearly refer to a specific noun or pronoun and agree with the nouns or pronouns they replace? (*See Chapter 36, Problems with Pronouns, pp. 638–60.*)

☐ Does the form of each modifier match its function in the sentence? (*See Chapter 37, Problems with Adjectives and Adverbs, pp. 661–73.*)

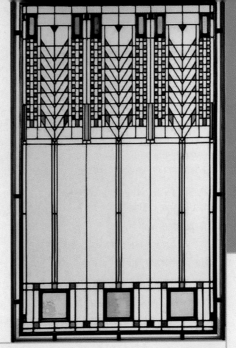

Frank Lloyd Wright's Robie House features 174 stained-glass windows. Sunlight brings out the clarity of each window's design; in turn, the designs—a variety of geometric, colorful patterns—transform the light.

I...believe that words *can* help us move or keep us paralyzed, and that our choices of language and verbal tone have something—a great deal—to do with how we live our lives and whom we end up speaking with and hearing.
—ADRIENNE RICH

Editing
for Clarity

Editing for Clarity

Answer these questions to test your familiarity with the topics covered in Chapters 32–37. For each example, select the choice that best replaces the highlighted words. If none of the choices is preferable to the example, select "no change." Check your work against the answer sheet at the back of the book, and pay particular attention to the sections in the chapters that correspond to the questions you get wrong.

1. The overthrow of the Kingdom of Hawaii was a landmark event in **the past history of the Hawaiian Islands.**
   a. no change
   b. the past of the Hawaiian Islands.
   c. the past of the Hawaii Islands.
   d. the history of the Hawaiian Islands.

2. The National Institute on Drug Abuse reported that fewer teenagers are smoking cigarettes **at this point in time in spite of the fact that the tobacco industry spends** millions of dollars targeting teens.
   a. no change
   b. at this point in time even though the tobacco industry spends
   c. now in spite of the fact that the tobacco industry spends
   d. now even though the tobacco industry spends

3. **There were millions of people who immigrated** to the United States in the late nineteenth and early twentieth centuries.
   a. There was millions of people who immigrated
   b. There are millions of people who immigrated
   c. Millions of people immigrated
   d. no change

4. The Republic of Senegal is **slightly smaller than North Dakota but larger than Ohio.**
   a. slightly smaller North Dakota but larger than Ohio.
   b. slightly smaller than North Dakota but larger Ohio.
   c. slightly smaller than North Dakota, but larger than Ohio.
   d. no change

5. Among the causes historians have proposed for the collapse of Minoan civilization are **an earthquake, volcanic eruption, and foreign invasion.**
   a. earthquake, volcanic eruption, and foreign invasion.
   b. an earthquake and a volcanic eruption and foreign invasion.
   c. an earthquake, a volcanic eruption, and a foreign invasion.
   d. no change

6. Some Americans argue that Mount Rushmore represents the country **more than the Statue of Liberty.**

   a. no change

   b. more than the Statue of Liberty does.

   c. more than the Statue of Liberty did.

   d. more than the Statue of Liberty represents.

7. **For Henry Ford used the assembly-line technique to mass produce** the Model T automobile.

   a. For Henry Ford used the assembly-line technique, he could mass produce

   b. For because Henry Ford used the assembly-line technique to mass produce

   c. Henry Ford used the assembly-line technique to mass produce

   d. no change

8. **The reason why the price of solar electric panels has risen is because demand for them has increased.**

   a. The price of solar electric panels has risen because demand for them has increased.

   b. The reason the price of solar electric panels has risen is because demand for them has increased.

   c. The price of solar electric panels has risen is because demand for them has increased.

   d. no change

9. **The Nineteenth Amendment is when women were granted** the right to vote.

   a. no change

   b. The Nineteenth Amendment granted women

   c. The Nineteenth Amendment is where women were granted

   d. The Nineteenth Amendment means women were granted

10. Full-time college students should spend at least six hours a week studying **if you want to succeed.**

    a. no change

    b. if they want to succeed.

    c. if he wants to succeed.

    d. if he or she wants to succeed.

11. Many Americans can trace their background to an ancestor **who arrives during the wave of immigration that began** in the late nineteenth century and ended in the early 1920s.

    a. no change

    b. who arrives during the wave of immigration that begins

  c. who arrived during the wave of immigration that began

  d. who arrived during the wave of immigration that begins

12. The geography teacher asked her students **if they knew which is the largest country in the world?**

  a. no change

  b. if they knew which country is the largest in the world?

  c. if they knew which country is the largest in the world.

  d. if they knew which is the largest country in the world.

13. Agamemnon, **the King of Mycenae, was the son of Atreus, brother of Menelaus, and led the Greek army during the Trojan War.**

  a. no change

  b. the King of Mycenae, was the brother of Menelaus, the son of Atreus, and led the Greek army during the Trojan War.

  c. ruling Mycenae, was the son of Atreus, brother of Menelaus, and led the Greek army during the Trojan War.

  d. the King of Mycenae, was the son of Atreus, the brother of Menelaus, and the leader of the Greek army during the Tojan War.

14. Past presidents of the Republic of Egypt include **Gamal Abdel Nasser (1956–1970) and Anwar al-Sadat (who governed from 1970 to 1981).**

  a. no change

  b. Gamal Abdel Nasser (1956–1970) and Anwar al-Sadat (who governed from 1970 to 1981).

  c. Gamal Abdel Nasser (1956–1970) and Anwar al-Sadat (who governed from 1970 to 81).

  d. Gamal Abdel Nasser (1956–1970) and Anwar al-Sadat (1970–1981).

15. Professional boxer Muhammad Ali **said, "I'm not the greatest; I'm the double greatest" to a reporter for the *New York Times*.**

  a. no change

  b. said to a reporter for the *New York Times,* "I'm not the greatest; I'm the double greatest."

  c. to a reporter from the *New York Times* said, "I'm not the greatest; I'm the double greatest."

  d. said, "I'm not the greatest; I'm the double greatest" to a *New York Times* reporter.

16. Now including the Museum of Natural History and the National Air and Space Museum, British scientist James Smithson bequeathed his wealth to the United States Government for the creation of the Smithsonian Institution, a network of museums and galleries in Washington, D.C.

a. Now including the National Air and Space Museum and the Museum of Natural History, British scientist James Smithson bequeathed his wealth to the United States Government for the creation of the Smithsonian Institution, a network of museums and galleries in Washington, D.C.

b. Now including the Museum of Natural History and National Air and Space Museum, British researcher James Smithson bequeathed his wealth to the United States Government for the creation of the Smithsonian Institution, a network of museums and galleries in Washington, D.C.

c. British researcher James Smithson bequeathed his wealth to the United States Government for the creation of the Smithsonian Institution, a network of museums and galleries in Washington, D.C., that now includes the Museum of Natural History and the National Air and Space Museum.

d. no change

17. Frank Lloyd Wright was an American architect. He is often considered the greatest American architect. He is known for the Prairie style. This style features low horizontal lines and extended eaves.

a. no change

b. Frank Lloyd Wright, an American architect, is often considered the greatest American architect. He is known for the Prairie style. This style features low horizontal lines and extended eaves.

c. Frank Lloyd Wright, often considered the greatest American architect, is known for the Prairie style, which features low horizontal lines and extended eaves.

d. Frank Lloyd Wright was an American architect. He is often considered the greatest American architect. He is known for the Prairie style, which features low horizontal lines and extended eaves.

18. During the 1800s, U.S. banks designed and printed their own currency, and this led to widespread counterfeiting.

a. no change

b. During the 1800s, U.S. banks designed and printed their own currency, which led to widespread counterfeiting.

c. During the 1800s, U.S. banks designed and printed their own currency, however this led to widespread counterfeiting.

d. During the 1800s, U.S. banks designed and printed their own currency, for this led to widespread counterfeiting.

679

19. Eight presidents were born in Virginia, and four were born in Massachusetts. **One was born in Arkansas. One was born in Connecticut.**

   a. no change

   b. One was born in Arkansas. Connecticut also was the birthplace of only one.

   c. One was born in Arkansas, and Connecticut was also the birthplace of only one.

   d. Arkansas and Connecticut, in contrast, were each the birthplace of only one president.

20. More than 830,000 people were killed by an earthquake in China in 1556.

   a. no change

   b. More than 830,000 people were killed in 1556 by an earthquake in China.

   c. In 1556, more than 830,000 people were killed by an earthquake in China

   d. An earthquake in China in 1556 killed more than 830,000 people.

38 Wordy Sentences

Clarity and conciseness go together. Writers are **concise** when they use as few words as needed to be clear and engaging. Wordiness thwarts clarity. Wordy sentences—sentences loaded with unnecessary words—can tire readers, making them struggle to decipher a writer's meaning.

A sentence does not have to be short and simple to be concise. Instead, every word in it must count, especially when the subject matter is complex or technical.

38a Identify and edit wordiness.

www.mhhe.com/ **nmhh**
For information on and practice avoiding wordiness, go to
Editing > Wordiness

Wordiness can be a natural by-product of the early stages of the writing process. As you come to grips with your subject, your task is to generate ideas and get them down, even if only roughly. Be on the lookout for wordiness, however, as you revise your work and hone your ideas.

To make your writing concise, be aware of the sources of wordiness described in this chapter and know how to counter them.

How to Make Your Writing More Concise

1. Recognize and eliminate wordy phrases and empty words.
2. Recognize and eliminate unnecessary repetition.
3. Recognize and revise constructions built around weak verbs and nouns derived from verbs.
4. Recognize opportunities to reduce clauses to phrases and phrases to single words.
5. Recognize opportunities to combine several repetitive sentences into one more concise sentence.

Wordiness and Grammar Checkers

Most computer grammar and style checkers recognize many wordy structures, but do so inconsistently. One style checker, for example, flagged most passive verbs and some *it is* and *there are* (expletive) constructions, but not others. It also flagged the redundant expression *true fact* but missed the equally redundant *round circle* and the empty phrase *it is a fact that.*

681

W

IDENTIFY AND EDIT
Wordy Sentences

To make your writing concise, ask yourself these questions as you edit your writing:

? *1. Do any sentences contain wordy or empty phrases such as at this point in time? Do any of them contain redundancies or other unnecessary repetitions?*

- ~~The fact is that at this point in time more~~ *More* women than men *now* attend college.

- Total college enrollments have increased steadily ~~upward~~ since the 1940s, but since the 1970s women have enrolled in greater numbers than men ~~have~~.

? *2. Can any clauses be reduced to phrases, or phrases to single words? Can any sentences be combined to reduce repetitive information?*

- ~~Reports that come from college~~ *College* officials indicate *report* that applications from women exceed those from men/~~This pattern indicates~~ , *indicating* that women will continue to outnumber men in college for some time to come.

? *3. Do any sentences include there is, or there are, or it is expressions; weak verbs; or nouns derived from verbs?*

- In 1970, *men outnumbered women in college by* ~~there were~~ more than 1.5 million. ~~more men in college than women.~~

- This trend ~~is a reflection of~~ *reflects* broad changes in gender roles throughout American society.

38b Eliminate wordy phrases and empty words.

1. Spotting Wordy Phrases

Certain common expressions use many words to say what only needs one. Make your sentences more concise by replacing these wordy phrases with appropriate one-word alternatives.

WORDY	Due to the fact that I have at this point in time driven my car more than three thousand miles, I should in the not-too-distant future schedule an appointment for the purpose of changing the oil.
CONCISE	Because I have now driven my car more than three thousand miles, I should schedule an oil change soon.

The following table lists some common wordy phrases and their concise alternatives.

WORDY PHRASES	CONCISE ALTERNATIVES
at this point in time	now
in this day and age	nowadays, today
at that point in time	then
in the not-too-distant future	soon
at all times	always
until such time as	until
in close proximity to	near
is necessary that	must
is able to	can
has the ability to	can
has the capacity to	can
due to the fact that	because
for the reason that	because
in spite of the fact that	although
in the event that	if
in order to	to
for the purpose(s) of	to
by means of	by

2. Recognizing empty words and phrases

Some phrases are empty, or meaningless, in that they provide little or no information. Examples include *the fact is, the process of,* and *to all intents and purposes.* Cutting **empty phrases** strengthens your writing.

➤ We had just begun ~~the process of~~ setting up our tent when the storm hit.

➤ ~~The fact is,~~ Geraldine Ferraro was the first woman to be nominated for vice president by a major party.

➤ The Nile is ~~to all intents and purposes~~ the longest river in the world.

You can often rephrase sentences to eliminate words like *manner, nature, character, way, type,* or *kind.*

➤ The mayor reacted ~~in a decisive manner.~~ *decisively.*

➤ The job ~~is the kind that~~ requires ~~a person with an honest~~ *honesty and candor.* ~~character who can communicate in a candid way.~~

Be on the alert, too, for opportunities to replace long descriptive phrases with brief, more vivid synonyms.

➤ The candidate ~~did not give a straight answer~~ *waffled* when asked about Medicare.

➤ The detectives saw no evidence ~~to suggest the death was not~~ *of homicide.* ~~from natural causes.~~

www.mhhe.com/
nmhh
For information on
and practice avoiding
redundancy, go to

Editing >
Eliminating
Redundancies

38c Eliminate unnecessary repetition.

1. Spotting redundancy

Words are **redundant** when they needlessly repeat information.

➤ She is writing a ~~fictional~~ historical novel ~~set in the past~~ about Anne Hutchinson and the settling of Rhode Island.

A historical novel *is* a work of fiction set in the past.

Be on the lookout for such commonplace redundancies as the following:

biography of the life	join together
blue in color	mix together
close proximity	past history
cooperate together	refer back
few in number	repeat again
final result	small in size
first and foremost	square (round, triangular) in shape
full and complete	underlying foundation

Sometimes, modifiers such as *very, rather,* and *really* and intensifiers such as *absolutely, definitely,* and *incredibly* do not add meaning to a sentence but are simply redundant. Delete them.

➤ **The ending ~~definitely~~ shocked us very much.**

For MULTILINGUAL STUDENTS

Redundancy and the Implied Meaning of English Words

Conciseness is not a matter of grammar but of style. Because sentences with redundancies may be perfectly grammatical, you may find it hard to spot them. In English, for example, the concept of *together* is implicit in the word *cooperate*—that is, cooperating is always something two or more parties do together. As a result, the phrase *cooperate together* is redundant.

➤ **The United States pledged to cooperate ~~together~~ with its major trading partners.**

As your knowledge of the implied meanings of English words grows, you will be better able to spot redundancies. Ask your teachers and peers for help in pointing out redundancies in your writing.

2. Reducing wordiness with elliptical constructions

Elliptical constructions allow you to omit otherwise grammatically necessary words from a sentence when their meaning and function are clear from the surrounding context.

➤ **The children enjoyed watching television more than ~~they enjoyed~~ reading books.**

685

➤   In ancient times, many astronomers knew ~~that~~ the earth was round but did not know ~~that~~ it revolved around the sun.

Note: Sometimes writers deliberately repeat words for emphasis when they could omit them. (*See Chapter 45: Sentence Variety and Emphasis, p. 747.*)

Exercise 38.1   Identifying and editing wordy or empty phrases and unnecessary repetition

Eliminate wordy or empty phrases and unnecessary repetition to make the following sentences concise.

EXAMPLE

~~The truth is that the time of the~~ ^The^ rainy season in Hawaii is

from ~~the month of~~ November to ~~the month of~~ March.

1. Charlotte Perkins Gilman was first and foremost known as a woman who was a champion of women's rights.
2. She was born on the date July 3, 1860, in the city of Hartford, which is in the state of Connecticut.
3. Gilman's "The Yellow Wallpaper," a novella about the holy matrimony of marriage and a state of madness, still speaks to contemporary readers in this present day and age.
4. The leading female heroine in Gilman's story is diagnosed by her physician husband as having an illness that is mental in origin.
5. Gilman wrote and published her book *Women and Economics* in the year 1898 and then published her book *Concerning Children* in the year 1900.

38d   Make your sentences straightforward.

Concise sentences are straightforward; they get to the point quickly instead of in a roundabout way. Roundabout sentences often result from expletive constructions and expressions built around static verbs like *to be* and *to have.*

1. Avoiding expletive constructions

An **expletive construction** is one that starts with the word *it* or *there* followed by a form of the verb *be*. In these constructions, the words *it* and *there* take the place of a subject that appears later in the sentence. These constructions can sometimes be effective. Consider, for example, the famous line from Shakespeare's *Hamlet*, "There are more things in heaven and earth, Horatio, than are dreamt of in your philosophy." In most cases, however, eliminating expletive constructions will make your sentences more concise.

ROUNDABOUT	There were millions of people who donated generously to help victims of the tsunami.
CONCISE	Millions of people donated generously to help victims of the tsunami.

2. Using strong verbs

As you edit your writing, look for roundabout expressions that combine a noun with a form of *be* or *have*. If the noun derives from a verb, replace the roundabout expression with the verb.

ROUNDABOUT	The stylistic similarities between "This Lime-Tree Bower" and "Tintern Abbey" are an indication that Coleridge had an influence on Wordsworth.
CONCISE	The stylistic similarities between "This Lime-Tree Bower" and "Tintern Abbey" indicate that Coleridge influenced Wordsworth.

The passive voice also lends itself to roundabout construction. Changing verbs from the passive to the active voice often results in stronger, more concise sentences.

ROUNDABOUT	The valley was surveyed by the archeologists for the purpose of locating sites that had been occupied by the Incas.
CONCISE	The archeologists surveyed the valley for Inca sites.

(For more on strong verbs, see Chapter 46: Active Verbs, pp. 749–52.)

38e Shorten clauses and phrases.

For conciseness and clarity, look for opportunities to simplify sentences by turning modifying clauses into phrases.

➤ The film *Dirty Pretty Things,* ~~which was~~ directed by Stephen Frears, portrays the struggles of illegal immigrants in London.

Also look for opportunities to reduce phrases to single words.

➤ Stephen Frears's film *Dirty Pretty Things* portrays the struggles of illegal immigrants in London.

38f Combine sentences.

Sometimes you can combine several short, repetitive sentences into a single more concise sentence.

WORDY	Little Red Riding Hood crossed the river. After that, she walked through the woods. Finally, she arrived at grandmother's house.
CONCISE	Little Red Riding Hood went over the river and through the woods to grandmother's house.
WORDY	Hurricane Floyd had a devastating effect on our town. The destruction resulted from torrential rains. Flooding submerged Main Street under eight feet of water. The rain also triggered mudslides that destroyed two houses.
CONCISE	Hurricane Floyd's torrential rains devastated our town, submerging Main Street under eight feet of water and triggering mudslides that destroyed two houses.

(*For more on combining sentences and clauses, see Chapter 42: Faulty Parallelism, pp. 710–18, and Chapter 44: Coordination and Subordination, pp. 729–39.*)

Exercise 38.2 Writing straightforward sentences

Use the techniques described in sections 38d–f to make each of the following passages into a single concise sentence.

EXAMPLE: ORIGINAL

The play opened on October 1. There were many reviews in which critics gave it a pan. The public loathed it too, which is why it closed after a run of less than two weeks.

EXAMPLE: REVISED

The play opened on October 1, but critics panned it, the public loathed it, and it closed after a run of less than two weeks.

1. There are many concerns that environmentalists have about whether genetically modified food products are absolutely safe for the environment.
2. Soybeans that are genetically engineered are very resistant to certain artificially made herbicides. These beans are also very resistant to certain artificially made insecticides.
3. These soybeans, which are resistant, permit the use of larger quantities of herbicides by farmers than before.
4. The herbicides kill surrounding plants. They also kill insects that are not considered pests, such as the Monarch butterfly.
5. There are also concerns from consumers about the handling of genetically modified soy crops. One of these concerns is that the genetically modified soy crops are not segregated from soy crops that have not been genetically modified.

Exercise 38.3   Chapter review: Wordy sentences

Use the techniques described in this chapter to make the following passage concise.

In this day and age, people definitely should take preventive precautions to prevent identity theft from happening to them. Identity thieves have the ability to use someone else's personal information to commit fraud or theft, such as opening a fraudulent credit card account. Identity thieves also have the capacity to create counterfeit checks. This type of theft is often done in such a clever manner that often the victim of identity theft never realizes that his or her identity has been stolen. People whose identity has been stolen should first and foremost contact the Federal Trade Commission (FTC) for the purpose of disputing fraudulent charges. There is also the fact that people should learn how they can minimize the chance that they will face the risk of becoming a victim of this type of crime.

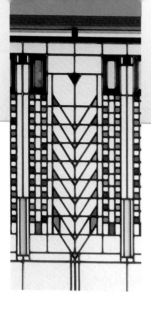

39 Missing Words

Just as wordiness muddies writing (*see Chapter 38*), omitting needed words obstructs its flow. When editing, make sure you have not omitted any words the reader needs to understand the meaning of your sentences.

39a Identify and edit problems with missing words.

www.mhhe.com/ **nmhh** For information and exercises on missing words, go to

Editing > Word Choice

Writers sometimes omit from sentences words that are needed to make the sentences clear or grammatically complete. The desire to avoid repetition or the mistaken assumption that the rest of the sentence conveys the required information is usually at the root of these omissions. Writers should be particularly alert for missing words in compound structures, in dependent clauses beginning with *that,* and in comparisons.

Situations in Which Needed Words Often Go Missing

1. Compound structures
2. Dependent clauses beginning with *that*
3. Comparisons

Here is an example that combines all three of these situations:

➤   *that*   *than Matrix II*   *claim*   *better than Matrix I*
    He claims *Matrix I* is better; I that *Matrix II* is.

Missing Words and Grammar Checkers

Computer grammar checkers are entirely unreliable at flagging most instances of the kinds of missing-word errors discussed in this chapter. In fact, one grammar checker failed to flag errors in any of the chapter's example sentences.

IDENTIFY AND EDIT
Missing Words

To avoid omissions that might confuse your readers, ask
yourself these questions as you edit your writing:

❷ *1. Are any additional words needed to make a sentence idiomatic and
grammatical?*

> ◆ Commuting in carpools, *by* train, or *by* bus can help reduce the
> nation's consumption of oil.
> ◆ My neighbor takes the bus, and I *take* the train.

❷ *2. Is the word* that *missing when it is needed for clarity?*

> ◆ Many companies suggest *that* their employees carpool or take mass
> transit to work.

❷ *3. Are all comparisons clear and complete?*

> ◆ Carpooling is more energy-efficient *than driving alone.*
> ◆ Driving alone is less energy-efficient than any *other* way of commuting
> to work.

39b Add words that are needed to make
compound structures complete and clear.

For conciseness, words can sometimes be omitted from compound
structures. In the following example, the second *is* can be omitted because the verb in the first part of the compound structure is also *is:*
The defendant's anger is extreme and his behavior violent.

   Do not leave out part of a compound structure unless both parts
of the compound are the same, however. If an idiom calls for different

691

For MULTILINGUAL STUDENTS

Obligatory Words in English

In English the subject and the verb are obligatory components of a sentence.

- Every English clause must have an explicit subject—a noun, phrase, pronoun, or filler word like *there* or *it*—even if the rest of the sentence seems unambiguously to imply the subject. The only exceptions are imperative sentences—commands—in which the subject, *you,* is understood.
- Every clause must have a verb, even if it is a linking verb (like *be*). Also, the verb must be complete (a main verb along with any helping verbs that are needed to express tense or voice).

prepositions in each part of a compound structure, both prepositions should appear in the sentence.

➤ **The gang members neither cooperated *with* nor listened to the authorities.**

> One cooperates *with* but listens *to,* so both prepositions are needed in this sentence.

➤ **The performers stood and sang for an hour without interruption.**

> In this case, both verbs require the same preposition, *for,* so it needs to appear only once.

Similarly, when grammar requires different forms of a word in each part of a compound, both forms should appear in the sentence.

➤ **The boss flies first class; the rest of us *fly* economy class.**

➤ **The coach declared that our team has never *been* and will never be defeated.**

Sometimes, to avoid ambiguity, you may need to repeat a word even when it serves the same function in both parts of a compound

structure.

➤ The author dedicated the book to her children and ^her teachers.

The repetition makes it clear that the children and the teachers are not the same people.

39c Include *that* when it is needed for clarity.

The subordinator *that* should be omitted only when the clause it introduces is short and the sentence's meaning is clear: *Faith Hill sings the kinds of songs many women love.* Usually, *that* should be included.

➤ The attorney argued ^that men and women should receive equal

pay for equal work.

39d Make comparisons clear.

www.mhhe.com/
nmhh
For information on
and practice avoiding
faulty comparisons,
go to
Editing > Faulty
Comparisons

To be clear, comparisons must be complete. If you have just said, "Peanut butter sandwiches are boring," you can say immediately afterward, "Curried chicken sandwiches are more interesting," but you cannot say in isolation, "Curried chicken sandwiches are more interesting." You need to name who or what they are more interesting than—in other words, you need to complete the comparison.

Check comparisons to make sure your meaning is clear. In the following example, does the writer mean that she loved her grandmother more than her sister did—or more than she loved her sister? To clarify, add the missing words.

➤ I loved my grandmother more than my sister. ^did

➤ I loved my grandmother more than ^I loved my sister.

When you use *as* to compare people or things, be sure to use it twice:

➤ Napoleon's temper was ^as volatile as a volcano.

Include the words *other* or *else* to clarify comparisons when the subject of the comparison belongs to the same category of people or things to which it is being compared.

➤ High schools and colleges stage *The Laramie Project* more

than any ^other play.

The sentence compares *The Laramie Project,* itself a play, with other plays.

➤ Professor Koonig has written more books than anyone in her *else*

department.

The sentence compares Professor Koonig with other members of her own department.

➤ *Lord of the Rings: Return of the King*, directed by New Zealander Peter Jackson, won more awards than any film *other*

in 2004.

Do not include *other* or *else,* however, when comparing people or things that belong to different categories.

➤ *Lord of the Rings: Return of the King*, directed by New Zealander Peter Jackson, won more awards than any ~~other~~ film directed by an American in 2004.

Use a possessive form when comparing attributes or possessions.

WEAK Plato's philosophy is easier to read than *that of Aristotle.*

BETTER Plato's philosophy is easier to read than *Aristotle's.*

Keep in mind that complex comparisons may require more than one addition to be completely clear.

➤ Smith's book is longer, but his account of the war is more *than Jones's book*

interesting than ~~Jones's.~~ *Jones's account*

39e Add articles (*a, an, the*) where necessary.

In English, omitting an article usually makes an expression sound odd, unless the omission occurs in a series of nouns.

➤ A dog that bites should be kept on leash. *a*

➤ He gave me books he liked best. *the*

➤ The classroom contained a fish tank, birdcage, and rabbit hutch.

Note: If the articles in a series are not the same, each one must be included.

➤ **The classroom contained an aquarium, ^abirdcage, and ^arabbit**
        ^   ^

hutch.

For MULTILINGUAL STUDENTS

For more information about the use of articles, consult Chapter 64: English Basics, pages 949–51.

Exercise 39.1   Chapter review: Editing for missing words

Read the following paragraphs carefully, and supply any missing words.

Most early scientists thought the speed of light was infinite. The Italian scientist Galileo never agreed nor listened to arguments of his contemporaries. He set up experiment to measure the speed of light between two hills that were a known distance apart. Although its results were ambiguous, Galileo's experiment was more influential than any experiment of his day.

Almost one hundred years later, the Danish astronomer Olaus Roemer devised a sophisticated experiment to measure speed of light. Roemer hypothesized the farther away planet Jupiter is from Earth, the longer its light will take. Knowing Jupiter's distance from Earth at various times of the year, Roemer calculated the speed of light at 141,000 miles per second. Roemer's result was closer than that of any earlier scientist to the actual speed of light, which is now known to be 186,281.7 miles per second in a vacuum.

According to Albert Einstein's theory of relativity, the speed of light has never and will never be exceeded. The speed of light is variable, however. For instance, it travels about twenty-five percent slower through water.

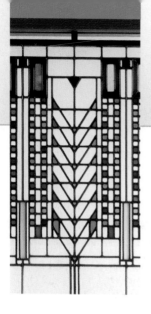

40 Mixed Constructions

When a sentence's parts do not fit together either grammatically or logically, the result is a **mixed construction.** Because they confuse readers, mixed constructions must be revised for clarity.

40a Identify and edit mixed constructions.

Mixed constructions occur when writers start a sentence one way and then, midway through, change grammatical direction. The writer of the following sentence begins with a prepositional phrase (a phrase introduced by a preposition such as *at, by, for, in,* or *of*) and then, midway through, tries to make that phrase into the subject. A prepositional phrase cannot be the subject of a sentence, however.

www.mhhe.com/
nmhh
For information on
and practice avoiding
mixed constructions,
go to

Editing > Mixed
Constructions

**MIXED-UP
SENTENCE** For family members who enjoy one another's company often decide on a vacation spot together.

The mixed construction obscures the exact meaning the writer wants to convey. Revising the sentence requires that the writer clarify his or her intent; different solutions will produce different effects. The most straightforward option, eliminating the preposition *for,* makes *family members* the subject of the verb *decide.* The result is a statement of fact about close families.

**REVISED
SENTENCE** Family members who enjoy one another's company often decide on a vacation spot together.

Perhaps the writer instead intended to recommend joint vacation planning as something for close families to consider. In that case, an alternative is to leave the opening as a prepositional phrase, change *decide* from a verb to a gerund (*deciding*) that serves as the subject, add the linking verb *is,* and provide a subject complement (*rewarding*) for the prepositional phrase to modify. (A **subject complement** is a word or word group that specifies or describes the subject of a linking verb.)

**REVISED
SENTENCE** For family members who enjoy one another's company, deciding together on a vacation spot is often rewarding.

In the following sentence, the dependent clause *when a* curandero *is consulted* cannot serve as the subject of the sentence.

MIXED-UP SENTENCE	In Mexican culture, when a *curandero* is consulted can address spiritual or physical illness.

One revision transforms the dependent clause into an independent clause with a subject and a predicate (a complete verb) that make sense together.

REVISED SENTENCE	In Mexican culture, a *curandero* can be consulted for spiritual or physical illness.

Here are two alternative revisions, each of which picks up on different words in the original, to slightly different effect in each case.

REVISED SENTENCE	In Mexican culture, when people suffer from spiritual or physical illness, they consult a *curandero*.

REVISED SENTENCE	In Mexican culture, the *curandero's* role is to address people's spiritual and physical illnesses.

Sometimes you may have to separate your ideas into more than one sentence to clarify the point you are trying to make. The writer of the following sentence is attempting to do two things at one time: contrast England and France in 1805 and define the difference between an oligarchy and a dictatorship.

MIXED-UP SENTENCE	In an oligarchy like England was in 1805, a few people had the power rather than a dictatorship like France, which was ruled by Napoleon.

By using two sentences instead of one, the writer makes both ideas clear.

REVISED SENTENCE	In 1805, England was an oligarchy, a state ruled by the few. In contrast, France under Napoleon was a dictatorship, a state ruled by one person.

Mixed Constructions and Grammar Checkers

As with missing words, computer grammar checkers are unreliable at detecting mixed constructions.

Note: The editing symbol for mixed constructions is *mix*.

40b Make sure predicates match their subjects.

A **predicate** is the complete verb along with any words that modify it, any objects or complements, and any words that modify them. A predicate must match a sentence's subject both logically and grammatically. When it does not, the result is **faulty predication.**

> **FAULTY PREDICATION**   The best kind of education for me would be a university with both a school of music and a school of government.

A university is an institution, not a type of education, so the sentence needs to be revised.

> **REVISED SENTENCE**   A university with both a school of music and a school of government would be best for me.

Avoid using the phrases *is where, is when,* and *the reason is . . . because.* These phrases may sound logical, but they usually result in faulty predication.

> **FAULTY PREDICATION**   Photosynthesis is where carbon dioxide, water, and chlorophyll interact in the presence of sunlight to form carbohydrates.

Photosynthesis is not a place, so *is where* is illogical. Also, to be grammatically correct, the linking verb *is* needs to be followed by a subject complement.

> **REVISED SENTENCE**   Photosynthesis is the production of carbohydrates from the interaction of carbon dioxide, water, and chlorophyll in the presence of sunlight.

Although *is because* may seem logical, it creates an adverb clause following the linking verb rather than the required subject complement.

> **FAULTY PREDICATION**   The reason the joint did not hold is because the coupling bolt broke.

To fix this kind of faulty predication, turn the adverb clause into a noun clause by changing *because* to *that,* or change the subject of the sentence.

>   *that*
> ➤ **The reason the joint did not hold is ~~because~~ the coupling bolt broke.**

or

>   *The*
> ➤ **~~The reason the~~ joint did not hold is because the coupling bolt broke.**

Exercise 40.1 Chapter review: Mixed constructions

Edit the following paragraph to eliminate mixed constructions. Some sentences may not need correction, and there may be several acceptable options for editing those that do need it.

Electrons spin around the nucleus of an atom according to definite rules. The single electron of a hydrogen atom occupies a kind of spherical shell around a single proton. According to the discoveries of quantum physics, states that we can never determine exactly where in this shell the electron is at a given time. The indeterminacy principle is a rule where we can only know the probability that the electron will be at a given point at a given moment. The set of places where the electron is most likely to be is called its orbital. By outlining a set of rules for the orbitals of electrons, the Austrian physicist Wolfgang Pauli developed the concept of the quantum state. Through using this concept permits scientists to describe the energy and behavior of any electron in a series of four numbers. The first of these, or principal quantum number, is where the average distance of the electron from the nucleus is specified. For the other quantum numbers describe the shape of the orbital and the "spin" of the electron. That no two electrons can ever be in exactly the same quantum state, according to Pauli's basic rule. The reason chemists use the four quantum numbers as a shorthand for each electron in an atom is because they can calculate the behavior of the atom as a whole.

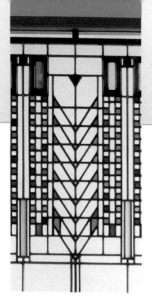

41 Confusing Shifts

When you are editing, look for jarring shifts in point of view, tense, mood, or voice that may confuse your readers. Keeping things consistent helps convey a clear message.

41a Identify and edit confusing shifts.

Confusing shifts occur in a variety of contexts and can involve many of the problems discussed in other chapters of this handbook. Shifts in person and number, for example, may involve errors in pronoun-antecedent agreement (*see Chapter 36: Problems with Pronouns, pp. 649–55*). Often, however, confusing shifts are just that—confusing—even though they occur in otherwise grammatically correct sentences.

In general, confusing shifts fall into four categories: inappropriate shifts in person and number, inappropriate shifts in verb tense, inappropriate shifts in verb mood and voice, and inappropriate shifts from indirect to direct quotations and questions.

Four Categories of Confusing Shifts

1. Inappropriate shifts in person and number
2. Inappropriate shifts in verb tense
3. Inappropriate shifts in verb mood and voice
4. Inappropriate shifts from indirect to direct quotations and questions

---

Confusing Shifts and Grammar Checkers

Because confusing shifts can occur in otherwise grammatical sentences, computer grammar checkers rarely flag them. Consider this blatant example:

The teacher entered the room and then roll is called.

Although the sentence shifts confusingly from past to present tense and from active to passive voice, it passed muster on at least one grammar checker.

41b Make your point of view consistent in person and number.

A writer has three points of view to choose from. First person (*I* or *we*) emphasizes the writer and is used in personal writing. Second person (*you*) focuses attention on the readers and is used to give them orders, directions, or advice. Third person (*he, she, it, one,* or *they*) is topic oriented and therefore prevalent in academic writing. Once you choose a point of view, you should use it consistently.

1. Correcting shifts in person

Writers sometimes make jarring shifts in person when they compose generalizations. For example, the writer of the following sentence initially shifted from the third person (*students*) to the second person (*you*), a common kind of confusing shift.

➤ **According to the new rules, students will be allowed access**

          they
to computers only if ~~you~~ arrive before 9 PM.

> *Note:* Do not use *you* unless you are addressing the reader directly. If you are writing *about* someone rather than *to* them, then use the third person.

2. Correcting shifts in number

Confusing shifts in number occur when writers switch from singular to plural or plural to singular for no apparent reason. To correct such shifts, you should usually choose the plural to avoid using *his or her* or introducing gender bias. (*See Chapter 36: Problems with Pronouns, pp. 651–53 and Chapter 48: Appropriate Language, pp. 772–75.*)

In the following sentence, the writer changed the singular noun *person* to the plural *people* to agree with the plural pronoun *they.*

    People are
➤ **~~A person is~~ often assumed to be dumb if they are attractive**

and smart if they are unattractive.

The alternative, changing the pronoun to the singular, would have resulted in gender bias or the awkward repetition of the phrase *he or she.*

Also be aware that confusing shifts in number can occur between nouns that are logically connected. As originally phrased, the following **701**

IDENTIFY AND EDIT
Confusing Shifts

shift

To avoid confusing shifts, ask yourself these questions as you edit your writing:

? *1. Does the sentence shift from one point of view to another? For example, does it shift from third person to second?*

♦ Over the centuries, millions of laborers helped build and
  maintain the Great Wall of China, and ~~if you were one, you~~
  most of them
  ~~probably~~ suffered great hardship as a result.

? *2. Are the verbs in your sentence consistent in the following ways:*

In tense (past, present, or future)?

♦ Historians call the period before the unification of China the
  Warring States period. It ~~ends~~ when the ruler of the Ch'in
  ended
  state conquered the last of his independent neighbors.

In mood (statements vs. commands or hypothetical conditions)?

♦ If a similar wall ~~is~~ built today, it would cost untold amounts
  were
  of time and money.

In voice (active vs. passive)?

♦ The purpose of the wall was to protect against invasion, but
  it also promoted
  commerce, ~~was promoted by it also.~~

? *3. Are quotations and questions clearly phrased in either direct or indirect form?*

♦ The visitor asked the guide ~~when~~ did construction of the
  , "When
  Great Wall begin?*"*

♦ The visitor asked the guide when ~~did~~ construction of the
  began.
  Great Wall ~~begin?~~

sentence suggests that the students have only one pencil among them. There are two ways to clarify the confusion.

> The students brought ~~a~~ soft lead ~~pencil~~ *pencils* to the exam.

or

> *Each student* ~~The students~~ brought a soft lead pencil to the exam.

Similarly, the following sentence, as originally phrased, suggests a group of job applicants might be sharing a single résumé. Again, two solutions are available.

> All of the applicants have ~~a~~ strong ~~résumé.~~ *résumés.*

or

> *Every applicant has* ~~All of the applicants have~~ a strong résumé.

Exercise 41.1   Making point of view consistent

Edit the following sentences so that they are consistent in person and number.

EXAMPLE

When people vote, ~~you~~ *they* participate in government.

or

When ~~people~~ *you* vote, you participate in government.

1. On November 30, 1974, archeologists discovered the 3.5 million-year-old skeleton of an early hominid (or human ancestor) you call Lucy.
2. If you consider how long ago Lucy lived, one might be surprised so many of her bones remained intact.
3. When an early hominid like Lucy reached full height, they were about three and a half feet tall.
4. When these early hominids were born, she could expect to live about thirty years.
5. Lucy and the other hominids who lived with her in what is today Ethiopia, Africa, all walked upright and could manipulate a tool with their dextrous hands.

41c Keep your verb tenses consistent.

Verb tenses show the time of an action in relation to other actions. Writers are expected to choose a time frame for their work—present, past, or future—and use it consistently, changing tense only when the meaning requires it. For example, the following sentence is about a *present* inquiry into *past* events and so requires a shift from present tense to past tense.

APPROPRIATE SHIFT IN TENSE

Our inquiry begins with a look at how the Germanic invasions affected the identity of the late Roman world.

The following sentence, in contrast, refers only to past events, but it shifts confusingly from present tense to past tense.

CONFUSING SHIFT IN TENSE

According to the traditional view, the medieval period begins when Rome fell.

REVISED

According to the traditional view, the medieval period began when Rome fell.

You may find yourself shifting confusingly between past and present tense when you are narrating dramatic events that are still vivid in your mind.

➤ **The wind was blowing a hundred miles an hour when**
               was   *fell*
  suddenly there ~~is~~ a big crash, and a tree ~~falls~~ into the

  living room.

You may also introduce inconsistencies when you are using the present perfect tense, perhaps because the past participle causes you to slip from present tense to past tense.

➤ **She has admired many strange buildings at the university**
          thinks   *looks*
  but ~~thought~~ that the new Science Center ~~looked~~ completely

  out of place.

41d Avoid unnecessary shifts in mood and voice.

Besides tense, verbs in a sentence also have a mood and a voice. There are three basic **moods:** the **indicative,** used to state or question facts,

CHARTING the TERRITORY

Present Tense and Literary Works

By convention, the present tense is used to write about the content of literary works. When you write about literary characters and events, be careful not to shift out of the present tense as you move from one sentence to another.

➤ **David Copperfield observes other people with a fine**

and sympathetic eye. He describes villains such as

Mr. Murdstone and heroes such as Mr. Micawber in

unforgettable detail. However, Copperfield ~~was~~ not
              is

himself an especially interesting person.

---

acts, and opinions; the **imperative,** used to give commands or advice; and the **subjunctive,** used to express wishes, conjectures, and hypothetical conditions. Unnecessary shifts in mood can confuse and distract your readers. Be on the lookout for shifts between the indicative and the subjunctive and between the indicative and the imperative.

www.mhhe.com/
nmhh
For information and
exercises on shifts in
verb tense and voice,
go to

Editing > Verb and
Voice Shifts

➤ **If he ~~goes~~ to night school, he would take a course in**
          could go

accounting.

➤ **The sign says that in case of emergency passengers should**

follow the instructions of the train crew and ~~don't~~ leave the
                                              should not

train unless instructed to do so.

Most verbs have two voices. In the **active voice** the subject does the acting; in the **passive voice** the subject is acted upon. Do not shift abruptly from one voice to the other, especially when the subject remains the same.

➤ **The Impressionist painters hated black. ~~Violet,~~ green, blue,**
                                        They favored violet,

pink, and red. ~~were favored by them.~~

Exercise 41.2 Keeping verbs consistent in tense, mood, and voice

Edit the following sentences so that the verbs are consistent in tense, mood, and voice unless meaning requires a shift. If a sentence is correct as is, circle its number.

EXAMPLE

The Silk Road, the famous trade route that linked Asia

followed
and Europe, ~~follows~~ the Great Wall of China for much
                    ^

of its length.

1. Many visitors who have looked with amazement at the Great Wall of China did not know that its origins reached back to the seventh century BCE.
2. In 221 BCE the ruler of the Ch'in state conquered the last of its independent neighbors and unifies China for the first time.
3. The Ch'in ruler ordered the walls the states had erected between themselves to be torn down, but the walls on the northern frontier were combined and reinforced.

FIGURE 41.1 **The Great Wall of China.**

4. Subsequent Chinese rulers extended and improved the wall until the seventeenth century CE, when it reached its present length of more than four thousand miles.
5. History shows that as a defense against invasion from the north, the wall was not always effective.
6. China was conquered by the Mongols in the thirteenth century, and the Manchus took control of the empire in the seventeenth century.
7. The wall, however, also served as a trade route and had helped open new regions to farming.
8. As a result, was it not for the wall, China's prosperity might have suffered.

41e Be alert to awkward shifts between direct and indirect quotations and questions.

Indirect quotations report what others wrote or said without repeating their words exactly. **Direct quotations** report the words of others exactly and should be enclosed in quotation marks. (*For more on punctuating quotations, see Chapter 54: Quotation Marks, pp. 857–59.*)

Shifts from one form of quotation to the other within a sentence can leave readers confused.

SHIFT: INDIRECT TO DIRECT QUOTATION	In his famous inaugural speech, President Kennedy called on Americans not to ask what their country could do for them but instead "ask what you can do for your country."
REVISED: INDIRECT	In his famous inaugural speech, President Kennedy called on Americans not to ask what their country could do for them but instead to ask what they could do for their country.
REVISED: DIRECT	In his famous inaugural speech, President Kennedy said, "My fellow Americans, ask not what your country can do for you; ask what you can do for your country."

Shifts from indirectly to directly posed questions are similarly confusing.

SHIFT: INDIRECT TO DIRECT QUESTION	The performance was so bad the audience wondered had the performers ever rehearsed.

REVISED:
INDIRECT

The performance was so bad the audience wondered whether the performers had ever rehearsed.

REVISED:
DIRECT

Had the performers ever rehearsed? The performance was so bad the audience was not sure.

Exercise 41.3 Chapter review: Confusing shifts

Edit the following passage, changing words as necessary to avoid confusing shifts.

From about the first to the eighth century CE the Moche civilization dominated the north coast of what is now Peru. The people of this remarkable civilization, which flourished nearly a thousand years before the better-known Inca civilization, are sophisticated engineers and skilled artisans. They built enormous adobe pyramids and a vast system of irrigation canals was created and maintained. Moche smiths forged spectacular gold ornaments as well as copper tools and weapons. The Moche potter sculpted realistic-looking portraits and scenes of everyday life onto clay vessels; they also decorated vessels with intricate drawings of imposing and elaborately garbed figures involved in complex ceremonies. One such scene, which appeared on many Moche vessels, depicted a figure archeologists call the Warrior Priest engaged in a ceremony that involves the ritual sacrifice of bound prisoners.

A question is what do these drawings represent. You wonder whether they depict Moche gods and mythological events, or do they represent actual figures from Moche society conducting actual Moche rituals? A dramatic discovery in 1987 provided an answer to these questions. In that year, archeologists have uncovered a group of intact Moche tombs at a site called Sipán. In one of the tombs were the remains of a man who had been buried clothed in stunningly rich regalia. As this outfit was carefully removed by the archeologists, they realized that it corresponded to the outfit worn by the Warrior Priest depicted on Moche pottery. If the warrior priest was just a mythological figure, then this tomb should not exist, but it did. In other words, the archeologists realized, the man in the tomb was an actual Moche Warrior Priest. The archeologists who excavated the tomb explain that the art "enabled us to . . . identify the status, rank and wealth of the principal individual buried in the tomb, as well as the role that he played in the ceremonial life of his people" (Alva and Donnan, 1993, p. 141).*

*Alva, W. and Donnan, C. B. (1993). *Royal Tombs of Sipán,* Los Angeles: Fowler Museum of Cultural History.

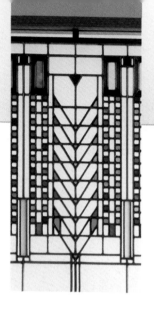

42 Faulty Parallelism

Parallelism is the presentation of equal (or parallel) ideas in the same (or parallel) grammatical form: individual terms with individual terms, phrases with phrases, and clauses with clauses. Effective parallelism can increase the clarity and impact of your writing.

➤ **Little Red Riding Hood went**

and { over the river / through the woods / to grandmother's house. } — *parallel phrases*

➤ **At Gettysburg in 1863, Lincoln said that the Civil War was being fought to make sure that government**

and { of the people, / by the people, / for the people } — *parallel phrases*

might not perish from the earth.

➤ **In the Declaration of Independence, Jefferson wrote, "We hold these truths to be self-evident:**

{ that all men are created equal; / that they are endowed by their Creator with certain unalienable rights; / that among these are } — *parallel clauses*

and { life, / liberty, / the pursuit of happiness." } — *parallel terms*

As you edit your writing, look for ways you can use parallelism to combine and give forceful expression to related ideas.

FIRST DRAFT

Claudius, Hamlet's uncle, strides confidently through the action of the play. His crown is ill-gotten, but he reaps its benefits. He smiles confidently. Those close to him are assured that he is indeed the rightful king.

www.mhhe.com/
nmhh
For information
and exercises on
parallelism, go to

Editing >
Parallelism

REVISED

Claudius, Hamlet's uncle, strides confidently through the action of the play, *reaping* the benefits of his ill-gotten crown, *smiling* confidently, and *assuring* those close to him that he is indeed the rightful king.

| **Exercise 42.1** | Identifying effective parallelism |

Underline the parallel elements in the following passage.

> I believe this government cannot endure permanently half slave and half free. I do not expect the Union to be dissolved— I do not expect the house to fall—but I do expect it will cease to be divided. It will become all one thing, or all the other. Either the opponents of slavery will arrest the further spread of it, and place it where the public mind shall rest in the belief that it is in the course of ultimate extinction; or its advocates will push it forward till it shall become alike lawful in all the states, old as well as new, North as well as South.
>
> —ABRAHAM LINCOLN, speech at the
> Republican State Convention,
> Springfield, Illinois, June 16, 1858

42a Identify and edit faulty parallelism.

Faulty parallelism occurs when items in a series, paired or contrasting items, or items in a list do not have the same grammatical form.

Situations in Which Faulty Parallelism Occurs

1. In sentences that present equivalent items in a series
2. In sentences that pair equivalent items with a conjunction or contrast them with a comparative expression
3. In outlines and headings, and in numbered and bulleted lists

---

Faulty Parallelism and Grammar Checkers

Computer grammar checkers cannot detect faulty parallelism because they cannot distinguish ideas that are equivalent and require parallel form from those that are not and do not.

42b Make items in a series parallel.

A list or series of equally important items should be parallel in grammatical structure. Phrases should balance phrases; clauses should balance clauses; and within phrases and clauses, equivalent elements should be of the same kind—nouns with nouns, for example, or verbs with verbs.

In the following sentence, the writer deleted *constructing* to make the last item in the series consistent with the rest of the items, which are all nouns or nouns modified by adjectives.

➤ **The development plan included apartment buildings, single-family houses, a park, and ~~constructing~~ two new schools.**

In the next sentence, the writer changed the last item in the series to give all three items the same form: action verb followed by direct object.

➤ **According to the Constitution, the president heads the executive branch of government, nominates the justices of the Supreme Court, and *commands* ~~is commander-in-chief of~~ the nation's armed forces.**

In the next sentence, the writer changed a noun to an adjective. Notice that the writer also decided to repeat the word *too* to make the sentence more forceful and memorable.

➤ **My sister obviously thought that I was too young, *too* ignorant, and *too troublesome.* ~~a troublemaker.~~**

IDENTIFY AND EDIT
Faulty Parallelism

//

To avoid faulty parallelism, ask yourself these questions as you edit your writing:

? 1. Are the items in a series in parallel form?

◆ The senator stepped to the podium, ~~an angry glance~~ *glanced angrily at* ~~shooting toward~~ her challenger, and began to refute his charges.

? 2. Are paired items in parallel form?

◆ Her challenger, she claimed, ~~had~~ not only *had* accused her falsely of accepting illegal campaign contributions, but ~~his contributions were from illegal sources also.~~ *also had accepted illegal contributions himself.*

? 3. Are the items in outlines and lists in parallel form?

FAULTY PARALLELISM

She listed four reasons for voters to send her back to Washington:
1. Ability to protect the state's interests
2. Her senority on important committees
3. Works with members of both parties to get things done
4. Has a close working relationship with the president

REVISED

She listed four reasons for voters to send her back to Washington:
1. *Her ability* to protect the state's interests
2. *Her seniority* on important committees
3. *Her ability* to work with members of both parties to get things done
4. *Her* close working *relationship* with the president

713

42c Make paired ideas parallel.

When you join ideas with a conjunction or distinguish between them with a comparative expression, you should word them in parallel form.

1. Pairing ideas with coordinating conjunctions

Coordinating conjunctions—*and, but, or, nor, for, so,* and *yet*—join elements of equal weight or function.

FAULTY PARALLELISM	The job requires initiative and leading others.
REVISED	The job requires *initiative* and *leadership*.
FAULTY PARALLELISM	Climbing the mountain was hard, but to descend was not much easier.
REVISED	*Climbing* the mountain was hard, but *descending* was not much easier.

2. Pairing ideas with correlative conjunctions

Correlative conjunctions are paired words—*not only . . . but also, both . . . and, either . . . or, neither . . . nor*—that link sentence elements of equal value. To be parallel, the expressions that follow each element in the pair should have the same form.

FAULTY PARALLELISM	Successful teachers must both inspire students and also challenging them is important.
REVISED	Successful teachers must both *inspire* and *challenge* their students.
FAULTY PARALLELISM	The school board concluded not only that the district should enlarge the existing elementary school but also build another one.
REVISED	The school board concluded that the district should *not only enlarge* the existing elementary school *but also build* another one.

3. Comparing ideas with *than* or *as*

To be parallel, ideas compared with expressions involving *than* or *as* should have the same grammatical form.

FAULTY PARALLELISM	Many people find that having meaningful work is more important than high pay.

REVISED	Many people find that *having meaningful work* is more important than *earning high pay*.
REVISED	Many people find that *meaningful work* is more important than *high pay*.

42d Repeat function words as needed to keep parallels clear.

Function words indicate the function of or relationship among other words in a sentence. They include articles (*the, a, an*), prepositions (*to, for,* and *by,* for example), subordinating conjunctions (*because, although,* and *that,* for example), and the word *to* in infinitives (*to eat, to grow*). You can omit repeated function words from parallel structures whenever the structures are clear without them, but you should include them otherwise. You may also want to include them for stylistic effect.

In the following sentence, the writer omitted the function word *to* from the second and third infinitives because the sentence is clear without the words.

➤ **Her goals for her retirement were to travel, ~~to~~ study art**

history, and ~~to~~ write a book about Michelangelo.

The writer of the next sentence, however, repeated the infinitive *to* in order to make clear where one goal ends and the next begins.

➤ **The project has three goals: to survey the valley for**

Inca-period sites, ⌃*to* excavate a test trench at each site the

survey locates, and ⌃*to* excavate one of those sites completely.

Exercise 42.2 Correcting faulty parallelism

Revise the following sentences to eliminate faulty parallelism.

EXAMPLE: ORIGINAL

Newlywed couples need to learn to communicate effectively and budget in a wise manner.

EXAMPLE: REVISED

Newlywed couples need to learn to communicate effectively and budget wisely.

1. Impressionism is a term that applies primarily to an art movement of the late nineteenth century, but the music of some composers of the era is also considered impressionist.
2. The early impressionists include Edouard Manet, Claude Monet, and Mary Cassatt, and also among them are Edgar Degas and Camille Pissarro.
3. Impressionist composers include Claude Debussy, and Maurice Ravel is considered an impressionist also.
4. Just as impressionism in art challenged accepted conventions of color and line, in music the challenge from impressionism was to accepted conventions of form and harmony.

FIGURE 42.1 *At the Opera,* an impressionist painting by Mary Cassatt.

5. Critics at first condemned both impressionist artists and impressionist music.
6. Women impressionist painters included Mary Cassatt from the United States and Berthe Morisot, who was French.
7. Among Monet's goals were to observe the changing effects of light and color on a landscape and record his observations quickly.
8. To accomplish these goals he would often create not just one but a series of paintings of a subject over the course of a day.

42e Make the items in outlines, headings, and lists parallel.

If you are writing a paper that includes headings or a formal outline of headings, make sure the items at each level of heading are consistent in emphasis and parallel in grammatical structure. (*See Chapter 3: Planning and Shaping the Whole Essay, pp. 50–53, for more on developing an outline and making headings parallel.*)

In the first-draft outline shown here, the writer mixed a phrase with a question in the first-level headings, and phrases with complete sentences in the second-level headings. In the revised outline, the writer opted for phrases throughout, with the phrases at each level of heading parallel in form with the others at the same level.

FIRST-DRAFT OUTLINE WITH FAULTY PARALLELISM

Germany's Path to Continuing Prosperity

I. Economic Realities
  A. Large gap between eastern and western Germany's GDP
  B. The public-sector deficit is ballooning.
  C. Lower than expected FDI inflows
  D. Steady increase in trade
II. What are Germany's Economic Prospects?
  A. Workforce and location attractive to investors.
  B. Negatives—labor costs, taxation rates, and regulations

REVISED OUTLINE

Germany's Path to Continuing Prosperity

I. Economic Realities
  A. Large gap between eastern and western Germany's GDP
  B. Ballooning public-sector deficits
  C. Lower than expected FDI inflows
  D. Steady increase in trade
II. Economic Prospects
  A. Positives—workforce and location
  B. Negatives—labor costs, taxation rates, and regulations

Items in a bulleted or numbered list should also be parallel.

NUMBERED LIST WITH FAULTY PARALLELISM

The plot can be reduced to seven main events:

1. Dorothy runs away from home but returns as a tornado strikes.
2. She is transported to Oz and gains the ruby slippers.
3. Befriends three fantastic creatures.
4. They met the Wizard, who sent them on a mission.
5. Dorothy confronts and destroys the Wicked Witch.
6. Dorothy and her friends learn that the Wizard is a fraud.
7. The return home.

REVISED LIST

The plot can be reduced to seven main events:

1. Dorothy runs away from home but returns as a tornado strikes.
2. She is transported to Oz and gains the ruby slippers.
3. She befriends three fantastic creatures.
4. They meet the Wizard, who sends them on a mission.
5. Dorothy confronts and destroys the Wicked Witch.
6. Dorothy and her friends learn that the Wizard is a fraud.
7. Dorothy returns home and is reunited with her family.

Exercise 42.3 Chapter review: Faulty parallelism

Edit the following passage so that parallel ideas are presented in parallel structures.

People can be classified as either Type A or Type B personalities depending on their competitiveness, how perfectionistic they are, and ability to relax. Type A people are often workaholics who not only drive themselves hard but also are driving others hard. In the workplace, employers often like Type A personalities because they tend to work quickly, punctually, and are efficient. However, because Type A people can characteristically also be impatient, verbally aggressive, or show hostility, they tend not to rise to top management positions as often as Type B people. Type A people also tend to be acutely aware of time, talking quickly, they interrupt when others are speaking, and try to complete other people's sentences. A Type B person in contrast takes the world in stride, walking and talking more slowly, and listens attentively. Type B people are better at dealing with stress and keep things in perspective, rather than being worried the way Type A people do.

People with traits that put them clearly on either end of the continuum between Type A and Type B should try to adopt characteristics of the opposite type. For example, to moderate some of their characteristic behaviors and reduce their risk of high blood pressure and heart disease, Type A people can use exercise, relaxation techniques, diet, and meditate. Understanding one's personality is half the battle, but implementing change takes time, discipline, and patience is needed.

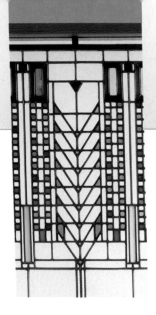

43 Misplaced and Dangling Modifiers

For a sentence to make sense, its parts must be arranged appropriately. When a modifying word, phrase, or clause is misplaced or dangling, readers get confused.

43a Identify and edit misplaced modifiers.

A **modifier** is misplaced when the reader cannot easily determine what it modifies or when it awkwardly disrupts the flow of a sentence. Be on the alert for **misplaced modifiers** as you revise your writing. Look in particular for modifiers that fall confusingly far from the expressions they modify, ambiguously modify more than one expression, or awkwardly disrupt the relationships among the grammatical elements of a sentence.

www.mhhe.com/
nmhh
For information and exercises on misplaced modifiers, go to

Editing > Misplaced Modifiers

> **Modifiers Are Misplaced When They**
>
> 1. Fall confusingly far from the expressions they modify
> 2. Ambiguously modify more than one expression
> 3. Awkwardly disrupt the relationships among the grammatical elements of a sentence

43b Put modifiers close to the words they modify.

For clarity, modifiers should come immediately before or after the words they modify. In the following sentence, the clause *after the police arrested them* modifies *protesters,* not *property.* Putting the clause before the word it modifies makes it clear that if any property destruction occurred, it occurred before—not after—the arrest.

> ➤ After the police arrested them, the
> ~~The~~ protestors were charged with destroying college
>   ^
> property. ~~after the police arrested them.~~
>   ^

Misplaced Modifiers and Grammar Checkers

Some computer grammar checkers reliably flag split infinitives but only occasionally flag other types of misplaced modifiers. One grammar checker, for example, flagged the split infinitive in this sentence:

The sign asks people to not walk on the grass.

It also caught the misplaced modifier in this sentence:

SAT scores may in comparison to other measures of academic potential be overrated.

It missed, however, the misplaced modifier *with a loud crash* in this sentence:

The valuable vase with a loud crash fell to the floor and broke into hundreds of pieces.

Like adverbial clauses, prepositional phrases used as adverbs are easy to misplace. The following sentence was revised to make it clear that the hikers were watching the storm from the porch.

➤ *From the cabin's porch, the* ~~The~~ hikers watched the storm gathering force. ~~from the cabin's porch.~~

43c   Clarify ambiguous modifiers.

Because adverbs can modify what precedes or what follows them, it is important that writers position adverbs carefully. Make sure not to place your adverbs ambiguously.

1. Moving squinting modifiers

A modifier that could describe either what precedes or what follows it is called a **squinting modifier** and should be repositioned for clarity. As originally written, the following sentence leaves unclear whether the historians in question are *objecting vehemently* or *arguing vehemently*. Changing the position of *vehemently* eliminates this ambiguity.

➤ Historians who object to this account *vehemently* ~~vehemently~~ argue that the presidency was never endangered.

721

IDENTIFY AND EDIT
Misplaced Modifiers

mm

To avoid misplaced modifiers, ask yourself these questions
as you edit your writing:

? 1. *Are all the modifiers close to the expressions they modify?*

> *At the beginning of the Great Depression, people*
> ◆ ~~People~~ panicked and all tried to get their money out of the
>   ^
> banks at the same time, forcing many banks to close. ~~at the~~
>   ^
> ~~beginning of the Great Depression.~~

? 2. *Are any modifiers placed in such a way that they modify more than one
expression? Pay particular attention to limiting modifiers such as* only,
even, *and* just.

> ◆ President Roosevelt *quickly* declared a bank holiday, ~~quickly~~ helping
>   ^   ^
> to restore confidence in the nation's financial system.
>
> ◆ Congress enacted many programs to combat the Depression
>   *only*
> ~~only~~ within the first one hundred days of Roosevelt's
>   ^
> presidency.

? 3. *Do any modifiers disrupt the relationships among the grammatical
elements of the sentence?*

> *Given how entrenched segregation was at the time, the*
> ◆ ~~The~~ president's wife, Eleanor, was a surprisingly
>   ^
> strong, ~~given how entrenched segregation was at the time,~~
> advocate for racial justice in Roosevelt's administration.

2. Repositioning limiting modifiers

Problems often occur with **limiting modifiers** such as *only, even, almost, nearly,* and *just.* When you edit, check every sentence that includes one of these modifiers. In the following sentence, does the writer
mean that vegetarian dishes are the only dishes served at dinner or
that dinner is the only time when vegetarian dishes are available?

722 Editing clears up the ambiguity.

AMBIGUOUS	The restaurant *only offers* vegetarian dishes for dinner.
REVISED	The restaurant *offers only* vegetarian dishes for dinner.

or

The restaurant *offers* vegetarian dishes *only* at dinner.

43d Move disruptive modifiers.

When you separate grammatical elements that belong together with a lengthy modifying phrase or clause, the resulting sentence can be difficult to read.

It is often acceptable to separate a subject from its verb with a long adjectival phrase that modifies the subject, as in the following sentence.

➤ **Descartes and Hume, two of Europe's most prominent philosophers, deal with the issue of personal identity in different ways.**

In contrast, a long adverbial phrase between subject and verb is almost always awkward. In the following sentence, the adverbial phrase beginning with *despite* initially came between the subject and verb, disrupting the flow of the sentence. With the modifying phrase at the beginning of the sentence, the edited version restores the connection between subject and verb.

➤ *Despite their similar conceptions of the self,* **Descartes and Hume, ~~despite their similar conceptions of the self,~~ deal with the issue of personal identity in different ways.**

An adverb or adverbial phrase that falls between a verb and its direct object is also likely to be disruptive.

➤ **Newton contested** *bitterly* ~~bitterly~~ **Leibniz's claim to have invented calculus.**

➤ **The *Jeopardy* contestant answered** *, without any apparent hesitation,* ~~without any apparent hesitation~~ **the question.**

43e Avoid splitting infinitives.

An **infinitive** couples the word *to* with the base form of a verb. In a **split infinitive,** one or more words intervene between *to* and the verb form. Avoid separating the parts of an infinitive with a modifier unless keeping them together results in an awkward or ambiguous construction.

In the following sentence, the word *not* awkwardly splits the infinitive *to disturb* and should be moved to precede it.

➤ The librarian asks us to ~~not~~ disturb other patrons.
$\qquad\qquad\qquad\quad$ *not*

In the next example, however, the modifier *successfully* should be moved, but the modifier *carefully* should probably stay where it is, even though it splits the infinitive *to assess. Carefully* needs to be close to the verb it modifies, but putting it between *have* and *to* would be awkward, and putting it after *assess* would cause ambiguity because readers might think it modifies *projected economic benefits.*

➤ To ~~successfully~~ complete this assignment students have to
$\qquad\qquad\qquad\qquad\qquad\qquad$ *successfully,*

carefully assess projected economic benefits in relation

to potential social problems.

Exercise 43.1 Repositioning misplaced modifiers

Edit the following sentences to correct any misplaced modifiers. If a sentence is acceptable as written, circle its number.

EXAMPLE

~~Global warming has received, although~~ long a cause for
$\qquad\qquad\qquad$ *Although*

concern among scientists and environmentalists, scant
$\qquad\qquad\qquad\qquad\qquad\qquad$ *global warming has received*

attention from some governments.

1. R. Buckminster Fuller developed during his career as an architect and engineer some of the most important design innovations of the twentieth century.
2. Fuller, a weak student, was expelled from Harvard.
3. Fuller resolved to dedicate his life to improving people's lives after suffering from a period of severe depression at the age of 32.

4. Fuller intended his efficient designs to not waste precious resources.
5. Those who doubted Fuller often were proved wrong.
6. Fuller is known as the inventor of the geodesic dome to most people today.
7. The geodesic dome is a spherical structure that is both lightweight and economical, which Fuller developed in the late 1940s.
8. Today there are more than 300,000 domes around the world based on Fuller's designs.
9. His contention that wind generators on high-voltage transmission towers could supply much of the electricity the United States needs, policy makers have largely ignored.
10. His twenty-eight books have sold more than a million copies, in which he wrote about a range of social, political, cultural, and economic issues.

43f Learn to identify and edit dangling modifiers.

A **dangling modifier** is a descriptive phrase that implies an actor different from the sentence's subject. When readers try to connect the modifying phrase with the subject, the results may be humorous as well as confusing.

The following sentence, for example, describes a *crowded beach* as *swimming.*

DANGLING MODIFIER	*Swimming toward the boat on the horizon,* the crowded beach felt as if it were miles away.

www.mhhe.com/ nmhh
For information and exercises on avoiding dangling modifiers, go to
Editing > Dangling Modifiers

Fixing a dangling modifier requires explicitly naming its implied actor, either as the subject of the sentence or in the modifier itself.

REVISED	Swimming toward the boat on the horizon, *I* felt as if the crowded beach were miles away.

or

As *I swam* toward the boat on the horizon, the crowded beach seemed miles away.

Note that you usually can not correct a dangling modifier simply by moving it. In the following sentence, for example, no matter where the modifying phrase falls, the sentence retains its unintended meaning, which is that the town had been struggling in the wilderness for weeks.

IDENTIFY AND EDIT
Dangling Modifiers

dm

To avoid dangling modifiers, ask yourself these questions when you see a descriptive phase at the beginning of a sentence:

? *1. What is the subject of the sentence?*

> ♦ Snorkeling in Hawaii, ancient sea turtles were an amazing sight.
>
> The subject of the sentence is *sea turtles.*

? *2. Could the phrase at the beginning of the sentence possibly describe this subject?*

> ♦ Snorkeling in Hawaii, ancient sea turtles were an amazing sight.
>
> No, sea turtles do not snorkel in Hawaii or anywhere else.

? *3. Who or what is the phrase really describing? Either make that person or thing the subject of the main clause, or add a subject to the modifier.*

> ♦ Snorkeling in Hawaii, *we saw* ancient sea turtles, ~~were~~ an amazing sight.
>
> ♦ *While we were snorkeling* ~~Snorkeling~~ in Hawaii, ancient sea turtles ~~were~~ *amazed us.* ~~an amazing sight.~~

DANGLING MODIFIER	*After struggling for weeks in the wilderness,* the town pleased them mightily.
STILL DANGLING	The town pleased them mightily *after struggling for weeks in the wilderness.*

The meaning will remain unclear until the implied actor in the modifying phrase is made explicit.

REVISED	After struggling for weeks in the wilderness, *they* were mightily pleased to come upon the town.

Dangling Modifiers and Grammar Checkers

Computer grammar checkers cannot distinguish a descriptive phrase that properly modifies the subject of the sentence from one that implies a different actor. As a result, they do not flag dangling modifiers. Writers must rely on their own judgment to identify and correct these modifiers.

Exercise 43.2   Correcting dangling modifiers

Edit the following sentences to correct any dangling modifiers. If a sentence is acceptable as is, circle its number.

EXAMPLE

Passengers ~~Entering the station, passengers~~ waited to board the train. that was entering the station

1. Admired by many women artists as a pioneer in the mostly male art world, Georgia O'Keeffe lived and worked without regard to social conventions or artistic trends.
2. One of the most admired American artists of the twentieth century, her color-saturated images of cactus flowers, bleached bones, and pale skies are widely reproduced.
3. Growing up in Wisconsin, art was always important to her.
4. Defending her gifted student to the principal, one of her teachers said, "When the spirit moves Georgia, she can do more in a day than you or I can do in a week."
5. Without informing her, some of O'Keeffe's drawings were exhibited by Alfred Steiglitz at his 291 Gallery.
6. Marrying in 1924, O'Keeffe and Steiglitz enjoyed one of the most fruitful collaborations of the modernist era.
7. Despite critical and financial success in the 1920s, New York City did not provide suitable subject matter for her paintings.
8. Vacationing with a friend in the summer of 1929, O'Keeffe discovered the stark natural beauty of Taos, New Mexico.

Exercise 43.3   Chapter review: Misplaced and dangling modifiers

Edit the following passage to eliminate any misplaced or dangling modifiers.

Henri Matisse and Pablo Picasso are considered often to have been the formative artists of the twentieth century. Although rivals for most of their careers, a traveling exhibit called "Matisse Picasso" exhibited their work side by side in museums in London, Paris, and New York.

Picasso's work may in comparison to Matisse's be more disturbing, and some say it is, in addition, more daring and experimental. Yet Matisse too, with his use of vivid colors and distorted shapes, was a daring innovator.

Looking for similarities, the works of both artists suggest an underlying anxiety. Yet each in different ways responded to this anxiety. Matisse painted tranquil yet often emotionally charged domestic scenes, whereas Picasso fought his inner fears with often jarringly disquieting images, by contrast.

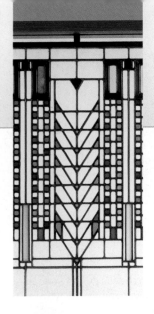

44 Coordination and Subordination

Coordination and subordination are tools for structuring sentences to clarify the relationships among the ideas you want to convey. Used effectively, these tools add grace and energy to your writing and help your readers follow your train of thought.

44a Identify coordination and subordination and use them effectively.

www.mhhe.com/ nmhh
For information and exercises on coordination and subordination, go to

Editing >
Coordination and Subordination

Coordination gives two or more ideas equal weight.

➤ The sky grew dark, and the wind began to howl.
equal ideas

➤ The newlyweds were poor but happy.
equal ideas

Subordination makes one idea depend on another and is therefore used to combine ideas that are not of equal importance.

subordinate idea   *main idea*

➤ Because the storm knocked the power out, we ate dinner by candlelight.

Coordination, Subordination, and Grammar Checkers

Computer grammar and style checkers can flag some of the problems associated with coordination and subordination, like errors in punctuation, for example, or excessively long sentences. Only a human, however, can evaluate relationships among ideas and decide how best to use coordination and subordination to structure those ideas in sentences.

729

> *Note:* The abbreviation used to flag faulty or excessive coordination is *coord*.
>
> The abbreviation used to flag inappropriate or faulty subordination is *sub*.

44b Use coordination to combine ideas of equal importance.

Coordination should be used only when two or more ideas deserve equal emphasis. You can use coordination to join phrases and words within clauses or to join two or more independent clauses.

1. To coordinate words and phrases within a clause, join them with a coordinating conjunction (*and, but, or, for, nor, yet,* or *so*).

   ➤ The auditorium was <u>huge</u> *and* <u>acoustically imperfect.</u>

2. To coordinate two or more independent clauses, use a comma plus a coordinating conjunction, insert a semicolon by itself, or insert a semicolon and a conjunctive adverb such as *moreover, nevertheless, however, therefore,* or *subsequently.* (For more on conjunctive adverbs, see Chapter 30: Parts of Speech, p. 547.)

   ➤ <u>The tenor bellowed loudly,</u> *but* <u>no one in the back could hear him.</u>

   ➤ <u>The days are getting shorter;</u> <u>winter is approaching.</u>

   ➤ <u>Jones did not agree with her position on health care;</u> *nevertheless,* <u>he supported her campaign for office.</u>

3. You can also coordinate words, phrases, and independent clauses with a correlative conjunction such as *not only . . . but also, both . . . and, either. . . or.*

   ➤ The scholarship included *not only* <u>full tuition</u> *but also* <u>money for living expenses.</u>

> ➤ ***Either*** Frodo will destroy the ring of power *or* Sauron
>
> will destroy Middle Earth.

44c Avoid faulty or excessive coordination.

1. Recognizing faulty coordination

When writers use coordination to join elements that are not logically equivalent or to join elements with an inappropriate coordinating word, the result is **faulty coordination.**

The following sentence, for example, is confusing because the writer has coordinated two ideas that are not equivalent.

FAULTY COORDINATION	The tortoise beat the hare, but the hare is a faster runner than the tortoise.

What the writer wants to say is that the tortoise won *despite* the hare's ability to run faster than the tortoise. The idea of the hare's speed is subordinate, not equal to, the idea of the tortoise's victory.

REVISED	The tortoise beat the hare even though the hare can run faster than the tortoise.

Each coordinating conjunction has a specific meaning. The conjunction *and,* for example, suggests equivalence, whereas the conjunction *but* suggests contrast. Be sure to use the conjunction that reflects the relationship between the elements you are coordinating.

FAULTY COORDINATION	The hare was fast, *and* victory went to the sure and steady tortoise.
REVISED	The hare was fast, *but* victory went to the sure and steady tortoise.

2. Avoiding excessive coordination

When writers use coordination to string together too many ideas at once, the result is **excessive coordination.**

EXCESSIVE COORDINATION	The speedy hare challenged the plodding tortoise to a race and immediately established a large early lead, but his initial burst of speed tired him and, feeling sure of himself, he decided to rest a bit before finishing the race, but he fell asleep, and the tortoise passed him and won, so the moral of the story is, "Sure and steady wins the race."

731

REVISED   The speedy hare challenged the plodding tortoise to a race. The hare established a large early lead, but his initial burst of speed tired him. Feeling sure of himself, he decided to rest a bit before finishing the race. He fell asleep, however, and the tortoise passed him and won. The moral of the story is, "Sure and steady wins the race."

44d Use subordination for ideas of unequal importance.

Subordination, not coordination, should be used to indicate that information is of secondary importance and to show its logical relation to the main idea.

➤ ~~The~~ *When the* police arrived, ~~and~~ the burglars ran away.

➤ The fourth set of needs to be met, ~~are~~ esteem needs, ~~and they~~ *includes* ~~include~~ the need for success, self-respect, and prestige.

To show the relationship between ideas of unequal importance, express the main idea in an independent clause and secondary ideas in subordinate clauses or phrases.

> *Note:* Commas often set off subordinate ideas, especially when the subordinate clause or phrase opens the sentence. (*For more on using commas, see Chapter 51: Commas, pp. 806–22.*)

1. Put secondary ideas in subordinate clauses introduced by a relative pronoun or a subordinating conjunction. The relative pronouns include *who, whom, that, which, whoever, whomever,* and *whose.*

   ➤ The blue liquid must be kept at room temperature. *, which will be added to the beaker later,* ~~It will be added to the beaker later.~~

   ➤ Thomas Jefferson *, who penned the phrase "All men are created equal,"* was a slaveholder. ~~He penned the phrase "All men are created equal."~~

Subordinating conjunctions include *after, although, because, if, since, when,* and *where. (For a fuller list of subordinating conjunctions, see Chapter 30: Parts of Speech, p. 546.)*

➤ **Christopher Columbus encountered the Americas in**

, although he
1492./ ~~He~~ never understood just what he had found.

After he   *, Wordsworth*
➤ **~~Wordsworth~~ wrote the opening four sections./ ~~He~~ put**

the work aside for two years.

2. Put secondary ideas in appositive phrases (*see Chapter 31: Sentence Basics, p. 560*).

, one of the founders of the women's rights movement in the United States,
➤ **Elizabeth Cady Stanton helped organize the Seneca**

Falls Convention of 1848. ~~She was one of the founders~~

~~of the women's rights movement in the United States.~~

3. Put secondary ideas in other modifying phrases or words.

Hoping for a better life, my
➤ **~~My~~ grandparents immigrated to the United States in**

the late nineteenth century. ~~They were hoping for a~~

~~better life.~~

powerful   *destructive, fast-moving*
➤ **The earthquake triggered a tsunami. ~~The earthquake~~**

~~was powerful. The tsunami was destructive and~~

~~fast-moving.~~

44e   Avoid faulty or excessive subordination.

1. Making major ideas the focus

Major ideas belong in main clauses, not in subordinate clauses or phrases where readers are unlikely to give them the attention they deserve. The writer revised the following sentence because the subject of the paper was definitions of literacy, not who values literacy.

SUBORDINATING WORDS and THEIR MEANINGS

Subordinating words fall into a variety of meaning categories. These include:

- **time**—*after, before, since, until, when, whenever, while*

  Before the race began, the hare was confident of victory.

- **place**—*where, wherever*

  The tortoise passed the spot *where* the hare lay sleeping.

- **identification**—*that, which, who, whose*

  The tortoise, *who* never stopped to rest, passed the hare.

- **cause or effect**—*as, because, since, so that*

  The hare lost *because* he fell asleep.

- **purpose**—*in order that, so that, that*

  The hare stopped *so that* he could rest and catch his breath.

- **condition**—*if, provided that, unless*

  If the hare hadn't stopped, he would have won.

- **contrast**—*although, as if, even though, though, whereas*

  The tortoise, *although* much the slower of the two contestants, won the race.

FAULTY SUBORDINATION	Literacy, which has been defined as the ability to talk intelligently about many topics, is highly valued by businesspeople as well as academics.
REVISION	Highly valued by businesspeople as well as academics, literacy has been defined as the ability to talk intelligently about many topics.

2. Choosing the right subordinating word

When you subordinate one idea to another, make sure to choose a subordinating word that properly and unambiguously expresses the logical relationship between the two ideas (*see the box "Subordinating Words and Their Meanings" on this page*).

The subordinating word *since* in the following sentence is ambiguous. Does it refer to time or cause? Revision clears up the confusion.

FAULTY SUBORDINATION	Since she won reelection, the mayor has acted on her plan to increase salaries for town officials.
REVISION	Since winning reelection, the mayor has acted to increase salaries for town officials.
	or
	Winning reelection has permitted the mayor to propose salary increases for town officials.

The writer of the next sentence has inappropriately used the relative pronoun *where,* which specifies location, to introduce a subordinate clause that refers to time.

FAULTY SUBORDINATION	*Where* time permits, students should take advantage of the city's museums and other cultural attractions.
REVISION	*When* time permits, students should take advantage of the city's museums and other cultural attractions.

3. Avoiding excessive subordination

Excessive subordination results from stringing together too many subordinate expressions at once. Like excessive coordination, it can leave readers confused. When a sentence seems overloaded, try separating it into two or more sentences.

EXCESSIVE SUBORDINATION	Big-city mayors, who are supported by public funds, should be cautious about spending taxpayers' money for personal needs, such as home furnishings, especially when municipal budget shortfalls have caused extensive job layoffs, angering city workers and the general public.
REVISED	Big-city mayors should be cautious about spending taxpayers' money for personal needs, especially when municipal budget shortfalls have caused extensive job layoffs. They risk angering city workers and the general public by using public funds for home furnishings.

735

For MULTILINGUAL STUDENTS

Language-Specific Differences in Coordination and Subordination

Coordination and subordination are universal features of human language; that is, every language permits them. Language communities differ, however, in the value they place on one or the other. The English rhetorical tradition prizes subordination and regards its use as evidence of stylistic maturity. The rhetorical traditions associated with other languages—Arabic and Persian, for example—stress coordination, favoring constructions that strike English-speaking readers as awkward. Be aware of these cultural preferences as you write, and try to achieve a balance of structural patterns that a sophisticated audience would find appealing.

Exercise 44.1 Using coordination and subordination

Combine the following sets of sentences, using coordination, subordination, or both to clarify the relationships among ideas.

> **EXAMPLE** **France was a major player in Europe's late-nineteenth-century imperial expansion. It began the conquest of Vietnam in 1858. By 1883 it controlled the entire country.**
>
> *France, a major player in Europe's late-nineteenth-century imperial expansion, began its conquest of Vietnam in 1858 and controlled the entire country by 1883.*

1. France divided Vietnam into three administrative regions. This was before World War II.
2. Most Vietnamese opposed French rule. Many groups formed to regain the country's independence.
3. Vietnam remained a French-administered colony during World War II. It was under Japanese control, however, from 1940 to 1945.
4. By the end of the war, a Communist group called the Viet Minh had emerged as Vietnam's dominant nationalist organization. Ho Chi Minh (1890–1969) was the leader of the Viet Minh.
5. In 1945 the Viet Minh declared independence. They took control of northern Vietnam. The French, however, regained control of the south. The British helped the French.

6. The French reached an agreement with Ho Chi Minh in 1946. The agreement would have made Vietnam an autonomous country tied to France.

7. The agreement broke down. War started. The French wanted to reassert colonial control over all of Vietnam. Ho Chi Minh wanted total independence.

8. The United States supported the French. Russia and China supported the Viet Minh.

9. The French suffered a major defeat at Dien Bien Phu in 1954. After that they realized they could not defeat the Viet Minh.

10. An agreement reached in Geneva left Vietnam divided into two regions. One region was the communist-controlled north. The other region was the noncommunist south.

Exercise 44.2 Avoiding inappropriate or excessive coordination and subordination

Rewrite the numbered passages that follow to eliminate inappropriate or excessive coordination or subordination. Do not hesitate to break up long strings of clauses into two or more sentences when it seems appropriate to do so.

EXAMPLE **The Industrial Revolution triggered economic and social upheavals, including changes in family structure, patterns of work, and the distribution of wealth, and in 1848, in the wake of these upheavals, the governments of France, Italy, and several central European countries were all threatened with revolution.**

The Industrial Revolution triggered economic and social upheavals, including changes in family structure, patterns of work, and the distribution of wealth. In 1848, in the wake of these upheavals, the governments of France, Italy, and several central Europe countries were all threatened with revolution.

1. During the early years of the Industrial Revolution, the many thousands of people who had left the countryside to move to Europe's fast-growing cities in search of work encountered poverty, disease, lack of sanitation, and exhausting, dangerous factory jobs, making cities breeding grounds for insurrection, and this threat of unrest increased after an international financial crisis in 1848 and the epidemic of bankruptcies and unemployment that followed it.

2. France's King Louis-Phillipe, hopelessly unpopular, abdicated the throne in February and the country was thrown into a revolution in which citizens set up barricades in the narrow streets of Paris, restricting the movement of government troops.

3. Revolutionary fervor also took hold in Vienna, the capital of the Austrian Empire, and at the same time, nationalist forces gained strength in Hungary and other regions of the empire, prompting Hungarian nationalists to demand autonomy from Vienna and radicals in Prague to demand greater autonomy for the empire's Slavic peoples.

4. By the middle of 1848, however, events had begun to turn against the revolutionaries, and the rulers of the Austrian Empire used divisions among the revolutionaries to reassert their power, and the Empire provided supplies and encouragement to Romanian nationalists who feared persecution in an independent Hungary.

44f Use coordination and subordination to combine short, choppy sentences.

Short sentences are easy to read, but several of them in a row can become so monotonous that meaning gets lost.

> **CHOPPY** My cousin Jim is not an accountant. Nevertheless he does my taxes every year. He suggests various deductions. These deductions reduce my tax bill considerably.

You can use subordination to combine a series of short, choppy sentences like these to form a longer, more meaningful sentence. Put the idea you want to emphasize in the main clause, and use subordinate clauses and phrases to include the other ideas. In the following revision, the main clause is italicized.

> **REVISED** Even though he is not an accountant, *my cousin Jim does my taxes every year,* suggesting various deductions that reduce my tax bill considerably.

If a series of short sentences includes two major ideas of equal importance, use coordination for the two major ideas and subordinate the secondary information. The following revision shows that Smith's and Johnson's opinions are equally important. The information about bilingual education is of secondary interest.

> **CHOPPY** Bilingual education is designed for children. The native language of these children is not English. Smith supports bilingual education. Johnson opposes bilingual education.

REVISED	Smith supports bilingual education for children whose native language is not English; Johnson, however, opposes bilingual education.

Exercise 44.3 Chapter review: Coordination and subordination

Edit the following passage to correct faulty coordination and subordination, and to eliminate choppy sentences and excessive coordination and subordination.

Germany and Italy were not always unified nations. For centuries they were divided into many city-states. They were also divided into many kingdoms, dukedoms, fiefdoms, and principalities. These city-states, kingdoms, dukedoms, fiefdoms, and principalities had maintained their autonomy for centuries.

Largely responsible for the unifications of Italy and Germany were two men. These men were Camillo di Cavour and Otto von Bismarck. Cavour became prime minister of the republic of Piedmont in 1852. Bismarck became chancellor of Prussia in 1862. Cavour was a practitioner of *realpolitik,* and *realpolitik* is a political policy based on the ruthless advancement of national interests. Bismarck was also a practitioner of *realpolitik.*

Cavour hoped to govern Piedmont in a way that would inspire other Italian states to join it to form a unified nation. Increasing the power of parliament, modernizing agriculture and industry, and building a railroad that encouraged trade with the rest of Europe, he also modernized the port of Genoa, updated the court system and installed a king, Victor Emmanuel, all of which made hopes for nationhood center on Piedmont. With the help of Napoleon III, Cavour engaged in a crafty political maneuver. Napoleon III was the emperor of France. Cavour induced Austria to attack Piedmont and then with French help defeated the Austrian armies, thus inspiring Modena and Tuscany to join Piedmont.

Bismarck used similar tactics in pursuit of unification as he prearranged French neutrality, and then he attacked and destroyed the Austrian army at Sadowa, and he eliminated Austrian influence in Prussia, and he paved the way for Prussian control of a large north German federation by 1867. Both men continued to use these tactics until they succeeded with the unification of Germany in 1871 and of Italy in 1879.

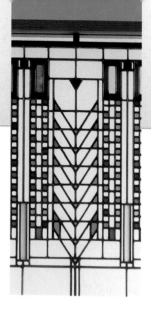

45 Sentence Variety and Emphasis

Just as listeners tune out a speaker who recites in a flat tone, with no variation in rhythm or pitch, so readers will tune out a writer whose sentences and paragraphs are uniform in length and structure. Monotonous writing, like the first of the two passages that follow, is a chore to read. Lively writing, like the second passage, keeps readers engaged and focused on the writer's arguments. The key to lively writing is variety.

MONOTONOUS

The Greek historian Herodotus called Egypt "the gift of the Nile." He might have called Harappan society "the gift of the Indus." He did not know about Harappan society, however. The Nile's waters come from rain and melting snow in towering mountains. The waters of the Indus come from rain and melting snow in the Hindu Kush and the Himalayas. The Himalayas have the world's highest peaks. The waters of both rivers charge downhill. They pick up enormous quantities of silt. They carry the silt for hundreds of kilometers. The waters lose force as they course through lowlands. As they do so, they deposit a burden of rich soil.

VARIED AND LIVELY

If the Greek historian Herodotus had known of Harappan society, he might have called it "the gift of the Indus." Like the Nile, the Indus draws its waters from rain and melting snow in towering mountains—in this case, the Hindu Kush and Himalayas, the world's highest peaks. As the waters charge downhill, they pick up enormous quantities of silt, which they carry for hundreds of kilometers. Like the Nile again, the Indus then deposits its burden of rich soil as it courses through lowlands and loses its force.

—from Bentley and Ziegler, *Traditions and Encounters,*
second edition, p. 91

Note: The abbreviation used to flag a passage that needs greater variety is *var.*

Variety, Emphasis, and Grammar Checkers

Monotony is not a grammatical error; variety and emphasis are issues of style, not syntax. A computer grammar checker might flag a very long sentence or a repeated word, but it can not decide whether the sentence is too long or whether the repetition is unwarranted.

45a Vary your sentence openings.

www.mhhe.com/
nmhh
For information and
exercises on sentence
variety, go to
Editing > Sentence
Variety

In a simple English sentence, the subject usually comes first. When you begin all the sentences in a passage with the subject, however, you risk losing your readers' attention. To open some of your sentences in a different way, try moving a modifier to the beginning.

Adverbial modifiers are words, phrases, or clauses that modify verbs, adjectives, and other adverbs, as well as whole phrases and clauses. You can often position them in a variety of places in a sentence, including the beginning.

➤ *Eventually,*
  Armstrong's innovations ~~eventually~~ became the standard.

➤ *In at least two instances, this*
  ~~This~~ money-making strategy backfired. ~~in at least two~~

  ~~instances.~~

➤ *After Glaser became his manager,*
  Armstrong no longer had to worry about business. ~~after~~

  ~~Glaser became his manager.~~

Adjectival modifiers are words and phrases that modify nouns. They include participles and participial phrases, which you can often place at the beginning of a sentence for variety. (*For more on participles and participial phrases, see Chapter 31: Sentence Basics, pp. 559–60.*)

➤ *Pushing the other children aside,*
  Joseph, ~~pushing the other children aside,~~ demanded that the

  teacher give him a cookie first.

741

➤ *Stunned by the stock market crash, many*
~~Many~~ brokers, ~~stunned by the stock market crash,~~

committed suicide.

➤ *Frustrated and running late for an important job interview, the*
~~The frustrated~~ driver, ~~running late for an important job~~

~~interview,~~ looked for a way around the traffic jam.

> *Caution:* If you decide to put a participial phrase at the beginning of a sentence, make sure that the phrase describes the explicit subject of the sentence or you will end up with a dangling modifier. (*See Chapter 43: Misplaced and Dangling Modifiers, pp. 725–27.*)

For MULTILINGUAL STUDENTS

Adverbial Modifiers and Subject-Verb Order

In standard English word order, the subject of a sentence precedes the verb. When certain adverbs come at the beginning of a sentence, however, they force changes in this order, usually requiring the subject to fall between a helping verb and the main verb. Adverbs that have this effect include *never, not since, seldom, rarely, in no case,* and *not until.*

	help main subj verb verb
FAULTY	Rarely Simon has tried harder at work than he did today.

	help main verb subj verb
REVISED	Rarely has Simon tried harder at work than he did today.

	subj verb
FAULTY	Never we expected such a difficult assignment.

	help main verb subj verb
REVISED	Never did we expect such a difficult assignment

Exercise 45.1 Varying sentence openings

Rewrite each sentence so that it does not begin with the subject.

> EXAMPLE **He would ask her to marry him in his own good time.**
>
> *In his own good time, he would ask her to marry him.*

1. Germany entered World War II better prepared than the Allies, as it had in World War I.
2. The Germans, gambling on a quick victory, struck suddenly in both 1914 and 1939.
3. The United States entered World War II in 1942.
4. World War II, fought with highly mobile armies, never developed into the kind of prolonged stalemate that had characterized World War I.
5. The productive power of the United States, swinging into gear by the spring of 1943, contributed to the Allied victory.

45b Vary the length and structure of your sentences.

Short, simple sentences will keep your readers alert, but only if they occur in a context that also includes longer, complex sentences. You may similarly tire readers with an uninterrupted succession of long, intricately structured sentences. Variety is the spice of life—and of writing.

As you edit your work, check to see if you have overused one kind of sentence structure. Are all or most of the sentences in a passage short and simple? If so, use coordination and subordination to combine some of the short sentences into longer, compound or complex sentences. (*For more on types of sentences, see Chapter 31: Sentence Basics, pp. 563–64; for more on coordination and subordination, see Chapter 44, pp. 729–39.*)

If, on the other hand, all or most of your sentences are long and complex, put at least one of your ideas into a short, simple sentence. Your goal is to achieve a good mix in a way that highlights your central ideas. Note, for example, the way a writer revised this paragraph from a personal essay both to make it flow better and to clarify the discussion of sharks that closes it.

> DRAFT
>
> I dived quickly into the sea. I peered through my mask at the watery world. It turned darker. A school of fish went by. The distant light glittered on their bodies and I stopped swimming. I waited

to see if the fish might be chased by a shark. I was satisfied that there was no shark and continued down.

REVISED I dived quickly into the sea, peering through my mask at a watery world that turned darker as I descended. A school of fish went by, the distant light glittering on their bodies. Concerned that a shark might be chasing them, I stopped swimming and waited. No shark appeared. I continued down.

45c Include a few cumulative and periodic sentences.

Cumulative sentences accumulate information. They begin with a subject and verb and then add detail in a series of descriptive participial or absolute phrases. Used effectively, cumulative sentences can make your writing more forceful and provide a graceful way to incorporate interesting detail. (*See Chapter 31: Sentence Basics, pp. 559–60 for more on participial and absolute phrases.*)

The following example, with the participial phrases italicized, illustrates the force a cumulative sentence can have.

➤ **The motorcycle spun out of control,** *plunging down the ravine, crashing through a fence,* **and** *coming to rest at last on its side.*

Besides making your writing more forceful, cumulative sentences can also be used to add details, as the following example shows.

➤ **Wollstonecraft headed for France,** *her soul determined to be free, her mind committed to reason, her heart longing for love.*

Periodic sentences provide another way to increase the force of your writing, while at the same time calling attention to key ideas. In a **periodic sentence,** the key word, phrase, or idea appears at the end, precisely where readers are most likely to remember it.

LACKLUSTER Young people fell in love with the jukebox in 1946 and 1947 and turned away from the horrors of World War II.

FORCEFUL In 1946 and 1947, young people turned away from the horrors of World War II and fell in love—with the jukebox.

LACKLUSTER	The test of power for writers is their ability to imagine what is not the self, to familiarize the strange and mystify the familiar.
FORCEFUL	The ability of writers to imagine what is not the self, to familiarize the strange and mystify the familiar, is the test of their power.

—Toni Morrison

Exercise 45.2   Constructing cumulative sentences

Combine the sentences in each numbered item that follows to create cumulative sentences.

EXAMPLE   **Europe suffered greatly in the fourteenth century. The Hundred Years War consumed France and England. Schism weakened Europe's strongest unifying institution, the Church. The Black Death swept away one third of the population.**

Europe suffered greatly in the fourteenth century, with the Hundred Years War consuming France and England; schism weakening the Church, Europe's strongest unifying institution; and the Black Death sweeping away one third of the population.

1. The Black Death started in China around 1333. It spread to Europe over trade routes. It killed one third of the population in two years. It proved to be one of the worst natural disasters in history.
2. It was a horrible time. Dead bodies were abandoned on the streets. People were terrified of one another. Cattle and livestock were left to roam the countryside.
3. It was all for themselves. Friends deserted friends. Husbands left wives. Parents even abandoned children.

Exercise 45.3   Constructing periodic sentences

Rewrite the sentences that follow so that the keywords (underlined) appear at the end.

EXAMPLE   **Prince Gautama <u>achieved enlightenment</u> while sitting in deep meditation under a Bo-tree after a long spiritual quest.**

Sitting in deep meditation under a Bo-tree after a long spiritual quest, Prince Gautama achieved enlightenment.   **745**

1. The Indus River in Pakistan was home to one of the earliest civilizations in the world, as were the Nile River in Egypt, the Tigris and Euphrates rivers in Iraq, and the Yellow River in China.
2. In 1921, archeologists discovered the remains of Harappa, one of the two great cities of the Indus civilization, which until then was unknown to modern scholars.
3. The Indus civilization, which flourished from about 2500 to 1700 BCE, had two main centers, Harappa and another city, Mohenjo-Daro.

45d Try an occasional inversion, rhetorical question, or exclamation.

Most of the sentences you write will be declarative in purpose, designed to make statements. Most of the time, those statements will follow the normal sentence pattern of subject plus verb plus object. Occasionally, though, you might try using an inverted sentence pattern or another sentence type, such as a rhetorical question or an exclamation. (*For more on sentence types, see Chapter 31: Sentence Basics, p. 549.*)

1. Using inversions

An **inversion** is a sentence in which the verb comes before the subject. In a passage on the qualities of various contemporary artists, the following inversion makes sense and adds interest.

➤ **Characteristic of Smith's work are bold design and original thinking.**

As the following example illustrates, poets often use inversion for dramatic effect.

➤ **Into the jaws of Death, / Into the mouth of Hell / Rode the six hundred.**

—from "The Charge of the Light Brigade"
by Alfred Lord Tennyson

Because many inversions sound odd, however, they should be used infrequently and carefully.

2. Using rhetorical questions

To get your readers to participate more actively in your work, you can ask them a question. Because you do not expect your audience to answer you, this kind of question is called a **rhetorical question.**

➤ **Players injured at an early age too often find themselves without a job, without a college degree, and without physical health. Is it any wonder that a few turn to drugs and alcohol, become homeless, or end up in a morgue long before their time?**

Rhetorical questions are attention-getting devices that work best in the middle or at the end of a long, complicated passage. Sometimes they can also help you make a transition from one topic to another. Avoid using them more than a few times in a paper, however, and never begin an essay with a broad rhetorical question, such as "Why should we study *Huckleberry Finn*?" or "How did the Peace Corps begin?" Such openings sound canned and may lead readers to suspect that you could not be bothered to think of something better.

3. Using exclamations

In academic writing, exclamations are rare, perhaps because they seem adolescent rather than adult. If you decide to use one for special effect, be sure that you want to express strong emotion about the idea and can do so without losing credibility with your readers.

➤ **Wordsworth completed the twelve-book *Prelude* in 1805, after seven years of hard work. Instead of publishing his masterpiece, however, he devoted himself to revising it—for 45 years! The poem, in a thirteen-book version, was finally published in 1850, after he had died.**

45e Repeat keywords for emphasis.

By repeating keywords within a parallel construction you can provide rhythmic emphasis to key points.

➤ **The costumes *were red*, the lights *were red*, and the props *were red*.**

➤ **[W]e here highly resolve . . . that government of *the people*, by *the people*, for *the people* shall not perish from the earth.**
—from Abraham Lincoln's Gettysburg Address

Use this strategy sparingly, however, so that it retains its power. Too much repetition makes writing dull. (*See Chapter 38: Wordy Sentences, pp. 684–86, and Chapter 42: Faulty Parallelism, pp. 710–15*). **747**

Exercise 45.4 Chapter review: Sentence variety

Revise the following passage for variety and emphasis using the strategies presented in this chapter.

The United Nations was established in 1945. It was intended to prevent another world war. It began with twenty-one members. Nearly every nation in the world belongs to the United Nations today.

The United Nations has four purposes, according to its charter. One purpose is to maintain international peace and security. Another is to develop friendly relations among nations. Another is to promote cooperation among nations in solving international problems and in promoting respect for human rights. Last is to provide a forum for harmonizing the actions of nations.

All of the members of the United Nations have a seat in the General Assembly. The General Assembly considers numerous topics. These topics include globalization, AIDS, and pollution. Every member has a vote in the General Assembly.

A smaller group within the United Nations has the primary responsibility for maintaining international peace and security. This group is called the Security Council. The Security Council has five permanent members. They are China, France, the Russian Federation, the United Kingdom, and the United States. The Security Council also has ten elected members. The General Assembly elects the members of the Security Council. The elected members serve for two-year terms.

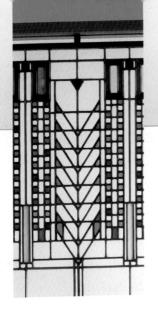

46 Active Verbs

Active verbs such as *run, shout, write,* and *think* are more direct and forceful than forms of the *be* verb (*am, are, is, was, were, been, being*) or passive-voice constructions. As you edit your work for clarity, pay attention to verb choice. The more active verbs you use, the stronger and clearer your writing will be.

www.mhhe.com/nmhh
For information and exercises on active verbs, go to
Editing > Verbs and Verbals

Active Verbs and Grammar Checkers

Computer grammar checkers generally do not flag weak uses of the *be* verb because they cannot tell when a usage is appropriate and when it clutters a sentence. Only a human writer can make that kind of judgment.

Some grammar checkers do flag most passive-voice sentences, but their suggestions for revising them can sometimes make things worse. Again, it requires a writer's judgment to determine how best—if at all—to revise a passive-voice sentence.

46a Consider alternatives to some *be* verbs.

Although it is not a strong verb, *be* does a lot of work in English. As a linking verb, a form of *be* can connect a subject with an informative adjective or a noun complement.

➤ **Germany *is* relatively poor in natural resources.**

➤ **Decent health care *is* a necessity, not a luxury.**

As a helping verb, a form of *be* can work with a present participle to indicate an ongoing action.

➤ **Macbeth *was* returning from battle when he met the three witches.**

Be verbs are so useful, in fact, that writers can easily overwork them. Watch for weak, roundabout sentences containing *be* verbs, and consider replacing those verbs with active verbs.

749

➤   The mayor's refusal to meet with our representatives ~~is a~~

demonstrates
~~demonstration of~~ his lack of respect for us, as well as for the
      ^

environment.

Exercise 46.1   Editing for overuse of *be* verbs

In the following sentences, replace the verb *to be* with active verbs.

EXAMPLE

puzzled
The contradictory clues ~~were a puzzle to~~ the detective.
                                          ^

1. Historians are generally in agreement that the Egyptians were the inventors of sailing around 3000 BCE.
2. Many years passed before mariners were to understand that boats could sail upwind.
3. The invention of the keel was an improvement in sailboat navigation.
4. Steamships and transcontinental railroads were contributing factors in the disappearance of commercial sailing ships.
5. Today, either diesel or steam engines are the source of power for most ships.

46b   Prefer the active voice.

Transitive verbs can be in the active or passive voice. In the **active voice,** the subject of the sentence acts; in the **passive voice,** the subject is acted upon.

ACTIVE   The Senate finally passed the bill.

PASSIVE   The bill was finally passed by the Senate.

The passive voice downplays the actors as well as the action, so much so that a passive-voice sentence may leave the actors entirely unspecified.

➤   **The bill was finally passed.**

Who or what passed the bill? The sentence does not tell us.

Unless you have a good reason to use the passive voice, prefer the active voice. It is more forceful, and it prevents the impression of evasiveness that results from leaving the actor in a sentence unidentified.

PASSIVE	Unfortunately, the soup was spilled in the client's lap.
ACTIVE	Unfortunately, I spilled the soup in the client's lap.

PASSIVE	Polluting chemicals were dumped into the river.
ACTIVE	Industrial Products Corporation dumped polluting chemicals into the river.

When the recipient of the action is more important than the doer of the action, however, the passive voice is the more appropriate choice.

➤ **After her heart attack, my mother was taken to the hospital.**

Mother and the fact that she was taken to the hospital are more important than who took her to the hospital.

CHARTING the TERRITORY

Passive Voice

The passive voice is often used in scientific reports to keep the focus on the experiment and its results rather than on the experimenters.

➤ **After the bacteria were isolated, they were treated carefully with nicotine and were observed to stop reproducing.**

The passive voice also appears in some forms of business writing, such as memos, when it is important to deliver information impersonally and objectively.

Note: The symbol for flagging a passive voice construction that should be changed to the active voice is *pass*.

Exercise 46.2 Editing to avoid the passive voice

Change the verbs in the following sentences from passive to active voice. In some cases you may have to give an identity to an otherwise unidentified actor. Circle the number of any sentence that is already in the active voice or that is better left in its passive-voice form.

EXAMPLE **The milk was spilled.**

Someone spilled the milk.

1. The remote islands of Oceania were settled by Polynesian sailors beginning in the early first millennium CE.
2. Around 500, Hawaii was reached.
3. By about 900, settlers had reached Easter Island, the most remote island in Polynesia.
4. New Zealand, the largest Polynesian island, was also the last to be settled.
5. These immensely long voyages were probably made by families of settlers in open, double-hulled sailing canoes.

Exercise 46.3 Chapter review: Active verbs

Minimize the use of the passive voice and the verb *to be* in the following paragraph.

The idea of a lighter-than-air balloon was first conceived by inventors in the Middle Ages. Not until October 15, 1783, however, was Pilatre de Rosier successful in ascending in a hot air balloon. Five weeks later, he and a companion were makers of history again, accomplishing the world's first aerial journey with a five-mile trip across the city of Paris. For the next century, lighter-than-air balloons were considered the future of human flight. Balloonists were able to reach heights of up to three miles and made long, cross-country journeys. In 1859, for instance, a balloonist was carried from St. Louis to Henderson, New York. Balloonists were unable, however, to control the movement of their craft. To overcome this deficiency, efforts were made to use hand-cranked propellers and even giant oars. The invention of the internal-combustion engine was what finally made it possible to create controllable, self-propelled balloons, which are known as airships. Hot air was replaced by hydrogen in the earliest airships. Hydrogen gas catches fire easily, however, and this was the doom of the airship as a major means of travel. In 1937, the German airship *Hindenburg* exploded as it was landing in New Jersey, a tragedy that was described by a radio announcer in a live broadcast. As a result, helium has replaced hydrogen in today's airships.

CHECKLIST

Editing for Clarity

As you revise, check your writing for clarity by asking yourself these questions:

☐ Are all sentences concise and straightforward? Are any overloaded in ways that make them difficult to read and understand? (*See Chapter 38: Wordy Sentences, pp. 681–89.*)

☐ Are all sentences complete? Are any necessary words missing from compounds or comparisons? (*See Chapter 39: Missing Words, pp. 690–95.*)

☐ Do the parts of each sentence fit together in a way that makes sense, or is the sentence mixed up? (*See Chapter 40: Mixed Constructions, pp. 696–99.*)

☐ Do the key parts of each sentence fit together well, or are there disturbing mismatches in person, number, or grammatical structure? (*See Chapter 41: Confusing Shifts, pp. 700–9, and Chapter 42: Faulty Parallelism, pp. 710–19.*)

☐ Are the parts of each sentence clearly and closely connected, or are some modifiers separated from what they modify? (*See Chapter 43: Misplaced and Dangling Modifiers, pp. 720–28.*)

☐ Are the focus, flow, and voice of the sentences clear, or do some sentences have confusing shifts or ineffective coordination and subordination? (*See Chapter 41: Confusing Shifts, pp. 700–9, and Chapter 44: Coordination and Subordination, pp. 729–39.*)

☐ Do sentence patterns vary sufficiently? Is the mixture of long and short sentences enough to keep the reader alert and interested? (*See Chapter 45: Sentence Variety and Emphasis, pp. 740–48.*)

☐ Are all verbs strong and emphatic, or are the passive voice, the verb *to be,* or other weak or too-common verbs overused? (*See Chapter 46: Active Verbs, pp. 749–52.*)

753

This detail of a Mayan vase shows a scribe at work. Scribes—who documented the deeds of rulers with carefully chosen words—were esteemed in the great Mayan cities that flourished on the Yucatan Peninsula from around 100 to 900 CE.

> The difference between the right word and the almost right word is the difference between lightning and the lightning bug.
> —MARK TWAIN

Editing for Word Choice

47 Dictionaries and Vocabulary

Words are the writer's fundamental tool. The more words you know and can use correctly, the more precise, compelling, and evocative your writing will be. Nothing surpasses wide and frequent reading as a way to increase your store of exact nouns, strong verbs, and striking adjectives. Obtain a good dictionary and make a habit of looking up new and unfamiliar words as you encounter them—you may even want to record the words and their meanings in a small notebook.

Ways to Increase Your Vocabulary

1. Keep a dictionary and a thesaurus handy.
2. Read widely.
3. Use context to infer the meaning of unfamiliar words.
4. Learn the meaning of common prefixes and suffixes.
5. Keep a journal of new words.

47a Make using the dictionary a habit.

A standard desk dictionary—such as the *Random House Webster's College Dictionary,* the *Webster's New World Dictionary,* or the *American Heritage College Dictionary*—contains 140,000 to 180,000 entries. Along with words and their definitions, most dictionaries provide additional information such as the correct spellings of important place names, the official names of countries with their areas and populations, and the names of capital cities. Biographical entries give birth and death years and enough information to explain each person's importance to society. Many dictionaries also include lists of abbreviations and symbols, names and locations of colleges and universities, titles and correct forms of address, and conversion tables for weights and measures.

Unabridged dictionaries, which you will find in the reference section of your college library, are more comprehensive than desk dictionaries and may consist of multiple volumes. They are especially valuable when you are analyzing literature or studying an English text from an earlier period. The most comprehensive unabridged dictionary is the *Oxford English Dictionary* (also known as the *OED*), a ten-volume work of 22,000 pages that contains more than 400,000 entries, including words no longer in use. Each entry begins with the earliest meaning and pronunciation of the word and charts changes and variations in usage over time.

All dictionaries include guides to their use, usually in the front. The guides explain the terms and abbreviations that appear in the entries as well as special notations such as *slang, nonstandard,* and *vulgar.*

Figure 47.1 shows a representative entry from the *Random House Webster's College Dictionary,* with each section of the entry highlighted and labeled. The labels refer to the kinds of information discussed on pages 758–60. Note that other dictionaries, although they all provide the same kind of information as in this example, may format or order that information differently.

| | Phonetic symbols showing pronunciation. | Word endings and grammatical abbreviations. |

Dictionary entry.

com•pare (kəmpâr´), *v.,* **-pared, -par • ing,** *n.* —*v.t.* **1.** to examine (two or more objects, ideas, people, etc.) in order to note similarities and differences. **2.** to consider or describe as similar; liken: *"Shall I compare thee to a summer's day?"* **3.** to form or display the degrees of comparison of (an adjective or adverb). —*v.i.* **4.** to be worthy of comparison: *Whose plays can compare with Shakespeare's?* **5.** to be in similar standing; be alike: *This recital compares with the one he gave last year.* **6.** to appear in quality, progress, etc., as specified: *Their development compares poorly with that of neighbor nations.* **7.** to make comparisons. —*n.* **8.** comparison: *a beauty beyond compare.* —*Idiom.* **9. compare notes,** to exchange views, ideas, or impressions. [1375–1425; late ME < OF *comperer* < L *comparāre* to place together, match, v. der. of *compar* alike, matching (see COM-, PAR)] —**com•par´er,** *n.* —**Usage.** A traditional rule states that COMPARE should be followed by *to* when it points out likenesses between unlike persons or things: *she compared his handwriting to knotted string.* It should be followed by *with,* the rule says, when it examines two entities of the same general class for similarities or differences: *She compared his handwriting with mine.* This rule, though sensible, is not always followed, even in formal speech and writing. Common practice is to use *to* for likeness between members of different classes: *to compare a language to a living organism.* Between members of the same category, both *to* and *with* are used: *Compare the Chicago of today with* (or *to*) *the Chicago of the 1890s.* After the past participle COMPARED, either *to* or *with* is used regardless of the type of comparison.

Definitions as transitive verb (*v.t.*).

Definitions as intransitive verb (*v.i.*).

Definition as a noun (*n.*).

Special idiomatic meaning.

Etymology.

Usage note.

Undefined word formed by adding a suffix to entry.

FIGURE 47.1 The entry for the word *compare* in the *Random House Webster's College Dictionary.*

757

LEARNING in COLLEGE

Using a Dictionary

- **Use the guide words.** At the top of each dictionary page are guide words (usually in bold type) that tell you the first and last words on the page. Because all the entries are in alphabetical order, you can locate the word you are seeking by looking for guide words that would appear before and after your word in an alphabetical listing.

- **Try alternate spellings.** If you cannot find a word on the first try, think of another way to spell it.

- **Use the pronunciation key.** The letters and symbols that indicate each word's pronunciation are explained in a separate section at the front or back of a dictionary. In some dictionaries, they are also summarized at the bottom of each right-hand page of entries. Pronouncing new words aloud will help you learn them.

- **Pay attention to the parts of speech in a definition.** The same word can have different meanings depending on how it is used in a sentence—that is, its part of speech.

- **Always test the meaning you find.** Before using an unfamiliar word in your writing, substitute the dictionary meaning for the word in your sentence and see if the sentence makes sense.

1. Spelling, word division, and pronunciation

Entries in a dictionary are listed in alphabetical order according to their standard spelling. In the *Random House Webster's College Dictionary,* the verb *compare* is entered as **com•pare.** The dot separates the word into its two syllables. If you had to divide the word *compare* at the end of a line, you would place the hyphen where the dot appears.

Phonetic symbols in parentheses following the entry show its correct pronunciation; explanations of these symbols appear on the bottom of each right-hand page in some dictionaries. The second syllable of *compare* receives the greater stress; when you pronounce the word correctly, you say "comPARE." In this dictionary, an accent mark (´) appears after the syllable that receives the primary stress.

Dictionaries usually do not give the plurals of nouns if they are formed by adding an *s,* unless the word is foreign (*gondolas, dashikis*). Dictionaries do note irregular plurals—such as *children* for *child.*

> *Note:* Some dictionaries list alternate spellings, always giving the preferred spelling first or placing the full entry under the preferred spelling only.

2. Word endings and grammatical labels

The abbreviation *v.* immediately after the pronunciation tells you that *compare* is most frequently used as a verb. The *-pared* shows the simple past and past participle form of the verb; the present participle form, *-paring,* follows, indicating that *compare* drops the final *e* when *-ing* is added. The next abbreviation, *n.,* indicates that *compare* can sometimes function as a noun, as in the phrase *beyond compare.*

Here is a list of common abbreviations for grammatical terms:

adj.	adjective	*prep.*	preposition
adv.	adverb	*pron.*	pronoun
conj.	conjunction	*sing.*	singular
interj.	interjection	*v.*	verb
n.	noun	*v.i.*	intransitive verb
pl.	plural	*v.t.*	transitive verb
poss.	possessive		

3. Definitions, word origins, and undefined run-on entries

In the sample entry for *compare,* the definitions begin after the abbreviation *v.t.,* which indicates that the first three meanings relate to *compare* as a transitive verb. A little farther down in the entry, *v.i.* introduces definitions of *compare* as an intransitive verb. Next, after *n.,* comes the definition of *compare* as a noun. Finally, the word *Idiom* signals a special meaning not included in the previous definitions. As an idiom, *compare notes* means "to exchange views, ideas, or impressions," not to examine how two sets of notes are alike and different.

Included in most dictionary entries is an etymology—a brief history of the word—set off in brackets. There we see the date of the first known use of the word in English together with the earlier words from which it is derived. *Compare* came into English between 1375 and 1425 and was derived from the Old French word *comperer,* which came from Latin. Etymological information can be useful to writers who need to define a word for their readers.

Most dictionaries also list, as undefined run-on entries, words formed by adding a suffix to the base word. The sample entry, for example, includes the noun *comparer* as a run-on entry.

4. Usage

A usage note concludes some main entries in the dictionary. In the sample entry for *compare,* the usage note discusses the differences between the expressions *compare to* and *compare with,* indicating in what circumstances each should be used.

CHARTING the TERRITORY

Specialized Dictionaries

In the library's reference section, you can usually find numerous specialized dictionaries such as biographical and geographical dictionaries; foreign language dictionaries; dictionaries of first lines of poems and of famous quotations; dictionaries of legal and medical terms; and dictionaries of philosophy, sociology, engineering, and other disciplines. These dictionaries can help you write an essay or simply expand your knowledge of various subjects. Ask the reference librarian to help you locate a useful specialized dictionary for your topic or field.

For MULTILINGUAL STUDENTS

Strategies for Dictionary and Thesaurus Use

Understanding a word requires more than knowing its meaning. It also requires knowing how and in what contexts to use the word appropriately. As you develop fluency in English, you may find it useful to keep on hand a usage guide like Michael Swanson's *Practical English Usage,* as well as one of the following ESL dictionaries:

> *Random House Webster's Dictionary of American English,*
>   *ESL / Learner's Edition*
> *Longman Advanced American Dictionary*
> *Oxford ESL Dictionary*

As an advanced learner of English, however, you should move beyond specialized ESL dictionaries and consult standard dictionaries. To achieve both precise and nuanced expression, you should also supplement the dictionary with a thesaurus. As you encounter new words, pay close attention to the context in which they are used—both grammatically and in relation to the meaning of surrounding words. As you read and write, be sensitive to subtleties of usage, and try to expand your understanding of words beyond their literal definitions.

47b Consult a thesaurus for words that have similar meanings.

The word *thesaurus* in Latin means "treasury" or "collection." A **thesaurus** is a dictionary of synonyms. Several kinds of thesauruses are available, many called *Roget's* after Peter Mark Roget (pronounced roZHAY), who published the first one in 1852. Today, thesauruses are included in most word-processing software packages.

Use a thesaurus when you are looking for the word that most precisely conveys your intended meaning or when you are looking for an alternative to a word you have overused. When choosing a word from a thesaurus, consider both the word's **denotation,** or primary meaning, and its **connotations,** the feelings and images associated with it (*see Chapter 49: Exact Language, pp. 777–81*). Do not choose a word just because you think it sounds smart or fancy.

Exercise 47.1 Using a dictionary and a thesaurus

Look up the following words in a thesaurus, and find two synonyms for each. Then, in each case, use a dictionary to find the definition of the original word and the two synonyms. Finally, use all three words—the original and both synonyms—in one or more sentences.

1. idea
2. pretty
3. good
4. say
5. look

47c Read for pleasure.

Whether you find it in a best-selling novel by Scott Turow or in a sophisticated magazine like the *Atlantic Monthly,* a new word you come across in something you read for fun or personal interest will stay with you at least as well as one you encounter in a text assigned for class. In college, each course will require you to learn the meanings of certain new words. Yet if you rely only on coursework to learn new words, you will deprive yourself of the easiest and most natural way to build vocabulary: reading for pleasure.

Reading Scott Turow's *The Burden of Proof,* for example, you would encounter words such as *putrefaction* (the rot or decay of organic matter), *craven* (fearful, cowardly), and *Anglophile* (an admirer of English ways). A recent issue of *Travel and Leisure* magazine contained *ribald* (indecent or irreverent in speech) and *riposte* (a sharp reply in speech or action). Even catalogs and advertisements can contain interesting words, such as *peerless* (unequaled), *cordovan* (a type of leather originally from Córdoba, Spain), and *tumultuous* (noisy and disorderly).

 TEXTCONNEX

Online "Word-a-Day" Services and Books of Curious Words

A number of Web sites will send you a daily e-mail containing an interesting or unusual word, its definition, origin, and even a sound clip demonstrating its pronunciation.

- Perhaps the best known of these sites is AWAD, or A.Word.A.Day, run by Anu Garg <www.wordsmith.org/words/today.html>.
- Merriam-Webster <www.m-w.com/cgi-bin/mwwod.pl> and the *Oxford English Dictionary* <www.oed.com/cgi/display/wotd> sponsor similar sites.
- For a comprehensive list of word-a-day sites, go to <dmoz.org/reference/dictionaries/vocabulary_lists/word-a-day>.

Anu Garg and Stuti Garg's book *A Word a Day* is a selection of words from the AWAD mailings. Other books such as William Espy's *Thou Improper, Thou Uncommon Noun* and Erin McKean's *Weird and Wonderful Words* can also be fun places to find new words.

Exercise 47.2   Learning new words

Scan a book, magazine, or Web site that interests you, and jot down ten words that are unfamiliar to you. Look up the words in a dictionary, and use each in a sentence.

47d Learn the meanings of new words by their context.

When reading for a class assignment, for work, or for pleasure, it is a good idea to have a dictionary nearby. Often, however, you may find you can deduce the meaning of an unfamiliar word—even without a dictionary—by examining the familiar words around it.

762

1. Embedded definitions

Textbooks and other academic materials often define specialized vocabulary or terms when they are first used in a sentence, as with the underlined words in the following examples.

➤ **<u>Fables</u> are brief stories that have an explicitly stated moral.**

➤ **One new form that emerged in the mid-seventeenth century was the <u>oratorio</u>, a vocal work with all the musical elements of an opera, but performed concert style, without staging or costumes.**

➤ **An entire week of rehearsal was spent on <u>blocking</u>— directing the actors' movements on the stage.**

➤ **Speaking in run-on sentences is a symptom of <u>mania</u> (a mental illness characterized by an exaggeratedly elevated mood, an inflated sense of self-importance, and profuse and rapidly changing ideas).**

2. Comparisons and other parallel constructions

Parallel constructions (*see Chapter 42: Faulty Parallelism, pp. 710–19*) often distinguish among or group together two or more terms or concepts, providing clues to the meaning of unfamiliar words. In the following sentence, for example, the word *although* sets up a contrast between *obedient and well-behaved* on the one hand and *recalcitrant* on the other, suggesting that *recalcitrant* is the opposite of *obedient and well-behaved.*

➤ **Although Jack was usually obedient and well-behaved, his brother was often recalcitrant.**

A list of examples can similarly suggest the meaning of new words. In the following sentence, the examples convey the sense of *cloying* as overly sentimental or excessively sweet.

➤ **Constant phone calls, daily offerings of roses and stuffed animals, and other cloying actions can repel the beloved.**

47e Learn new words by analyzing their parts.

You may be able to deduce the meaning of an unfamiliar word if you can recognize the meaning of its parts. Many words consist of a prefix

COMMON PREFIXES

PREFIX	MEANING	EXAMPLES
a-	without	amoral, atonal
ab-	away from, off	abduct, abbreviate
ad-	toward, near	adverb, adjoin
anti-	against	antiwar, antidote
bi-	two	bisect, bicycle
co-, com-, con-	with, together	cosign, combine, condescend
contra-, counter-	against, opposite	contradict, counteract
de-	from, against	detach, demerit
deci-, deca	ten	decimal, decameter
dis-	remove from, negate	disappear, disavow
du-	two	duplicate, duplicity
ex-	from, beyond	exit, external
extra-	beyond	extraordinary, extrasensory
il-, im-, in-, ir-	not	illegal, impossible, incomplete, irrational
inter-	between, among	interaction, intersect
mal-	bad	malfunction, malcontent

or suffix (or both) attached to a root word, as in *preview* (*pre* + *view*) or *viewer* (*view* + *er*). Others may consist of two or more root words joined together as a compound word, as in viewpoint (*view* + *point*). Learning how prefixes and suffixes modify base words will help you decode unfamilar words.

1. Prefixes

A **prefix** is a syllable that attaches to the beginning of a root word, creating a new word with its own meaning. For example, the prefix *semi-,* meaning "half," joins with *circle* to produce *semicircle,* which means "half-circle." Similarly, the prefix *extra,* meaning "beyond,"

PREFIX	MEANING	EXAMPLES
mis-	wrong	mistake, misuse
mono-	one, same	monotone, monorail
multi-	many	multicultural, multimedia
non-	no, not	nonsense, noncombatant
pre-	before	preview, predate
post-	after	postgraduate, postscript
pro-	in front of, for	prologue, pro-business
quad-, quar-	four	quadrilateral, quarter
re-	again, back	restart, recline
semi-	half	semicircle, semiprecious
sub-	under	submarine, substandard
super-	above	superscript, supersonic
syn-, sym-	together	synchronize, symphony
trans-	across	transatlantic, translate
tri-	three	triangle, tricycle
un-	not	unhappy, undo
uni-	one	uniform

joins with *ordinary,* to produce *extraordinary,* which means "beyond the ordinary." See the box above for a list of common prefixes and their meanings.

2. Suffixes

Suffixes are syllables that are attached to the ends of words. They usually modify the meaning of a word by changing it from one part of speech to another. With different suffixes, for example, the adjective *pure* becomes the adverb *purely* and the noun *purity.* Similarly, the noun *fear* becomes the adjective *fearless* and, with the addition of a second suffix, the noun *fearlessness.* See the box on the next page for a list of common suffixes and their meanings.

COMMON SUFFIXES

SUFFIX	MEANING	EXAMPLES
-able	capable of, given to	miser<u>able</u>, laugh<u>able</u>
-al	pertaining to	natur<u>al</u>, season<u>al</u>
-ance, -ence	act, process, or quality of	continu<u>ance</u>, differ<u>ence</u>
-ant	characterized by, one who	observ<u>ant</u>, assist<u>ant</u>
-ary	pertaining to	legend<u>ary</u>, monet<u>ary</u>
-dom	quality or state	wis<u>dom</u>, free<u>dom</u>
-en	made of, make	wood<u>en</u>, tight<u>en</u>
-ful	full of	plenti<u>ful</u>
-hood	quality, state, or sharing a quality or state	mother<u>hood</u>, neighbor<u>hood</u>
-ion	act or process of	creat<u>ion</u>, motivat<u>ion</u>
-ish	related to	child<u>ish</u>, self<u>ish</u>
-ism	principles of, practice of, quality of	Marx<u>ism</u>, hero<u>ism</u>
-ist	one concerned with	Marx<u>ist</u>, lobby<u>ist</u>
-ity	quality or state of	abnormal<u>ity</u>, insan<u>ity</u>
-ize	make or subject to	privat<u>ize</u>, penal<u>ize</u>
-ness	quality or state of	kind<u>ness</u>, fond<u>ness</u>
-less	without	friend<u>less</u>, fear<u>less</u>
-ly	in the manner or way of	ghost<u>ly</u>, glad<u>ly</u>
-ment	action or process	commit<u>ment</u>, indict<u>ment</u>

Exercise 47.3   Chapter review: Dictionaries and vocabulary

Look for compounds and use context and your knowledge of prefixes and suffixes to infer the meaning of the underlined words in the following passage. Write down your inferred definitions; then check them against a dictionary and write down the dictionary definition that most closely matches the meaning of the words as they are used in the passage.

    The <u>Enlightenment</u> ideals promoted by the American and French <u>revolutions</u>—freedom, equality, and popular sovereignty—appealed to <u>peoples</u> throughout Europe and the

Americas. In the Caribbean and South America, they inspired revolutionary movements: slaves in the French colony of Saint-Domingue rose against their overlords and established the independent republic of Haiti, and Euro-American leaders mounted independence movements in Central America and South America. The ideals of the American and French revolutions also encouraged social reformers to organize broader programs of liberation. Whereas the American and French revolutions guaranteed political and legal rights to white men, social reformers sought to extend these rights to women and slaves of African ancestry. During the nineteenth century, all European and Euro-American states abolished slavery, but former slaves and their descendants remained an underprivileged and often oppressed class in most of the Atlantic world. The quest for women's rights also proceeded slowly during the nineteenth century.

—from Bentley and Ziegler,
Traditions and Encounters

48 Appropriate Language

Language is appropriate when it fits your topic, purpose, and audience. You have already had a great deal of experience fitting language to your audience and the rhetorical situation. Consider, for example, how differently you would describe an unpleasant work experience to a close friend as opposed to a potential employer during a job interview. A more formal choice of words would obviously be appropriate in the business setting.

You may also have witnessed someone using language that subtly discriminates against a group of people, and you may have felt how inappropriate that language was.

In academic and professional writing, **standard English** is the form of English that can be understood by everyone and is considered clear and appropriate. Standard English has evolved over time by consensus among writers, editors, teachers, and others who study language, and it is the language this book focuses on. In academic and professional situations, language that is overly formal and pretentious can be just as inappropriate as overly informal language. The guidelines presented in this chapter are intended to help you develop a notion of appropriateness that you can tailor to your writing situation.

www.mhhe.com/
nmhh
For information
and exercises on
appropriate language,
go to

Editing >
Word Choice

48a Avoid slang, regional expressions, and nonstandard English in college writing.

1. Avoiding Slang

Slang is a very informal and playful type of language that is used within a social group or discourse community (see *Charting the Territory: Discourse Communities on the next page*). There is, for example, surfer slang (*aggro, gremmies, landshark*), coffeehouse slang (*cap, skinny, whipless*), and even publishing slang (*comp, slush pile, dead matter*). Teen slang is the most extensive and short-lived (remember *awesome?*), serving to bond a generation. In college papers, however, slang terms and the hip tone that goes with them should be avoided.

SLANG	In *Heart of Darkness,* we hear a lot about a *dude* named Kurtz, but we don't see the *guy* much.
REVISED	In *Heart of Darkness,* Marlow, the narrator, talks almost continually about Kurtz, but we meet Kurtz himself only at the end.

CHARTING the TERRITORY

Discourse Communities

People who share certain interests, knowledge, and customary ways of communicating constitute a **discourse community.** Members of the discourse community of baseball fans, for example, talk and write about *switch-hitters, batting averages,* and *earned-run averages*—terms that may be unfamiliar to people outside the community. Each of us belongs to several discourse communities, in and out of school. Historians, literary critics, economists, astronomers, pilots, surgeons, lovers of fishing, and thousands of others have their own discourse communities. The more familiar you are with a discourse community, the more you will know about the language that is appropriate in that community.

2. Avoiding nonstandard dialects and regional expressions

American English consists of numerous **dialects** and varieties of the language that are distinguished from other varieties by differences in vocabulary, pronunciation, and grammar. A dialect is used by a particular social, geographic or ethnic group, as in Cajun English, New York English, and Black English. In American colleges, professions, and businesses, the dominant dialect is standard English. If you speak a dialect that varies from standard English, be aware of the differences for those occasions when standard English is preferred. Common nonstandard words are labeled as such in the dictionary.

Dialects particular to a geographic area may contain **regionalisms,** or expressions unique to that region. Examples of regionalisms are *memberize* for "recall," *y'all* for "all of you," and *pockeybook* for "purse." Use regionalisms in writing only when you are sure that your audience will understand and appreciate them. Regionalisms are not appropriate for college papers.

48b Use an appropriate level of formality.

College writing assignments usually call for a style that avoids the extremes of the colloquial and the pretentious. Language that is appropriate to informal conversation but not precise enough for academic writing is known as **colloquial** language. It may be labeled "colloquial" or "informal" in the dictionary. Slang and regionalisms also fall within the category of informal language.

COLLOQUIAL	Shakespeare's character Hamlet sure has a mixed bag of emotions.

769

REVISED Shakespeare's character Hamlet is racked by conflicting emotions.

Pretentious or **stilted language** is language that is overly formal. It forces readers to work hard at decoding its meaning—and eventually readers lose interest. Pretentious language is overly abstract, wordy, and lacking in concrete detail. Avoiding pretentious language does not mean avoiding all long or complex words, but rather choosing such a word only when it communicates your meaning more precisely than a simpler word.

PRETENTIOUS Romantic lovers are characterized by a preoccupation with a deliberately restricted set of qualities in the love object that are viewed as means to some ideal end.

REVISED People in love tend to idealize the beloved.

48c Avoid jargon.

When specialists communicate with one another, they often use technical language that can sound incomprehensible to nonspecialists. Such language is appropriate in many contexts and has a place in college writing. Without it, no one could write a lab report, an economic analysis, or a philosophical argument. Technical language becomes a problem, however, when it is used in an inappropriate context.

Jargon is technical language used in an inappropriate context, that is, when it does not fit a writer's purpose and audience. If you want to be understood, you should not use discourse that is appropriate for specialists when you are writing for a wider audience. Jargon puts people off, making them feel like outsiders.

JARGON Pegasus Technologies, a leading B2C solutions provider, developed a Web-based PSP system to support standard off-line brands in meeting their loyalty-driven marketing objectives via the Internet space.

REVISED Pegasus Technologies developed a system for businesses that helps them create Web sites to run contests and other promotions for their customers.

If you need to use technical terms when writing for nonspecialists, be sure to define them.

> Armstrong's innovative singing style featured "scat,"
> a technique that combines "nonsense syllables [with]
> improvised melodies" (Robinson 425).

48d Avoid most euphemisms and all doublespeak.

Although most writers strive to be clear and direct, euphemisms and
doublespeak have another goal: to cover up the truth. **Euphemisms**
substitute nice-sounding words like *correctional facility* and *passing
away* for such harsh realities as *prison* and *death*. On some occasions,
a euphemism like *passing away* may serve a useful purpose; for example, you may wish to avoid upsetting a grieving person. Usually,
however, words should not be used to evade or deceive.

Doublespeak is the deceitful use of language. Its purpose is not
to prevent hurt feelings but to confuse or mislead readers. As the following example shows, doublespeak obscures facts.

> A revenue enhancement program will be implemented in
> response to last year's negative gains.

The writer tries to obscure bad news by using *revenue enhancement* instead of *tax* or *price hike* and *negative gains* instead of *deficit* or *loss*.

Exercise 48.1 Editing for informal language, pretentious language,
jargon, and euphemisms

Edit the following sentences so that they are suitable for college writing.

1. With the invention of really cool steel engraving and mechanical
   printing presses in the nineteenth century, publishers could
   make tons of books like practically overnight.
2. France was the womb of nineteenth-century realism, a fecund
   literary land that gave birth to those behemoths of realism
   Stendahl, Balzac, and Flaubert.
3. Flaubert really hated the bourgeoisie because he thought they
   never thought about anything but cash, stuff, and looking good
   in front of others.
4. Flaubert's *Madame Bovary* is the story of this really bored pro-
   vincial chick who dreams of being a fancy lady, cheats on her
   husband, and then does herself in.
5. Intense class antagonisms, combined with complex currents
   of historical determinism, extending back into the ancient

traditions of serfdom and the czar, may precisely index the factors constitutive of the precipitant flowering of the Russian novel in the nineteenth century.

6. The present writer's former belief that nineteenth century literature is incomprehensible is no longer operational.

48e Do not use biased or sexist language.

Words can wound. Ethnic and religious groups, people with disabilities, gay men and lesbians, and workers in some occupations often object to the way people talk and write about them. Always review your writing to see if it is unintentionally biased. Be on the lookout for subtle stereotypes that demean, ignore, or patronize people on the basis of gender, race, religion, national origin, ethnicity, physical ability, sexual orientation, occupation, or any other human condition. Revise for inclusiveness.

1. Avoiding stereotypes

A **stereotype** is a society's simplified image or generalization about a racial, ethnic, or social group. Stereotypes are never completely true and can in fact be grossly misrepresentative. Even when positive, stereotypes lump individuals together and should be avoided.

➤ ~~Although the~~ *The* Browns are Irish ~~Catholics, there are only~~ *an* *Catholic family with* two

children. ~~in the family.~~

➤ ~~Because Asian students are whizzes at math, we~~ *We* all wanted

~~them~~ *math whizzes* in our study group.

2. Avoiding sexist language

Sexist clichés and stereotypes **Sexist language** demeans or stereotypes women and men, but women are usually the explicit targets. For example, many labels and clichés imply that women are not as able or as mature as men. Consider the meaning of words or phrases like *the weaker sex, the fair sex, the little woman, my better half, working mother, lady lawyer, housewife, poetess,* and *coed.*

Avoiding bias means more than simply not using derogatory words and slurs. It also means avoiding subtle stereotypes. For example, not all heads of state are or have to be men. Secretaries can be either women or men.

BIASED	Wives of heads of state typically have their own administrative staffs.
REVISED	Spouses of heads of state typically have their own administrative staffs.

BIASED	We advertised for a new secretary because we needed another girl in the office.
REVISED	We advertised for a new secretary because we had too much work for the staff on hand.

Women and men should be referred to in parallel ways: ladies and gentlemen (not ladies and men), men and women, husband and wife. Names should also be given parallel treatment: Virginia Woolf and Lytton Strachey, or Woolf and Strachey, not Virginia and Strachey.

The generic **he**   Traditionally, the pronoun *he* and other masculine pronouns—*he, him, his, himself*—have been used generically to refer to unspecified individuals of either gender. This convention subtly takes women out of the picture as members of society and is no longer acceptable. Whenever possible, replace the masculine pronouns *he, him, his,* and *himself* when they are being used generically to refer to both women and men. One satisfactory way to replace masculine pronouns is to use the plural.

BIASED	Everybody had his way.
REVISED	We all had our way.

Some writers alternate *he* and *she, him* and *her.* This strategy may be effective in some writing situations, but switching back and forth can also be distracting. The constructions *his or her* and *he or she* are acceptable, as long as they are not used excessively or more than once in a sentence.

AWKWARD	Each student in the psychology class was to choose a different book according to his or her interests, to read the book overnight, to do without his or her normal sleep, to write a short summary of what he or she had read, and then to see if he or she dreamed about the book the following night.
REVISED	Each student in the psychology class was to choose an interesting book, read it overnight without getting a normal night's rest, write a short summary of the book the next morning, and then see if he or she dreamed about the book the following night.

773

The construction *his/her* and the unpronounceable *s/he* are not acceptable in academic writing.

> *Note:* Using the neuter impersonal pronoun *one* can sometimes help you avoid masculine pronouns. *One* can make your writing sound stuffy, however, so it is usually better to try another option.
>
> **STUFFY** The American creed holds that if one works hard, one will succeed in life.
>
> **REVISED** The American creed holds that those who work hard will succeed in life.

(*For more on editing to avoid the generic use of* he, him, his, *or* himself, *see Chapter 36: Problems with Pronouns, pp. 651–53.*)

For MULTILINGUAL STUDENTS

Biased Language

English speakers are sensitive to language that may stereotype or offend groups of people. As an educated user of English, you should be aware of potential pitfalls in the forms and connotations of words. Regardless of the usage norms in your native language, you should generally avoid gender stereotyping in the names of jobs. Use plural forms of pronouns to make generalizations about human traits or activities (for example, by replacing the generic *mankind* with terms like *humanity* or *humankind*).

The generic man Just as *he* and *him* have been used generically to represent both males and females, the syllable *man* as a word or suffix has been used generically to refer to all humanity. Today, however, the use of *man* to represent both men and women should be avoided. Also, choose substitutes for words that contain *man* but could apply to both men and women (*see the "Gender-Neutral Alternatives" box on the next page*).

BIASED The chairman of the department reviews grant applications.

REVISED The department chair reviews grant applications.

GENDER-NEUTRAL ALTERNATIVES to GENDER-SPECIFIC TERMS: SOME EXAMPLES

GENDER-SPECIFIC TERM	GENDER-NEUTRAL ALTERNATIVE
chairman	chair, chairperson
congressman	representative, member of Congress
fireman	firefighter
forefathers	ancestors
man, mankind	people, humans, humanity
man-made	artificial
policeman	police officer
postman	mail carrier
salesman	sales representative
spokesman	spokesperson
-ess (poetess, actress, stewardess, etc.)	poet, actor, flight attendant

Exercise 48.2 Editing to eliminate biased language

Identify the biased language in each of the following sentences, and rewrite each sentence using the suggestions in section 48e.

EXAMPLE

flight attendants
Because ~~stewardesses~~ travel so much, child care is an issue

for them.

1. Man is fast approaching a population crisis.
2. Each of us must do his part to reduce the production of greenhouse gases.
3. Every housewife should encourage her children to make recycling a habit, and every corporate chief executive officer should encourage his employees to carpool or take mass transit whenever possible.
4. Congressmen should make conservation and environmental protection legislative priorities.
5. If he tried, the average motorist could help reduce our dependence on oil.

Exercise 48.3 Chapter review: Appropriate language

Edit the following passage to make the language appropriate for a college paper.

The writer of novels Henry James had many illustrious forefathers. His grandfather William traversed the Atlantic in 1789 with little more than a Latin grammar book and a desire to see the battlefields of the Revolutionary War. When William James met his maker in 1832, he left an estate worth $3 million, or about $100 million in today's cash. This little something was to be divided among eleven children and his better half, Catherine Barber James. William's fourth kid, Henry, who is often referred to as the elder Henry James so's that he is not confused with the novelist, became a lecturer and writer on metaphysics. His big thing was the doctrines of the Swedish mystic Emanuel Swedenborg. Although some thought the elder Henry James a few plates short of a picnic, his work was very well known and influential during his lifetime.

49 Exact Language

To communicate clearly, you need to put words in the right order in well-formed sentences and paragraphs, but you also need to choose the right words. As you revise, be on the lookout for problems with **diction,** or word choice. Do the words you have chosen reflect your intended meaning as precisely as they should?

> *Note:* The editing symbol for questionable word choice is *WW,* which is an abbreviation for "wrong word."

Selecting the right word involves two aspects of its meaning. A word has a primary (or explicit) meaning, called its **denotation,** and a secondary (or implicit) meaning, called its **connotation.**

49a Avoid misusing words.

www.mhhe.com/
nmhh
For information and exercises on exact language, go to

Editing >
Word Choice

A word's denotation is what you would find if you looked up the word in a dictionary. Be careful not to misuse words that have similar but distinct denotations.

> ➣ The medication ~~effects~~ *affects* concentration but has no ~~affect~~ *effect* on

> appetite.

> ➣ Murdock ~~flaunted~~ *flouted* the no-smoking rule.

Consult a dictionary or the Glossary of Usage in Chapter 50 for help with commonly misused terms.

In college, your vocabulary will grow as you learn more about various subjects and ways of talking about them. You can expect some growing pains, however, including mistakes in your use of new terms and unfamiliar words. You can reduce such mistakes by consulting a dictionary whenever you include an unfamiliar word in your writing.

➤   The aristocracy ~~exuded~~ *exhibited* numerous vices, including greed and ~~license.~~ *licentiousness*

Also, check your course textbooks for glossaries that can help you use new terms properly.

Exercise 49.1   Avoiding the misuse of words

In the following sentences, replace any of the underlined words that are misused with a word with an appropriate denotation, and circle those that are properly used. For help, consult a dictionary or the Glossary of Usage in Chapter 50.

EXAMPLE

Computer software and computer hardware ~~compliment~~ *complement* ~~one another.~~ *each other.*

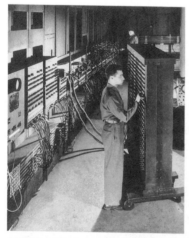

FIGURE 49.1 The incredible shrinking computer. Almost any of today's laptop computers (right) has more computing power than the first general-purpose digital computer (left), the massive ENIAC (Electronic Numerical Integrator and Calculator).

1. The nineteenth-century Englishman Charles Babbage was probably the first person to conceive of a general-purpose computing machine, but the ability to build one <u>alluded</u> him.
2. Because she was able to <u>imply</u> the <u>kinds of</u> instructions that would work with Babbage's machine, some historians <u>cite</u> Ada Lovelace, daughter of the poet Byron, as the first computer programmer.
3. <u>Incredulous</u> as it may seem, the first general-purpose digital electronic computer was 100 feet long and 10 feet high but had less computing power than one of today's inexpensive laptop computers.
4. The U.S. government was the <u>principle</u> source of funding for some of the most important advances in computing after World War II.
5. Without the invention of the transistor, today's small, powerful computing devices would not have been <u>plausible</u>.

49b Choose words with suitable connotations.

To use words effectively, you need to know their connotations as well as their denotations. Connotations come from the feelings and images people associate with a word, so they influence what readers understand a writer to be saying.

Consider, for example, the following three statements:

Murdock *ignored* the no-smoking rule.
Murdock *disobeyed* the no-smoking rule.
Murdock *flouted* the no-smoking rule.

Even though the three sentences depict the same event, each sentence describes Murdock's action somewhat differently. If Murdock *ignored* the rule, it may simply have been because he did not know or care about it. If he *disobeyed* the rule, he must have known about it and consciously decided not to follow it, but what if he *flouted* the rule? Well, then there was probably a look of disdain on his face as he made sure that others would see him ostentatiously puffing away at a cigarette.

As you revise, consider replacing any word whose connotations do not exactly fit what you want to say.

➤ The players' union should ~~request~~ *demand* that the NFL amend its

pension plan.

If you cannot think of a more suitable word, consult a print or an online thesaurus (*see Chapter 47*) for **synonyms,** words with similar meanings. Keep in mind, however, that most words have connotations that allow them to work in some contexts but not in others. To find out more about a synonym's connotations, look up the word in a dictionary.

For MULTILINGUAL STUDENTS

Connotation and Usage Problems

Most students whose first language is not English consider vocabulary use a major challenge in analyzing and responding to academic texts. Even though you may learn the meaning of a word, you may have trouble using it correctly in your speaking and writing. Certain types of word combinations are determined by conventional use rather than by their literal meaning (for example, you *do* homework, but you *make* a plan).

Conscious or unconscious translation from your native language will always be part of your learning, but you should try to study English words and phrases in context, with sensitivity to their connotations. It helps to keep a dictionary close by (*see Chapter 47: Dictionaries and Vocabulary, pp. 756–60*).

Synonyms and Your Word Processor's Thesaurus

Many word-processing programs include a thesaurus that lets you replace a word with a synonym at the click of a mouse. As with a print or an online thesaurus, however, it is up to you to make sure that the connotations of the synonym you choose are appropriate to the context in which you are using it.

Exercise 49.2   Choosing words with suitable connotations

Use a dictionary or thesaurus to list as many synonyms as you can for each of the underlined words in the passages that follow. Discuss why you think the authors chose the underlined words.

1. Space and time capture the imagination like no other scientific subject. . . . They form the arena of reality, the very fabric of the cosmos. Our entire existence—everything we do, think, and experience—takes place in some region of space during some interval

of time. Yet science is still <u>struggling</u> to understand what space
and time actually are.

—BRIAN GREENE, *The Fabric of the Cosmos*

2. On Waverly Street, everybody knew everybody else. It was only
   one short block, after all—a narrow strip of patched and re-
   patched pavement, bracketed between a high stone cemetery
   wall at one end and the commercial <u>clutter</u> of Govans Road at the
   other. The trees were <u>elderly</u> maples with lumpy, <u>bulbous</u> trunks.
   The <u>squat</u> clapboard <u>houses</u> seemed mostly front porch.

—ANNE TYLER, *Saint Maybe*

49c Include specific and concrete words.

In addition to general and abstract terms, clear writers use words that
are specific and concrete. Such words can help your readers grasp your
particular message.

General words name broad categories of things, such as *trees,
books, politicians,* or *students*. **Specific words** name particular kinds
of things or items, such as *pines, Victorian novels, Republicans,* or *college sophomores*.

Abstract words name qualities and ideas that do not have physical properties, such as *charity, beauty, hope,* or *radical*. **Concrete
words** name things we can sense by touch, taste, smell, hearing, and
sight, such as *velvet, vinegar, smoke, screech,* or *sweater*.

By creating images that appeal to the senses, specific and concrete words can help make your writing more precise.

VAGUE	The trees were affected by the bad weather.
PRECISE	The small pines shook in the gale.

VAGUE	Their generosity helped the library.
PRECISE	Their $5 million gift paid for the library's new online catalog.

As you edit, make sure that you have developed your ideas with
specific and concrete details. Also check for overused, vague terms—
such as *factor, thing, good, nice,* and *interesting*—and replace them
with more specific and concrete alternatives.

➤ The protesters were charged with ~~things~~ they never ~~did~~.
^crimes ^committed

Exercise 49.3 | Including specific and concrete words

Draw on your own knowledge, experience, and imagination to rewrite the following paragraph with invented details described in specific and concrete language.

EXAMPLE

Niagara Falls is an awe-inspiring sight.

The waters of the Niagara River flow over the edge of the half-mile-wide, crescent-shaped Horseshoe Falls and plunge with a roar to the bottom of the cataract two hundred feet below.

Last summer I worked as an intern at a company in a field that interests me. The work was hard and the hours were long, but I gained a lot of experience. At first I was assigned only routine office work. As I learned more about the business, however, my employers began to give me more interesting tasks. By the end of the summer I was helping out on several high-priority projects. My employers liked my work and offered me another internship for the following summer.

49d Use standard idioms.

An **idiom** is a customary expression whose meaning does not relate in a predictable way to the meaning of the words it is composed of. As customary expressions, idioms are not always logical and are not easily translated from one language to another, or even from one dialect to another. Often they involve expressions with prepositions. We are not capable *to* but capable *of;* we do not go *with* the car but *in* the car or simply *by* car; we do not abide *with* a rule but *by* a rule. We might meet someone *at* the train station or, a bit later, *on* the train. In some parts of the United States, people wait *in* line to go to a movie; in other parts, they wait *on* line.

Some verbs, called **phrasal verbs,** include a preposition to make their meaning complete. These verbs often have an idiomatic meaning that changes significantly when the attached preposition changes.

Henry *made up* with Gloria.
Henry *made off* with Gloria.
Henry *made out* with Gloria.

If you are not sure which preposition to use with a verb, consult the box on idiomatic expressons on pages 783–84 or look up the main word in a dictionary.

For MULTILINGUAL STUDENTS

For more on phrasal verbs and idiomatic expressions, see Chapter 66: Identifying and Editing Common Errors, pages 974–77.

COMMON IDIOMATIC EXPRESSIONS in ENGLISH

Common Adjective + Preposition Combinations

afraid of: fearing someone or something
anxious about: worried
ashamed of: embarrassed by someone or something
aware of: know about
content with: having no complaints about; happy about
fond of: having positive feelings for
full of: filled with
grateful to (someone) (for something): thankful; appreciative
interested in: curious; wanting to know more about
jealous of: feeling envy toward
proud of: pleased about
responsible to (someone) (for something): accountable; in charge
satisfied with: having no complaints about
suspicious of: distrustful of
tired of: had enough of; bored with

Common Verb + Preposition Combinations

apologize to: express regret for actions
arrive at (an event at a specific location): come to a building or a house (*I arrived at the Louvre at ten.*)
arrive in (a place): come to a city/country (*I arrived in Paris.*)
blame for: hold responsible; accuse
complain about: find fault; criticize
concentrate on: focus; pay attention
congratulate on: offer good wishes for success
consist of: contain; be made of
depend on: trust
explain to: make something clear to someone
insist on: be firm
laugh at: express amusement
look up: visit
rely on: trust

(continued)

smile at: act friendly toward
take care of: look after; tend
thank for: express appreciation
throw at: toss an object toward someone or something without
    expecting that the object will be caught
throw to: toss something to someone to catch
throw (something) away: discard
throw (something) out: discard; present an idea for consideration
worry about: feel concern; fear for someone's safety or well-being

Common Particles (verb + preposition combinations that create
verb phrasals, expressions with meanings that are different from
the meaning of the verb itself)

break down: stop functioning
bring up: mention in conversation; raise a child
call off: cancel
call up: contact by telephone
catch up on: get up-to-date information on
catch up with: reach the same place as
drop in on: visit unexpectedly
drop off: deliver
fill out: complete
find out: discover
get away with: avoid discovery
get off (your chest): tell a long-concealed secret or problem
get off (the couch): stand up
get over: recover
give up: surrender; stop work on
leave out: omit
look down on: despise
look forward to: anticipate
look into: research
look up: check a fact
look up to: admire
put up with: endure
run across: meet unexpectedly
run out: use up
send off: say goodbye to
stand up for: defend
take after: resemble
take off: leave the airport (a plane); miss time from work
turn down: reject

49e Create suitable figures of speech.

Figurative language, or **figures of speech,** are imaginative expressions, usually comparisons, that modify the literal meaning of other words. Two of the most common figures of speech are similes and metaphors.

A **simile** is a comparison that contains the word *like* or *as.*

➤ **His smile was like the sun peeking through after a rainstorm.**

A **metaphor** is an implied comparison. It treats one thing or action, such as a critic's review, as if it were something else, in this case, an extreme method of clearing land.

➤ **The critic's slash-and-burn review devastated the cast.**

Because it is compressed, a metaphor is often more forceful than a simile.

Other common figures of speech include personification, hyperbole, and hyperbole's counterpart, understatement. **Personification** is a form of metaphor in which human qualities are attributed to objects, animals, or abstract ideas.

➤ **The stormy sea tossed the little boat cruelly about.**

Hyperbole is deliberate exaggeration.

➤ **The speech was endless.**

Understatement is exaggeratedly restrained comparison.

➤ **The speech was certainly more engaging than a recitation of the phone book.**

Figurative comparisons can make your prose more vivid, but only if they suit your subject and purpose. Clumsy or inappropriate comparisons distract readers and obscure meaning. Be careful to avoid **mixed metaphors**; if you use two or more comparisons together, make sure they are compatible. Not only does the following sentence mix three incompatible figures (a mineral, running, and a ship), but two of the three are also unsuitable (running a race, boarding a ship).

| MIXED | His presentation of the plan was so *crystal clear* that in a *burst of speed* we decided *to come aboard.* |
| REVISED | His clear presentation immediately convinced us to support the plan. |

Exercise 49.5 Recognizing figures of speech

Identify and explain the figures of speech (simile, metaphor, personification, hyperbole, and understatement) in the following passages.

EXAMPLE

A miss is as good as a mile.

This expression is a simile suggesting that an error is an error, whether small ("a miss") or large ("a mile").

1. Her voice is full of money.
   —F. Scott Fitzgerald, *The Great Gatsby*

2. She runs the gamut of emotions from A to B.
   —Quip attributed to Dorothy Parker and said to be about the actress Katharine Hepburn

3. The farm was crouched on a bleak hillside, whence its fields, fanged with flints, dropped steeply to the village of Howling a mile away.
   —Stella Gibbons, *Cold Comfort Farm*

4. America is woven of many strands; I would recognize them and let it so remain. . . . Our fate is to become one, and yet many.
   —Ralph Ellison, *Invisible Man*

5. Our military forces are one team—in the game to win regardless of who carries the ball.
   —Omar Bradley, *Testimony to the Committee on Armed Services, House of Representatives, October 19, 1949*

6. The hardest thing in the world to understand is the income tax.
   —Albert Einstein

7.   We are such stuff
   As dreams are made on, and our little life
   Is rounded with a sleep.
   —Shakespeare, *The Tempest, IV, i, 149*

49f Avoid clichés.

A **cliché** is an overworked expression or figure of speech. The moment we read the first word or two of a cliché, we know how it will end. If someone says, "She hit the nail on the _____," we expect the next word to be *head.* We have heard this expression so often that it no longer creates a vivid picture in our imagination.

It is usually best to rephrase a cliché as simply as you can in plain language.

CLICHÉ   When John turned his papers in three weeks late, he had to *face the music.*

BETTER   When John turned his papers in three weeks late, he had to *accept the consequences.*

The list that follows gives some common clichés to avoid.

SOME COMMON CLICHÉS

acid test
agony of suspense
beat a hasty retreat
beyond the shadow
    of a doubt
blind as a bat
blue as the sky
brave as a lion
brutal murder
bustling cities
calm, cool, and
    collected
cold, hard facts
cool as a cucumber
crazy as a loon
dead as a doornail
deep, dark secret
depths of despair
doomed to
    disappointment
every dog has his
    day
face the music
few and far
    between

flat as a pancake
gild the lily
give 110 percent
green with envy
heave a sigh of
    relief
hit the nail on the
    head
in this day and age
ladder of success
last but not least
live from hand to
    mouth
livid with rage
the other side of
    the coin
paint the town red
pale as a ghost
pass the buck
pick and choose
poor but honest
poor but proud
pretty as a picture
primrose path
proud possessor

quick as a flash
quiet as a church
    mouse
rise and shine
rise to the occasion
sadder but wiser
shoulder to the
    wheel
sink or swim
smart as a whip
sneaking suspicion
sober as a judge
straight and narrow
tempest in a teapot
tired but happy
tried and true
ugly as sin
untimely death
walking the line
wax eloquent
white as a ghost
white as a sheet
worth its weight
    in gold

Exercise 49.6   Chapter review: Exact language

Edit the following passage for misused words, clichés, and ineffective figures of speech. Also, when appropriate, replace abstract and general words with concrete and specific words.

During the boom times of the 1920s, making money in the stock market was like shooting fish in a barrel. Conjecture in stocks was so intense that the price of a share could double overnight.

Poorly regulated, the markets sometimes fell prey to foul play by unscrupulous businesses. Brokers would inflate the price of a stock by staging rumors about a company; they would then sell out their own shares of the stock for a profit before the public discovered that the rumors were fragrant lies.

The stock market crashed to the bottom of the barrel in 1929, pulling the rug out from under the prosperous Twenties. Many speculators who had procured stocks on credit went bankrupt, followed by the financial institutions that had provided the speculators with capitol.

The Great Depression came on fast and furious after the crash. The prolonged financial slump had climbed to new heights by 1932, when the country voted out Herbert Hoover. Franklin D. Roosevelt was elected as the champion of workers and the down-and-out. The new president instigated a legislative program known as the New Deal that sought to ease the affects of the Depression. It was not until World War II boasted production dramatically that the U.S. economy at long last regained its footing.

50 Glossary of Usage

Although the meanings of some words change over time, clear communication is enhanced when change takes place slowly and meanings remain relatively constant. The following words and expressions are often confused (such as *advice* and *advise*), misused (such as *etc.*), or considered nonstandard (such as *could of*). Consulting this list will help you use these words more precisely.

www.mhhe.com/
nmhh
For an online glossary
of usage with
exercises, go to

Editing >
Word Choice

a, an Use *a* with a word that begins with a consonant sound: *a cat, a dog, a one-sided argument, a house.* Use *an* with a word that begins with a vowel sound: *an apple, an X ray, an honor.*

accept, except *Accept* is a verb meaning "to receive willingly": *Please accept my apologies. Except* is a preposition meaning "but": *Everyone except Julie saw the film.*

adapt, adopt *Adapt* means "to adjust or become accustomed to": *They adapted to the customs of their new country. Adopt* means "to take as one's own": *We adopted a puppy.*

advice, advise *Advice* is a noun; *advise* is a verb: *I took his advice and deeply regretted it. I advise you to disregard it, too.*

affect, effect As a verb, *affect* means "to influence": *Inflation affects our sense of security.* As a noun, *affect* means "a feeling or an emotion": *To study affect, psychologists probe the unconscious.* As a noun, *effect* means "result": *Inflation is one of the many effects of war.* As a verb, *effect* means "to make or accomplish": *Inflation has effected many changes in the way we spend money.*

agree to, agree with *Agree to* means "consent to"; *agree with* means "be in accord with": *They will agree to a peace treaty, even though they do not agree with each other on all points.*

ain't A slang contraction for *is not, am not,* or *are not, ain't* should not be used in formal writing or speech.

all/all of, more/more of, some/some of Except before some pronouns, the "of" in these constructions can usually be eliminated. *All France rejoiced. Some students cut class.* But: *All of us wish you well.*

all ready, already *All ready* means "fully prepared." *Already* means "previously." *We were all ready to go out when we discovered that Jack had already ordered a pizza.*

all right, alright The spelling *alright* is an alternate, but many educated readers still think it is incorrect in standard written English. *He told me it was all right to miss class tomorrow.*

789

all together, altogether *All together* expresses unity or common location. *Altogether* means "completely," often in a tone of ironic understatement. *At the NRA convention, it was altogether startling to see so many guns set out all together on one table.*

allude, elude, refer to *Allude* means "to refer indirectly": *He alluded to his miserable adolescence. Elude* means "to avoid" or "to escape from": *She eluded the police for nearly two days.* Do not use *allude* to mean "to refer directly": *The teacher referred* [not *alluded*] *to page 468 in the text.*

almost, most *Almost* means "nearly." *Most* means "the greater part of." Do not use *most* when you mean *almost. He wrote to me about almost* [not *most*] *everything he did. He told his mother about most things he did.*

a lot *A lot* is always two words. Do not use *alot.*

A.M., AM, a.m. These abbreviations mean "before noon" when used with numbers: 6 A.M., 6 a.m. Be consistent in the form you choose, and do not use the abbreviations as a synonym for *morning: In the morning* [not *a.m.*]*, the train is full.*

among, between Generally, use *among* with three or more nouns, *between* with two. *The distance between Boston and Knoxville is a thousand miles. The desire to quit smoking is common among those who have smoked for a long time.*

amoral, immoral *Amoral* means "neither moral nor immoral" and "not caring about moral judgments." *Immoral* means "morally wrong." *Unlike such amoral natural disasters as earthquakes and hurricanes, war is intentionally violent and therefore immoral.*

amount, number Use *amount* for quantities that cannot be counted; use *number* for quantities that can be counted. *The amount of oil left underground in the United States is a matter of dispute, but the number of oil companies losing money is tiny.*

an *See* a, an.

anxious, eager *Anxious* means "fearful": *I am anxious before a test. Eager* signals strong interest or desire: *I am eager to be done with that exam.*

anymore, any more *Anymore* means "no longer." *Any more* means "no more." Both are used in negative contexts. *I do not enjoy dancing anymore. I do not want any more peanut butter.*

anyone/any one, anybody/any body, everyone/every one, everybody/every body *Anyone, anybody, everyone,* and *everybody* are indefinite pronouns: *Anybody can make a mistake.* When the pronoun *one* or the noun *body* is modified by the adjective *any* or *every,* the words should be separated by a space: *A good mystery writer accounts for every body that turns up in the story.*

as Do not use *as* as a synonym for *since, when,* or *because. I told him he should visit Alcatraz since* [not *as*] *he was going to San Francisco. When* [not *as*] *I complained about the meal, the cook said he did not like to eat there himself. Because* [not *as*] *we asked her nicely, our teacher decided to cancel the exam.*

as, like In formal writing, avoid the use of *like* as a conjunction: *He sneezed as if* [not *like*] *he had a cold. Like* is perfectly acceptable as a preposition that introduces a comparison: *She handled the reins like an expert.*

at Avoid the use of *at* to complete the notion of *where:* not *Where is Michael at?* but *Where is Michael?*

awful, awfully Use *awful* and *awfully* to convey the emotion of terror or wonder (awe-full): *The vampire flew out the window with an awful shriek.* In writing, do not use *awful* to mean "bad" or *awfully* to mean "very" or "extremely."

awhile, a while *Awhile* is an adverb: *Stay awhile with me. A while* is an article and a noun. Always use *a while* after a preposition: *Many authors are unable to write anything else for a while after they publish their first novel.*

being as, being that Do not use *being as* or *being that* as synonyms for *since* or *because. Because* [not *being as*] *the mountain was there, we had to climb it.*

belief, believe *Belief* is a noun meaning "conviction"; *believe* is a verb meaning "to have confidence in the truth of." *Her belief that lying was often justified made it hard for us to believe her story.*

beside, besides *Beside* is a preposition meaning "next to" or "apart from": *The ski slope was beside the lodge. She was beside herself with joy. Besides* is both a preposition and an adverb meaning "in addition to" or "except for": *Besides a bicycle, he will need a tent and a pack.*

between, among See *among, between.*

better Avoid using *better* in expressions of quantity: *Crossing the continent by train took more than* [not *better than*] *four days.*

bring, take Use *bring* when an object is being moved toward you, *take* when it is being moved away: *Please bring me a new disk and take the old one home with you.*

but that, but what In expressions of doubt, avoid writing *but that* or *but what* when you mean *that: I have no doubt that* [not *but that*] *you can learn to write well.*

can, may *Can* refers to ability; *may* refers to possibility or permission. *I see that you can rollerblade without crashing into people, but nevertheless you may not rollerblade on the promenade.*

can't hardly This double negative is ungrammatical and self-contradictory. *I can* [not *can't*] *hardly understand algebra. I can't understand algebra.*

capital, capitol *Capital* refers to a city; *capitol* refers to a building where lawmakers meet. *Protesters traveled to the state capital to converge on the capitol steps. Capital* also refers to wealth or resources.

censor, censure *Censor* means "to remove or suppress material." *Censure* means "to reprimand formally." *The Chinese government has been censured by the U.S. Congress for censoring newspapers.*

cite, sight, site The verb *cite* means "to quote or mention": *Be sure to cite all your sources in your bibliography.* As a noun, the word *sight* means "view": *It was love at first sight. Site* is a noun meaning "a particular place": locations on the Internet are referred to as *sites.*

compare to, compare with Use *compare to* to point out similarities between two unlike things: *She compared his singing to the croaking of a wounded* *frog.* Use *compare with* for differences or likenesses between two similar things: *Compare Shakespeare's* Antony and Cleopatra *with Dryden's* All for Love.

complement, compliment *Complement* means "to go well with": *I consider sauerkraut the perfect complement to sausages. Compliment* means "praise": *She received many compliments on her thesis.*

conscience, conscious The noun *conscience* means "a sense of right and wrong": *His conscience bothered him.* The adjective *conscious* means "awake" or "aware": *I was conscious of a presence in the room.*

continual, continuous *Continual* means "repeated regularly and frequently": *She continually checked her computer for new e-mail. Continuous* means "extended or prolonged without interruption": *The car alarm made a continuous wail in the night.*

could of, should of, would of Avoid these ungrammatical forms of *could have, should have,* and *would have.*

criteria, criterion *Criteria* is the plural form of the Latin word *criterion,* meaning "standard of judgment." *The criteria are not very strict. The most important criterion is whether you can do the work.*

data *Data* is the plural form of the Latin word *datum,* meaning "fact." Although *data* is often used informally as a singular noun, in writing, treat *data* as a plural noun: *The data indicate that recycling has gained popularity.*

differ from, differ with *Differ from* expresses a lack of similarity; *differ with* expresses disagreement. *The ancient Greeks differed less from the Persians than we often think. Aristotle differed with Plato on some important issues.*

different from, different than The correct idiom is *different from.* Avoid *different than. The east coast of Florida is very different from the west coast.*

discreet, discrete *Discreet* means "tactful" or "prudent." *Discrete* means "separate" or "distinct." *What is a discreet way of telling them that these are two discrete issues?*

disinterested, uninterested *Disinterested* means "impartial": *We expect members of a jury to be disinterested. Uninterested* means "indifferent" or "unconcerned": *Most people today are uninterested in alchemy.*

don't, doesn't *Don't* is the contraction for *do not* and is used with *I, you, we, they,* and plural nouns. *Doesn't* is the contraction for *does not* and is used with *he, she, it,* and singular nouns. *You don't know what you're talking about. He doesn't know what you're talking about either.*

due to, because of *Due to* is an overworked and often confusing expression when it is used for *because of.* Use *due to* only in expressions of time in infinitive constructions or in other contexts where the meaning is "scheduled." *The plane is due to arrive in one hour. He is due to receive a promotion this year.*

each and every Use one of these words or the other but not both. *Every cow came in at feeding time. Each one had to be watered.*

each other, one another Use *each other* in sentences involving two subjects and *one another* in sentences involving more than two. *Husbands and wives should help each other. Classmates should share ideas with one another.*

eager, anxious *See* anxious, eager.

effect, affect *See* affect, effect.

e.g., i.e. The abbreviation *e.g.* stands for the Latin words meaning "for example." The abbreviation *i.e.* stands for the Latin for "that is." *Come as soon as you can, i.e., today or tomorrow. Bring fruit with you, e.g., apples and peaches.* In formal writing, replace the abbreviations with the English words: *Keats wrote many different kinds of lyrics, for example, odes, sonnets, and songs.*

either, neither Both *either* and *neither* are singular: *Neither of the two boys has played the game. Either of the two girls is willing to show you the way home. Either* has an intensive use that *neither* does not, and when it is used as an intensive, *either* is always negative: *She told him she would not go either.*

elicit, illicit The verb *elicit* means "to draw out." The adjective *illicit* means "unlawful." *The detective was unable to elicit any information about other illicit activity.*

elude, allude *See* allude, elude, refer to.

emigrate, immigrate *Emigrate* means "to move away from one's country": *My grandfather emigrated from Greece in 1905. Immigrate* means "to move to another country and settle there": *Grandpa immigrated to the United States.*

eminent, imminent, immanent *Eminent* means "celebrated" or "well known": *Many eminent Victorians were melancholy and disturbed. Imminent* means "about to happen" or "about to come": *In August 1939, many Europeans sensed that war was imminent. Immanent* refers to something invisible but dwelling throughout the world: *Medieval Christians believed that God's power was immanent through the universe.*

etc. The abbreviation *etc.* stands for the Latin *et cetera,* meaning "and others" or "and other things." Because *and* is included in the abbreviation, do not write *and etc.* In a series, a comma comes before *etc.,* just as it would before the coordinating conjunction that closes a series: *He brought string, wax, paper, etc.* In most college writing, it is better to end a series of examples with a final example or the words *and so on.*

everybody/every body, everyone/every one *See* anyone/any one. . . .

except, accept *See* accept, except.

expect, suppose *Expect* means "to hope" or "to anticipate": *I expect a good grade on my final paper. Suppose* means "to presume": *I suppose you did not win the lottery on Saturday.*

explicit, implicit *Explicit* means "stated outright." *Implicit* means "implied, unstated." *Her explicit instructions were to go to the party without her, but the implicit message she conveyed was disapproval.*

farther, further *Farther* describes geographical distances: *Ten miles farther on is a hotel. Further* means "in addition" when geography is not involved: *He said further that he did not like my attitude.*

fewer, less *Fewer* refers to items that can be counted individually; *less* refers to general amounts. *Fewer people signed up for indoor soccer this year than last. Your argument has less substance than you think.*

first, firstly *Firstly* is common in British English but not in the United States. *First, second, third* are the accepted forms.

flaunt, flout *Flaunt* means "to wave" or "to show publicly" with a delight tinged with pride and even arrogance: *He flaunted his wealth by wearing overalls lined with mink. Flout* means "to scorn" or "to defy," especially in a public way, seemingly without concern for the consequences: *She flouted the traffic laws by running through red lights.*

former, latter *Former* refers to the first and *latter* to the second of two things mentioned previously: *Mario and Alice are both good cooks; the former is fonder of Chinese cooking, the latter of Mexican.*

further, farther *See* farther, further.

get In formal writing, avoid colloquial uses of *get,* as in *get with it, get it all together, get-up-and-go, get it,* and *that gets me.*

good, well *Good* is an adjective and should not be used in place of the adverb *well. He felt good about doing well on the exam.*

half, a half, half a Write *half, a half,* or *half a* but not *half of, a half a,* or *a half of. Half the clerical staff went out on strike. I want a half-dozen eggs to throw at the actors. Half a loaf is better than none, unless you are on a diet.*

hanged, hung People are *hanged* by the neck until dead. Pictures and all other things that can be suspended are *hung.*

hopefully *Hopefully* means "with hope." It is often misused to mean "it is hoped." *We waited hopefully for our ship to come in* [not *Hopefully, our ship will come in*].

i.e., e.g. *See* e.g., i.e.

if . . . then Avoid using these words in tandem. Redundant: *If I get my license, then I can drive a cab.* Better: *If I get my license, I can drive a cab. Once I get my license, I can drive a cab.*

illicit, elicit *See* elicit, illicit.

imminent, immanent *See* eminent, imminent, immanent.

immigrate, emigrate *See* emigrate, immigrate.

immoral, amoral *See* amoral, immoral.

implicit, explicit *See* explicit, implicit.

imply, infer *Imply* means "to suggest something without stating it directly": *By putting his fingers in his ears, he implied that she should stop singing. Infer* means "to draw a conclusion from evidence": *When she dozed off in the middle of his declaration of eternal love, he inferred that she did not feel the same way about him.*

in, in to, into *In* refers to a location inside something: *Charles kept a snake in his room. In to* refers to motion with a purpose: *The resident manager came in to capture it. Into* refers to movement from outside to inside or from separation to contact: *The snake escaped by crawling into a drain. The manager ran into the wall, and Charles got into big trouble.*

incredible, incredulous The *incredible* cannot be believed; the *incredulous* do not believe. Stories and events may be *incredible;* people are *incredu-*

lous. Nancy told an incredible story of being abducted by a UFO over the week-
end. We were all incredulous.

infer, imply *See* imply, infer.

inside of, outside of The "of" is unnecessary in these phrases: *He was out-*
side the house.

ironically *Ironically* means "contrary to what was or might have been expected." It should not be confused with *surprisingly,* which means "unexpected," or with *coincidentally,* which means "occurring at the same time or
place." *Ironically, his fast ball lost speed after his arm healed.*

irregardless This construction is a double negative because both the prefix *ir-* and the suffix *-less* are negatives. Use *regardless* instead.

it's, its *It's* is a contraction, usually for *it is* but sometimes for *it has: It's often*
been said that English is a difficult language to learn. Its is a possessive pronoun: *The dog sat down and scratched its fleas.*

kind, kinds *Kind* is singular: *This kind of house is easy to build. Kinds* is
plural and should be used only to indicate more than one kind: *These three*
kinds of toys are better than those two kinds.

lay, lie *Lay* means "to place." Its main forms are *lay, laid,* and *laid.* It generally has a direct object, specifying what has been placed: *She laid her book on*
the steps and left it there. Lie means "to recline" and does not take a direct object. Its main forms are *lie, lay,* and *lain: She often lay awake at night.*

less, fewer *See* fewer, less.

like, as *See* as, like.

literally *Literally* means "actually" or "exactly as written": *Literally thousands*
gathered along the parade route. Do not use *literally* as an intensive adverb when
it can be misleading or even ridiculous, as here: *His blood literally boiled.*

loose, lose *Loose* is an adjective that means "not securely attached." *Lose* is
a verb that means "to misplace." *Better tighten that loose screw before you lose*
the whole structure.

may, can *See* can, may.

maybe, may be *Maybe* is an adverb meaning "perhaps": *Maybe he can get*
a summer job as a lifeguard. May be is a verb phrase meaning "is possible": *It*
may be that I can get a job as a lifeguard, too.

moral, morale *Moral* means "lesson," especially a lesson about standards of
behavior or the nature of life: *The moral of the story is do not drink and drive.*
Morale means "attitude" or "mental condition": *Office morale dropped sharply*
after the dean was arrested.

more/more of *See* all/all of. . . .

more important, more importantly The correct idiom is *more impor-*
tant, not *more importantly.*

most, almost *See* almost, most.

myself (himself, herself, etc.) Pronouns ending with *-self* refer to or intensify other words: *Jack hurt himself. Standing in the doorway was the man*
himself. When you are unsure whether to use *I* or *me, she* or *her, he* or *him* in

a compound subject or object, you may be tempted to substitute one of the *-self* pronouns. Don't do it. *The quarrel was between her and me* [not *myself*]. (*Also see Chapter 36: Problems with Pronouns on pp. 640–42.*)

neither, either *See* either, neither.

nohow, nowheres These words are nonstandard for *anyway, in no way, in any way, in any place,* and *in no place.* Do not use them in formal writing.

number, amount *See* amount, number.

off of Omit the *of: She took the painting off the wall.*

one another, each other *See* each other, one another.

outside of, inside of *See* inside of, outside of.

plus Avoid using *plus* as a substitute for *and: He had to walk the dog, do the dishes, empty the garbage, and* [not *plus*] *write a term paper.*

practicable, practical *Practicable* is an adjective applied to things that can be done: *A space program that would land human beings on Mars is now practicable. Practical* means "sensible": *Many people do not think such a journey is practical.*

precede, proceed *Precede* means "come before;" *proceed* means "go forward." *Despite the heavy snows that preceded us, we managed to proceed up the hiking trail.*

previous to, prior to Avoid these wordy and somewhat pompous substitutions for *before.*

principal, principle *Principal* is an adjective meaning "most important" or a noun meaning "the head of an organization" or "a sum of money": *Our principal objections to the school's principal are that he is a liar and a cheat. Principle* is a noun meaning "a basic standard or law": *We believe in the principles of honesty and fair play.*

proceed, precede *See* precede, proceed.

quote, quotation *Quote* is a verb: *The author quotes extensively from Shakespeare. Quotation* is a noun: *The author begins each chapter with a quotation from one of Shakespeare's plays.*

raise, rise *Raise* means "to lift or cause to move upward." It takes a direct object—someone raises something: *I raised the windows in the classroom. Rise* means "to go upward." It does not take a direct object—something rises by itself: *We watched the balloon rise to the ceiling.*

real, really Do not use the word *real* when you mean *very: The cake was very* [not *real*] *good.*

reason is because This is a redundant expression. Use either *the reason is that* or *because: The reason he fell on the ice is that he cannot skate. He fell on the ice because he cannot skate.*

refer to *See* allude, elude, refer to.

relation, relationship *Relation* describes a connection between things: *There is a relation between smoking and lung cancer. Relationship* describes a connection between people: *The brothers have always had a close relationship.*

respectfully, respectively *Respectfully* means "with respect": *Treat your partners respectfully. Respectively* means "in the given order": *The three Williams she referred to were Shakespeare, Wordsworth, and Yeats, respectively.*

rise, raise *See* raise, rise.

set, sit *Set* is usually a transitive verb meaning "to establish" or "to place." It takes a direct object, and its principal parts are *set, set,* and *set: DiMaggio set the standard of excellence in fielding. She set the box down in the corner. Sit* is usually intransitive, meaning "to place oneself in a sitting position." Its principal parts are *sit, sat,* and *sat: The dog sat on command.*

shall, will *Shall* was once the standard first-person future form of the verb *to be* when a simple statement of fact was intended: *I shall be twenty-one on my next birthday.* Today, most writers use *will* in the ordinary future tense for the first person: *I will celebrate my birthday by throwing a big party. Shall* is still used in questions. *Shall we dance?*

should of *See* could of, should of, would of.

site, sight, cite *See* cite, sight, site.

some Avoid using the adjective *some* in place of the adverb *somewhat: He felt somewhat* [not *some*] *better after a good night's sleep.*

some of *See* all/all of. . . .

somewheres Use *somewhere* or *someplace* instead.

stationary, stationery *Stationary* means "standing still": *I worked out on my stationary bicycle. Stationery* is writing paper: *That stationery smells like a rose garden.*

suppose, expect *See* expect, suppose.

sure Avoid confusing the adjective *sure* with the adverb *surely: The dress she wore to the party was surely bizarre.*

sure and, sure to *Sure and* is often used colloquially. In formal writing, *sure to* is preferred: *Be sure to* [not *Be sure and*] *get to the wedding on time.*

take, bring *See* bring, take.

that, which Many writers use *that* for restrictive (i.e., essential) clauses and *which* for nonrestrictive (i.e., nonessential) clauses. *The bull that escaped from the ring ran through my china shop, which was located in the square.* (*Also see* Chapter 51: Commas, pp. 817–19.)

their, there, they're *Their* is a possessive pronoun: *They gave their lives. There* is an adverb of place: *She was standing there. They're* is a contraction of *they are: They're reading more poetry this semester.*

this here, these here, that there, them there When writing, avoid these nonstandard forms.

to, too, two *To* is a preposition; *too* is an adverb; *two* is a number. *The two of us got lost too many times on our way to his house.*

try and, try to *Try to* is the standard form: *Try to* [not *try and*] *understand.*

uninterested, disinterested *See* disinterested, uninterested.

use, utilize *Utilize* seldom says more than *use,* and the simpler term is almost always better: *We must learn how to use the computer's zip drive.*

verbally, orally To say something *orally* is to say it aloud: *We agreed orally to share credit for the work, but when I asked her to confirm it in writing, she refused.* To say something *verbally* is to use words: *His eyes flashed anger, but he did not express his feelings verbally.*

wait for, wait on People *wait for* those who are late; they *wait on* tables.

weather, whether The noun *weather* refers to the atmosphere: *She worried that the weather would not clear up in time for the victory celebration. Whether* is a conjunction referring to a choice between alternatives: *I can not decide whether to go now or next week.*

well, good *See* good, well.

which, who, whose *Which* is used for things, *who* and *whose* for people. *My fountain pen, which I had lost last week, was found by a child who had never seen one before, whose whole life had been spent with ballpoints.*

whether, weather *See* weather, whether.

will, shall *See* shall, will.

would of *See* could of, should of, would of.

your, you're *Your* is a possessive pronoun: *Is that your new car? You're* is a contraction of *you are: You're a lucky guy.*

CHECKLIST

Editing for Word Choice

Words are the building blocks of all writing. Keep the following questions in mind to be sure that you understand words as you encounter them in your reading and that you use them effectively and appropriately in your writing:

☐ Do you have a dictionary at hand to learn the meaning of unfamiliar words you encounter in your reading? Do you have a thesaurus at hand to find the most appropriate word to convey your meaning to your readers? Have you tried to infer the meaning of unfamiliar words from contextual clues? (*See Chapter 47: Using Dictionaries and Building Vocabulary, pp. 756–67.*)

☐ Is your language appropriate to the assignment? Does it include any evasive euphemisms or misleading doublespeak? Does it include any inappropriate slang expressions, regionalisms, or jargon? Have you used any stereotyping, biased, or sexist expressions? (*See Chapter 48: Appropriate Language, pp. 768–76.*)

☐ Have you chosen words with the appropriate connotations for their context? Have you confused any words with others that have similar but distinct denotations? (*See Chapter 49: Exact Language, pp. 777–88 and Chapter 50: Glossary of Usage, pp. 789–98.*)

☐ Have you enriched your language with specific and concrete words and suitable figures of speech? Have you avoided clichés? (*See Chapter 49: Appropriate Language, pp. 756–88.*)

Musical notation includes punctuation-like symbols that composers use to indicate stops or pauses as well as to cue changes in dynamics, key, and tempo.

No steel can pierce the human heart so chillingly
as a period at the right moment.
—ISAAC BABEL

Sentence
Punctuation

Sentence Punctuation

Answer these questions to test your familiarity with the topics covered in Chapters 51–56. For each example, select the choice that best replaces the highlighted words. If none of the choices is preferable to the example, select "no change." Check your work against the answer sheet at the back of the book, and pay particular attention to the sections in the chapters that correspond to the questions you get wrong.

1. During photosynthesis, water and carbon dioxide **are converted into oxygen and light is converted** into stored energy.

   a. are converted into oxygen; and light is converted

   b. are converted into oxygen, and light is converted

   c. are converted into oxygen and, light is converted

   d. no change

2. Tourists who want a glimpse of ancient Rome should visit **the Colosseum, the Arch of Constantine and the Pantheon.**

   a. the Colosseum, the Arch of Constantine, and the Pantheon.

   b. the Colosseum; the Arch of Constantine, and the Pantheon.

   c. no change

   d. the Colosseum; the Arch of Constantine; and the Pantheon.

3. New Zealand is an **island not a continent.**

   a. no change

   b. island, not a continent.

   c. island; not a continent.

   d. island, not, a continent.

4. World War I began in **August, 1914.**

   a. August 1914.

   b. no change

   c. August; 1914.

   d. August: 1914.

5. The two teams that have won the Super Bowl title **five times, are the** San Francisco 49ers and the Dallas Cowboys.

   a. five times are the

   b. no change

   c. five times, are, the

   d. five times; are the

6. Most European countries now **use the euro, however, the United Kingdom** continues to use its own currency, the pound sterling.

   a.   no change

   b.   use the euro, however the United Kingdom

   c.   use the euro; however, the United Kingdom

   d.   use the euro, however; the United Kingdom

7. Fashion trends are cyclical. Short skirts came into fashion **during the 1960s, they reappeared** in the 1990s.

   a.   no change

   b.   during the 1960s and they reappeared

   c.   during the 1960s and, they reappeared

   d.   during the 1960s; they reappeared

8. The three most commonly spoken languages in the world are Mandarin, spoken by approximately 885 million people; Spanish, spoken by approximately 332 million **people; and English,** spoken by approximately 322 million people.

   a.   people, and English,

   b.   people and; English,

   c.   no change

   d.   people; and, English,

9. Although Venus is the **planet nearest to Earth; astronomers** know very little about it.

   a.   planet nearest to Earth: astronomers

   b.   planet nearest to Earth, astronomers

   c.   planet nearest to Earth astronomers

   d.   no change

10. **Three British policies that contributed to the American Revolution:** the increased regulation of colonial trade, the increased regulation of westward expansion, and the imposition of new colonial taxes.

   a.   no change

   b.   Three British policies that contributed to the American Revolution;

   c.   Three British policies that contributed to the American Revolution,

   d.   Three British policies contributed to the American Revolution:

803

11. The ratio of teachers to students at the school **is 1:5.**

    a. is 1,5.

    b. is 1;5.

    c. is 1-5.

    d. no change

12. The best way to lose weight **is: to eat less** and exercise more.

    a. is, to eat less

    b. is to eat less

    c. is; to eat less

    d. no change

13. "Nobody can be exactly like me," Tallulah Bankhead **once said, "Sometimes** even I have trouble doing it."

    a. once said: "Sometimes

    b. once said "Sometimes

    c. no change

    d. once said. "Sometimes

14. "I don't care what is written about me **so long as it isn't true." quipped Dorothy Parker.**

    a. so long as it isn't true" quipped Dorothy Parker.

    b. so long as it isn't true," quipped Dorothy Parker.

    c. so long as it isn't true", quipped Dorothy Parker.

    d. no change

15. Athena, Aphrodite, **and Zeus—these are Greek deities** who were adopted by the Romans.

    a. and Zeus, these are Greek deities

    b. and Zeus; these are Greek deities

    c. and Zeus these are Greek deities

    d. no change

16. Swiss psychologist Jean Piaget—**author of *The Psychology of the Child*—he is best known** for his theory of cognitive development.

    a. author of *The Psychology of the Child,* he is best known

    b. author of *The Psychology of the Child*—he is best known

    c. no change

    d. author of *The Psychology of the Child*—is best known

17. According to the style guidelines of the **American Psychological Association, (APA), an e-mail message** should be cited as a personal communication.

    a. no change

    b. American Psychological Association, APA, an e-mail message

    c. American Psychological Association (APA), an e-mail message

    d. American Psychological Association, (APA) an e-mail message

18. Hamlet says to Horatio, **"He [Hamlet's father] was a man,** take him for all in all, I shall not look upon his like again."

    a. no change

    b. "He (Hamlet's father) was a man,

    c. "He, [Hamlet's father] was a man,

    d. "He, [Hamlet's father], was a man,

19. Adopted by the Seneca Falls Convention in 1848, the "Declaration of Sentiments" asserts, "We hold these truths to be **self-evident: that all men and women are created equal. . ."**

    a. self-evident: that all men and women are created equal. . .".

    b. self-evident: that all men and women are created equal. . . ."

    c. self-evident: that all men and women are created equal..."

    d. no change

20. **"What causes a tsunami" the professor asked?**

    a. "What causes a tsunami?" the professor asked.

    b. "What causes a tsunami," the professor asked?

    c. no change

    d. "What causes a tsunami?", the professor asked.

51 Commas

An unedited paper may have two different types of comma errors: missing commas and unnecessary commas. In the first section of this chapter, we review when a comma is needed and when it is optional. The section beginning on page 830 covers common misuses of commas.

COMMON USES OF THE COMMA

www.mhhe.com/
nmhh

For information and exercises on commas, go to

Editing > Commas

Commas are the most frequently used punctuation mark, clarifying meaning within sentences by setting off certain sentence elements. Although it is tempting to think that commas indicate a pause for breath, reading a sentence aloud and adding commas in places where you pause is not a reliable way to punctuate your sentences.

Editing to Add Commas Where Needed

- Use a comma to separate coordinated independent clauses. (*See 51a.*)

                    coordinating
    independent clause,   conjunction   + independent clause
    ➤ **Prices rose steadily,**   **but**   **profits still fell.**

- Use commas to separate items in a series and coordinate adjectives. (*See 51b–c.*)

              item,   item,   item
    ➤ **The gift should be unique, inexpensive, and returnable.**

              adjective, adjective
    ➤ **He described her as a beautiful, talented child.**

- Use a comma to set off an introductory element from an independent clause. (*See 51d.*)

        introductory element,   independent clause
    ➤ **Mysteriously,**   **the image reappeared.**

    (continued)

Editing to Add Commas Where Needed (*continued*)

- Use commas to set off nonessential elements that interrupt, interject, or modify. (*See 51e–g.*)

  beginning of sentence,   nonessential phrase,   end of sentence
  ➤ **The flower garden, untended for years, produced only weeds.**

- Use a comma to separate a direct quotation from the phrase that signals it. (*See 51h.*)

  direct quotation
  ➤ **Mead said, "I am glad that I am alive."**

- Use commas to separate parts of dates, addresses, titles, and numbers. (*See 51i.*)

  city,   state,   day, year
  ➤ **They traveled to Orlando, Florida, on January 5, 2005.**

- Use a comma to take the place of an omitted word or to prevent misreading. (*See 51j.*)

  omitted word: *had*
  ➤ **The punch bowl had a crack and the crystal glass, a chip.**

51a Place a comma before a coordinating conjunction that joins two independent clauses.

An independent clause is a group of words that could stand alone as a sentence (*see 33c, p. 590*). When a coordinating conjunction (*and, but, for, nor, or, so, yet*) is used to join two independent clauses, put a comma before the coordinating conjunction.

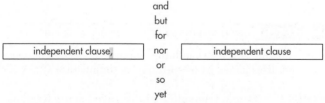

➤ **He felt a pain in his knee, and he began to play cautiously.**

Note: Do not place a comma between the coordinating conjunction and the second independent clause. (*see 51m, p. 832*).

Commas and Grammar Checkers

Because many decisions about comma use involve context and judgment calls, computer grammar checkers are of very limited value in helping you spot errors in your use of commas. Grammar checkers usually do not highlight missing commas following introductory elements or between independent clauses joined by a coordinating conjunction such as *and*. They also cannot judge whether a sentence element is essential or nonessential. Rely on yourself, not a grammar checker, to apply these rules and make these decisions.

If you are joining two long clauses that contain commas, using a semicolon instead of a comma and a coordinating conjunction between the two clauses can make your sentence clearer for readers.

➤ **After his knee surgery, he needed almost a year to**

    ;   *however,*

    recover, but once his doctor gave her approval, he

    began to play with his old skill, enthusiasm, and nerve.

If you are joining two short clauses, the comma is optional unless it is needed for clarity.

➤ **I ran and they cheered.**

Do not use a comma with a coordinating conjunction that joins word groups that cannot stand alone as sentences (*see 51l, p. 832*).

Exercise 51.1   Using commas with coordinating conjunctions

Edit the following sentences, adding commas as needed between independent clauses joined by a coordinating conjunction.

    EXAMPLE   **Organ transplants have saved many lives, so**

                              people should consider filling out a donor card.

1. Surgeons began attempting organ transplants in the early-twentieth century but the first successful transplant did not take place until 1954.

2. The transplant was from one identical twin to another and the twin who received the organ—a kidney—lived for eight years after the operation.
3. Recently, surgeons have transplanted hands and face transplants are on the horizon.
4. Face transplants raise ethical issues so this type of operation is controversial.
5. Some organs for transplant operations come from live donors but most organs come from cadavers.

Exercise 51.2 Combining sentences with commas and coordinating conjunctions

Use a comma and a coordinating conjunction to combine each set of sentences into one sentence. Vary your choice of conjunctions.

EXAMPLE **The experiment did not support our**

, yet we
hypothesis. We considered it a success.
        ^

1. Asperger's syndrome and autism, although they are both classified as autism spectrum disorders, are not the same. Asperger's syndrome is often confused with autism.
2. People with Asperger's syndrome have normal IQs. They are unable to interact with others in a social setting.
3. Children with this disorder often engage in solitary, repetitive routines. In school they may have difficulty working in groups.
4. People with Asperger's syndrome also have a difficult time with nonverbal communication. They may be unable to read other people's body language.
5. The public has only recently become aware of Asperger's syndrome. Drugs that can cure this neurobiological disorder have yet to be developed.

51b Use commas between items in a series.

A comma should appear between each of three or more items in a series.

➤ **Three industries that have been important to New England**
        first item,   second item,   third item
are shipbuilding, tourism, and commercial fishing.

Occasionally, separating the items in a sentence with commas only—omitting *and, or,* or another coordinating conjunction before the last item—can help you add emphasis: *Her coat was thin, muddy, torn.*

Commas clarify which items are part of the series. In the following example, the third comma clarifies that the hikers are packing lunch *and* snacks, not chocolate and trail mix for lunch.

> **CONFUSING** For the hiking trip, we needed to pack lunch, chocolate and trail mix.
>
> **CLEAR** For the hiking trip, we needed to pack lunch, chocolate, and trail mix.

Items in a series can consist of words, phrases, or clauses. If the items in a series contain commas, separate the items with semicolons instead of commas (*see 52d, p. 839*).

➤ **During the play's three acts, the characters gather at a deserted, lonely house by the seashore; discover that one of their number, an obnoxious business executive, has been murdered; and call on the hero, an off-duty police officer, to help them solve the mystery.**

When three or more items within a sentence are preceded by numbers or letters, they are treated as items within a series.

➤ **The hawks that have built their nest on a ledge of this building prey on (1) squirrels, (2) pigeons, and (3) other small birds.**

CHARTING the TERRITORY

Commas in Journalism

If you are writing for a journalism course, you may be required to leave out the final comma that precedes *and* in a series, just as magazines and newspapers usually do. Follow the convention that your instructor prefers.

51c Use commas between coordinate adjectives.

Two or more adjectives placed side by side before a noun or pronoun are either coordinate or cumulative. **Coordinate adjectives** act individually to modify a noun or pronoun; each adjective should be separated from the next one with a comma.

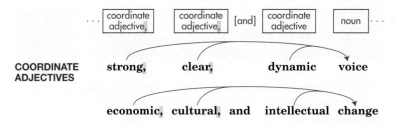

COORDINATE ADJECTIVES

strong, clear, dynamic voice

economic, cultural, and intellectual change

Cumulative adjectives act as a set: the first cumulative adjective modifies the following adjective or adjectives as well as the noun or pronoun. Because they act as a set, cumulative adjectives are not separated by commas.

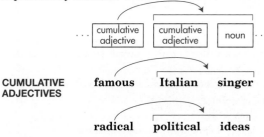

CUMULATIVE ADJECTIVES

famous Italian singer

radical political ideas

If you are not sure whether a comma should separate two or more adjectives, try changing the order of the adjectives or putting the word *and* between them. If the sentence sounds wrong, then do not add a comma.

➤   adj   adj   noun
Luciano Pavarotti is a famous Italian tenor; he is known for
  adj   adj   adj   noun
his strong, clear, dynamic voice.

In the example above, we could say that Pavarotti had a clear, strong, dynamic voice, but it would be awkward to say that he is an Italian famous tenor.

Note that the comma is placed between the coordinate adjectives, not between the adjective and the noun.

➤   adj   adj   noun
I'm tired of that boring, monotonous/ song.

Also note that a comma is not used between two coordinate adjectives joined by *and* or between a number and an adjective.

➤   adj   adj
He addressed a crowd of loud/ and excited supporters.

➤ **The scientist focused her attention on the two/ black bears under a tree.**   **811**

IDENTIFY AND EDIT
Commas with Coordinate Adjectives

Follow these steps if you have trouble determining whether commas should separate two or more adjectives that precede a noun:

✱ *1. Identify the adjectives.*

> **PROBLEM SENTENCE**
> Ann is an [excellent art] teacher and a [caring generous] mentor.
>
> Note that nouns such as *art* can also be used as adjectives.

✱ *2. Try changing the order of the adjectives or putting the word* and *between them. Then read the adjectives and noun to yourself. How do they sound?*

> **PROBLEM SENTENCE**
> Ann is an [art excellent] teacher and a [generous caring] mentor.
>
> We could say that Ann is a generous caring mentor, but it would be awkward to say that she is an art excellent teacher.

> **PROBLEM SENTENCE**
> Ann is an [excellent and art] teacher and a [caring and generous] mentor.
>
> We could say that Ann is a caring and generous mentor, but it would be awkward to say that she is an excellent and art teacher.

✱ *3. If the phrase sounds wrong, the adjectives are cumulative and don't need a comma between them. If the phrase sounds right, the adjectives are coordinate and require a comma. If need be, correct the original sentence.*

> Ann is an excellent art teacher and a caring, generous mentor.
> ⌄

Exercise 51.3   Using commas with series of nouns and adjectives

Edit the following sentences, adding commas as needed to separate items in a series and coordinate adjectives. Some sentences may be correct; circle their numbers.

EXAMPLE   **One part of the wall was covered with pictures**

              of leaping, prancing animals.
                     ⌄

FIGURE 51.1 An image of a horse painted around 15,000 years ago on the wall of a cave in Lascaux, France.

1. Scholars have studied prehistoric cave paintings for almost a century.
2. Paintings have been found in North America Europe Africa and Australia.
3. Paintings found in southeastern France contain images of animals birds and fish.
4. Some scholars believe that the cave painter may have been a rapturous entranced shaman.
5. We can picture the flickering dazzling torchlight that guided the painter's way through dank dark passageways.
6. Mixing colors with their saliva and blowing the paint onto the wall with their breath must have given the cave painters feelings of creative power supernatural control and expressive glory.

51d Use a comma after an introductory word group that is not the subject of the sentence.

Like an overture, an introductory word group must be distinct from, yet clearly attached to, what follows. A comma both attaches an introductory word, phrase, or clause to and distinguishes it from the rest of the sentence.

introductory word,	rest of sentence

➤ *Finally,* the speeding car careened to the right.

introductory phrase,	rest of sentence

➤ *Reflecting on her life experiences,* **Washburn was satisfied.**

introductory clause,	rest of sentence

➤ *Until he noticed the handprint,* the detective had no clues.

Do not add a comma after a word group that functions as the subject of the sentence, however. Be especially careful with word groups that begin with *-ing* words.

subject

➤ **Persuading Washington lawmakers is one of a lobbyist's**

main tasks.

introductory word group   subject
➤ **Persuading Washington lawmakers, lobbyists pursue the**

interests of their clients.

A comma is also not used following the opening phrase in an inverted sentence, where the subject follows the verb (*see 51o, pp. 833–34*).

verb   subject
➤ **In the bushes lurked a poisonous snake.**

When the introductory phrase is less than five words long and there is no danger of confusion without a comma, the comma is optional.

➤ *For several hours* we rode on in silence.

Exercise 51.4   Using commas with introductory word groups

Edit the following sentences, adding commas as needed after introductory word groups. Some sentences may be correct; circle their numbers.

EXAMPLE   **During the early Middle Ages, Western Europeans**
                                   ^

remained fairly cut off from the East.

1. After the year 1000 CE Europeans became less isolated.
2. To the Holy Lands traveled Western pilgrims and merchants in a steady stream.

3. Increasingly aware of the rich civilizations beyond their borders Europeans began to enter into business relationships with the cities and countries in the East.
4. Establishing contact with the principal ports of the eastern Mediterranean and Black seas allowed merchants to develop a vigorous trade.
5. As this trade expanded across the Mediterranean world Western Europeans were able to enjoy spices and other exotic products.
6. In the thirteenth and fourteenth centuries European missionaries and merchants traveled to China, India, and the Near East.

Exercise 51.5 Combining sentences with commas and introductory word groups

Combine the following sentences into one sentence using the suggestions in parentheses. Revise the wording of the sentences as necessary.

EXAMPLE

<u>Some researchers are</u> studying short-term *To*

, *some researchers*

memory. They conducted an experiment that

tested the results of pressure on students'

memory. **(introductory phrase)**

1. The researchers are Dr. Sian Bellock of Miami University of Ohio and Dr. Thomas Carr of Michigan State. An article about their work appeared in the *New York Times*. (introductory phrase)
2. They administered two math tests to two groups of students. The experiment took place recently. (introductory word)
3. One test was a low-pressure situation. The other test was a high-pressure situation. (introductory clause)
4. Strong students performed well on the low-pressure test. They did not perform as well on the high-pressure test. (introductory clause)
5. Other students had lower scores on the first test. Their performance on the second test was about the same as on the first. (introductory phrase)
6. The results were a surprise. They suggest that high-pressure situations interfere with the short-term memories of the strongest students. (introductory word)

51e Use a comma or commas to set off nonessential (nonrestrictive) elements.

Nonessential, or **nonrestrictive,** elements add information to a sentence but are not required for its basic meaning to be understood. They are set off with commas. They can also be set off with dashes or parentheses. (*See 55c on pp. 864–65 and 55f on pp. 867–68.*)

> | main part of sentence, | | nonrestrictive element |
> |---|---|---|
>
> ➤ **Robert's essay won the contest,** *which was sponsored by the local paper.*

> The words *which was sponsored by the local paper* give more information about the contest, but they do not tell you more about Robert's essay, which is what the sentence is about.

> | first part of sentence, | nonrestrictive element, | rest of sentence |
> |---|---|---|
>
> ➤ **Robert's essay,** *which was about charter schools,* **won the contest.**

> The words *which was about charter schools* tell you more about the essay, but they do not tell you which essay the sentence is about.

Essential, or **restrictive,** elements identify who or what the writer is describing. Readers need these elements to understand the sentence's meaning so they are not set off with commas.

> | first part of sentence | restrictive element | rest of sentence |
> |---|---|---|
>
> ➤ **The essay** *that was about charter schools* **won the contest.**

> The words *that was about charter schools* tell you which essay the sentence is about and are essential to conveying the sentence's meaning: that the essay on charter schools was the winner.

In the first two examples, the commas help you see that the words they set off are an aside—a piece of additional information. In the third example, the words are more than an aside. They identify the essay for the reader. Therefore, they are restrictive and are not set off with commas.

Sometimes the addition of a comma or commas can subtly change a sentence's meaning, as in the next pair of sentences.

> ➤ **The customers, demanding a refund, lined up by the register.**

> The commas set off a phrase that gives us additional information about all of the customers in question: they are demanding a refund.

➤ **The customers demanding a refund lined up by the register.**

We can assume that out of all the customers in the store only the group named—those demanding a refund—lined up by the register.

In this case, the context would determine whether to enclose *demanding a refund* with commas. Notice how a preceding sentence can affect the meaning of the sentence in question and determine whether a comma is needed:

➤ **Two customers with angry looks on their faces approached the checkout counter. The customers, demanding a refund, lined up by the register.**

➤ **The store opened at the usual time. The customers demanding a refund lined up by the register.**

If you are unsure if an element is restrictive or nonrestrictive, imagine the sentence without it. Would the reader know which person, place, or thing you are describing? Would the basic meaning of the sentence remain unchanged? If so, the element is nonrestrictive and should be set off with commas.

1. Commas with nonrestrictive clauses

A **clause** is a group of words with a subject and a verb. **Adjective clauses,** which begin with *who, whom, whose, which, that, when, where,* or *why,* are dependent clauses that modify a noun or pronoun in an independent clause. **Adverb clauses,** which can begin with *when* or *where* or with a subordinating conjunction (*see 31i, pp. 561–62*), modify a verb in an independent clause. Adjective or adverb clauses can be nonrestrictive or restrictive.

An adjective clause is nonrestrictive and should be set off with commas when it does not identify the person, place, or thing that is being described, even if it supplies important information.

nonrestrictive

➤ **Odysseus, *who is constantly tested on his epic voyage,* returns**

home after a twenty-year absence.

The phrase *who is constantly tested on his epic voyage* does not identify the noun it modifies, *Odysseus,* even though it does tell us something important about him.

IDENTIFY AND EDIT
Commas with Nonrestrictive Words
or Word Groups

Follow these steps if you have trouble deciding whether a
word or word group should be set off with a comma or commas:

1. *Identify the word or word group that may need to be set off with commas. Pay special attention to words that appear between the subject and verb.*

> PROBLEM
> SENTENCE
>
> Dorothy Parker [a member of the famous Algonquin
> subj
> verb
> Round Table] wrote humorous verse as well as short
> stories.
>
> PROBLEM
> SENTENCE
>
> subj   verb
> Her poem ["One Perfect Rose"] is a lament about a
> well-intentioned gift that falls short.

2. *Read the sentence to yourself without the word or word group. Does the basic meaning stay the same, or does it change? Can you tell what person, place, or thing the sentence is about?*

> SENTENCE
> WITHOUT
> THE WORD
> GROUP
>
> Dorothy Parker wrote humorous verse as well as
> short stories.
>
> The subject of the sentence is identified by name, and the
> basic meaning of the sentence does not change.
>
> SENTENCE
> WITHOUT
> THE WORD
> GROUP
>
> Her poem is a lament about a well-intentioned gift
> that falls short.
>
> Without the words "One Perfect Rose" we cannot tell what
> poem the sentence is describing.

3. *If the meaning of the sentence stays the same without the word or word group, set it off with commas. If the meaning changes, the word or word group should not be set off with commas.*

> ◆ Dorothy Parker, a member of the famous Algonquin Round
>   ∧
> Table, wrote humorous verse as well as short stories.
> ∧
>
> ◆ Her poem "One Perfect Rose" is a lament about a well-
> intentioned gift that falls short.
>
> The sentence is correct. Commas are not needed to enclose "One
> Perfect Rose."

An adjective clause is restrictive—not set off with commas—when it is essential to the meaning of the noun it modifies.

➤ **I had read many studies on the subject, but the studies**
restrictive
***that Johnson recommended* were the most helpful.**

> Without the adjective clause, the sentence does not make sense: *I had read many studies on the subject, but the studies were the most helpful.* The adjective clause identifies the studies the writer thinks were helpful and is essential to the meaning of the sentence.

> *Note:* Use *that* only with restrictive adjective clauses. *Which* can introduce either restrictive or nonrestrictive adjective clauses. Some writers prefer to use *which* only with nonrestrictive clauses.
>
> ➤ **I had read many studies on the subject, but the studies**
> *that*
> ~~which~~ **Johnson recommended were the most helpful.**

An adverb clause at the beginning of a sentence is considered an introductory word group and should be set off with a comma (*see 51d, pp. 813–14*). Adverb clauses that are within or at the end of sentences are usually essential to the meaning of the sentence and are not set off with commas.

restrictive
➤ **Ruiz refused the prize *because he objected to the judging***

process.

> The clause *because he objected to the judging process* tells why Ruiz did what he did and is therefore essential.

However, some adverb clauses are nonessential, or nonrestrictive.

nonrestrictive
➤ **Ruiz, *when asked why he refused the prize,* cited his**

objections to the judging process.

> The sentence's meaning would be the same without the nonrestrictive clause: *Ruiz cited his objections to the judging process.*

Adverb clauses beginning with *although, even though, though,* and *whereas* present a contrasting thought and are usually nonrestrictive.

nonrestrictive
➤ **Ruiz will not accept the prize, *even though it is a great honor.***

2. Commas with nonrestrictive phrases

Phrases that modify nouns and verbs can also be restrictive or nonrestrictive. An **adjective phrase** begins with a preposition (for example, *at, by, for, with*) or a verbal (a verb form with an *-ing, -ed,* or *-en* ending that can have various functions within a sentence). Nonrestrictive adjective phrases are set off with commas.

nonrestrictive adjective phrase
➤ **Some people,** *by their faith in human nature or their general*

 goodwill, **bring out the best in others.**

The sentence would have the same basic meaning without the nonrestrictive phrase (*Some people bring out the best in others*).

A restrictive adjective phrase identifies the noun it modifies and should not be set off with commas.

restrictive adjective phrase
➤ **People** *fighting passionately for their rights* **can inspire**

 others to join a cause.

The adjective phrase lets readers know which people the writer means.

3. Commas with nonrestrictive appositives

Appositives are nouns or noun phrases that rename nouns or pronouns and generally appear right after the word they rename. They can appear at the beginning, in the middle, or at the end of a sentence. Nonrestrictive appositives supply extra information about the noun or noun phrase, but they do not identify or limit it. Nonrestrictive appositives are set off with commas.

nonrestrictive
➤ **One researcher,** *the widely respected R. S. Smith,* **has shown**

 that a child's performance on IQ tests is not reliable.

The noun *researcher* is limited by the word *one*, and the appositive, *the widely respected R. S. Smith,* provides additional information about that one researcher, including his name.

Restrictive appositives indicate which person, place, or thing is being named. They are not set off with commas.

restrictive
➤ **The researcher** *R. S. Smith* **has shown that a child's**

 performance on IQ tests is not reliable.

The meaning of the noun *researcher* is restricted to the name *R. S. Smith.*

Exercise 51.6 Using commas with nonrestrictive elements

Edit the following sentences, adding commas as needed to set off non-restrictive clauses, adjective phrases, and appositives. Some sentences may be correct; circle their numbers.

EXAMPLE The brain, connected by nerves to all the other

parts of the body, seems to be the seat of the

mind, an abstract term for the workings of

the brain.

1. The mind-body problem under debate for centuries concerns the relationship between the mind and the body.
2. Prehistoric peoples must have observed that when a person died the body remained and the mind departed.
3. Since the time of the ancient Greeks the prevailing opinion has been that the mind and the body are separate entities.
4. Plato the Greek philosopher is often credited with originating the concept of mind-body dualism.
5. The French philosopher René Descartes described the mind and the body as independent.
6. Descartes's influential theories helped lay the foundation for scientific rationalism which views nature as a vast machine.

Exercise 51.7 Combining sentences with commas
and nonrestrictive word groups

Combine the following sentences into one sentence using the suggestions in parentheses. Revise the wording of the sentences as necessary.

EXAMPLE Brazil, is the largest country on the South

American continent/, Brazil has an area of more

than three million square miles. (nonessential

appositive)

1. The people in Brazil speak Portuguese. Brazil was formerly a colony of Portugal. (essential clause)

2. Peru is famous for its spectacular scenery. The Amazon River snakes through the northeastern part of the country and the Andes Mountains stretch along its coast. (nonessential phrase)
3. Argentina is in the southern part of South America. It exports beef to the United States and other countries. (nonessential clause)
4. The coast of Venezuela is on the Caribbean Sea. Venezuela is north of the equator. (nonessential phrase)
5. A number of islands dot the Caribbean Sea. They are north of Venezuela. (essential phrase)
6. Chile stretches from the central part of South American to its southern tip. Chile is the longest country in South America. (nonessential appositive)

51f Use a comma or commas with transitional expressions, parenthetical expressions, contrasting comments, and absolute phrases.

1. Transitional Expressions
Transitional expressions show the relationship between ideas in two or more clauses or sentences and make the sentence in which they appear clearer. Conjunctive adverbs (*however, therefore, moreover*) and other transitional phrases (*for example, on the other hand*) are usually set off by commas when used at the beginning, in the middle, or at the end of a sentence. You can also use a dash or dashes (*see 55c, on pp. 864–65*) or, in some cases, parentheses (*see 55f, on pp. 867–68*) to set off transitional expressions. (*For a list of transitional expressions, see Chapter 33, p. 592.*)

➤ **Brian Wilson,** *for example,* **was unable to cope with the pressures of touring with the Beach Boys.**

➤ *As a matter of fact,* **he had a nervous breakdown shortly after a tour.**

➤ **He is still considered one of the most important figures in rock and roll,** *however.*

When a transitional expression connects two independent clauses, use a semicolon before and a comma after it.

➤ **The Beatles were a phenomenon when they toured the United States in 1964; *subsequently,* they became the most successful rock band of all time.**

Short expressions such as *also, at least, certainly, instead, of course, then, perhaps,* and *therefore* do not always need to be set off with commas.

➤ **I found my notes and *also* got my story in on time.**

2. Parenthetical expressions

Parenthetical expressions are like whispered asides or a shrug in a conversation. The information they provide is relatively insignificant and could easily be left out. Therefore, they are set off with a comma or commas.

➤ **Human cloning, *so they say,* will be possible within a decade.**

➤ **The experiments would take a couple of weeks, *more or less.***

3. Contrasting comments

Contrasting comments beginning with words such as *not, unlike,* or *in contrast to* should be set off with commas.

➤ **As an actor, Adam Sandler is a talented comedian, *not a tragedian.***

> *Exception:* Contrasting comments that begin with *but* are often not set off with commas: *He was poor but honest.*

4. Absolute Phrases

Absolute phrases usually include a noun (*sunlight*) followed by a participle (*shining*) and are used to modify whole sentences. Set them off with commas.

➤ **The snake slithered through the tall grass, *the sunlight shining now and then on its green skin.***

823

51g Use a comma or commas to set off words of direct address, *yes* and *no,* mild interjections, and tag sentences.

Like nonrestrictive phrases and clauses, words that interrupt a sentence are set off by commas because they are not essential to the sentence's meaning.

direct address
➤ **We have finished this project, *Mr. Smith,* without any help**

from your foundation.

➤ ***Yes,* I will meet you at noon.**

interjection
➤ **We must leave, *sadly,* this evening.**

A **tag sentence** is a normal sentence with a phrase or question attached (or "tagged") on the end. Use a comma to set off the tag. When the tag is a question, end the sentence with a question mark.

tag
➤ **This is the right key, *I think.***

tag
➤ **This is the right door, *don't you think?***

Exercise 51.8 Using commas to set off other nonessential sentence elements

Edit the following sentences, adding commas where they are needed to set off nonessential sentence elements.

EXAMPLE **Yes, I will go with you to dinner; however, I must**

leave by ten, not a minute later.

1. Millions of viewers watch reality-based television shows. Cultural critics however argue that shows such as *The Swan, Survivor,* and *The Bachelor* exploit human greed and the desire for fame.
2. These shows so the critics say take advantage of our insecurities.
3. The participants who appear on these shows are average, everyday people not actors.
4. *The Swan* follows its subjects contestants hoping to beat out their competitors through drastic weight loss and multiple plastic surgeries.

5. The message is always the same: You too can be rich and famous Average Jane or Joe.
6. Yes many of these shows hold the promise that anyone can win a million dollars and gain instant notoriety.
7. These shows of course are extremely enjoyable.
8. Their entertainment value is why we watch them don't you think?

51h Use a comma or commas to separate a direct quotation from the phrase that signals it.

Commas are used with quotation marks to set off a quotation from the words that identify its source, such as *she said* or *Robert Rubin maintains. (See Chapter 54: Quotaton Marks, pp. 849–54, for more on punctuating quotations.)*

➤ **Irving Howe declares, "Whitman is quite realistic about the place of the self in an urban world" (261).**

➤ **"Whitman is quite realistic about the place of the self in an urban world," declares Irving Howe (261).**

Exception: If the words that introduce the quotation form a complete sentence, you can use a colon instead of a comma to introduce the quotation, especially if it is long.

➤ **Thomas Paine inspired the colonists with a famous rallying cry: "These are the times that try men's souls. The summer soldier and the sunshine patriot will, in this crisis, shrink from the service of their country; but he that stands it *now,* deserves the love and thanks of man and woman."**

If the quoted sentence is interrupted, use commas to set off the interrupting words.

➤ **"When we interpret a poem," DiYanni says, "we explain it to**

ourselves in order to understand it."

If you are quoting more than one sentence and interrupting the quotation between sentences, the interrupting words should end with a period.

➤ **"But it is not possible to give to each department an equal**

power of self defence," James Madison writes in *The*

***Federalist No. 51*. "In republican government the legislative**

authority, necessarily, predominates."

A comma is not needed if the quotation ends with a question mark or an exclamation point.

➤ **"Where are my glasses?" she asked in a panic.**

➤ **"I don't know!" he replied angrily.**

Commas are not used to separate indirect quotations or paraphrases from the source of the quotation.

➤ **Irving Howe notes, that Whitman realistically depicts the**

urban self as free to wander (261).

Exercise 51.9   Using commas to set off direct quotations

Edit the following sentences to correct problems with the use of commas. Some sentences may be correct; circle their numbers.

> **EXAMPLE**   **"Nothing I studied was on the test," she moaned**
>
> **to her friends.**

1. Professor Bartman entered the room and proclaimed "Today we will examine Erikson's eight stages of human development."
2. "Who may I ask has read the assignment," he queried.
3. "Patricia" he hissed "please enlighten the rest of the class."
4. "What would you like to know?" she asked.

5. Now smiling, he replied "Begin by telling us what the eight stages are."

6. She explained that the first stage is when infants must learn to trust that their needs will be met.

51i Use commas with parts of dates and addresses, with people's titles, in numbers, and in parts of correspondence.

1. Dates
Use a comma or paired commas in dates when the month, day, and year are included or when the day of the week is followed by the date. Do not use commas when the day of the month is omitted or when the day appears before the month.

➤ **On March 4, 1931, she traveled to New York.**

➤ **She traveled to New York on March 4, 1931.**

➤ **On Wednesday, March 4, she traveled to New York.**

➤ **In March 1931 she traveled to New York.**

➤ **On 4 March 1931 she traveled to New York.**

When a season appears with a year, a comma is not needed: *spring 2006*.

2. Addresses
Use a comma or commas to set off the parts of an address or the name of a state, but do not use a comma preceding a zip code.

➤ **He lived at 1400 Crabgrass Lane, Garrison, New York.**

➤ **At Cleveland, Ohio, the river changes direction.**

➤ **Here is my address for the summer: 63 Oceanside Drive,**

  Apt. 2A, Surf City, New Jersey 06106.

3. People's titles or degrees
Put a comma between the person's name and the title or degree when it comes after the name. If the sentence continues, place another comma after the title or degree.

827

➤ **Luis Mendez, MD, gave her the green light to resume her**

exercise regimen.

If an abbreviation such as *Jr.* or a roman numeral such as *II* follows
a name, it is not necessary to set it off with a comma or commas.

➤ **The show was hosted by Milton Clark Jr.**

4. Numbers

When a number has more than four digits, use commas to mark off
the numerals by hundreds—that is, by groups of three beginning at
the right.

➤ **Andrew Jackson received 647,276 votes in the 1828**

presidential election.

If the number is four digits long, the comma is optional.

➤ **The survey had 1856 [or 1,856] respondents.**

Exceptions: Street numbers, zip codes, telephone numbers, page
numbers (p. 2304), and years (1828) do not include commas.

Within text, you should use a comma to separate two numbers
that appear together, whether the numbers are spelled out or given
as numerals: *ten feet, six inches; page 15, paragraph 4; act 3, scene 1.*

For MULTILINGUAL STUDENTS

Long Numbers

In some other languages, periods, not commas, are used to mark
off numerals by hundreds. In American English, however, periods
indicate decimals only; commas are used in long numbers.

5. Parts of correspondence

Add a comma after the greeting in an informal letter and after the closing in any kind of letter.

➤ **Dear Aunt Di,**

➤ **Sincerely yours,**

➤ **With best wishes,**

A colon follows the greeting in a business letter.

➤ **Dear Professor Chodoff:**

51j Use a comma to take the place of an omitted word or phrase or to prevent misreading.

When a writer omits one or more words from a sentence to create an effect, a comma is often needed to make the meaning of the sentence clear for readers. In the following example, the second comma substitutes for the phrase *he found*.

➤ **Under the tree he found his puppy, and under the car,**

his cat.

Commas are also used to keep readers from misunderstanding a writer's meaning when words are repeated or might be misread.

➤ **Many birds that sing, sing first thing in the morning.**

➤ **Any offbeat items that can be, are sold at auction sites on the**

World Wide Web.

It is often better, however, to revise the sentence and avoid the need for the clarifying comma.

➤ **Many songbirds sing first thing in the morning.**

➤ **A wide variety of offbeat items are sold at auction sites on**

the World Wide Web.

Exercise 51.10 │ Editing for conventional and stylistic uses of commas

Edit the following sentences, adding commas where they are needed.

> **EXAMPLE**   **Before work she visits her father, and after**
>
> **work, her mother.**
>   ^

1. Families lured west by the Homestead Act of 1862 were promised "free land," and with this land the opportunity for a new life.
2. Any belongings that could be were piled into Conestoga wagons for the long journey west.
3. The journey from Missouri to Oregon, a 2000-mile trip, was made by some 150000 people during the mid-nineteenth century.
4. Born in Wisconsin on February 7 1867, children's book author Laura Ingalls Wilder traveled with her family throughout the West, settling in various places.
5. In October 1880 Wilder and her family were living in De Smet South Dakota; they experienced the first of a series of blizzards that lasted until May 1881.
6. Mary Anne Miller PhD wrote her dissertation on the pioneer experience.

COMMON MISUSES OF THE COMMA

Just as a correctly used comma can clarify the meaning of a sentence, an incorrectly used comma can confuse readers. Comma errors result when writers place commas between grammatical elements that belong together.

51k Do not use commas to separate major elements in an independent clause.

Do not use a comma to separate a subject from its verb or a verb from its object.

➤ **Reflecting on one's life,/ is necessary for emotional growth.**

  The subject, reflecting, should not be separated from the verb, is.

➤ **Washburn resolved,/ that she would succeed.**

  The verb, *resolved,* should not be separated from its direct object, the subordinate clause *that she would succeed.*

Editing to Eliminate Unnecessary Commas

- Delete commas that separate a subject from a verb or a verb from an object. (*See 51k.*)

  subject   verb   object
  ➤ **Kahn's homage to his father,/ contains,/ moments**

  of humor.

- Delete commas that separate compound word groups unless the word groups are independent clauses. (*See 51l.*)

  subject   subject   verb   verb
  ➤ **Evan,/ and Sam were drinking tea,/ and reading in**

  my room.

- Delete a comma that follows a preposition or a coordinating or subordinating conjunction. (*See 51m.*)

  sub conj   prep
  ➤ **Although,/ he is a famous actor, he is in,/ emotional**

  limbo.

- Delete commas that set off restrictive elements. (*See 51n.*)

  restrictive clause
  ➤ **The knowledge,/ that Pete had lied,/ was hard for her**

  to bear.

- Delete a comma after an introductory phrase if the phrase begins an inverted sentence. (*See 51o.*)

  ➤ **In the heart of the forest,/ lives Baba Yaga.**

- Delete a comma that falls before the first or after the last item in a series. In a series of adjectives, also delete a comma placed between the last adjective and the noun it modifies. (*See 51p.*)

  ➤ **The shelf held,/ a kettle, a pot, and a dusty, greasy,/ pan.**

- Delete commas that appear with other punctuation, with some exceptions. (*See 51q.*)

  ➤ **"Isn't my home cooking better than any restaurant's?,/"**

  asked her cousin.

51l Do not use commas to separate compound word groups unless the word groups are independent clauses.

A comma should not be used between word groups joined with a co-ordinating conjunction (such as *and*) unless each word group could stand alone as a sentence.

➤ **Injuries were so frequent that he became worried,/ and**

  started to play more cautiously.

  Here, *and* joins two verbs (*became* and *started*), not two independent clauses.

➤ **He is worried that injuries are more frequent,/ and that he**

  will have to play more cautiously to avoid them.

  Here, *and* joins two subordinate clauses—both beginning with the word *that*—not two independent clauses.

51m Do not place commas after prepositions or conjunctions.

A comma should not be placed after a preposition or a conjunction unless you are inserting a parenthetical phrase. Avoid the common error of placing a comma after *although, such as, like,* and *than.*

➤ **The *duomo* in Siena was begun in the thirteenth century,**

  and,/ it was used as a model for other Italian cathedrals.

➤ **Puppets were used in the stage version of *The Lion King* to**

  represent many different animals, although,/ human actors

  were still needed to operate them.

➤ **Stage designers may create one spectacular element for a**

  show, such as,/ the huge crystal chandelier in *Phantom of*

  the Opera.

51n Do not use commas to set off restrictive modifiers, restrictive appositives, or slightly parenthetical words or phrases.

Words that are necessary to identify the noun or pronoun they describe should not be set off with commas. (*For more on restrictive modifiers, see 51e, pp. 816–20.*)

restrictive clause
➤ The applicants *who had studied for the admissions test* were

restless and eager for the exam to begin.

restrictive appositive
➤ The director *Michael Curtiz* was responsible for many great

films in the 1930s and 1940s, including *Casablanca.*

Concluding adverb clauses that begin with *after, as soon as, before, because, if, since, unless,* and *when* are usually essential to a sentence's meaning and should not be set off with commas.

➤ I am eager to test the children's IQ again *because significant variations in a child's test score indicate that the test itself may be flawed.*

If setting off a brief parenthetical remark with commas would draw too much attention to the remark and interrupt the flow of the sentence, then the commas can be left out.

➤ Science is *basically* the last frontier.

> *Note:* An adverb clause that appears at the beginning of a sentence is an introductory element and is usually followed by a comma: *Until we meet, I am continuing my work on the budget.* (*See 51d, pp. 813–14, and 51e, pp. 816–20.*)

51o Do not use a comma after a phrase that begins an inverted sentence.

Although commas are used to set off introductory phrases (*see 51d, pp. 813–14*), do not use them after a phrase that appears at the beginning of an inverted sentence. A sentence is "inverted" when the verb precedes the subject.

➤ **Deep in the jungle/ prowls a tiger.**

verb   subject

51p Do not place a comma before the first or after the last item in a series. Do not place a comma between an adjective and a noun, even in a series of coordinate adjectives.

Use commas to separate items in a series but never before the first item in the series. Do not place a comma after the final item in a series either, unless another comma rule calls for its use (for example, if the series falls at the end of an introductory word group or independent clause).

➤ **He wanted to record/ country music, blues, ballads, and gospel/ on the same album.**

➤ **He has long, ropy, arms and/ small, close-set/ eyes.**

Exception: If a nonrestrictive appositive consists of a series of items, you can set it off with commas.

➤ **He wanted to record four types of music, country music, blues, ballads, and gospel, on the same album.**

Often, however, dashes are a better option in this situation (*see 55c, pp. 864–65*).

51q Do not use a comma to repeat the function of other punctuation.

A comma is never used before an opening parenthesis. It is used after a closing parenthesis only when another comma rule applies. In the following example, the comma following the closing parenthesis sets off the introductory clause.

➤ **When they occupy an office cubicle/ (a relatively recent invention), workers need to be especially considerate of their neighbors.**

When a question mark or an exclamation point ends a quotation, a comma is unnecessary.

➤ **"Why did Rome fall?/" he asked the class.**

Commas are never placed next to dashes.

➤ **I saw her/—what a surprise—/with my brother.**

Exercise 51.11 Editing for misused commas

Edit to eliminate unnecessary or disruptive commas in the following sentences. Some of the commas are correctly placed.

EXAMPLE **The Constitution, which was ratified in 1789, reflects the colonial and/ revolutionary experi- ence of the thirty-nine men/ who signed it.**

1. The colonies revolted against British rule, but English tradition provided ideas about, government, power, and freedom, that were expressed in the Declaration of Independence and, later in the Constitution.
2. The Constitution was, in part, designed to confine power, and limit government.
3. To this end, the Framers, (the name given to the creators of the Constitution), confined government to certain expressly granted powers, and denied certain specific powers.
4. The Bill of Rights was added, to the Constitution to guarantee freedom of, speech, assembly, and other individual liberties.
5. However, the separation of powers, was the most significant provision, according to some political scientists.
6. Each of the three branches of government, acts as a check on the others, in an arrangement that, has, in fact, prevented abuses of power.
7. In *Marbury v. Madison,* the Supreme Court assumed authority to review legislation, and executive actions, and to declare them unconstitutional, and invalid.

8. The Framers respected self-government, but distrusted, popular majorities.
9. Presidential voting, direct election of senators, and primary elections, strengthen the majority's influence, and are rooted in ideas deeply held by Americans,—that the people must have substantial control.
10. In this balancing of interests, lies the genius, power, and strength of the Constitution.

Exercise 51.12 Chapter review: Commas

Edit the following passage, adding and deleting commas as needed.

Every society has families but the structure of the family varies from, society to society. Over time the function of the family, has changed so that in today's postindustrial society for instance the primary function of the family is to provide "emotional gratification" according to Professor Paula Stein noted sociologist of Stonehall University New Hampshire. In a recent interview Stein also said "Images of the family tend to be based on ideals not realities." To back up this claim Stein pointed to, a new as yet unpublished survey of more than 10000 married American couples, that she and her staff conducted. Expected to be released in the October 17 2003 edition of the *Weekly Sociologist,* the survey indicates that the biggest change has been the increase in the variety of family arrangements including singles single parents and childless, couples. Most Americans marry for love they say, but research portrays courtship as an analysis of costs benefits assets and liabilities, not unlike a business deal.

Virtually all children, are upset by divorce, but most recover in a few years while others suffer lasting serious, problems. Despite the high rate of divorce which reached its height in 1979, Americans still believe in the institution of marriage as indicated by the high rate of remarriages that form *blended families.* "Yes some see the breakup of the family as a social problem or the cause of other problems but, others see changes in the family as adaptations to changing social conditions as I do" concluded the professor.

52 Semicolons

Semicolons are used to join statements that are closely related and grammatically equivalent. They are also used to mark major breaks within some sentences that contain commas.

Semicolons and Grammar Checkers

Computer grammar checkers catch some comma splices that can be corrected by adding a semicolon between the two clauses, and they also catch some incorrect uses of the semicolon. They cannot tell you when a semicolon *could* be used for clarity, however, nor can they tell you if a semicolon is the best choice. Rely on your own judgment, not a grammar checker, when deciding whether to add a semicolon to a sentence.

52a Use a semicolon to join independent clauses.

www.mhhe.com/
nmhh
For information
and exercises on
semicolons, go to

Editing >
Semicolons

A semicolon is an effective way to link two clauses if readers are able to see the relationship between the two without the help of a coordinating conjunction. Each clause in this example has a subject and a verb and could stand alone as a sentence, but the writer chose a semicolon to mark the close relationship between the statements.

➤ **Tracy Kidder wanted to write about architecture; *House* is the result.**

Sometimes, the close relationship is a contrast.

➤ **Philip had completed the assignment; Lucy had not.**

Semicolons are useful when repairing comma splices and run-on sentences (*see Chapter 33, pp. 590–91*).

52b Use semicolons with transitional expressions that connect independent clauses.

Transitional expressions, including transitional phrases (*after all, even so, for example, in addition, on the contrary*) and conjunctive adverbs (*consequently, however, moreover, nevertheless, then, therefore*), indicate the way in which two clauses are related to each other. When a transitional expression appears between two clauses, it is preceded by a semicolon and usually followed by a comma.

➤ **Sheila had to wait until the plumber arrived; consequently, she was late for the exam.**

If the transitional expression is a short word such as *then*, the comma is often omitted. In academic writing, however, it is usually best to include it.

Note: The semicolon always appears between the two clauses, even when the transitional expression appears in another position within the second clause. Wherever it is placed, the transitional expression is usually set off with a comma or commas.

➤ **My friends are all taking golf lessons; my roommate and I, however, are more interested in tennis.**

➤ **My friends are all taking golf lessons; my roommate and I are more interested in tennis, however.**

Joining two independent clauses with a comma and a transitional expression results in a comma splice (*see Chapter 33, pp. 584–86*).

52c Use care when placing a semicolon before a conjunction.

A comma is the correct punctuation before a coordinating conjunction (*and, but, for, nor, or, so, yet*) that joins independent clauses.

➤ **Forsythia blooms in the early spring, *but* azaleas bloom later.**

However, if the independent clauses contain internal commas, a semicolon can help the reader identify where the clauses begin and end.

> **The closing scenes return to the English countryside, recalling the opening; *but* these scenes are bathed in a different, cooler light, suggesting that memories of her marriage still haunt her.**

If you are in doubt, it is always correct to use a comma before a coordinating conjunction.

52d Use a semicolon to separate items in a series when the items contain commas.

Typically, commas are used to separate items in a series.

> **The committee included Curtis Youngblood, Roberta**
>
> **Collingwood, and Darcy Coolidge.**

Semicolons can take the place of commas when the items within the series contain other commas. The semicolons mark the breaks between the items, and the commas mark breaks within them.

> **The committee included Dr. Curtis Youngblood, the county**
>
> **medical examiner; Roberta Collingwood, the director of**
>
> **the bureau's criminal division; and Darcy Coolidge, the**
>
> **chief of police.**

Exception: This rule is an exception to the general principle that there should be a full sentence (independent clause) on each side of a semicolon.

Exercise 52.1 Editing using semicolons

Use semicolons to correct any comma splices and run-on sentences in the following items. (*See Chapter 33 for a detailed discussion of common splices and run-ons.*) Also add semicolons in place of commas in sentences that contain two independent clauses with internal commas joined by a coordinating conjunction or a series with internal commas (*see 52c and 52d*).

EXAMPLE The witness took the stand/; the defendant,

meanwhile, never looked up from her notepad.

1. The Pop Art movement flourished in the United States and in Britain in the 1960s it was a reaction to the abstract art that had dominated the art scene during the 1950s.
2. Pop artists were inspired by popular culture and consumerism, for example, they painted advertisements, comic strips, super-market products, and even dollar bills!
3. The artists' goal was to transform ordinary daily experiences into art, they also wanted to comment on the modern world of mass production.
4. Pop artist Andy Warhol used silkscreening techniques to create identical, mass-produced images on canvas, so the result was repeated images of Campbell's soup cans and Coca-Cola bottles, as well as famous people like Marilyn Monroe, Elvis Presley, and Jacqueline Kennedy.
5. Other pop artists include Roy Lichtenstein, who is best known for his depiction of cartoons, Richard Hamilton, who is famous for his collages of commercial art, and David Hockney, whose trade-mark theme is swimming pools.
6. These artists all attained great fame in the art world however, many people did not accept their work as real art.

Exercise 52.2 Combining sentences with semicolons

Use a semicolon to combine each set of sentences into one sentence. Add, remove, or change words as necessary. Use a semicolon and a transitional expression between clauses for at least two of your revised sentences. More than one answer is possible for each item.

EXAMPLE A recent *New York Times* article discusses new

discoveries/ ~~These discoveries are~~ about

the
personality in animals/; ~~Some~~ scientists ~~are~~

quoted in the article. ~~The scientists~~ are studying

personality traits in hyenas and wild birds.

1. Some scientists are studying a European bird related to the chickadee. The scientists are at the Netherlands Institute of Ecology. They are conducting experiments with this bird.
2. Another scientist has studied hyena populations. His name is Dr. Samuel Gosling. Dr. Gosling asked handlers to rate the hyenas using a questionnaire. He adapted a version of a questionnaire used for humans.
3. These studies and others indicate that animals display personality traits. These traits include boldness and shyness. Bold birds quickly investigate new items in their environment. Shy birds take more time.
4. Bold birds have an advantage over shy birds in some situations. They do not have an advantage in other situations.
5. Some experts on human personality are sceptical. They doubt that animals have the same personality traits that humans do. Scientists who study personality in animals need to be careful to avoid anthropomorphism. That is the tendency to attribute human characteristics to animals.

52e Edit to correct common semicolon errors.

Writers sometimes use semicolons when commas or colons are needed. Avoid these common errors.

1. Do not use a semicolon to join independent clauses linked by a coordinating conjunction unless the clauses contain commas.

   ➤ **Women in the nineteenth century wore colorful**

   coordinating conjunction
   clothes⁣⸴ but their clothes look drab in black-and-

   white photographs.

2. Do not use a semicolon to join an independent clause to a dependent clause.

   dependent clause
   ➤ *Although cats seem tame⸴* **they can be fierce hunters.**

   Some instructors consider the dependent clause in the uncorrected version of this sentence to be a type of sentence fragment. (*For help with fragments, see Chapter 32, pp. 572–83.*)

3. Do not use a semicolon to join an independent clause to a phrase.

➤ He has always hated birthday parties̸, *even as*

a child.

> phrase

➤ Foremost among the German competition horses
> appositive
is the Hanoverian̸, *a great show-jumping breed.*

4. Do not use a semicolon to introduce a list or a quotation. A colon should usually be used for this purpose. (*See Chapter 53, pp. 843–48, for more on using colons.*)

➤ My day was planned̸: *a morning walk, an afternoon*
> list

in the library, and an evening with friends.

➤ Boyd warns of the difficulty in describing Bach̸:
> quotation
"Even his physical appearance largely eludes us."

You can also use a dash to introduce a list. (*See Chapter 55, pp. 863–66, for more on dashes.*)

An occasional semicolon adds variety to your writing. Too many semicolons can make your writing seem monotonous, however. If you have used three or more semicolons in a paragraph, you should edit your sentences to eliminate most of them. (*For help with sentence variety, see Chapter 45, pp. 740–48.*)

Exercise 52.3 | Chapter review: Semicolons

Edit the following passage, using semicolons as appropriate to join independent clauses or separate items in a list. Delete any incorrectly used semicolons, and supply the correct punctuation.

EXAMPLE **Professional writers need to devote time every**

day to their writing̸ because otherwise they can

lose momentum. Some writers carve out a few

hours in the morning; others wait for the

stillness of night.

DNA fingerprinting is a technique that can be used to identify a person accurately, it is also known as DNA profiling. DNA is present in cells and can be isolated from the following; blood, skin, hair, and sweat. DNA fingerprinting can be used to diagnose inherited disorders in fetuses and newborn babies; it can be used to study and research genetic disorders; it is also a key tool in determining paternity or maternity. Criminal identification and forensics rely on DNA fingerprinting to connect suspects to biological evidence; and it has proven a very precise method by which to convict suspects.

DNA fingerprinting may eventually become a means of personal identification, it would work as a kind of genetic bar code. Many people like Tim Smith express their discomfort with this idea; "It sounds like something out of a science fiction movie." Although it may seem like science fiction; the U.S. armed services has already started a program to collect DNA fingerprints to make it easy to identify casualties. This may appear to be a practical way to keep track of people, ensuring clear identification in an emergency situation; but it is a controversial issue, causing some people to rethink joining the military or even to leave the military because they do not want to have their DNA filed in a databank.

Information derived from DNA fingerprinting should be more private than other medical information for several reasons: it includes information about a person's future, such as possible genetic illnesses, the DNA code has not yet been fully broken, making it likely that further research will reveal even more information, and a person's DNA is connected to family, potentially revealing information about parents, siblings, and children. Luckily, it would be expensive and very time-consuming to isolate, analyze, and file the DNA information for all human beings; so picture IDs and Social Security numbers are here to stay for at least a while longer.

53 Colons

Colons function within sentences to introduce elements, and they also have other conventional uses.

Colons and Grammar Checkers

Computer grammar checkers may point out when you have used a colon incorrectly. Because colons are usually optional, however, most of the time you will need to decide for yourself whether a colon is your best choice in a sentence.

www.mhhe.com/
nmhh
For information and
exercises on colons,
go to

Editing > Colons

53a Use a colon after a complete sentence to introduce a list, an appositive, or a quotation.

Like an announcer on a television show, a colon draws the reader's attention to what it is introducing. It is used after a complete sentence (independent clause) to introduce lists, appositives (nouns or noun phrases that appear right after the word they rename), and quotations.

> <small>independent clause</small>   <small>list</small>
> **Several majors interest me: biology, chemistry, and art.**

> <small>independent clause</small>   <small>appositive</small>
> **She shared with me her favorite toys: a spatula and a pot lid.**

> <small>independent clause</small>   <small>quotation</small>
> **He said the dreaded words: "Let's just be friends."**

Note: If you introduce a quotation with a signal phrase such as *he said* or *Morrison comments* instead of a complete sentence, you should use a comma, not a colon, before the quotation.

When you use a colon to introduce a sentence element, make sure that it is preceded by an independent clause (a clause with a subject and a verb that can stand alone as a sentence).

lacks a complete verb—not an independent clause

INCORRECT   **Three kinds of futility dealt with in the novel:**

pervasive poverty, lost love, and inescapable

aging.

independent clause

CORRECT   **Three kinds of futility are dealt with in the**

novel: pervasive poverty, lost love, and

inescapable aging.

The words *the following* or *as follows* often appear at the end of the introductory sentence.

➤ **The three ingredients are as follows: *graham crackers,***
                                        ^

   marshmallows, and chocolate bars.

53b Use a colon when a second closely related independent clause elaborates on the first one.

The colon can be used to link independent clauses when the second clause restates or elaborates on the first. Use a colon between two independent clauses of this sort when you want to emphasize the second clause.

➤ **I can predict tonight's sequence of events: my brother will**
                                               ^

   arrive late, talk loudly, and eat too much.

Note: When a complete sentence follows a colon, the first word may begin with either a capital or a lowercase letter. Whatever you decide to do, though, you should use the same style throughout your document.

53c Use colons to indicate ratios, to indicate times of day, for city and publisher citations in bibliographies, to separate titles and subtitles, and in business letters.

➤ **The ratio of armed to unarmed members of the gang was 3:1.**

➤ **He woke up at 6:30 in the morning.**

➤ **New York: McGraw-Hill, 2006**

➤ *Possible Lives: The Promise of Public Education in America*

➤ **Dear Mr. Worth:**

In some situations, such as in the military, time is expressed in four digits without a colon: *1500 hours* instead of 3:00.

CHARTING the TERRITORY

Biblical Citations

Colons are often used to separate biblical chapters and verses (John 3:16), but the Modern Language Association (MLA) recommends using a period instead (John 3.16).

53d Edit to eliminate unnecessary colons.

Do not use a colon to separate sentence parts that belong together, such as a verb and its object or complement or a preposition and its object or objects.

verb   complement
➤ **The elements in a good smoothie are: yogurt, fruit, and honey.**

preposition   objects
➤ **Some feel cancer can be prevented by: diet, exercise,**

and screening.

Do not use a colon after *such as, for example,* or *including,* even when you are introducing a list.

846

➤ **I am ready for a change,** *such as⁄* **a new job or a new**

apartment.

Expressions like *that is* and *namely,* which often precede appositives, should follow the colon: *He had a next-to-impossible goal: namely, a career in the major leagues.*

Do not use a colon between a phrase or a dependent clause and an independent clause. Some instructors consider this error to be a sentence fragment. (*For help with fragments, see Chapter 32, pp. 572–83.*)

➤ N̶o̶ such luck: the doctor was not at home.
  I had no

➤ **Before the children go to lunch⁄,** W̶e̶ **will observe their**
  we

interactions.

Do not use a second colon in a sentence.

➤ **He was taken in by** a̶ ̶n̶e̶w̶ ̶c̶o̶n̶: **the Spanish lottery scam:**

the victim is told that he or she has won a big prize and

is asked to send financial information to the officer of a fake

Spanish company.

Exercise 53.1   Chapter review: Colons

Edit the following passage by adding or deleting colons.

> EXAMPLE   **The director of the soup kitchen is considering**
>
> **ways to raise funds, for example⁄ a bake sale,**
>
> **car wash, or readathon.**

Ciguatera is a form of food poisoning, humans are poisoned when they consume reef fish that contain toxic substances called ciguatoxins. These toxins accumulate at the end of the food chain: large carnivorous fish prey on smaller herbivorous fish. These smaller fish feed on ciguatoxins, which are produced by microorganisms that grow on the surface of marine algae. Ciguatoxins are found in certain marine fish, snapper, mackerel, barracuda, and grouper. People should avoid eating fish from reef waters, including: the tropical and subtropical waters of the Pacific and Indian oceans and the Caribbean Sea.

Some people think that ciguatera can be destroyed by: cooking or freezing the fish. People who consume reef fish should avoid eating: the head, internal organs, or eggs. People who eat contaminated fish experience gastrointestinal and neurological problems: vomiting, diarrhea, numbness, and muscle pains. Most physicians offer the same advice, "Eat fish only from reputable restaurants and dealers."

54 Quotation Marks

www.mhhe.com/
nmhh
For information and
exercises on quotation
marks, go to

Editing >
Quotation Marks

As an academic writer, you are engaged in a dialogue with the work of other scholars, and you will often need to incorporate their words into your papers. Parts 3 and 4 discuss the process of researching and documenting sources. This chapter covers the use of quotation marks—as well as the punctuation marks that appear with them—to present other people's written and spoken words in your papers. It also presents other uses of quotations marks.

As you proofread your papers, bear in mind that every opening quotation mark (") must be accompanied by a closing mark (") and vice versa. A missing closing quotation mark is all too easy to overlook.

> *Note:* You should credit the source of direct quotations using the documentation style appropriate to your audience. Most of the examples in this chapter are not fully documented because they are not meant to illustrate documentation styles; that advice is given in detail in Part 4: Documenting across the Curriculum.

54a Use quotation marks to indicate the exact words of a speaker or writer.

Direct quotations from written material may include whole sentences or only a few words or phrases.

➤ In *Angela's Ashes,* Frank McCourt writes, "Worse than the ordinary miserable childhood is the miserable Irish childhood."

➤ Frank McCourt believes that being Irish worsens what is all too "ordinary"—a "miserable childhood."

> *Note:* Do not use quotation marks to set off an **indirect quotation,** which reports what a speaker said but does not use the exact words.
>
> ➤ He said that ~~"~~he didn't know what I was talking about.~~"~~

849

> ## Quotation Marks and Grammar Checkers
>
> Computer grammar checkers cannot determine where a quotation should begin and end. In addition, grammar checkers will not point out many errors in the use of quotation marks with other marks of punctuation. For example, a grammar checker did not highlight the error in the placement of the period in the following sentence.
>
> ➤ **Barbara Ehrenreich observes, "There are no Palm Pilots, cable channels, or Web sites to advise the low-wage job seeker".** [The period should come before the closing mark.]

54b Use quotation marks to set off brief direct quotations and lines of dialogue.

Quotation marks are used to incorporate brief direct quotations within the main body of your text. Longer direct quotations are set off from the main text by indenting them (*see 54d*).

1. Using signal phrases to introduce quotations

If you introduce a quotation with a signal phrase such as *he said* or *she noted,* add a comma after the phrase and use a capital letter to begin the quotation.

➤ **Hamilton says, "That is the miracle of Greek mythology—**

   a humanized world."

If the phrase follows the quotation, add a comma at the end of the quotation, before the closing quotation mark. (If the quotation ends in a question mark or an exclamation point, however, do not add a comma.) Capitalize the first letter of the quotation even if the first word does not begin a sentence in the original source.

➤ **"The only white people who came to our house were welfare**

   workers and bill collectors," James Baldwin wrote.

   If you interrupt a quoted sentence with a signal phrase, place quotation marks around both parts of the quoted sentence and set the signal phrase off with commas. Note that the first word of the second part of the quoted sentence is not capitalized.

➤ **"The first thing that strikes one about Plath's journals,"**

writes Katha Pollitt in *the Atlantic*, "is what they leave out."

To interrupt a quotation of two or more sentences with a signal phrase, attach the signal phrase to the first sentence with a comma and put a period after it. The next sentence begins with an opening quotation mark and a capital letter.

➤ **"There are at least four kinds of doublespeak," William Lutz**

observes. "The first is the euphemism, an inoffensive or

positive word or phrase used to avoid a harsh, unpleasant,

or distasteful reality."

2. Using complete sentences to introduce quotations
When you are introducing a quotation with a complete sentence, use a colon.

➤ **Hamilton credits the Greeks with a shift in the portrayal of**

gods: "Until then, gods had no semblance of reality."

3. Integrating quotations into your sentence
When a quotation is integrated into a sentence's structure, treat the quotation as you would any other sentence element, adding a comma or not as appropriate.

➤ **Saying that the moth "now knew death," Woolf contemplates**

its strangeness.

➤ **Hoagland has described the essay as a work that "hangs**

somewhere on a line between two sturdy poles."

4. Quoting dialogue
When you are quoting dialogue between two or more speakers, you should usually begin a new paragraph to indicate a change in speaker. **851**

"I don't know what you're talking about," he said. "I did listen to everything you told me."

"If you had been listening, you would know what I was talking about."

If a speaker continues for more than a paragraph, begin each subsequent paragraph with quotation marks, but do not insert a closing quotation mark until the end of the quotation.

54c Use single quotation marks, slashes, ellipses, and brackets with direct quotations as required.

Along with the quotation marks indicating that material comes from another source, you may also need to use single quotation marks, slashes, ellipses, and brackets when quoting. The box that follows indicates where you can find detailed coverage of these four marks in this text.

Punctuation Mark	Use in Direct Quotation	Section (*Page No.*)
Single quotation marks ' '	Enclose a quotation within a quotation	54e (*p. 854*)
Slash /	Mark line division within a poetry quotation	55k (*p. 876*)
Ellipses . . .	Mark missing words within a quotation	55j (*pp. 872–76*)
Brackets [ ]	Show changes, additions, or comments from an outside source within a quotation	55i (*pp. 870–72*)

54d Set off long quotations in indented blocks rather than using quotation marks.

If you are using a long quotation, set it off from the text as an **extract,** or a **block quotation.** If you are following MLA style, a quotation of five typed lines or more of prose or four or more lines of a poem should be treated as a block quotation. If you are following APA style, a quotation of forty words or more should be set off in this way. Always double-space the lines in a block quotation, as well as the lines above and below it. The lines of a block quotation should be indented one inch (ten spaces) in MLA style and one-half inch (five spaces) in APA style. (*For more information, on these styles, see Chapters 24 and 25.*)

Do not surround a block quotation with quotation marks. However, if the passage that you are quoting contains quotation marks, include them exactly as they appear in the passage. If your quotation is more than one paragraph long, indent the first line of each new paragraph an extra quarter inch (three spaces) if you are following MLA style and one-half inch (five spaces) if you are following APA style. The following examples are in MLA style.

PROSE EXTRACT

As Carl Schorske points out, the young Freud was passionately interested in classical archeology:

> He cultivated a new friendship in the Viennese professional
> elite--especially rare in those days of withdrawal--with
> Emanuel Loewy, a professor of archeology. "He keeps me
> up till three o'clock in the morning," Freud wrote
> appreciatively to Fleiss. "He tells me about Rome." (273)

Colon used to introduce quotation.

Quotation marks for quotation within passage.

POETRY EXTRACT

In the following lines from "Crossing Brooklyn Ferry," Walt Whitman celebrates the beauty of the Manhattan skyline and his love for the city:

> Ah what can ever be more stately and admirable
>   to me than mast-hemm'd Manhattan?
> River and sunset and scallop-edg'd waves of flood-tide?
> The sea-gulls oscillating their bodies, the hay-boat
>   in the twilight, and the belated lighter?
> What gods can exceed these that clasp me by
>   the hand, and with voices I love call me promptly
>   and loudly by my nighest name as I approach? (92–95)

Colon used to introduce quotation.

Indent turned lines an extra ¼ inch (3 spaces).

853

When quoting poetry, represent the formatting, spelling, capitalization, and punctuation of the original work.

> Ferlinghetti's interpretation of Klimt's painting leads him to this
> conclusion:

Formatting of
poem follows
the original.

> She
>
> will not open
>
> He
>
> is not the One (59–62)

> *Note:* Writers often end the sentence introducing a quotation
> with a colon, but it is not a requirement. You may end the sentence with a period. If your instructor allows, you may even
> introduce the quotation with the beginning of a sentence that
> the quotation completes. If you do so, the quotation should not
> begin with a capital letter unless the first word is a proper noun.

54e Use single quotation marks to enclose a quotation
within a quotation.

Unless you are using a block quotation, set off a quotation within a
quotation with a pair of single quotation marks.

➤ **Kenneth Burke notes with displeasure that his "procedures**

 have been characterized as 'intuitive' and 'indiosyncratic.'"

> *Note:* In the unlikely event that you need to include quotation
> marks within an already embedded quotation or title, use
> double quotation marks again: *"I agree with the article titled*
> *'The "Animal Rights" War on Medicine.'"*

Exercise 54.1 Using double and single quotation marks

Below is a passage from the Seneca Falls Declaration (1848) by Elizabeth Cady Stanton, followed by a numbered series of quotations from this passage. Add, delete, or replace quotation marks to quote from the passage accurately. Some sentences may be correct; circle their numbers.

> The history of mankind is a history of repeated injuries and usurpations on the part of man toward woman, having in direct object the establishment of an absolute tyranny over her. To prove this, let facts be submitted to a candid world.
>
> WHEREAS, The great precept of nature is conceded to be that "man shall pursue his own true and substantial happiness." Blackstone in his *Commentaries* remarks that this law of Nature being coeval with mankind, and dictated by God himself, is of course superior in obligation to any other. It is binding over all the globe, in all countries and at all times; no human laws are of any validity if contrary to this, and such of them as are valid, derive all their force, and all their validity, and all their authority, mediately and immediately, from this original; therefore,
>
> RESOLVED, That such laws as conflict, in any way, with the true and substantial happiness of woman, are contrary to the great precept of nature and of no validity, for this is "superior in obligation to any other."

EXAMPLE　　**As Elizabeth Cady Stanton points out, "The**

great precept of nature is conceded to be that

'man shall pursue his own true and substantial

happiness.'"

1. "The history of mankind is a history of repeated injuries and usurpations on the part of man toward woman," Elizabeth Cady Stanton asserts, "having in direct object the establishment of an absolute tyranny over her."
2. To prove this, writes Stanton, let facts be submitted to a candid world.
3. Stanton argues that men have oppressed women throughout history.
4. Stanton contends "that all laws are subject to natural laws."
5. Stanton resolves "that such laws as conflict, in any way, with the true and substantial happiness of woman, are contrary to the great precept of nature and of no validity, for this is "superior in obligation to any other.""

54f Use quotation marks to enclose titles of short works such as articles, poems, and stories.

The titles of long works, such as books, are usually put in italics or underlined (*see Chapter 60, pp. 916–17*). The titles of book chapters, essays, most poems, and other short works are usually put in quotation marks.

For when to use quotation marks with titles in a works-cited or references list, see the chapter in Part 4: Documenting across the Curriculum that covers the documentation style you are using.

Note: If quotation marks are needed within the title of a short work, use single quotation marks: "The 'Animal Rights' War on Medicine."

TITLES THAT SHOULD BE ENCLOSED in QUOTATION MARKS

- **Essays**
  "Once More to the Lake"
- **Songs**
  "Seven Nation Army"
- **Short poems**
  "Daffodils"
- **Short stories**
  "The Tell-Tale Heart"
- **Articles in periodicals**
  "Scotland Yard of the Wild" (from *American Way*)
- **Book chapters or sections**
  "The Girl in Conflict" (Chapter 11 of *Coming of Age in Samoa*)
- **Part of a Web site**
  "Explainer" (part of the *Slate* site)
- **Episodes of radio and television programs**
  "I Can't Remember" (on *48 Hours*)
- **Titles of unpublished works, including student papers, theses, and dissertations**
  "Louis Armstrong and Joe Glaser: More Than Meets the Eye"

  Do not, however, use quotation marks to enclose the title of your own paper on your title page.

54g Use quotation marks to indicate that a word or phrase is being used in a special way.

Occasionally, you can use quotation marks around a word or phrase that someone else uses, or has used, in a way that you or your readers may not agree with.

➤ **The "worker's paradise" of Stalinist Russia included**

   slave-labor camps.

Quotation marks used in this way function as raised eyebrows do in conversation and should be used sparingly. Do not use quotation marks to distance yourself from slang, clichés, or trite expressions. Avoid those expressions altogether.

   Words cited as words and words that you are defining can also be put in quotation marks, although the more common practice is to italicize them. (You should be consistent throughout your paper.)

➤ **The words "compliment" and "complement" sound alike but**

   have different meanings.

➤ **"Chatter," the communications intercepted by an**

   intelligence agency, needs to be interpreted to be useful.

You should enclose a word you are defining in quotation marks only when you introduce and explain it, not afterward.

   Use quotation marks to give the English translation of a word in another language.

➤ *Merci* **means "thank you."**

   Finally, do not enclose well-known nicknames in quotation marks: *President Bill Clinton*, not *President "Bill" Clinton.*

54h Place punctuation marks within or outside quotation marks, as convention and your meaning require.

As you edit, check closing quotation marks and the punctuation that appears next to them to make sure that you have placed them in the correct order.

857

1. Periods and commas
Place the period or comma before the final quotation mark, even when the quotation is brief. When single and double quotation marks appear together, both should be placed after the period or comma (*see the example in 54e on p. 854*).

➤   **"Instead of sharing an experience the spectator must come to grips with things," Brecht writes in "The Epic Theatre and Its Difficulties."**

However, place the period or comma after a parenthetical citation.

➤   **Brecht wants the spectator to "come to grips with things" (23).**

2. Question marks and exclamation points
Place a question mark or an exclamation point after the final quotation mark if the quoted material is not itself a question or an exclamation.

➤   **How does epic theater make us "come to grips with things"?**

Place a question mark or an exclamation point before the final quotation mark when it is part of the quotation. No additional punctuation is needed after the closing quotation unless there is a parenthetical citation.

➤   **"Are we to see science in the theater?" Brecht was asked.**

➤   **Brecht was asked, "Are we to see science in the theater?"**

➤   **Brecht was asked, "Are we to see science in the theater?" (27).**

3. Colons and semicolons
Place colons and semicolons after the final quotation mark.

➤   **Dean Wilcox cited the items he called his "daily delights":**

a free parking space for his scooter at the faculty club,

a special table in the club itself, and friends to laugh with

after a day's work.

4. Dashes

Place a dash outside either an opening or a closing quotation mark, or both, if it precedes or follows the quotation or if two dashes are used to set off the quotation.

➤ **One phrase—"time is running out"—haunted me.**

Place a dash inside either an opening or a closing quotation mark if it is part of the quotation.

➤ **"Where is the—" she called. "Oh, here it is. Never mind."**

Exercise 54.2   Using quotation marks with other punctuation

Edit the following sentences to correct problems with the use of quotation marks with other punctuation. Some sentences may be correct; circle their numbers.

EXAMPLE   **In June 1776, Richard Henry Lee proposed that**

the Continental Congress adopt a resolution

that "these united Colonies are, and of right

ought to be, free and independent States.",/

1. "We hold these truths to be self-evident", wrote Thomas Jefferson in 1776.
2. Most Americans can recite their "unalienable rights:" "life, liberty, and the pursuit of happiness."
3. According to the Declaration of Independence, "whenever any form of government becomes destructive to these ends, it is the right of the people to alter or to abolish it."!
4. The signers of the Declaration of Independence contended that the "history of the present King of Great Britain is a history of repeated injuries and usurpations, all having in direct object the establishment of an absolute tyranny over these states."
5. What did the creators of this document mean by a "candid world?"

859

6. Feminists and civil rights advocates have challenged the Declaration's most famous phrase "—all men are created equal"—on grounds that these "unalienable rights" were originally extended only to white men who owned property.

54i Edit to correct common errors in using quotation marks.

Writers are sometimes overzealous in their use of quotation marks or unsure about how to use end punctuation with the closing mark. Watch out for the following errors in particular.

1. Do not use quotation marks to distance yourself from slang, clichés, or trite expressions. Avoid overused or slang expressions in college writing. If your writing situation permits slang, however, do not enclose it in quotation marks.

➤ **Californians are reputed to be very ⸢laid back.⸣**

Revising the sentence is usually a better solution:

➤ **Californians have a reputation for being relaxed**

and carefree.

2. Do not use quotation marks for indirect quotations.

➤ **He told his boss that ⸢the company lost its largest**

account.⸣

Another way to correct this sentence is to change to a direct quotation.

➤ **He said to his boss, "We just lost our largest account."**

3. Do not add another question mark or exclamation point to the end of a sentence that concludes with a quotation ending in one of those marks.

➤ **What did Juliet mean when she cried, "O Romeo,**

Romeo! wherefore art thou Romeo?"⸮

If you quote a question within a sentence that makes a statement, place a question mark before the closing quotation mark and a period at the end of the sentence.

➤ **"What was Henry Ford's greatest contribution to the**

Industrial Revolution?" he asked.

4. Do not use quotation marks to enclose the title of your own paper on the title page or above the first line of the text.

➤ **"Edgar Allan Poe and the Paradox of the Gothic"**

If you use a quotation or the title of a short work in your title, though, put quotation marks around that quotation or title.

➤ **Edgar Allan Poe's "The Raven" and the Paradox of**

the Gothic

Exercise 54.3   Chapter review: Quotation marks

Edit the following passage to correct problems with the use of quotation marks.

On August 28, 1963, Dr. Martin Luther King Jr. delivered his famous 'I Have a Dream' speech at the nation's Lincoln Memorial. According to King, "When the architects of our republic wrote the magnificent words of the Constitution and the Declaration of Independence, they were signing a promissory note to which every American was to fall heir". King declared that "this note was a promise that all men, yes, black men as well as white men, would be guaranteed the unalienable rights of life, liberty, and the pursuit of happiness." This promissory note, however, came back "marked "insufficient funds."" King's speech, therefore, was designed to rally his supporters to "make justice a reality."

Unlike the more militant civil rights leaders of the 1950s, King advocated nonviolence. This stance is why King said that the 'Negro community' should not drink "from the cup of bitterness and hatred" and that they should not use physical violence.

King's dream was uniquely American: "I have a dream that one day this nation will rise up and live out the true meaning of its creed: 'We hold these truths to be self-evident: that all men are created equal.'" King challenged all Americans to fully embrace racial equality. Nearly fifty years later, we must ask ourselves if King's dream has in fact become a reality. Are "all of God's children, black men and white men, Jews and Gentiles, Protestants and Catholics . . . able to join hands and sing in the words of the old Negro spiritual, "Free at last! free at last! thank God Almighty, we are free at last!?""

55 Dashes, Parentheses, and Other Punctuation Marks

Like commas, dashes and parentheses are used to set off information within a sentence. Dashes emphasize and parentheses de-emphasize the set-off material.

➤ **Our neighbors have taken up bird-watching, an ideal pastime for nature-starved city dwellers.**

➤ **We were surprised that Jim—a man who never owned a pair of sneakers—spends hours in the park.**

➤ **Carrie (who now lives in Florida) introduced them to the hobby.**

Brackets are also used to set off information from an outside source within a quotation or to set off material within parentheses. Ellipses indicate that words have been deleted from a quotation, and slashes indicate line breaks in quotations from poetry, among other uses.

Other Punctuation Marks and Grammar Checkers

All of the punctuation marks covered in this chapter involve judgment calls on the writer's part. Computer grammar checkers will not tell you when you might use a pair of dashes or parentheses to set off material in a sentence, for example. They may catch some errors in the use of these marks, but in general you will need to proofread your work to make sure that you are using these marks correctly.

55a Use the dash provided by your word-processing program, or form it by typing two hyphens.

A typeset dash, sometimes called an em dash, is a single, unbroken line about as wide as a capital M (—). Most word-processing programs **863**

www.mhhe.com/
nmhh
For information and
exercises on dashes,
go to

Editing > Dashes

provide the em dash as a special character or will convert two hyphens to an em dash as an autoformat function. Otherwise, you can make a dash on the keyboard by typing two hyphens in a row (--) with no space between them. Do not put a space before or after the dash. A handwritten dash should be about as long as two hyphens.

55b Use a dash to highlight an explanation or a list that begins or ends a sentence.

A dash indicates a very strong pause and emphasizes what comes immediately before or after it.

➤ **I think the Comets will win the tournament—*their goalie has***

the best record in the league.

➤ ***Coca-Cola, potato chips, and brevity—*these are the marks of**

a good study session in the dorm.

Do not break up an independent clause with a dash.

➤ **Haydn, Mozart, Beethoven—are the most famous composers**

and

of the classical period.

55c Use a dash or two dashes to insert—and highlight— a nonessential phrase or an independent clause within a sentence.

Dashes are especially useful for inserting clarifying information such as a definition, an example, or an appositive (a word or phrase that renames a noun) into a sentence.

DEFINITION   **In addition to the trumpet, he played the**

cornet—*a wind instrument smaller than a*

trumpet, with three valves.

EXAMPLE   **All finite creatures—*including humans—*are**

864   **incomplete and contradictory.**

APPOSITIVE **Located in east London, Smithfield Market—*a***

huge meat market—has a long history.

Make sure that the word or words set off with dashes appear next to the word they are clarifying.

> *found*
> **On a day hike we ~~found~~—my sisters and I—a wounded owl.**

A dash or pair of dashes can also be used to insert a contrast.

CONTRAST **Watercolor paint is easy to buy—*but hard to***

master.

Independent clauses can also be inserted into a sentence using dashes.

> **The first rotary gasoline engine—*it was made by Mazda*—**
>
> **burned 15 percent more fuel than conventional engines.**

If the clause you are adding is a question or an exclamation, the question mark or exclamation point should precede the second dash: *I never imagined—how could I?—that he would return.* When editing, make sure that your sentence is clear and complete without the material within brackets.

> **Because we wanted the tickets so badly—it was the last**
>
> **performance of the season—~~so~~ we stood in line for hours.**

The two parts of the original sentence (without the inserted material) do not fit together: *Because we wanted the tickets so badly so we stood in line for hours.* Removing *so* fixes the problem.

55d Use a dash or dashes to indicate a sudden break in tone, thought, or speech.

> **Breathing heavily, the archeologist opened the old chest**
>
> **in wild anticipation and found—old socks and an empty**
>
> **soda can.**

➤ **His last words were "There's nothing here except—"**

> *Note:* Commas, semicolons, and periods should never appear beside dashes. An opening or a closing quotation mark sometimes appears next to a dash, as in the preceding example, but the two marks should never overlap.

55e Do not overuse dashes.

Used sparingly, dashes can be effective, but too many dashes make your writing disjointed.

CHOPPY	After we found the puppy—shivering under the porch—we brought her into the house—into the entryway, actually—and wrapped her in an old towel—to warm her up.
SMOOTHER	After we found the puppy shivering under the porch, we brought her into the house—into the entryway, actually—and wrapped her in an old towel to warm her up.

Exercise 55.1 Using dashes

Insert or correct dashes where needed in the following sentences.

EXAMPLE	Women ⎯ once shut out of electoral office ^ altogether ⎯ have made great progress in recent ^ decades.

1. Patsy Mink, Geraldine Ferraro, Antonia Novello, and Madeleine Albright all are political pioneers in the history of the United States.
2. Patsy Mink the first Asian-American woman elected to the U.S. Congress served for twenty-four years in the U.S. House of Representatives.
3. Geraldine Ferraro she was a congresswoman from Queens, New York became the first female vice presidential candidate when she was nominated by the Democratic Party in 1984.

FIGURE 55.1 Dr. Antonia Novello testifying during her confirmation hearing.

4. Antonia Novello—former U.S. Surgeon General—was the first woman—and the first Hispanic—to hold this position.
5. Madeleine Albright, the first female Secretary of State, has observed, "To understand Europe, you have to be a genius-or French."

55f Use parentheses to enclose supplementary information.

Parentheses are useful when you want to insert additional—but nonessential—information about a sentence element. Parentheses can enclose an explanation, an example, a brief but pertinent digression,

www.mhhe.com/
nmhh
For information
and exercises on
parentheses, go to

Editing >
Parentheses

or an abbreviation. Parentheses are always used in pairs (an opening and a closing parenthesis).

EXPLANATION   The last four telephone bills (September to December) have each been more than fifty dollars.

EXAMPLE   Every household is filled with items (buttons, for example) that people will never use but will not throw away.

DIGRESSION   Envious of the freedoms adults enjoy, few children realize (I never did) how stressful adult life can be.

ABBREVIATION   When quoting poetry in the style of the Modern Language Association (MLA), put the line numbers in parentheses following the quotation.

Caution: Enclose information in parentheses only occasionally in your writing. If you notice that you have used parentheses more than once or twice in a paper, ask yourself whether, in each case, the information they enclose could be deleted or incorporated into your sentence without the parentheses.

55g   Use parentheses to enclose numbers or letters, according to convention.

Parentheses are used to enclose numbers or letters that label items in a list that is part of a sentence.

➤ **He wants the sales data to be updated in (1) the monthly report, (2) the quarterly forecast, and (3) the annual budget.**

Do not use parentheses to enclose the numbers or letters in a list set up so that each entry starts a new line.

Parentheses are also used to enclose page numbers and other reference information in the MLA, APA, and CSE name-year documentation styles (*see Part 5 for details*). They are also used in business writing to enclose a numeral following a spelled-out number and, in some disciplines, to set off alternate forms of a measurement.

➤ **The contract will terminate in sixty (60) days.**

868 ➤ **I added the compound to 2 liters (2.114 quarts) of water.**

55h Learn the conventions for capitalization and punctuation with parentheses.

1. The first word of a sentence that stands by itself within parentheses should begin with a capital letter, and the sentence should conclude with a period, a question mark, or an exclamation point.

> ➤ **Folktales and urban legends often reflect the concerns of a particular era. (The familiar tale of a cat accidentally caught in a microwave oven is an example of this phenomenon.)**

2. The first word of a sentence in parentheses that appears within another sentence should not begin with a capital letter unless the word is a proper noun. The sentence should not end with a period, a comma, or a semicolon. However, it can end with a question mark or an exclamation point.

> ➤ **John Henry (he was the man with the forty-pound hammer) was a hero to miners fearing the loss of their jobs to machines.**

> ➤ **The most popular major in this school a decade ago was business administration (although wasn't psychology a close second?).**

> ➤ **Dirt absorbs light and uses more energy (clean your light bulbs!).**

3. Do not use any punctuation before the opening parenthesis within a sentence. To decide if any punctuation should follow the closing parenthesis, imagine the sentence without the parenthetical material.

> ➤ **As he walked past/ (dressed, as always, in his Sunday best), I got ready to throw the spitball.**
> ^

➤ He walked past (never noticing me behind the statue)/
on his way to the assembly.

4. Quotation marks should never surround parentheses.

➤ His first poem *("Eye")* was also his most famous.

Exercise 55.2 Using parentheses

Insert parentheses where needed in the following sentences, and correct any errors in their use.

EXAMPLE   During leap year, February has twenty-nine (29)
days.

1. German meteorologist Alfred Wegener he was also a geophysicist proposed the first comprehensive theory of continental drift.
2. According to this geological theory, 1 the earth originally contained a single large continent, 2 this land mass eventually separated into six continents, and 3 these continents gradually drifted apart.
3. Wegener contended that continents will continue to drift. They are not rigidly fixed. The evidence indicates that his predictions are accurate.
4. The continents are moving at a rate of one yard .09144 meters per century.
5. The movement of the continents, (slow though this movement may be), occasionally causes earthquakes along fault lines such as the famous San Andreas Fault in California.

55i When quoting, use brackets to set off material that is not part of the original quotation

Brackets set off information you add to a quotation that is not part of the quotation itself. Use brackets to add significant information that is needed to make the quotation clear.

➤ **Samuel Eliot Morison has written, "This passage has attracted a good deal of scorn to the Florentine mariner [Verrazzano], but without justice."**

In this sentence, the writer is quoting Morison, but Morison's sentence does not include the name of the "Florentine mariner." The writer places the name—Verrazzano—in brackets so that readers will know his identity.

Information that explains or corrects something in a quotation is also bracketed.

➤ **Vasco da Gama's man wrote in 1487, "The body of the church [it was not a church but a Hindu shrine] is as large as a monastery."**

Brackets are also used around words that you insert within a quotation to make it fit the grammar, style, or context of your own sentence. If you replace a word with your own word in brackets, ellipses are not needed.

➤ **At the end of *Pygmalion*, Henry Higgins confesses to Eliza Doolittle that he has "grown accustomed to [her] voice and appearance."**

To make the quote fit properly into the sentence, the writer inserts the bracketed word *her* in place of *your.*

If you change the first letter of a word in a quotation to a capital or lowercase letter, enclose the letter in brackets: *Ackroyd writes, "[F]or half a million years there has been in London a pattern of habitation and hunting if not of settlement."*

If you are adding ellipses to a passage that already contains ellipses, you can distinguish them from the ellipses that appear in the original by using brackets. (*See 55j on ellipses.*)

If you need to set off words within material that is already in parentheses, use brackets: (*I found the information on a Web site published by the National Institutes of Health [NIH].*)

Note: Brackets may be used to enclose the word *sic* (Latin for "thus") after a word in a quotation that was incorrect in the original. If you are following MLA style, the word *sic* should not be underlined or italicized when it appears in brackets. The three other styles covered in this book (APA, Chicago, and CSE) put *sic* in italics.

➤ **The critic noted that "the battle scenes in *The Patriot* are realistic, but the rest of the film is historically inacurate [sic] and overly melodramatic."**

Sic should be used sparingly because it can appear pretentious and condescending, and it should not be used to make fun of what someone has said or written.

55j Use ellipses to indicate that words have been omitted from a quotation or that a thought is incomplete.

If you wish to shorten a passage you are quoting, you may omit words, phrases (such as the one highlighted in the quotation that follows), or even entire sentences. To show readers that you have done so, use three spaced periods (. . .), called *ellipses* or an *ellipsis mark*.

FULL QUOTATION

Just before noon on April 23, 1838, the *Sirius,* a small paddle-wheel steam packet nineteen days out of Cork, limped across the Upper Bay, its coal supply all but exhausted, and made landfall to the cheers of a great crowd gathered at the Battery. A scant four hours later, a second steamer, twice as big and half again as fast, hove into view, belching black smoke. This was the *Great Western,* fourteen days out of Bristol. She had been chasing *Sirius* across the Atlantic, and the sight of her churning toward the city touched off even more exuberant rejoicing, as it was now doubly clear that New York had established a maritime steam link to Europe.

—EDWIN G. BURROWS AND MIKE WALLACE,
Gotham: A History of New York City to 1898, p. 649

EDITED QUOTATION

In their account of the boom in transatlantic trade in the mid-nineteenth century, Burrows and Wallace describe its beginning:

"Just before noon on April 23, 1838, the Sirius, a small paddlewheel steam packet . . . made landfall to the cheers of a great crowd gathered

at the Battery" (649).

Some instructors may ask you to use brackets to enclose any ellipses that you add, to indicate that the elision is yours and was not in the original source.

EDITED QUOTATION (ALTERNATE STYLE, WITH BRACKETS)

In their account of the boom in transatlantic trade in the mid-

nineteenth century, Burrows and Wallace describe its beginning:

"Just before noon on April 23, 1838, the Sirius, a small paddlewheel

steam packet [. . .] made landfall to the cheers of a great crowd

gathered at the Battery" (649).

The following guidelines will help you use ellipses correctly for the different kinds of omissions you may need to make. All quotations are cited in the style recommended by the Modern Language Association (MLA). (*For guidance in using MLA style, see Chapter 24; for guidance in using the APA, Chicago, and CSE styles to cite sources, see Chapters 25 and 26.*)

1. If you are leaving out the end of a quoted sentence, the three ellipsis points are preceded by a period to end the sentence. (*See also item 4 below.*)

END OF A QUOTED SENTENCE OMITTED

In describing the arrival in New York of the first transatlantic steamers on

page 649, Burrows and Wallace note that "four hours later, a second

steamer, twice as big and half again as fast, hove into view. . . ."

Note that ellipses are not needed at the beginning of the quotation because the lowercase letter *f* makes it clear that the first part of the sentence has been left out.

To add a parenthetical reference after the ellipses at the end of a sentence, place it after the quotation mark but before the final period.

EDITED QUOTATION WITH PARENTHETICAL REFERENCE

In describing the arrival in New York of the first transatlantic steamers,

Burrows and Wallace note that "four hours later, a second steamer, twice

as big and half again as fast, hove into view . . ." (649).

2. If you are leaving out a sentence or sentences, use three ellipsis points preceded by a period.

ENTIRE SENTENCE OMITTED

Burrows and Wallace recount the arrival of the second steamer:

> A scant four hours later, a second steamer, twice as big and half
> again as fast, hove into view, belching black smoke. . . . She had
> been chasing Sirius across the Atlantic, and the sight of her
> churning toward the city touched off even more exuberant
> rejoicing, as it was now doubly clear that New York had
> established a maritime steam link to Europe. (649)

3. If you are leaving out the last part of one sentence and the first
   part of the next, use three ellipses points.

PARTS OF TWO ADJACENT SENTENCES OMITTED

Burrows and Wallace describe a joyful scene: "This was the Great
Western, . . . and the sight of her churning toward the city touched
off even more exuberant rejoicing, as it was now doubly clear that
New York had established a maritime steam link to Europe" (649).

Note that the comma after *Western* has been retained because it is needed
before the coordinating conjunction *and,* which is joining two independent
clauses. Commas and other punctuation marks that are not needed in the
new sentence can be dropped.

4. If you are leaving out the last part of a sentence and one or more
   of the sentences that follow it, use three ellipsis points followed by
   a period.

**LAST PART OF ONE SENTENCE AND ONE OR
MORE SUBSEQUENT SENTENCES OMITTED**

"[A] second steamer, twice as big and half again as fast, hove into
view. . . . She had been chasing Sirius across the Atlantic, and the sight
of her churning toward the city touched off even more exuberant
rejoicing . . ." (Burrows and Wallace 649).

Note that ellipses are not needed at the beginning of the quotation
because the letter *A* in brackets indicates that the first part of the
sentence has been omitted. At the end of the quotation, the sentence
period follows the parenthetical citation, and the three ellipsis points
represent the omission of the end of the quoted sentence.

Note: If the quotation begins with a capitalized word, rather than with a lowercased word or one starting with a bracketed capital letter, ellipses should precede the first word of the quotation so that readers will know that the first part of the sentence has been left out.

> The arrival of the steamers in 1838 meant that ". . . New York had established a maritime steam link to Europe" (Burrows and Wallace 649).

5. Ellipses are usually not needed to indicate an omission when you are quoting only a word or phrase.

PHRASE QUOTED—NO ELLIPSES

According to Burrows and Wallace, the arrival of the two steamers caused "exuberant rejoicing" in the city (649).

6. To indicate the omission of an entire line or more from the middle of a poem or a paragraph or more from a prose quotation, insert a line of spaced periods. (Otherwise, the rules for omitting words from a poetry quotation are the same as those given in items 1–5.)

Shelley seems to be describing nature, but what is really at issue is the seductive nature of desire:

> See the mountains kiss high Heaven.
>
> And the waves clasp one another:
>
> . . . .
>
> And the sunlight clasp the earth,
>
> And the moonbeams kiss the sea:
>
> What is all this sweet work worth
>
> If thou kiss not me? (1-2, 5-8)

   Ellipses should be used only as a means of shortening a quotation, never as a device for changing its fundamental meaning or for creating emphasis where none exists in the original.

   You can also use ellipses to leave a thought or statement hanging or to suggest that a series continues.

INCOMPLETE THOUGHT

She glared at me and said, "If I have to come over there one more time . . ."

INCOMPLETE SERIES

The chores were seemingly endless. Feed the animals, make breakfast, wash the dishes, make the beds, sweep the floors . . . and then do it all over again the next day.

55k Use a slash to show line breaks in quoted poetry, to separate options or combinations, and in electronic addresses.

When quoting two or three lines of poetry within a sentence, use a slash to show where each line of poetry ends. Add a space before and after the slash.

QUOTATION WITH SLASHES

In "The Tower," Yeats makes his peace with "All those things whereof / Man makes a superhuman / Mirror-resembling dream" (163-65).

Reproduce the capitalization and punctuation of the original poetry, but add a period if necessary to end your sentence. If you leave out the end of the last line you are quoting, add ellipses (*see 55j*). Do not use slashes in block quotations or extracts of poetry. (*see 55d*).

You should also use slashes to mark divisions in Internet addresses (URLs) and in fractions.

➤ **www.mheducation.com/college.html**

➤ **3/4, 1 2/3**

Note: There is a space, not a hyphen, between the *1* and the *2/3*.

Slashes are also used to indicate a choice or combination.

➤ **credit/noncredit**   **owner/operator**   **and/or**

Note: Although this use of the slash is common in business writing, it is discouraged in academic writing, especially in the humanities.

Exercise 55.3 Using brackets, ellipses, and slashes

Insert brackets, ellipses, and slashes where needed in the following sentences, and correct any errors in their use. Refer to the following excerpts from a poem and an essay.

> The lights begin to twinkle from the rocks;
> The long day wanes; the slow moon climbs, the deep
> Moans round with many voices. Come, my friends.
> 'T is not too late to seek a newer world. (54–57)
>
> —from *Ulysses* by Alfred, Lord Tennyson

> Now when I had mastered the language of this water and had come to know every trifling feature that bordered the great river as familiarly as I knew the letters of the alphabet, I had made a valuable acquisition. But I had lost something, too. I had lost something which could never be restored to me while I lived. All the grace, the beauty, the poetry had gone out of the majestic river!
>
> —from "Two Views of the Mississippi" by Mark Twain

EXAMPLE   **The speaker in the poem *Ulysses* longs to seek "/ / / a newer world" (57).**

1. Ulysses is tempted as he looks toward the sea: "The lights begin to twinkle from the rocks; The long day wanes . . ." (54–55).
2. In "Two Views of the Mississippi," Mark Twain writes that "I had mastered the language of this water. I had made a valuable acquisition."
3. Twain regrets that he "has lost something"—his sense of the beauty of the river.
4. In Tennyson's poem, "the deep the ocean / moans round with many voices" (55–56).
5. In *Ulysses* the ocean beckons with possibilities; in "Two Views of the Mississippi," the river has become too familiar: "All the grace had gone out of the majestic river!"

Exercise 55.4 Chapter review: Dashes, parentheses, and other punctuation marks

Edit the following passage by adding or deleting dashes, parentheses, brackets, ellipses, and slashes. Make any other additions, deletions, or changes that are necessary for correctness and sense. Refer to the following excerpt as necessary.

This is a book about that most admirable of human virtues—courage.

. . . .

Some of my colleagues who are criticized today for lack of forthright principles—or who are looked upon with scornful eyes as compromising "politicians"—are simply engaged in the fine art of conciliating, balancing and interpreting the forces and factions of public opinion, an art essential to keeping our nation united and enabling our Government to function.

—JOHN F. KENNEDY, *Profiles in Courage,* pp. 1, 5

John Fitzgerald Kennedy—the youngest man to be elected U.S. president—he was also the youngest president to be assassinated. He was born on May 29, 1917, in Brookline, Massachusetts. Kennedy was born into a family with a tradition of public service; his father, Joseph Kennedy, served as ambassador to Great Britain. (his maternal grandfather, John Frances Fitzgerald, served as the mayor of Boston.)

Caroline, John Fitzgerald Jr., and Patrick B. (Who died in infancy) are the children of the late John F. Kennedy. Kennedy's background, a Harvard education, military service as a lieutenant in the navy, and public service as Massachusetts senator—helped provide John F. Kennedy with the experience, insight, and recognition needed to defeat Richard Nixon in 1960.

Even before being elected U.S. president, Kennedy received the Pulitzer Prize for his book *Profiles in Courage* 1957. According to Kennedy, "This *Profiles in Courage* is a book about that most admirable of human virtues—courage" 1. "Some of my colleagues," Kennedy continues, "who are criticized today for lack of forthright principles / are simply engaged in the fine art of conciliating. . . ." 5.

During Kennedy's presidency, Americans witnessed 1 the Cuban missile crisis, 2 the Bay of Pigs invasion, and 3 the Berlin crisis. Most Americans—we hope—are able to recognize Kennedy's famous words—which were first delivered during his Inaugural Address: "Ask not what your country can do for you—ask what you can do for your country."

56 End Punctuation: Periods, Question Marks, and Exclamation Points

Periods, question marks, and exclamation points mark the ends of statements, commands, questions, and exclamations. Periods are also used in abbreviations.

www.mhhe.com/nmhh
For information and exercises on end punctuation, go to

Editing >
End Punctuation

End Punctuation and Grammar Checkers

Computer grammar checkers will catch a few errors in the use of end punctuation, such as use of a period instead of a question mark at the end of a question. For the most part, though, you cannot rely on your grammar checker to recognize these errors. You will need to check your writing carefully for problems with end punctuation.

56a Use a period after most statements, indirect questions, polite requests, and mild commands.

STATEMENT

There are more than one thousand periods in this book.

STATEMENT CONTAINING A QUOTATION

"What is the word count?" she asked.

STATEMENT CONTAINING AN INDIRECT QUESTION

She asked me where I had gone to college.

POLITE REQUEST

Please go with me to the lecture.

MILD COMMAND

Take a vitamin every day.

56b   Use a period in abbreviations according to convention.

A period or periods are used with the following common abbreviations, which end in lowercase letters.

Mr.	Dr.	Mass.
Ms.	i.e.	Jan.
Mrs.	e.g.	

If an abbreviation is made up of capital letters, however, the periods are optional. Be consistent throughout your document.

RN (or R.N.)

MD (or M.D.)

BA (or B.A.)

PhD (or Ph.D.)

Periods are omitted in abbreviations for organizations, famous people, states in mailing addresses, and acronyms (words made up of the initial letters of their parts).

FBI	JFK	MA	NATO
CIA	LBJ	TX	NAFTA
NASA			

When in doubt, consult a dictionary. (*For more on abbreviations, see Chapter 58.*)

When an abbreviation ends a sentence, the period at the end of the abbreviation serves as the period for the sentence. If a question mark or an exclamation point ends the sentence, place it *after* the period in the abbreviation.

➤   **When he was in the seventh grade, we called him "Stinky,"**

     but now he is William Percival Abernathy, Ph.D.!

56c   Do not use a period at the end of a sentence within a sentence.

Omit the period when a sentence is contained within parentheses or quotation marks.

➤ **I rapped on Mai's door (she is usually home), but no one answered.**

➤ **"I'm not home," came the reply.**

56d Use a question mark after a direct question.

➤ **Who wrote *The Old Man and the Sea*?**

Occasionally, a question mark changes a statement into a question.

➤ **You expect me to believe a story like that?**

You can end a polite question with either a period or a question mark, but be consistent within your paper.

➤ **Will you please go with me to the lecture.**

➤ **Will you please go with me to the lecture?**

When questions follow one another in a series, each one can be followed by a question mark even if the questions are not complete sentences, as long as the meaning is understood. You begin each question in the series with a capital or a lowercase letter.

➤ **What will you contribute? Your time? Your talent? Your money?**

➤ **What will you contribute? your time? your talent? your money?**

Use a question mark in parentheses to indicate a questionable date, number, or word, but do not use it to convey an ironic meaning or to indicate that you are not certain of a fact.

➤ **Chaucer was born in 1340 (?) and lived until 1400.**

➤ **His yapping dog had recently graduated from obedience ~~(?)~~ training.**

➤ Franklin Roosevelt was elected president four (?) times.

Note: Do not use a question mark after an indirect quotation, even if the words being indirectly quoted were originally a question.

➤ He asked her if she would be at home later?.

56e Use exclamation points sparingly to convey shock, surprise, or a forceful command.

➤ Stolen! The money was stolen! Right before our eyes, somebody snatched my purse and ran off with it.

➤ Watch out for the flying glass!

Note: Using numerous exclamation points throughout a document actually weakens their force. As much as possible, try to convey emotion with your choice of words and your sentence structure instead of with an exclamation point.

➤ Jefferson and Adams both died on the same day in 1826, exactly fifty years after the signing of the Declaration of Independence!.

The fact that the sentence reports is surprising enough without the addition of an exclamation point.

Although you might use an exclamation point within parentheses (!) to convey an ironic or sarcastic meaning in your personal writing, this use is inappropriate in academic writing.

56f Place a question mark or an exclamation point within a sentence if your meaning requires it.

➤ The wait seems endless (how long has it been?), but he

will return.

➤ He has been gone so long—will he ever return?—that I have

almost forgotten his voice.

➤ "Will you wait for me?" he asked.

➤ "Never!" I answered.

(For more on inserting questions and exclamations within sentences, see Chapters 54 and 55.)

56g Do not add a comma or an additional end mark after a period, a question mark, or an exclamation point.

➤ William earned a Ph.D./

➤ Is it you who asked, "Will he be home soon?"?

➤ "It isn't true!/ " she exclaimed.

56h Make sure that the end mark concludes a complete sentence.

Punctuating a dependent clause or phrase as if it were a sentence results in a sentence fragment. Make sure that your sentence has a subject and a complete verb and does not start with a subordinating word. *(For more on sentence fragments, see Chapter 32.)*

SENTENCE FRAGMENT	Although it was clearly marked on the label.
SENTENCE FRAGMENT	Driving all over town in search of a present?

Exercise 56.1   Chapter review: End punctuation

Insert periods, question marks, and exclamation points in the following passage. Delete any unnecessary commas.

Do you realize that there is a volcano larger than Mt St Helens Mt Vesuvius Mt Etna Mauna Loa is the largest volcano on Earth, covering at least half the island of Hawaii The summit of Mauna Loa stands 56,000 feet above its base This is why Native Hawaiians named this volcano, the "Long Mountain" Mauna Loa is also one of the most active volcanoes on the planet, having erupted thirty-three times since 1843 (most people do not think of a volcano as dormant) Its last eruption occurred in 1984 Most people associate a volcanic eruption with red lava spewing from the volcano's crater, but few people realize that the lava flow, and volcanic gases are also extremely hazardous Tourists like to follow the lava to where it meets the sea, but this practice is dangerous because of the steam produced when the lava meets the water So, the next time you visit an active volcano, beware

FIGURE 56.1 Tourists watching lava from Mauna Loa flow into the sea.

CHECKLIST

Editing for Sentence Punctuation

As you revise, check your writing for proper punctuation by asking yourself these questions:

☐ Are commas used appropriately to separate or set off coordinated independent clauses; items in a series and coordinate adjectives; introductory sentence elements; nonessential sentence elements; direct quotations; and the parts of dates, addresses, titles, and numbers? (*See Chapter 51: Commas, pp. 806–29.*) Are any commas mistakenly used with sentence elements that should not be separated or set off? (*See Chapter 51: Commas, pp. 830–36.*)

☐ Are semicolons used appropriately to join independent clauses and to separate items in a series when the items contain commas? (*See Chapter 52: Semicolons, pp. 837–43.*)

☐ Are colons used appropriately after a complete sentence to introduce a list, an appositive, or a quotation; after one independent clause to introduce a second that elaborates on the first; and in business letters, ratios, and bibliographic citations? (*See Chapter 53: Colons, pp. 844–48.*)

☐ Are quotation marks used appropriately with other punctuation to identify brief direct quotations, dialogue, and the titles of short works? Are single quotation marks used appropriately to identify quotations within quotations? (*See Chapter 54: Quotation Marks, pp. 849–62.*)

☐ Are brackets and ellipses used correctly to identify elisions and interpolations within quotations? Are dashes and parentheses used appropriately to insert or highlight nonessential information within a sentence? (*See Chapter 55: Dashes, Parentheses, and Other Punctuation Marks, pp. 863–78.*)

☐ Are periods used appropriately at the end of sentences and in abbreviations? Are question marks and exclamation points used appropriately at the end of sentences and within quotations? (*See Chapter 56: End Punctuation, pp. 879–84.*)

The great twelfth century inventor al-Jazari designed many innovative, mechanical devices. This plan for a water-operated automaton documents the engineering behind one invention's design; each working part relies on the precise placement of others.

PART

11

It wasn't a matter of rewriting but simply of tightening up all the bolts.

—Marguerite Yourcenar

Mechanics
and Spelling

Mechanics and Spelling

Answer these questions to test your familiarity with the topics covered in Chapters 57–63. For each example, select the choice that best replaces the highlighted words. If none of the choices is preferable to the example, select "no change." Check your work against the answer sheet at the back of the book, and pay particular attention to the sections in the chapters that correspond to the questions you get wrong.

1. Many of the fashions of the **roaring twenties** have come back into vogue.

   a. no change

   b. Roaring twenties

   c. roaring Twenties

   d. Roaring Twenties

2. Before becoming a **mayor, Clint Eastwood acted in many Westerns** and detective movies.

   a. Mayor, Clint Eastwood acted in many Westerns

   b. Mayor, Clint Eastwood acted in many westerns

   c. mayor, Clint Eastwood acted in many westerns

   d. no change

3. Students today rarely read such literary classics as J.D. Salinger's **The Catcher In The Rye.**

   a. The Catcher in the Rye.

   b. no change

   c. The Catcher in The Rye.

   d. The Catcher In the Rye.

4. "As you simplify your life," wrote Henry David **Thoreau, "The laws of the universe** will be simpler."

   a. Thoreau, "the laws of the Universe

   b. Thoreau: "The laws of the universe

   c. no change

   d. Thoreau, "the laws of the universe

5. *The Common Sense Book of Baby and Child Care,* by **pediatrician Dr. Benjamin Spock, MD,** had a profound influence on American childcare practices.

   a. no change

   b. pediatrician Benjamin Spock, MD,

   c. pediatrician Dr. Benjamin Spock MD,

   d. pediatrician DR. Benjamin Spock, MD,

6. The study of martial arts (**e.g., kung fu, karate, judo, tae kwon do, etc.**) is popular in the United States.

   a. (for example, kung fu, karate, judo, tae kwon do, etc.)

   b. (e.g., kung fu, karate, judo, tae kwon do, and so forth)

   c. (for example, kung fu, karate, judo, and tae kwon do)

   d. no change

7. Most people know that **three is a prime number, but they may not know that 109** is also a prime number.

   a. no change

   b. three is a prime number, but they may not know that one hundred nine

   c. 3 is a prime number, but they may not know that one hundred nine

   d. 3 is a prime number, but they may not know that 109

8. The final score was **twenty to three.**

   a. no change

   b. twenty to 3.

   c. 20 to three.

   d. 20 to 3.

9. **"Charlie and the Chocolate Factory,"** by Roald Dahl, has been made into a movie.

   a. no change

   b. "Charlie And The Chocolate Factory."

   c. *Charlie and the Chocolate Factory,*

   d. *Charlie* and the *Chocolate Factory.*

10. **Homo erectus preceded Homo sapiens.**

    a. "Homo erectus" preceded "Homo sapiens."

    b. *Homo erectus* preceded *Homo sapiens.*

    c. 'Homo erectus' preceded 'Homo sapiens.'

    d. no change

11. Movies such as ***Star Wars* and *E.T. the Extra-Terrestrial*** appeal to both children and adults.

    a. no change

    b. Star Wars and E.T. the Extra-Terrestrial

    c. "Star Wars" and "E.T. the Extra-Terrestrial"

    d. 'Star Wars' and 'E.T. the Extra-Terrestrial'

889

12. Studies show that children **whose** parents read to them do better in school.

    a. who is

    b. who's

    c. who'se

    d. no change

13. Oddly, the **chief-of-staffs position** was given to a person with little experience.

    a. no change

    b. chief-of-staff position

    c. chief-of-staff's position

    d. chief's-of-staff position

14. The driver believed that the accident was caused by a malfunction in the **bus's brake system.**

    a. bus brake system.

    b. bus' brake system.

    c. no change

    d. bus'es brake system.

15. The reporter returned home after spending two years in **several war torn countries.**

    a. no change

    b. several wartorn countries.

    c. several war-torn countries.

    d. several war, torn countries.

16. The Nobel Peace Prize recipient's speech was **awe-inspiring.**

    a. no change

    b. awe inspiring.

    c. awe, inspiring.

    d. awe—inspiring.

17. Ralph Waldo Emerson's essay on **self reliance** reflects American individualism.

    a. no change

    b. self-reliance

    c. self, reliance

    d. self—reliance

18. Many soft drinks are **caffienated.**

    a. no change

    b. caffeinated

19. some people prefer **stationery** bikes to treadmills.

    a. no change

    b. stationary

20. The Sahara **Desert** is the world's largest subtropical **desert.**

    a. no change

    b. Dessert; dessert.

57 Capitalization

Many rules for the use of capital (uppercase) letters have been fixed by custom, such as the convention of beginning each sentence with a capital letter, but the rules sometimes change. As you revise your drafts, check to make sure you are using capital letters appropriately in the following types of words:

- Proper nouns (names), words derived from proper nouns, brand names, and certain abbreviations (*see 57a, p. 893*)
- People's titles (*see 57b, p. 895*)
- Names of areas and regions (*see 57c, p. 896*)
- Names of races, ethnic groups, and sacred things (*see 57d, p. 896*)
- Titles of works of literature, art, and music; documents; and courses (*see 57e, p. 897*)
- The first word of a sentence (*see 57f, p. 898*)
- The first word of a quotation (*see 57g, p. 898*)
- The first word of an independent clause after a colon (*see 57h, p. 899*)

Capitalization and Grammar Checkers

Grammar checkers will flag words that should be capitalized or lowercased by convention, but they will not flag proper nouns unless the noun is stored in the program's dictionary, and they will not necessarily point out a noun that can be either proper or common, depending on the context. For example, a grammar checker flagged the capitalization error in the first sentence (should be *North America*) but not the second (should be *Buffalo*):

Maria is going to study the mammals of north America.

The Darwin Martin House, designed by Frank Lloyd Wright, is located in buffalo, New York.

Editing tip: The abbreviation *cap* indicates that a letter should be capitalized. (Professional editors and proofreaders also add three lines under the letter to mark it for capitalization.) The abbreviation *lc* indicates that a letter should be lowercased rather than capitalized. (Professional editors and proofreaders also add a slash mark through the letter to mark it as lowercase.)

57a Capitalize proper nouns (names), words derived from them, brand names, certain abbreviations, and call letters.

www.mhhe.com/
nmhh
For information
and exercises on
capitalization, go to

Editing >
Capitalization

Proper nouns are the names of specific people, places, or things, names that set off the individual from the group, such as the name *Jane* instead of the common noun *person.* Capitalize proper nouns, words derived from proper nouns, brand names, abbreviations of capitalized words (including *acronyms,* abbreviations that form words), and the call letters of radio and television stations.

PROPER NOUNS	Ronald Reagan, the Sears Tower, the Internet
WORDS DERIVED FROM PROPER NOUNS	Reaganomics, Siamese cat, *but* french fries, simonize
BRAND NAMES	Apple Computer, Kleenex
ABBREVIATIONS AND ACRONYMS	FBI (government agency), A&E (cable television network), NATO (international alliance)
CALL LETTERS	WNBC (television), WMMR (radio)

TYPES and EXAMPLES of PROPER and COMMON NOUNS

People: John F. Kennedy, Ruth Bader Ginsburg, Albert Einstein
Nationalities, ethnic groups, and languages: English, Swiss, African Americans, Arabs, Chinese, Turkish
Places: the United States of America, Tennessee, the Irunia Restaurant, the Great Lakes, *but* my state, the lake

(continued)

893

TYPES and EXAMPLES of
PROPER and COMMON NOUNS (continued)

Organizations and institutions: Phi Beta Kappa, Republican Party (Republicans), Department of Defense, Cumberland College, the North Carolina Tarheels, *but* the department, this college, my hockey team

Religious bodies, books, and figures: Jews, Christians, Baptists, Hindus, Roman Catholic Church, the Bible, the Koran *or* Qur'an, the Torah, God, Holy Spirit, Allah, *but* a Greek goddess, a biblical reference

Scientific names and terms: *Homo sapiens, H. sapiens, Acer rubrum, A. rubrum,* Addison's disease, Cenozoic era, Newton's first law, *but* the law of gravity

Names of planets, stars, and other astronomical bodies: Earth (as a planet) *but otherwise* the earth, Mercury, Polaris *or* the North Star, Whirlpool Galaxy, *but* a star, that galaxy, the solar system

Computer terms: the Internet, the World Wide Web *or* the Web, *but* search engine, a network, my browser

Days, months, and holidays: Monday, Veterans Day, August, the Fourth of July, *but* yesterday, spring and summer, the winter term

Historical events, movements, periods, and documents: World War II, Impressionism, the Renaissance, the Jazz Age, the Declaration of Independence, the Constitution of the United States, *but* the last war, a golden age, the twentieth century, the amendment

Academic courses and subjects: English 101, Psychology 221, a course in Italian, *but* a physics course, my art history class

Note: Although holidays and the names of months and days of the week are capitalized, seasons, such as summer, are not. Neither are the days of the month when they are spelled out.

➤ Why would *Valentine's Day,* the day representing love and romance, fall in *winter*—and in the coldest month of the year at that?

➤ She will be available to meet with you on Sunday, the *seventh* of March.

CHARTING the TERRITORY

Capitalization Rules in the Disciplines

Just as different disciplines have their own guidelines for capitalizing elements in a works-cited or reference list, they also have guidelines for capitalizing specialized vocabulary. In scientific names, for example, the genus is capitalized, but the species is not: *Homo sapiens.* The names of higher divisions—phylum, class, order, family—are capitalized: *Felidae.* In musical chord notation, a capital *M* stands for "major"; a lowercase *m* stands for "minor." When you are reading primary sources in a discipline, observe how specialized terminology is treated, and consult a discipline-specific style guide when in doubt.

57b Capitalize a person's title when it appears before a proper name but not when it is used alone.

Capitalize titles when they come before a proper name, but do not capitalize them when they appear alone or after the name.

TITLE USED BEFORE A NAME

Every Sunday, *Aunt Lou* tells fantastic stories.

Everyone knew that *Governor Grover Cleveland* of New York was the most likely candidate for the Democratic nomination.

TITLE USED ALONE

My *aunt* is arriving this afternoon.

TITLE USED AFTER A NAME

The most likely candidate for the Democratic nomination was Grover Cleveland, *governor* of New York.

Exceptions: If the name for a family relationship is used alone (without a possessive such as *my* before it), it should be capitalized.

➤ I saw *Father* **infrequently during the summer months.**

Most writers do not capitalize the title *president* unless they are referring to the President of the United States: "The *president* of this university has seventeen honorary degrees." Usage varies, but be consistent. If you write "the President of the University," you should also write "the Chair of the History Department."

For MULTILINGUAL STUDENTS

Capitalizing the Pronoun I

Unlike other languages, English requires you to capitalize the first person singular pronoun (*I*). All other pronouns are lowercase, unless they start a sentence or are part of the title of a work.

➤ When *I* get home, *I* will call my doctor for the test results and let you know what she says.

57c   Capitalize names of areas and regions.

Names of geographical regions are generally capitalized if they are well established, like *the Midwest* and *Central Europe*. Names of directions, as in the sentence *Turn south,* are not capitalized.

> **CORRECT**   *East* meets *West* at the summit.

> **CORRECT**   You will need to go *west* on Sunset Road.

Note: The word *western,* when used as a general direction or the name of a genre, is not capitalized. It is capitalized when it is part of the name of a specific region.

                                           western
➤ The river flows through the ~~Western~~ part of the state.

   western
➤ The ~~Western~~ *High Noon* is one of my favorite movies.

    Western
➤ I visited ~~western~~ Europe last year.

57d   Follow standard practice for capitalizing names of races, ethnic groups, and sacred things.

The words *black* and *white* are usually not capitalized when they are used to refer to members of racial groups because they are adjectives that substitute for the implied common nouns *black person* and *white person*. However, names of ethnic groups and races are capitalized: *African Americans, Italians, Asians, Caucasians.*

> *Note:* In accordance with current APA guidelines, most social scientists capitalize the terms *Black* and *White,* treating them as proper nouns.

Many religious terms, such as *sacrament, altar,* and *rabbi,* are not capitalized. The word *Bible* is capitalized (though *biblical* is not), but it is never capitalized when it is used as a metaphor for an essential book.

➤ **His book *Winning at Stud Poker* used to be the *bible* of gamblers.**

57e Capitalize titles of works of literature, works of art, musical compositions, documents, and courses.

Capitalize the first and last word of a title and subtitle. Capitalize all the words within the title or subtitle *except* articles (*a, an,* and *the*), the *to* in infinitives, prepositions, and coordinating conjunctions. (However, if you are using APA style, capitalize any word that has four or more letters.) Capitalize all words in a hyphenated word unless the additional word is a preposition (*Hands-on*), a conjunction or an article (*Peaches-and-Cream, Dime-a-Dozen*), or a second number (*Twenty-five*). Capitalize the word that follows a colon or semicolon in a title.

Book: *Two Years before the Mast*

Play or film: *The Taming of the Shrew*

Building: the Eiffel Tower

Ship or aircraft: the *Titanic* or the *Concorde*

Painting: the *Mona Lisa*

Article or essay: "On Old Age"

Poem: "Ode on a Grecian Urn"

Music: "The Star-Spangled Banner"

Document: the Bill of Rights

Course: Economics 206: Macro-Economic Analysis

TextConnex

Emphasis in E-Mail

When you are writing an e-mail message, you may be tempted to use all capital letters for emphasis when italics are not available. Although capital letters are sometimes used this way in print documents, they are not always welcome in online chat rooms and electronic mailing list postings, where participants may feel that they are equivalent to shouting. Also, strings of words or sentences in capital letters can be difficult to read. If you want to emphasize a word or phrase in an online communication, put an asterisk before and after it instead.

➤ **I *totally* disagree with what you just wrote.**

57f Capitalize the first word of a sentence.

A capital letter is used to signal the beginning of a new sentence.

➤ **Robots reduce human error, so they produce uniform products.**

Sentences in parentheses also begin with a capital letter unless they are embedded within another sentence.

➤ **Although the week began with the news that he was hit by a car, by Thursday we knew he was going to be all right. (It was a terrible way to begin the week, though.)**

➤ **Although the week began with the news that he was hit by a car (it was a terrible way to begin the week), by Thursday we knew he was going to be all right.**

57g Capitalize the first word of a quoted sentence but not the first word of an indirect quotation.

➤ **She cried, "Help!"**

➤ **He said that jazz was one of America's major art forms.**

The first word of a quotation from a printed source is capitalized if the quotation is introduced with a phrase such as *she notes* or *he concludes.*

➤ **Jim, the narrator of *My Ántonia,* concludes, "Whatever we had missed, we possessed together the precious, the incommunicable past" (324).**

When a quotation from a printed source is treated as an element in your sentence, not a sentence on its own, the first word is not capitalized.

➤ **Jim took comfort in sharing with Ántonia "the precious, the incommunicable past" (324).**

If you need to change the first letter of a quotation to fit your sentence, enclose the letter in brackets.

➤ **The lawyer noted that "[t]he man seen leaving the area after the blast was not the same height as the defendant."**

If you interrupt the sentence you are quoting with an expression such as *he said,* the first word of the rest of the quotation should not be capitalized.

➤ **"When I come home an hour later," she explained, "the trains are usually less crowded."**

Many authors in earlier centuries and some writers today—especially poets—use capital letters in obsolete or eccentric ways. When quoting a text directly, reproduce the capitalization used in the original source, whether or not it is correct by today's standards.

➤ **Blake's marginalia include the following comment: "Paine is either a Devil or an Inspired Man" (603).**

57h Capitalizing the first word of an independent clause after a colon or in a series of short questions is optional.

If the word group that follows a colon is not a complete sentence, do not capitalize it. If it is a complete sentence, you can capitalize it or not, but be consistent throughout your document.

➤ **The question is serious: do you think the peace process has a chance?**

or

➤ **The question is serious: Do you think the peace process has a chance?**

In a series of one- or two-word questions that follow a complete sentence, you can capitalize the first word of each question or not, as long as you are consistent.

➤ **When are you available? Next week? Next month?**

or

➤ **When are you available? next week? next month?**

Note, however, that incomplete questions like these are not usually appropriate in academic writing.

57i Capitalize the first word of each item in a formal outline.

Capitalize the first word of each item in an outline, whether or not the item is a complete sentence. If the items are complete sentences, remember to add a period at the end of each one.

    I. Evidence of the last Ice Age in New England and the Middle Atlantic States
       A. Glacial deposits in Cape Cod
       B. Terminal moraines on Long Island
       C. The Finger Lakes in central New York

57j Be consistent about the capitalization of the first word of items in numbered lists.

Lists can either run in with your text or be displayed. In either case, you are required to capitalize the first word of each item if the items are complete sentences. In run-in lists, do not capitalize the first letter of items in a list if they are not sentences. In displayed lists, capital letters are optional for items that are not sentences, but you need to be consistent. If the lead-in to the list is a complete sentence, it can end with a colon. If it is not, you should incorporate the list into your sentence.

RUN-IN LIST WITH PHRASES

There are three ways to register: (1) by mail, (2) by telephone, and (3) in person on the day classes begin.

or

The three ways to register are (1) by mail, (2) by telephone, and (3) in person on the day classes begin.

DISPLAYED LIST WITH PHRASES

There are three ways to register:

1. By mail	*or*	1. by mail
2. By telephone		2. by telephone
3. In person on the day classes begin		3. in person on the day classes begin

It is preferable to introduce a displayed list with a complete sentence ending in a colon. Items in a displayed list do not need to end in periods unless they are complete sentences.

Note that the items in each list are parallel grammatically. (*For more on parallel structure, see Chapter 42: Faulty Parallelism, pp. 710–19.*)

57k Capitalize the first word in the greeting and closing of a letter.

Dear Mr. Morrison:

Sincerely,

Yours truly,

Exercise 57.1   Chapter review: Capitalization

Edit the following passage, changing letters to capital or lowercase as necessary.

Perhaps the most notable writer of the 1920s is F. Scott Fitzgerald. He was born on September 24, 1896, in St. Paul, Minnesota, to Edward Fitzgerald and Mary "mollie" McQuillan, who were both members of the catholic church. After attending Princeton university and embarking on a career as a writer, Fitzgerald married southern belle Zelda Sayre from Montgomery, Alabama. Together, he and his Wife lived the celebrated life of the roaring twenties and the jazz age.

Fitzgerald wrote numerous short stories as well as four novels, *This Side of Paradise, The Beautiful and Damned, The Great Gatsby,* and *Tender is the night. The Great Gatsby,* which he finished in the Winter of 1924 and published in 1925, is considered Fitzgerald's most brilliant and critically acclaimed work. readers who have read this novel will remember the opening words spoken by Nick Carraway, the narrator in the story: "in my younger and more vulnerable years my father gave me some advice that i've been turning over in my mind ever since. 'Whenever you feel like criticizing anyone,' he told me, 'Just remember that all the people in this world haven't had the advantages that you've had.'"

FIGURE 57.1 **The cover of the first edition of *The Great Gatsby.***

58 Abbreviations and Symbols

Abbreviations and symbols are used in the body of scientific and technical reports. Abbreviations are also used in lists of works cited or references for all types of academic papers. However, in nontechnical writing you should avoid using abbreviations or symbols, except in the situations explained in this chapter.

www.mhhe.com/
nmhh
For information
and exercises on
abbreviations, go to

Editing >
Abbreviations

Editing tip: The abbreviation *abbr* indicates a problem with the use of abbreviations.

Abbreviations and Grammar Checkers

Computer grammar or spelling checkers may flag an abbreviation, but they generally can not tell you if your use of it is acceptable or consistent within a piece of writing.

58a Abbreviate familiar titles that precede or follow a person's name.

Some abbreviations appear before a person's name (*Mr., Mrs., Dr.*) and some follow a proper name (*Jr., Sr., MD, Esq., PhD*). Abbreviations that follow a person's name often indicate academic or professional degrees or honors.

Punctuation tips: Periods are used with most abbreviations that end in lowercase letters: *Mr., Ms., Jr.* If the abbreviation is made up of capital letters, however, the periods are optional: *RN* or *R.N.; PhD* or *Ph.D.; MD* or *M.D.* In most cases, when an abbreviation follows a person's name, a comma is placed between the name and the abbreviation. In the case of *Jr.,* however, the comma between the name and abbreviation is optional (*see Chapter 51: Commas, p. 828*).

TITLES BEFORE NAMES	Mrs. Jean Bascom
	Dr. Epstein
TITLES AFTER NAMES	Robert Robinson, Jr.
	Elaine Less, CPA, LLD

Do not use two abbreviations that represent the same thing: *Dr. Peter Joyce, MD.* Use either *Dr. Peter Joyce* or *Peter Joyce, MD.*
Spell out titles used without proper names.

doctor.
➤ **Mr. Carew asked if she had seen the d̶r̶.**
                                          ^

Academic titles such as *PhD* can appear by themselves, however.

➤ **Elena earned her PhD in biochemistry.**

For MULTILINGUAL STUDENTS

Reading Abbreviations in Standard American English

Learning how to read abbreviations in standard American English can be puzzling—to native speakers as well as multilingual students—because no universal logic governs the way they are pronounced. In general, however, they fall into five types.

1. **Acronyms**—abbreviations composed of the initial letters of words or syllables—**that are read as individual letters,** such as *ATM* (*automated teller machine*), *ID* (*identification*), *IBM* (*International Business Machines*), and *UN* (*United Nations*)
2. **Acronyms that are read as words,** such as NATO (*North Atlantic Treaty Organization*) and *AIDS* (*acquired immunodeficiency syndrome*)
3. **Acronyms that are sometimes read as the phrases they represent and sometimes as individual letters,** such as *FYI* (*for your information*) and *AKA* (*also known as*)
4. **Abbreviations that are consistently read as full words,** such as *Dr.* or *Mr.*
5. **Clippings**—words used in a shortened form, usually informally—such as *lab* (for *laboratory*), *exam* (for *examination*), and *memo* (for *memorandum*)

To avoid confusion, identify an abbreviation for your audience word by word the first time you use it. For a list of common abbreviations, consult your English dictionary.

58b Use abbreviations only when you know your readers will understand them.

If you use a technical term or the name of an organization, a country, or a government agency in a report, you may abbreviate it as long as your readers are likely to be familiar with the abbreviation.

FAMILIAR
ABBREVIATION
The EPA has had a lasting impact on the air quality in this country.

UNFAMILIAR
ABBREVIATION
After you have completed them, take these
the Human Resources and Education Center.
forms to ~~HREC.~~
                        ^

Write out an unfamiliar term or name the first time you use it, and give the abbreviation in parentheses.

➤ **The Student Nonviolent Coordinating Committee (SNCC)**

was far to the left of other civil rights organizations, and

its leaders often mocked the "conservatism" of Dr. Martin

Luther King, Jr. SNCC quickly burned itself out and

disappeared.

> *Note:* In the body of a paper, you can use *U.S.* as an adjective (*U.S. Constitution*) but not as a noun (*I grew up outside of the United States*).

> *Punctuation tip:* Periods are omitted in abbreviations for organizations, certain famous people, states in mailing addresses, and acronyms (words made up of initials): *FBI, CIA, APA, JFK, LBJ, TX, NASA, NATO, NAFTA, WWII.* The periods in the abbreviations for the United States of America are optional: *U.S.A. (U.S.) or USA (US).*

TEXTCONNEX

Digital Age Abbreviations and Acronyms

CD	compact disc
CD-ROM	compact disc read-only memory
DVD	digital videodisc
FTP	file transfer protocol
HTML	hypertext markup language
http	Hypertext transfer protocol
KB	kilobyte
MB	megabyte
MOO	multiuser domain, object-oriented
URL	uniform resource locator
www	World Wide Web

58c Abbreviate words typically used with times, dates, and numerals, as well as units of measurement in charts and graphs.

Abbreviations or symbols associated with numbers should be used only when accompanying a number: *3 p.m.*, not *in the p.m.*; *$500,* not *How many $ do you have?* The abbreviation *B.C.* ("before Christ") follows a date; *A.D.* ("in the year of our Lord") precedes the date. The alternative abbreviations *B.C.E.* ("before the Common Era") and *C.E.* ("Common Era") can be used instead of *B.C.* or *A.D.*, respectively.

> 6:00 p.m. *or* 6:00 P.M. *or* 6:00 PM
>
> 9:45 a.m. *or* 9:45 A.M. *or* 9:45 AM
>
> 498 B.C. *or* 498 B.C.E. *or* 498 BCE
>
> A.D. 275 *or* 275 C.E. *or* 275 CE
>
> 6,000 rpm
>
> 271 cm

Note: Be consistent. If you use *a.m.* in one sentence, do not switch to *A.M.* in the next sentence.

In charts and graphs, abbreviations and symbols such as = for *equals,* *in.* for *inches,* % for *percent,* and *$* with numbers are acceptable because they save space.

58d Use abbreviations in mailing addresses.

Abbreviations such as *St.*, *Ave.*, and *Apt.* are used in mailing addresses on correspondence. The following list gives the postal abbreviations for states and territories in the United States and provinces and territories in Canada.

United States

AK	Alaska	MN	Minnesota	VA	Virginia
AL	Alabama	MO	Missouri	VT	Vermont
AR	Arkansas	MS	Mississippi	WA	Washington
AZ	Arizona	MT	Montana	WI	Wisconsin
CA	California	NC	North Carolina	WV	West Virginia
CO	Colorado	ND	North Dakota	WY	Wyoming
CT	Connecticut	NE	Nebraska		
DC	District of Columbia	NH	New Hampshire		

Canada

DE	Delaware	NJ	New Jersey	AB	Alberta
FL	Florida	NM	New Mexico	BC	British Columbia
GA	Georgia	NV	Nevada	MB	Manitoba
GU	Guam	NY	New York	NB	New Brunswick
HI	Hawaii	OH	Ohio	NL	Newfoundland and Labrador
IA	Iowa	OK	Oklahoma	NS	Nova Scotia
ID	Idaho	OR	Oregon	NT	Northwest Territories
IL	Illinois	PA	Pennsylvania	NU	Nunavut
IN	Indiana	PR	Puerto Rico	ON	Ontario
KS	Kansas	RI	Rhode Island	PE	Prince Edward Island
KY	Kentucky	SC	South Carolina	QC	Québec
LA	Louisiana	SD	South Dakota	SK	Saskatchewan
MA	Massachusetts	TN	Tennessee	YT	Yukon Territory
MD	Maryland	TX	Texas		
ME	Maine	UT	Utah		
MI	Michigan				

58e Become familiar with abbreviations used in research citations.

Depending on the documentation style they are using, writers of research papers may use the following abbreviations in the list of works cited or references at the end of the paper or in explanatory notes. Refer to Chapters 24–26 or to a discipline-specific style manual (*see p. 367 for a list*) for guidelines about using abbreviations for this purpose.

Names

anon.	anonymous	dir.	director, directed by
ed., eds.	editor(s), edited by, edition	illus.	illustrator, illustrated by
gen. ed.	general editor	trans.	translator, translated by
comp.	compiler, compiled by		

Parts of Publications

app.	appendix	introd.	introduction
ch.	chapter	l., ll.	line, lines
col., cols.	column, columns	n, nn	note, notes
cont.	contents	no.	number
div.	division	n. pag.	no pagination
fig.	figure	p., pp.	page, pages
ff.	following (pages or lines)	par., pars.	paragraph, paragraphs
fwd.	foreword	pref.	preface
illus.	illustration	pt.	part
		sec., secs.	section, sections

Types of Publications

bk.	book	rev.	revision, revised, *or* review, reviewed
bull.	bulletin		
diss.	dissertation	rept.	reprint *or* report
ed.	edition	ser.	series
jour.	journal	supp.	supplement
mag.	magazine	vol., vols.	volume, volumes
ms., mss.	manuscript, manuscripts		

Months of Publication

Jan.	January	Sept.	September
Feb.	February	Oct.	October
Mar.	March	Nov.	November
Apr.	April	Dec.	December
Aug.	August		

Publishers

P	Press	Soc.	Society
U	University	n.p.	no place of publication or no publisher
UP	University Press		
GPO	Government Printing Office		

Other Abbreviations

b.	born	esp.	especially
©	copyright	n.d.	no date of publication
c. *or* ca.	about (*circa*)	v. *or* vs.	versus
d.	died		

58f Avoid Latin abbreviations in formal writing.

Latin abbreviations can be used in notes or works-cited lists, but in formal writing it is usually a good idea to avoid even common Latin abbreviations (*e.g., et al., etc.,* and *i.e.*). Instead of *e.g.,* use *such as* or *for example.*

cf.	compare (*confer*)	i.e.	that is (*id est*)
e.g.	for example, such as (*exempli gratia*)	N.B.	note well (*nota bene*)
		viz.	namely (*videlicet*)
et al.	and others (*et alii*)		
etc.	and so forth, and so on (*et cetera*)		

58g Avoid inappropriate abbreviations and symbols.

Days of the week (*Sat.*), places (*TX* or *Tex.*), the word *company* (*Co.*), people's names (*Wm.*), disciplines and professions (*econ.*), parts of speech (*v.*), parts of written works (*ch., p.*), symbols (@), and units of measurement (*lb.*) are all spelled out in formal writing.

➤ The *environmental* (not *env.*) engineers from the Paramus Water *Company* (not *Co.*) are arriving in *New York City* (not *NYC*) this *Thursday* (not *Thurs.*) to correct the problems in the *physical education* (not *phys. ed.*) building in time for *Christmas* (not *Xmas*).

Exceptions: If an abbreviation such as *Inc., Co.,* or *Corp.* is part of a company's official name, then it can be included in formal writing: *Time Inc. announced these changes in late December.* The ampersand symbol (&) can also be used but only if it is part of an official name: *Church & Dwight.*

Exercise 58.1 Chapter review: Abbreviations and symbols

Spell out any inappropriate abbreviations in this passage of nontechnical writing.

In today's digital-savvy world, a person who has never used a computer with access to the WWW and a Motion Pictures Experts Group Layer 3 (MP3) player would be surprised to find that anyone can download and groove to the sounds of "Nights in White Satin" by the 1960s rock band the Moody Blues at 3 AM without ever having to have spent $ for the album *Days of Future Past.* However, music listeners should understand that such file sharing, commonly known as "file swapping," is illegal and surrounded by controversy. The Recording Industry Association of America (RIAA), which represents the U.S. recording industry, has taken aggressive legal action against such acts of online piracy, etc. E.g., in a landmark case in 2004, U.S. District Judge Denny Chin ruled that ISPs must identify those subscribers who share music online, at least in the states of NY, NJ, and CT. As the nature of music recordings changes with the proliferation of digital music services & file formats, this controversy is far from being resolved, at least not this yr.

59 Numbers

Numbers appear in all types of academic writing but they are handled differently in a nontechnical context than in a technical context. Academic writing in the humanities is usually nontechnical; academic writing in the sciences and in business is often technical.

Editing tip: The abbreviation *num* indicates a problem with the way a number is expressed in a sentence. (Professional editors and proofreaders sometimes circle a number that should be spelled out and write *sp* in the margin.)

59a In nontechnical writing, spell out numbers up to one hundred and round numbers greater than one hundred.

www.mhhe.com/
nmhh
For information
and exercises on
numbers, go to
Editing > Numbers

➤ The principal announced that *twenty-five* students failed the exam, but more than *two hundred* passed.

When you are using a great many numbers or when spelling out a number would take more than two words, use numerals.

➤ This regulation affects nearly *10,500* taxpayers, substantially more than the *200* originally projected. Of those affected, *2,325* filled out the papers incorrectly and another *743* called the office for help.

Round numbers larger than one million are expressed in numerals and words: *8 million, 2.4 trillion.*

Use all numerals rather than mixing numerals and spelled-out words for the same type of item in a passage.

➤ We wrote to 130 people but only ~~sixteen~~ 16 responded.

> *Exception:* When two numbers appear together, spell out one
> and use numerals for the other: *two 20-pound bags.*

When you are writing about more than one type of item, you can spell
out numbers for one type and use numerals for the other, as long as
you are consistent.

➤ The two football teams battled to a 28-28 tie, so the game
   went into overtime. The Raptors won with a 3-point field
   goal and then went on to defeat the other three teams
   in the league.

> *Punctuation tip:* Use a hyphen with two-word numbers from
> twenty-one through ninety-nine, whether they appear alone
> or within a larger number: *fifty-six, one hundred twenty-eight.*
> A hyphen also appears in two-word fractions (*one-third, five-
> eighths*) and in compound words made up of a spelled-out
> number or numeral and another word (*forty-hour work week,
> 5-page paper*).

59b   In technical and business writing, use numerals for
exact measurements and all numbers greater than ten.

➤ The endosperm halves were placed in each of 14 small glass
   test tubes.

➤ A solution with a GA_3 concentration ranging from 0 g/ml to
   10^5 g/ml was added to each test tube.

➤ With its $1.9 trillion economy, Germany has an important
   trade role to play.

59c   Always spell out a number that begins a sentence.

If a numeral begins a sentence, spell out the numeral or reword the
sentence.

   Twenty-five
➤ ~~25~~ children are in each elementary class.
   ^

   Each elementary class has
912 ➤ 25 children, ~~are in each elementary class.~~
   ^   ^

Reword sentences that start with numbers to avoid mixing numerals and spelled-out numbers for the same type of quantities.

➤ *Boarding the vessel were 22*
~~Twenty-two~~ men and 300 women. ~~boarded the vessel.~~

59d Use numerals for dates, times of day, addresses, and similar kinds of conventional quantitative information.

Dates: October 9, 2002; 1558–1603; A.D. 1066 (*or* AD 1066); *but* October ninth, May first

Time of day: 6 A.M. (*or* AM *or* a.m.); but a quarter past eight in the evening; three o'clock in the morning

Addresses: 21 Meadow Road, Apt. 6J, Grand Island, NY 14072

Percentages: 73 percent; 73%

Fractions and decimals: 21.84; 0.05; 6½; *but* two-thirds (*not* 2-thirds); a fourth

Measurements: 100 miles per hour (*or* 100 mph); 9 kilograms (*or* 9 kg); 38° F; 15° Celsius; 3 tablespoons; 4 liters (*or* 4 l); 18 inches (*or* 18 in.)

Volume, chapter, page: volume 4 (*or* Volume 4); chapter 8 (or Chapter 8); page 44 (or p. 44)

Scenes, lines in a play: *Hamlet,* act 2, scene 1, lines 77–84

Scores and statistics: 0 to 3; 98–92; an average age of 35

Amounts of money: 10¢ (*or* 10 cents); $125, $2.25, $2.8 million (*or* $2,800,000)

Serial or identification numbers: batch number 4875; 1520 on the AM dial

Telephone numbers: (716) 555-2174

Note: In nontechnical writing, spell out the names of units of measurement (*inches, liters*) in text. You can use abbreviations (*in., l*) and symbols (%) in charts and graphs to save space.

Numbers and Grammar Checkers

Computer grammar checkers cannot help you decide if a number should be expressed in figures or spelled out. You need to learn and apply the rules for numbers of the discipline in which you are working.

For MULTILINGUAL STUDENTS

Dates and Decimals

In American English, the day usually follows the month in dates: *May 9, 2005; 5/9/05*. Decimals are preceded by a period (*one-tenth = 0.1*), and commas are used within whole numbers longer than four numerals (*twenty-two thousand three = 22,003*). In four-digit numbers, the comma is optional: *4,010* or *4010*.

Exercise 59.1   Chapter review: Numbers

Edit the sentences that follow to correct errors in the use of numbers. Some sentences are correct; circle their numbers.

EXAMPLE   I have ~~five hundred forty-six dollars~~ in my

$546

bank account.

1. The soccer team raised one thousand sixty seven dollars by selling entertainment booklets filled with coupons, discounts, and special promotions.
2. 55% of the participants in the sociology student's survey reported that they would lie to a professor in order to have a late assignment accepted.
3. In one year alone, 115 employees at the company objected to their performance appraisals, but only twenty-four filed formal complaints.
4. When preparing a professional letter, set the margins at 1 inch.
5. Eighty-five applicants hoped to win the four-year scholarship, but only one person was awarded full tuition and living expenses.
6. Four out of 5 children who enter preschool in Upper East County already know the alphabet.
7. The motorcycle accident occurred at a half past 4 in the morning on the interstate highway, but paramedics did not arrive until six thirty AM.
8. The horticulturist at the nursery raises more than 200 varieties of orchids.

60 Italics (Underlining)

To set off certain words and phrases, printers have traditionally used *italics,* a typeface in which the characters slant to the right. Now any word-processing program can produce italics. If italics are not available, however, you can underline words that would be type-set in italics. Your instructor may prefer that you use underlining rather than italics, especially if you are following the MLA style of documentation (*see Chapter 24: MLA Documentation Style, pp. 374–426*).

www.mhhe.com/
nmhh
For information
and exercises on
italics, go to
Editing > Italics

➤ **Tom Hanks gives one of his best performances in *Saving Private Ryan.***

➤ **Tom Hanks gives one of his best performances in <u>Saving Private Ryan.</u>**

Editing tip: The abbreviation *ital* indicates that italics are needed. (Professional editors and proofreaders also mark words to be italicized by underlining them.) The abbreviation *rom,* which stands for roman (or regular) type, indicates that an italicized word or words should not be italicized. (Professional editors and proofreaders also circle words to be changed from italics to roman.)

Italics and Grammar Checkers

Computer grammar checkers cannot help you decide if you have used italics or underlining appropriately. You will need to learn how to apply to your own work the rules found in this chapter or required by the discipline in which you are working.

TEXTCONNEX

Italics and Underlining

Depending on the software you are using, italics or underlining may not be available for your e-mail messages. To indicate underlining, put an underscore mark or an asterisk before and after what you would italicize or underline in a manuscript: *Tom Hanks gives one of his best performances in _Saving Private Ryan_.*

To create Web sites, many people use hypertext markup language (HTML). In HTML, underlining indicates a hypertext link. If your work is going to be posted on the World Wide Web, use italics for titles instead of underlining to avoid confusion.

60a Italicize (underline) titles of lengthy works or separate publications.

Italicize (or underline) titles of long works or works that are not part of a larger publication. The box on the next page provides a guide.

In titles of lengthy works, *a, an,* or *the* is capitalized and italicized (underlined) if it is the first word, but *the* is not treated as part of the title in names of newspapers and periodicals in MLA or Chicago style: the *New York Times.* If you are following APA or CSE style, however, you should treat *the* as part of the title.

Court cases may also be italicized or underlined, but legal documents are not.

➤ In *Brown v. Board of Education of Topeka* **(1954), the U.S. Supreme Court ruled that segregation in public schools is unconstitutional.**

➤ **He obtained a writ of habeas corpus.**

Do not italicize or underline punctuation marks that follow a title unless they are part of the title:

➤ **I finally finished reading *Moby Dick*!**

Exceptions: Do not use italics or underlining when referring to the Bible and other sacred books.

WORKS THAT SHOULD BE ITALICIZED (or UNDERLINED)

Books (including textbooks)
The Color of Water
The Art of Public Speaking

Magazines and journals
Texas Monthly
College English

Newspapers
Chicago Tribune

Comic strips
Dilbert

Plays, films, and television series
Death of a Salesman
On the Waterfront
The American Experience

Long musical compositions
Beethoven's *Pastoral Symphony* (*but* Beethoven's Symphony no. 6—the title consists of the musical form, a number, and/or a key)

Choreographic works
Balanchine's *Jewels*

Artworks
Edward Hopper's *Nighthawks*

Web sites
The Motley Fool

Software
Microsoft PowerPoint

Long poems
Odyssey

Pamphlets
Gorges: A Guide to the Geology of the Ithaca Area

Quotation marks are used for the titles of short works, including essays, newspaper and magazine articles and columns, short stories, and short poems. Quotation marks are also used for the titles of unpublished works when they are referred to within texts, including student papers, theses, and dissertations. (*See Chapter 54, p. 856, for more on quotation marks with titles.*)

60b Italicize (underline) the names of ships, trains, aircraft, and spaceships.

Italicize the name of a specific ship, aircraft, or spaceship, but do not italicize any abbreviations used with the name, such as HMS or SS. Model names and numbers (such as Boeing 747) are not italicized.

Queen Mary 2   *Orient Express*   *Spirit of St. Louis*   *Apollo 11*

60c Italicize (underline) foreign terms.

➤ **In the Paris airport, we recognized the familiar no smoking sign: *Défense de fumer.***

Many foreign words have become so common in English that everyone accepts them as part of the language. Terms such as rigor mortis, pasta, and sombrero, for example, do not require italics or underlining.

60d Italicize (underline) scientific names.

The scientific (Latin) names of organisms, consisting of the genus and species, are always italicized.

➤ **Most chicks are infected with *Cryptosporidium baileyi*, a parasite typical of young animals.**

> *Note:* Although the whole name is italicized, only the genus part of the name is capitalized.

60e Italicize (underline) words, letters, and numbers referred to as themselves.

For clarity, italicize words or phrases used as words rather than for the meaning they convey. (You may also use quotation marks for this purpose.)

➤ **The term *romantic* does not mean the same thing to the Shelley scholar as it does to the fan of Danielle Steele's novels.**

Letters and numbers used alone should also be italicized.

➤ **The word *bookkeeper* has three sets of double letters: double *o*, double *k*, and double *e*.**

➤ **Add a *3* to that column.**

60f Use italics (underlining) sparingly for emphasis.

Sometimes writers are tempted to italicize words to show the kind of emphasis they would give the word in speaking. An occasional word in italics helps you make a point. Too much emphasis, however, may mean no emphasis at all.

WEAK   You don't *mean* that your *teacher* told the whole *class* that *he* did not know the answer *himself*?

REVISED   Your teacher admitted that he did not know the answer? That is amazing.

Note: If you add italics or underlining to a quotation, indicate the change in parentheses following the quotation.

➤ **Instead of promising that no harm will come to us, Blake only assures us that we "need not *fear* harm" (emphasis added).**

Exercise 60.1   Chapter review: Italics

Edit the following passage, underlining the words that should be italicized and circling the italicized words that should be roman.

Today, thousands of people in the United States practice *yoga* for its physical, spiritual, and mental benefits. The word *yoga,* originating from the Sanskrit root yuj, means the union of the body, spirit, and mind. Although there are many styles of *yoga,* people who want a gentle introduction to *yoga* should practice Iyengar yoga, a style developed by B.K.S. Iyengar of India, which uses props such as blocks, belts, and pillows to help the body find alignment in asanas (poses) and prana-yama (breathing). Those people who want to learn more about Iyengar yoga are encouraged to read the following books

919

written by the master himself: *Light on Yoga, Light on Prana- yama,* The *Art of Yoga,* The *Tree of Yoga,* and *Light on the Yoga Sutras of Patanjali.* Those who want to learn about the general benefits of *yoga* can find numerous articles, such as "*Yoga and Weight Loss,*" by doing a general online search. All forms of *yoga* promise the *diligent* and *faithful* practitioner increased *strength, flexibility,* and *balance.*

FIGURE 60.1 **A yoga class.**

61 Apostrophes

Apostrophes show possession (*the dog's bone*) and indicate omitted letters in contractions (*don't*). They are also used in such a wide variety of other ways that they can be confusing. Keep track of the uses that give you trouble, and when in doubt, consult this chapter.

> **Editing tip:** The abbreviation **ap** indicates a problem with the use of apostrophes.

Apostrophes and Grammar Checkers

Spelling and grammar checkers can help you catch some errors in the use of apostrophes. For example, a spelling checker may sometimes highlight *its* used incorrectly instead of *it's* or an error in a possessive (for example, *Englands' glory*) but often gets it backwards. Spelling and grammar checkers also miss many apostrophe errors, so you should double-check all words that end in *-s* in your work.

61a Use apostrophes to indicate possession.

www.mhhe.com/
nmhh
For information
and exercises on
apostrophes, go to

Editing >
Apostrophes

For a noun to be possessive, two elements are usually required: (1) someone or something is the possessor and (2) someone, something, or some attribute or quality is possessed.

POSSESSOR	PERSON, THING, ATTRIBUTE, QUALITY, VALUE, OR FEATURE POSSESSED	POSSESSION
woman	son	the woman's son
Juanita	shovel	Juanita's shovel
child	bright smile	a child's bright smile

921

Sometimes the thing possessed precedes the possessor.

> thing possessed   possessor
> ➤ **The motorcycle is the student's.**

Sometimes the sentence may not name the thing possessed, but its identity (in this case, *house*) is clearly understood by the reader.

> ➤ **I saw your cousin at Nick's.**

Note: You can also indicate possession using the preposition *of: the bright smile of a child.*

---

1. Deciding whether to use an apostrophe plus -s or use only an apostrophe

Making singular nouns possessive   To form the possessive of all singular nouns, add an apostrophe plus -s to the ending: *baby's*. Even singular nouns that end in -s form the possessive by adding -'s: *bus's*.

Note: If a singular noun with more than two syllables ends in -s and adding -'s would make the word sound awkward, it is acceptable to use only an apostrophe to form the possessive: *Socrates', Dickens', Moses', Jesus'*. Whatever your choice, be consistent.

Making plural nouns ending in -s possessive   To form the possessive of a plural noun that ends in -s, add only an apostrophe to form the possessive: *subjects', babies'*.

Making plural nouns that do not end in -s possessive   To form the possessive of a plural noun that does not end in -s add an apostrophe plus -s to form the possessive: *men's, cattle's*.

Making indefinite pronouns possessive   To form the possessive of most indefinite pronouns, such as *no one, everyone, everything,* or *something,* add an apostrophe plus -s: *no one's, anybody's*.

Note: Adding -'s makes some indefinite pronouns sound awkward. In those cases, use *of* to form the possessive: *the wishes of a few, the parents of both.*

Forming Possessives

IF THE WORD IS A(N)	ADD	EXAMPLE
singular noun	-'s	horse's Moore's
plural noun ending in -s	-'	horses' Moores'
plural noun not ending in -s	-'s	children's
indefinite pronoun	-'s	everybody's

2. Using the apostrophe in tricky situations

Multiple possessors   To express joint ownership by two or more people, use the possessive form for the last name only; to express individual ownership, use the possessive form for each name.

➤   **Felicia and Elias's report**

➤   **The city's and the state's finances**

Compound words   To form the possessive of compound words, add an apostrophe plus -s to the last word in the compound.

➤   **My father-in-law's job**

➤   **The editor-in-chief's responsibilities**

Proper names   To form the possessive of proper names, follow the rules given above, with some exceptions. Some place or organizational names that include a possessive noun lack an apostrophe. In these cases, follow the established style rather than adding an apostrophe.

➤   **Kings Point**

➤   **Department of Veterans Affairs**

> *Note:* To form the possessive of buildings, machines, and other inanimate objects, use *of* if adding -'s sounds awkward: *the window of the house* (not *the house's window*).

923

Exercise 61.1 Using apostrophes to form the possessive

Write the possessive form of each word. The first one has been done for you.

Word(s)	**Possessive**
the press	*the press's*
nobody	
newspapers	
Monday and Tuesday classes (individual ownership)	
deer	
women	
someone	
Edward	
trade-off	
well-worn footpath	
United States	
this year and last year combined population (joint ownership)	

61b Use apostrophes to form contractions.

A contraction is a shortened word or group of words formed when some letters or sounds are omitted. In a contraction, the apostrophe serves as a substitute for the omitted letters.

we've = we have   weren't = were not   here's = here is

In informal writing, apostrophes can also substitute for omitted numbers in a decade: *the '90s.* It is usually better to spell out the name of the decade in formal writing, however: *the nineties.*

CHARTING the TERRITORY

Contractions in Academic Writing

Although the MLA and APA style manuals allow contractions in academic writing, some instructors think that they are too informal. Check with your instructor before using contractions in a paper.

61c Distinguish between contractions and possessive pronouns.

The following pairs of **homonyms** (words that sound alike but have different meanings) often cause problems for writers. Note that the apostrophe is used only in the contraction.

CONTRACTION	POSSESSIVE PRONOUN
it's (it is or it has)	its
It's too hot.	The dog scratched *its* fleas.
you're (you are)	your
You're a lucky guy.	Is that *your* new car?
who's (who is)	whose
Who's there?	The man *whose* dog was lost called us.
they're (they are)	their*
They're reading poetry.	They gave *their* lives.

*The adverb *there* is also confused with *their* and *they're*: *She was standing there.*

Exercise 61.2 Distinguishing between contractions and pronouns

Underline the correct word choice in each sentence.

EXAMPLE Transcendentalists have had a strong influence on American thought; (there/they're/their) important figures in our literary history.

1. In the essay "The Over-soul," Ralph Waldo Emerson describes the unity of nature by cataloging (it's/its) divine, yet earthly, expressions, such as waterfalls and well-worn footpaths.
2. Emerson states that you must have faith to believe in something that supersedes or contradicts (your/you're) real-life experiences.
3. (Who's/Whose) the author of the poem at the beginning of Emerson's "Self-Reliance"?
4. Emerson believes that (there/they're/their) are ways to live within a society without having to give in to its pressures.
5. According to Emerson, people should occasionally silence the noise of (there/they're/their) inner-voices and learn to listen to the world's unconscious voice.
6. Emerson also believes that, in the end, (it's/its) the individual— and the individual alone—who must decide his or her own fate.

925

61d An apostrophe can be used with -s to form plural numbers, letters, abbreviations, and words used as words.

An apostrophe plus -s ('s) can be used to show the plural of a number, a letter, or an abbreviation. Underline or italicize single letters but not the apostrophe or the -s.

➤ **He makes his 2's look like 5's.**

➤ **_Committee_ has two _m_'s, two _t_'s, and two _e_'s.**

➤ **Professor Morris has two Ph.D.'s.**

> *Exceptions:* If an abbreviation does not have periods, the apostrophe is not necessary (*RPMs*). The apostrophe is also not necessary to form the plural of dates (*1990s*).

If a word is used as a word rather than as a symbol of the meaning it conveys, it can be made plural by adding an apostrophe plus -s. The word should be italicized or underlined but not the -'s.

➤ **There are twelve _no_'s in the first paragraph.**

> *Note:* Style guides vary, and the *MLA Handbook for Writers of Research Papers,* for example, no longer recommends using apostrophes to form plurals of this sort, except for plurals of letters treated as letters.
>
> MLA STYLE   **He makes his 2s look like 5s.**
>
> MLA STYLE   **Committee has two m's, two t's, and two e's.**
>
> Note the use of underlining instead of italics in MLA style.

61e Watch out for common misuses of the apostrophe.

Never use an apostrophe with -s to form a plural noun.

➤ **The ~~teacher's~~ asked the girls and boys for their attention.**
  teachers

(*See Chapter 63, pp. 935–36, for more on forming plural nouns.*)

Never use an apostrophe with -*s* to form the present tense of a verb used with a third-person singular subject (*he, she, it,* or a singular noun).

➤ **A professional singer** ~~need's~~ *needs* **to practice different vocal**

techniques.

Never use an apostrophe with the possessive form of a pronoun such as *hers, ours,* or *theirs.*

➤ **That cat of** ~~our's~~ *ours* **is always sleeping!**

(*See 61c for advice on distinguishing contractions* [*it's*] *from possessive pronouns* [*its*].)

Exercise 61.3 Chapter review: Apostrophes

Edit the following passage by adding and deleting apostrophes and correcting any incorrect word choices.

Transcendentalism was a movement of thought in the mid- to late 1800s that was originated by Ralph Waldo Emerson, Henry David Thoreau, and several other's who's scholarship helped to shape the democratic ideals of their day and usher America into it's modern age. Emerson, a member of New Englands' elite, was particularly interested in spreading Transcendentalist notion's of self-reliance; he is probably best known for his essay "Self-Reliance," which is still widely read in todays' universities. Most people remember Thoreau, however, not only for what he wrote but also for how he lived: its well known that—for a while, at least—he chose to live a simple life in a cabin on Walden Pond. Altogether, one could say that Emerson's and Thoreau's main accomplishment was to expand the influence of literature and philosophy over the development of the average Americans' identity. With a new national literature forming, people's interest in they're self-development quickly increased as they began to read more and more about what it meant to be American. In fact, one could even say (perhaps half-jokingly) that, today, the success of home makeovers on television and the popularity of self-help books might have a lot to do with Emerson's and Thoreau's ideas about self-sufficiency and living simply—idea's that took root in this nation more than a hundred years ago.

62 Hyphens

Hyphens are used to form compound words and to indicate that a word is being broken at the end of a line. Unlike a dash (-- or —), which is used *between* words, a hyphen (-) is used *within* words.

> **Editing tip:** The abbreviation *hyph* indicates a problem with the use of a hyphen. Professional editors and proofreaders usually indicate that a hyphen is needed with a caret and two lines (=) to distinguish the hyphen from a dash.
>
> ➤ **He was a self employed worker for most of his life.**

Hyphens and Grammar Checkers

Spelling and grammar checkers will generally not help you find problems in the use of hyphens. Your dictionary is your best guide.

www.mhhe.com/
nmhh
For information
and exercises on
hyphens, go to

Editing > Hyphens

62a Use hyphens to form compound words and to avoid confusion.

Think of hyphens as bridges. A hyphen joins two nouns to make one compound word. Scientists speak of a *kilogram-meter* as a measure of force, and professors of literature talk about the *scholar-poet*. The hyphen lets us know that the two nouns work together as one. As compound nouns come into general use, the hyphens between them tend to disappear: *firefighter, thundershower.*

A dictionary is the best resource when you are unsure about whether to use a hyphen. The dictionary sometimes gives writers several options, however. For example, you could write *life-style* or *life style* or *lifestyle* and be correct in each case, according to the *Random House Webster's College Dictionary.* If you cannot find a compound word in the dictionary, spell it as two separate words. Whatever spelling you choose, be consistent throughout your document.

62b Use hyphens to join two or more words to create compound adjective or noun forms.

A hyphen can link words to form a compound adjective.

accident-prone
quick-witted

Hyphens often help clarify adjectives that come before the word they modify. If you say, "She was a quick thinking person," you might mean that she was quick and that she was also a thinking person. If you say "She was a quick-thinking person," though, your meaning is unmistakable: she thought rapidly. Modifiers that are hyphenated when they are placed *before* the word they modify are usually not hyphenated when they are placed *after* the word they modify.

➤ It was a *bad-mannered* reply.

➤ The reply was *bad mannered.*

Do not use a hyphen to connect an *-ly* adverb to the word it modifies. The fact that the word is an adverb makes the relationship between the words clear.

➤ They explored the newly⁄discovered territories.

Hyphens are also used in nouns designating family relationships and compounds of more than two words.

brother-in-law
stay-at-home
stick-in-the-mud

Note: Compound nouns with hyphens generally form plurals by adding *-s* or *-es* to the most important word.

attorney at-law/attorneys-at-law
mother-in-law/mothers-in-law
court-martial/courts-martial

In a pair or series of compound nouns or adjectives, add suspended hyphens after the first word of each item.

➤ **The child care center accepted *three-*, *four-*, and *five-year-olds*.**

Some proper nouns that are joined to make an adjective are hyphenated.

the Franco-Prussian war
of Mexican-American heritage

62c Use hyphens to spell out fractions and compound numbers.

Use a hyphen when writing out fractions or compound numbers from twenty-one through ninety-nine.

three-fourths of a gallon
thirty-two
twenty-five thousand

Note: Use a hyphen to show inclusive numbers: *pages 198-205.*

62d Use a hyphen to attach some prefixes and suffixes.

Use a hyphen to join a prefix and a capitalized word.

un-American	pre-Columbian
mid-August	neo-Nazi

A hyphen is sometimes used to join a capital letter and a word.

T-shirt	V-six engine

The prefixes *all-*, *ex-*, *quasi-*, and *self-* and the suffixes *-elect*, *-odd*, and *-something* generally take hyphens.

all-purpose	self-sufficient	thirty-something
ex-convict	president-elect	
quasi-scientific	fifty-odd	

Most prefixes, however, are not attached by hyphens unless a hyphen is needed to show pronunciation, avoid double letters (anti-immigration), or to reveal a special meaning that distinguishes the word from the same word without a hyphen: *recreate* (play) versus *re-create* (make again). Check a dictionary to be sure you are using the standard spelling.

62e Use hyphens to divide words at the ends of lines.

When you must divide words, do so between syllables, but pronunciation alone cannot always tell you where to divide a word. If you are unsure about how to break a word into syllables, consult your dictionary.

➤ **My writing group had a very fruitful *collab-oration*. [not *colla-boration*]**

Never leave just one or two letters on a line.

➤ **He seemed so sad and vulnerable and so *discon-nected* from his family. [not *disconnect-ed*]**

Compound words such as *hardworking, rattlesnake,* and *bookcase* should be broken only between the words that form them: *hard-working, rattle-snake, book-case.* Compound words that already have hyphens, like *brother-in-law,* are broken after the hyphens only.

> *Note:* Never hyphenate an abbreviation or acronym (CIA) or a one-syllable word.

TEXTCONNEX

Dividing Internet Addresses

If you need to divide an Internet address between lines, divide it after a slash. Do not divide a word within the address with a hyphen; readers may assume the hyphen is part of the address.

Exercise 62.1 Chapter review: Hyphens

Edit the following passage, adding and deleting hyphens as necessary.

We need only to turn on the television or pick up a recent issue of a popular fashion or fitness magazine to see evidence of modern society's obsession with images of thinness. Few actors, models, or celebrities fail to flaunt their thinly-trimmed waist-lines, regardless of their gender. Not surprisingly, more than ten million females and almost one million males in the United States are currently battling eating disorders such as anorexia nervosa and bulimia nervosa. A person who is anorexic fears gaining weight, and thus en-gages in self starvation and excessive weight loss. A person who is bulimic binges and then engages in self-induced purging in order to lose weight. Although we are often quick to assume that those with eating disorders suffer from low self-esteem and have a history of family or peer problems, we cannot ignore the role that the media play in encouraging eating disorders, particularly when thin-ness is equated with physical attractiveness, health and fitness, and success over-all. We need to re-member the threat of these eating disorders the next time we hear a ten year old girl tell her mommy that she "can't afford" to eat more than one half of her peanut butter and jelly sandwich.

63 Spelling

Frequent or even occasional misspellings can make your readers suspect that you are careless or ignorant, and you will then have to work twice as hard to convince them to take your ideas seriously. Proofread your writing carefully. Misspellings creep into the prose of even the best writers.

www.mhhe.com/
nmhh
For information
and exercises on
spelling, go to
Editing > Spelling

Unfortunately, pronunciation is at best an unreliable guide to spelling in English. Words can have similar patterns of letters but be pronounced in different ways, or different patterns can be pronounced in the same way. For example, the following words, all containing the pattern *-ough,* are each pronounced differently: *thought, cough, through, bough.* On the other hand, these words, each with a different pattern, are pronounced in the same way in American English: *bite, fight, height.*

Rather than relying on pronunciation, use the following strategies to help you improve your spelling.

- Become familiar with the major rules of spelling (*see 63a, pp. 934–38*).

- Learn to distinguish **homonyms**—words that are pronounced alike but have different meanings and spellings (*see 63b, p. 938*).

- Be aware of commonly misspelled words, and keep your own list of words that give you trouble (*see 63c, p. 938*).

- Keep a good college dictionary at hand. If you are not sure how to spell a word, try looking up different combinations of letters, based on how you pronounce the word, until you hit the right one. You can also try typing a synonym for the problem word into your word-processing program's thesaurus to see if the word you are looking for is listed as an alternative.

- Compile a list of the words that you frequently misspell. Include tricks to help you remember how to spell particular words. For example, there is "a rat" in *separate,* and there are two double letters, "cc" and "mm," in *accommodate.*

933

Editing tip: The abbreviation *sp* is used to indicate a spelling error. The best time to check your draft for spelling errors is after you are happy with the style and content of your writing. First, check any words that your computer software's spell-checker has highlighted, and then print out a draft to go over again. Read this draft very slowly. Some people find it helpful to use a ruler to focus on one line at a time or to read the draft from the final sentence to the first as a way of making sure to pay attention to individual words. Circle each spelling that you are unsure of. Then, when you have checked the entire paper, look up each circled word in a dictionary.

Spelling Checkers

Computer spell-checkers are helpful tools. The most recent versions of some commonly used word-processing programs automatically correct obvious misspellings as you type them. Spell-checkers will also give you a list of possible substitutes for a highlighted word if you right-click on the word. All spell-checkers have limitations, however. They cannot tell how you are using a particular word. If you write *their* but mean *there,* a spell-checker cannot point out your mistake. Spell-checkers also cannot point out many misspelled proper nouns. To catch these kinds of errors, you need to proofread your work carefully yourself.

63a Learn the rules that generally hold for spelling, as well as their exceptions.

1. Placing *i* before *e*

Use *i* before *e* except after *c* or when the combination is sounded like *a,* as in *neighbor* and *weigh.*

I BEFORE *E*	believe, relieve, chief, grief, wield, yield
EXCEPT AFTER *C*	receive, deceive, ceiling, conceit
EI SOUNDED LIKE *A*	weight, freight, eight, rein
EXCEPTIONS	caffeine, codeine, foreign, forfeit, height, leisure, seize, weird

2. Forming plurals

Most plurals are formed by adding -*s*. Some others are formed by adding -*es*.

When to Form the Plural with -*es*

SINGULAR ENDING	PLURAL ENDING
-s, -sh, -x, -z, "soft" -ch bus, bush, fox, buzz, peach	**-es** buses, bushes, foxes, buzzes, peaches
consonant + o hero, tomato	**-es** heroes, tomatoes EXCEPTION: solo/solos
consonant + y beauty, city	**change y to i and add -es** beauties, cities EXCEPTION: a person's name— Kirby/the Kirbys
-f, -fe leaf, knife, wife	**change f to v and add -s or -es** leaves, knives, wives EXCEPTION: Words that end in -ff and some words that end in -f (staff, roof) form the plural by adding only an -s (staffs, roofs).

Most plurals follow standard rules, but some have irregular forms (child/children, tooth/teeth). Some words with foreign roots create plurals in the pattern of the language they come from, as do these words.

addendum/addenda
alumna/alumnae
alumnus/alumni
analysis/analyses
crisis/crises
criterion/criteria

datum/data
medium/media
phenomenon/phenomena
stimulus/stimuli
thesis/theses

Some nouns with foreign roots have both irregular and regular plural forms (*appendix/appendices/appendixes*). As in other cases where you have options, you should be consistent in using the spelling you choose.

Note: Some writers now treat *data* as though it were singular, but the preferred practice is still to recognize that *data* is plural and takes a plural verb.

➤ The *data are* clear on this point: events have made the pass/fail course obsolete.

Compound nouns with hyphens generally form plurals by adding *-s* or *-es* to the most important word.

> attorney-at-law/attorneys-at-law
> mother-in-law/mothers-in-law
> court-martial/courts-martial

For some compound words that are spelled as one word, the same rule applies (*passersby*); for others, it does not (*cupfuls*). Consult a dictionary if you are not sure.

If both words in the compound are equally important, add *-s* to the second word: *singer-songwriters.*

A few words such as *fish* and *sheep* have the same forms for singular and plural. To indicate that the word is plural, you need to add a word or words that indicate quantity: *five fish, a few sheep.*

For MULTILINGUAL STUDENTS

American and British Spelling

Standard British spelling differs from American spelling for some words—among them *color / colour, canceled / cancelled, theater / theatre, realize / realise,* and *judgment / judgement.*

3. Adding suffixes

Although suffixes are simply added to the end of most words, sometimes a spelling change is required (*see the box on the next page*).

Words ending in *-cede, -ceed,* and *-sede* frequently cause spelling problems. Most words that end with this sound use the spelling *-cede* (*recede, concede, precede, intercede*); the following four words are the only exceptions:

> exceed   succeed
> proceed   supersede

Note: Adding a prefix such as *re-, un-, de-,* or *anti-* does not change the spelling of the word the prefix is attached to (*reunion, unintended, destabilized, antidepressant*), although a hyphen may be needed for clarity (*recreate / re-create, anti-inflammatory*).

SPELLING CHANGES with SUFFIXES

Adding suffixes to words that end in a silent -e

If the suffix begins with a vowel (as in *-ed, -ing, -er, -est*), drop the final *-e*, and then add the suffix.

force/forced   surprise/surprising   remove/removable

EXCEPTIONS: Keep the silent *-e* if it is needed to clarify the pronunciation (*mile / mileage, be / being*), if the word would be confused with another word without the *-e* (*dyeing*), or if the *-e* is needed following *c* or *g* to keep the sound of the consonant the same (*manageable, traceable*).

In a few words the *-e* is dropped when the suffix begins with a consonant.

true/truly   judge/judgment
argue/argument   acknowledge/acknowledgment

Adding suffixes to words that end in a consonant + y

Change the *y* to an *i* and add the suffix.

happy/happiness   hungry/hungrier   apply/applied

EXCEPTION: Do not change the *y* to an *i* when adding the suffix *-ing* (*apply/applying, enjoy/enjoying, cry/crying*) or when adding *-s* to a proper name ending in *-y* (*Ballys*).

Adding suffixes to words that end in one vowel + a consonant

(but only when the consonant ends a one-syllable word or a stressed syllable—*refer,* not *glower*)

Double the final consonant and add the suffix.

grip/gripping stun/stunning refer/referred transmit/transmitted

EXCEPTION: bus/busing

Adding the suffix -ly to words that end in -ic

Add *-ally.*

logic/logically   terrific/terrifically   static/statically

Exercise 63.1 Practicing spelling rules

Write the correct plural form for each of the following words. Consult the preceding rules or a dictionary, as needed.

Bentley	hoof	trophy
president-elect	potato	index
life	fungus	Sidney
box	brother-in-law	self
appendix	stereo	nucleus

Exercise 63.2 Practicing spelling rules

Some words in the following list are misspelled. Circle each of the misspelled words, and write the correct spelling next to it.

either	boxxing	hopping
hygiene	supplyed	nieghbor
dealer	neither	worried
buying	divorced	tring
exced	managable	receipt

63b Learn to distinguish words that are pronounced alike but spelled differently.

Homonyms are words that sound alike but have different meanings and different spellings. Many are commonly confused, so you should check them when you are proofreading your work. The box that begins on the next page contains a list of common homonyms as well as words that are almost homonyms. For more complete definitions, consult the Glossary of Usage (*Chapter 50, pp. 789–98*) and a dictionary.

Exercise 63.3 Distinguishing homonyms

Review the list of common homonyms, and highlight the words that give you trouble. Then write each word in a sentence.

63c Check for commonly misspelled words.

Words that are exceptions to standard spelling rules are commonly misspelled. The words in the box on pages 941–44 often give writers trouble.

COMMON HOMONYMS and NEAR HOMONYMS

accept (to take willingly); **except** (to leave out; but for)

adapt (to change); **adopt** (to take as one's own)

advice (an opinion); **advise** (to give an opinion)

affect (to influence; a feeling); **effect** (to make; a result)

aisle (passage between seats); **isle** (island)

all ready (prepared); **already** (by this time)

allude (to hint at); **elude** (to escape or avoid)

allusion (indirect reference); **illusion** (unreal image or faulty idea)

altar (a platform used in worship); **alter** (to change somewhat)

amoral (neither moral nor immoral); **immoral** (violating morals)

are (form of *be*); **hour** (sixty minutes); **our** (possessive of *we*)

ascent (the act of rising up); **assent** (to agree to)

assistance (help); **assistants** (helpers)

bare (to reveal; naked); **bear** (to carry; an animal)

belief (conviction); **believe** (to have faith)

beside (by the side of); **besides** (in addition, other than)

board (a piece of lumber; a group; to enter a vehicle); **bored** (uninterested)

brake (to stop); **break** (to separate into parts)

buy (to purchase); **by** (next to)

capital (punishable by death; uppercase letter; city); **capitol** (the building)

censer (incense container); **censor** (to remove objectionable material); **censure** (to blame)

choose (to select); **chose** (past tense of *choose*)

cite (to quote or refer to); **sight** (a spectacle; the sense); **site** (a place)

clothes (attire); **cloths** (fabric)

coarse (rough); **course** (a path; a series of classes)

complement (something that completes); **compliment** (praise)

conscience (knowledge of right and wrong); **conscious** (to be aware)

council (an advisory group or meeting); **counsel** (to give advice)

descent (downward movement); **dissent** (to disagree, disagreement)

desert (a dry, sandy place; to leave); **dessert** (an after-dinner course)

device (a scheme; a piece of equipment); **devise** (to invent)

discreet (showing good judgment); **discrete** (distinct)

dominant (commanding, having influence); **dominate** (to control)

elicit (to bring forth); **illicit** (illegal)

emigrate (to move from a country); **immigrate** (to move to a country)

(continued)

COMMON HOMONYMS
and NEAR HOMONYMS (continued)

eminent (highly ranked); **imminent** (about to happen); **immanent** (inherent)

envelop (to surround); **envelope** (stationery)

fair (beautiful; lawful; acceptable); **fare** (payment for travel; to go; food or drink)

farther (related to geographical distances); **further** (in addition)

flaunt (to show off); **flout** (to ignore in a showy way)

forth (forward); **fourth** (numerical place)

gorilla (large primate); **guerrilla** (unconventional soldier)

hear (to perceive by listening); **here** (at this place)

hole (an opening); **whole** (complete, in one piece)

it's (it is, it has); **its** (possessive of *it*)

know (to be aware of); **no** (negative)

lay (to place); **lie** (to recline)

lead (to guide); **led** (past tense of *lead*)

lessen (to make less); **lesson** (something learned)

lightning (flashing light in a storm); **lightening** (to make lighter)

loose (not securely attached); **lose** (to misplace)

meat (flesh of an animal); **meet** (to come together, encounter)

moral (lesson); **morale** (attitude or mental condition)

of (derived from, coming from); **off** (opposite of *on*)

passed (past tense of *pass*); **past** (former time)

patience (self-control); **patients** (people under medical care)

peace (quiet; harmony); **piece** (part of)

personal (private); **personnel** (employees)

plain (simple); **plane** (aircraft; a tool for leveling wood)

practicable (can be done); **practical** (sensible)

precede (to go before); **proceed** (to go by; to carry on)

presents (gifts); **presence** (being at hand)

principal (chief); **principle** (a basic truth; a sum)

rain (precipitation); **reign** (to govern as a monarch); **rein** (leather strap that controls an animal)

raise (to lift something); **raze** (to tear down); **rise** (to go upward)

respectfully (with respect); **respectively** (in the given order)

right (correct); **rite** (part of a ceremony); **write** (to compose)

road (street); **rode** (past tense of *ride*)

scene (part of or place in a story); **seen** (past tense of *see*)

sense (a meaning; to be aware of); **since** (after, because)

stationary (not moving); **stationery** (writing paper)

straight (unbending; honest); **strait** (a narrow channel)

than (used in comparisons); **then** (related to time sequence)

their (possessive of *they*); **there** (place); **they're** (they are)

threw (past tense of *throw*); **through** (from one end to another); **thorough** (complete)

to (indicating movement); **too** (also); **two** (number)

waist (body part); **waste** (discarded material)

weak (not strong); **week** (seven days)

wear (to use as clothing); **where** (place); **were** (past tense form of *be*)

weather (atmospheric condition); **whether** (if it is or was true)

which (what one); **witch** (sorcerer)

who's (who is); **whose** (possessive of *who*)

you're (you are); **your** (possessive of *you*)

A SAMPLING of COMMONLY MISSPELLED WORDS

A	appearance	bureaucracy
absence	appreciate	business
acceptable	appropriate	
accessible	approximately	**C**
accidentally	arguing	calculator
accommodate	argument	calendar
accomplish	arrest	carrying
accuracy	assassination	ceiling
accustomed	atheist	cemetery
achieve	athlete	certain
actually	audience	changeable
address	average	changing
admission		characteristic
adolescent	**B**	chief
aggressive	bargain	chocolate
amateur	basically	chose
analysis	beginning	coarse
analyze	belief	column
angel	believe	commercial
anonymous	beneficial	commitment
apology	boundary	committee
apparent	breath	competent

(*continued*)

A SAMPLING of COMMONLY MISSPELLED WORDS (continued)

competition
conceive
concentrate
consistency
consistent
continuous
controlled
controversial
convenience
convenient
coolly
courteous
criticism
criticize
cruelty
curiosity
curious
curriculum

D
decision
definitely
descendant
description
desirable
despair
desperate
destroy
develop
difference
different
disappear
disappoint
disapprove
disastrous
discipline
discriminate
discussion
disease
dissatisfied
divide
divine

E
easily
ecstasy
efficient
eighth
embarrass
emphasize
enemy
entirely
environment
equipment
equipped
especially
essential
exaggerate
exercise
existence
experiment
explanation

F
familiar
fascinate
favorite
February
finally
foreign
fulfill

G
gauge
generally
government
grammar
guarantee
guard
guidance

H
happily
harass
height

heroes
humorous
hungry
hurriedly
hypocrisy
hypocrite

I
ideally
imaginary
imagine
imitation
immediately
incidentally
incredible
independence
individual
individually
influential
initiate
innocuous
inoculate
integrate
intelligence
interest
interference
irrelevant
irresistible
irreverent
irritable
irritated

J
jealousy
judgment

K
kindergarten
knowledge

L
laboratory

A SAMPLING of COMMONLY MISSPELLED WORDS

leisure
license
lieutenant
likelihood
livelihood
luxurious
luxury
lying

M
magazine
maintenance
manageable
marriage
mathematics
meant
medicine
miniature
mirror
mischievous
missile
misspelled
mortgage
muscle
mysterious

N
naturally
necessary
neighbor
niece
noticeable
noticing
nuclear
nuisance
numerous

O
occasion
occasionally
occur
occurred
occurrence

official
omission
omitted
opponent
opportunity
opposite
ordinary
originally

P
parallel
paralleled
parliament
particularly
peaceable
peculiar
perception
performance
permanent
permissible
personnel
persuade
physical
physiology
pitiful
playwright
poison
politician
possession
practical
practically
preference
prejudice
preparation
prevalent
privilege
probably
process
processes
professor
prominent
pronunciation
psychology

purpose
pursue
pursuing
pursuit

Q
quandary
questionnaire
quizzes

R
really
rebel
receive
recognize
recommend
referred
relief
relieve
religious
remembrance
reminisce
repetition
representative
resemblance
restaurant
rhyme
rhythm
ridiculous

S
sacrifice
sacrilegious
satellite
scarcity
schedule
secretary
seize
separate
several
shining
significance

(continued)

A SAMPLING of COMMONLY MISSPELLED WORDS *(continued)*

similar	**T**	unnecessary
sincerely	technical	usually
sophomore	technique	
specimen	temperature	**V**
sponsor	tendency	vacuum
strategy	thorough	vengeance
strenuous	together	villain
studying	tomatoes	visible
succeed	tomorrow	
sufficient	tragedy	**W**
summary	twelfth	Wednesday
superintendent	tyranny	weird
supersede		wholly
suppress	**U**	woman
surely	unanimous	women
surprise	unconscious	writing
suspicious	undoubtedly	written

Exercise 63.4 Commonly misspelled words

Highlight the words in the preceding list that give you trouble. In a list or spelling log, write down other words you often misspell. Try to group your errors. Do they fall into patterns—errors with suffixes or plurals, for example? Errors with silent letters or doubled consonants?

Exercise 63.5 Chapter review: Spelling

Edit the following passage, correcting any misspelled words. In addition to applying the spelling rules in this chapter, you may need to consult a dictionary.

> Most people will agree that scientists need to find cures for Alzheimer's and Parkinson's diseases, yet many individals are opposeed to stem cell research because of it's controversal use of human embryoes. The procedure that many people, including many goverment officials and law makers, oppose is somatic cell nucclear transfer, commonly known as therapeutic cloning. This tecnique involves creating and then harvesting

embryoes for there stem cells. These cells can develop into any type of tissue in the body and perhaps regenerate mature organs. The results of this type of research might prove benefical.

Some people confuse therapeutic cloning with reproductive cloning, a procedure that creates embryoes for human reproduction rather than for medical research. People who oppose therapeutic cloning beleive that this procedure cannot be done ethicly because the embryo, an early stage of human life, is eventually destroyeed. Opponents argue on morale grounds that therapeutic cloning will lead to human cloning. Others assert that therapeutic cloning can produce genetic abnormalities, witch few people are willing to except. What position does your conscious allow you to support?

CHECKLIST

Editing for Mechanics and Spelling

As you revise, check your writing for mechanics and spelling by asking yourself these questions:

☐ Are words and letters capitalized according to convention and context? (*See Chapter 57: Capitalization, pp. 892–902.*)

☐ Are abbreviations capitalized and punctuated in a consistent way? Are Latin abbreviations and non-alphabetic symbols used appropriately? (*See Chapter 58: Abbreviations and Symbols, pp. 903–10.*)

☐ Are numbers either spelled out or represented with numerals according to the conventions of the type of writing (nontechnical or technical) you are engaged in? (*See Chapter 59: Numbers, pp. 911–14.*)

☐ Are italics (or underlining) used appropriately for emphasis and to identify the titles of works, foreign words, and words used as words? (*See Chapter 60: Italics and Underlining, pp. 915–20.*)

☐ Are apostrophes used appropriately to indicate possession and to form contractions? Are any apostrophes misused to make a noun plural? (*See Chapter 61: Apostrophes, pp. 921–27.*)

☐ Are hyphens used appropriately to form compound words, in spelled-out numbers, and with certain prefixes and suffixes? (*See Chapter 62: Hyphens, pp. 928–32.*)

☐ Have you learned the rules for spelling (and their exceptions) and checked a dictionary for any words whose spelling you are unsure of? (*See Chapter 63: Spelling, pp. 933–45.*)

Language is a city to the building of which every
human being brought a stone.

—RALPH WALDO EMERSON

Guide
for Multilingual
Writers

64a Learn the characteristics of English nouns and their modifiers.

1. Reviewing noun types

To use an English noun properly, you need to know its basic characteristics and how it functions in a sentence. English nouns fall into a variety of overlapping categories, including:

- count and noncount
- proper and common
- concrete and abstract

(For a brief overview of these and other noun categories, see Chapter 30: Parts of Speech, pp. 534–36.)

www.mhhe.com/
nmhh
For information and
exercises on English
for multilingual
students, go to
Editing >
Multilingual/ESL
Writers

2. Recognizing the difference between count and noncount nouns

Recognizing the difference between count and noncount nouns can help you choose the correct article (*a, an,* and *the*) or quantifier (*some, many, three, a few,* for example) for each noun.

Count nouns   **Count nouns**—nouns that name specific, countable things—can be either singular or plural. Plural forms can be regular or irregular. In regular nouns, the ending *-s* signals the plural form:

shoe	shoes
clock	clocks
grandmother	grandmothers
preference	preferences

Irregular plurals take a variety of forms:

man	men		
woman	women	mouse	mice
child	children	deer	deer
ox	oxen	species	species
loaf	loaves	syllabus	syllabi
knife	knives		

Because irregular plurals take so many different forms, always check a dictionary when you are unsure of the correct form for a particular word.

Noncount nouns **Noncount nouns** refer to categories of people, places, things, or ideas that cannot be counted. Because they cannot be counted, noncount nouns, even those that end in *-s,* are always singular, never plural.

The most common noncount nouns fall into one of the following categories:

- Abstract nouns: *advice, bravery, capitalism, confusion, courage, fortitude, greed, patience, peace*
- Certain classes of concrete nouns
  - Collections of individual items: *clothing, furniture, homework, jewelry, luggage, makeup*
  - Fields of study: *astronomy, chemistry, linguistics, physics*
  - Games: *baseball, chess, football, hockey, poker, soccer*
  - Diseases: *cholera, diabetes, pneumonia*
  - Natural substances and phenomena: *air, blood, cold, dust, heat, rain, weather*

Note: Many nouns can be either count or noncount depending on the context in which they appear.

➤ *Baseball* [the game: noncount] **is never played with two baseballs** [the object: count] **at the same time.**

➤ **The suspect's** *hair* [noncount] **is brown, and the two** *hairs* [count] **found at the scene of the crime are also brown.**

---

3. Using articles appropriately with count, noncount, and proper nouns

In English, articles must accompany nouns in many situations. You need to be aware of the conventions that govern the use of articles, especially if English conventions differ from those of your native language or if articles do not exist in your native language.

Articles in English express three basic meanings:

- Indefinite (indicating nonspecific reference)
- Definite (indicating specific reference)
- Generic (indicating reference to a general category)

Indefinite and definite meaning   A noun has indefinite meaning, or nonspecific reference, when it is first mentioned. To express indefinite meaning with count nouns, use the **indefinite article** (*a, an*) for singular forms and no article for plural forms.

➤   **I bought *a* new computer.**

➤   **I bought new computers.**

Note: Noncount nouns *never* take the indefinite article.

    Knowledge
➤   ~~A knowledge~~ **is a valuable commodity.**

To express definite meaning, or specific reference, use the **definite article** (*the*) with noncount nouns and both singular and plural count nouns. A noun has definite meaning in a variety of situations:

1. When the noun identifies something previously mentioned

    ➤   **I was driving along Main Street when *a* car** [nonspecific reference] **pulled up behind me. *The* car** [specific reference to the previously mentioned car] **swerved into the left lane and sped out of sight.**

    ➤   **Knowledge** [nonspecific] **is a valuable commodity. *The* knowledge** [specific] **I gained in college, for example, helped me get a good job.**

2. When the noun identifies something familiar or known from the context

    ➤   **We could not play today because *the* soccer field was wet.**

3. When the noun identifies a unique subject

    ➤   ***The* moon will be full tonight.**

4. When the noun is modified by a superlative adjective

    ➤   **We purchased *the* most economical appliance.**

5. When information in modifying phrases and clauses makes the noun definite

    ➤   ***The* goal *of this discussion* is to explain article use.**

    ➤   ***The* book *that we studied in this course* is about medieval art.**

Generic meaning   A noun is used generically when it is meant to represent all the individuals in the category it names. Singular count nouns used generically can take either an indefinite or a definite article depending on context.

➤ *A student* **can use the Internet to research** *a topic* **efficiently.**

➤ *The university* **is** *an institution* **with roots in ancient times.**

Plural nouns used generically take no article.

➤ **As** *people* **live longer, they need more medical services.**

➤ *Psychologists* **believe that** *children* **should reduce the amount of time they spend watching television.**

Articles and proper nouns   Most proper nouns take no article.

➤ ~~The~~ **Arizona is a dry state.**

Some proper nouns, however, do take the definite article.

➤ **New York City has five boroughs: Manhattan, Staten Island, Brooklyn, Queens, and** *the* **Bronx.**

➤ *The* **Civil War was a watershed event in American history.**

Some other exceptions are the names of structures, names that include the word *of,* and many countries with names that are two or more words long.

➤ *the* **White House**

➤ *the* **Wizard of Oz**

➤ *the* **United States**

4. Using quantifiers appropriately with count and noncount nouns

Because noncount nouns are singular only and refer to things that cannot be counted, they require different quantifiers than count nouns, which refer to countable entities and can be plural. Following is a list of some quantifiers for noncount and count nouns, as well as some quantifiers that can be used with both.

▪ **With noncount nouns only:** *much, a great deal of, little, a little*

➤ **We did not spend** *much time* **studying for the exam.**

➤ *Little time* **remains before the paper is due.**

➤ **The coach gave us** *a little advice* **before the game.**   **951**

- **With count nouns only:** *many, several, a number of, a couple of, few, a few*

  ➤ We did not spend *many hours* studying for the exam.

  ➤ *Few days* remains before the paper is due.

  ➤ The coach gave us *a few suggestions* before the game.

- **With either count or noncount nouns only:** *all, a lot of, any, some*

  ➤ *All homework* must be handed in by Monday.

  ➤ *All assignments* must be handed in by Monday.

  ➤ We don't have *any luggage.*

  ➤ We don't have *any suitcases.*

  ➤ The book has *some information* that relates to your topic.

  ➤ The book has *some ideas* that relate to your topic.

Exercise 64.1 Classifying nouns

Identify the category of each noun (common or proper, count or non-count) and give its singular or plural form, if applicable.

EXAMPLE

patience *(common, noncount, singular only)*

1. research
2. basis
3. luggage
4. fascination
5. idea
6. the Rocky Mountains

Exercise 64.2 Using quantifiers

In the following passages, choose the appropriate quantifiers from the options in parentheses. If there is more than one acceptable option, choose the one that best fits the context.

1. The airline industry has been facing (much/many) challenges lately. The high cost of fuel and services has left many companies nearly bankrupt. Major airlines are now turning to the government and even to their employees for (some/little/a little) help. They cannot expect to get as (many/much) understanding as they want, in either case.

2. Estate sales attract (many/much) bargain shoppers and collectors. Early arrivals can find (a great deal of/a number of) items, including, for example, (much/a lot of) jewelry, (some/many) furniture, and (much/many) antiques. The resale value of such items is unpredictable, however, so buyers cannot count on getting rich from their finds.

3. A recent United Nations report shows that the impact of natural disasters has increased dramatically in recent years. In the 1990s, three times as (much/many) people were affected by catastrophes as in the previous decade. One reason for the increase is that (many/much) more people than before now live in the cities and coastal areas that are vulnerable to storms and earthquakes.

4. Long road trips can be taxing on families with small children. Psychologists have (a little/a few) tips to make these trips easier. These tips include planning (much/plenty of) activities for the car, packing (a great deal of/several) toys, bringing (some/any/little/a little) music to listen to, and trying to leave early in the morning so the children can sleep through the first (few/little) hours of the trip.

Exercise 64.3 Using articles in context

Correct the errors in article use in the following passage.

In his book *Travels with Charley,* John Steinbeck describes the journey he took that helped him discover his country. The Hurricane Donna struck New York state and delayed the beginning of the long-planned trip. While author was traveling in the New England, weather became cold, and leaves turned their fall colors. On his way, he met farmer who had a Yankee face and the Yankee accent. Steinbeck discovered that the best way to learn about local population was to visit local bar or church. He also saw many people fleeing New England to escape winter. Many shops were closed, and some had signs saying they would be closed until following summer. As he traveled through states, he noticed the changes in the language. These differences were apparent in road signs. A trouble arose when he was not allowed to cross Canadian border because he did not have vaccination certificate for his dog, Charley. Steinbeck and his companion were later able to resume their trip without the further problems.

5. Working with English adjectives

English adjectives do not change form to agree with the form of the nouns they modify. They stay the same whatever the number or gender of the noun.

➤ **Juan is an *attentive* father. Alyssa is an *attentive* mother. They are *attentive* parents.**

Adjectives usually come before a noun, but they can also occur after a linking verb.

➤ **We had a *delicious* meal.**

➤ **The food at the restaurant was *delicious*.**

Be aware, however, that the position of an adjective can affect its meaning. The phrase *my old friend,* for example, can refer to someone with whom the speaker has had a long friendship (*a friend I have known for a long time*) or to an aged friend (*my friend who is elderly*). In the sentence *My friend is old,* in contrast, *old* has only one meaning—elderly.

When two or more adjectives modify a noun cumulatively, they follow a sequence—determined by their meaning—that is particular to English logic:

1. Adjectives that express subjective evaluation: *cozy, intelligent, outrageous, elegant, original*

2. Adjectives of size and shape: *big, small, huge, tiny, tall, short, narrow, thick, round, square*

3. Adjectives of color: *yellow, green, pale*

4. Adjectives of origin and type: *African, Czech, Gothic*

5. Nouns used as adjectives: *brick, plastic, glass, stone*

6. NOUN

Here are some examples:

SUBJECTIVE EVALUATION	SIZE AND SHAPE	COLOR	ORIGIN AND TYPE	NOUN AS ADJECTIVE	NOUN
cozy		red		brick	cottage
			African		statues
ugly		orange		plastic	chairs
	arched		Gothic	stained-glass	windows

Exercise 64.4   Working with English adjectives

Correct any errors in adjective placement or agreement in the following sentences. Some of the sentences may be correct as written.

EXAMPLE

huge brick
The houses in the development were all ~~brick huge~~
mansions.

1. House hunting can be a time-consuming activity and frustrating.
2. Prospective home buyers are bombarded with images of spacious, elegant houses.
3. Multiple bedrooms, bathrooms fully equipped, and gardens landscaped are becoming standard features of suburban new properties.
4. The kitchens are filled with shiny surfaces and hi-tech numerous gadgets.
5. Many American young families cannot afford those expensive properties.

64b   Learn the characteristics of English pronouns.

The pronoun system in English is less complex than those of many other languages. For instance, English has few pronoun case forms. Some features of English pronouns, however, may present problems for the multilingual learner.

■ The second-person pronouns *you* and *your/yours* have only one form for both singular and plural referents.

➤ *You* **are my** *friend.*

➤ *You* **are my** *friends.*

➤ *Your car* **is parked in the driveway. The** *car* **is** *yours.*

➤ *Your cars* **are parked in the driveway. The** *cars* **are** *yours.*

■ In English, the gender and number of a pronoun is determined by the gender and number of the noun or pronoun it replaces (its antecedent). (In some other languages, possessive pronouns take the gender and number of the nouns they modify.)

➤ **Daria bought her daughter a red bike and** ~~his~~ **son** *her*

  a yellow bike.

➤ **The school is planning a bike tour in Vermont for** ~~their~~ **students.** *its*

Exercise 64.5 Reviewing pronoun usage and reference

Correct the errors in pronoun usage and reference in the following sentences.

EXAMPLE

  This book is ~~her~~, not mine. *hers*

1. The American college today often has a large international population and must deal with issues of ethnicity and national allegiance among their students.
2. Hoping to educate better citizens for an increasingly interconnected world, schools are emphasizing international relations in its programs.
3. Students should care about the future of the world, not just about the future of theirs careers.
4. That woman's mother is from Belgium and his father is from Mexico.

64c Learn the characteristics of English verb phrases.

English verbs require **auxiliary (helping) verbs** in many situations to provide information about time (tense) and the characteristics of an action.

1. Using helping verbs to form tenses

Many English tenses consist of a form of the helping verbs *have* or *be* combined with either the *-ing* or the *-ed* form of the main verb. In these tenses:

- The subject agrees with the helping verb, not the main verb.

  ➤ She ~~have~~ *has* traveled to many places.

- The helping verb should never be omitted.

  ➤ She *is* traveling to South America next summer.

(For a complete discussion of English tenses and how to form them, see Chapter 35: Problems with Verbs, pp. 623–32.)

2. Understanding modal auxiliaries

In addition to those required for tense formation, English has a variety of helping verbs, known as **modals,** that express an attitude to the action or circumstances of a sentence:

can	must	will
could	ought to	would
may	shall	
might	should	

- These verbs do not change form to indicate person or number.
- They do not carry tense.
- They are followed directly by the base form of the verb without *to*.

  ➤ We *must* ~~to~~ study now.

Some verbal expressions ending in *to* also function as modals, including *have to*, *be able to,* and *be supposed to.* These **phrasal modals** behave more like ordinary verbs than true modals, changing form to carry tense and agree with the subject.

Modals are used to do the following:

- **Ask for permission:** *may, might, can, could*
  May (*Might* / *Can* / *Could*) I come at five o'clock?

- **Make a polite request:** *would*
  Would you please open the door?

- **Express ability:** *can, am* / *is* / *are able to; was* / *were able to*
  I *can* (*am able to*) take one piece of luggage.

- **Express possibility:** *may, might*
  She *may* (*might*) return this afternoon.

- **Express expectation:** *should*
  I *should* finish my project today.

- **Express necessity:** *must* (*have to*)
  I *must* (*have to*) pass this test.

- **Express prohibition:** *must* + *not*
  You *must not* go there.

- **Express logical deduction:** *must* (*has to*)
  He *must* (*has to*) be there by now.

- **Express intention:** *will* (*shall*)
  I *will* (*shall*) go today.

3. Including linking verbs

In some languages, linking verbs (verbs like *be, seem, look, sound, feel, appear, remain*) may sometimes be omitted, but not in English.

> *look/seem/appear. . .*
> **They happy.**
>   ^

> *am*
> **I Jonathan.**
>   ^

Exercise 64.6   Using modals, other helping verbs, and linking verbs

Correct any errors in the use of modals, other helping verbs, and linking verbs in the following sentences.

EXAMPLE

> *had*
> **We been hoping that we could ~~to~~ visit California before**
>   ^
>
> **we graduated.**

1. Do you know where you and Erica will to go on vacation this summer?
2. We hoping to go to Europe, but it too expensive to travel there now.
3. You should to look online. You can to find great deals there.
4. I have been looking all over the Internet, but I not found any cheap hotels.
5. Have you thought about camping? My sister did able to save a lot of money by camping when she traveling around Europe last summer.
6. That is a great idea! Are there any campsites she can suggests in Spain and Portugal?
7. I am not sure if she went to Portugal, but she must been to Spain. Let me ask her.
8. That is excellent. I just hope I will not have buy too much camping gear.
9. I have a lot of gear, and I am sure Erica coulds borrow some of my sister's things.
10. Thanks so much! I have a feeling we going to have a great vacation after all.

4. Understanding verbals

Verbals are words derived from verbs that function as nouns or modifiers. They do not indicate tense and cannot function alone as complete verbs. There are three kinds of verbals:

- Past and present **participles** used as adjectives or in adjective phrases

  ➤ *Reading as much as they could,* **the students learned many new words.**

  The participial phrase *reading as much as they could* modifies *students.*

  ➤ *Exhausted by the race,* **the candidate withdrew.**

  The participial phrase *exhausted by the race* modifies *candidate.*

- **Gerunds,** or present participles used as nouns or in noun phrases

  ➤ **Intensive *reading* enriches your vocabulary.**

  The gerund *reading* is the subject of the sentence.

  ➤ **The conductor criticized his *singing* because it was off-key.**

  The gerund *singing* is the object of the sentence.

▪ **Infinitives** used as nouns or in noun phrases

➤ ***To graduate* on time became unlikely for her after she got sick.**

The infinitive *to graduate* is the subject of the sentence.

➤ **He managed *to complete* his dissertation in six months.**

The infinitive phrase *to complete his dissertation* is the object of the sentence.

Note: The present participle is the *-ing* form of a verb. In regular verbs, the past participle ends in *-ed,* but it takes many forms in irregular verbs. (*See the list of irregular verb forms in Chapter 35: Problems with Verbs, pp. 615–16.*)

An infinitive is the word *to* plus the base form of the verb: *to be, to learn, to graduate, to complete.*

Remember that English sentences require a complete verb that indicates tense. A participle alone cannot be a complete verb, so an expression that includes a participle but no helping verb or verbs is considered a fragment, not a complete sentence.

➤ **He** *is* **writing an essay.**

➤ **She** *has* **written an essay.**

Be aware of this strict rule, especially if your first language sometimes allows the omission of helping verbs. (*For more on fragments and how to avoid them, see Chapter 32: Sentence Fragments, pp. 572–83.*)

Gerunds after a preposition   A gerund, not an infinitive, follows a preposition:

➤ **I look forward to** ~~work~~ *working* **on the project with you instead of** ~~to do~~ *doing* **it alone.**

Present versus past participle   Although both present and past participles can function as adjectives, present-participle adjectives differ from past-participle adjectives in ways that can be difficult for multilingual writers to distinguish. To use these forms properly, keep the following in mind:

- Present-participle adjectives usually modify nouns that are the agent of an action.

  ➤ **This problem is *confusing*.**

  The present participle *confusing* modifies *problem,* which is the agent, or cause, of the confusion.

- Past-participle adjectives usually modify nouns that are the recipient of an action.

  ➤ **The students are *confused* by the problem.**

  The past participle *confused* modifies *students,* who are the recipients of the confusion the problem is causing.

Here are some other present- and past-participle pairs that often cause trouble for multilingual writers:

amazing	amazed	frightening	frightened
annoying	annoyed	interesting	interested
boring	bored	satisfying	satisfied
depressing	depressed	shocking	shocked
embarrassing	embarrassed	surprising	surprised
exciting	excited	tiring	tired
fascinating	fascinated		

Exercise 64.7 Choosing the correct participle

Underline the correct participle from each pair in parentheses.

EXAMPLE

The (tiring/<u>tired</u>) students celebrated the end of final exams.

1. I spent a busy week (preparing/prepared) for the art history final.
2. The review material is very (boring/bored).
3. The term paper I am writing for the class is on a (challenging/challenged) topic: twentieth-century painting.
4. I am especially (interesting/interested) in the paintings of Picasso.
5. I will be (relieving/relieved) when I have finished the paper and handed it in.
6. Most students have already submitted their (completing/completed) papers.
7. I am so (exciting/excited) that the semester is almost over.

Gerunds versus infinitives Verbs in English differ as to whether they can be followed by a gerund, an infinitive, or either. Some verbs, like *avoid,* can be followed by a gerund but not an infinitive.

➤ We avoided ~~to climb~~ ^climbing^ the mountain during the storm.

Other verbs, like *attempt,* can be followed by an infinitive but not a gerund.

➤ We attempted ~~reaching~~ ^to reach^ the summit when the weather cleared.

Others can be followed by either a gerund or an infinitive with no change in meaning.

➤ We began climbing.

➤ We began to climb.

Still others have a different meaning when followed by a gerund than they do when followed by an infinitive. Compare these examples:

➤ She stopped eating.
  She was eating, but she stopped.

➤ She stopped to eat.
  She stopped what she was doing, in order to eat.

You need to learn these obligatory verb-verbal combinations as you would any other aspect of new vocabulary. The lists here provide common examples of each type of verb.

Some verbs that take only an infinitive

afford	hurry	promise
appear	intend	refuse
attempt	learn	request
choose	manage	seem
claim	mean	tend
decide	need	threaten
expect	offer	want
fail	plan	wish
hope	prepare	would like

Some verbs that take only a gerund

admit	finish	recommend
advise	forgive	regret
avoid	imagine	resist
consider	look forward to	risk
defend	mention	suggest
deny	mind	support
discuss	practice	tolerate
enjoy	propose	understand
feel like	quit	urge

Some verbs that can take either a gerund or an infinitive

An asterisk (*) indicates those verbs for which the choice of gerund or infinitive affects meaning.

begin	love	stop*
continue	prefer	try*
hate	remember*	
like	start	

Exercise 64.8 Using gerunds versus infinitives after verbs

Underline the correct choice—gerund or infinitive—in each pair in parentheses.

EXAMPLE

Most people hope (to work/working) in rewarding jobs.

1. In the past, people were expected (to stay/staying) at the same job for a long time, ideally for their whole career.
2. Today, people tend (to change/changing) careers several times before retiring.
3. People who are not happy with their careers attempt (to find/finding) other jobs that interest them more.
4. Others, who regret (not to get/not getting) undergraduate or graduate degrees when they were younger, go back to school.
5. Some people even look forward to (to change/changing) jobs every few years to avoid boredom.
6. So, if you do not like your job, stop (to complain/complaining) and do something about it.

65 English Sentence Structure

65a Learn the requirements of English word order.

English has strict rules of word order in sentences. These rules can present difficulties for multilingual students.

1. Understanding word order in declarative sentences

Declarative sentences provide information (declare something) about their subjects.

The English word order for declarative sentences with a transitive verb is subject–verb–object (or S–V–O) (*See the box "For Multilingual Students: English Word Order" in Chapter 31, p. 552.*)

	V S O
FAULTY WORD ORDER	Wrote Clara Schumann a piano concerto.

	S V O
REVISED	Clara Schumann wrote a piano concerto.

Stated subject All English sentences and clauses except commands (discussed later) must have an explicitly stated subject.

➤ The teacher told us to review sentence structure. ~~Said~~ we *She said*

would have a quiz on it next week.

Unlike in some other languages, however, in English a pronoun cannot duplicate the subject.

➤ The teacher ~~she~~ told us to review sentence structure.

Word order in verb phrases Helping verbs always precede the main verb in verb phrases.

➤ I have been sick lately. *(hv) (mv)*

The negative word *not* usually precedes the main verb and follows the first helping verb in a verb phrase.

>   *not*
> ➤ I have been ~~not~~ sick lately.

Word order of indirect and direct objects   Some transitive verbs—including *ask, bring, find, get, give, hand, lend, offer, pay, promise, read, send, show, teach, tell, write*—can take an indirect object as well as a direct object. The **direct object** receives the action of the verb; the **indirect object** is the beneficiary of the action.

    The indirect object usually precedes the direct object.

	ind obj	dir obj
➤ The students sent	**their parents**	**an e-mail message.**
➤ The students sent	**them**	**an e-mail message.**

The indirect object can follow the direct object if it is introduced by a preposition such as *to* or *for*.

>   *to*
> ➤ The students sent an e-mail message their parents.

> *Exception:* If the indirect object is a noun and the direct object is a pronoun, the indirect object cannot come before the direct object.
>
>   *to their parents*
> ➤ The students sent ~~their parents~~ it.

    Some verbs, such as *analyze, describe, mention,* and *say,* do not take an indirect object before the direct object.

>   *to her friend*
> ➤ She mentioned ~~her friend~~ the news.

>   *for us*
> ➤ The scientist analyzed ~~us~~ the compound.

2. Understanding word order in questions

Questions can take a variety of forms. In most of them the S–V word order of declarative sentences is reversed, and the verb, or part of it, precedes the subject.

> ▪ For simple forms of the verb *be,* put the subject before the verb.
>
> She *was* on time for the   *Was* she on time for
> meeting.   the meeting?

- For other simple verbs, begin the question with a form of *do* followed by the subject and then the main verb.

You *noticed* the change in the report.   *Did* you *notice* the change in the report?

- For verbs consisting of a main verb with one or more helping verbs, put the subject after the first (or only) helping verb.

He *is pleased* with the results.   *Is* he *pleased* with the results?

You *have been waiting* a long time.   *Have* you *been waiting* a long time?

The guests *have arrived*.   *Have* the guests *arrived*?

- Questions that begin with question words like *how, what, who, when, where,* or *why* follow the same patterns.

When did the guests *arrive*?

Where have you *been* hiding?

- When the question word is the subject, however, the question follows the S–V word order of a declarative sentence.

What happened last night?

Who spilled the milk?

3. Understanding word order in commands

In commands, or imperative sentences, the subject, which is always *you,* is omitted.

➤ [you] **Read the instructions before using this machine.**

➤ [you] **Do not enter.**

➤ [you] **Do not touch this chemical—it is hazardous.**

Exercise 65.1   Understanding word order in declarative sentences, questions, and commands

Find and correct the errors in the following sentences. Some sentences have more than one error.

EXAMPLE

the ring
Frodo ~~the ring~~ **carries to Mount Doom.**

1. J. R. R. Tolkien he wrote the three books of *The Lord of the Rings.*
2. You have read them yet?
3. What the books are about?

4. The books describe us the world of Middle Earth.

5. Gandalf gives to Frodo a magical ring.

6. The movies are good?

7. The movies won many Oscars?

8. You tell me your opinion of the movies after you see them.

4. Understanding word order in reported speech

Changing a direct quotation (someone else's exact words) to an indirect quotation (a report of what the person said or wrote) often requires changing many sentence elements. When the quotation is a declarative sentence, however, the subject-before-verb word order does not change.

DIRECT QUOTATION   The instructor said, "You have only one more week to finish your papers."

INDIRECT QUOTATION   The instructor told the students that they had only one more week to finish their papers.

Changing a direct question to an indirect question, however, does require a word order change: from the V–S pattern of a question to the S–V pattern of a declarative sentence.

DIRECT QUESTION   The instructor always asks, "Are you ready to begin?"

INDIRECT QUESTION   The instructor always asks [us] if we are ready to begin.

In an indirect quotation of a command, a pronoun or noun takes the place of the command's omitted subject, *you,* and is followed by the infinitive (*to*) form of the verb.

DIRECT QUOTATION: COMMAND   The instructor always says, "[*you*] Write down the assignment before you leave."

INDIRECT QUOTATION: COMMAND   The instructor always tells *us* to write down the assignment before we leave.

In indirectly quoted negative imperatives, the word *not* comes before the infinitive.

DIRECT   The instructor said, "Do not forget your homework."

INDIRECT   The instructor reminded us *not* to forget our homework.

967

5. Placing adverbs

An adverbial modifier should never come between the verb and the direct object in a sentence.

➤ She finished ~~quickly~~ the exam. ^{quickly}

or

➤ She ^quickly^ finished ~~quickly~~ the exam.

➤ She presented ~~with great eloquence~~ the issue. ^{with great eloquence}

Adverbs can come after, but usually not before, the first helping verb in a verb phrase.

➤ They ~~gradually~~ are ^gradually^ moving into their new home.

Note that adverbs of frequency (*sometimes, often, never*) usually fall between the subject and the predicate.

➤ She *sometimes* writes articles for this magazine.

When adverbs occur at the very beginning of a sentence, they usually show special emphasis.

➤ *Sneakily,* she hid the letter under her bed.

Certain adverbs—mostly negatives like *never, rarely,* and *seldom*—change the normal subject-before-verb word order when they appear at the beginning of a sentence.

➤ Rarely ^is^ the weather ~~is~~ so cold in California.

(*See the box "For Multilingual Students: Adverbial Modifiers and Subject-Verb Order" in Chapter 45, p. 742.*)

65b Use subordinating and coordinating words correctly.

1. Distinguishing the different functions of *that*

The word *that* can introduce a subordinate clause either as a relative pronoun or as a subordinating conjunction.

➤ **The house *that* they decided to buy needs a lot of renovation.**

The relative pronoun *that* replaces the noun *house.*

➤ **The Bakers said *that* their new house needed a lot of renovation.**

The subordinating conjunction *that* introduces a noun clause that is the direct object of the sentence.

2. Using either subordination or coordination

Do not use both subordination and coordination together to combine the same two clauses, even if the subordinating and coordinating words are similar in meaning. Some examples include use of *although* or *even though* with *but* and use of *because* with *therefore.*

FAULTY   *Although* I came early, *but* the tickets were already sold out.

REVISED   *Although* I came early, the tickets were already sold out.

or

I came early, *but* the tickets were already sold out.

FAULTY   *Because* Socrates is human, and humans are mortal, *therefore,* Socrates is mortal.

REVISED   *Because* Socrates is human, and humans are mortal, Socrates is mortal.

or

Socrates is human, and humans are mortal; *therefore,* Socrates is mortal.

3. Distinguishing *because* and *for*

The word *for,* when used as a subordinating conjunction, has the same meaning as *because. For* is more formal, however, and is used less frequently.

FORMAL SOUNDING   He did not respond to the employment ad *for* he knew he had little chance of getting the job.

PREFERRED   He did not respond to the employment ad *because* he knew he had little chance of getting the job.

Exercise 65.2   Using English word order

Find and correct the errors in the following sentences. Some sentences
have more than one error.

EXAMPLE

**Because they worry about food so much, ~~therefore~~
Americans may have more eating-related problems
than people in other developed countries.**

1. As Michael Pollan in the *New York Times Magazine* writes,
   Americans have become the world's most anxious eaters.
2. Researchers have found that Americans they worry more about
   what they eat than people do in other developed countries.
3. Therefore, tend to enjoy their food less and associate a good meal
   with guilty pleasure.
4. Paradoxically, this worrying does not stop regularly many
   Americans from overeating.
5. The report also tells to readers that it is not uncommon for
   people to visit the gym after overeating.
6. The people of many other nations take pleasure in eating and
   turn often a meal into a festive occasion.
7. Although they relish their meals, but they are less prone to
   obesity or eating disorders than Americans.
8. Some scientists speculate that the people of these nations therefore are less obese because they cook with more healthful ingredients than Americans.
9. The question arises, however, whether might people's attitude
   toward eating be as important to good health as what they eat?

66 Identifying and Editing Common Errors

For multilingual students one of the main sources of errors in written English is native language interference, or the inappropriate transfer of usages from different languages into English. It helps to be aware of the similarities and differences between English and your native language (for example, in vocabulary, tense formation, word order, and article use) especially when you are editing your writing.

Interference can be both lexical (involving the meaning and structure of words) and syntactic (involving the structure of sentences).

66a Beware of misleading cognates.

Because English evolved from several different languages, you may find that some English words are very similar to words in your native language (and indeed have a similar origin). Explore these **cognates,** but do not rely on them. You will find many to be false friends: you turn to them for support, but they let you down because they have a different meaning in English than in your native language.

Here are some examples:

ENGLISH WORD	MEANING IN ENGLISH	COGNATES IN OTHER LANGUAGES AND THEIR MEANING
assist	help	Spanish *asistir:* attend
attend	be present at	French *attendre:* wait for
demand	request forcefully, claim	French *demander:* request, ask a question of
fabric	cloth	German *fabrik:* factory
library	a place where books can be borrowed	French *librairie,* Spanish *librería,* Italian *libreria,* Portuguese *livraria:* bookstore

(*continued*)

ENGLISH WORD	MEANING IN ENGLISH	COGNATES IN OTHER LANGUAGES AND THEIR MEANING
passionate	emotional	French *passionnant:* fascinating
sympathetic	compassionate	French *sympathique,* Spanish, *simpático,* Italian *simpatico:* nice, friendly

➤ She ~~demanded~~ ^{asked} her instructor for an extension on her

term paper.

➤ We bought our textbooks at the campus ~~library~~ ^{bookstore}.

66b Express quantity appropriately.

As discussed in Chapter 64 (*section 64a*), some quantifiers can be used with count nouns only, some with noncount nouns only, and some with both count and noncount nouns. Certain quantifiers differ subtly in the quantity of a thing they designate. Here are some examples, arranged on a scale from small amount to large amount:

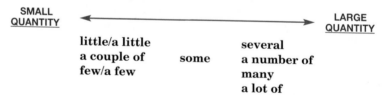

SMALL QUANTITY			LARGE QUANTITY
little/a little a couple of few/a few	some	several a number of many a lot of	

The quantifiers *a few* and *few* for count nouns and *a little* and *little* for noncount nouns all indicate a small quantity. In contrast to *a few* and *a little,* however, *few* and *little* have the negative connotation of "hardly any."

➤ **The problems are difficult, and we have *few* options for solving them.**

The outlook for solving the problems is gloomy.

➤ **The problems are difficult, but we have *a few* options for solving them.**

The outlook for solving the problems is hopeful.

➤ **We have *little time* to find a campsite before sunset.**

The campers might have to spend the night in the open by the side of the trail.

➤ **We have *a little time* to find a campsite before sunset.**

The campers will probably find a place to pitch their tent before dark.

66c Understand adverb formation.

The usual way to form an adverb is to add the ending *-ly* to the corresponding adjective. The adjective *quick,* for example, becomes the adverb *quickly,* and the adjective *happy* becomes the adverb *happily.*

However, there are exceptions to this rule.

1. Not all adverbs end in *-ly.*

Adjective	Adverb
good	well
fast	fast
hard	hard

Note: Adding *-ly* to *hard* does produce an adverb, but one that has a different meaning than the adverb *hard.*

Hardly means "almost not at all."

➤ **He *hardly* works.**

He is lazy.

Hard, in contrast, means "with great exertion."

➤ **He works *hard.***

He works a lot.

2. Some words that end in *-ly* are adjectives, not adverbs. Examples include *friendly, lovely, manly.*

3. Adverbs such as *seldom* and *often* do not have corresponding adjectives.

When in doubt about the meaning or form of an adverb, consult your dictionary. (*For more on adverb usage, see Chapter 37: Problems with Adjectives and Adverbs, pp. 661–73.*)

Exercise 66.1 Avoiding lexical pitfalls: False friends, quantifiers, and adverb formation

Correct the errors in lexical usage in the following sentences. Note that to identify the errors in some of them, you will need to refer to Chapter 64.

EXAMPLE

Although the field hands work hardly all day, they make a little money.

1. A great deal of reports in the press point out that the spread of infections in hospitals has reached almost epidemic proportions.
2. The best way for hospital staffs to prevent the spread of infections is to follow meticulous hygiene procedures.
3. Hospital workers are demanded to wash their hands often.
4. They should wash their hands after the interaction with every patients.
5. Otherwise, there is a little hope of stopping the spread of infections.
6. On the other hand, no matter how hardly they try, hospital workers cannot completely eliminate the risk of infection.
7. Hospital visitors also need to take few precautions to avoid health risks to themselves and patients.
8. To avoid contact with dangerous microbes, for example, visitors should touch as little surfaces as possible while in the hospital.
9. Visitors should also wash their hands carefully after all visit.
10. In the end, however, patients and visitors have to rely mostly on their immune systems to ward off infection.

66d Manage English prepositions.

The relationship between prepositions and the words they accompany is often arbitrary. In standard English, for example, people ride *in* cars but *on* trains. They eat a romantic dinner *by* candlelight, but they cook it *on* a stove *with* gas. As a result, the use of prepositions is among the most difficult aspects of English for multilingual students to master.

Some of the most troublesome combinations are those with verbs and with adjectives. Whenever you learn a new adjective or verb, you should also learn the preposition or prepositions that are commonly used with it. Here are some examples:

SOME VERB-AND-PREPOSITION COMBINATIONS

approve of	compare with/to	distinguish from
base on	consist of	focus on
believe in	contribute to	insist on
combine with	depend on	prefer to

SOME ADJECTIVE-AND-PREPOSITION COMBINATIONS

afraid of	content with	proud of
associated with	familiar with	sorry for
aware of	famous for	tired of
capable of	interested in	worried about

66e Master phrasal verbs.

In some cases, adding one or two prepositions to a verb changes the verb's meaning. These verb-preposition combinations are called **phrasal verbs.**

PHRASAL VERB	DEFINITION	EXAMPLE
turn away	avert, refuse	The refugees were *turned away* at the border.
turn off	disconnect, stop	Who *turned off* the lights?
turn on	connect, start	I overslept because I forgot to *turn on* the alarm.
turn down	reject	The company *turned down* her job application.

Phrasal verbs are of two kinds: separable and inseparable. A phrasal verb is **separable** if a direct object can come between the verb and the preposition or after the preposition:

➤ *Put your books away.*

➤ *Put away your books.*

Note: If the direct object of a separable phrasal verb is a pronoun, it must come between the verb and the preposition.

   them
➤ *Put away* ~~them.~~

975

SOME SEPARABLE PHRASAL VERBS

ask out	give up	put off
call back	hand in	start over
call off	hand out	take off
cross out	pick up	throw away
fill in	put away	try on
fill out	put back	write down
give back	put down	

A phrasal verb is **inseparable** if no other word can come between the verb and the preposition:

➤ I *ran into* Mark on the street.

SOME INSEPARABLE PHRASAL VERBS

call on	get on	look out
come across	get out	pass out
drop in (on)	get over	run into
drop out (of)	get through	run out (of)
get back	grow up	speak up
get in	keep on	watch out (for)
get off		

66f Learn the meaning of idioms.

Idioms are expressions whose meaning cannot be understood from the meaning of the individual words they are composed of. They are usually phrases that may consist of several different categories of words. Learn the whole structure of an idiom as you would learn any other vocabulary word.

Here are some common idioms:

IDIOM	MEANING
be in seventh heaven	be elated
be on the ball	be intelligent
child's play	easy
get something off one's chest	confess
get the ball rolling	start a project
get to the point	do not digress
hit the sack	sleep
hold one's tongue	keep silent

(continued)

IDIOM	MEANING
make ends meet	live within one's income
odds and ends	miscellaneous things
on the tip of one's tongue	almost remembered
pain in the neck	aggravating
pay through the nose	pay a painfully large amount of money
push one's luck	risk losing what one has gained by trying too hard for something
scared stiff	terrified
talk nonsense	be illogical
be in a fix	be in difficulty
make headway	make progress
stir things up	provoke action

Note that many idioms, including many of those listed here, are also clichés and should be avoided in formal writing.

Exercise 66.2 Avoiding lexical pitfalls: Prepositions, phrasal verbs, and idioms

Fill in the missing preposition in each sentence.

EXAMPLE

High school students often worry _about_ **getting into the college of their choice.**

1. High school teenagers are aware _____ the difficulty of getting into a good college.
2. Not only do they have to excel _____ their studies, but they also have to have many extracurricular interests.
3. Students try to distinguish themselves _____ other students through their activities.
4. They participate _____ dance, language, or art clubs; they try out for sports teams; or they work on the yearbook.
5. Sometimes they insist _____ doing things they do not particularly enjoy, just to make their college applications look impressive.
6. The pressures of college applications combined _____ schoolwork, homework, and extracurricular activities can be very stressful.
7. Teachers feel sorry _____ students, who often become overworked and overextended.

977

8. Students need to find balance and realize that getting ____ a college cannot be their only focus.

9. They should enjoy high school and be content ____ their daily accomplishments.

66g Avoid errors in subject-verb agreement.

There is a special relationship between the subject and the verb in an English sentence. The subject and verb—in most cases adjacent to one another—are the core of the sentence and must agree in person and number. The following steps will help assure subject-verb agreement in your sentences.

1. Identify the subject. Determine its person (first, second, or third) and number (singular or plural). Remember that in regular nouns the ending -s signals the plural form (see 64a). In other cases, identifying whether a subject is singular or plural can present problems:

   ■ Nouns with irregular plurals (see 64a)

   ■ Nouns without singular forms (*trousers, binoculars*)

   ■ Noncount nouns, which are always singular

   ■ Subjects accompanied by quantifiers

   ■ Indefinite pronouns, most of which are always singular, but some of which are always plural, and some of which can be singular or plural depending on context (see *Chapter 34: Subject-Verb Agreement, pp. 608–9*)

   ■ Gerunds and infinitives, which are always singular

   ■ The word *what,* which is always singular when it is the subject of a question

   ■ The filler subject *there,* which can be either singular or plural depending on the subject it fills in for

     ➤ There *are* some *tools* for this experiment.

     ➤ There *is* new *equipment* in the lab.

     ➤ There *is* no *tolerance* for discrimination in our society.

2. Study and apply the general rules for subject-verb agreement.

   ■ For the simple present tense of regular verbs, a third-person singular or noncount subject takes the base form of the verb with the ending -s or -es. All other subjects take the base form with no ending.

> The *student writes* well.

> The new lab *equipment works* well.

> College *students write* frequently.

> *I/you/we/they write* frequently.

■ The verb *be* has three present tense forms (*am, are,* and *is*) and two past tense forms (*was* and *were*).

> *I am* often early for class.

> The *student is* often late for meetings.

> The *teacher was* late yesterday.

> The *teachers/we/you/they were* never late for class.

> The *students/we/you/they are* never late for class.

■ In all tenses formed with auxiliary verbs, including all passive-voice verbs, the subject agrees with the auxiliary verb.

> The *teacher has* graded all the papers.

> The *students have* completed the assignment.

> The *student is* applying for a scholarship.

> The *teachers were* grading papers all week.

> The *homework is/was* completed by the student.

> The *assignments are/were* submitted by all the students.

(For a detailed discussion of subject-verb agreement, tense formation, and voice, see Chapter 34: Subject-Verb Agreement, pp. 597–612, and Chapter 35: Problems with Verbs, pp. 613–37.)

Exercise 66.3 Avoiding syntactic pitfalls: Subject-verb agreement

Find and correct the errors in the following sentences.

EXAMPLE

The price of digital cameras ~~are~~ *is* falling.

1. Obesity in children and adolescents are becoming a major problem around the world.
2. Statistics reveals that more than fifteen percent of children and adolescents are obese.

3. There is several causes for obesity, some of which are subject to individual control and some of which are not.
4. Genetics are not subject to individual control.
5. The many controllable causes of obesity includes lack of exercise, sedentary behavior, and poor eating habits.
6. Socioeconomic status can trigger obesity because healthful food also tend to be relatively expensive.
7. The environment in which people live affect their diet and the amount of exercise they get.
8. Preventing obesity in children are not easy.
9. Collaboration between schools and families are needed to create an active and healthy environment for children.
10. Everyone agree that the consequences of obesity in adulthood can be deadly, so it is critical to diagnose and treat this problem early.

66h Avoid errors in pronoun reference.

In English, a pronoun must agree with its antecedent (the noun it refers to) in number and gender. In addition, the antecedent for the pronoun you are using should be clear and located close enough to it to avoid any ambiguity. (*For a detailed discussion of pronoun reference, see Chapter 36: Problems with Pronouns, pp. 649–60.*)

Exercise 66.4 Avoiding syntactic pitfalls: Pronoun reference

Find and correct the errors in the following sentences.

EXAMPLE

its
The computer has become ubiquitous since ~~their~~ invention more than fifty years ago.

1. Cafés are finding modern ways to attract its customers.
2. A coffee drinker no longer needs to bring their friends to a café to have a conversation.
3. Internet access allows customers to bring his computer instead.
4. Instead of hearing the conversations of other people, the customer hears their fingers clicking on keyboards.
5. Providing Internet access is a clever marketing idea because when someone is on the Internet, they are likely to stay at the café a long time and buy more coffee than they otherwise would.

6. In addition, comfortable couches provide the customer with a homey ambience that makes them reluctant to leave.

7. At cafés that offer free Internet access, one can expect to see a group of students working on their computer.

8. Students can get a cup of coffee, surf the Web, and pay for it online with a credit card.

9. So it is not surprising to see a person at a café laughing aloud while typing furiously on her laptop.

10. The computer probably cannot replace face-to-face interaction, but they can put people all over the world in instant communication with one another.

66i   Avoid errors in word order.

When constructing a sentence, check for the following aspects of word order:

- The inclusion of a subject (obligatory) and, depending on the type of sentence, the order of subject and verb (*see 65a*)
- The logical placement of adjectives (*see 64a*)
- The correct placement of objects (direct and indirect) and modifiers (adverbs) (*see 65a*)

Exercise 66.5   Editing for word order

Correct any word order errors in the following paragraph.

EXAMPLE

the Tour de France
Lance Armstrong won seven times ~~the Tour de France~~.
                                    ^

During even good times, credit card debt is a burden heavy to carry. Financial advisers stress always that people should stop adding to their debt and begin rapidly paying it down while they have the option. When asked what would they do if they knew they would be laid off in six months, most people say they would start slashing expenses. Consuming less and buying less are both ways reasonable to reduce outflow. Every household needs a pool of money to keep it afloat during hard times when the income stream dries temporarily up. That fund needs to hold enough to pay the bills and keep on the table food for at least six months. Having enough money tucked away to survive for half a year can soften the blow of unemployment because buys precious time for a job search.

66j Understand tense sequence in reported speech.

As pointed out in Chapter 65 (*p. 967*), changing a direct quotation to an indirect quotation often requires changes in many sentence elements. In addition to the changes in word order discussed in Chapter 65, these include changes in tense sequence.

If the verb that introduces the quotation is in the present tense, the tense of the indirect quotation is the same as the tense of the direct quotation.

DIRECT He says, "I believe you."

INDIRECT He says that he believes me.

However, if the introductory verb is in the past, the tense of the indirect quotation shifts in the following ways:

- The simple present becomes the simple past:

  DIRECT He said, "I believe you."

  INDIRECT He said that he believed me.

- The simple past and the present perfect become the past perfect:

  DIRECT She said, "We saw the movie."

  DIRECT She said, "We have seen the movie."

  INDIRECT She said that they had seen the movie.

- The future becomes future-in-the-past:

  DIRECT She said, "We will see the movie tomorrow."

  INDIRECT She said that they would see the movie tomorrow.

- The past perfect remains the same:

  DIRECT They said, "We had hoped the movie would be better."

  INDIRECT They said that they had hoped the movie would be better.

66k Avoid double negation.

In English, negative meaning is expressed either by negating the verb with *not* or by using another negative word like *no, nothing, never,* or *hardly*—but not both. Unlike many languages, standard English does not permit two negatives in one sentence.

➤ The students ~~did not have~~ *had* no homework.

or

➤ The students did not have ~~no~~ *any* homework.

Exercise 66.6 Understanding tense sequence in direct and reported speech

Change direct speech to reported (indirect) speech, and reported speech to direct speech.

EXAMPLES

DIRECT **Roosevelt said to the American people, "The only thing we have to fear is fear itself."**

REPORTED **Roosevelt told the American people that the only thing they had to fear was fear itself.**

1. "Class, we will discuss Jane Austen's novel *Pride and Prejudice*," said the professor.
2. She explained that before *Pride and Prejudice,* Jane Austen had published another novel titled *Sense and Sensibility.*
3. "There are four other novels by Jane Austen, but *Pride and Prejudice* is the most popular," said the professor.
4. The professor asked if anyone had read any of the other novels, such as *Emma* or *Sense and Sensibility.*
5. "I saw the movies when they came out," a student answered.
6. A student asked if Austen's other novels had themes similar to those in *Pride and Prejudice.*
7. The professor replied that the themes of family and society were prevalent in all of Austen's novels.
8. "Have we seen hints of her characteristic satirical tone in the first several chapters of *Pride and Prejudice*?" asked the professor.
9. A student replied that Mrs. Bennett was an example of satire directed at the women of the period.
10. "Austen also presents a satire of marriage in the characters of Mr. and Mrs. Bennett," another student added.

CHECKLIST

Self-Editing for Multilingual Students

As a multilingual writer, think of errors as signals to help keep you oriented toward your learning goals. As you edit, try to look past occasional lapses in grammar to see if you can detect patterns in your mistakes—that is, recurring errors in structure.

This checklist will help you identify the types of errors that can confuse your readers. Check the rules for those items that you have trouble with, and study them in context to avoid future errors.

As you edit a sentence, ask yourself these questions:

☐ Do the subject and verb agree? (*See Chapters 34: Subject-Verb Agreement and 35: Problems with Verbs, as well as 66g.*)

☐ Is the form of the verb or verbs correct? (*See Chapters 34: Subject-Verb Agreement and 35: Problems with Verbs, as well as the coverage of verb phrases in Chapter 64.*)

☐ Is the tense of the verb or verbs appropriate and correctly formed? (*See Chapters 34: Subject-Verb Agreement and 35: Problems with Verbs, as well as the coverage of verb phrases in Chapter 64 and tense formation in Chapter 66.*)

☐ Do all pronouns agree with their referents, and are the referents unambiguous? (*See Chapter 36: Problems with Pronouns, as well as the coverage of pronouns in Chapters 64 and 66.*)

☐ Is the word order correct for the sentence type (for example, declarative or interrogative)? Is the word order of any reported speech correct? (*See Chapter 65.*)

☐ Is the sentence complete (not a fragment)? Is the sentence a run-on or a comma splice? (*See Chapters 32: Sentence Fragments and 33: Comma Splices and Run-on Sentences.*)

☐ Are articles and quantifiers used correctly? (*See Chapter 64.*)

☐ Is the sentence active or passive? (*See Chapter 31: Sentence Basics, Chapter 35: Problems with Verbs, and Chapter 46: Active Verbs.*)

☐ Are the words in the sentence well chosen? (*See Chapter 48: Appropriate Language and Chapter 49: Exact Language.*)

☐ Is the sentence punctuated correctly? (*See the chapters in Part 10: Sentence Punctuation and Part 11: Mechanics and Spelling.*)

ABBREVIATIONS

ALB.	ALBANIA
AUST.	AUSTRIA
BELG.	BELGIUM
BOS.	BOSNIA AND HERZEGOVINA
BULG.	BULGARIA
DEN.	DENMARK
DOM. REP.	DOMINICAN REPUBLIC
CRO.	CROATIA
CZECH.	CZECH REPUBLIC
EST.	ESTONIA
GER.	GERMANY
HUNG.	HUNGARY
LAT.	LATVIA
LITH.	LITHUANIA
LUX.	LUXEMBURG
MAC.	MACEDONIA
NETH.	NETHERLANDS
ROM.	ROMANIA
RUSS.	RUSSIA
S. M.	SERBIA AND MONTENEGRO
SLOVK.	SLOVAKIA
SLOVN.	SLOVENIA
SWITZ.	SWITZERLAND
U. A. E.	UNITED ARAB EMIRATES

Thursday 5:00 p.m.	**Thursday 7:00 p.m.**	**Thursday 8:00 p.m.**	**Thursday 9:00 p.m.**	**Friday 1:00 a.m.**	**Friday 2:00 a.m.**	**Friday 3:00 a.m.**	**Friday 4:00 a.m.**	**Friday 4:30 a.m.**	**Friday 8:00 a.m.**	**Friday 9:00 a.m.**	**Friday 10:00 a.m.**
San Francisco, USA	Chicago, USA Mexico City, Mexico	Montreal, Canada New York, USA Havana, Cuba Santiago, Chile	Sao Paulo, Brazil Buenos Aires, Argentina	Dublin, Ireland Lisbon, Portugal	Stockholm, Sweden Berlin, Germany Rome, Italy Cape Town, South Africa	Cairo, Egypt	Moscow, Russia Baghdad, Iraq	Tehran, Iran Kabul, Afghanistan	Shanghai, China Manila, Philippines Singapore	Tokyo, Japan	Sydney, Australia

Many multilingual students encounter problems when they try to transfer their thoughts from one language into another. For example, some languages, like Russian and Chinese, do not include articles such as *a*, *an*, and *the* (English: *The flowers are beautiful*); other languages, such as Arabic and French, do not use definite articles to introduce a profession (English: *Here is the doctor*); still others, such as Spanish, include articles to indicate a generalization, whereas English does not (English: *time flies*). More tips for multilingual writers appear in the many *For Multilingual Students* boxes found throughout this handbook and in the three-chapter guide for multilingual writers in Part 12, but here is a quick reference for dealing with some of the common issues that come up when you are transferring your first language into English.

Nouns and Pronouns

Count and Noncount Nouns

Count nouns name persons, places, or things that can be counted. Count nouns can be singular or plural.

Noncount nouns name a class of things. Usually, noncount nouns have only a singular form.

COUNT	NONCOUNT
cars	information
table	furniture
child	humanity
book	advice

Pronouns

Common Problem: Personal pronoun restates subject.

| INCORRECT | My sister, *she* works in the city. |
| CORRECT | My sister works in the city. |

Pronouns replace nouns. They stand for persons, places, or things and can be singular or plural.

Personal pronouns act as subjects, objects, or words that show possession.

Subject pronouns: I, we, you, he, she, it, one, they, who

Object pronouns: me, us, you, him, her, it, one, them, whom

Possessive pronouns: my, mine, our, ours, your, yours, his, her, hers, its, their, theirs, whose

Relative pronouns introduce dependent clauses.

Relative pronouns: that, whatever, which, whichever, who, whoever, whom, whomever, whose

| EXAMPLE | His sister, *who* lives in Canada, came to visit. |

Articles

Common Problem: Article is omitted.

| INCORRECT | Water is cold. I bought watch. |
| CORRECT | *The* water is cold. I bought *a* watch. |

Using Articles with Count and Noncount Nouns

Definite article (*the*): used for specific reference with all types of nouns.

The car I bought is red. [*singular count noun*]

The dogs howled at the moon. [*plural count noun*]

The furniture makes the room appear cluttered. [*noncount noun*]

Do not use *the* before most singular proper nouns, such as names of people, cities, languages, and so on.

~~The~~ Dallas is a beautiful city.

Indefinite articles (*a, an*): used with singular count nouns only.

Use *a* before a word that begins with a consonant sound.

a pencil

a sports car

a tropical rain forest

Use *an* before a word that begins with a vowel sound.

an orange

an hour

an instrument

Do not use an indefinite article with a noncount noun.

Water
~~A water~~ is leaking from the faucet.

No article: Plural count nouns and noncount nouns do not require *indefinite* articles. Plural count nouns and noncount nouns do not need *definite* articles when they refer to all of the items in a group.

Plural count nouns and noncount nouns

Every night I hear ~~a~~ dogs barking.

I needed to find ~~an~~ information in the library.

Plural count nouns

| SPECIFIC ITEM | *The* dogs next door never stop barking. |
| ALL ITEMS IN A GROUP | Dogs make good pets. |

Noncount nouns

| SPECIFIC ITEM | *The* jewelry she wore to the party was beautiful. |
| ALL ITEMS IN A GROUP | Jewelry is expensive. |

Verbs

Common Problem: *be* verb is left out.

| INCORRECT | He sleeping now. She happy. |
| CORRECT | He *is* sleeping now. She *is* happy |

Verb Tenses

Tense refers to the time of action expressed by a verb.

Present tense (base form or form with -s ending): action taking place now.

I *sleep* here. She *sleeps*. We *sleep* late every weekend.

Past tense (-d or -ed ending): past action.

I *laughed*. He *laughed*. They *laughed* together.

Future tense (*will* + base form): action that is going to take place.

I *will go* to the movie. He *will run* in the marathon. You *will write* the paper.

Present perfect tense (*have* or *has* + past participle): past action that was or will be completed.

I *have spoken*. He *has washed* the floor. We *have made* lunch.

Past perfect tense (*had* + past participle): past action completed before another past action.

I *had spoken*. She *has been* busy. They *had noticed* a slight error.

Future perfect tense (*will* + *have* + past participle): action that will begin and end in the future before another action happens.

I *will have eaten*. She *will have danced* in the recital by then. You *will have taken* the train.

Present progressive tense (*am*, *are*, or *is* + present participle): continuing action.

I *am writing* a novel. He *is working* on a new project. They *are studying* for the test.

Past progressive tense (*was* or *were* + present participle): past continuing action.

I *was cleaning* the house. She *was working* in the yard. You *were making* dinner.

Future progressive tense (*will* + *be* + present participle): future continuing action

I *will be traveling* to Europe. She *will be sightseeing* in New York. They *will be eating* together tonight.

Present perfect progressive tense (*have* or *has* + *been* + present participle): past action that continues in the present.

I *have been practicing*. He *has been sleeping* all morning. They *have been coming* every weekend.

Past perfect progressive tense (*had* + *been* + present participle): continuous action completed before another past action.

I *had been driving* for six hours. She *had been reading* when I arrived. They *had been singing*.

Future perfect progressive tense (*will* + *have* + *been* + present participle): action that will begin, continue, and end in the future.

I *will have been driving* for ten hours. He *will have been living* there for three years. You *will have been studying* for the test all afternoon.

Sentence Structure

Subjects and Verbs

English requires both a subject and a verb in every sentence or clause.

S   V   S   V
She slept.   He ate.

Direct and Indirect Objects

Verbs may be followed by *direct* or *indirect objects*. A *direct object* receives the action of the verb.

S   V   DO
He drove the car.

An *indirect object* is the person or thing to which something is done.

S   V   IO   DO
She gave her sister a birthday gift.

The United States is one of only a few countries in the world that have not converted to the International System of Units (SI), otherwise known as the modern metric system. You will encounter this system of measurement in all science courses. Following is a helpful conversion chart for many common units of metric measurement. (Source: Merriam-Webster online dictionary and the U.S. Metric Association Web site)

Length

1 kilometer (km) = 0.62 mile
1 hectometer (hm) = 328.08 feet
1 decameter (dam) = 32.81 feet
1 meter (m) = 39.37 inches
1 decimeter (dm) = 3.94 inches
1 centimeter (cm) = 0.39 inch
1 millimeter (mm) = 0.039 inch
1 micrometer (μm) = 0.000039 inch

Area

1 square kilometer (sq km *or* km^2) = 0.3861 square mile
1 hectare (ha) = 2.47 acres
1 are (a) = 119.60 square yards
1 square centimeter (sq cm *or* cm^2) = 0.155 square inch

Volume

1 cubic meter (m^3) = 1.307 cubic yards
1 cubic decimeter (dm^3) = 61.023 cubic inches
1 cubic centimeter (cu cm *or* cm^3, *also* cc) = 0.061 cubic inch

Capacity (liquid)

1 decaliter (dal) = 2.64 gallons
1 liter (l) = 1.057 quarts
1 cubic decimeter (dm^3) = 1.057 quarts
1 deciliter (dl) = .21 pint
1 centiliter (cl) = 0.338 fluid ounce
1 milliliter (ml) = 0.27 fluid dram
1 microliter (μl) = 0.00027 fluid dram

Mass and Weight

1 metric ton (t) = 1.102 short tons
1 kilogram (kg) = 2.2046 pounds
1 hectogram (hg) = 3.527 ounces
1 decagram (dag) = 0.353 ounce
1 gram (g) = 0.035 ounce
1 decigram (dg) = 1.543 grains
1 centigram (cg) = 0.154 grain
1 milligram (mg) = 0.015 grain
1 microgram (μg) = 0.000015 grain

This fourteenth-century map features Mansa Musa, the greatest ruler of the Empire of Mali in West Africa. During his reign, Mali prospered as a hub of trade and learning.

The adequate study of culture, our own and those on the opposite side of the globe, can press on to fulfillment only as we learn today from the humanities as well as from the scientists.

—RUTH BENEDICT

Further
Resources
for Learning

Timeline of World History

ca. 3000 BCE City of Babylon is founded; cuneiform script, the earliest known fully developed system of writing, emerges in ancient Mesopotamia.

3000

2500–2001 BCE Bow and arrow is first used in warfare; cotton is cultivated in Peru.

ca. 2660–1640 BCE Old and Middle Kingdoms of Egypt. Pyramids and grand monuments such as the Great Sphinx of Giza are built as royal tributes and burial structures.

2000 BCE *Gilgamesh,* ancient Mesopotamian epic, is composed (fullest extant *written* text of this epic dates from **seventh century BCE**): theme is futile human quest for immortality.

2000

ca. 1950 BCE Irrigation systems are in use in Chinese agriculture.

ca. 1850 BCE Oldest surviving Egyptian mathematics text shows that decimal system was in use.

1792–1750 BCE Rule of Babylonian king Hammurabi produces an orderly arrangement of written laws—the Hammurabi Code—among the first in the ancient world.

1200 BCE Olmec culture flourishes in Mexico (until **ca. 400 BCE**).

ca. 1000–80 BCE Varna system— precursor of caste system—evolves in India.

1000

776 BCE First recorded Olympic games are held at Olympia in Greece.

ca. 750 BCE *Iliad*—the earliest surviving example of Greek literature— and *Odyssey* are composed (ascribed to Homer).

700

Literary and cultural developments and events

Historical events

Advances in science and technology

Changes in everyday life

Break in timeline

600

551–479 BCE Life of Confucius, China's greatest philosopher.

ca. 500 BCE Many Old Testament books are transcribed.

ca. 500 BCE Greeks adopt Ptolemaic model of cosmos, in which the sun revolves around the earth.

399 BCE Greek philosopher Socrates is tried and executed for corruption of youth.

387 BCE Greek philosopher Plato founds the Academy.

350 BCE Aristotle, student of Plato, writes *Poetics*, founds rival school, Lyceum; earliest portion of *Mahabharata* (Sanskrit heroic epic) is composed mid-century.

ca. 250 BCE Archimedes, founder of mathematical physics, writes *Measurement of the Circle* (includes concept of π).

215 BCE Construction of Great Wall of China begins.

23–13 BCE Roman poet Horace composes *Odes*.

30 Jesus is crucified by the Romans in Jerusalem.

ca. 560–480 BCE Life of Buddha (Siddhartha), founder of Buddhism.

508 BCE Athens becomes the world's first democracy.

500

461–429 BCE Reign of Pericles ushers in flowering of Athenian culture: Aeschylus, *Oresteia* (**458 BCE**); Sophocles, *Antigone* (**ca. 442–441 BCE**) and *Oedipus the King* (**ca. 429 BCE**); Euripides, *Medea* (**431 BCE**); Aristophanes, *Lysistrata* (**411 BCE**); Plato, *Republic* (**ca. 406 BCE**).

400

404 BCE Golden age of Periclean Athens ends with fall of Athens to Sparta.

356–323 BCE Life of Alexander the Great, king of Macedonia, who conquers the Persian Empire

300

ca. 300 BCE Euclid writes *Elements*, seminal work of elementary geometry.

ca. 250 BCE *Ramayana* (Sanskrit heroic epic) is composed mid-century.

200

ca. 200 BCE–500 CE Roman Empire encompasses the entire Mediterranean region.

100

0

27–19 BCE Roman poet Virgil composes the epic poem *Aeneid*.

8 Ovid composes *Metamorphoses*, a 15-volume poem based on Greek and Roman myths.

ca. 65–85 New Testament Gospels are composed.

300

ca. 300 Large towns exist in inland Niger Delta, later to develop into the Empire of Ghana in west Africa.

400

413–26 St. Augustine writes *City of God,* interpreting history in light of Christianity.

410 Visigoths sack Rome.

478 First Shinto shrine is built in Japan.

500

550–900 Mayan civilization reaches Late Classical phase: art, architecture, and writing flourish at Tikal and dozens of other city-states.

600

ca. 650–750 *Beowulf,* Old English epic, is composed.

622 Mohammed, founder of Islam, flees from Mecca to Medina, transforms Islam into religious and secular empire.

651–5 Koran or Qu'ran, the holy book of Islam, is codified.

718 Muslims are in control of most of Iberian peninsula; some Muslim influence remains until Christian forces gain control in **1492** with taking of Granada.

700

900 **960–1279** Song Dynasty in China: flowering of arts and scholarship.

1000

ca. 978–1026 Life of Lady Shikibu Murasaki, Japanese author of *Tale of Genjii,* considered by many to be the world's first novel.

ca. 1100 *Song of Roland*, French epic poem, is composed.

1100 **1096–1291** The Crusades, nine military expeditions in which European Christians attempted to reconquer the Holy Land (Palestine) from the Muslims, take place.

1200

ca. 1200 Zen Buddhism travels from China to Japan, becomes influential in Japanese politics, painting, landscape, and culture, especially in the tea ceremony.

ca. 1290–1918 Ottoman Empire, Muslim Turkish state comprising Anatolia, modern southeastern Europe, and the Arab Middle East and North Africa, is established.

1300 **ca. 1300–1650** Renaissance in Europe: "rebirth" of arts and culture.

1307–21 Dante Alighieri composes *La Divina Commedia*, an epic poem describing his imaginary journey through heaven and hell.

1312–27 Empire of Mali in West Africa reaches its height under Mansa Musa, builder of the Great Mosque at Timbuktu.

1350

1347–51 "Black Death," an epidemic of the bubonic plague, rages in Europe, eventually claiming 25–50% of the population.

ca. 1370–1400 English poet Chaucer composes *The Canterbury Tales*, a collection of 24 tales with dramatic links.

ca. 1350–1400 Great Zimbabwe, a fabled stone city that controlled a large part of southeast Africa in medieval times, reaches its height.

1400

1431 Joan of Arc, leader of French army against the British in the Hundred Years' War, is burned at the stake for heresy by the British.

ca. 1438–1532 Inca Empire, largest native empire of the Americas, reaches its height in Central and South America; expansion ends with the Spanish invasion led by Pizarro.

1453 Constantinople falls to Ottoman Turks, marking the end of the Byzantine Empire.

1450

ca. 1455 Gutenberg Bible set and printed; Gutenberg's invention of movable type leads to book printing boom in Europe.

1484 Botticelli paints *Birth of Venus* for the Medici family of Florence.

ca. 1492 Christopher Columbus lands in the Bahamas.

1500

1499 Amerigo Vespucci lands in South America.

1503 Leonardo da Vinci, painter, inventor, and scientist, paints *Mona Lisa*.

1508–12 Michelangelo paints the ceiling of the Sistine Chapel in Rome.

1513 Niccolo Machiavelli writes *The Prince*, arguing for pragmatism over virtue in a ruler.

1517 Martin Luther's 95 *Theses* introduces the Protestant Reformation in Europe.

1520 Gold, silver, and chocolate are brought from the Americas to Spain.

1532 Sugar cane is cultivated in Brazil.

1593–99 Shakespeare's sonnets are published, followed by *Hamlet* (**1600–1**) and *Othello* (**1604**).

1599 Globe Theater is built in London.

1600

1603 Kabuki is first performed in Japan by female entertainer Okuni.

1605 Miguel de Cervantes Saavedra writes his masterpiece *Don Quixote.*

1609 Tea is first shipped to Europe from China.

1611 King James Bible is published, becomes most popular version for more than three centuries.

1619 African captives are brought to Jamestown, Virginia, to be servants; slave system develops over the next 80 years.

1631–48 Taj Mahal, premier example of Mogul architecture, is built in Agra, India.

1637 René Descartes, called by some the founder of modern philosophy, writes *Discourse on Method* (from which comes "*Cogito, ergo sum*": "I think; therefore, I am").

1651 Thomas Hobbes writes *Leviathan,* portraying human life in a state of nature as "nasty, brutish, and short" and offering as a remedy a social contract in which the ruler's power—for the sake of expediency—is absolute.

1608 Galileo Galilei invents astronomical telescope, provides evidence to support Nicolaus Copernicus's theory that the earth and planets revolve around the sun.

1614 Pocahontas, Native American princess, marries tobacco planter John Rolfe.

1625

1620 Pilgrims sail for America and found Plymouth Colony.

1632 Rembrandt van Rijn, prolific Dutch painter, paints his first major portrait, *The Anatomy Lesson of Dr. Tulp.*

1642–1648 English Civil War pits Parliamentary forces under Oliver Cromwell against Charles I: Charles I is defeated and beheaded in **1649.**

1650

1667 John Milton writes *Paradise Lost,* an epic poem describing man's "first disobedience" and the promise of his redemption.

1675

1687 Isaac Newton publishes *Principia,* in which he codifies laws of motion and gravity not modified until the twentieth century.

ca. 1688–1790 The Enlightenment, an intellectual movement committed to secular views based on reason, takes hold in Europe.

1690 John Locke publishes *Essay Concerning Human Understanding,* in which he espouses an empiricist view of philosophy (limiting true knowledge to what can be perceived through the senses or through introspection).

1700

ca. 1701 Peter the Great begins westernization of Russia.

1740

ca. 1740s Culmination of the Baroque era in music: Vivaldi, *The Four Seasons;* Bach, *Brandenberg Concertos;* Handel, *Messiah.*

1750

1755–73 Samuel Johnson publishes *Dictionary of the English Language.*

Johann Sebastian Bach

1760

1767–87 Sturm und Drang ("Storm and Stress"), a literary and intellectual movement in Germany that prefigures Romanticism (**ca. 1789–1825** in England).

1761 Jean-Jacques Rousseau publishes *The Social Contract,* in which he praises the natural goodness of human beings but insists on the need for society to attain true happiness.

1769 James Watt patents a steam engine.

1770

ca. 1770 Industrial Revolution begins, fueled by steam power: first steam-driven cotton factory (**1789**) and first steam-powered rolling mill open in England (**1790**).

1775-81 American Revolution: hostilities begin at Lexington and Concord, Massachusetts, in 1775, although the Continental Congress will not officially vote for independence until 1776.

1776 "Declaration of Independence" is approved by the Continental Congress on July 4.

1780

Adam Smith publishes *Causes of the Wealth of Nations,* advocates regulation of markets through supply and demand and competition.

1781 Immanuel Kant publishes *Critique of Pure Reason,* an attempt at reconciling empiricism and rationalism, and for many the single most important work of modern philosophy.

1780s–90s Height of the Classical era in music: Mozart writes the opera *Don Giovanni* (**1787**); Haydn establishes the form of the symphony with *The Clock Symphony* (**1794**).

1788 Bread riots occur in France

1789 William Blake's *Songs of Innocence,* followed by *Marriage of Heaven and Hell* (**1790**) and *Songs of Experience* (**1794**), ushers in early Romanticism in England; Olaudah Equiano's *The Interesting Narrative of the Life of Olaudah Equiano, or Gustaus Vassa, the African,* one of the first slave narratives, is published.

1790

1789–99 French Revolution transforms France from a monarchy to a modern state.

1792 Mary Wollstonecraft publishes *A Vindication of the Rights of Woman,* an early work of feminism.

1793 Queen Marie Antoinette and King Louis XVI of France are guillotined.

ca. 1795–1825 English Romantic poetry flourishes with the work of William Wordsworth (**1770–1850**), Lord Byron (**1788–1824**), Percy Bysshe Shelley (**1792–1822**), and John Keats (**1795–1821**).

1798 Thomas Malthus's *An Essay on the Principle of Population* stirs interest in birth control and concerns about overpopulation.

1799 Rosetta Stone is found in Egypt, making it possible to decipher hieroglyphics; perfectly preserved mammoth is found in Siberia.

1800

1800 Alessandro Volta produces first battery of zinc and copper plates.

1803 Beethoven composes *Third Symphony (Eroica),* marking the start of his dramatic middle period.

1804–6 Lewis and Clark expedition from St. Louis to the Pacific fuels westward expansion in the USA.

1804 Napoleon becomes emperor of France.

1807 Hegel publishes *Phenomenology of Spirit,* which introduces the concept of "master-slave" dialectic.

1808 Goethe publishes *Part 1* of *Faust,* a drama about a man who sells his soul for knowledge and power.

1810

1812 Noah Webster's *American Dictionary of the English Language* helps standardize spelling of American English.

1813 Mexico declares independence from Spain, becomes a republic in **1824.**

1813 Jane Austen publishes her novel *Pride and Prejudice.*

1815 Napoleon is defeated by British and Prussian forces at Waterloo.

1818 Mary Shelley publishes horror classic *Frankenstein.*

1820

ca. 1821 Cherokee leader Sequoya codifies the Cherokee alphabet.

1823 Monroe Doctrine closes Western Hemisphere to colonial settlements by Europe.

ca. 1825 Katsushika Hokusai, great Japanese printmaker, creates *Mt. Fuji on a Clear Day.*

1830

1830–42 Auguste Comte, founder of philosophical positivism, writes *The Course of Positive Philosophy,* advocates application of scientific method to social problems.

1830 Church of Jesus Christ of Latter-day Saints (Mormons) is founded by Joseph Smith.

1831 Nat Turner leads a group of fellow slaves in the largest slave revolt in North America.

1833 Charles Babbage designs an "analytical engine," prototype of the modern computer.

1836 Samuel Colt puts his revolver into mass production, revolutionizes manufacture of small arms.

1837 Ralph Waldo Emerson, American transcendentalist, delivers "The American Scholar," an address expressing American literary independence.

1837–1901 Queen Victoria reigns in England, Ireland, and India.

1838 Charles Dickens publishes *Oliver Twist,* the first of many novels that sharply criticize abuses brought on by the Industrial Revolution in England.

1839 Daguerreotypes, forerunners of modern photographs, are developed by L. M. Daguerre and J. N. Niepce in France.

1840

1840s Rise of Romantic movement in France, Germany, and Italy.

1841 First university degrees granted to women in USA.

1843 Søren Kierkegaard, Christian existentialist philosopher, publishes *Either / Or.*

1843 Richard Wagner composes *The Flying Dutchman,* an opera expressing his ideal of the *Gesamtkunstwerk* ("total work of art").

1844 Samuel Morse invents the telegraph.

1847 Charlotte Brontë publishes *Jane Eyre*; Emily Brontë publishes *Wuthering Heights;* Anna Brontë publishes *Agnes Grey.*

1850

1848 Seneca Falls Convention for Women's Suffrage is held in USA; Karl Marx and Friedrich Engels write *Communist Manifesto*, a pamphlet exhorting workers to unite against capitalist oppressors.

1855 Walt Whitman publishes first edition of *Leaves of Grass,* creates a new American style for poetry.

1857 French poet Charles Baudelaire publishes *Flowers of Evil,* one of the seminal works of modern poetry.

1859 Charles Darwin publishes *On the Origin of Species,* establishes theories of evolution and natural selection ("survival of the fittest").

ca. 1860 Louis Pasteur invents pasteurization process, advances germ theory of infection, discovers rabies and anthrax vaccines (**1880s**).

1860

1860–65 Emily Dickinson writes most of her poetry; creates a new rhythm and vernacular for American verse.

1861–65 U.S. Civil War pits northern against southern states.

1863 "Emancipation Proclamation" frees all slaves in states rebelling against the federal government.

1865 U.S. President Abraham Lincoln is assassinated.

1865–69 Leo Tolstoy publishes *War and Peace,* an epic of the Napoleonic invasion of Russia.

1867 Universal Exposition in Paris introduces Japanese art to the West.

1867–94 Publication of Karl Marx's *Capital,* a political and economic treatise providing the theoretical basis of socialism.

1869 U.S. transcontinental railroad is completed.

1870

1868 Overthrow of Tokugawa Shogunate, followed by the Meiji Restoration and establishment of a new government, signals emergence of Japan as a major world power.

1874 First exhibition of French Impressionism in Paris is held; notable exponents include Monet, Renoir, Pissarro, Degas, and Cassatt.

1875 Alexander Graham Bell invents the telephone.

1877 Thomas Edison invents the phonograph.

1879 Thomas Edison invents the light bulb.

1880

1878 In Boston, Mary Baker Eddy founds Church of Christ, Scientist, a religion emphasizing divine healing.

1883-85 Friedrich Nietzsche writes *Thus Spake Zarathustra,* which expounds on the concept of *Übermensch* (superman).

1890

1889 Eiffel Tower is built for Paris Exposition.

1893 Fabian Society, a socialist group that includes Irish playwright George Bernard Shaw, is established.

1893 X rays are discovered.

1895 Louis and Auguste Lumière project brief motion pictures on a screen to a paying audience in Paris; based on Thomas Edison's technology, their Cinématographe became the prototype of the movie camera.

ca. 1895 Charles "Buddy" Bolden, New Orleans cornet player and band leader, begins playing improvised music later known as jazz.

1898 Marie and Pierre Curie isolate radium and polonium.

1900

1903 Orville and Wilbur Wright make their debut power-driven flight near Kitty Hawk, North Carolina.

1907 Albert Einstein first publishes equation $E = mc^2$, deduced from his theory of special relativity, ushering in revolution in physics and astronomy.

1907 Pablo Picasso's *Les Demoiselles d'Avignon*, first Cubist painting, ushers in new artistic aesthetic.

1908 Henry Ford introduces the Model T; demand for cars induces the company to introduce assembly-line technique.

1910

1910 International Psychoanalytic Association is founded by Sigmund Freud and others; Freud's theories of the unconscious begin to gain popular recognition.

1913 *The Rite of Spring,* ballet with groundbreaking music by Igor Stravinsky and choreography by Vaslav Nijinsky, is first performed.

1914 Serbian nationalist assassinates heir to the Austro-Hungarian Empire in Sarajevo, sparking World War I.

1915 Margaret Sanger opens the first birth control clinic in USA.

1914–21 James Joyce writes *Ulysses,* a masterpiece of modernist literature; publication in USA is delayed until **1933** because of obscenity charges.

1915 British passenger ship *Lusitania* sunk by German submarine, fueling American sympathy for war efforts of Britain, France, and Russia.

1917 USA enters World War I; Russian Revolution: Bolsheviks led by Vladimir Lenin seize power.

1918 Romanian poet Tristan Tzara writes manifesto for Dada, avant-garde artistic movement established in part in reaction to the senseless slaughter of World War I.

1918–19 Influenza epidemic kills 22 million worldwide.

1920

1918 Treaty of Versailles ends World War I; death toll approaches 15 million worldwide; race riots rock major U.S. cities.

1920 Nineteenth Amendment to the U.S. Constitution grants women suffrage.

ca. 1920 Arnold Schoenberg invents 12-tone system of musical composition.

1922 First fascist government formed by Benito Mussolini in Italy.

1924 Joseph Stalin succeeds Lenin as head of Soviet Union.

1920s Harlem Renaissance: flowering of African American literature and the arts, particularly jazz, centered in New York City.

1927 Martin Heidegger publishes *Being and Time,* a founding work of existentialist philosophy; Martha Graham, pioneer of modern dance, opens a dance studio in New York.

1929 Virginia Woolf, central to the Bloomsbury literary group, publishes feminist work *A Room of One's Own.*

1930

1930s The Great Depression, precipitated by a stock market crash in **1929,** begins in USA and spreads abroad; in response, President Roosevelt introduces "New Deal" measures based on Keynesian economics.

1933 Adolf Hitler becomes chancellor of Germany, gradually assumes dictatorial power.

1927 Charles Lindbergh makes first solo, nonstop transatlantic flight; Werner Heisenberg develops Uncertainty Principle, which, together with Theory of Relativity, becomes basis of quantum physics; first successful transmission of an image via "television" occurs.

1931 Incompleteness Theorem is developed by the mathematician and philosopher Kurt Gödel.

1936–39 Spanish Civil War.

1935 African American Jesse Owens wins four gold medals in track at the Berlin Olympics.

1940

1939 World War II begins shortly after Germany's invasion of Poland; Hitler's Nazis begin program of extermination of "undesirable" elements, including dissidents, homosexuals, Gypsies, and especially Jews; 6 million Jews die in the ensuing Holocaust.

1941 Japan bombs Pearl Harbor, and USA enters World War II.

1943 Jean-Paul Sartre, existentialist philosopher, publishes *Being and Nothingness.*

1945 USA drops atomic bombs on Hiroshima and Nagasaki, Japan—World War II ends; United Nations is formed; Soviet Union occupies Eastern Europe.

1947 India and Pakistan gain independence from Britain.

1948 Mahatma Gandhi, Indian nationalist and spiritual leader, is assassinated; Pakistan-India wars ensue.

1949 Communists seize mainland China; Mao Zedong becomes first chairman of the People's Republic of China.

1950

1949 Simone de Beauvoir publishes *The Second Sex,* a groundbreaking study of women's place in society.

1950–55 Jonas Salk develops polio vaccine.

1950s–70s Height of the "Cold War," in which USA and Soviet Union face off—mutual military buildup and threat of nuclear annihilation create a "balance of power."

1953 J. D. Watson and F. H. C. Crick determine the structure of DNA, launching the modern study of genetics.

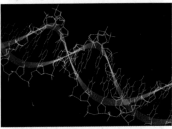

1956 Soviet Union crushes revolt in Hungary.

1959 Cuban Revolution: Fidel Castro overthrows Batista regime.

1962 Cuban missile crisis—Soviet missile-building in Cuba precipitates tense standoff with USA, ultimately resolved through diplomacy; César Chávez organizes the National Farm Workers Association (NFWA).

1960

1961 Berlin Wall erected; USA stages failed "Bay of Pigs" invasion of Cuba.

1964 U.S. involvement in Vietnam War escalates with Tonkin Gulf Resolution; Malcolm X is assassinated in New York; Watts riots roil Los Angeles.

1966 Mao Zedong's Cultural Revolution begins, aiming to revitalize communist zeal; Black Panther Party is founded in Oakland, California.

1968 Martin Luther King, Jr. is assassinated in Memphis, Tennessee.

1969 American astronaut Neil Armstrong becomes first man to walk on the moon.

1963 Martin Luther King, Jr., delivers "I Have a Dream" speech to crowd of 250,000 at the Lincoln Memorial;

President John F. Kennedy is assassinated in Dallas.

1971 East Pakistan (now Bangladesh) declares independence from West Pakistan.

1970

1974 President Richard Nixon resigns as a result of the Watergate scandal.

1973 *Gulag Archipelego* by Alexander Solzhenitsyn is published in Paris; it is a massive study of Soviet penal system based on author's firsthand experience.

1975 Bill Gates and Paul Allen build and sell their first computer product, creating Microsoft.

1975 Wave of former colonies—Mozambique, Surinam, Papua New Guinea—gain independence.

1975–79 Vaccination programs against smallpox eradicate the disease worldwide.

1979 Islamic revolution in Iran: Shah flees, Khomeini comes to power.

1980

1981 First cases of acquired immune deficiency syndrome (AIDS) in the USA are reported in New York and California.

1982 Benoit Mandelbrot publishes *The Fractal Geometry of Nature,* contributing to chaos theory.

1986 Chernobyl nuclear power plant disaster spreads fallout over Soviet Union and parts of Europe.

1989 Prodemocracy protests in Tiananmen Square, China, are quashed by government crackdown; Berlin Wall is demolished; Eastern Europe is democratized.

1990

1991 Soviet Union is dissolved, making way for looser confederation of republics.

1995 Internet boom hits—number of people online grows exponentially.

2000

2000 Initial sequencing of human genome completed.

2001 Hijacked planes fly into 110-story World Trade Center Towers in New York City and the Pentagon in Washington, D.C.—thousands die; USA invades Afghanistan and later Iraq in "war on terrorism."

2004 Massive Indian Ocean tsunami devastates coastal communities from Indonesia to Somalia.

2005 Voters in France and Holland reject the proposed constitution for the European Union.

2005 Hurricane Katrina overwhelms U.S. Gulf coast and forces the evacuation of New Orleans.

Selected Terms from across the Curriculum

Your professors will explain the vocabulary and concepts that are specific to the study of particular disciplines, but they might assume you understand certain terms that commonly appear in academic **discourse.** *As you look at the sampling that follows, feel free to jump around among the words printed in bold, each of which has its own entry.*

alienation (from the Latin *alius,* "other") Being estranged from one's society or even from oneself. First used in psychology, the term was adapted by Karl **Marx** (1818–1883) in his writings on the relationship of workers to the products of their labor. In the twentieth century, **existentialist** philosophers used the word to mean an individual's loss of a sense of self, his or her *authenticity,* amid the pressures of modern society. *See also* **Marxism.**

Apollonian From *Apollo,* Greek god of prophecy, music, medicine, and poetry, often identified with the sun. Today Apollonian describes works of art or other cultural products characterized by clarity, harmony, and restraint. *See also* **Dionysian.**

archetype A model after which other things are patterned. The psychoanalyst Carl Jung (1875–1961) used the term to denote a number of universal symbols—such as the Mother or the universal Creator—that inhabit the **collective unconscious.**

Aristotelian Relating to the writings of Aristotle (384–322 BCE), Greek philosopher and author of works on logic, ethics, rhetoric, and the natural sciences. Aristotle established a tradition that values **empirical** observation, **deductive reasoning,** and science. This tradition can be contrasted with **Platonic idealism.**

arithmetic progression *See* **geometric progression.**

bell curve In statistics and science, a graph showing a normal distribution of results—in other words, a distribution in which the greatest number of results are grouped in the middle. If a math test is graded on a bell curve, for instance, most students will receive B's and C's, whereas only a few will receive A's or F's.

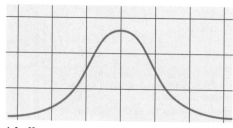

A bell curve.

Plotted on a graph, the curve will evoke the shape of a bell.

Big Bang Theory A **hypothesis** about the origins of the universe: some 14 billion years ago, all the matter in the universe was concentrated in one almost infinitely dense point, which then exploded, dispersing matter in all directions at tremendous velocity. The Big Bang Theory implies a universe of finite size and age.

binary oppositions Paired terms conventionally treated as stable and logical opposites, such as *light/dark* and *man/woman.* Certain **postmodern** trends in philosophy and literary theory, notably **deconstruction,** seek to expose the "artificiality" of these and other **constructs** that shape the way we see the world. *See also* **structuralism.**

black hole From astronomy, a region in space-time where matter is infinitely dense and dimensionless and where the gravitational field is so strong that nothing can escape from it. The term is often used metaphorically to indicate something that is limitless or unresolvable.

Boolean logic (after the English mathematician George Boole, 1815–1864) A specialized algebra developed for the analysis of logical statements, used extensively in the development of the modern computer. A computer performs everything from simple math to Internet searches by means of Boolean logic, which uses **variables** and operators such as AND, OR, NOT, IF, THEN, and EXCEPT.

bourgeois Of or relating to the middle **class.** Although it originally referred to the artisans and craftsmen of medieval French towns, the term came into wide use with the Industrial Revolution, which created the modern middle class, and it is used in **Marxist** analysis to represent the capitalist class. *Bourgeois* commonly connotes an excessive concern with respectability and material goods.

canon Originally referring to a code of laws established by the church, the canon now typically refers to a collection of books deemed necessary for a complete education. What works are *canonical* is often debated and has changed over time. Current debate tends to focus on the exclusion from the canon of works by and about women and people of color. *See also* **multiculturalism.**

capitalism An economic system that emerged during the Industrial Revolution of the nineteenth century and offered private individuals the ownership of industry as well as unregulated market freedom. Today capitalism includes **Keynesian economic** models that allow government to regulate industry, particularly regarding such concerns as the minimum wage, tariffs, and taxes.

case study An intensive investigation and analysis of a person or group; often the object of study is proposed as the model of a certain phenomenon. Originally used in medicine, the term is now also common in psychology and business. Among the most famous and widely imitated case studies are those of Sigmund **Freud** (1856–1939), who used them to expound his theory of psychoanalysis. In business, a case study denotes a detailed examination of a corporation or enterprise with a view to determining the causes of its success or failure.

chaos theory A branch of mathematics used to describe highly complex phenomena such as weather or the flow of blood through the body. Chaos theory starts with the recognition that minute changes in a system can have large and unpredictable results. The *butterfly effect,* for instance, states that the flap of a butterfly's wings in China could theoretically cause a hurricane in New York. *See also* **iteration.**

class A term denoting social and/or economic standing in society (*upper class, lower class, middle class; working class, professional class, leisure class*). Karl **Marx** (1818–1883) argued that class conflict is economically based and

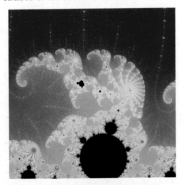

An image generated from the Mandelbrot set, an aspect of chaos theory.

so necessarily occurs between the working class and the capitalist class (those who control the means of production). Many have argued that economic standing alone does not determine class and that factors such as family, cultural background, and education play significant roles. *See also* **bourgeois, proletariat.**

classical   Originally used to describe the artistic and literary conventions of ancient Greece and Rome. *Classical* (or *classicism / neoclassicism*) is also used for periods and products in the sciences, social sciences, philosophy, and music marked by straightforwardly rational models that describe the workings of the universe and human society as logical and ultimately harmonious. *See also* **modernism, postmodernism.**

coefficient   In mathematics, a coefficient is a number or symbol multiplying a **variable** in an algebraic term, such as the 4 in $4x$. In the physical sciences, a coefficient is the numerical measure of a physical or chemical **constant.** In general usage, *coefficient* can denote factors working together to produce a result, as in "Jobs and longer prison terms are *coefficients* in the prevention of crime."

collective unconscious   In the psychology of Carl Jung (1875–1961), the elements of the **unconscious** that are common to all humans. In the same way that each human body shares many features with others while at the same time being unique, the collective unconscious represents the general framework of the human unconscious, within which each individual's unconscious mind presents a unique pattern. *See also* **archetype.**

colonialism   A policy by which a nation extends and maintains political and military control over a territory, often reducing it to a state of dependence. Begun as a way of acquiring resources such as spices, precious metals, and slaves, later instances of colonialism—such as the U.S. occupation of the Philippines from 1898 to 1946—have served mostly political or strategic purposes. *Postcolonial* refers to a state (or a cultural product or even a state of mind) that reflects former colonial occupation. *See also* **imperialism.**

constant   In mathematics, science, and general usage, a factor that does not change. A mathematical or scientific constant is a quantity assumed to have a fixed value within a specific context. In physics, for example, the speed of light in a vacuum is 186,000 miles per second and is denoted by the constant c. Thus, in Einstein's famous equation $E = mc^2$, c is a constant and m, standing for any mass, is a **variable.**

construct (*noun*)   Something that is shaped by culture ("constructed") but sometimes assumed to be "natural." For example, some might hold that the idea of gender ("maleness" and "femaleness") is a construct rather than the essential or inborn quality that past generations often assumed it to be.

contingent   In logic, that which is true only under certain circumstances. In common usage, contingent often connotes that which has happened or can happen only as a result of a long, perhaps improbable sequence of events. Whenever you think, "It could easily have been different," you are feeling a sense of *contingency.*

correlation   In statistics, a number that describes the relationship between two variables. In a *positive correlation,* the variables increase in tandem—for example, the higher a student's IQ, the better his or her scholastic performance.

In a *negative correlation,* one variable increases while the other decreases—for example, the more green tea consumed, the lower the incidence of cancer.

counterculture *See* **culture.**

cross section A sample meant to be representative of a whole population. *See also* **longitudinal.**

culture Knowledge, beliefs, behavior, arts, institutions, and other products of work and thought that characterize a society. Within a dominant culture there may exist many *subcultures:* groups of particular ethnicity, age, education, employment, inclination, or other factors. A *counterculture* is a form of subculture whose values and lifestyle reject those of the dominant culture. *See also* **relativism.**

Darwinism British naturalist Charles Darwin's (1809–1882) theory of the historical evolution of species based on *natural selection,* or "the survival of the fittest." Where insects living within the bark of trees constitute a major food source, for instance, birds with longer, more pointed beaks tend to survive longer and produce more offspring, who then pass on longer, sharper beaks to ensuing generations.

deconstruction A method of literary criticism whose best-known theorist, Jacques Derrida (1930–2004), postulated that texts rest on **binary oppositions** such as *nature/culture, subject/object,* and *spirit/matter* that have been incorrectly assumed to be "true"; in exposing this fallacy, Derrida revealed the illogic of texts thought to be logical and coherent. Although often associated with **postmodernism** and the debate about the **canon,** deconstruction is in a philosophical sense a radical form of skepticism. In more common usage, to *deconstruct* something is to analyze it intensively, exposing it as (perhaps) something unexpected.

deductive reasoning Reasoning to a conclusion based on a previously held principle. *Inductive reasoning,* on the other hand, is the process of deriving a conclusion based on data. **Empiricism** holds that all knowledge is derived from sense experience by induction, whereas *rationalism* claims that knowledge can be deduced from certain a priori (presumptive) claims.

demographics (from the Greek *demos,* "people," and *graphia,* "writing") The quantitative study of human populations. A demographic study of a city might include the rate at which its population is growing, the size and distribution of its middle **class,** or the number of its families who have access to the Internet.

determinism In philosophy and science, the doctrine that every event is *determined,* or entirely shaped by earlier events, and that given complete knowledge of prior events and the laws that govern them, all future events can be predicted. Something described as *overdetermined* is thought to be shaped by more than one equally significant cause. Usually contrasted with **free will,** determinism is a feature of eighteenth- and nineteenth-century **classical** thought. In science, determinism has come to be opposed by the *indeterminism* of **quantum physics.**

dialectic In philosophy, history, and the humanities, the use of logical oppositions as a means of arriving at conclusions about ideas or events. *Dialectical reasoning* is most often associated with the philosophies of Georg Hegel (1770–1831) and Karl **Marx** (1818–1883). According to Hegel, any human idea or *thesis* (for example, the sun circles the earth) naturally gives rise to an opposing idea or *antithesis* (the earth circles the sun), and these ideas resolve into a new idea or *synthesis* (the earth revolves around the sun but in an ellipse). Hegel's famous *master/slave dialectic* describes a seeming paradox: a slave holds power over his master because the master could not hold power without the slave. Marx extended dialectical reasoning in his theory of dialectical **materialism,** which analyzes not opposing ideas but contradictory **class** interests.

Dionysian   That which embodies creativity, intuition, and, by extension, ecstasy, orgiastic release, and the irrational. The term is most often associated with the philosophy of Friedrich **Nietzsche** (1844–1900), where it opposes the **Apollonian.**

discourse (from the French *discours*, "speech" or "talk") *Discourse* is most often used in English to denote verbal expression in general, without distinguishing between writing and speech. *Discourse* can also refer to habits of expression characteristic of a particular community or to the content of that expression ("The *discourse* of experimental science does not often allow the use of the personal pronoun *I*").

disfranchise (also **disenfranchise**) Literally, to deprive of the right to vote; more loosely, to *disfranchise* means to deny rights or exclude from privileges, most often those associated with citizenship: "The rioters in Oklahoma felt themselves to have been effectively *disfranchised* by post–World War I economic and political change."

ecosystem   A principal unit of study in ecology, the science of the relationships between organisms and their environments. All parts of an ecosystem are interdependent, and even small perturbations of one part (such as might be caused by pollution) can have profound effects on all of the other parts—a phenomenon often studied in **chaos theory.**

ego   **Freudian** term for the "I" of mental functioning—that is, the capacity for realistic assessment of the needs of the self and the means of fulfilling these needs. *See also* **id, superego, repression, projection, unconscious.**

empiricism (from the Greek *empierikos*, "experienced") A philosophical trend, developed in large part by the philosophers John Locke (1632–1704) and David Hume (1711–1776), that data derived from experience or the senses are the ultimate source of knowledge, as opposed to reason, tradition, or authority. *Empirical* data are data gained through observation or experiment. Especially in medicine and psychology, *empirical* is often contrasted with *theoretical*. In its emphasis on observation and experience, empiricism is a conceptual cousin of **inductive reasoning** and **Aristotelianism.**

Enlightenment   An intellectual movement committed to secular views based on reason that established itself in Europe in the eighteenth century (ca. 1688–1790).

epistemology   The study of the nature of knowledge, its foundations and limits.

ethos (Greek for "character, a person's nature or disposition") The spirit or code of behavior peculiar to a specific person or group of people—for example, "part of the college student ethos is to stay up late drinking cola and eating Captain

Crunch." Ethos is one of the parts of Aristotle's **rhetorical triangle (ethos-logos-pathos**): in order to argue effectively, a speaker or writer must communicate a persuasive ethos, that is, a credible **persona** and a coherent perspective.

existentialism A strain in philosophy that emphasizes the isolation of the individual in an indifferent universe and stresses the individual's freedom (and responsibility) to determine his or her own existence. Having roots in the philosophies of Friedrich **Nietzsche** (1844–1900) and Martin Heidegger (1889–1976), existentialism was extremely influential in France after World War II, where French intellectuals like Jean-Paul Sartre (1905–1980) and Albert Camus (1913–1960) argued that by making conscious choices and taking responsibility for one's acts, one could overcome the otherwise absurd nature of the universe.

extrapolation In mathematics and computer science, the estimation of an unknown value using projections based on known information. For example, one might *extrapolate* the total number of votes cast for a political candidate nationwide based on a representative **sample.** *Interpolation,* on the other hand, is the estimation of an unknown value made by comparing known values that are closely related or nearby. The size of a colony of ants in June, for example, might be *interpolated* based on the numbers for May and July.

fascism (from the Italian *fascio,* "group") A name for the form of government established by Benito Mussolini (1883–1945) in Italy and Adolf Hitler (1889–1945) in Germany. Arising in response to economic and political upheaval in Europe after World War I, both governments centralized authority under a dictator, exerted strong economic controls, suppressed opposition through censorship and terror, and implemented belligerent nationalist and racist policies.

Mussolini and Hitler.

feminism The principle that women should enjoy the same political, economic, social, and cultural rights and opportunities as men. Mary Wollstonecraft's *A Vindication of the Rights of Woman* (1792) was a pioneering feminist work. The *suffrage movement,* which demanded that women be granted the right to vote, emerged following the first women's rights convention in Seneca Falls, New York, in 1848, and had achieved its goal in the United States and Europe by the early twentieth century. The *women's movement* that began in the 1960s initiated a new wave of feminism that focused on rectifying political, economic, social, and cultural inequalities between women and men. The many feminist thinkers who emerged from the women's movement have had a lasting impact in many academic fields, from the social sciences and humanities to the natural sciences.

formalism An approach to literary and art criticism that emphasizes rigorous attention to the structural elements and techniques of a work and deemphasizes the historical or social contexts in which the work was created and its relationship to other works.

Freudian Relating to the theories of Sigmund Freud (1856–1939), the Viennese neurologist who invented psychoanalysis. A Freudian interpretation focuses on the unconscious emotional dynamics that are played out in a particular situation; in the study of literature, a Freudian interpretation focuses on such dynamics as they are represented in the **text.** *See also* **ego, id, superego, repression, projection, unconscious.**

game theory (also sometimes called *decision theory*) A mathematical method for analyzing situations of conflict or competition so as to determine a winning strategy. Game theory is useful not only in *true games* such as poker but also in business management, economics, and military strategy. *See also* **zero sum game.**

geometric progression A sequence of numbers determined by multiplying or dividing each number in succession by a **constant.** For example, *1, 4, 16, 64, 256* is a geometric progression with a constant multiplier, or **coefficient,** of 4. *Arithmetic progressions* proceed more slowly by adding or subtracting a constant: for example, *1, 4, 7, 10, 13* is an arithmetic progression with a constant *addend* of 3.

gestalt (German for "form" or "structure") The recognition of the whole of something that precedes the notice of any of its parts. In psychology, *Gestalt theory* asserts that psychological phenomena are irreducible and cannot be derived from the simple total of sensations a person experiences.

globalization The process by which communication and transportation technologies have made the world seem smaller and more interconnected. In economics, *globalization* refers to the way these advances have made national borders far less relevant in determining markets. The *anti-globalization* movement aims to protect workers from exploitation by multinational corporations, to prevent job loss among domestic workers, and to counter cultural homogenization. The presence of a McDonald's in Beijing is a good example of the effects of globalization.

hegemony Generally, the dominance of one nation or state over its neighbors. The Italian Marxist Antonio Gramsci (1891–1937) and his followers often used the term to refer to the dominance of the capitalists over the working **class.** *Hegemony* is now also used to describe a theory that has dominance in a particular field of study: "Dualism has long exercised hegemony in Western thought."

humanism (also *secular humanism*) A movement traditionally associated with Renaissance philosophers who deemphasized the role of religion or God in society while celebrating the achievements of human beings. There are *humanistic* branches of psychology, theology, and other disciplines that move the role of the human individual to the forefront of their studies.

hypothesis A statement that can be shown to be true or false either experimentally (in science) or through the use of logic (in other disciplines). For example, a simple hypothesis is that light is necessary for the survival of a certain plant. This hypothesis could be proved or disproved by the simple experiment of trying to grow the plant in a dark closet.

icon In **semiotics,** a **sign** that looks like what it refers to. A picture of the globe used to signify the earth or a line drawing of a suitcase indicating where to go to get your luggage at an airport are icons. Historically, an icon was a small picture of a religious figure, usually Jesus or the Virgin Mary.

id In **Freud**'s model of mental functioning, the raw desires and instincts of the individual, whose impulses are mediated by both the reality-testing capacities of the **ego** and the socializing function of the **superego**. *See also* **unconscious, projection, repression.**

idealism In philosophy and psychology, the notion that the mind determines ultimate reality, an idea that can be traced to **Plato** (428–347 BCE).

ideology A set of beliefs about the world (and often how it can be changed) espoused by an individual, group, or organization; a systematized worldview. **Capitalism,** for example, is an ideology. In the work of the Marxist critic Louis Althusser (1918–1990), an *ideology* is that which allows the individual to find his or her place and sense of self-worth within a given society.

imperialism One country's imposition of political and economic rule upon other countries. The British annexation of several countries in Africa in the nineteenth century is an example of this brand of imperialism. Today the term has been broadened to include the exportation of dominant cultural products and values. For example, some people in Europe and other parts of the world see the influx of American films into their markets as a form of *cultural imperialism. See also* **colonialism.**

inductive reasoning *See* **deductive reasoning.**

interpolation *See* **extrapolation.**

iteration Generally, the process of repeating steps over and over. In computer science, *iteration* refers to a computer's repeated looping through a set of programming instructions until it reaches the program's goal. In **chaos theory,** *iteration* involves getting data from an equation and repeatedly plugging the results back into the equation.

Keynesian economics The theory of economics developed by John Maynard Keynes (1883–1946), distinguished by the belief that government must intervene in the marketplace in order to promote stability and growth, specifically by increasing the money supply during economic downturns. *See also* **laissez-faire.**

laissez-faire (French for "allow to act") Generally, noninterference in the affairs or conduct of others. In economic and political theory, the idea that governments should not intervene in markets. The concept is based on the **classical** economic theory developed by Adam Smith (1723–1790) and others, which argues that an "invisible hand"—supply and demand, and competition—is sufficient to guide economic markets. *See also* **Keynesian economics.**

logos (Greek for "word") In Aristotle's **rhetorical triangle,** the topic of the argument or argument itself.

longitudinal A study in which the same group of subjects is examined over a long period of time. A *longitudinal study* could, for example, be conducted to test the rate of obesity over time among a certain group of schoolchildren.

Marxism The economic and political doctrine put forth by Karl Marx (1818–1883) and Friedrich Engels (1820–1895). Its basic teachings center around the **class** struggle between the **proletariat** (the working class) and the **bourgeoisie** (capitalists, those who own the *means of production*). Marxism predicts that in time the working class will inevitably revolt, wresting the means of production from the bourgeoisie and ceding them to the state, which will distribute goods equitably. A classless society will result.

materialism In philosophy, the belief that physical matter is all that exists and that so-called higher phenomena—for example, thought, feeling, mind, will—are wholly dependent on and **determined** by physical processes. Since the **Enlightenment,** almost all scientists have been materialists. In history and economics, the dialectical materialism of Karl **Marx** (1818–1883) held that **cultural** phenomena are determined wholly by economic conditions.

mean (also *average*) The sum of a set of numbers divided by the number of terms in the set. For example, the mean of the set (1, 2, 3) is 2 because its sum (6) divided by the number of terms (3) equals 2.

median The middle term in an ordered set of numbers. For example, the median of the ordered set (2, 6, 10, 12, 15) is 10 because there are two numbers (2 and 6) below 10 and two (12 and 15) above 10.

meta- A prefix often used to suggest "moving beyond," "going up a level," or "transcending." Thus, *metaphysics* is the branch of philosophy that deals with questions that cannot be resolved by physical observation, such as whether God exists. Similarly, *metapsychology* deals not with perception, emotion, or cognition per se, but rather with how such things are discussed and defined. **Freud**'s division of the psyche into **id, ego,** and **superego** is an example of metapsychology.

modernism Often used in opposition to classicism or neoclassicism when denoting periods in the sciences, social sciences, philosophy, and music, *modernism* as a trend in thought represents a break with the certainties of the past, among them a confidence that everything can be known. *Modern* science has been characterized by highly counterintuitive theories such as **relativity**—according to which there is no absolute way to measure time—and **quantum physics**—according to which you can know the speed or the position of a subatomic particle but never both. In literature, the **stream of consciousness** and/or *free association* style of *modernist* writers like Virginia Woolf (1882–1941) and James Joyce (1882–1941) broke decisively with the storytelling conventions of the late-nineteenth-century, or Victorian, novel. Thus, some

Virginia Woolf.

critics believe that **postmodernism** is really only the development of a trend begun in the modernist era.

multiculturalism The view that many cultures, not just the dominant one, should be given attention in the classroom and in broader society. The debate on multiculturalism is related to the debate on the **canon.**

nature-nurture controversy A debate about whether genetic (*nature*) or environmental (*nurture*) factors have the upper hand in determining human behavior. Experimental studies involving fraternal and identical twins raised together and apart have been undertaken to investigate the issue, but fundamental questions about method and the small **samples** involved have left the question unresolved. This debate pervades countless topics studied in the social sciences, among them questions of gender difference, intelligence, poverty, crime, and childhood development.

Nietzschean Following the ideas of Friedrich Nietzsche (1844–1900), a pioneering **existentialist** philosopher. Nietzsche believed that overemphasis on the Christian belief in the afterlife had led people away from what is real in the world. Nietzsche used the term *superman* (*Übermensch* in German) to apply to those who found the strength to cast aside these traditional social and moral values, using their **will to power**. *See also* **Apollonian, Dionysian.**

object/subject In philosophy and psychology, the *subject* does the observing or experiencing, while the *object* is that which is observed or experienced. Throughout history, this philosophical dualism has been studied, refined, and debated extensively. In **Freudian** and post-Freudian psychology, an *object* is an external person or thing that gratifies an infant and is therefore loved.

objective Pertaining to that which is independent of perception or observation, as opposed to *subjective,* which pertains to that which is determined by perception or observation. The old philosophical puzzle—If a tree falls in the woods, and no one is there to hear it, does it make a sound?—plays upon the notions of philosophical *objectivity* and *subjectivity.*

Oedipus complex The psychological notion expounded by Sigmund **Freud** (1856–1939) that describes the unconscious sexual longing of a son for his mother and his unconscious wish to kill his father, his rival for possession of the mother. The name is a reference to Sophocles' play *Oedipus Rex.* Freud also wrote of the *Electra* complex, which describes the similar sexual longing of a daughter for her father.

ontology Generally, the study of being and human consciousness.

paradigm A theoretical framework that serves as a foundation for a field of study or branch of knowledge. Darwinian evolution, Newtonian physics, and Aristotle's chemistry are all examples of scientific paradigms. *Paradigm shifts* designate the transition from one paradigm to another, usually with a profoundly transformative effect. For example, the shift from Newtonian physics to quantum physics might be termed a *paradigm shift.*

pathos (Greek for "suffering, experience, emotion") In Aristotle's **rhetorical triangle,** the feelings evoked in the audience by an argument.

persona (Latin for "mask") An assumed or public identity (as distinct from the *inner self*); a character adopted for a particular purpose; in literature, the voice or character of the speaker.

placebo effect A psychological process wherein subjects in medical research respond to an inactive compound, often a sugar pill, as if it contained active ingredients intended to treat a disease or condition.

Platonic Following the teachings of the Greek philosopher Plato (428–347 BCE), Platonic **idealism** is a system that attempts to show a rational relationship between the individual, the state, and the universe, governed by what is good, true, and beautiful. Basic tenets of this seminal branch of philosophy are that only a reflection of the truth can be perceived and that the gap between the ideal and its reflection motivates human consciousness. It can be contrasted with the **Aristotelian** tradition, which values empirical observation and scientific reasoning. In common usage, a *platonic relationship* is a close friendship that does not have a sexual component.

pluralism   In everyday language, a condition of society in which multiple religions, ethnicities, and subcultures coexist peacefully. *Pluralism* can also refer to any philosophical system that proposes that reality is made up of a number of distinct entities. The pragmatist William James (1842–1910) and the analytic philosopher Bertrand Russell (1872–1970) were prominent *pluralist* thinkers.

postcolonial   *See* **colonialism.**

postmodernism   A cultural trend that seeks to expose the artificiality of the **constructs** that defined earlier periods of cultural production while confessing—indeed, in some cases even boasting of—an inability to replace them with an authentic substitute. One of the hallmarks of *postmodern* cultural products is *pastiche,* or *collage,* a form that borrows from other trends and emphasizes the disjuncture between disparate elements. *See also* **modernism.**

praxis   Often used as a substitute for *practice* in ordinary usage, and opposed to **theory.** In the work of Antonio Gramsci (1891–1937), the "philosophy of praxis" outlined the refinements to Marxism that were necessary to make it relevant in the twentieth century.

projection   In **Freudian** psychology, a mechanism by which the individual, unable to come to terms with his or her own fears and desires, imagines that these unwelcome impulses exist outside of him- or herself. *See also* **id, ego, superego, repression, unconscious.**

proletariat   In **Marxism,** the *proletariat* is the downtrodden working **class,** who will revolt against the **bourgeois,** or capitalist, class, seizing from its members the means of production (factories and other industrial concerns).

quantum physics   A theoretical branch of physics that deals with the behavior of atoms and subatomic particles. The work of such pioneers as Max Planck (1858–1947), Niels Bohr (1885–1962), and later Werner Heisenberg (1901–1976) has had a profound impact on the way we understand such things as the relationships between matter and energy. *See also* **relativity.**

relativism   The belief that the meaning and value of all things are determined by their *context*—their relationship to other things in that time and place—rather than that things have inherent or absolute meaning or worth. *Moral relativism* is the idea that different people, groups, nations, or cultures have differing ideas about what constitutes good and evil and that those differences must be respected. *Cultural relativism* is the position that there is no absolute point of view from which one set of cultural values or beliefs can be deemed intrinsically superior to any other. *See also* **culture, humanism.**

relativity   In physics, the theory expounded by Albert Einstein (1879–1955), which states that all motion is relative and that energy and matter are convertible. The famous formulation $E = mc^2$ equates energy (E) with matter (m) multiplied by the speed of light (c) squared. Einstein's work directly challenged two cornerstones of **classical** physics—that motion is an absolute and that energy and matter are two completely different entities.

repression In **Freudian** psychology, the process that keeps unacceptable desires, fears, and other troubling material (such as memories of traumatic experiences) from reaching (or returning to) consciousness. *See also* **unconscious, projection.**

rhetoric In classical times, the art of public speaking. Currently, the term more broadly encompasses *language* or *speech,* often in a derogatory context (as in "The mayor's speech was so much empty *rhetoric*"), as well as the study of writing and the effective use of language.

Albert Einstein.

rhetorical triangle Aristotle's description of the context of argument, consisting of **ethos** (roughly, the character of the speaker), **logos** (the topic of the argument or the argument itself), and **pathos** (the feelings evoked in the audience).

sample A subset or selection of a group from a population. In a *random sample,* each subject is chosen in ways that replicate pure chance, and all members of the population have an equal chance of being selected for the sample.

scientific method A process involving observations of phenomena and the conducting of experiments to test ideas suggested by those observations. The development of the scientific method, a specialized form of trial and error, ushered in the scientific revolution of the seventeenth century. Francis Bacon (1561–1626), René Descartes (1596–1650), and especially Galileo Galilei (1564–1642) are most often credited with developing its constituent procedures: (1) choosing a question or problem (for example, what causes yellow fever); (2) developing a **hypothesis** (the disease is caused by a bacteria or virus transmitted by mosquitoes); (3) conducting observations and experiments (noting **correlations** between mosquito populations and incidence of yellow fever); (4) examining and interpreting the data (high correlations exist between incidence of yellow fever and that of the *A. aegypti* mosquito); (5) affirming, revising, or rejecting the hypothesis; and (6) deriving further experiments and hypotheses from it (microscopically examining the bodies of *A. aegypti* and yellow fever victims to try to find a virus or bacteria present in both).

secular Not having to do with religion or the church; deriving its authority from nonreligious sources. *See also* **humanism.**

semiotics The theory and study of **signs** and symbols. According to semiotics, meaning is never inherent but is always a product of social conventions, and **culture** can be analyzed as a series of **sign** systems. *See also* **structuralism.**

sign In **semiotics,** a constituent of a text—that is, any cultural product, including but not limited to language and human behavior—that derives its meaning only by means of its differentiation from surrounding signs. A recurring word in a poem can function as a sign, as can a wink or a nod; the meaning of each of these signs can be derived only from the study of their context.

skepticism The belief that nothing can be held true until grounds are established for believing it to be true. René Descartes (1596–1650), one of the founders of modern philosophy, expressed this attitude in his famous statement *"Cogito, ergo sum"* ("I think, therefore I am").

sociobiology The study of human behavior within an evolutionary/biological context. E. O. Wilson's *Sociobiology: The New Synthesis* (1975) provoked a controversial debate over the extent to which social behavior has a biological basis. *See also* **Darwinism.**

Socratic method Repeated questioning to arrive at implicit truths, a teaching method used by the Greek philosopher Socrates (470?–399? BCE), who influenced **Plato.**

solipsism Philosophical theory that the self is the only thing that can be known and verified and therefore is the only reality.

somatic (from the Greek for "body") Relating to the body. A *psychosomatic* illness is a physical condition that has a psychological origin.

standard deviation A measure of the degree to which data diverge from the **mean.** A high standard deviation means a greater range of results. Thus, in a **bell curve,** a tall, skinny curve represents a smaller standard deviation than does a wide, flat one.

statistical significance A value assigned to a research result as a measure of how likely it is that the result reflects mere chance. The higher the statistical significance, the less likely it is that chance determined the outcome. The results of studies employing large numbers of subjects typically have a higher statistical significance than do those from studies of a small number of subjects.

stream of consciousness A **modernist** literary technique in which the writer renders the moment-by-moment progress of a character's or narrator's thoughts. Among those writers who have used the technique are James Joyce (1882–1941) in *Ulysses,* Virginia Woolf (1882–1941) in *Mrs Dalloway,* and Marcel Proust (1871–1922) in *Remembrance of Things Past.*

structuralism An analytical method, today often subsumed under **semiotics,** that is used in the social sciences, the humanities, and the arts to examine underlying deep structures in a **text** by close investigation of its constituent parts (often termed **signs**). For example, in *narratology* (the study of narratives), myths, folktales, novels, paintings, and even comic books are reduced to their essential structures, from which are derived the rules that govern the different ways in which these narratives tell their stories. In *structural* approaches, the individual works under study are commonly considered less important than the universal structures that underlie them. This tendency has opened the approach to charges of anti-**humanism.** Michel Foucault (1926–1984) and other *poststructuralists* have challenged structuralists' belief in the possibility of revealing essential structures of knowledge and reality through this type of study. *See also* **semiotics, deconstruction, formalism, sign.**

subculture *See* **culture.**

subjective *See* **objective.**

sublimation A psychological concept describing the redirection of unacceptable feelings or impulses into socially acceptable behavior. For example, one might say that working long hours *sublimates* the desire to engage in adulterous exploits.

sublime Inspiring awe; impressive; moving; of high spiritual or intellectual worth. Michelangelo's painting on the ceiling of the Sistine Chapel is often cited as an example of the *sublime* in art; in nature, mountains such as Kilimanjaro have been described as *sublime.*

The ceiling of the Sistine Chapel.

superego In the **Freudian** model of mental functioning, the mental agent responsible for keeping the desires of the **id** and the antisocial impulses of the **ego** in check. Religion and the law are two institutions that Freud identified as manifestations of the superego in society. *See also* **repression, projection.**

symbiosis In biology, a prolonged association and interdependence of two or more organisms, usually to their mutual benefit. *Parasitism* occurs when one organism benefits at the expense of another. In general usage, *symbiotic* is used metaphorically to denote a mutual dependency and benefit between people, organisms, or ideas.

taxonomy Any set of laws and principles of classification. Originating in biology, taxonomy includes the theory and principles governing the classification of organisms into categories such as species and phyla. Today a literary critic might compose a "taxonomy of literary styles."

teleology In philosophy, religion, history, and the social sciences, an explanation or theory that assumes movement or development toward a specific end. For instance, Christianity is profoundly *teleological* because it looks toward the second coming of Christ.

text In common academic usage, anything undergoing rigorous intellectual examination and analysis. Although commonly associated with printed or written works, texts may also be oral works such as speeches, visual works such as paintings, everyday objects like toys, and even human behavior. Analysis of such cultural products is often called "reading the text," even if the text is not a written work. *See also* **semiotics, sign.**

theory A statement devised to explain a collection of facts or observations; also, the systematic organization of such statements. Theory is commonly contrasted with *practice* or **praxis.**

topography The physical features of a region. In cartography and surveying, maps and charts are the graphic representations of topography.

totem/totemic (from the Ojibwa, a Native American tribal language) A bird, animal, or plant or a natural phenomenon that has a special meaning for an individual or social group and with which the individual or group claims a special relationship.

trope A figure of speech. In literary criticism, the term is often used to refer to any technique that recurs in a **text.** Comparing women's faces to flowers is a common trope in Renaissance poetry.

typology The systematic study and classification of individuals in a group according to selected characteristics. In psychology, Carl Jung (1875–1961) developed a personality typology that uses characteristics such as extraversion and introversion. The Myers-Briggs assessment tools, based on Jung's typologies, are used in psychotherapy and employment settings. *See also* **archetypes.**

uncertainty principle An important theory in **quantum physics** formulated by German physicist Werner Heisenberg (1901–1976) that places an absolute, theoretical limit on the accuracy of certain pairs of simultaneously recorded measurements. The significance of this principle is that it prevents scientists from making absolute predictions of the future state of certain systems. Heisenberg's principle has been applied to philosophy, where it is called the *indeterminacy principle.*

unconscious In the **Freudian** theory of the mind, the repository for repressed desires, fears, and memories. Ordinarily inaccessible to the conscious mind, the repressed material in the unconscious nevertheless has a powerful impact on conscious behavior and thoughts. *See also* **id, ego, superego, projection, repression.**

variable In mathematics, a variable is a term capable of assuming any set of values. In algebra, it is represented by a symbol such as x, y, p, or q. In experimental research, the *dependent variable* is measured for change precipitated by an *independent variable* determined by the experimenter. A *random variable* is a numerical value determined by chance-driven experiment or phenomenon. The value can be predicted according to the laws of probability but is usually not known until after the experiment has been completed.

will to power (from Friedrich **Nietzsche**'s *Thus Spake Zarathustra,*) The capacity to overcome the dictates of conventional morality in order to achieve a level of experience beyond the reach of the "common herd." The key quality of Nietzsche's *superman* (*Übermensch*), the will to power manifests itself in creativity, independence, and originality. The association of this concept with Nazism has long made Nietzsche's ideas the focus of heated debate. *See also* **Apollonian, Dionysian, Nietzschean.**

zero sum game Any competitive situation where a gain for one side results in a loss for the other side. This term originated in **game theory** but is now in common use. In a *zero sum economy,* any economic gain is offset by an economic loss.

Test Yourself
Answer Key

and

Quick Guide

On the following pages are the answers to the Test Yourself exercises that begin Parts 6, 7, 8, 10 and 11 of this handbook. Use a coin to scratch off the silver coating that covers the answer to each question. The numbers in parentheses refer you to the chapters and sections of the handbook to turn to for help with questions you answer incorrectly.

In addition, on the middle two pages of this answer key is a Quick Guide to help—in the handbook and on *Catalyst*— with identifying and editing specific problems with grammar, clarity, word choice, and punctuation.

Test Yourself Answer Key

PART 6 Grammar Basics

1. ▪	(See 30a)	**11.** ▪ (See 30g)
2. ▪	(See 30a)	**12.** ▪ (See 31a)
3. ▪	(See 30b)	**13.** ▪ (See 31a)
4. ▪	(See 30b)	**14.** ▪ (See 31b)
5. ▪	(See 30c)	**15.** ▪ (See 31c)
6. ▪	(See 30c)	**16.** ▪ (See 31c)
7. ▪	(See 30d)	**17.** ▪ (See 31c)
8. ▪	(See 30e)	**18.** ▪ (See 31f)
9. ▪	(See 30f)	**19.** ▪ (See 31i)
10. ▪	(See 30g)	**20.** ▪ (See 31j)

PART 7 Editing for Grammar Conventions

1. ■ (See 32d)
2. ■ (See 32c)
3. ■ (See 32c)
4. ■ (See 32c)
5. ■ (See 33e)
6. ■ (See 33e)
7. ■ (See 33d)
8. ■ (See 33e)
9. ■ (See 34c)
10. ■ (See 34i)
11. ■ (See 34f)
12. ■ (See 35c)
13. ■ (See 35i)
14. ■ (See 35k)
15. ■ (See 36j)
16. ■ (See 36m)
17. ■ (See 36r)
18. ■ (See 37e)
19. ■ (See 37g)
20. ■ (See 37h)

Quick Guide

Identifying and editing: A quick guide to help in *The New McGraw-Hill Handbook* and *Catalyst* (**www.mhhe.com/nmhh**)

If you need help identifying and editing problems with . . .	see these chapters or chapter sections in the text	follow this click path in *Catalyst*
Abbreviations	58	Editing > Abbreviations
Adjectives	37	Editing > Adjectives and Adverbs
Adverbs	37	Editing > Adjectives and Adverbs
Apostrophes	61	Editing > Apostrophes
Biased language	48e	Editing > Word Choice
Capitalization	57	Editing > Capitalization
Clauses	31i, 32d	Editing > Phrases and Clauses
Clichés	49f	Editing > Clichés, Slang, Jargon
Colloquialisms	48a	Editing > Word Choice
Colons (:)	53	Editing > Colons
Comma splice	33	Editing > Comma Splices
Commas (,)	51	Editing > Commas
Comparative adjectives and adverbs	37g	Editing > Adjectives and Adverbs
Confusing shifts	41	Editing > Verb and Voice Shifts
Coordination	44	Editing > Coordination and Subordination
Dangling modifiers	43f	Editing > Dangling Modifiers
Dashes (—)	55	Editing > Dashes
Direct quotations	41e, 51h, 54	Editing > Quotation Marks
Exclamation points (!)	56e	Editing > End Punctuation
Helping verbs	35f, 35g, 35i	Editing > Verbs and Verbals
Hyphens	62	Editing > Hyphens
Idioms	49f, 66f	Editing > Word Choice
Indirect quotations	41e, 54a	Editing > Quotation Marks
Intransitive verbs	31c	Editing > Verbs and Verbals
Irregular verbs	35a, 35b	Editing > Verbs and Verbals
Italics and underlining	60	Editing > Italics
Jargon	48c	Editing > Clichés, Slang, Jargon
Linking verbs	31c, 34h	Editing > Verbs and Verbals
Misplaced modifiers	43a–43e	Editing > Misplaced Modifiers
Missing words	39	Editing > Word Choice
Mixed constructions	40	Editing > Mixed Constructions

If you need help identifying and editing problems with . . .	see these chapters or chapter sections in the text	follow this click path in *Catalyst*
Numbers	51i, 59	Editing > Numbers
Parallelism	42	Editing > Parallelism
Parentheses ( )	55f–55h	Editing > Parentheses
Parts of speech	30	Editing > Parts of Speech
Periods (.)	56a–56c	Editing > End Punctuation
Phrases	31d–31h	Editing > Phrases and Clauses
Pronoun case	36a–36j	Editing > Pronouns
Pronoun reference	36p–36t	Editing > Pronoun Reference
Pronoun-antecedent agreement	36k–36o	Editing > Pronoun-Antecedent Agreement
Question marks (?)	56d	Editing > End Punctuation
Quotation marks ("")	54	Editing > Quotation Marks
Redundancy	38c	Editing > Eliminating Redundancies
Regular verbs	35a	Editing > Verbs and Verbals
Restrictive vs. nonrestrictive modifiers	51e, 51n	Editing > Commas
Run-on sentences	33	Editing > Run-on Sentences
Semicolons (;)	52	Editing > Semicolons
Sentence fragments	32	Editing > Sentence Fragments
Sentence patterns	31c	Editing > Sentence Types
Sentence predicate	31c	Editing > Sentence Types
Sentence structures	31j	Editing > Sentence Variety
Sentence subject	31b, 34	Editing > Sentence Types
Sentence types	31j	Editing > Sentence Types
Sentence variety	45	Editing > Sentence Variety
Sexist language	36m, 48e	Editing > Word Choice
Slang	48a	Editing > Clichés, Slang, Jargon
Spelling	47, 63	Editing > Spelling
Subject complement	31c, 34h	Editing > Adjectives and Adverbs
Subject-verb agreement	34	Editing > Subject-Verb Agreement
Subordination	44	Editing > Coordination and Subordination
Transitive verbs	31c	Editing > Verbs and Verbals
Usage	49, 50	Editing > Word Choice
Verb forms	35	Editing > Verbs and Verbals
Verb mood	35k, 41d	Editing > Verbs and Verbals
Verb tense	35g	Editing > Verbs and Verbals

Test Yourself Answer Key

PART 8 Editing for Clarity

1. ■ (See 38c)
2. ■ (See 38b)
3 ■ (See 38d)
4. ■ (See 39d)
5. ■ (See 39e)
6. ■ (See 39d)
7. ■ (See 40a)
8. ■ (See 40b)
9. ■ (See 40b)
10. ■ (See 41b)

11. ■ (See 41c)
12. ■ (See 41e)
13. ■ (See 42b)
14. ■ (See 42b)
15. ■ (See 43b)
16. ■ (See 43f)
17. ■ (See 44f)
18. ■ (See 44d)
19. ■ (See 45b)
20. ■ (See 46b)

annotation (7d.2) The process of taking notes on the who, what, how, an[d] why of a work while reading or examining it carefully.

antecedent (30c; 34i; 36k) The noun that a pronoun replaces. In the sen[-] tence *Katya, who was at the concert, saw her picture in the paper,* the ant[e-] cedent of the pronouns *who* and *her* is *Katya.*

APA documentation style (25) The documentation style developed [by] the American Psychological Association and used in many of the behavior[al] and social sciences.

application letter (29c) A letter to a potential employer that usually acco[m-] panies an applicant's résumé and highlights the information on the résumé th[at] demonstrates the applicant's suitability for the job he or she is seeking.

appositive (31g; 36e; 51e) A noun or noun phrase that appears next to [a] noun or pronoun and renames it: *My friend Max, the best dancer on campu[s], is a chemistry major.*

archive (19) A cataloged collection of documents, manuscripts, or oth[er] materials, possibly including receipts, wills, photographs, sound recording[s] and other kinds of media.

argument (2c; 10) An attempt to persuade others to accept a point of view [or] a position on a contentious issue through logic and the marshalling of eviden[ce.]

articles (30d; 64a) The words *a, an,* and *the. A* and *an* are **indefinite art[i-] cles;** *the* is a **definite article.**

audience (2e) The intended readership for a piece of writing.

auxiliary verb (30a; 35f) See *helping verb.*

bias (10b.2) In argument, a sometimes unstated positive or negative inclina[-] tion that affects and limits a writer's objectivity.

blog or **weblog** (1b.3; 14a; 14f) A personal online journal.

body (3c) In writing, the middle section where the main idea is developed i[n] a series of paragraphs, each making a point that is supported by specif[ic] details.

Boolean operators (16d) Terms used in search engines for refining key[-] word searches.

brainstorming (3a.3) A technique for developing ideas about a topic.

browser (14e) Software that allows users to view material on the Worl[d] Wide Web.

call number (16g) A number based on a classification system for shelvin[g] books in libraries. Books on the same topic have similar call numbers and ar[e] shelved together.

case (30c.4; 36a–f) The form of a noun or pronoun that determines the gram[-] matical role it plays in a sentence. See *pronoun case.*

chartjunk (5g) Distracting visual details in a chart or graph.

chat room (3a.9, 16i) An online site, usually devoted to a specific topic, i[n] which people can engage in real-time discussions.

Chicago documentation style (26a–d) A style of documentation rec[-] ommended by the *Chicago Manual of Style* and used in the humanities.

PART 10 Sentence Punctuation

1. ▪ (See 51a)	8. ▪ (See 52d)	15. ▪ (See 55b)
2. ▪ (See 51b)	9. ▪ (See 52e)	16. ▪ (See 55c)
3. ▪ (See 51f)	10. ▪ (See 53a)	17. ▪ (See 55h)
4. ▪ (See 51i)	11. ▪ (See 53c)	18. ▪ (See 55i)
5. ▪ (See 51o)	12. ▪ (See 53d)	19. ▪ (See 55j)
6. ▪ (See 52a)	13. ▪ (See 54b)	20. ▪ (See 56a)
7. ▪ (See 52a)	14. ▪ (See 54b)	

PART 11 Mechanics and Spelling

1. ▪ (See 57a)	8. ▪ (See 59d)	15. ▪ (See 62a)
2. ▪ (See 57b/c)	9. ▪ (See 60a)	16. ▪ (See 62b)
3. ▪ (See 57e)	10. ▪ (See 60d)	17. ▪ (See 62d)
4. ▪ (See 57g)	11. ▪ (See 60a)	18. ▪ (See 63a)
5. ▪ (See 58a)	12. ▪ (See 61c)	19. ▪ (See 63b)
6. ▪ (See 58f)	13. ▪ (See 61a)	20. ▪ (See 63b)
7. ▪ (See 59a)	14. ▪ (See 61a)	

Glossary of Key Terms

This glossary defines key terms used in this handbook to discuss learning, writing, researching, and editing. It includes all the terms that appear in the book in bold type. The references in parentheses that follow the term indicate the chapters or chapter sections in which the terms are discussed.

absolute phrase (31h) A phrase made up of a noun or pronoun and a participle that modifies an entire sentence: *Their heads hanging, the boys walked off the field.*

abstract and concrete (30b; 49c) Kinds of language. An **abstract** word names qualities and concepts that do not have physical properties, such as *idea* or *beauty*. A **concrete** word names things that can be perceived with the senses, such as *chocolate* or *jacket*.

abstract noun (30b) See *noun*.

acronym (58a) An abbreviation composed of the initials of an organization and sometimes pronounceable as if it were a word, such as *NASA* (National Aeronautics and Space Administration) or *OSHA* (Occupational Safety and Health Administration).

active voice (31c.3; 35l; 41d) The form of a transitive verb in which the subject of the sentence is doing the acting. See *voice*.

adjective (30d; 37) A word that modifies a noun or pronoun with information specifying, for example, which one, what kind, or how many: *a delicious orange.*

adjective clause (or **relative clause**) (31i.1; 51e) A dependent clause that begins with a relative pronoun or adverb (such as *who, whom, whose, which, that, where*) and modifies a noun or pronoun (see *adjective*): *The house that I grew up in eventually sold for a million dollars.*

adjective phrase (51e) A phrase that begins with a preposition or verb and modifies a noun or pronoun: *The game lasting 21 innings was by far t longest of the season.*

adverb (30e; 37) A word that modifies a verb, an adjective, or anot adverb with information specifying, for example, when, where, how, how of how much, to what degree, or why: *She was terribly unhappy.*

adverb clause (31i.2; 51e) A dependent clause, usually introduced by ordinating word (such as *after, because,* or *when*), that modifies a verb, an tive, or another adverb (see *adverb*): *After he lost the tennis match, Rodri straight to the gym.*

agreement (34, 36) The appropriate pairing in number, person, an of one word to another. See *pronoun-antecedent agreement* and *sut agreement.*

analogy (4d.7) A comparison that points out the similarities be often very different things, such as a heart and a pump or an eye era. A well-structured analogy can make something unfamiliar s and provide insight into difficult concepts.

analysis (7d) An aspect of critical reading that involves exa in detail, in particular by breaking it down into significant par ing how those parts relate to each other.

chronological organization (4c.1) In writing, the arrangement of information about events according to the sequence in which the events occurred.

citation (21a; 22c; 24; 25; 26) The identification and acknowledgment of the source of information or ideas presented in a paper.

claim (10b.2) An assertion about a topic. In an argument paper, claims should be backed by reasons and evidence. See *Toulmin method.*

classification (4d.3) In writing, a method of organizing information by grouping it into categories.

clause (31d; 51e) A group of related words containing a subject and a predicate. An **independent (main) clause** can stand on its own as a sentence: *We can have a picnic.* A **dependent (subordinate) clause** cannot stand on its own as a sentence: *We can have a picnic if it doesn't rain.*

cliché (49f) An overworked expression or figure of speech.

clipping (58a) The use of a shortened form of a word, usually informally, such as *exam* for *examination.*

clustering or mapping (3a.4) A brainstorming technique for discovering connections among ideas by writing a topic in the center of a page and then clustering related topics and subtopics around the central term as they come to mind.

cognate (66a) A word in English that is similar to a word in another language and has a similar origin.

coherence (5f.3) The quality of a piece of writing that links ideas from sentence to sentence and from paragraph to paragraph clearly and logically.

collaborative learning (5a.1) A process in which classmates work together to review and make constructive suggestions on one another's work.

collaborative writing (2g) Writing coauthored by two or more people.

collective noun (30b.5; 34e) See *noun.*

colloquial (48b) Language that is appropriate to informal conversation but not precise enough for academic writing.

comma splice (33a) An error in which two independent clauses are joined by a comma without a coordinating conjunction.

common noun (30b.1) See *noun.*

comparative degree (37g) See *comparison.*

comparison (37g) The form of an adjective or adverb that indicates its degree or amount. The **positive degree** is the simple form and involves no comparison: *large, difficult* (adjectives); *far, confidently* (adverbs). The **comparative degree** compares two things: *larger, more difficult; farther, more/less confidently.* The **superlative degree** compares three or more things, indicating which is the greatest or the least: *largest, most difficult; farthest, most/least confidently.*

comparison and contrast (4d.6) In writing, an organizational strategy that involves pointing out similarities and differences among items. See *subject-by-subject* and *point-by-point comparison.*

complement (31c) A word or group of words that follow a linking verb to explain or define the subject of a sentence. See *subject complement* and *object complement*.

complete predicate (31c) See *predicate*.

complete subject (31b) See *subject*.

complete verb (32a; 35f) A main verb and any helping verbs needed to indicate tense, person, and number.

complex sentence (31j) See *sentence*.

compound predicate (31c.2; 32c.7) Two or more predicates connected by a conjunction.

compound sentence (31j) See *sentence*.

compound-complex sentence (31j) See *sentence*.

compound structures (36c) Words or phrases joined by *and, or,* or *nor*.

compound subject (31b.2; 34d) See *subject*.

concise (38) Of writing, employing as few words as needed to be clear and engaging.

conclusion (3c) The closing section of a paper. A good conclusion gives readers a sense of completion and often offers a final comment on the thesis.

concrete (30b; 49c) See *abstract and concrete*.

concrete noun (30b) See *noun*.

conjunction (30g) A word that joins words, phrases, or clauses and indicates their relation to each other. **Coordinating conjunctions** (such as *and, but, or, nor, for, so, yet*) join words or ideas of equal weight or function: *The night grew colder, but the boys and girls kept trick or treating.* **Correlative conjunctions** (such as *both . . . and, neither . . . nor, not only . . . but also*) link sentence elements of equal value, always in pairs: *She knew that either her mother or her father would drive her to the airport.* **Subordinating conjunctions** (such as *after, although, as if, because, if, when*) introduce dependent or subordinate clauses, linking sentence elements that are not of equal importance: *They waltzed while the band played on.*

conjunctive adverb (30g.4) A word or expression such as *for example, however,* or *therefore* that indicates the relation between two clauses. Unlike conjunctions, conjunctive adverbs are not grammatically strong enough on their own to hold the two clauses together, requiring the clauses to be separated by a period or semicolon: *The night grew colder; however, the boys and girls kept trick or treating.*

connotation (49) The secondary, or implicit, meaning of a word that derives from the feelings and images it evokes.

contraction (61b) A shortened word formed when two words are combined and letters are replaced with an apostrophe: *doesn't* for *does not*.

coordinate adjectives (51c) Two or more adjectives that act individually to modify a noun or pronoun: *Her speech was brief, clear, and engaging.*

coordinating conjunction or coordinator (30g.1; 42c) See *conjunction*.

coordination (44a–b) In a sentence, the joining of elements of equal weight. See also *subordination.*

copyright (20a) The legal right to control the reproduction of any original work—a piece of writing, a musical composition, a play, a movie, a computer program, a photograph, or a work of art.

correlative conjunction (30g.2) See *conjunction.*

count noun (30b.2) See *noun.*

counterargument (10c.4) In an argument paper, a substantiated claim that does not support the writer's position.

critical response paper (7e) A paper that synthesizes the writer's response to another work. A critical response paper typically begins with a summary of the work followed by a thesis that encapsulates the writer's response to the work and then an elaboration on the thesis.

critical reading (7) A process for systematically and thoughtfully approaching a text to understand its literal and implicit meaning and arrive at a judgment about it. The process typically involves previewing the text, reading and analyzing it, and synthesizing and evaluating it.

CSE documentation style (26e–j) A style of documentation developed by the Council of Science Editors and used in the sciences.

cumulative adjectives (51c) Adjectives that act as a set and should not be separated by a comma. The first adjective modifies the following adjective or adjectives as well as the noun or pronoun: *world-famous American sculptor.*

cumulative sentence (45c) A sentence that begins with a subject and verb and then accumulates information in a series of descriptive modifiers: *The reporters ran after the film star, calling out questions and shoving each other aside.*

dangling modifier (43f) A modifier that confusingly implies an actor different from the sentence's subject: *Being so valuable, thousands of people flooded into California during the gold rush.*

database (16e.2) A collection of information available either in print or electronically.

deductive reasoning (10b.1; p. FR-21) A method of reasoning based on claims structured such that if the premises are true, the conclusion must be true: *All humans are mortal, and Socrates is a human, so Socrates must be mortal.*

definite article (64a) See *articles.*

definition (4d.4) In writing, an organizational strategy based on the explanation of concepts a reader must understand to grasp the ideas that follow.

degree (37g) See *comparison.*

demonstrative pronoun (30c.5) A pronoun such as *this, that, these,* and *those* that points out nouns and pronouns that come later: *This is the house that Jack built.*

denotation (49) The primary, or dictionary, definition of a word.

dependent or **subordinate clause** (31i) See *clause.*

description (4d.2) In writing, an organizational strategy based on the presentation of vivid details describing sight, sound, taste, smell, or touch.

descriptive adjective (30d) An adjective that names a quality or attribute of a noun or pronoun: _beautiful_ sunset.

dialect (48a) A variant of a language that is used by a particular social, geographical, or ethnic group.

diction (49) Word choice.

direct address (51g) A construction that includes a word or phrase that names the person or group being spoken to: _Are you coming, Vinny?_

direct object (31c.3) See _object._

direct question (41e) A sentence that asks a question and concludes with a question mark. Contrast with _indirect question._

direct quotation (21b.5; 41e; 54a) The reproduction of the exact words someone else has spoken or written. In academic writing, direct quotations are enclosed in quotation marks or, if long, set off in a separate block of text.

discipline (1a.1) A specialized branch of academic study or area of inquiry.

discourse community (48a) A group of people who share certain interests, knowledge, and customary ways of communicating.

discussion list or **electronic mailing list** (16i) A group of people interested in a particular topic linked in networked e-mail conversation. A list can be open (anyone can join) or closed (only certain people can join).

division (4d.3) A form of classification that involves breaking a subject into its parts. See _classification._

documentation (22c; 24–26) The acknowledgment in full citations in a paper of the source of any words or ideas that come from others.

document design (6) The arrangement of text and visuals in a paper or other document. The goal of good document design is to showcase the work effectively for its purpose and audience.

do/say plan (3c.2) An informal but detailed outline that lays out what the writer will introduce, support, and conclude.

doublespeak (48d) The deceitful use of language to obscure facts and mislead readers.

drafting (4) A stage of the writing process that involves developing and honing a paper through a series of versions.

editing (5) A stage of the writing process in which writers polish sentences and paragraphs for correctness, clarity, and effectiveness.

electronic portfolio (6d) See _portfolio._

elliptical clause (31i.4; 38c) A clause in which one or more grammatically necessary words is omitted because their meaning and function are clear from the surrounding context: _I like New York more than_ [_I like_] _Los Angeles._

empty phrase (38b) A phrase that provides little or no information: _The fact is, the planets revolve around the sun._

ethos (10c.6; p. FR-22) See _logos, ethos, pathos._

euphemism (48d) An innocuous word or phrase that substitutes for a harsh, blunt, or offensive alternative: *pass away* for *die.*

evaluation (15a) A judgment about a set of facts or a situation.

evidence (10b.1) The facts, statistics, anecdotes, and expert opinions writers use to support their claims.

excessive coordination (44c) The use of coordination to string together too many ideas at once.

excessive subordination (44e) The use of subordination to string together too many subordinate expressions at once.

exclamatory sentence (31a) A sentence that expresses strong emotion and ends with an exclamation point.

expletive construction (38d) The use of *there, here,* or *it* in the subject position of a sentence, followed by a form of *be: Here are the directions.* The subject follows the verb.

extract or **block quotation** (54d) A long direct quotation that is not enclosed by quotation marks but is set off from the text.

fact (15a) Objective information that can be measured, observed, or independently verified.

fair use (20a) The provision of copyright law that permits the reproduction, in some circumstances, of limited portions of a copyrighted work for news reporting or for scholarly or educational purposes.

fallacies (10b.3) Mistakes in logic or reasoning.

faulty coordination (44c) The use of coordination to join sentence elements that aren't logically equivalent, or to join elements with an inappropriate coordinating word.

faulty parallelism (42a) An error that results when items in a series, paired ideas, or items in a list do not have the same grammatical form.

faulty predication (40b) An illogical, ungrammatical combination of subject and predicate.

field research (19c) Research that involves eliciting information through direct observations, interviews, or surveys.

figurative language or **figure of speech** (49e) An imaginative expression, usually a comparison, that amplifies the literal meaning of other words. See also *hyperbole, irony, metaphor, personification, simile,* and *understatement.*

file (14a) In computer technology, a collection of information in computer-readable form.

focused freewriting See *freewriting.*

fonts (6c.2) The variations available in size and form (bold and italic, for example) of a particular typeface. See *typeface.*

formal outline (3c.2) An outline that classifies and divides the information a writer has gathered by organizing main points, supporting ideas, and specific details into separate levels of subordination.

fragment (32) See *sentence fragment.*

freewriting (3a.2) A method for developing ideas by writing down whatever comes to mind about a topic. Ideas that emerge from freewriting can become the subject of further exploration in **focused freewriting,** or freewriting that begins with a point or a specific question.

function word (42d) A word, such as an article, a preposition, or a conjunction, that indicates the relationship among other words in a sentence: *I called the company for days but never got through.*

funnel opener (4f) An introduction that begins with broad assertions and then narrows in focus to conclude with a statement of the writer's thesis.

fused sentence (33a) See *run-on sentence.*

gender (36j–m; 64b) The classification of nouns and pronouns as masculine (*he, father*), feminine (*she, mother*), or neuter (*it, painter*).

generalization A broad statement without details.

general word (49c) A word that names a broad category of things, such as *trees* or *students.*

generic noun (36m; 64a) A noun used to represent anyone and everyone in a group: *the average voter; the modern university.*

genre (2d) A category of writing. In literary writing, for example, genres include story, play, and poem; in nonfiction writing, genres include letter, essay, review, and report.

gerund (31f) The present participle (*-ing*) form of a verb used as a noun: *Most college courses require writing.* See *verbal.*

gerund phrase (31f.2; 34j) A word group consisting of a gerund followed by objects, complements, or modifiers: *Walking to the mailbox was my grandmother's only exercise.*

GIF (14e) See *JPEG.*

grammar (30) A description of the rules and conventions for combining the elements of a language into meaningful sentences.

grounds (10b.2) In argument, the reasons and evidence presented in support of a claim. See *Toulmin method.*

help sheets (16a) In libraries, documents that provide information about the location of both general and discipline-specific resources, both in print and online.

helping or **auxiliary verb** (30a; 35f) Verbs that combine with main verbs to indicate a variety of meanings, including tense, mood, voice, and manner. Helping verbs include forms of *be, have,* and *do* and the modal verbs *can, could, may, might, shall, should,* and *will.* See *modal verb.*

hit (16f) In online keyword searches, a link yielded by a search.

home page (14e) The opening page of a Web site.

homonyms (63b) Words that sound alike but have different meanings and different spellings, such as *bear* and *bare.*

HTML/XML (14e) Hypertext markup language and extensible markup language used to code text so that it appears as a formatted Web page in a browser.

HTTP (14e) Hypertext transfer protocol, a format for breaking down a document for transmission over the Internet.

hyperbole (49e) Deliberate exaggeration. See *figurative language.*

hypertext essay (14c) A multimedia essay with embedded links that take readers to other files, including text, image, audio, and video files.

hypothesis (15c.4; p. FR-24) A proposed explanation for a particular set of observations or provisional answer to a research question that is subject to testing and revision during the course of research.

idiom (1c.2; 49d; 66f) An expression whose meaning is established by custom and cannot be determined from the dictionary definition of the words that compose it: *Boston Red Sox fans were in seventh heaven when their team finally won the World Series in 2004.*

image interpretation (14b) A paper that combines an image with the writer's interpretation of that image.

imperative mood (41d) Of verbs, the mood that expresses commands, directions, and entreaties: *Please don't leave.* See *mood.*

imperative sentence (31a) A sentence in the imperative mood.

indefinite article (64a) See *articles.*

indefinite pronoun (30c.7; 34f; 36m) A pronoun such as *someone, anybody, nothing,* and *few* that does not refer to a specific person or item.

independent clause (31d) See *clause.*

index (16e.2) A catalog of articles published in periodicals; an alphabetical list, usually appearing at the end of a book, that lists the topics covered in the book and the pages on which those topics are discussed.

indicative mood (35k; 41d) Of verbs, the most common mood, used to make statements (*We are going to the beach*) or ask questions (*Do you want to come along?*). See *mood.*

indirect object (31c.3; 65a) See *object.*

indirect question (41e) A sentence that reports a question and ends with a period: *My mother often wonders if I'll ever settle down.* Contrast with *direct question.*

indirect quotation (41e; 54a) A sentence that reports, as opposed to repeating verbatim, what someone else has said or written. Indirect quotations are not enclosed in quotation marks.

inductive reasoning (10b.1; p. FR-25) A method of reasoning that involves deriving a general conclusion from specific facts. When using inductive reasoning, a writer presents evidence (facts and statistics, anecdotes, and expert opinion) to convince reasonable people that the writer's argument is probably true.

infinitive (31f) A verbal consisting of the base form of a verb preceded by *to: to run, to eat.* See *verbal.*

infinitive phrase (31f.3) An infinitive, plus any subject, objects, or modifiers, that functions as an adverb, adjective, or noun: *When I was a child, I longed to be a famous soprano.*

informative report (2c; 8a) Writing that passes on what the writer has learned about a subject.

instant messaging (IM) (16i) An online medium for real-time communication.

intellectual property (20a) A work under copyright or some other legal protection, such as patent or trademark.

intensive pronoun (30c) A pronoun ending with the suffix *-self* or *-selves* that adds emphasis to the noun or pronoun it follows. It is grammatically optional: *I myself couldn't care less.*

interjection (30h) A forceful expression, usually written with an exclamation point: *Hey! Beat it!*

interpret (7d) To explain the meaning of something.

interpretation (15a) The determination of implications and meanings, for example, in a painting, a short story, or a political speech.

interpretive analysis (2c; 9) A kind of writing that explores the meaning of documents, cultural artifacts, social situations, and natural events.

interrogative pronoun (30c.6) A pronoun (*who, whose, whom, which, what, whatever*) used to ask questions.

interrogative sentence (31a) A sentence that poses a direct question.

in-text citation or **parenthetical citation** (24–26) Source information placed in parentheses in the body of a paper.

intransitive verb (31c.3; 35c) A verb that describes an action or a state of being and does not take a direct object: *The tree fell.*

introduction (3c) A paragraph or series of paragraphs that begins an essay.

invention techniques (3a) Prewriting strategies for exploring ideas about a topic.

inversion (45d) In sentences, a reversal of standard word order, as when the verb comes before the subject: *Up jumped the cheerleaders.*

irony The use of words to imply the opposite of their literal meaning: *Aren't you cheerful this morning!* (to a grumpy roommate). See *figurative language.*

irregular verb (35a) A verb that forms the past tense and past participle other than by adding *-ed.*

jargon (48c) One group's specialized, technical language used in an inappropriate context; that is, used with people outside the group or when it does not suit a writer's purpose.

journal (3a) A place to record one's thoughts in writing.

JPEG and **GIF** (14e) File formats for digitally coding photographs and other visuals that are recognized by Web browsers.

keyword (16b.1) A term entered into an online search engine to find sources—books, journal articles, Web sites—of needed information.

keyword search (16c) An online search conducted by entering keywords into a search engine.

limiting modifier (43c) A word such as *only, even, almost, really,* and *just* that qualifies the meaning of another word or word group.

limiting sentence (4c.2) A statement that seems to oppose a paper's main idea, allowing the writer to bring in a different perspective.

link (14c) A connection from one electronic file to another, or from one place to another in the same file.

linking verb (31c.3; 34h; 35f; 37f) A verb that joins a subject to its subject complement. Forms of *be* are the most common linking verbs: *They are happy.* Others include *look, appear, feel, become, smell, sound,* and *taste: The cloth feels soft.*

logos, ethos, pathos (10c.6; pp. FR-22 and FR-25) Greek words for the qualities of *thought, character,* and *feeling* that the writer of an argument paper conveys to the audience he or she is attempting to persuade.

main verb (30a) The part of a verb phrase that carries the principal meaning.

mechanics (57–62) Conventions regarding the use of capital letters, italics, abbreviations, numbers, and hyphens.

metaphor (49e) An implied comparison between two unlike things: *Your harsh words stung my pride.* See *figurative language.* Compare to *simile.*

misplaced modifier (43a) A modifier placed confusingly far from the expression it modifies, that ambiguously modifies more than one expression, or that awkwardly disrupts the relationships among the grammatical elements of a sentence.

mixed construction (40) A sentence with parts that do not fit together logically or grammatically.

mixed metaphor (49e) A confusing combination of two or more incompatible or incongruous metaphoric comparisons: *His fortune burned a hole in his pocket and trickled away.*

MLA documentation style (24) The documentation style developed by the Modern Language Association and used in the arts and humanities.

modal verb (30a.3) A helping verb that signifies the manner, or mode, of an action: *You should get ready for your guests.*

modifier (37; 43) A word or group of words functioning as an adjective or adverb to describe or limit another word or group of words.

mood (35k) The form of a verb that reveals the speaker or writer's attitude toward the action of a sentence. The **indicative mood** is used to state or question facts, acts, and opinions: *The wedding is this weekend. Did you get your suit pressed?* The **imperative mood** is used for commands, directions, and entreaties: *Take your dirty dishes to the kitchen.* The **subjunctive mood** is used to express a wish or a demand or to make a statement contrary to fact: *If I were rich, I would travel the world by boat.*

multimedia writing (14) Writing that combines words with images, video, or audio into a single composition.

narration (4d.1) In writing, a strategy for developing a paragraph or essay based on the retelling of events, usually in chronological order.

navigation bar (14e.5) A grouping of links on a Web page that makes it easy to move to other pages and back again.

netiquette (1b.3) A new word, formed from a combination of *Internet* and *etiquette,* that refers to good manners in cyberspace.

networked classroom (1b.3) A classroom in which each student works at one of a group of linked computers.

noncount noun (30b.2; 64a) See *noun.*

nonrestrictive element (51e) A nonessential element that adds information to a sentence but is not required for understanding its basic meaning.

noun (30b) A word that names a person, place, thing, or idea: *David, Yosemite, baseball, democracy.* **Common nouns** name a general class and are not capitalized: *teenager, dorm, street.* **Proper nouns** name specific people, places, or things and are capitalized: *Shakespeare, London, Globe Theater.* **Count nouns** name specific items that can be counted: *muscle, movie, bridge.* **Noncount nouns** name nonspecific things that cannot be counted: *advice, air, time.* **Concrete nouns** name things that can be perceived by the senses: *wind, song, man.* **Abstract nouns** name qualities and concepts that do not have physical properties: *love, courage, hope.* **Collective nouns** are singular in form but name groups of people or things: *crew, family, audience.*

noun clause (31i.3) A dependent clause that functions as a noun: *They told me where to meet them.*

noun phrase (31e) A noun plus all of its modifiers.

number (30a.1) The form of a verb, noun, or pronoun that indicates whether it is singular or plural.

object (31c) A noun or pronoun that receives or is influenced by the action reported by a transitive verb, a preposition, or a verbal. A **direct object** receives the action of a transitive verb or verbal and usually follows it in a sentence: *Tom and I watched the sunrise together.* An **indirect object** names for or to whom something is done: *Tom promised me a pancake breakfast afterward.* The **object of a preposition** usually follows a preposition and completes its meaning: *We drove into town together.*

object complement (31c.3) A word or group of words that follows an object in a sentence and describes or renames it: *I call my cousin Mr. Big.*

object of a preposition (30f) See *object.*

objective case (36) See *pronoun case.*

objective stance (8b.3) The fair presentation of differing views without indicating a preference for one view or the other. Contrast with *subjective stance.*

paragraph (4b) A set of sentences that work together to develop an idea or example.

parallel construction (47d) See *parallelism.*

parallelism (42) The presentation of equal ideas in the same grammatical form: individual terms with individual terms, phrases with phrases, and clauses with clauses. The use of parallelism results in **parallel constructions.**

parenthetical citation or reference (24–26) See *in-text citation.*

paraphrase (21b.3) The restatement of source material in different words and in a different form from the original, and usually more succinctly and in less detail.

participial phrase (31f.1) A word group that consists of a participle and any objects or modifiers and functions as an adjective: *Jumping the fence, the dog ran down the street.*

participle (31f; 35a) The *-ing* (present participle) or *-ed* (past participle) form of a verb. (In regular verbs, the past tense and the past participle are the same.) Participles are used with helping verbs in verb phrases (*They are walking slowly.*) and as verbals (*Walking is good exercise.*). See *verb phrase* and *verbal.*

parts of speech (30) The eight primary categories to which all English words belong: verbs, nouns, pronouns, adjectives, adverbs, prepositions, conjunctions, and interjections.

passive voice (31c.3; 35l; 41d) The form of a transitive verb in which the subject of the sentence is acted upon. See *voice.*

pathos (10c.6; pp. FR-22 and FR-27) See *logos, ethos, pathos.*

peer review (1b.4; 5a.1) A structured process in which students respond to each other's work at different stages in the writing process.

perfect tenses (35g.3) See *tense.*

periodic sentence (45c) A sentence in which the key word, phrase, or idea appears at the end: *Despite a massive investment, the assembling of a stellar cast, and months of marketing hype, the movie flopped.*

periodical (16e.1) A regularly published newspaper, magazine, or scholarly journal.

person (30a.1; 34) The form of a verb or pronoun that indicates whether the subject of a sentence is speaking or writing (*first person*), is spoken or written to (*second person*), or is spoken or written about (*third person*).

personal pronoun (30c.1; 36) A pronoun that stands for a specific person or thing. The personal pronouns are *I, me, you, he, his, she, her, it, we, us, they,* and *them.*

personification (49e) The attribution of human qualities to objects, animals, or abstract ideas. See *figurative language.*

phrasal verb (49d, 66e) A verb that combines with a preposition to make its meaning complete and often has an idiomatic meaning that changes when the preposition changes: *look out, dig into.*

phrase (31d) A group of related words that lacks either a subject or a predicate or both and cannot stand alone as an independent sentence. Phrases function within sentences as nouns, verbs, and modifiers.

plagiarism (20; 21) The use of someone else's words, ideas, or other original work without acknowledging its source. Plagiarism is, in effect, the theft of someone else's intellectual property.

planning (3) The early stage of writing, when a writer generates ideas, develops a thesis, plans a structure, and considers the use of visuals.

plural (30b.3) Referring to more than one. See *number.*

point-by-point comparison (4d.6) The comparison of two items one feature at a time. A point-by-point comparison of two photographs might first discuss the subject of each, then the composition of each, then the use of color, and so forth. See *subject-by-subject comparison.*

portfolio (6) A collection of one's writing for presentation to others, such as potential employers. An **electronic portfolio** is a portfolio in electronic form and can include video, audio, and image files as well as text files.

positive degree (37g) See *comparison.*

possessive case (30b.6; 36) See *pronoun case.*

possessive noun (30b.6) A noun that indicates possession or ownership: *Jesse's, America's.*

possessive pronoun (30c.2) A pronoun that indicates ownership: *mine, ours.*

predicate (31c; 40b) In a sentence, the verb and its objects, complements, or modifiers. The predicate reports or declares (*predicates*) something about the subject. The verb itself, including any helping verbs, constitutes the **simple predicate.** The simple predicate together with its objects, complements and modifiers constitutes the **complete predicate.**

premise (10b.1) A statement or assertion that supports an argument's conclusion.

preposition (30f) A word that precedes a noun, pronoun, or noun phrase (the *object of the preposition*) and allows the resulting **prepositional phrase** to modify another word or word group in the sentence.

prepositional phrase (30f) A preposition and its object: *We went home after completing our exams.*

present tense (35a) See *tense.*

presentation software (14d) An electronic replacement for the traditional kinds of visual aids speakers have used to accompany oral presentations. Software like Microsoft's PowerPoint makes it possible to incorporate audio, video, and animation as well as text and still visuals into a presentation.

pretentious or **stilted language** (48b) Language that is overly formal or full of fancy phrases, making it inappropriate for academic writing.

previewing (7b) Scanning a text for basic information about its author, title, and contents in preparation for further critical examination.

prewriting activities (3a) See *invention techniques.*

primary research (15a; 19) Research that involves working in a laboratory, in the field, or with an archive of raw data, original documents, or authentic artifacts to make firsthand discoveries.

primary source (7b) A firsthand (primary) account of an event or research. Examples of primary sources include letters, contemporary newspaper accounts of events, a researcher's lab notes, and historical data like that found in census records.

progressive tense (35g.4) See *tense.*

pronoun (30c; 36) A word that takes the place of a noun.

pronoun-antecedent agreement (36) The appropriate pairing in number, person, and gender of a pronoun to its antecedent: *Judi loved her tiny apartment.*

pronoun case (36) The form of a pronoun that reflects its function in a sentence. Most pronouns have three cases: **subjective** (*I, she*), **objective** (*me, her*), and **possessive** (*my, hers*).

pronoun reference (36) The nature of the relationship—clear or ambiguous—between a pronoun and the word it replaces.

proofreading (5i) The process of checking the final draft of a piece of writing to make sure it is free of mistakes.

proper adjective (30d) An adjective formed from a proper noun, such as *Britain/British*.

proper noun (30b.1; 57a) See *noun*.

protocol (14e) A set of rules controlling data exchange between computers.

purpose (2c) A writer's goal: for example, to inform, to interpret, or to argue.

quantifier (64a) Words that tell how much or how many: *a few, some, many*.

questionnaire (19c.3) A series of questions structured to elicit information from respondents in a survey.

quotation (21b; 21d; 41e; 54a–e) A restatement, either directly (verbatim) or indirectly of what someone has said or written. See *direct quotation* and *indirect quotation*.

reciprocal pronouns (30c.8) Pronouns such as *each other* or *one another* that refer to the separate parts of a plural antecedent: *They helped <u>one another</u> escape from the flooded city.*

redundancy (38c) Unnecessary repetition.

reflexive pronoun (30c.3) A pronoun ending in *-self* or *-selves* that refers back to the sentence subject: *They asked <u>themselves</u> if they were doing the right thing.* Reflexive pronouns, unlike intensive pronouns, are grammatically necessary. See *intensive pronoun*.

regionalism (48a) An expression common to the people in a particular region.

regular verb (35a) A verb that forms its past tense and past participle by adding *-d* or *-ed* to the base form.

relative clause (31i.1; 51e) See *adjective clause*.

relative pronoun (30c.4) A pronoun such as *who, whom, which,* or *that* used to relate a relative (adjective) clause to an antecedent noun or pronoun: *The woman <u>who</u> came in second is a friend of ours.*

research journal or **research log** (21b.2) A tool for keeping track of your research.

research project (15b) A project that involves conducting research, evaluating the results of the research, and writing a paper in which sources are accurately cited and documented.

restrictive element (51n) A word, phrase, or clause with essential information about the noun or pronoun it describes. Restrictive elements are not set off by commas: *The house <u>that Jack built</u> is sturdy.*

résumé (29b) A brief summary of one's education and work experience.

review of the literature (8d) An informative report on the current state of knowledge in a specific area.

revising (5) A stage of the writing process in which the writer reviews the whole paper and its parts, adding, deleting, moving, and editing text as necessary.

rhetoric (p. FR-29) The study of the effective use of language as determined by a writer's or speaker's audience and purpose.

rhetorical question (45d) A question asked for effect, with no expectation of an answer.

run-on sentence or **fused sentence** (33a) An error in which two independent clauses are joined together without punctuation or a connecting word.

scientific method (10b.1) The method by which scientists gather data from experiments, surveys, and observations to formulate and test hypotheses.

scratch outline (3c.2) A simple list of points, without the levels of subordination found in more complex outlines.

search engine (16c) Software that searches for information on the Internet or online databases.

secondary research (15a; 19) Research that involves investigating what other people have learned and written about a field or topic. Contrast with *primary research*.

secondary source (7b) A source with information derived from the study of primary sources (or other secondary sources). Textbooks and encyclopedia articles are examples of secondary sources. Contrast with *primary source*.

sentence (31j) A subject and predicate not introduced by a subordinating word that fit together to make a statement, ask a question, give a command, or express an emotion. A **simple sentence** is composed of only one independent clause: *I am studying.* A **compound sentence** contains two or more coordinated independent clauses: *I would like to go to the movies, but I am studying.* A **complex sentence** contains one independent clause and one or more dependent clauses: *If you try to make me go to the movies, I'll be really annoyed.* A **compound-complex sentence** contains two or more coordinated independent clauses and at least one dependent clause: *I'm staying home to study because I'm failing the course, but I'd much rather go to a movie.*

sentence fragment (32) An incomplete sentence that is treated as if it were complete, with a capital letter at the beginning and a closing punctuation mark.

sentence outline (3c.2) A formal outline in which each topic and subtopic is stated in a full sentence.

sequence of tenses (35g) The choice of verb tenses within the clauses and phrases of a sentence to reflect the logical relationship in time among the actions each expresses.

server (14e) A computer that links other computers in a network.

sexist language (48e) Language that demeans or stereotypes women or men based on their sex.

signal phrase (21d.1) A phrase that indicates who is being quoted. *In his memoir, my grandfather wrote, "My father was the first to leave Romania."*

simile (49e) A comparison, using *like* or *as,* of two unlike things: *His eyes were like saucers.* See *figurative language.*

simple predicate (31c.1) See *predicate.*

simple sentence (31j) See *sentence.*

simple subject (31b) See *subject.*

simple tense (35e) See *tense.*

singular (30b.4) Referring to one. See *number.*

slang (48a) An informal and playful type of language used within a social group or discourse community and generally not appropriate for academic writing.

spatial organization (4c.1) The arrangement of details about a subject in a paragraph according to the way they appear to the viewer: from top to bottom, outside to inside, east to west, and so on.

specific word (49c) A word that names a particular kind of thing or item, such as *pines* or *college senior.*

split infinitive (43e) One or more words interposed between the two words of an infinitive: *The team hoped to immediately rebound from its defeat.*

squinting modifier (43c) A modifier misplaced such that it is not clear whether it describes what precedes it or what follows it. It should be repositioned for clarity.

standard English (48) The form of English characteristic of most academic discourse and expected in most academic writing.

stereotype (48e) A simplified image or generalization about the members of a racial, ethnic, or social group.

storyboard (3c) A comic strip-like sketch that outlines major changes of action in a film or video scene sequence.

subject (31b) The words that name the topic of a sentence, which the predicate makes a statement about. The **simple subject** is the pronoun or noun that identifies the topic of a sentence: *The dog was in the yard.* The **complete subject** includes the simple subject and its modifiers: *The big black dog was in the yard.* A **compound subject** contains two or more subjects connected by a conjunction: *The dog and cat faced each other across the fence.*

subject-by-subject comparison (4d.6) The comparison of two items as a whole, beginning with a description of the relevant features of one, followed by a discussion of the features of the other. See *point-by-point comparison.*

subject complement (30d; 31c.3; 34h; 36d; 37f; 40a) A word or word group that follows a linking verb and renames or specifies the sentence's subject. It can be a noun or an adjective.

subject directory (16f) In an Internet search, a hierarchical listing of subject categories, beginning with broad categories and branching to increasingly specific subcategories. Subject directories provide an alternative to keyword searches.

subject-verb agreement (34) The appropriate pairing, in number and person, of a subject and a verb: *The student looks confused; The students look confused.*

subjective case (36) See *pronoun case.*

subjective stance (8b.3) The presentation of an issue from a personal point of view or reflecting personal preference. Contrast with *objective stance.*

subjunctive mood (35k) Of verbs, the mood used to express a wish or a request or to state a condition contrary to fact: *I wish I were home.* See *mood.*

subordinating conjunction or **subordinator** (30g.3) See *conjunction.*

subordination (44a; 44d) In a sentence, the joining of a secondary (subordinate) element to the main element in a way that shows the logical relationship between the two: *Although we shopped for hours, we didn't find a dress for the party.*

summary (7d.2; 21b.4) A brief synthesis, in a writer's own words and form, of the main points of a source written by someone else.

superlative degree (37g) See *comparison.*

survey (19c.3) A research tool common in the social sciences in which subjects are asked to respond to a questionnaire.

synchronous communication (16i) Real-time online exchanges between individuals. See *chat room, instant messaging.*

synonyms (49b) Words with similar meanings, such as *scowl* and *frown.*

syntax (30) The rules for forming grammatical sentences in a language.

synthesize (7e) To bring together and make connections between things. Synthesis is an important element in critical thinking, reading, and writing.

tag sentence (51g) A sentence with a phrase or question attached at the end. *It's hot today, isn't it?*

template (14d.3) In presentation software, a predesigned slide format, usually provided with the software.

tense (35g) The form of a verb that indicates its time of action, whether present, past, or future. There are three **simple tenses:** present (*I laugh*), past (*I laughed*), and future (*I will laugh*). The **perfect tenses** indicate actions that were or will be completed by the time of another action or time: *I have spoken* (present perfect); *I had spoken* (past perfect), *I will have spoken* (future perfect). The **progressive forms** of the simple and perfect tenses indicate ongoing action: *I am laughing* (present progressive), *I was laughing* (past progressive), *I will be laughing* (future progressive), *I have been laughing* (present perfect progressive), *I had been laughing* (past progressive), *I will have been laughing* (future progressive).

thesis (3b) A paper's central idea.

thesis statement (3b) The statement that asserts a paper's central idea.

tone (2f) The writer's voice, communicated through content, style, and word choice.

topic (2b) The subject of a paper.

topic outline (3c.2) A formal outline in which each topic and subtopic is stated in words and phrases.

topic sentence (4b.2) The sentence that announces a paragraph's main idea.

Toulmin method (10b.2) A method of analyzing arguments based on **claims** (assertions about a topic), **grounds** (reasons and evidence), and **warrants** (assumptions that link the grounds to the claims).

transition (5f.3) The connection of one idea to another in writing.

transitional expression (5f.3) A word or phrase that links one idea to another.

transitional sentence (5f.3) A sentence that refers to the previous paragraph and at the same time moves an essay on to the next point.

transitive verb (31c.3; 35c) A verb that takes a direct object. *He bought a new bike last week.*

tree diagram (3c.2) A method of planning a paper's organization by showing the relationship between topics and subtopics (but not the sequence of topics) in a branching structure.

typeface (6c.2) A design established by printers for the letters in the alphabet, numbers, punctuation marks, and special characters.

understatement (49e) An exaggeratedly restrained comparison. See *figurative language.*

URL (14e) (uniform resource locator) A Web address.

usenet news group (16i) An Internet news group in which messages are posted to a computer that hosts the group and distributes the postings to subscribers.

unity (5f) The clear relationship between the main idea of a paragraph and the evidence that supports it.

verb (30a) A word that reports an action, condition, or state of being. Verbs change form to indicate person, number, tense, voice, and mood.

verb phrase (30a; 31e) A main verb plus its helping verbs: *Louie is helping with the party preparations.*

verbal (31f; 35j; 64c) A word formed from a verb that functions as a noun, an adjective, or an adverb, not as a verb.

verbal phrase (31f) A verbal plus an object, complement, or modifier.

virtual classroom (1b.3) A class conducted entirely online so that students can participate wherever they are.

voice (31c.3; 35l; 46) The form of a verb used to indicate whether the subject of a sentence does the acting or is acted upon. In the **active voice,** the subject acts: *The crowd sang "Take Me Out to the Ballgame."* In the **passive voice,** the subject is acted upon: *"Take Me Out to the Ballgame" was sung by the crowd.*

warrant (10b.2) An unstated assumption that underlies an argument's claim and the grounds that support it. See *Toulmin method.*

Weblog (14a) See *blog.*

Web page (14a) A page on the World Wide Web.

Web site (14a) A site on the Web usually consisting of written work, links, and graphics.

white space (6c.1) The area of a document that does not contain type or graphics.

wiki (16i) Internet sites designed to allow participants to comment on and modify one another's work.

working bibliography (21a) A preliminary list of books, articles, pamphlets, Web sites, and other sources that seem likely to help answer a research question.

writing process (2a) The activities writers engage in as they undertake and complete a writing project. These activities include understanding the assignment, generating ideas, drafting, revising, and designing and producing the finished work.

writing situation (2a) The characteristics of a particular writing project, including its genre, topic, purpose, audience, tone, length, due date, and format.

Credits

Text Credits

P. 4: Adapted from Robert S. Feldman, *Strategies for Success in College and Life,* Second Edition, p. 92. Copyright © 2003 The McGraw-Hill Companies, Inc. Reprinted by permission of The McGraw-Hill Companies, Inc.; **p. 9:** From Herbert F. Spirer, Louise Spirer and Abram J. Jaffee, *Misused Statistics,* 2nd and Revised Edition, 1987. Reprinted by permission of Taylor and Francis Books, Inc.; **p. 14:** Created in PageOut by Dr. Susan P. Sullivan, Professor of Accounting, University of Massachusetts Dartmouth. Copyright © McGraw-Hill Companies, Inc. Used with permission; Microsoft® Internet Explorer used by permission of Microsoft Corporation; **p. 15:** Reprinted by permission of The McGraw-Hill Companies, Inc.; **p. 18:** Definition of "haze." Copyright © 2000 by Houghton Mifflin. Reprinted by permission from *The American Heritage Dictionary of the English Language,* Fourth Edition; **p. 19:** Definition of "pig out." *ESL Learner's Edition, Random House Webster's Dictionary of American English* 1997; Definition of "academic." *ESL Learner's Edition, Random House Webster's Dictionary of American English* 1997; **p. 24:** With permission from Amazonia Images and Terra; **p. 30:** From Dana Payne, Keeper at Woodland Park Zoo. Reprinted by permission of Dana Payne; **p. 31:** From "Python Molurus" by Dr. Susan Evans, NSF Digital Library, University of Texas, Austin. Reprinted by permission; **p. 43:** Reprinted by permission of Google; **p. 45:** From Elaine Maimon and Janice Peritz, *A Writer's Resource,* p. 70. Copyright © 2003 The McGraw-Hill Companies. Reprinted by permission of The McGraw-Hill Companies, Inc.; **p. 59:** Gary Klass, "Presenting Data" http://lilt.ilstu.edu/gmklass. Reprinted by permission of Gary Klass; **p. 61:** R. V. Clark and D. B. Cornish. "Modeling Offenders' Decisions: A Framework for Research and Policy." *Crime and Justice 6,* Michael Tonry and Norval Morris, eds., p. 169. Reprinted by permission of University of Chicago Press; **p. 66:** From J. D. Fast, "After Columbine: How People Mourn Sudden Death," *Social Work,* Vol. 48, No. 4, 2003, p. 485. Copyright © 2003 National Association of Social Workers, Inc. Reprinted with permission; **p. 66:** From Damian Robinson, "Riding Into the Afterlife," *Archaeology,* Vol. 57, Number 2, March/April 2004. Copyright © 2004 by The Archaeological Institute of America. Reprinted with permission; **p. 67:** From Jill J. Suiter, Rebecca Powers and Rachel Brown, "Avenues to Prestige Among Adolescents," *Adolescence,* Summer 2004. Reprinted by permission; **p. 68:** From Robert Faust, "Integrated Pest Management Programs Strive to Solve Agricultural Problems," *Agricultural Research,* November 2004. Reprinted with permission; **p. 68:** From Mark Chapell, et al., "Bullying in College by Students and Teachers," *Adolescence,* Spring 2004. Reprinted by permission; **p. 68:** From Yang Guorong, "Transforming Knowledge Into Wisdom," *Philosophy East and West,* Volume 52, Number 4, October 2002, pp. 441–458. Reprinted with permission from University of Hawaii Press; **p. 69:** From Ross Greene, et al., "Are Students with ADHD More Stressful to Teach?" *Journal of Emotional and Behavioral Disorders,* Summer 2002. Reprinted with permission from Pro-Ed; **p. 71:** From Michelle M. Ducharme, "A Lifetime in Production," *Newsweek,* September 9, 1996, p. 17. Reprinted by permission of the author; **p. 74:** From Robert Reich, "The Future of Work," *Harper's,* April 1989, 26. Copyright © 1989 by Robert Reich. Reprinted by permission of the author; **p. 77:** From Jerry Bentley and Herbert F. Ziegler, *Traditions and Encounters,* 2nd Edition, p. 1049. Copyright © 2003 The McGraw-Hill Companies. Reprinted by permission of The McGraw-Hill Companies, Inc.; **p. 79:** Chart: "Morning News Viewership: All Networks," http://www.stateofthenewsmedia.org/narrative_networktv_audience.asp?cat=3&media=4. Reprinted by permission of Nielson Media Research; **p. 86:** From Ross N. Hoffman, "Controlling Hurricanes," *Scientific American,* October 2004, p. 69. Copyright © 2004 Scientific American, Inc. All rights reserved; **pp. 86, 87:** From David Keys, "Rethinking the Picts," *Archaeology,* Vol. 57, Number 5, 2004. Copyright © 2004 by The Archaeological Institute of America. Reprinted with permission; **p. 88:** From Susan Woods, "Untreated Recovery from Eating Disorders." *Adolescence,* Summer 2004. Reprinted by permission; **p. 88:** From Ken Belson, "Saved, and Enslaved, by the Cell," *The New York Times,* October 10, 2004, p. 12. Direct quote by Kenneth J. Gergen

ginia Center for Digital History. http://valley.vcdh.virginnia.edu; **p. 327:** Reprinted
by permission of Oxfam America; **p. 334:** Courtesy of the Louis Armstrong Archives,
Queens College; **p. 350:** Courtesy of Libraries of The City University of New York;
p. 351: Courtesy of New Orleans Online. (photo) Courtesy of the Louis Armstrong
Archives, Queens College; **pp. 353, 354:** From J. Bradford Robinson. "Scat Sing-
ing" in *The New Grove Dictionary of Music and Musicians, Second Edition* (29
Volumes), edited by John Tyrrell, Executive Editor. Copyright © 2003 Oxford Uni-
versity Press, Inc. Used by permission of Oxford University Press, Inc.; **pp. 354–355:**
From John Ephland. From "Down Beat Jazz 101: The Very Beginning," *Down Beat
Magazine,* http://www.downbeat.com/default.asp?sect=education&subsect=jazz.
Reprinted with permission; **p. 356:** From Mario A. Charles. "The Age of a Jazzwoman: Valaida Snow, 1900–1956." *The Journal of Negro History,* 80.4 (1995): 183.
Reprinted by permission of the author; **p. 378:** Title Page and Copyright Page
from *Louis Armstrong: An Extravagant Life* by Lawrence Bergreen. Copyright
© 1997 by Lawrence Bergreen. Used by permission of Broadway Books, a division
of Random House, Inc.; **p. 379:** First page of article and journal table of contents
from Brent Edward Hayes, "Louis Armstrong and the Syntax of Scat," *Critical
Inquiry,* 28 (2002): 618–649. Reprinted with permission from University of
Chicago Press; **p. 379:** Lyrics from "Heebie Jeebies" by Boyd Atkins. Copyright ©
1926, 1954 by MCA Music Publishing. All rights administered by Universal Music
Corporation/ASCAP. Used by permission. All rights reserved; **p. 380:** Image produced by ProQuest Information and Learning Company. Inquiries may be made to:
ProQuest Information and Learning Company, 300 North Zeeb Road, Ann Arbor,
MI 48106–1346, USA. Tel: 734-761-7400; email: info@proquest.com; web page:
www.il.proquest.com. Reprinted with permission; **p. 431:** Title page and copyright
page from *Exploring Agrodiversity* by Harold Brookfield, 2001. Reprinted by per-
mission of Columbia University Press; **p. 432:** Excerpt and table of contents page
from *A Voice in the Wilderness* by Jack Epstein, 2001. Reprinted by permission of
Latin Trade Magazine; **p. 433:** Image courtesy of EBSCO Host; **p. 458:** Fig. 1
From *Hamburger Connection Fuels Amazon Destruction: Cattle Ranching and
Deforestation in Brazil's Amazon* by D. Kaimowitz, B. Mertens, S. Wunder &
P. Pacheco, 2002, Center for International Forestry Research. Used with permission; **p. 740:** From Jerry Bentley & Herbert Ziegler, *Traditions and Encounters,*
Second Edition, p. 91. Copyright © 2003 The McGraw-Hill Companies. Reprinted
by permission of The McGraw-Hill Companies, Inc.; **p. 757:** Definition of "com-
pare" from *Random House Webster's Dictionary of American English.* Copyright
© 1997 by Random House, Inc. Reprinted with permission; **pp. 766, 767:** From
Jerry Bentley & Herbert Ziegler, *Traditions and Encounters,* Second Edition, p.
820. Copyright © 2003 The McGraw-Hill Companies. Reprinted by permission of
The McGraw-Hill Companies, Inc.; p. **854:** From Lawrence Ferlinghetti, "Short
Story on a Painting by Gustav Klimt" in *Endless Life: Selected Poems.* Copyright
© 1976 by Lawrence Ferlinghetti. Reprinted by permission of New Directions
Publishing Corp; **p. 876:** From W. B. Yeats, "The Tower" reprinted with the permission of Scribner, an imprint of Simon & Schuster Adult Publishing Group,
from *The Collected Works of W. B. Yeats, Volume I: The Poems, Revised,* edited by
Richard J. Finneran. Copyright © 1928 by The Macmillan Company; copyright
renewed © 1956 by Georgie Yeats.

Photo Credits

Part Opener 1: © Royalty-free/CORBIS; **p. 10 top and bottom:** © John Althouse;
p. 42: © Seth Joel/CORBIS; **p. 62:** Space Science and Engineering Center/Univer-
sity of Wisconsin-Madison; **p. 72:** © Cheryl Diaz Meyer/Dallas Morning News/
CORBIS; **p. 73:** © CORBIS/SYGMA; **p. 76:** © Bettmann/CORBIS; **p. 123:** © 2000
by Sebastião Salgado/Amazonas Images/Contact Press Images.
Part Opener 2: © Philadelphia Museum of Art/CORBIS; **p. 146:** Courtesy, ACLU;
p. 153: Courtesy, ACLU; **p. 154:** © Lynsey Addario/CORBIS; **p. 181:** Stephanie
Berger for The New York Times; **p. 188:** Image: © Andy Warhol Foundation/
CORBIS Artwork: © The Andy Warhol Foundation for the Visual Arts/CORBIS;

Index

Index for Multilingual Writers

For MULTILINGUAL STUDENTS

Abbreviations and Symbols
for Editing and Proofreading

abbr	Faulty abbreviation **58**		*p*	Punctuation error
ad	Misused adjective or adverb **37**		,	Comma **51a–j**
agr	Problem with subject-verb or pronoun agreement **34, 36k–o**		no ,	Unnecessary comma **51k–q**
appr	Inappropriate word or phrase **48, 49**		;	Semicolon **52**
art	Incorrect or missing article **39e, 64a**		:	Colon **53**
awk	Awkward		'	Apostrophe **61**
cap	Faulty capitalization **57**		" "	Quotation marks **54**
case	Error in pronoun case **36a–j**		. ? !	Period, question mark, exclamation point **56**
cliché	Overused expression **49f**		— ( ) [ ]	Dash, parentheses,
coh	Problem with coherence **5f**		. . . /	brackets, ellipses, slash **55**
com	Incomplete comparison **39d**		*para*	Problem with a paraphrase **20,21b, d**
coord	Problem with coordination **44**		*pass*	Ineffective use of passive voice **351, 46b**
cs	Comma splice **33**			
d	Diction problem **48, 49**		*pn agr*	Problem with pronoun agreement **36k–o**
dev	More development needed **4b–d**		*quote*	Problem with a quotation **20, 21b–d, 54d, i**
dm	Dangling modifier **43f**			
doc	Documentation problem		*ref*	Problem with pronoun reference **36p–t**
	APA **25**		*rep*	Repetitious words or phrases **38c**
	Chicago **26a–d**		*run-on*	Run-on (or fused) sentence **33**
	CSE **26e–j**		*sexist*	Sexist language **36m, 48e**
	MLA **24**		*shift*	Shift in point of view, tense, mood, or voice **41**
emph	Problem with emphasis **44, 45e,60f**			
exact	Inexact word **49**		*sl*	Slang **48a**
exam	Example needed **4d**		*sp*	Misspelled word **63**
frag	Sentence fragment **32**		*sub*	Problem with subordination **44**
fs	Fused (or run-on) sentence **33**		*sv agr*	Problem with subject-verb agreement **34**
hyph	Problem with hyphen **62**			
inc	Incomplete construction **39**		*t*	Verb tense error **35g–j**
intro	Stronger introduction needed **4f**		*trans*	Transition needed **5f**
ital	Italics or underlining needed **60**		*usage*	See Glossary of Usage **50**
jarg	Jargon **48c**		*var*	Vary your sentence structure **45**
lc	lowercase letter needed **57**		*vb*	Verb problem **35**
mix	Mixed construction **40**		*w*	Wordy **38**
mm	Misplaced modifier **43a–e**		*ww*	Wrong word **49**
mng	Meaning not clear		//	Parallelism needed **42**
mood	Error in mood **35k**		#	Add a space
ms	Error in manuscript form **6**		∧	Insert
	APA **25d, e**		↻	Close up space
	Chicago **26d**		x	Obvious error
	MLA **24e, f**		??	Unclear
num	Error in number style **59**			
¶	Paragraph **4**			

Resources for Writers in *The New McGraw-Hill Handbook*